# Speaking in God's Name

RELATED TITLES PUBLISHED BY ONEWORLD

*Al-Farabi: His Life, Works and Influence*, Majid Fakhry, ISBN 1–85168–302–X
*Approaches to Islam in Religious Studies*, Richard C. Martin, ISBN 1–85168–268–6
*As Through a Veil*, Annemarie Schimmel, ISBN 1–85168–274–0
*Averroes: His Life, Works and Influence*, Majid Fakhry, ISBN 1–85168–269–4
*A Concise Encyclopedia of Islam*, Gordon D. Newby, ISBN 1–85168–295–3
*The Faith and Practice of Al-Ghazálí*, William Montgomery Watt, ISBN 1–85168–062–4
*Faith and Reason in Islam*, Averroes, translated with an introduction by Ibrahim Najjar, ISBN 1–85168–263–5
*The Formative Period of Islamic Thought*, William Montgomery Watt, ISBN 1–85168–152–3
*Islam and the West*, Norman Daniel, ISBN 1–85168–129–9
*Islam: A Short History*, William Montgomery Watt, ISBN 1–85168–205–8
*Islam: A Short Introduction*, Abdulkader Tayob, ISBN 1–85168–192–2
*Islamic Philosophy, Theology and Mysticism*, Majid Fakhry, ISBN 1–85168–252–X
*The Legacy of Arab–Islam in Africa*, John Alembillah Azumah, ISBN 1–85168–273–2
*The Mantle of the Prophet*, Roy Mottahedeh, ISBN 1–85168–234–1
*Muhammad: A Short Biography*, Martin Forward, ISBN 1–85168–131–0
*Muslim Women Mystics*, Margaret Smith, ISBN 1–85168–250–3
*On Being a Muslim*, Farid Esack, ISBN 1–85168–146–9
*Progressive Muslims: On Justice, Gender and Pluralism*, Edited by Omid Safi, ISBN 1–85168–316–X
*The Qur'an and its Exegesis*, Helmut Gätje, ISBN 1–85168–118–3
*The Qur'an: A Short Introduction*, Farid Esack, ISBN 1–85168–231–7
*Quran, Liberation and Pluralism*, Farid Esack, ISBN 1–85168–121–3
*Revival and Reform in Islam*, Fazlur Rahman, edited and with an introduction by Ebrahim Moosa, ISBN 1–85168–204–X
*A Rumi Anthology*, Reynold A. Nicholson, ISBN 1–85168–251–1
*Rumi: Past and Present, East and West*, Franklin D. Lewis, ISBN 1–85168–214–7
*Sufism: A Short Introduction*, William C. Chittick, ISBN 1–85168–211–2
*What Muslims Believe*, John Bowker, ISBN 1–85168–169–8

# Speaking in God's Name

## Islamic Law, Authority, and Women

Khaled Abou El Fadl

ONEWORLD
OXFORD

SPEAKING IN GOD'S NAME

Oneworld Publications
(Sales and Editorial)
185 Banbury Road
Oxford, OX2 7AR
England
www.oneworld-publications.com


Reprinted 2003, 2005


A CIP record for this title is available
from the British Library

ISBN 1–85168–262–7

Cover design by Design Deluxe, Bath
Typeset by LaserScript Ltd, Mitcham, UK
Printed and bound in Britain by Bell & Bain Ltd, Glasgow

This work is dedicated to my students,
past, present, and future, with much hope.

# Contents

# Preface

It is often maintained that Islamic jurisprudence is the heart and kernel of the Islamic religion. Traditionally, Islamic jurisprudence has been the arena in which the conditions, dynamics, and meanings of the relationship between God and human beings were explored. It is certainly true that Islamic jurisprudence is one of the crowning achievements of Islamic civilization; it is the repository of a subtle, complex, and illimitably rich intellectual heritage.[1] Admittedly, however, I do not believe that, for the most part, this richness has survived the trauma of colonialism and modernity. In fact, I fear that today the remnants of the classical Islamic jurisprudential heritage are verging on extinction. Furthermore, I think that one of the most poignant manifestations of this unfortunate reality is the spread of a trenchant authoritarianism in contemporary Islamic legal determinations. The epistemology and normative premises that guided the development and flourishing of the classical jurisprudential process are now defunct, and whereas the classical jurisprudential tradition, I think, faithfully projected basic constitutional premises that were anti-authoritarian in character, the same cannot be said about the current reality.

This book does not present an anthropological or sociological study of Islamic legal practice in the modern age. This is a work of legal theory and not a work on anthropology or sociology. The basic aim of this book is to present a conceptual framework for the idea of authority, and for identifying an abuse of authority in Islamic law. I am not referring here to institutional authority, but to persuasive or moral authority. As such, the primary focus of this book is on the notion of the authoritative in Islamic law, in contrast to the authoritarian. At a broader level, this book explores the idea of speaking for God without pretending to be God or, at least, without being perceived, for all practical purposes, as God. Dealing with God's law inevitably involves an intricate balance between the sovereignty of the Divine, human determinacy, and morality.

Working from within the Islamic legal tradition, I offer a normative proposal for achieving this balance. I am sure that some will argue that it is impossible to attempt to represent God's law without descending into one form of authoritarianism or another, and that hoping to achieve the balance that I am proposing is at best naive. Nevertheless, I believe this is a separate issue, and I do not deal with the challenges or the meaning of secularism in this book. The focus of this book is more narrow; I assume the relevance and desirability of the Islamic juristic tradition, I analyze its theory of authority, the misuse and misrepresentation of this theory in the contemporary setting, and I propose solutions for resisting the authoritarian tendencies in the practice of Islamic law.

The book is divided into seven chapters and a conclusion. The first chapter, named the 'Induction' identifies the central themes and the basic assumptions of the work. I did not name this chapter the 'introduction' because it is not intended simply as an explanatory note for the rest of the book. Properly speaking, it makes no formal introductions but extends an invitation or inducement to become intellectually, and emotionally, involved with this book's investigations. It does so by raising a series of questions and by sharing with the reader some of the author's own assumptions and intellectual dilemmas. Many readers, justifiably, skip reading the introduction and start with the first chapter. In this work, the induction is a necessary invitation to the rest of the work. The second chapter explores the idea of the authoritative in Islamic law by analyzing the notion of Divine sovereignty, the role of deference in the construction of authority, and the function of jurists. The third chapter functions as a summary transition into the fourth and fifth chapters. Chapters Four and Five are somewhat abstract and detailed, and so the third chapter has been written in deference to those who might not be interested in the finer points of my argument. Although Chapter Three is not an adequate replacement for the fourth and fifth chapters, the reader may want to jump from the third to the sixth and seventh chapters. The fourth and fifth chapters study the role of the text in the determination of meaning. In this context, I set out the theory and conditions for the authoritativeness of jurists in Islam, and the process pursuant to which one can say that the jurists have abused their authority. The second, third, fourth, and fifth chapters lay the foundations for a critical analysis of particular abusive legal practices in modern Islam, which is the task of the sixth and seventh chapters. The sixth and seventh chapters present case studies in the construction of the authoritarian in modern Islamic legal practice. Most of the case studies focus on *responsa* dealing with legal issues related to women. I have chosen these *responsa* in particular because, more than any others, they demonstrate the misuse and abuse of God's authority in order to impose a suffocating patriarchy upon Muslim society. Furthermore, I think that gender-related issues present some of the most difficult and complicated challenges to contemporary Islamic law, and it is imperative that Muslim legal specialists start to develop coherent and critical ways of dealing with these issues. Importantly, however, this book does not belong to the genre of gender studies or feminist jurisprudence. I do not have the competence to engage these discourses. In addition, my primary aim in this work is to develop a conceptual framework for analyzing Islamic legal determinations according to their own frame of reference. In the Islamic context, gender studies and feminist jurisprudence raise controversies that I am not eager to engage. I leave this to more resolute hearts.

This book has had a rather long and, at times, unpleasant history. It started out about five years ago as a short essay criticizing a misogynist legal *responsum* issued by a Muslim organization in the United States. At that time, what troubled me the most about the *responsum* was the fact that it presented a determination that was demeaning and degrading to women as the indisputable and unchallengeable will of God. My training in the classical legal tradition allowed me to recognize the remarkable amount of evidence ignored or suppressed by that organization, and, yet, it seemed to me that too many Muslims in the United States were willing to accept the *responsum* as the one and only will of God. The more I thought about and investigated the dynamics of Islamic law in the United States, the more I was troubled by the superficiality, frivolity, and even, at times dishonesty of these discourses. There was no coherence, no method, no principled approaches, and no jurisprudence. Islamic juristic discourse in the United States consisted of a battle between the *ḥadīth*-hurlers – each party surveys the traditions of the Prophet to find something that can be hurled at the opposite party, and the other parties, naturally, do the same. Very few of the proclaimed scholars of Islamic law in the United States seemed to have any interest in developing a systematic and critical discourse on God's law. Frankly, it appeared to me that Islamic law had become the pastime activity of intellectually challenged and, otherwise, stolid individuals. For the most part, I was wrong.

The problem was not the state of Muslim pseudo-intellectualism in the United States – the problem was much larger. The problem was the disintegration and abandonment of the traditional premises upon which Islamic law was constructed, without their replacement with a viable alternative. Most of the determinations of the various *ḥadīth*-hurling parties in the United States mirrored and relied on the discourses of various factions in the Muslim world as a whole. So, for instance, legal determinations by some organizations in the United States that exhibited a psychotic contempt of women were mere transplants of the determinations of influential Muslim organizations in some Muslim countries. Put simply, the methodological shortcomings were endemic to Muslim legal discourses at large.

As a result of this thought process, I expanded the short essay into a modest and rather bashful book entitled, *The Authoritative and Authoritarian in Islamic Discourses: A Case Study*, published by an Islamic press. The book used a case study method by focusing on the *responsum* of a particular Muslim organization as a way of raising the larger issues related to despotism in the practice of contemporary Islamic law. That book was eventually translated into Arabic by Professor ʿĀdil ʿAṣfūr at Ain Shams University in Cairo. This was the beginning of a rather interesting journey. The English book received enthusiastic support by some Muslim intellectuals, but was demonized in many other contexts, with the usual unpleasant encounters for the author and publisher. The book was banned in some influential Muslim countries, and as a result, was never published in Arabic. I am not claiming any heroism; in truth, it is the publisher of the English book, Quill Publishers (formerly Dar Taiba), and the publishers that attempted to print the book in Arabic who withstood the brunt of the consequences. Although the English book immediately sold out, the publisher, because of its brave stand, sustained considerable collateral financial losses. At this point, Ebrahim Moosa, a formidable Muslim intellectual and scholar, urged me to expand and develop the earlier book into a full-length study, and kindly introduced me to Oneworld Publications. As a result, this book was born.

This book is quite different from *The Authoritative and Authoritarian.* Other than the fact that this book is three times as long, I have dropped all references to the USA-based Muslim organization and its *responsum*, and I have developed a more comprehensive approach to the issue of authority in Islamic law. Importantly, I have changed my mind about several issues discussed in the first book, hopefully, for the better. In developing the theory of the authoritative and authoritarian, I have added an analysis of a group of *responsa* by one of the most influential, if not the most influential, legal institutions in the Arabic-speaking Muslim world. As I have noted in the conclusion, I am not thrilled about criticizing the determinations of such an influential organization but I can find no alternative. Those who read Chapters Six and Seven will understand what I mean. I am hoping to set a higher and more demanding, principled standard for Islamic juristic discourses in the modern age. I do not, however, intend to belittle or demean anyone. Nothing I say in this book should be taken as a form of casting doubts upon the piety of the jurists of this, or any other, organization. Their piety is something that is between them and God, and it has no relevance for the discussion in this book.

This project has had a five-year period of growth, and during this period, I have accumulated such an enormous debt of gratitude to so many people, I have no realistic hope of paying it back. The least I can do is mention their names and thank them, but this hardly does justice to them. I thank the numerous individuals who supported my research through the years and took the trouble to engage, criticize, and enlighten me. Among them, I thank Professor Hossein Modarressi who supervised my work at Princeton, and who taught me that no standard is too high or too demanding when studying Islamic law. I also thank Ṭāriq al-Bishrī, the Egyptian jurist, for his helpful comments, and *Shaykh* Yūsuf al-Qarḍāwī for trying to defend the banned Arabic book. In addition, I thank Waheed Hussein, at Harvard, who is a troublemaker, and philosopher, and who aimed a stream of insults at some of my ideas in crowded and noisy Cambridge cafés. I have not risen to his standards in this work, but I have learned a great deal from him – insults and all. I cannot express sufficient gratitude to my colleagues at the UCLA School of Law who are always supportive and a delight to work with. Stephen Bainbridge, Taimie Bryant, Stephen Gardbaum, Jerry Kang, Herbert Morris, Stephen Munzer, Arthur Rosett, and Richard Steinberg have discussed or read and commented on various parts of this work, and their invaluable critical insights have kept me alert and, hopefully, coherent. I had the privilege of working with a group of highly motivated, industrious, and intelligent students who helped in incalculable ways. I thank my students Anver Emon, Hisham Mahmoud, Jihad Turk, and Mairaj Syed who graciously withstood my numerous, sometimes unreasonable, demands. I would like to single out Anver Emon and Hisham Mahmoud because they went well beyond the call of duty. I am also extremely thankful to the staff of the UCLA Law Library who facilitated the work of my research assistants by kindly and patiently putting up with endless requests. In particular, I thank Kim Coss, Gabriel Juarez, Ann Lucas, Sangeeta Pal, and Brett Roller. They diligently and competently obtained sources for me from the various University of California libraries, and from all over the country.

The UCLA School of Law has provided an unfailingly supportive and friendly environment that continues to facilitate all my work. I am particularly grateful to Dean Jonathan Varat, Associate Dean Robert Goldstein, and Associate Dean Myra Saunders for providing me with research funds, and for generously allowing me to hire competent assistants who have proved invaluable for my work. I also thank Azmeralda and Omar Alfi for their continued belief and support for my work.

I am thankful to Khalid al-Saleh, the owner of Quill publishers, for believing in the early work and for his sacrifices, and to Ebrahim Moosa for his encouragement and for commending me to Oneworld Publications. I commend Oneworld Publications and its competent staff for adopting this project, and for publishing some of the most important and provoking books on Islamic thought in our age. I am also extremely grateful to the Oneworld readers, Muhammad Fadel and Denise Spellberg. I benefited enormously from their thorough and insightful comments. I would like to thank Cluny Sheeler, who copy-edited the manuscript.

Finally, I express my illimitable gratitude to Grace, my wife, for reading and commenting on the full text, and for her unbounded support. I also thank Naheed Fakoor who read and helped edit the text, and who provided me with a constant supply of coffee and tea throughout the writing process. I cannot forget to mention my mother, Afaf, and father, Medhat, who instilled in me the love of knowledge, and who taught me to equate God and morality. Forever in their debt.

*NOTE*

1 Schacht, *An Introduction to Islamic Law*, p. 1.

# 1 Induction

only God knows what's in your heart?

At the conclusion of a characteristically fascinating passage, the Qur'ān proclaims: "No one can know the soldiers of God except God" (*wa mā ya'lamu junūda rabbika illā huwa*).[1] The statement sounds rather decisive but it is also teasingly ambiguous. Who are these soldiers? Does it make any sense to even pose this question to the reader if only God knows God's soldiers? What should the reader understand from this statement? That God knows what humans cannot know? That the reader should not try to search and identify God's soldiers, or that the reader should not fancy himself/herself to be God's soldier? As a prelude to this statement the Qur'ān speaks of a Hellfire guarded by nineteen angels. As if anticipating the reader's mind, the Qur'ān elaborates upon the significance of the number nineteen. The Qur'ān explains that God has decreed that only angels may guard Hellfire. As for the specific number nineteen, the Qur'ān states, the unbelievers will be cast into doubt because they will see no sound reason that nineteen angels, as opposed to eighteen or twenty, should guard Hell. But the "People of the Book" (Christians and Jews), the Qur'ān contends, will be reassured and comforted, and the believers (presumably the Muslims) will only increase in faith. The Qur'ān does not explain the reason for this avowed comfort or increase in faith; it simply goes on to state that part of the reason for this revelation is so that the People of the Book and the believers will be assured and not suffer the pangs of doubt. The Qur'ān adds that those whose hearts are diseased will say, "What did God intend by this *mathal*?" *Mathal* could mean symbol, parable, metaphor, or simile. After affirming that God has the power to lead people astray or guide them, the Qur'ān concludes by stating that none can know the soldiers of God except God, and that "verily, this is a reminder to humankind."[2]

This Qur'ānic passage highlights several intriguing problems of interpretation. As a prelude to the analysis, we ought to ask, what is humankind being reminded of, and what or who defines this memory? If the passage reflects a private dialogue between a one-time author and a one-time reader, how is this private dialogue relevant to anything beyond its own particular dynamics? More importantly, what is the methodological process by which we go about investigating the meaning of the text? It appears as if the Qur'ānic verse invites the reader to join an ongoing conversation that started a long time ago, and so the question becomes, to what extent can or should the reader even attempt to join this conversation?

A reader implementing a reasonable reading of the text will probably understand that there are nineteen angels guarding Hell, and that the unbelievers responded to this revelation with a certain amount of jeering. But a reader will not necessarily know why this revelation will increase the faith of believers or provide assurance to the People of the Book. Possibly, this verse is historically specific; possibly it is the product of a particular context and specific debate that is now lost to us forever. However, it is also possible that the text is invoking a sign for a deeper meaning or set of associations. Perhaps the passage is an invitation to those whom Umberto Eco aptly describes as the "followers of the veil" to investigate the signs that point to the discrete and deeper meaning of things.[3] This method of interpretation has had its strong proponents in the Kabbalistic tradition in Judaism, mystical Christianity, and Ṣūfī Islam.[4] Under this approach, the number nineteen might hold the secret to an esoteric truth that is discoverable only by the truly knowledgeable.[5] The esoteric possibilities are confirmed by the fact that the passage employs the word *mathal*, which could mean a sign or symbol. Nonetheless, the passage concludes by ascribing to the text the function of remembrance – the discourse serves as a reminder to human beings. Can readers be reminded of the esoteric if the esoteric is not readily accessible? Another possibility is that the text is not opening itself to interpretation but simply affirming the supremacy of God's knowledge and futility of human endeavors to make sense of this knowledge. Believers, whether People of the Book or Muslims,[6] will be comforted by this awareness but unbelievers will respond with skepticism and doubt. This creates an ambiguity as to the meaning of the statement that only God knows God's soldiers. Does this statement prescribe a sense of unquestioning submission to God's knowledge – a knowledge that is ascertainable only by transmission and mechanical absorption? Alternatively, does it mean that there are, in fact, soldiers of God, but these soldiers are only known to God and that God's knowledge can be investigated but can never be ascertained or fully acquired? If it is the former, then effectively the text denies the reader access to the process that constructs and generates meaning from a text. If it is the latter, then this passage is a wonderful negation of authoritarian interpretive methods.

To put the issue differently, does this Qur'ānic passage open or close the text to interpretation? Umberto Eco has suggested that open texts operate at the level of suggestion and the stimulation of constructive interpretive activity. In contrast, closed texts aim to define and closely limit the interpretive activity of the reader.[7] In stating that only God knows God's soldiers, does the text stimulate and validate the constructive efforts of the reader, or does it, effectively, take the meaning of the text away from the reader and deposit it in the exclusive domain of the author? We will have more to say about this issue later, but for now it is important to note that we have two distinct, but not exclusive, possibilities. If only God knows God's soldiers, the reader may conclude that only God has the power to define and identify God's soldiers, and that human beings must search the divine text for any possible identification of these soldiers. The role of the reader becomes fairly mechanical; after a close reading, the reader will conclude that God identifies the nineteen angels as God's soldiers and that is the end of the interpretive process. Alternatively, the passage may suggest or stimulate more complex constructions. For instance, the reader may reason that the passage has a more general and timeless dynamic. The passage is not a private conversation limited to a specific contextual setting, rather it is a more inclusive and accessible conversation with a wider and more transcendental application. The reader may argue that since only God knows God's soldiers, it might follow that human beings cannot conclusively ascertain whether a specific individual or set of individuals are, in fact, God's soldiers. If the passage is read normatively, it might mean that any person may aspire to be a soldier of God, and that she or he can strive with the utmost exertion to achieve this status, but such a person will never know if they succeeded in achieving the esteemed position of being God's chosen soldier. Assuming that God's soldiers enjoy a delegated divine-authority, the reader can argue that everyone, in principle, has access to God's authority, but no one, in fact, is assured of receiving it. Since no one is assured of receiving it and God's knowledge is not accessible to human beings, then a reasonable person can never rest assured that any human being has, in fact, reached the exalted status of being God's chosen soldier.

I should confess that I have always understood this Qur'ānic verse to be a negation of the authoritarian – it denied any human being the claim that he or she is a soldier of God endowed with God's authority. A person can strive, hope, and aspire to be God's soldier, but no person may claim that they have, in fact, achieved this status. My understanding, however, raises difficult issues concerning the relationships between the reader, the text, and the author of the text. To what extent do I, as the reader, decide the meaning of the text? To what extent are my sensibilities and subjectivities determinative in constructing the text's meaning? May I or should I submit the text to my use, and permit my needs to be determinative in constructing a meaning for the text? If the peculiarities of the reader are determinative, what then happens to the intent of the author? Should the reader focus on the intent of the author and consider the author's intent determinative as to the meaning of the text? Isn't this more respectful towards the author, especially when the author is divine? But how can the intent of the author be ascertained if the author's motives are not accessible?

One can argue that the author has deposited and entrusted the authorial intent to the objectified medium of language – a medium that is accessible to human beings. But, then, are the semiotics of the language purely the product of the subjectivities of the author or does the medium partly, or wholly, re-formulate the authorial intent by forcing the author's subjectivities to yield to the structure and logic of the language? Does it make sense to talk of the author's subjectivities in the case of a divine authorship? Can we properly speak of divine subjectivities or even of intent? If God chose to communicate through an objective linguistic medium how will this medium interact with human subjectivities or even idiosyncrasies? As explained above, the Qur'ānic passage seems to assume a specific historical context that might have been familiar to a certain group of readers at a certain point in time. But when and to what extent does the text become independent and autonomous from the host of subjectivities, whether authorial or historical, that once generated the text? If, for a contemporary reader, the context is significant but unreachable, does this mean that the author or text has delegated the meaning to the reader, or that the reader may use the text in whichever way he/she deems fit? Every reader brings his/her own historical context to bear upon the context, so what are the appropriate dynamics between the historical context that generated the text in the first place and the historical context of the reader? Finally, as a reader, to what extent am I bound or limited by the communities of meaning that have been generated around the text? For instance, if Qur'ānic exegesis over a period of fourteen-hundred years chooses an interpretation of the verse that is decidedly different from my own, should that limit or direct my own interpretive efforts?[8]

These types of questions will be familiar to students of literary criticism but are largely unfamiliar to specialists in Islamic law. The "citizenship" of these questions, however, is not nearly as important as the fact that they raise several issues directly pertinent to the purpose of this book. As will be discussed later, these types of questions about the role of the author, the text, and the reader help bring into focus some of the tensions that exist in the Islamic interpretive tradition. Foremost among these tensions, is the uncomfortable relationship between the authoritativeness of the text, and the threat of authoritarian constructions of the text. For the purposes of this book, understanding the role and purpose of ambiguity in the authoritative texts of Islam is of pivotal importance. Much of the analysis of this book will deal with the extent to which ambiguity is part of the intended meaning of the authoritative text, and, at a more basic level, the extent to which ambiguity is purposeful in the processes and dynamics of Islamic law.

This study presents an analysis of the use of legal authority in contemporary Islamic discourses. I do not intend to analyze or generalize about all Islamic discourses; this would be empirically impractical and probably unwise. Rather, I focus on certain types of legal discourses that I characterize as authoritarian. As will be elaborated upon later, I am using the word "authoritarian" in a very specific sense. At this point, I should note that authoritarianism, as used here, refers to a hermeneutic methodology that usurps and subjugates the mechanisms of producing meaning from a text to a highly subjective and selective reading. Later, I will argue that the selective subjectivity of the authoritarian hermeneutic involves equating between the authorial intent and the reader's intent, and renders the textual intent and autonomy, at best, marginal.[9] Furthermore, in order to make the textual intent irrelevant and to abrogate the autonomy of the text, I argue that the selectively subjective reader will inevitably commit an act of misrepresentation or fraud as well as violate other conditions, as explained later.

This study does not address the political authoritarianism that seems to prevail in many Muslim countries. But readers of this book may draw whatever inferences they wish about the influence of authoritarian hermeneutics on social and political institutions in Muslim countries. This book cannot empirically verify the extent to which authoritarian methodologies of interpretation are prevalent in Muslim societies. Nevertheless, as a result of my personal involvement, as a Muslim and jurist, with Islamic communities in and outside the United States, I must admit that my own sense is that authoritarian hermeneutics have become rampant in contemporary Muslim societies. My impression is that this type of hermeneutics seems to have become widespread post-1975.

This book does not focus on case law adjudications or positive legislation in Muslim countries. Case law and positive law are the products of complex processes emerging from within the political structures and political dynamics prevalent in particular Muslim countries. Furthermore, case law and legislation in Muslim countries are heavily influenced by a synchronistic process that reconciles between French civil and American law, and Islamic law. This synchronistic process is not necessarily informative as to the mechanics of religious hermeneutics in Muslim countries. Nevertheless, as discussed later, there is at least one respect in which the transplanting of the civil law system to Muslim societies has seriously impacted on the development of Islamic law in the contemporary age.[10] The civil law system relies on centralized hierarchical structures that implement avowedly consistent and theoretically coherent systems of law.[11] The foundational instruments of the civil law system are systematic codes that articulate the general principles of law, and the specific commands that flow from the general principles. In the twentieth century, most Middle Eastern legal scholars were trained in the civil law system either in their own countries or abroad. These scholars, for a variety of social reasons, brought their training and intellectual orientations to bear upon the construction of Islamic law. Consequently, they often attempted to search the Islamic legal tradition for systematic conceptual frameworks. Furthermore, they tended to re-construct and distill the amorphous Islamic legal tradition into a set of clear and precise rules quite similar to a civil law code. Aside from purposeful attempts at systematic codification of Islamic law such as the *Majallah*, the training and intellectual cultures of these scholars exercised a subtle, but clearly discernable, impact upon their approach to Islamic law.[12] At times, this amounted to superimposing an awkwardly-fitting set of paradigms upon the Islamic legal tradition.[13] Although this trend so far has gone unnoticed, and it is fascinating in its own right, this study does not focus on it. I do believe that it is quite possible that this trend did exercise a corrupting, and perhaps authoritarian, influence on Islamic law in the contemporary age, but I have not chosen to fully analyze it. Instead, I focus this study on contemporary approaches that lay claim to a greater sense of doctrinal purity and authenticity. I center the analysis on approaches that claim to represent the authentic Islamic tradition and claim not to be corrupted by influences foreign to the Islamic legal tradition. Consequently, I have chosen to concentrate on a representative selection of *responsa* or legal opinions issued by an influential religious institution and a group of prominent traditional jurists in the Islamic world. Most of the selected *responsa* deal with legal issues relating to women. The primary purpose of this book, however, is not to evaluate the merits of the legal discourses on women in Islam or to brand contemporary Islamic discourses as authoritarian or non-authoritarian. Rather, this book aims to produce a critical analysis of the anatomy of authoritarian legal interpretive practices.

The methodology of this book is analytical and normative; I write as an insider to the Islamic legal tradition. It is appropriate to disclose that I believe in the divine origin of the Qurʾān and in the prophecy of Muḥammad, and I also believe that authoritarian methodologies of interpretation corrupt the integrity of Islamic texts and mute their voice. I also believe that authoritarian methodologies are bound to erode the effectiveness and dynamism of Islamic law. Consequently, after identifying the anatomy of authoritarian discourses, I present a normative proposal to uphold the authoritativeness of the text and limit the authoritarianism of the reader. As an insider to the Islamic tradition, I do not write as a social scientist who is simply observing and describing trends and tendencies. I am writing as a jurist who is evaluating the doctrines of his relevant legal community and proposing avenues for normative improvement. Admittedly, the way I identify and analyze legal problems is influenced by my training in and commitment to a legal process that might be described as traditional (or post-traditional) rather than a desire to validate any particular legal results. Implicit in my approach is a claim to authenticity, but as will become apparent later, I do not believe in a single or exclusive authenticity. I do believe, however, in authenticities, and I do claim that the authenticity that I present here is qualitatively superior to other authenticities discussed in this study.

This study makes a set of assumptions that should be laid out at the very beginning. I do believe in the authenticity of the Qurʾān as God's uncorrupted and immutable Word. Furthermore, I do believe that the Qurʾān is worth exploring, studying and, in one sense or another, following. I do not hold this belief as a social scientist who notes that the Qur'ān deserves to be studied because of the sociological fact that most Muslims hold it in high regard. The sociological reality is irrelevant for my purposes. I study the Qur'ān as a jurist who believes in the object of his study, very much akin to a Rabbi studying the Talmud or an American constitutional scholar analyzing the American Constitution. The constitutional scholar might believe in the normative vision of the good life that the Constitution lays out, but such a scholar may argue that the medium of language employed in the text of the Constitution does not match the vision of the good life adopted by the concept of the Constitution.

As compared to the Qur'ān, I do take a more critical approach to the *Sunnah* (the reported sayings and actions) of the Prophet. I do not make the assumption that every report recorded in the *Sunnah* is authentic or that the *Sunnah* necessarily reflects the authorial voice or intent of the Prophet. I do make the assumption that the intent and precedent of the Prophet should be determinative, but this assumption comes with many qualifiers that will become apparent later. I realize, of course, that for many Muslims, this is extremely controversial, if not worse, but I shall defend my point of view. Finally, I do make the assumption that the Islamic legal tradition and the Islamic legal process represent a search for the Divine Will, and that the Divine Will is worth searching for. I will explain the basis for this assumption, but, as is discussed later, I consider this to be an article of faith not verifiable or provable by rational means.

I will have an opportunity to elaborate further upon the methodology of this work, but for now it is important to emphasize one more point. The legal process, which I refer to above, involves a dialectical engagement with God. God, in one form or another, speaks to human beings, and human beings engage God's speech through interpretation and praxis. The dialectic is experienced both at the level of abstract interpretation and at the level of use and action. There is a thesis, antithesis and eventual synthesis. Arguably, the synthesis is not final or permanent but simply a temporary stage until such synthesis is challenged by a new thesis and so on. The authoritarian interpretive process, however, will either adopt a thesis that it transforms into a final truth or will reach a synthesis that it will consider final and unchangeable. Put differently, the authoritarian interpretive process believes that it hears God loud and clear, does not struggle with much ambiguity, and if it engages in the dialectical process at all, it will cut this process short.

*NOTES*

1 ʿAlī, trans., *The Meaning of the Holy Qur'ān* (hereafter, Qur'ān), 74:31. I have consulted Yūsuf ʿAlī's translation, but all translations presented in this book reflect my own understanding of the original.

2 Qur'ān, 74:31.

3 On the idea of followers of the veil and over-interpretation see Eco, "Overinterpreting Texts," in *Interpretation and Overinterpretation*, ed. Collini, pp. 45–66.

4 On the use of signs in interpretation see Eco, *The Limits of Interpretation*, pp. 8–21. Of course, I am not contending that only the mystic traditions developed this system of interpretation.

5 This seems to be the sense in which ʿAbdullah Yūsuf ʿAlī understood the verse. See, his translation, p. 1560 n. 5794. However, in the following footnote, 5795, ʿAlī seems to argue against this point, and suggests that it is perhaps better to avoid thinking about such questions.

6 Technically, Muslims, along with Jews and Christians, are among the People of the Book. But this verse seems to draw a distinction between Muslims and other believers.

7 Eco, *The Role of the Reader*, pp. 47–65; Eco, *The Open Work.*

8 For instance, Qurʾānic exegetes interpret the verse in question to mean that there are nineteen angels guarding Hellfire, and only God can know that fact. They do not ascribe a further meaning to the verse as I do. See, al-Zamakhsharī, *al-Kashshāf ʿan Ḥaqāʾiq*, 4:183–184; al-Bayḍāwī, *Anwār al-Tanzīl*, 5:160; Ibn Kathīr, *Mukhtaṣar Tafsīr Ibn Kathīr*, ed. Muḥammad ʿAlī al-Ṣābūnī, 3:570; al-Nasafī, *Tafsīr al-Nasafī*, 4:310; al-Shawkānī, *Fatḥ al-Qadīr*, 5:402; al-Ṭabarī, *Tafsīr al-Ṭabarī*, eds. Bashshār ʿAwwād Maʿrūf and ʿIṣām Fāris al-Ḥarastānī, 7:403–404; al-Qurṭubī, *al-Jāmiʿ li Aḥkām al-Qurʾān*, 10:52–53; Quṭb, *Fī Ẓilāl al-Qurʾān*, 6:3757–3758; al-Huwwāriyy, *Tafsīr Kitāb Allāh al-ʿAzīz*, 4:437; al-Ḥijāzī, *al-Tafsīr al-Wāḍiḥ*, 2:549–550; al-Anṣārī, *Tajrīd al-Bayān li Tafsīr*, 2:785; Abū al-Nūr, *al-Muntakhab fī Tafsīr al-Qurʾān al-Karīm*, 866.

9 By textual intent I mean that the text has a will independent of the intent of the author or reader. This "will" is embodied in the mechanics of language and symbolism used by the text. It also includes the texture, shape, form and socio-historical role played by the text. Of course, this is an interpretive fiction that anthropomorphizes the text, and gives an integral role to the text, equal to the role of the author and reader.

10 For a study on the practice of legal borrowing and its impact on the development of the law see, Watson, *Legal Transplants.*

11 Watson, *The Making of the Civil Law*, pp. 23–38, 83–98; Merryman et al, *The Civil Law Tradition, Europe, Latin America, and East Asia* pp. 975–979; Merryman, *The Civil Law Tradition, An Introduction to the Legal System of Western Europe and Latin America* pp. 45, 61–67.

12 Part of the nineteenth-century Ottoman *Tanzimat* reforms, the *Majallah* was completed in 1876. With the French Civil Code as a primary model, the *Majallah* codified Islamic law using the organization and structure of European civil codes. For more on the *Majallah*, see S.S. Onar, "The Majalla," in *Law in the Middle East*, vol. 1, *Origin and Development of Islamic Law*, eds. Khadduri and Liebesny, pp. 292–308; Liebesny, "Impact of Western Law in the Countries of the Near East," *George Washington Law Review* 22 (1953): pp. 127–141; Coulson, *A History of Islamic Law*, pp. 151–152; Cleveland, *A History of the Modern Middle East*, pp. 81–82; For an example of civil law approaches to Islamic law, see, Chehata, *Études de Droit Musulman* and *Théorie Générale de L'Obligation en Droit Musulman Hanéfite*; ʿal-Sanhūrī, *Maṣādir al-Ḥaqq fī al-Fiqh al-Islāmī*; ʿAwdah, *al-Tashrīʿ al-Jināʾī al-Islāmī Muqārinan.*

13 For a pronounced example of this see, Comair-Obeid, "Particularity of the Contract's Subject-Matter in the Laws of the Arab Middle East," *Arab Law Quarterly* 11, no. 4 (1996): pp. 331–349, the author attempts to superimpose civil law conceptual categories upon Islamic law, however, sensing that her efforts did not make much sense, she complains that Islamic contract law lacks a general theory.

# 2 The authoritative

*Background note*

Growing up in an Islamic Sunnī religious culture, one is frequently reminded by one's teachers that there is no church in Islam, and that no person, or set of persons, embodies God's Divine authority. The picture conveyed and repeated is one of egalitarianism and the accessibility of God's truth to all. Muslims strive to discover the Divine Will but no one has the authority to lay an exclusive claim to it. In this context, one often encounters the famous report attributed to the Prophet that every *mujtahid* (a person who applies original analysis and independent judgment to legal issues) is correct. If the *mujtahid* is correct in his or her *ijtihād* (the exercise of independent or original analysis on legal issues), he or she receives two bounties, and if he or she is wrong, he or she receives one.[1] In other words, one must try without fear of failure; one is rewarded for the success and the failure. The idea conveyed and constantly reinforced as part of the Islamic ethos is that Islam rejects elitism and emphasizes that truth is equally accessible to all Muslims regardless of race, class, or gender. The teachers will also emphasize that in Islam each and every person is solely responsible for his or her own actions and beliefs. No teacher, parent or ruler will be able to absolve his or her followers of their sins in the Hereafter. Because accountability is individual and no one may carry the burden of another, the net result is a diversity of consciences, beliefs, and actions. On the Final Day, each person will suffer only for his or her sins; no one will be made to suffer for the sins of another.[2] In addition, potentially every Muslim may be the bearer of God's truth. Consequently, it is this notion of individual and egalitarian accessibility of the truth that results in a rich doctrinal diversity in Islam.

A student commencing the study of the Islamic legal heritage is immediately struck by the complexity of doctrines, diversity of opinions and enormous amounts of disputations over a wide range of issues. Early on, the student learns that other than the main jurisprudential schools – the Ḥanafī, Mālikī, Shāfiʿī, Ḥanbalī, Jaʿfarī, Zaydī, Ibāḍī, and Ismāʿīlī – there are many extinct schools such as the schools of Ibn Abī Laylā, Sufyān al-Thawrī, al-Ṭabarī, al-Layth b. Saʿd, al-Awzāʿī, Abū Thawr, Dāwūd b. Khalaf (the Ẓāhirīs), and many more. Even in one school, such as the Ḥanafī school, there can be several trends, such as the positions of Zafar, Abū Yūsuf, and al-Shaybānī. Often, a student is taught that classical Muslim jurists frequently maintained that there is a long-established tradition of disputation, debate and disagreement that started from the age of the Companions of the Prophet and continued therefrom.[3] Furthermore, the student is taught that a major contributing factor to the diversity of Islamic legal schools is the acceptance and reverence given to the idea of *ikhtilāf* (disagreement and diversity).[4] One of the first books I was assigned to read in Islamic law, for example, had the enchanting title, *The Disagreement [ikhtilāf] of the Scholars is a Mercy for the Nation.*[5] This title is extracted from the famous *ḥadīth* attributed to the Prophet providing that the disagreement of the *ummah* is a source of mercy.[6] The book itself was a rather simplistic recounting of the positions of the different schools on a variety of legal issues. But the book and the traditions on which it relies reflect the fact that in addition to the idea of accessibility, the expectation of disagreement is firmly supported by Muslim sources. Not only is disagreement to be expected, but it is actually a positive reality to be embraced and encouraged. Early on, the student will also learn that when the Abbasid caliph al-Manṣūr (d. 158/775) offered to adopt *al-Muwaṭṭaʾ* of al-Imām Mālik b. Anas (d. 179/796) as the uniform law of the land, Mālik refused, arguing that there were many established juristic practices in different areas of the Muslim world and there was no legitimate reason to impose legal uniformity upon the various territories. Reportedly, Mālik argued that no one jurist or juristic tradition may have an exclusive claim over the divine truth, and hence, the caliph may not legitimately support one school to the exclusion of the others.[7] Furthermore, the student will be instructed in Abū Ḥanīfah's (d. 150/767) famous statement, "I believe that my opinions are correct but I am cognizant of the fact that my opinions may be wrong. I also believe that the opinions of my opponents are wrong but I am cognizant of the fact that they may be correct."[8] The basic idea is that a fair-minded person should not lose sight of the fact that his opinions could quite possibly be wrong and the opinions of others quite possibly correct. Yet, these various egalitarian doctrines do not go unopposed.

The same teachers who take great pride in the ethos of diversity and egalitarianism will also insist on the existence of an orthodoxy in Islam and the need for unity and uniformity. The orthodoxy is represented not only by a set of basic and common theological beliefs but also by a quite specific and detailed set of laws. So, for example, the question of whether women may lead prayer or whether women must cover their hair will often be declared closed to discussion or study. Often, the very same teachers who lectured on the doctrines of accessibility, egalitarianism and diversity will lecture endlessly about the dangers of *bidaʿ* (innovations), *fitan* (sing. *fitnah*, discord or divisiveness) and the evils of intellectualism and theological disputations (*ʿilm al-kalām*). One is repeatedly reminded that Islam is simple and that the *ummah* must reflect this simplicity. Similarly, the same teachers who proudly asserted the absence of a church in Islam will insist that the doctrines of Islam are, for the most part, unitary, cohesive, and self-evident. In this context, those teachers will resort to invoking *ijmāʿ* (consensus) and argue that most of the doctrines of Islam are agreed upon and are well-established. "*Al-Islām al-dīn al-samiḥ*" (Islam is the simple religion), they proclaim as they warn against the dangers of breaking with consensus or engaging in disputations.[9] At times, they will go so far as to declare that whoever violates a consensus is an apostate or unbeliever. Furthermore, depending on the orientation of the teacher, he may insist that the *Shīʿah* or *Ṣūfīs*, for example, are out of the pale of Islam. In other words, the ethos of egalitarianism and diversity coexist, often uncomfortably, with the ethos of structure, order, stability and unity. There is an undeniable degree of pride taken in the idea of accessibility and openness, but also anxiety about the dismantling of the authoritativeness of the Islamic intellectual inheritance.

The problem is only exacerbated by concerns over the infiltration and dismantling of the Islamic intellectual heritage by Western values and foreign systems of thought.[10] Some of my teachers, for instance, tended to brand the use of non-customary or unfamiliar methods of analysis as part of the Western cultural invasion. Admittedly, some of these methods did, in fact, originate with Western writers. At other times, however, at least from my point of view as a student, I would sincerely believe that my method was simply original and unprecedented, and was honestly my own. Nevertheless, the method would be stigmatized as Western simply because it was unprecedented or different.[11]

These kinds of social dynamics would hardly come as a surprise to students of the Muslim world and the legacy of modernity.[12] A number of commentators have already observed that the tension between modernity and tradition has taken a particularly exasperated form in the Muslim world.[13] My point is not to rehash these same sociological observations but to focus on the paradigms of authority in the theology of Islam.

It is certainly true that Sunnī Islam does lack a formal institutional and hierarchical structure of authority. There is no authoritative center other than God and the Prophet, but both God and the Prophet are represented by texts. In effect, it is the text that stands as the authoritative center in Islam. The Qur'ān often criticizes Christians and Jews for treating their priests and rabbis as mini-Gods, of sorts, instead of submitting to God alone.[14] This Qur'ānic polemic against the role of priests and rabbis has made the theoretical role of any religious authority rather dubious. During the Prophet's lifetime, there was no question that he was recognized as the authoritative voice representing the Divine Will. He was considered the direct recipient of God's revelation, and therefore, he effectively became the point of authority for the early Muslim community. However, with the death of the Prophet, the early Muslim community experienced its first serious crisis of legitimacy and authority. The first caliph Abū Bakr (d. 13/634) became engulfed in a civil war, the second, ʿUmar b. al-Khaṭṭāb (d. 23/644), and the third, ʿUthmān b. ʿAffān (d. 35/656), were assassinated, and the fourth, ʿAlī b. Abī Ṭālib (d. 40/661), confronted several serious rebellions and was eventually assassinated as well.[15] These rebellions had underlying economic and social causes, but they also reflected a crisis of legitimate authority. Early Muslims debated and fought over who become the repository of legitimate authority after the Prophet. There were several candidates to receive this rather formidable authority. The candidates included the Prophet's tribe Quraysh, the Prophet's family, the Prophet's close friends and Companions, any ruler or leader, regardless of how he came to power, and the Muslim community at large.[16] Regardless of the underlying political reasons fueling each of these conceptual candidates, a variety of theological justifications was offered in support of each potential recipient of the Prophet's effective authority. By the second/eighth century, the most serious and formidable candidate had emerged as a coherent and systematic contender: the law of God, the *Sharīʿah*, as constructed, articulated, and represented by a specialized body of professionals known as the *fuqahāʾ* (the jurists). It is fair to say that from the very beginning of Islam, the precedents of the Prophet and the Companions as well as the Qurʾānic laws formed the nucleus that would eventually give rise to a specialized juristic culture in Islam. But it is only after the development of the juristic corps and the development of a technical legal culture with its specialized language, symbols, and structures that Islamic law acquired consistent institutional representation. By the fourth/tenth century, the authoritativeness of the Prophet had become firmly and undeniably deposited in the idea or concept of Islamic law and in the representatives of Islamic law, the jurists of Islam.[17]

I am not arguing that, from a socio-historical point of view, Muslim jurists became the exclusive voice of authoritative legitimacy throughout Islamic history. Rather, it is more useful to think in terms of various "legitimacies" in Islamic history – political, communal, custom-based, tribal, economic, military and those obtained from belonging to organized and structured Ṣūfī orders based on mystical visions or truth. The jurists had become the repositories of a literary, text-based legitimacy. Their legitimacy based itself on the ability to read, understand, and interpret the Divine Will as expressed in texts that purported to embody the Divine Will. The Divine Will is embedded, and perhaps concealed, in the texts and it is the function of the jurists to locate and explore that Will. The jurists did institutionalize their charismatically based power into law guilds with sophisticated formal and hierarchical structures, and these legal guilds did, in fact, levy substantial coercive power at different points in Islamic history.[18] Importantly, state judges were often jurists trained and certified by these legal guilds. Typically, a judge would remain loyal to his legal guild during his tenure in the judiciary, and would often return to teaching in the guild after retiring or after being forced to retire.[19] Nonetheless, many jurists refused to serve in the judiciary, believing that this compromised their scholarly independence and loyalty to their law guilds. Islamic history is replete with examples of jurists who were persecuted for their refusal to accept any judicial or governmental positions.[20]

Muslim jurists' rhetorical and moral power was grounded in the fact that they could plausibly argue that ruler and ruled are normatively bound by God's law. The legitimacy of any political or social institution should and must be evaluated according to its compliance with God's law. God's law is not based on collective customary practices, pure reason or rationality, political expediency, or social utility. All of these elements may aid the textual search for God's law, but they may not by themselves be sufficient causes for God's law.[21] God's law must rightly be based on God's literal and immutable speech, the Qur'ān, and the precedent of God's last Prophet, the *Sunnah.*

There were various doctrinal manifestations of this basic idea. For instance, the jurists distinguished between a legitimate Islamic government (caliphate) and other forms of government by the fact that an Islamic government is based on and bound by *Sharīʿah* law while other governments are based on whimsical despotism (*hawā*).[22] Furthermore, Muslim jurists often espoused legal doctrines that were restrictive of the discretionary powers of rulers. For example, the jurists argued that the rights of human beings (*ḥuqūq al-ādamiyyīn*) are retained exclusively by human beings, and that rulers have no power of dispensation over such rights. These rights often included contractual rights or rights of compensation for injuries. The idea espoused by the jurists was that a ruler does not have the legitimate power to forgive, waive, or transfer such rights without the consent of the holder of the right.[23] The jurists often maintained that if any people, including rulers, usurp or violate the rights of any person, no amount of repentance will suffice. God will forgive the sin only if the usurped property is returned or another form of restitution is made to the victim.[24] Importantly, however, it is not reason or the state of nature, but texts, that endowed people with rights or denied them such rights. I, however, do not wish to overstate the case for textual dependence; Muslim jurists were often innovative and competent enough to use the text as an enabling device to go beyond the text, while at the same time exalting and honoring the sanctity and value of the text. The *Sharīʿah* often represented a normative conceptual ideal of the just and good life that is embedded, and at times hidden, in the text. So, for example, in the following passage the famous Ḥanbalī jurist Ibn Qayyim al-Jawziyyah (d. 751/1350–1) conveys a representative sense of adoration and reverence for the idea of *Sharīʿah* by stating:

> The *Sharī'ah* is God's justice among His servants, and His mercy among His creatures. It is God's shadow on this earth. It is His wisdom which leads to Him in the most exact way and the most exact affirmation of the truthfulness of His Prophet. It is His light which enlightens the seekers and His guidance for the rightly guided. It is the absolute cure for all ills and the straight path which if followed will lead to righteousness ... It is life and nutrition, the medicine, the light, the cure and the safeguard. Every good in this life is derived from it and achieved through it, and every deficiency in existence results from its dissipation. If it had not been for the fact that some of its rules remain [in this world] this world would become corrupted and the universe would be dissipated ... If God would wish to destroy the world and dissolve existence, He would void whatever remains of its injunctions. For the *Sharī'ah* which was sent to His Prophet ... is the pillar of existence and the key to success in this world and the Hereafter.[25]

Significantly, Ibn al-Qayyim goes on to argue that any injustice that might occur from the application of God's law must be ascribed to a faulty interpretation of the text. A faithful and accurate interpretation cannot and should not lead to an empirical injustice.[26]

Often the jurists conveyed the notion of the supremacy of *Sharī'ah* law through intriguing and multi-layered anecdotal reports. For instance, Ibn al-Jawzī (d. 597/1201) relates that the Buyid ruler 'Aḍud al-Dawlah (r. 338/944–372/983) once fell in love with a slave-girl and found himself increasingly preoccupied by her. The ruler ordered that the girl be drowned so that he might be able to focus his attention on more fruitful endeavors. Ibn al-Jawzī comments on this by saying: "This is clear and obvious insanity because killing a Muslim without fault is not allowed. And, his [the ruler] belief that it is permissible to do so is *kufr* (an act of disbelief). Perhaps the caliph (ruler) did not believe that this was permissible but thought that his actions were justified by *maṣlaḥah* (an act justified by the pursuit of public welfare). But [it is clear] that no *maṣlaḥah* may be justified if it contravenes the *Sharī'ah*."[27] We cannot verify the historicity of this incident but that is beside the point. Anecdotal reports such as this served an emotive and symbolic point; they are intended to invoke apprehension and fear of a life lived without the safeguards of *Sharī'ah* and subject only to the whims of rulers. Other anecdotal reports are more ambiguous and negotiative in nature. For example, consider the following report related by the Ḥanafī jurist 'Uthmān b. 'Alī al-Zayla'ī (d. 743/1343): "It is reported that 'Iṣām b. Yūsuf (an early jurist) came to the *amīr* (prince) of Balah, and found that the *amīr* had captured a thief. The *amīr* turned to 'Iṣām and asked, 'How do you propose we go about investigating this case?' 'Iṣām responded, 'The burden of proof is upon the claimant and the accused has the right to take an oath denying the charges.' The *amīr*, however, said, 'Bring me a whip,' and he beat the thief until the thief confessed and returned all the stolen property. 'Iṣām then commented, 'I have never seen an injustice more similar to justice than this (*mā ra'aytu ẓulman ashbah bi al-'adl minhu*)!'"[28] The reader of this report is left unsure what to take from it. The jurist appears reserved, just, process-oriented, and rather measured. The prince appears haughty and rash but he gets results. Does the report mean that the prince's actions were justified or unjustified? What is the precendential value of this report? It is not clear but this lack of clarity is exactly the point – the ambiguous space gives the jurist room for maneuverability and affords negotiative leverage.

Throughout the classical period Muslim jurists played a rather dynamic negotiative role in society. They often acted as a medium between the various social structures and political structures.[29] They were at times allied to the government and at other times allied to social forces, and often represented the interests and concerns of one to the other.[30] That is why it is fair to say that the juristic culture in Islam was semi-autonomous – influenced by the paradigms and institutions of the law, influenced by a variety of social forces and political powers but not entirely shaped by any of them.[31] Significantly, Muslim jurists did not make a direct claim to power despite their position as the representatives to the Divine Law. They argued that the rulers should consult with and rely on the jurists as they formulated and executed the law, but did not claim that they (the jurists) should govern or rule society directly. The rulers should obey the jurists because the jurists are the upholders of God's law, and the governed should obey the rulers to the extent that they obey God's law. For instance, Ibn al-Qayyim states:

> Properly speaking, the rulers (*al-umarāʾ*) are obeyed [only to the extent] that their commands are consistent with the [articulations] of the religious sciences (*al-ʿilm*). Hence, the duty to obey [the rulers] derives from the duty to obey the jurists (*fa ṭāʿatuhum tabaʿ li ṭāʿat al-ʿulamāʾ*). [This is because] obedience is due only in what is good (*maʿrūf*), and what is required by the religious sciences (*wa mā awjabahu al-ʿilm*). Since the duty to obey the jurists is derived from the duty to obey the Prophet, then the duty to obey the rulers is derived from the duty to obey the jurists [who are the experts on the religious sciences]. Furthermore, since Islam is protected and upheld by the rulers and the jurists alike, this means that the laity must follow [and obey] these two [i.e. the rulers and jurists].[32]

Importantly, in terms of the development of Islamic law, the adjudications or regulations of rulers had no precedential value as far as the jurists were concerned.[33] Regulations or adjudications by rulers might have binding force in their immediate and present context, but they were not integrated in the formal doctrines of Islamic jurisprudence. Only the *responsa* (*fatāwā*) issued by jurists and systematic writings by law professors were considered to be legitimate articulations of the Divine Law. Legal adjudications by prominent Muslim judges would, at times, be incorporated into the formal codex of Islamic laws, but only because these judges had proven themselves as legal scholars, and not necessarily because of their official position.[34] As a result, Muslim juristic sources did not, for the most part, preserve the regulations or adjudications of the various rulers of the Islamic empires, but they did meticulously preserve the opinions and precedents of numerous prominent, and not so prominent, legal scholars throughout Islamic history.[35] This partly accounts for the amorphous and evolutionary nature of Islamic law, which is contained in thousands of volumes recording the cumulative juristic wisdom of many centuries. This also emphasizes the fact that Islamic law developed through a cumulative, evolutionary, and often dialectical process. A jurist within a certain legal guild would write a commentary on a text or systematically extract principles and rules from a specific text. Other jurists would write a commentary on the work of their predecessor but in doing so they would incorporate the latest opinions and adjudications of other contemporaneous and prominent jurists within the same guild or even outside the guild. The commentator would elaborate upon, or often personally disagree, or note the disagreement of, some jurists with the doctrines of the original author. This evolutionary process would continue with each successive generation until a jurist, quite often the most learned and prominent within a guild, would write a legal hornbook (*mukhtaṣar*) synthesizing and summarizing the development of the law up to that point.[36] The hornbook would be used as an aid and quick reference to judges and students of law.[37] But then later jurists would write commentaries on the hornbook incorporating the latest evolving law, and the process would commence all over again.[38]

As explained later, the epistemology, structure, and dynamics that supported this evolving process of law are now largely dead. Islamic jurists do not play the same functions of mediation in the contemporary age that they played in the past. There are a variety of reasons for the disintegration of the traditional dynamics of Islamic jurisprudence. Primary among those reasons is the increasing centralization of state power, the nationalization of the private endowments (*awqāf*) that supported and funded the law guilds, the withering away of law guilds and their replacement with state-owned secular law schools, the adoption of the civil law system into a large number of Muslim countries, the development of enormous hegemonic state bureaucracies that co-opted and transformed many jurists into salaried employees, and the experience of colonialism that often methodically dismantled the traditional institutions of Islamic law under the guise of the imperative of modernization.[39] It is difficult to assess whether this process started with the centralized structure of the Ottoman Empire, the adoption of the Ḥanafī School of law as the official law of the empire, or the increasing reliance on *qānūn* (secular positive law) and *faramāns* (edicts) as the main legislative mechanism of the Ottoman rulers. But there is no doubt that the movement to dismantle the traditional mechanisms of Islamic law were given a great momentum in the age of colonialism and in the post-colonial age with the emergence of what Amos Perlmutter called the praetorian state in many Muslim countries.[40] With the widespread reception of centralized European civil law into Muslim societies, there was an inevitable marginalization of Islamic law and increasing shrinkage of the jurisdiction of Islamic courts. More importantly, as noted earlier, even the so-called reformers of Islamic law were educated in the civil law system and were heavily influenced by paradigms and theories of civil law jurists. Contemporary works on Islamic law written by lawyers, rather than activists, are replete with citations to French legal theorists and European jurisprudential theories of law. In the late nineteenth and twentieth centuries, the idea of modernizing Islamic law was often equated with the perceived need for codification. Significantly, even when there was no realistic hope that the codifications formulated by these lawyers would ever be enacted into positive state law, these lawyers continued their individual efforts nevertheless. Consequently, when one reads modern treatises on Islamic law it often feels as if one is reading a treatise on French law with the complexity and diversity of the Islamic legal heritage distilled into a set of code-like imperative commands. There are some Muslim countries such as Saudi Arabia, Sudan, and Pakistan that did not formally adopt the civil law system and either adopted a version of the British common law system or purported to continue to apply traditional Islamic law. However, this did not mean the survival of the epistemology and structure of classical Islamic law. Even in those states there was an increasing centralization of state powers and public control over the means of production of religious discourse manifested in the public ownership of mosques (*masjids*), the abolition of private religious endowments (*awqāf*), public ownership of law schools, and the placing of Islamic jurists on the state payroll. Furthermore, these states increasingly relied on statutory legislation or executive regulations in generating enforceable law.

Again, I am at risk of overstating the case because there are notable exceptions to what is stated above. For example, jurists such as Rashīd Riḍā (d. 1355/1935), ʿAbd al-Ḥalīm Maḥmūd (d. 1399/1978), Maḥmūd Shaltūt, (d. 1384/1963), *Shaykh* Muḥammad al-Ghazālī (d. 1410/1989), Shāh Walī Allāh (d. 1176/1762), or Muḥammad Zakariyyā al-Kāndahlawī (d. 1389/1968) employed the traditional methodologies of classical Islamic law with impressive creativity and originality.[41] However, one should note that the existence of these admirable jurists does not alter the overwhelming reality that the traditional role of Muslim jurists as mediators among the various forces in society has been substantially restricted and fundamentally altered.[42] Furthermore, in the post-1975 era with the substantial rise in the price of oil, the Muslim world experienced, and continues to experience, the re-emergence and near dominance of the puritan Wahhābī movement.[43] Although I cannot empirically verify this claim, my own distinct impression is that the symbolisms, logic, and language of the Wahhābī movement are exceedingly widespread in the Muslim world. As will be seen later on, the method and processes of the Wahhābī school are quite dissimilar to the methods and processes of classical Islamic law. While it would be an exaggeration to claim that the Wahhābī movement is affirmatively hostile to the juristic tradition of classical Islam, the Wahhābīs tend to regard this tradition as unnecessarily complex and messy. The Wahhābī movement hardly celebrates differences of opinions or juristic diversity. With the spread of the Wahhābī influence in the Muslim world, the impact of the jurists mentioned above weakened considerably. It is difficult to evaluate whether these jurists have been marginalized, but the casual observer will notice that they are often considered heretical innovators in many contemporary circles.[44] In any case, as demonstrated in this study, the least one can say is that while there is no doubt that the Islamic jurisprudential heritage is complex and diverse, there is also no doubt that there are tremendous pressures in contemporary Islam to deny and negate this complexity.

## *The notion of authority*

Before proceeding to explore the construction of the authoritative in the Islamic context, it would be helpful to clarify the sense in which I am using the terms authority and authoritativeness.[45] I start out by distinguishing between coercive authority and persuasive authority. Coercive authority is the ability to direct the conduct of another person through the use of inducements, benefits, threats, or punishments so that a reasonable person would conclude that for all practical purposes they have no choice but to comply. Persuasive authority involves normative power. It is the ability to direct the belief or conduct of a person because of trust. To use R. B. Friedman's helpful terminology, the distinction I am making is partly between "being in authority" versus "being an authority."[46] According to Friedman, being "in authority" means occupying some official or structural position that empowers a person to issue commands or directives. Persons in authority obtain compliance with their commands by displaying the marks or insignia of authority that communicate to others that they are entitled to issue such a directive or command. There is no "surrender of private judgment" in this case because a person may disagree with the person in authority and yet feel that there is no choice but to comply. The private conscience is not affected by surrendering to those in authority – it is simply that the private conscience is rendered irrelevant because of the recognition that those in authority ought to be obeyed. Put simply, you may disagree with the command but you comply anyway because you recognize the authority of the person.

Obeying "an authority" involves a different dynamic. Here, a person surrenders private judgment in deference to the perceived special knowledge, wisdom or insight of an authority. In Friedman's words, it "is this special knowledge that constitutes the vindication of the layman's deferential acceptance of the authority's utterances even though he does not or even cannot comprehend the grounds on which those utterances rest."[47] In other words, deferring to someone *in* authority involves deferring to someone's official position or capacity, but deferring to someone who is *an* authority involves deferring to someone's perceived expertise. The distinction is the difference between deferring to a police officer and deferring to one's plumber.

Importantly, Friedman argues that deferring to someone who is *an* authority involves what he calls an "epistemological presupposition." The person who is *an* authority and the person deferring to him will both share an epistemological framework as to a certain field of knowledge. Friedman states:

> [T]he claim that a person should defer to the superior knowledge or insight of another person presupposes that such knowledge or insight is in principle available – at least to some humans. And, in turn, the person who defers must share with his authority this same "epistemological" framework which defines what sorts of things are accessible to the human mind or to human experience, even though he is himself debarred from that knowledge or experience through lack of the requisite learning, wisdom, grace, revelation, opportunity, etc.[48]

As discussed below, I would add to Friedman's analysis that the shared epistemological presuppositions could include a common belief in a heritage or tradition.[49] Importantly, Friedman notes that deference to authority necessarily means a surrendering or transference of independent judgment and reasoning. The person who surrenders judgment forgoes the opportunity to personally examine and evaluate the merits of the thing he or she is asked to do or believe. Such deference necessarily means that one transfers reason to another person's will or judgment as opposed to inquiring into the substantive value of what the authority is commanding one to do or believe. Friedman explains this point:

> From this standpoint, then, it is the contrast between authority and persuasion through rational argument ... that is essential to the delineation of the distinctive kind of dependence on the will or the judgment of another person involved in an authority relationship. That is, the crucial contrast is between the case in which one man influences another to adopt some course of action by helping him to see the merits of that particular action and the case in which no reasons have to be given to a person to gain his compliance with a prescription because he "accepts" the person who prescribes it.[50]

Friedman's analysis partly turns on distinguishing between the surrender of judgment where one obeys without scrutinizing or understanding the justifications for a command, and persuasion where a person seeks to understand, reflect and decide on a course of action. According to Friedman, if one has to evaluate the substance and merits of a pronouncement before considering it authoritative "then the distinction between an authoritative utterance and advice or rational persuasion will have collapsed."[51] Hannah Arendt makes a similar distinction between authority and persuasion. In her view, authority is incompatible with persuasion. "Where arguments are used, authority is left in abeyance."[52] Authority, for Arendt, is what makes people obey without demanding to be persuaded.[53] Considering Arendt's understanding of the nature of authority, it is not surprising that she concludes that authority has vanished in the modern age along with the weakening of the belief in religion and tradition.[54]

While the distinction between being *in* authority and being *an* authority is intuitively sensible, Friedman and Arendt end up adopting a view of authority that is too restrictive. It seems unreasonable to equate the notion of authority with the practice of blind obedience. I, for example, accept the authority of my plumber and doctor. I accept them as authorities because I do not have the time, will or capacity to learn either plumbing or medicine. Furthermore, individuals might accept me as an authority on Islamic law because they perceive me to be more experienced or learned in the subject. I do not consider my plumber or doctor to be "in authority" because I am generally free to ignore their advice or to find alternatives. They do not have coercive power over me. As to those who might consider me an authority on Islamic law, I do not have coercive power over them either. They are free to ignore my counsel or find another source of information. Yet, I am extremely dissatisfied with my plumber or doctor if they fail to satisfy my ego by giving me adequate justifications for any course of action they might recommend to me. Likewise, individuals who choose to consult me on Islamic law are not satisfied if I do not adequately explain my reasoning on a legal issue. Does the fact that I expect an explanation from my plumber and doctor mean that I do not recognize them as authorities? Or, does the fact that my clients or colleagues expect to be persuaded that Islamic law requires the performance of a particular act mean that I am not considered an authority in my field? One final example: in a classroom I am both *in* authority and *an* authority to my students. However, the practices of anonymous grading and student written evaluations of the teacher, in many ways, weaken my coercive power over my students. Assuming that my coercive powers are seriously eroded, an assumption that I think is justified, what does the fact that I am "in authority" exactly mean? Assuming that I have no coercive powers, and that the students are aware of this fact, does it make sense to speak in terms of me having authority over my students? The answer is yes, but only to the extent that I have directive normative powers over my students. These directive normative powers could be supported by a variety of factors: the students trust that the school hires competent professors, the students reasonably expect and trust that if I like them I will support their job applications, or the students trust that professors, generally speaking, are experts in the fields they choose to teach. Importantly, however, the students are not transferring or surrendering their judgment to me. They are simply delegating a certain amount of trust to me and granting me the benefit of their judgment. That is why when students ask questions, generally speaking, a yes or no response will not do. They will rightly expect an explanation of my reasoning as a condition for continued delegation of their trust. If I continually fail to explain the reasoning behind my analysis, I eventually lose their trust and my authority as a teacher is eroded. Similarly, if my plumber and doctor explain their directives to me, I will tend to think that they are competent people and that they deserve my trust. On the other hand, if they issue directives without an explanation that sounds reasonable to me I will distrust them. I will tend to think that their inadequate explanations conceal ignorance, arrogance, dishonesty or ulterior motives.

I am not arguing that Friedman's concept of authority is necessarily flawed. I prefer to use the expression "coercive authority" rather than "in authority" because it is not always clear what is an official position or what powers a person "in authority" may possess. In underdeveloped countries, for instance, some officials "in authority" are obeyed because they have coercive powers while there are many officials that are safely ignored or disobeyed because one can obtain the benefits they offer through other means, including unlawful methods. As a professor, I am often not sure if I am "in authority," and if I am, what actual coercive powers I possess. As to authoritativeness, I agree with Friedman that absolute authoritativeness will often involve an unqualified surrender of judgment. However, my point is that the proffering of persuasive arguments is not necessarily inconsistent with the state of being *an* authority. Being an authority or being authoritative necessarily involves the element of trust, and any behavior consistent with justifying this trust, including the offering of persuasive arguments, will preserve or bolster such an authority.

This point is rather nicely illustrated in the Qur'ānic narrative. After God has chosen Abraham as a prophet, and after Abraham has brought the prophecy to his people, Abraham asks God for a demonstrative proof of His powers. Abraham requests that God show him how He can bring the dead back to life. Hearing Abraham's request, God asks Abraham, "Have you not [yet] believed Abraham?" Abraham responds by saying, "Yes I have, but I want to reassure my heart." At this point, God demonstrates His powers by resurrecting dead birds.[55] Furthermore, the Qur'ān repeatedly offers explanations, arguments or proofs addressed to the "already-believing", commenting that God offers this to them so that they will trust in God. One can hardly claim that these types of discourse constitute a negation or dilution of the Qur'ān's authoritativeness.

Persuasive authority does not necessarily involve the complete surrender of judgment or an unconditional surrender of autonomy. In fact, a complete surrender of judgment or autonomy often turns into a coercive form of authority. So, for instance, if someone brainwashes me or places me under hypnosis so that I obey without asking for reasons or justifications, it is fair to say that this person exercises coercive authority over me. I do not consider this person to be an authority to me because my slavish subjugation does not allow me to demand to be persuaded or convinced. The loss of my sense of self-responsibility – the fact that I have completely abdicated any sense of responsibility for my own welfare – leads one to reasonably suspect that I am under the spell of coercive authority. If, in fact, I do feel that my will and judgment have become irrelevant, that I ought to submit myself completely, and that I should abandon any sense of self-responsibility to the person who is an authority, this sounds more like domination and not authoritativeness.

At a minimum, persuasive authority involves the exercise of influence and normative power upon someone.[56] Persuasive authority influences people to believe, act or refrain from acting in a certain fashion by persuading them that this is what ought to be. It influences people to believe that acting according to a certain directive is consistent with their sense of self-responsibility.[57] In terms of the mechanics of persuasion, Joseph Raz's expression "exclusionary reasons" is useful.[58] Typically, a person will have a variety of reasons for performing or not performing an act. All things being equal, such a person will not have any particular reason to prefer one reason over another. In other words, many different, and often conflicting, inducements will exist for a person to do or not do something. An exclusionary reason will create some justification for picking a certain reason or set of reasons and excluding all other reasons. For instance, I might have a variety of reasons for eating or not eating something. It might taste good, it will increase my weight, it belongs to someone else, I need the nutrition, the food is not healthy, or it will displease God. An exclusionary reason is the reason that I will consider the most compelling, and the reason that leads me to exclude all other countervailing reasons.[59]

If I evaluate the various reasons and then decide that, everything considered, I prefer one reason to all others, I have not necessarily relied on the authoritative. Simply because I evaluated the various reasons, and preferred one reason over all others does not, by itself, mean that the preferred reason necessarily has exclusionary power. A reason has exclusionary power when it causes a person to defer to it, or to at least presumptively trust it, and when it prevails upon a person to suspend the process of evaluating any other countervailing reasons. In summary, an exclusionary reason is often the result of an encounter with the authoritative. I will close this section with a rather lengthy quote from the legal philosopher John Finnis. Finnis's description of the authoritative, other than being the most intellectually satisfying, will later prove very helpful in constructing the idea of the authoritarian in Islamic discourses. Finnis states:

> A person treats something (for example, an opinion, a pronouncement, a map, an order, a rule ...) as authoritative if and only if he treats it as giving him sufficient reason for believing or acting in accordance with it *notwithstanding* that he himself cannot otherwise see good reason for so believing or acting, or cannot evaluate the reasons he can see, or sees some countervailing reason(s), or would himself otherwise (i.e. in the absence of what it is that he is treating as authoritative) have preferred not so to believe or act. In other words, a person treats something as authoritative when he treats it as ... an exclusionary reason, i.e. a reason for judging or acting in the absence of understood reason, or for disregarding at least some reasons which are understood and relevant and would in the absence of the exclusionary reason have sufficed to justify proceeding in some other way ... This is the focal meaning of authority, whether that authority be speculative (the authority of learning or genius) or practical (the authority of

> good taste, or practical experience, or office ...), and whether the authority be ascribed to a man, or to his characteristics, or to his opinion or pronouncements, or to some opinion or prescription which has authority for reasons other than that its author(s) had authority (e.g. ... custom or convention).[60]

## *The authoritative in Islam*

### HISTORICAL DEBATES ON GOD'S SOVEREIGNTY

God, God's book, and the Prophet are authoritative in Islam – in fact, they are the only authorities that count. This statement has the comforting advantage of being crisp and clean but without explanations and qualifiers it is largely unintelligible. Muslims confronted this realization early on in Islamic history. ʿUthmān b. ʿAffān (r. 23–35/644–656), the third caliph after the death of the Prophet, confronted a serious uprising after he was accused of failing to govern by *shūrā* (rule by consultation) and of ruling by personal whim instead of according to God's law.[61] The uprising against ʿUthmān eventually led not only to his assassination but also to a series of insurrections generally known in Islamic literature as the grand *fitnah*. ʿAlī b. Abī Ṭālib (r. 35–40/656–661), ʿUthmān's successor, confronted rebellions by at least three main parties – a Syrian group led by ʿUthmān's cousin Muʿāwiyah (d. 60/680), a Qurayshī party led by the Prophet's wife ʿĀʾishah bint Abī Bakr (d. 58/678), and a rebellion by factions of the religious puritans known as the Qurrāʾ (the readers and reciters of the Qurʾān). Eventually, these puritan rebels became known as the Khawārij (the secessionists).[62] The doctrinal arguments of the Khawārij are important for our purposes. Initially, they supported ʿAlī as the legitimate ruler and fought on his side against the ʿĀʾishah faction in the Battle of the Camel (35/656). They also supported ʿAlī against the Muʿāwiyah faction in the Battle of Ṣiffīn (37/657). When ʿAlī agreed, however, to resolve his conflict with Muʿāwiyah through arbitration, the Khawārij broke off with, and eventually assassinated, him. The rallying cry of the Khawārij was "all sovereignty belongs to God" (*al-ḥākimiyyah li Allāh*). By accepting arbitration, they argued, ʿAlī had betrayed God by accepting the judgment of human beings rather than the judgment of God. The fact that sovereignty belongs to God, they contended, meant that the law of God, as enshrined in the Qurʾān, had to be enforced. Arbitrating a dispute, however, effectively meant that sovereignty was improperly delegated to human beings, and God's sovereignty violated.[63]

The reports on the polemics between the Khawārij and ʿAlī are fascinating because they directly deal with the meaning of God's sovereignty. In one such report ʿAlī purportedly hears the Khawārij proclaim, "All rule belongs to God alone" (*inna al-ḥukm li Allāh*). ʿAlī responds,

> This statement is correct but what they [the Khawārij] intend by it is wrong. It is true that all rule belongs to God, but these people claim that the act of governing

> belongs to God as well. The truth is that there is no escape from the fact, that for better or worse, people will have to rely on rulers ... Through rulers taxes are collected, the enemy is resisted, roadways are protected and the right of the weak is taken from the strong until the virtuous can enjoy peace and can be protected from the oppression of the wicked.[64]

In another report, members of the Khawārij state: "'Alī followed the judgment of people while judgment [should] belong to God alone." In response to this accusation, 'Alī gathered the people and brought a large copy of the Qur'ān. He touched the Qur'ān and proclaimed, "O, Qur'ān speak to the people" (i.e. inform the people of God's judgment). The people gathered around 'Alī exclaimed, "What! 'Alī, do you mock us? It is but paper and ink, and it is we (human beings) who speak on its behalf." At this point, 'Alī stated, "the Qur'ān is written in straight lines between two covers. It does not speak by itself. [In order for the Qur'ān to speak] it needs interpreters, and the interpreters are human beings."[65]

The historicity of these statements is beside the point. What is material is that they demonstrate that the issue of the implications of God's sovereignty was present and debated in the early Muslim community. In fact, these types of reports constitute a specific type of genre in Islamic discourses. The genre is structurally and substantively distinguishable in that the reports tend to have a similar narrative structure and they tend to problematize the meaning of God's sovereignty. For instance, in a report attributed to the jurist Abū Bakr b. al-'Arabī (d. 543/1148), we observe the same type of narrative structure and the same kind of skepticism expressed about the meaning of God's sovereignty. It was reported that the Wazīr criticized literalist puritanical approaches to legal interpretation by saying:

> As to their claim that the only relevant issue [in legal interpretation] is God's word, that is certainly true, but I would say: "the real challenge is discerning what God actually said." As to their claim that sovereignty belongs solely to God (*lā ḥukm illā li Allāh*) that we will not concede. It is a part of God's law that He delegates sovereignty to people in interpreting what God said. That is why the Prophet said, "If you lay siege to a fortress, do not agree to allow the people in the fortress to surrender according to the terms of the law of God because you [and they] do not know what is the law of God. Have them surrender according to your law [or terms]."[66]

These reports did not indicate a reluctance to accept the immutability or power of God. Rather, the phrase "sovereignty belongs to God" was co-opted into a resistance discourse. It was used as a cry for justice, fairness, mercy or any other intangible normative value. However, since God's sovereignty is represented by human beings who interpret and implement this sovereignty, effectively, this slogan became a rallying cry not for God, but for a specific political cause.

## SOVEREIGNTY AND OBEDIENCE IN THE QURʾĀN

The polemics discussed above were not solely the by-product of socio-economic pressures and political conflicts in early Islam. The text of the Qurʾān, itself, sets many of these debates into motion. The discourses of the Qurʾān repeatedly raise the issue of God's sovereignty and the imperative of obedience to God. For one, the rallying cry of the Khawārij, itself, is a close paraphrasing of the Qurʾān. So, for instance, the Qurʾān states, "The Command is for none but God. God has commanded that you worship none but God. That is the right religion, but most people do not understand."[67] Elsewhere, the Qurʾān states, "Jacob said ... None can command except God. In God I place my trust, and let all that [can] trust place their trust in God."[68] Furthermore, the Qurʾān specifically commands Muslims to apply the commands of God, and juxtaposes such commands with the whims of people. God commands the Prophet to judge according to the law of God and not to follow the whims of human beings.[69] At one point it states, "We [God] have sent down to you the Book [the Qurʾān] in truth so that you might judge between people according to what God has taught you. So do not be an advocate for those who betrayed their trust."[70] On other occasions, the Qurʾān informs Muslims that they must resolve all disputes by referring them to God and God's Prophet. In fact, the Qurʾān asserts that those who refuse to submit their disputes to the judgment (*qaḍāʾ*) of God and God's Prophet are not true believers.[71] Emphasizing this point, the Qurʾān remarks, "It is not fitting for any believer, whether man or woman, when God and God's Prophet have decided something to have any choice but to submit. If anyone disobeys God and God's Messenger, that person is clearly on the wrong path."[72]

The point here is not to delve into the interpretations of this genre of Qurʾānic verse but simply to emphasize that the polemics of the Qurʾān do appear incessantly to demand submission to God's judgment, law or rule.[73] But, as discussed below, the idea of submission to God raises a host of challenging issues, which partly relate to the ability to verify that a specific command is in fact coming, directly or indirectly, from God or God's Prophet. This is a matter of historical verification and authentication – how do we know that the command (most often preserved in some text) before us was in fact produced by God or God's Prophet? To put it bluntly, how do we know that someone did not lie and attribute something to God or God's Prophet that they did not in fact say? I will call this a matter of competence (authenticity).[74] Another issue raised is that of the determination of the meaning of the specific command. This is partly a matter of understanding and interpretation, but it is also a matter of ascertaining the "use" of the command. Put differently, the interpretive process will seek not only to understand the meaning of words and phrases but also the ways that the meaning should be used in application. I will call this a matter of determination. Finally, there is also the issue of who bears the responsibility for ascertaining and resolving the issues of competence and determination. What is the process and the institutional format for deciding authenticity, meaning and application? Is this left to the individual discretion of the followers of the religion or does it take some compulsory institutional form? I will call this an issue of agency.

The debates between ʿAlī and the Khawārij clearly involve notions of determination and agency with both sides appearing to hold very different conceptions of these issues. According to the Khawārij, the law of God is precisely determinable, both in the sense of its meaning and application. ʿAlī, however, does not consider the law of God to be easily determinable, and, therefore, he ends up conceding a much larger role to human agency. Importantly, however, the agency is deposited in the ruler or the arbitrators who ultimately get to decide the determination of the law. The Khawārij, on the other hand, do not appear to recognize the agency of either ruler or arbitrators. Their conception of agency is individual and personal: regardless of the determination by the ruler or arbitrator, the truth is the truth, and it should be ascertainable by any pious and just Muslim.[75]

I will address the issues of competence and determination in Chapter Two of this study, but for now it is important to note that all three issues (competence, determination, and agency) play a significant role in the construction of the authoritative in Islamic discourses. Assuming that whatever comes from God and God's Prophet is authoritative, there still remains a host of ambiguities that must be dealt with before the idea of Divine authoritativeness can assume any concrete meaning. The idea of Divine authoritativeness is laden in the very word Islam, which means complete submission to God – the acceptance of God as the sole master without any partners. In Qur'ānic discourses, submitting oneself to anything or anyone other than God is considered an act of *shirk* (associating partners with God).[76] This means not only that Muslims must be willing to obey the commands of God but also that they cannot submit to anyone else. Importantly, the Qur'ān repeatedly affirms the notion of individual responsibility and accountability.[77] As noted earlier, in the Hereafter, no person will be held liable for the sins of another, and no person will be able to absolve another of his or her sins.[78] This doctrine is, for the most part, consistent with the notion of the absence of a church in Islam. No person may unconditionally surrender or completely entrust his or her responsibilities and obligations towards God to another human being. In principle, each person must investigate and ascertain God's law, and then proceed to faithfully comply with it. No person may surrender his or her judgment and sense of self-responsibility to another when ascertaining and complying with God's commands.

On several occasions, the Qur'ān refers to the fact that God has made human beings the *khulafā'* on earth. *Khulafā'* could mean inheritors, viceroys or agents, but the basic idea seems to be that human beings were made the representatives of God on earth.[79] For instance, the Qur'ān states, "God has made you vicegerents [of God] in the earth. So whosoever rejects God, his [or her] rejection is against himself [or herself]."[80] Therefore, in Qur'ānic discourses, God is sovereign but this sovereignty can only be exercised through human agents who act on God's behalf. The human agents are bound to faithfully execute the intent of the Principal (i.e. God). The Qur'ānic verses cited above seem to indicate that the Principal here is not a disinterested party. Put differently, it does not seem that the human beings acting on behalf of God are independent agents authorized to exercise their own judgment in all matters and subject to the Principal only for the results of their work. While human beings are God's agents, they are restricted agents, bound by a set of specific instructions issued by the Principal. They may not act beyond this delegation and must, therefore, ascertain two things. Firstly, are the instructions truly, in fact, from God? And secondly, what do the instructions say?

The Qur'ānic idea of agency raises two distinct questions. First, are human beings the agents of God collectively or individually and severally? Second, what is the scope of, or how detailed are, the instructions issued to the agents? If accountability is individual and non-transferable, is it fair to assume that every person is God's agent in some form or another? If every individual is, in fact, God's agent, does this mean that every individual is obligated to search for, understand and implement the instructions of the Principal? If the response is affirmative, then how accessible, broad or detailed are these instructions?

These questions have engaged Muslim theologians for centuries and it is fair to say that a single response or set of responses has not emerged as the orthodox position. As alluded to above, early on, the Umayyad caliphs, in particular, claimed that agency lies exclusively with the caliphs. They argued that they are God's representatives and shadow on earth, and also that the nature of their agency is discretionary and unrestricted. The jurists of Islam, on the other hand, did not contend that they were God's chosen agents, but they did argue that they were the party qualified to understand God's instructions and so, effectively, they stood as a medium between God and human beings. The jurists argued that while human beings, in general, are God's agents, only those willing and able to understand the instructions of the Principal are rightfully equipped to mediate between God and humanity. Nevertheless, this historically based response does not address normatively the issues of the scope and accountability of this presumed agency, and to these I now turn.

As discussed above, the Qur'ān repeatedly commands that people obey the law of God, and, at times, speaks of the law of God as a set of specific and detailed instructions. Interestingly, however, the Qur'ān often speaks of the law of God as basically constituted of the imperative of justice. Typically, it states that God commands people to establish justice, or it dictates that the Prophet or Muslims implement God's law by enforcing justice.[81] The imperatives of justice (*'adl*) and equity (*qisṭ*), especially if substantive instead of procedural, reinforce the subjectivity anticipated by God's commands. What I mean by the subjectivity of God's commands is that justice and equity, as ultimate goals, tend to endow the agent with a considerable amount of discretion. If, for instance, I instruct my agent to do whatever is necessary to reach an equitable and just result, this type of agency is much broader than if I instruct my agent to perform specifically defined tasks. Importantly, the authoritativeness of the principal and the authority of the principal are different in each situation. Even more, the authority granted to the agent will partly depend on the Islamic conception of justice. Is the Islamic conception of justice intuitive or text-based? My purpose here is not to provide a thorough accounting of the idea of justice in the Qur'ān, but simply to point out that there is a tension in the Qur'ānic discourse between the idea of a restricted agency and the general imperative of justice.[82] Furthermore, I want to point out that the Qur'ān dictates the imperative of justice both as an individual and collective responsibility. Meaning, the obligation of justice must be discharged by the individual and by society at large. This poses the question of what is the proper balance between the demand on the individual and the demand on the collectivity? What if the individual firmly believes that the collectivity is in error in its conception or application of justice? Consistently with the idea of individual responsibility, can or should the individual stand by principle and refuse to obey the collectivity? I will later argue that an individual should, in fact, do so but in the form of what I call a "faith-based objection."

Another factor that the Qur'ān throws into the equation for authoritativeness is the idea of the suspended judgment. Often the Qur'ān appears to recognize that not all disputes or disagreements are resolvable, except in the Hereafter. As discussed, the Qur'ān commands that all disputes be resolved by referring to the Book or the law of God, and it also commands the establishment of justice as a normative value. But it also appears to recognize that not all disputes are resolvable on this earth, and hence, asserts that when human beings return to God (i.e. in the Hereafter) He will resolve all their disagreements. In one passage the Qur'ān states, "And you will all return to Me, and I will judge between you of the matters wherein you dispute."[83] The notion of suspended judgment coexists in the Qur'ān with the idea that the Divine books were sent to resolve matters on which human beings disagree. So, for example, the Qur'ān states:

> Humankind was but one single nation and God sent the messengers with glad tidings and warnings. And with them, God sent the Book to judge between people in matters wherein they disagreed, but the People of the Book did not disagree amongst themselves after the clear signs came to them except through selfish contumacy. God by His grace guided the believers to the truth concerning that wherein they disagree for God guides whom God wills to the straight path.[84]

Elsewhere, the Qur'ān conveys the same basic idea, "We did not send the Book to you except so that you will be able to make clear to them those things on which they disagree, and that it should be a guide and a mercy to those who believe."[85] Here, the Book has the power to resolve disagreements and to locate the straight path. Interestingly, however, there seems to be *de jure* and *de facto* recognition of disagreements. As to the *de jure*, the Qur'ān not only recognizes but even commands that the People of the Book rule or adjudicate according to what God has decreed to them. The Qur'ān rhetorically asks the Prophet, "But why do they [the Jews] come to you [Prophet] for decisions when they have their own law?"[86] As to Christians, the Qur'ān asserts, "Let the People of the Gospel judge by what God has revealed to them. If any do fail to judge according to what God has revealed they are truly iniquitous."[87] The disagreements or differences between the law of Muslims and non-Muslims appear to be legitimate, and appear to receive *de jure* recognition. Elsewhere, the Qur'ān speaks of disagreements and differences as a *de facto* reality, but goes on to intimate that such differences are part of the Divine plan. For instance, consider the following three verses: "If your Lord had so willed, He could have made humankind one people, but they will not cease to dispute [and disagree] except those whom your Lord has bestowed His mercy upon. *And, for this did God create humankind*;"[88] "Humankind was but one nation, but they differed later. *Had it not been for a Word sent by your Lord, their differences would have been settled between them*;"[89] "O humankind! We created you from male and female and made you into nations and tribes *so that you may get to know each other.* The most honored of you in the sight of God, is the most righteous of you, and God knows everything."[90]

The least one can say about these verses is that the Qur'ān tells a multi-layered and rather nuanced story about individual responsibility, the law, justice, and the expectation of differences. I do not want to draw any strong conclusions from the discourse cited above because its meanings are debatable, and because definitive conclusions would not be material to this study. Suffice it to say that in terms of understanding agency and the authority of the agent, the Qur'ān seems to leave much open to interpretation. If the agency is collective, then what is the meaning of individual and personal accountability? But if the agency is personal and individual, does this mean that the nation and community have no collective delegation? Who are the viceroys of God? Who are the soldiers of God and how can they be identified? What is the charge of the agency – is it to live by the law of God or is it a wider charge demanding the establishment of justice? Does the recognition of the inevitability of disagreement constitute a tacit recognition of the individualistic nature of the agency, and the results of its implementation? Assuming that disagreement is expected, is it justified and legitimate? Was the Book sent to resolve human disputes because it is the text that is the legitimate repository of all authority? Is it the text, symbolized by the word "Book," and only the text, that is authoritative and all else is tentative? Is the suspension of judgment until the Hereafter a tacit recognition that people will not be able to agree on the meaning of the text or the meaning of justice? Importantly, is the Qur'ān saying that God will resolve all disputes between Muslims and non-Muslims in the Hereafter, or is it saying that all disputes, theological, legal, and moral, will be resolved in the Hereafter? Finally and most importantly, is the sovereignty of God (*ḥākimiyyah*) represented by the fact that

God will resolve all disputes in the Hereafter? Or, is this sovereignty represented in the text, or in individuals, or in the abstraction of justice (the abstract concept of justice)? Or, is God's sovereignty represented by a human collectivity and if so, which collectivity?

## AUTHORITY IN ISLAM

A variant of the idea of suspension of judgment ended up playing a significant role in the development of Islamic jurisprudence, and in the emergence of the idea of diversity in Islamic law. In fact, the idea of suspension of judgment developed a strong sectarian following in early Islam exemplified by the sect known as the Murji'ah.[91] The Murji'ah argued that as to all major points of disagreement between Muslims, judgment, on this earth, should be suspended until the Hereafter when God will resolve all disputes. The Murji'ah emerged partly as a reaction to the puritanism of the Khawārij and the early civil wars between ʿAlī and his opponents. The doctrine of *irjāʾ* (suspension of judgment) became the earmark of political pacifism and moral relativism, and that is primarily why the Umayyads championed *Murjiʾī* thought.[92] Nevertheless, the Murjiʾah as a sect did not thrive in Islamic history, and they were replaced by more judgmental schools such as the Ashʿariyyah and the Muʿtazilah.[93] Both the Muʿtazilah and Ashʿariyyah were theological schools of thought, and while each has left an undeniable imprint on jurisprudence, Muslim jurists have resolved the issue of authority in Islam in a way that is conceptually distinct from the approach of these schools.

Before analyzing the issue of authority further, a methodological point is in order. At this point, it is important to clarify whether we will proceed in a normative fashion unburdened by the Islamic juristic tradition or whether we will proceed normatively but from within the Islamic juristic tradition. There are several methodological alternatives open to us. We could analyze the issue of authority from a normative rational point of view. In other words, we could look at the authority of God and human beings and their interrelationship from a purely rational or philosophical perspective. We could define our rational premises and then proceed in terms of what makes rational sense in light of our premises. We could even argue that from a normative point of view, a particular determinative value such as rationality, justice, well-being, or any other core value is the authoritative standard according to which we must construct our notion of authority in Islam. For instance, we might ascertain that justice is the determinative core value and then evaluate whether the Qurʾān can or does uphold or better fulfill this core value. If it does not then we would conclude that the Qurʾān is not authoritative or should not be authoritative.

Another alternative is to choose a hermeneutic approach. We could, for instance, take the Qurʾānic text, as a text, define what we consider to be determinative of meaning – the author, the text, the reader or all or none of them – and proceed to develop a theory of authority based on our reading of it. Continuing this approach, we would take the relevance of the Qur'ān as a given, and proceed with a close reading of the text in search for as conception of authority.

In the approaches outlined above, we need not pay much attention to the juristic theory of authority except perhaps to deconstruct it as irrational, unjust, hermeneutically unsound or naive. An alternative approach, and it is the approach that I adopt, is to accept the juristic tradition as part of the relevant community of meaning, if not the relevant community and to work normatively from within that tradition. The reader will observe that in addressing the matter of authority in Islam, I will focus exclusively on the juristic tradition and its particular conception of authority. The critical reader will also realize that this focus is not necessarily logical, for I could have focused on sociological practices and social constructions of authority, or I could have focused on interpreting the Qur'anic conception of authority and looked at the issue of authority from a philosophical perspective. Considering the alternatives, my focus on juristic culture warrants some justification.

It is my contention that the juristic concept of authority has become a firmly embedded part of Islamic dogma. As far as Islamic law is concerned, it is the juristic paradigms and categories that dominate all normative discourses on Islamic orthodoxy. To the extent that someone disagrees with this basic contention, my analysis will be irrelevant or unimportant to that person. Also, my purpose in this study is to identify what I have called authoritarian tendencies. As I argue later, these authoritarian tendencies co-opt the Islamic juristic tradition but essentially misrepresent and corrupt it in an unabashed result-oriented process. In other words, it is these authoritarian tendencies that invoke and utilize the persuasive effect of the juristic tradition, and, thus, force it into the realm of the relevant and authoritative. My interest is to engage exponents of authoritarian tendencies in Islam on their own terms not on terms that are irrelevant, or beside the point, for them. Furthermore, as I noted earlier, I accept, as a theological matter, the truth of the Islamic message. This means that I am starting off from a point that I consider to be authoritative as a matter of belief and conscience. I would like to add that as a matter of intellectual conviction, I believe the Islamic juristic heritage *should* be a part of a restrictive community of meaning when interpreting and reading legally relevant Islamic texts. This arises from an intellectual conviction in the value of tradition and precedent in forming both communities of meaning and cultures of authority. This means that as a normative matter, I am starting out with an assumption in favor of the relevance and authoritativeness of the Islamic juristic tradition. This is not qualitatively different from a Jewish scholar starting an analysis assuming the relevance and importance of rabbinic discourses on the Talmud, or a constitutional scholar starting an analysis assuming the relevance and importance of juristic discourses on the American Constitution. Nonetheless, it is important to note that accepting the relevance and authoritativeness of the Islamic juristic tradition does not mean accepting its qualitative superiority on all matters. As I argue later, with regard to certain moral determinations, one might be ethically bound to dissent from the communities of meaning constructed through tradition. I will elaborate this point when I address the issue of textual determinacy, and the anatomy of the authoritarian.

Islam's central organizational document, the Qur'ān, does not clearly resolve the issue of authority in Islam. There is no question that the Qur'ān regards itself and regards God as authoritative on most matters, but the Qur'ān does clearly explicate the dynamics of the interrelationship and appropriate balance between God, the text, the collectivity, and the individual. Admittedly, this is not the way that Muslim jurists understood the Qur'ānic discourses. They argued that the Qur'ān does in fact delineate the proper dynamics of authority. They contended that there is no question that accountability and liability in the Hereafter is personal and individual, and that the individual is personally responsible for ascertaining and implementing God's law. God's law represents the abstract notion of God's Will, but the nature and purpose of this Will, as will be seen later, is subject to debate. The individual's pursuit and implementation of the Divine Will is a manifestation of a person's submission to God. God's law as an abstraction is called the *Sharīʿah* (literally, the way), while the concrete understanding and implementation of this Will is called the *fiqh* (literally, the understanding).[94] The *Sharīʿah* is God's Will in an ideal and abstract fashion, but the *fiqh* is the product of the human attempt to understand God's Will. In this sense, the *Sharīʿah* is always fair, just and equitable, but the *fiqh* is only an attempt at reaching the ideals and purposes of *Sharīʿah* (*maqāṣid al-Sharīʿah*). According to the jurists, the purpose of *Sharīʿah* is to achieve the welfare of the people (*taḥqīq maṣāliḥ al-ʿibād*), and the purpose of *fiqh* is to understand and implement the *Sharīʿah.*[95]

The conceptual distinction between *Sharīʿah* and *fiqh* was the product of a recognition of the inevitable failures of human efforts at understanding the purposes or intentions of God. Human beings, the jurists insisted, simply do not possess the ability to encompass the wisdom of God. Consequently, every understanding or implementation of God's Will is necessarily imperfect because, as the dogma went, perfection belongs only to God. Muslim jurists had a particularly humble way of acknowledging this assertion. They would often write at the conclusion of their legal discussions the phrase, "And, God knows best" (*wa Allāhu aʿlam*). Symbolically, this meant that while the jurist was submitting his or her efforts for consideration, ultimately, only God knows what is right and wrong. This invocation was much more than a rhetorical device – it was an articulation of the very epistemological foundation of Islamic law. It ultimately justified the practice of juristic diversity and the culture of juristic disputations. In fact, the Islamic juristic tradition is replete with similar statements expressing the same epistemological idea. For instance, Muslim jurists repeatedly cited the traditions attributed to the Prophet stating, "Every *mujtahid* (jurist who strives to find the correct answer) is correct" or "Every *mujtahid* will be [justly] rewarded."[96]

Every adult Muslim, man or woman, is obligated to understand and implement the *Sharīʿah.* Accountability is personal and individual, and no single person or institution may or can represent the Divine Will. Hence the individual is directly responsible for seeking and learning the way of God – the *Sharīʿah.* In this context, Muslim jurists would often quote the tradition attributed to the Prophet stating that, "Seeking knowledge (*ṭalab al-ʿilm*) is a mandatory obligation upon every Muslim."[97] Importantly, although Muslim jurists did not explicitly contend that the "knowledge" addressed in this tradition is exclusive to religious knowledge (*ʿilm al-dīn*), they did argue that the effort to attain knowledge of the Divine Will is superior to any other form of learning.[98] The mark of the search for the Divine Will is the *dalīl* (pl. *adillah*). A *dalīl* is the indicator, pointer, mark or evidence of the Divine Will. God, for the purpose of edification, and in order to test human beings, and as a sign of His mercy and compassion, demanded that human beings exert an effort in seeking the evidence of His Will (*badhl al-juhd fī ṭalab al-dalīl* or *ṭalab al-ʿilm*). God, the jurists argued, placed indicators (*adillah*) pointing toward God's Way. God placed these indicators specifically so that human beings will engage them in an (*al-ṣirāṭ al-mustaqīm*). The purpose of the search, however, is not simply to locate the Path, but is the very act of engagement, and the very involvement with the Will of God. A large number of jurists even argued that the reason for the search is the search, and not necessarily to locate the Straight Path at all. In other words, the search *is* the Straight Path.

Because of the centrality of this discourse in Islamic law and the importance of the tradition maintaining that "every *mujtahid* is correct," this point warrants more attention. Muslim jurists debated whether this tradition meant that every *mujtahid* is potentially correct. Arguably, this tradition means that while every *mujtahid* is potentially correct, only one point of view ultimately reaches the right answer. The other points of view are in the end wrong, but those who try are rewarded for the effort. The reward or the knowledge of the correct answer cannot be attained on this earth, but will only be attained in the Hereafter. Alternatively, however, this tradition could mean that truth is relative and every *mujtahid* is ultimately correct, not in attaining the correct result, but in seeking the Divine Will.[99] As discussed later, truth here relates to the object or purpose of the Divine Will. God, it is argued, does not seek an objective or singular truth. God wishes human beings to search and seek for the Divine Will. Truth adheres to the search – the search itself is the ultimate truth. Consequently, correctness is measured according to the sincerity of the individual's search.

In this context, Muslim jurists discussed whether the *taklīf* (legal or religious obligation imposed on the person) is to find the truth or to simply perform the *ijtihād.* If one is obligated to perform the *ijtihād,* and is ultimately not responsible for missing the truth, then the emphasis is on the process and the results are left to God to assess and evaluate. Furthermore, if the emphasis is on the process, then a duty of utmost diligence, exertion, and even exhaustion in investigating the sources is mandated. It is not sufficient that one happens to find the truth accidentally. Rather, one is evaluated on the sincerity of the attempt and the exhaustiveness of the search for the truth.[100] It is through this search that God tests the vigilance and diligence of God's servants. It is the willingness to submerge oneself into this search that is the true sign of a life lived in submission to God. Mere compliance with the law is a sign of the submission of the will and body, but engaging in the search is a sign of the total submission of the will, body and intellect.

Furthermore, the wealth and complexity of the indicators exemplify the vast expanse of God's Wisdom. The diversity of the indicators is at the heart of the suitability of the *Sharīʿah* for all times and places. The fact that the indicators are not usually precise, clear or one-dimensional allows humans to read the indicators in light of the demands of the time and place. So, for example, one of the founding fathers of Islamic jurisprudence, al-Shāfiʿī (d. 204/820) had one set of legal opinions that he thought properly applied in Iraq, and a different set of opinions that he thought applied in Egypt.[101] Purportedly, al-Shāfiʿī read the Divine indicators to require different results in Iraq and Egypt. Furthermore, we see the same kind of reasoning reflected in Mālik b. Anas' (d. 179/795) argument that different juristic methods have developed in different parts of the Muslim world, and that it would be wrong to try to unify or consolidate the various methods into one.[102] This reasoning is also the genesis of the Islamic legal maxim that states, "It may not be denied that laws will change with the change of circumstances" (*la yunkar taghayyur al-aḥkām bi taghayyur al-zamān* or *al-aḥwāl*).[103] Following this logic, the jurists could argue that the *Sharīʿah* is immutable and unchangeable, but the understanding and implementation of the *Sharīʿah* (i.e. the *fiqh*) is, in fact, changeable and evolving.[104]

One of the significant debates confronting early juristic Muslim culture focused on the nature of *dalīl* or *adillah* (indicator or indicators). If God communicates the *Sharīʿah* through indicators, what is the nature of these indicators? Of course, there are many conceptual possibilities – God's signs or indicators could manifest themselves through reason and rationality (*ʿaql* and *ra'y*), intuitions (*fiṭrah*), human custom and practice (*ʿurf* and *ʿādah*), or the text (*naṣṣ*).[105] As several Western scholars have noted, which of these could legitimately be counted as avenues to God's Will was hotly debated, especially in early Islam. Some scholars such as Joseph Schacht have erroneously argued that early Muslim jurists initially were not very interested in the text (*naṣṣ*), and were much more prone to use custom and reason (*ra'y*).[106] Many of these scholars have claimed that it was only through the efforts of the jurist al-Shāfiʿī that Islamic law became text-based. Nevertheless, this view has been adequately refuted, and there remains little doubt concerning the centrality of the text from the very inception of Islamic legal history. Furthermore, Schacht and others have exaggerated al-Shāfiʿī's role in defining the centrality of the text in the development of Islamic jurisprudence.[107] In the first two centuries of Islam, one clearly observes a much greater reliance on custom, practice, and unsystematic reasoning. Both the juristic schools of Medina and Kūfah incorporated what they perceived to be the established practice of local Muslims, but both schools also struggled with the role of the text, its authenticity and its meaning. Importantly, early Muslim jurists struggled with methodologies by which they could avoid the use of what they called whim (*hawā*) in the development of the law. Whim, or a life led according to whim, is repeatedly condemned in the Qur'ān. In Qur'ānic discourse, *hawā* is consistently contrasted to justice, righteousness, and the Law.[108] Those who worship their whims instead of God, the Qur'ān states, are truly the misguided ones.[109] Muslim jurists struggled with ways to differentiate between law based on whim (*ḥukm al-hawā*) and law based on what they considered to be legitimate indicators of the Divine Will. Early Muslim jurists did not undertake a close hermeneutic analysis of the meaning of the term *hawā* in the Qur'ān, but they did utilize the idea of *hawā* as a rhetorical symbol against the idea of lawlessness. Apparently, what the early jurists thought is particularly problematic about the idea of whim was its unpredictability and idiosyncrasy. Whimsicalness was seen as the exact antithesis of the kind of disciplined and reflective life led in pursuit of the Divine Way. Importantly, as far as the law is concerned, the earmark of legal legitimacy became consistency, authoritative reference, and predictability. Increasingly, the text and the precedent of each school became the source of legitimacy in juristic thinking, and the use of pure logical reasoning and unverified empirical references became increasingly suspect. References to customary practices or general notions of equity (preference or *istiḥsān*) were seen as opening the door to idiosyncratic judgments that easily could disintegrate into whim. This does not mean that reason or equity played no role in the development of Islamic law.[110] In fact, Islamic jurisprudence divided all indicators into a rational proof (*dalīl ʿaqlī*) and a textual proof (*dalīl naṣṣī*), and in the case of Shīʿī jurisprudence, reason remained one of the main sources of the law. Some late jurists such as Fakhr al-Dīn al-Rāzī (d. 606/1210), Sayf al-Dīn al-Āmidī (d. 631/1233), Tāj al-Dīn al-Subkī (d. 771/1370), and Ibn ʿAqīl (d. 513/1119) extensively employed systematic reasoning in developing their juristic theories. In fact, in the case of jurists such as al-Subkī and Ibn ʿAqīl, it would be accurate to say that methodologically, they became the embodiment of the Latin maxim *ratio est radius divini luminis* (reason is a ray of divine light). Some jurists such as Ibn ʿĀbidīn (d. 1252/1836) and al-Shāṭibī (d. 790/1388) systematically integrated custom as a source of law.[111] In addition, many Islamic schools of thought accepted *istiḥsān* or *istiṣlāḥ* (preference on the basis of equity or public interest) as legitimate sources of law.[112] However, reason, custom, equity or public interest became concepts fettered and limited by the juristic method. They occupied roles carefully defined by the overall structure of the law. It is accurate to say that, in most circumstances, they were regarded as aids to textual interpretation, and not as independent sources of the law.[113]

A couple of examples will clarify this point. Reason was primarily used in the context of *qiyās* (rule by analogy). With this method, the jurist would use carefully defined analytical skills in deducing the operative cause or *ratio legis* (the element that triggers the law into action – *ʿillah* in Arabic) of a particular textual law. Confronted by an unprecedented case for which there is no law on point, the jurist would extend the ruling in a previous case (*aṣl*) to the new case (*farʿ*), but only if both cases share the same operative cause.[114] The derivation of the operative cause of a ruling (*istikhrāj ʿillat al-ḥukm*) was important not only because it had become the method by which the law was extended to cover new cases, but also because it became one of the primary instruments for legal change. If the operative cause changes or no longer exists, the law, in turn, must change. The Islamic legal maxim *al-ʿillah tadūr maʿa al-maʿlūl wujūdan wa ʿadaman* became substantially the same as the Latin maxim providing that the law is changed if the reason of the law is changed (*mutata legis ratione mutatur et lex*).

Reason was also used in the methodology of *istiḥsān*, which became a method by which a jurist would follow a certain precedent that was not directly on point instead of another precedent that was directly on point for purposes of achieving equity. But this exercise of preference was not a matter of a simple exercise of discretion. Rather, the jurists developed a set of limiting criteria that were intended to make the process of exercising a preference more systematic and accountable.[115]

Naturally, it is open to debate whether these various juristic methods actually restrained the discretion of jurists or whether they actually determined the results from one case to another. Nonetheless, at least in theory, the text represented by the Qurʾān and *Sunnah* achieved a clear rhetorical supremacy over discretionary methods of analysis. Furthermore, the juristic methods did force jurists to justify their decisions according to a language and a symbolic reference that is accessible and accountable at least to other jurists. Idiosyncratic decisions that could not be justified by reference to a restrictive community of meaning shared by the other jurists would be rejected and marginalized by the juristic culture. I am not implying that the determinations of the jurists were largely result-oriented and that juristic methodologies were used primarily as after-the-fact justifications for predetermined results. This type of generalization about the mechanics of the juristic culture would be inaccurate. As I have argued elsewhere, determinations in a juristic culture are often the result of imperatives dictated by political and socio-economic conditions, and the result of constraints imposed by the methods and practices of the juristic culture itself.[116] At a very minimum, the methodologies of the Muslim juristic culture compelled the jurists to explain their legal determinations according to a linguistic practice that is both accessible and accountable to those who are proficient in it.[117]

The average Muslim, however, cannot be expected to gain proficiency in the linguistic practices of the juristic culture.[118] As noted above, accountability and legal responsibility are personal and individual. Furthermore, Muslim jurists had concluded that as far as life on this earth is concerned, ignorance of the law, in most cases, does not relieve a person from the obligation to follow the law.[119] As to the Hereafter, whether ignorance of the law will count as an excuse depends, to a large measure, on the degree of diligence exhibited by the individual in attempting to learn the law. In other words, a person is liable in the Hereafter for negligence in learning the law, for following his or her whim instead of the law, or for arrogantly assuming that the law is whatever they want the law to be. In the Hereafter, God judges people on their efforts and sincerity, but this is because God knows the subjectivities and the inner feelings of people (*yaʿlam khafāyā al-ṣudūr*). On this earth, however, humans will have to judge each other by objective standards and, therefore, ignorance of the law cannot exempt a person from liability.

In theory, the pursuit of indicators and the understanding of the Way are accessible to all Muslims. In theory, there is no formal bar to becoming a jurist except the attainment of requisite knowledge of the linguistic practices and conceptual categories of the juristic culture. Importantly, Muslim jurists did develop a rather elaborate system of legal guilds, certifications, and insignia of investiture to symbolize that a particular person had attained the requisite knowledge to speak as a jurist.[120] Such a person had to master the Qurʾān, attain knowledge of the abrogated and abrogating verses in the Qurʾān (*nāsikh* and *mansūkh*), of Qurʾānic interpretation (*tafsīr*), of the occasions of revelation of Qurʾānic verses (*asbāb al-nuzūl*), and a knowledge of the science of traditions of the Prophet (*ʿilm al-ḥadīth*). Also required were an ability to undertake the authentication of sources (*tanqīḥ*), and an ability to weigh a variety of relevant legal factors pertinent to the deduction of the law, and then to identify the most influential among these factors (*tarjīḥ*). Furthermore, a jurist could specialize in jurisprudential theory, the positive laws alone, or the most favored opinions within a particular school among many other possible specialities. By the sixth/twelfth century a person could need more than fifteen years of undergraduate and graduate study before he could qualify as a professor of law.[121]

Muslim jurists also created a conceptual distinction between a jurist who is qualified to imitate and follow precedent (*muqallid*) and a jurist who is qualified to break with precedent and articulate new normative legal doctrines (*mujtahid*). *Taqlīd*, or being bound by precedent, was seen as the normative presumption of the law, and as a doctrine, *taqlīd* recognized the institutional fact that jurists are normally trained in already existing legal opinions and precedents. For a jurist to be able to perform *ijtihād* (a break with precedent to generate original and unprecedented law) the jurist had to have a superior amount of training. *Taqlīd*, as a doctrine, played an important symbolic role in creating predictability and loyalty within each of the legal guilds (*madhhab*, pl. *madhāhib*).[122] However, it is doubtful that the dichotomy between *taqlīd* and *ijtihād* was as clear or decisive as some contemporary scholarship has claimed. It is likely that *taqlīd* was asserted as a legal presumption of continuity. It effectively constituted a demand upon jurists to explain or justify changes if they were introducing novel elements in the law. Importantly, however, jurists regularly introduced innovations and changes in the law while claiming that they were, in fact, adhering to precedent or the true spirit of a precedent.[123] Muslim jurists could, and did, introduce considerable developments in legal doctrine without having to assert that they were introducing unprecedented changes in legal doctrine. This is not simply a matter of convenience or bad faith. Rather, in legal cultures, opinions that assert a continuity of doctrine have a greater claim to legitimacy and authoritativeness than novel doctrines that represent a clear and sharp break with the established doctrines of a legal system.[124] Therefore, while one finds in Islamic sources assertions about the closing of the doors of *ijtihād* by the fourth/tenth century, this was nothing more than a rhetorical device employed to resist the chaotic proliferation in new schools of thought and legal opinions.

One characteristic of the Islamic legal experience has been its irrepressible pluralism. In the first centuries of Islam, there was a proliferation in the number of legal schools of thought, each one named after its symbolic founder. By the fourth/tenth century, for reasons that are not entirely clear, a large number of these schools became extinct leaving less than ten in the *Sunnī* sect and less than five in the Shiʿī sect. Nonetheless, there continued to be a remarkable diversity in legal opinions and trends even within each of the surviving schools. The broad range of diversity, was such that it was fairly difficult to ascertain the predominant view within a particular legal guild, let alone being able to establish a predominant view in Islamic juristic thought as a whole. This pluralism was partly due to the epistemology of Islamic law that emphasized the multiplicity of God's indicators and that refused to invest a single institution with the task of elucidating or discovering the law of God. Although, as mentioned above, there were curriculums and systems of certification and promotion within each of the legal guilds, these guilds, for the most part, lacked a compulsory process by which they could censure or punish rebellion or heterodoxy. Often the legal guild would have to convince the state to become its enforcement mechanism by stepping in to punish a defiant jurist. However, this typically took a considerable investment of energy and time, and the state was not always interested in playing the role of the policeman for a legal guild.[125] A particular jurist would have formal power either as a professor over his students or as a judge with compulsory powers over litigants. A jurist might also yield power indirectly by being an adviser and trustee of the ruling class. However, this is not what established the reputation and authoritativeness of a particular jurist. Even more, the certifications and investitures bestowed by a legal guild upon a jurist would not necessarily establish the persuasive authority of a jurist. Rather, it was the charisma, learning, teaching, writing, and creativeness of a jurist that would establish his reputation among his peers and the laity.[126] It is not clear what exact role the laity played in establishing the authoritativeness of a jurist; this matter needs considerable socio-historical investigation. But one notices that the biographies of jurists written in pre-modern Islam would consistently comment on jurists whose classes were attended by large numbers of students and auditors, and on jurists whose funerals were attended by sizeable masses of people.[127] This is evidence that the popularity of a jurist among the laity was taken as an indication of success.[128] At the same time, official governmental positions or high-ranking positions within a legal guild did not guarantee the persuasive authority of a jurist. Islamic history is full of examples of jurists who occupied such high-ranking positions, but who did not have a persuasive impact upon their peers or the laity.[129]

This populist element in the evolvement of Islamic jurisprudence contributed to sustaining an ethos of pluralism and diversity. But, the methodologies of Islamic law, themselves, contributed equally to this ethos. With the possible exception of the doctrine of *ijmāʿ* (consensus), which we will address later, Islamic legal methodologies rarely spoke in terms of legal certainties (*yaqīn* and *qaṭʿ*). The linguistic practice of the juristic culture spoke in terms of probabilities or the preponderance of evidence (*ghalabat al-ẓann*). As mentioned earlier, Muslim jurists asserted that only God possesses perfect knowledge – human knowledge is tentative; it must rely on the weighing of competing factors and the assertion of judgment based on an assessment of the balance of evidence. Therefore, for example, Muslim jurists devoted considerable energy developing the field of *tarjīḥ* (preponderance), which was referred to above. The field of *tarjīḥ* (pl. *tarjīḥāt*)[130] dealt with the method by which a jurist would investigate the preponderance of the evidence from a set of conflicting indicators. Because of the importance of this issue for our discussion on the construction of the authoritarian, I will produce a fairly lengthy list to exemplify the type of factors the jurists considered in reaching a *tarjīḥ* decision. Furthermore, this list will give the reader a sense of the complexity of the juristic analytical process in pre-modern Islam. In producing this list, I have relied on Bernard Weiss' admirable synthesis in this field but have introduced changes to make the list more accessible to the reader, and to reflect my own understanding of works on *uṣūl al-fiqh* (Islamic jurisprudence) that Weiss might not have consulted.[131]

It is important to note that the field of *tarjīḥ* does not deal with reconciling between contradictory evidence or opinions. Rather, this field sets out methodological rules for determining the relative weight to be given to seemingly contradictory pieces of evidence. The process of reconciling between conflicting evidence (*al-ta'līf* or *al-tawfīq bayn al-mukhtalif*) through interpretation is a different discipline with its own set of methodological rules. For instance, assume that we have two traditions attributed to the Prophet, one that provides that melodic singing while reciting the Qur'ān is prohibited while the second affirmatively commands Muslims to melodically sing the Qur'ān.[132] *Tarjīḥ* would investigate which of the two traditions was more authentic and would determine, considering the totality of evidence, which was the ultimate rule of law. The process of reconciliation (*ta'līf*) would ascertain or assume the authenticity of both traditions and then proceed to interpret these traditions in such a fashion as to remove the appearance of inconsistency or contradiction. *Tarjīḥ*, on the other hand, does not engage in fictions of interpretation in order to resolve apparent contradictions but attempts to ascertain which substantive position is supported by the weight of the evidence.

The first issue posed by conflicting evidence may relate to the transmitter of the text. In other words, given the existence of different texts transmitted by different people, which transmitters are considered more authoritative than the others? This has to do with what I called earlier the competence of the text. In other words, it relates to the way that authenticity impacts upon the competence of the text. What follows are some of the rules:

1) A text with a greater number of transmitters outweighs a text with a smaller number of transmitters. Legally relevant texts, especially texts relating to the adjudications of the Prophet and his Companions, are transmitted by reporters who claim to have seen an event or heard so-and-so say such-and-such. The greater the number of reporters and transmitters of a tradition, the greater the likelihood that the tradition is authentic, and the greater the weight it should be given in legal analysis.
2) A text whose transmitter is well-known for his or her trustworthiness (*'adālah*) outweighs a text whose transmitter is not well-known for this quality; or a text whose transmitter is more known for his trustworthiness outweighs a text whose transmitter is less known for this quality. This is not an issue of whether the transmitter is trustworthy or not, but a matter of scale and proportionality based on the overall socio-historical reputation of a transmitter. This also does not preclude the possibility that a lesser-known transmitter, under a particular set of circumstances, might be considered more reliable than a famous transmitter if there is evidence to support such a conclusion.
3) A text whose transmitter is more known for his or her intelligence, knowledge, piety, diligence or meticulousness should be given more weight than a transmitter who is less known for these qualities.
4) A text whose transmitter who, at the time of transmitting a text, depended more on his memory from a teacher carries more weight than a text whose transmitter is known to have depended more on written material without a teacher.
5) A text whose transmitter is known to have acted consistently with what he or she transmitted outweighs a text whose transmitter is known to have acted contrary to the dictates of his or her transmission.

6) A text whose transmitter had direct experience of that which the text is about outweighs a text whose transmitter has not had this experience.
7) A text whose transmitter is known to have had more demanding standards in accepting reports outweighs a text whose transmitter is known to have had less demanding standards.
8) A text whose transmitter was personally involved in the event reported should be given more weight than a text whose transmitter is reporting with no first hand knowledge. The closer the transmitter to the actual experience, the more weight he or she should be given.
9) A text whose transmitter became a Muslim earlier in life outweighs a text whose transmitter became a Muslim later in life. Similarly, a text whose transmitter was closer to the Prophet during his life or who was one of the more prominent Companions should be given more weight.
10) A text whose transmitter is more versed in *fiqh* outweighs a text whose transmitter is less versed in *fiqh*. Similarly, a text whose transmitter was more intelligent or wiser should be given greater weight.

These are just a few of the balancing factors listed by the jurists that relate to the transmitter of the text. Samples of balancing factors that relate to the transmission, itself, are as follows:

1) A text whose authenticity is guaranteed by the scale of its transmission (*al-khabar al-mutawātir*) outweighs a text whose authenticity depends on the trustworthiness of the individual transmitters (*al-khabar al-wāḥid*). In other words, a text that has been transmitted by many people should be given more weight than one that has been transmitted by fewer people.
2) A text whose transmission can be traced all the way back to a direct witness (that is, a Companion of the Prophet who witnessed the event) outweighs a text whose transmission can be traced back only to a member of the second generation after the Prophet (*tābiʿīn*).
3) A text that is transmitted by identifiable transmitters, one from the other, outweighs a text that is simply in circulation but is not accompanied by a chain of such transmitters. In other words, a text that is considered popularly known (*mashhūr*) should be given less weight than a text that has a historical chain of transmission, even if lesser known.
4) A text found in a book that has a wide reputation for reliability (such as the books of al-Bukhārī and Muslim) outweighs a text found in a book that does not have as wide a reputation for reliability (such as the *Sunan* of Abū Dāwūd).
5) A text whose transmission is through direct recitation by one transmitter to another outweighs a text whose transmission is through some other means (for example, through study of books, attainment of licenses to recite based on examination, etc.). Similarly, a text that has been personally authenticated

by a teacher or is transmitted in the handwriting of a teacher outweighs a text that has simply been entrusted to a student or is transmitted in the handwriting of a student.

6) A text that transmits the actual words of the Prophet outweighs a text that transmits the Prophet's meaning but not his actual words.
7) A text that has been transmitted by a woman sitting behind a veil (*ḥijāb*) is given less weight than a text transmitted by a woman not sitting behind a veil.
8) A text that has been transmitted in different versions is given less weight than a text that has been transmitted in a single version.
9) A text whose authenticity is disagreed upon is given less weight than a text whose authenticity is agreed upon.
10) A text whose context and circumstances is known is given more weight than a text whose context or circumstances is not known.
11) A text that reports the words of the Prophet should be given more weight than a text that reports the actions of the Prophet.
12) A text that reports the words of the Prophet should be given more weight than a text that reports an incident in which the Prophet was silent.
13) A text that is reported by a single transmitter but that does not have widespread public consequences is given more weight than a text that is reported by a single transmitter but that does have widespread public consequences.
14) A text that is reported by a transmitter that might have personal interest in the transmission is given less weight than a text that is reported by a transmitter that might have less personal interest in the transmission.

Balancing the evidence and reaching a preponderance of belief may relate to the meaning or the understanding of the text instead of authenticity. What follows is a sample of the methodological rules that relate to interpretation or the determination of meaning:

1) A positive command (do such-and-such) outweighs a negative command (do not do such-and-such).
2) A grant of freedom of action (*mubīḥ*) outweighs a command.
3) An assertion (*khabar*) outweighs a command.
4) An assertion outweighs a granting of freedom of action.
5) An expression that has a single literal meaning outweighs a homonym.
6) An expression that is clear and precise outweighs an expression that is figurative.
7) A complete expression outweighs an elliptical expression.
8) An expression that is accompanied by an emphasizer (*mu'akkid*) outweighs an expression that is not.
9) Congruent-implication outweighs counter-implication.

10) A specific expression outweighs a general expression.
11) A definite plural (for example, "the thieves") outweighs a common noun with definite article (for example, "the thief") as an indication of general reference.
12) A text that signifies both a rule and the occasioning factor behind it outweighs a text that signifies only a rule.
13) A saying of the Prophet (or saying expressing a consensus) outweighs a deed.
14) A saying corroborated by a deed outweighs a mere saying.
15) A text that includes additional matter or elaborations outweighs a text that omits this matter.
16) The linguistic meaning of words outweighs their legal meaning unless there is evidence that the text intended the legal meaning of words.
17) What is known to occur in human experience outweighs what normally does not occur in human experience.
18) Interpretations that produce rational results outweigh interpretations that do not produce rational results.
19) Texts that set out non-contingent results outweigh texts that set out contingent results.
20) Texts that identify the operative cause of the law outweigh texts that do not do so.
21) A text that transmits claims of specific injunctions outweighs a text that transmits claims of a consensus because we do not know if the consensus ever took place.
22) A consensus of the entire community that includes the jurists outweighs a consensus of jurists alone.
23) A consensus of the Companions of the Prophet outweighs a consensus of the following generations.
24) An established or uncontested consensus of a past generation outweighs an evolving or contested consensus of a living generation. Similarly, a consensus of a living generation that is uncontested and firmly established outweighs the consensus of a past generation that is contested.
25) If the community is divided into two opinions on a certain matter, but there is a claim of consensus that a third opinion or alternative point of view is excluded from consideration, and there is a claim of consensus that the third opinion is *not* excluded from consideration, the claim of non-exclusion outweighs the claim of exclusion.
26) The consensus of jurists who are specialized in jurisprudential theory (*uṣūl*) outweighs the consensus of jurists who are specialized in positive laws (*furūʿ*) alone.
27) The opinions of jurists who are specialists in jurisprudential theory outweigh the opinions of jurists who are specialists in positive law even if the opinions of the former group include the views of innovators.

28) The view of a qualified specialist in jurisprudential theory (*uṣūlī*) outweighs the views of a jurist who is a specialist in positive laws (*furūʿī*) even if the *uṣūlī* is an innovator (*mujtahid mubtadiʿ*).
29) An opinion that guards against cases of legitimate doubt outweighs an opinion that does not. So, for instance, an opinion that would guard against criminal punishments in cases of doubt outweighs an opinion that imposes punishments even in cases of doubt.

Balancing of evidence and reaching a preponderance of belief may relate to what the texts signify in terms of specific legal rules or principles. What follows is a sample:

1) A rule that forbids, outweighs one that allows freedom of action.
2) A rule that forbids, outweighs one that imposes an obligation.
3) A rule that requires more, outweighs a rule that requires less.
4) A normative rule takes precedence over a non-normative rule.
5) A rule that imposes what is reasonable, outweighs a rule that imposes what is unreasonable.
6) A rule that is rationally acceptable outweighs a rule that is rationally unacceptable.
7) A rule that imposes more, outweighs a rule that imposes less.
8) A rule that exculpates outweighs a rule that inculpates.
9) A rule that avoids punishments outweighs a rule that imposes punishments.
10) A rule that recognizes the validity of legal acts (for example, sales and contracts) outweighs a rule that invalidates legal acts.
11) A rule that does not result in hardship outweighs a rule that does result in hardship.
12) A rule that has limited consequences, outweighs a rule that has broad consequences.
13) The greater the consequences of a rule, the more certitude there should be about its authenticity and correctness.
14) A rule that is more cautious, outweighs a rule that is less cautious of committing something forbidden.
15) A rule that is the product of less interpretation, outweighs a rule that is the product of more interpretation.
16) A rule that is supported by the Qurʾān outweighs a rule that is not supported by the Qurʾān.
17) A rule that has been followed and implemented by the Companions of the Prophet and/or the founders of the four main Sunnī schools (al-Shāfiʿī, Mālik, Aḥmad b. Ḥanbal, and Abū Ḥanīfah) outweighs a rule that is not similarly supported.
18) A rule that is accompanied by an explanation or justification outweighs a rule that is not accompanied by an explanation or justification.

19) A rule that establishes freedom (*ḥurriyyah*) outweighs a rule that negates freedom (e.g. a rule that emancipates slaves or supports the freedom of divorce).
20) A rule that is supported by reason outweighs a rule that is not supported by reason.
21) A rule that begets facility and ease outweighs a rule that does not.
22) A rule that supports public or general interests outweighs a rule that supports private or specific interests.
23) A rule that furthers the objective of the law in achieving the welfare of human beings (*taḥqīq maṣāliḥ al-ʿibād*) outweighs a rule that does not further that objective.

Balancing of evidence and reaching a preponderance of belief may relate to conflicts between analogies. As noted above, analogy involves the extension of an original rule or case (*al-aṣl*) to a new case (*al-farʿ*). What follows are some of the rules that apply when weighing between conflicting analogies:

1) An analogy involving an original rule (*aṣl*) that is certain outweighs an analogy involving an original rule that is merely probable.
2) An analogy involving an original rule whose non-abrogation is agreed upon outweighs an analogy involving an original rule whose abrogation is disputed.
3) An analogy performed according to the systematic methodologies of analogy outweighs an analogy not performed according to the systematic methodologies of analogy.
4) An analogy involving an original rule whose operative cause (*ʿillah*) is agreed upon by those jurists who accept the use of analogy outweighs an analogy whose operative cause is not agreed upon by those jurists who accept analogy.
5) An analogy involving a probable (*ẓannī*) original rule that conforms to systematic methodologies of analogy outweighs an analogy involving a certain (*qaṭʿī*) original rule that does not conform to these systematic methodologies.
6) An analogy involving a probable original rule on whose operative cause there is agreement outweighs an analogy involving a certain original rule on whose operative cause there is disagreement.
7) An analogy involving an original rule based on certain evidence but the evidence of the operative cause of which is weak, outweighs an analogy involving an original rule based on weak evidence but the operative cause of which there is certain evidence.
8) As a general matter, the stronger the evidence identifying the operative cause of a rule, the stronger the rule by analogy. Therefore, an analogy involving a more probable operative cause outweighs an analogy involving a less probable operative cause.

9) An analogy involving an original rule based on less reliable evidence but the operative cause of which is agreed upon, outweighs an analogy involving an original rule based on more reliable evidence but the operative cause of which is controversial.
10) An analogy involving an original rule the operative cause of which was extracted from revealed texts, outweighs an analogy involving an original rule the operative cause of which was inferred by reasoning.
11) An analogy involving an original rule the operative cause of which was explicitly stated by the text, outweighs an analogy involving an original rule the operative cause of which was not explicitly stated by the text.
12) An analogy involving an operative cause that has been subjected to the method of elimination of alternatives, outweighs an analogy involving an operative cause that has been ascertained through the test of suitability.
13) An analogy involving an operative cause that has been ascertained through the method of elimination of alternatives, outweighs an analogy involving an operative cause that has been ascertained through the method of concomitance.
14) An analogy involving a determinate operative cause outweighs an analogy involving an indeterminate operative cause.
15) An analogy involving a simple operative cause outweighs an analogy involving a complex operative cause that has a number of features.
16) An analogy involving an operative cause that has been ascertained by reference to the purpose of the law relating to the requirement of achieving the welfare of human beings (*taḥqīq maṣāliḥ al-ʿibād*), outweighs an analogy involving an operative cause that has been ascertained with reference to some other kind of legal purpose.
17) An analogy involving an operative cause intended to serve the public welfare outweighs an analogy involving an operative cause intended to serve other purposes.
18) An analogy involving an operative cause, the ascertainment of which is explained and justified, outweighs an analogy involving an operative cause that is not similarly explained and justified.
19) An ascertainment of an operative cause that is supported by numerous citations outweighs an ascertainment of an operative cause that is not supported by many citations.
20) The greater the similarity between the operative cause in an original rule and the operative cause in a new rule, the more authoritative the analogy.
21) An analogy based on an operative cause that can apply to a variety of new cases outweighs an analogy based on an operative cause that applies only to specific cases.
22) An analogy based on an operative cause that exculpates in cases of doubt outweighs an analogy based on an operative cause that inculpates despite the existence of doubt.

23) An operative cause that relates to a human necessity outweighs an operative cause that relates to a need or luxury. An operative cause that relates to a human need outweighs an operative cause that relates to a luxury.
24) An operative cause that relates to something essential and basic in religion outweighs an operative cause that relates to an ancillary matter in religion.
25) An operative cause that relates to the preservation of human life outweighs an operative cause that relates to the protection of religion.
26) An operative cause that relates to the rights of human beings (*ḥuqūq al-ʿibād*) outweighs an operative cause that relates to the rights of God (*ḥuqūq Allāh*).
27) An operative cause that is supported by rational proofs outweighs an operative cause that is not supported by rational proofs.
28) An operative cause that is intended to alleviate hardship outweighs an operative cause that is not intended to do so.[133]

The rules outlined above are not intended to be determinate factors; they are rules of thumb intended to guide the process of balancing between competing factors. Naturally, this process does not produce uniformity of results and it is not intended to do so. Additionally, in setting out these rules, the jurists would often engage in disputations with interlocutors, and freely admit that there are disagreements over the appropriateness of one rule or another. The end result was a considerable degree of pluralism in legal determinations. Muslim jurists did develop a doctrine of *taṣḥīḥ* (literally correction) according to which a jurist would consider determinations of *tarjīḥ* by a variety of jurists within a certain school, and consolidate these determinations into a set of prevailing opinions or attempt to identify the most correct opinions.[134] In the process of *taṣḥīḥ*, a jurist would also try to identify the weakest or most marginal opinions within a legal guild, and thus contribute to the ejection of these opinions from the evolutionary process of the legal guild. Nonetheless, this was a subjective analytical process that could be accepted or rejected by other jurists. Perhaps if the jurist performing the *taṣḥīḥ* was sufficiently high-ranking and was highly regarded within a particular legal guild, his efforts would be given more weight, but the fact remained that, like *tarjīḥ*, *taṣḥīḥ* relied on the evaluation of a variety of analytical factors and a subjective balancing process. In fact, from a methodological point of view, *taṣḥīḥ* was just another form of, or perhaps an institutionally higher level of, *tarjīḥ*.

The subjectivity and indeterminacy of the Islamic juristic process did not pose an epistemological problem. The various methodological tools of Islamic jurisprudence, and we have addressed only a few of them, were designed to produce accountability and not uniformity. By forcing them to set out their evidence and methodological processes, jurists could be engaged and held accountable. Therefore, Muslim jurists would often follow the discussion on *tarjīḥ* and the balancing of evidence with a discussion on the ethics of disputation – the acceptable manners for jurists to dispute and argue over issues (*adab al-munāẓarah* or *al-jadal wa al-munāẓarah*).[135] Other than the fact that the competence of a jurist in the art of disputation would often augment and promote a jurist's reputation, the field of the ethics of disputation reaffirmed the linguistic *practice* of the juristic culture – a culture that valued the process of disputation more than the results.

This does not mean that Muslim jurists were not concerned with results or that they believed that all opinions are equally valid or plausible. In fact, they were quite concerned about the point at which pluralism becomes chaotic fragmentation, and as will be seen below, attempted to establish an epistemology of consolidation and unification. In spite of its indeterminacies, the jurists saw the juristic method, as legitimate because of its reliance on indicators and its accountability. If God's Will is manifested in text, then methodologies that systematically engage the text outweigh any non-text based process. Muslim jurists repeatedly express this idea, and so, for example, *Imām al-Ḥaramayn* al-Juwaynī (d. 478/1085), citing al-Shāfiʿī, argues that all human conduct and events are subject to God's legislation. Asserting that there can be no event or matter that is not subject to the rule of *Sharīʿah* he states:

> All meanings [of things or events], if based on systematic principles and disciplined by text, become subject to the limitations set by the Legislator. But if one does not require that [meanings] be founded on systematic principles, then there will be no disciplined limitations and the matter will get out of hand. The law of *Sharīʿah* will be subject only to the vagaries of opinions, and will be based on pursuing the wisdom of the wise. As a result, the wise will become like prophets who do not have to base their insights on systematic principles. This would degrade the dignity of the *Sharīʿah*, and every person will do and think whatever he pleases without any limitations. And, then every age, place and culture will invent whatever it wants (and attribute it to the *Sharīʿah*).[136]

In the absence of an established hierarchical structure that would possess the formal authority to legitimate the results of the juristic process, Muslim jurists placed much emphasis on the duty of diligence. Diligence and adherence to systematic jurisprudential methods would be the earmark of legitimacy. A jurist was obligated to exert the utmost effort in searching for God's law while following systematic principles of analysis. The Arabic terminology used in this context was *badhl al-juhd*, *badhl al-wusʿ*, *jahd al-qarīḥa*, or *istifrāgh al-wusʿ* which, in this context, basically meant expending every possible effort in conscientiously and diligently searching and evaluating the indicators, and then applying systematic analytical principles in reaching a result.[137] The symbolic construct here is one of not just exertion, but exhaustion – if the jurist is negligent in the search and the analysis, he is committing a sin and will be held liable in the Hereafter.[138] Furthermore, if material damage results from the issuance of negligent *responsa* or adjudications a jurist may be held financially liable.[139] There was no formal process for de-certification or de-investiture, and save for the rare occurrence of a trial for heresy, the main force against negligent jurists was the censure of their peers or the refusal of a judge to accept their *responsa* as authoritative in adjudications. Jurists often did engage in polemics against each other, accusing each other of ignorance or lack of diligence.[140] We do not have extensive socio-legal studies demonstrating the impact of such peer censure upon the social position of a jurist. Most of the anecdotal evidence that we do have involves the persecution of particularly gifted jurists by petty colleagues who were motivated by professional jealousies.[141]

Muslim jurists also defended the position and integrity of the juristic culture against outside competitors. They often engaged in polemics against self-declared *Sharīʿah* experts or those who the jurists considered to be pretenders in the field. We do not know much about these pretenders other than the fact that they apparently employed the symbols of the linguistic practice of the juristic culture. In an example of one of these polemics, found in the *Fatāwā al-Hindiyyah*, an unnamed set of individuals are berated for pretending to be jurists:

> Know that some men become resentful and despairing. [These men] find themselves failures in society and become restless and bored, and are overcome by insecurities, ignorance and a deficient intellect. Their afflictions only increase when idiots surround these men and listen to them. Then these men, pretending to be jurists, fill their mouths with the words of jurists, and spew out phrase after phrase. Neither do they understand nor do their followers understand the meaning and implications of what they are saying. It is better for the rational man to guard his mouth against imitating the jurists for the ignorant only fall flat on their faces.[142]

Interestingly, Muslim jurists also refused to consider as jurists those who acquired by rote memory, or otherwise, a knowledge of the raw materials (the Qur'ān and *Sunnah*), but did not master or implement the juristic methods of analysis. This often resulted in tensions between the jurists and the literalist narrators of traditions (*ahl al-ḥadīth*) whose analytical process, for the most part, consisted of the mechanical process of matching traditions with problematic factual situations. This methodology basically consisted of restructuring all contemporaneous factual situations so that they would fit into a mold that was literally addressed by an inherited Prophetic tradition. This, of course, was fed by a myth that the Qur'ān and *Sunnah* already addressed every possible factual situation or problem that might ever arise. Therefore, the legal process of these traditionists primarily consisted of essentializing every factual scenario so that a literal reading of the text could resolve the problem.[143] The representatives of the juristic culture did not consider these traditionists as legitimate legal scholars. Often the jurists would brand the traditionists as the "pharmacists" of Islam while describing themselves as the "doctors" of Islam. In one such example, we find that those who gather and memorize the traditions but do not study the juristic sciences were likened to pharmacists who gather medicines but have no idea how to diagnose a disease or to dispense the appropriate medicine to the appropriate patient. It is only with the study of the juristic sciences that proper applications of the law may be made.[144]

The issue at this point, is how did the juristic tradition reconcile itself with the notion of individual responsibility and accountability? There is a pronounced tension between the notion of a legal system that is not subject to the vagaries of undisciplined subjectivities, and the idea of individual accountability before God and the idea of accessibility of God's law. Assuming that God made His Way discoverable only through a complex matrix of indicators, and assuming that God demanded systematic discipline, diligence, and exertion in the pursuit of the indicators, how does one understand the idea of individual responsibility and accountability? The jurists are expected to live a life absorbed in the search and understanding of the Divine indicators, but where does this leave the laity that may not have the time or capacity to personally pursue or analyze the indicators?

The response to these issues will consist of two parts. The first part is to describe the classical arguments of the jurists. The second part will consist of re-articulating the classical conception in a way that will be helpful in understanding what I have described as the authoritarian process in modern Islamic legal discourses.

Muslim jurists referred mainly to two Qur'ānic verses in addressing the issues raised above. The first verse states, "The believers should not go forth all together. In every expedition [there should be] a group that remains behind so that they could devote themselves to studies in religion and admonish their people when they return to them, and thus they may learn to guard themselves (against evil or ignorance)."[145] The second Qur'ānic reference is part of a verse that simply states, "if you do not know, ask the people of religion" (*ahl al-dhikr*).[146] The people of religion, in this context, could mean the people of knowledge or the people of piety or the people endowed with special knowledge of the Message. The basic idea conveyed in these verses, the jurists argued, is the expectation that not everyone can or should be a specialist in the Way of God – there must be a group that will dedicate itself to the knowledge of the Way.[147] This group will act as the reference point for their people in advising them on the affairs of religion, which necessarily includes the law. But because of the absence of Church in Islam, and for the reasons explained above, the role of the people of religion is primarily advisory. We will address the issue of the enforcement of the law later, but at this point it is sufficient to note that it is the task of the state to give effect to and implement the law. In the language of the jurists, religion is the heart of the matter and the state is its guard (*ḥirāsat al-dīn*).[148] As to the normative role of the jurists, their task is summarized by the Qur'ānic verse, "Remind them [the people] for you are nothing but a reminder [to the people]. You do not control them."[149]

The laity does not have the time, the training or, perhaps, the capacity to thoroughly study and analyze the indicators.[150] Nevertheless, this does not excuse people from bearing responsibility before God for their own decisions and conduct. The responsibility of the laity is to imitate the jurists, (perform *taqlīd*), but not blindly. Rather the laity is responsible for diligently investigating which of the jurists and juridical schools to follow. To simplify somewhat, the responsibility of the jurists is to diligently investigate the law, and the responsibility of the laity is to diligently investigate the jurists. The laity must ascertain the qualifications of the jurist they are consulting and choose the jurist, not on the basis of whim (*hawā*), but on the basis of rational thought and conviction. If they are negligent in doing so, they incur sin before God. Furthermore, if a layperson is in doubt or has a reason to be troubled about a particular ruling, he or she should ask the jurist for evidence. Upon considering the evidence to the best of his or her ability, a layperson should form a preponderance of belief about the correctness of the ruling.[151] Such a layperson should not reject the evidence as a matter of personal taste or whim, but on the basis of contrary evidence offered by another jurist. Importantly, however, most jurists condemned the practice of crossing school lines if one is shopping for a convenient result. This means that laypeople are free to select from any of the systematic schools of thought, and may freely switch from one school to another. But the switching of schools, or the crossing of school lines, should not be done for improper reasons. The improper reasons include trying to find the easiest or least demanding legal opinion, or case-by-case result-oriented selections, or switching in order to gain some earthly benefit such as political or social promotion. If a person switches from one school to another, it must be done because the person is convinced that the new school better approximates the Divine Will. Once he or she selects the appropriate school, a person should continue to follow it until he or she forms a preponderance of belief that another school outweighs the former school. The reason that a person should pick a particular school and continue to adhere to it is that each school of thought adopts a set of systematic principles of analysis, and a layperson is obligated to remain systematic in adherence to this law. Significantly, a person may go to any jurist within a particular school of thought as long as such a person is satisfied that the jurist is qualified to perform the juristic function that he is being asked to perform.[152]

Rearticulating and restructuring the juristic conception of the basis of their authority can help us develop a normative conception of the authoritative in Islam. It is important to take note of the fact that the authoritativeness of the jurists is not based on what we might call extra-rational powers. Jurists do not have the power to forgive, absolve, or bless, and no jurist has a monopoly over the truth. Jurists are not privy to the Divine Will by virtue of a sacramental act of investiture or ordination. The authoritativeness of jurists is derived from a perceived mastery over a body of knowledge, and a perceived adherence to a systematic methodology. In a sense, the extent of a jurist's authoritativeness is in direct proportion to his or her ability to objectify the analytical process, and avoid the perception of whimsical subjectivity. As discussed above, in Islamic theology God is the Sovereign and Legislator. God is both of these things, not in the sense of being the maker of the Law, but the founder of the Law. God is the Founding Master, so to speak, of a conceptual abstraction known as the Way, and a non-abstract and concrete set of indicators. Since, after the death of the Prophet, human beings are no longer the recipients of direct and personal communication from God, individuals must investigate the Divine Will through a medium. In Islamic jurisprudence, the medium is most often a text.[153] The text documents the experience of revelation, and this experience counts as the primary precedent guiding the search for the Divine Will. The experience of revelation as documented in texts is in itself a demonstrative indicator for the Divine Way. The experience of revelation does contain a certain amount of specific and quite detailed laws, but these laws do not embody the Way. What does embody the Way are the ethos of experience, the normativities of precedent, and the demonstrative dynamics of a revelation that has now ended. The indicators are the constituent elements of the revelatory episode in the life of Islam, but the ethos of that episode is the search – the process of engaging the indicators in order to live a conscientious and reflective life in the pursuit of the Divine.[154]

Accepting the Qur'ān and *Sunnah* as foundational sources of legitimacy is a logical conclusion if one accepts, as a matter of faith, that the Qur'ān is the literal unexpurgated word of God and if one accepts the Qur'ān as a source of guidance towards God's Way. It is logical if one accepts that the *Sunnah* does document part of the demonstrative revelatory experience and that God intended this documentation to have normative value for human beings. In my view, it is logical to accept the Qur'ān and *Sunnah* as the foundation of legitimacy but it does not necessarily follow that they are the exclusive sources of legitimacy. One can make a reasoned argument that God's indicators may be found in values embodied by God's attributes such as the Merciful, Compassionate and the Just. Part of God's indicators could be certain natural processes in life or creation, perhaps such as history, intuition or rational thought. Furthermore, it is possible rationally to conclude that respect for all basic forms of human good is a fundamental and natural law of God, and that whatever is necessary in order to fulfill this respect is part of God's indicators.[155] One can also argue that God's indicators must be pursued not just through rigor and discipline, but that the search for the indicators must be founded on an a priori systematic moral view. Arguably, it is not sufficient to have a systematic methodology of research and investigation, without a substantive moral understanding of the nature of God's Way – for instance, is the nature of God's Way about beauty, justice, compassion, dignity or something else?[156]

I will return to this point later, although to deal fully with this issue requires a separate book. The important point at this juncture is that, like God's

Sovereignty, the Qur'ān and *Sunnah* do not speak without agents, and the agents are, for better or worse, human beings. The authoritativeness of God is invariably represented and negotiated by human beings. And, because human agency is unavoidable, the negotiative process will inevitably involve an intricate balance between an authoritativeness and an authoritarianism. The authoritativeness of the agents is derivative. Importantly, the authoritativeness is derived not only from God (the Principal) or the text (the instructions of the Principal), but from fellow agents. Since all human beings are accountable to God (the Principal), and since all human beings are commanded to follow the Principal's instructions, it is reasonable to assume that human beings are God's agents.[157] It should be recalled that the Qur'ān itself intimates that human beings were made the viceroys of God. Yet, some of these agents (the believing, pious Muslims who I will call the common agents) yield their will or partly surrender their judgment to a special group or a certain *strata* of agents (the jurists). They do so because, and only because, they consider this special group to be an authority. The special group is an authority because of its perceived competence and special understanding of the Principal's instructions. The special group (the jurists) are authoritative not because they are in authority – the formal position is irrelevant – but because of the social perception of being authorities on the set of instructions (indicators) that point to God's Way.[158] The common agents consider the determinations of the special agents as exclusionary reasons for disregarding alternative courses of action that, in the absence of the exclusionary reasons, would have been reasonable alternatives to discharge their obligations towards the Principal. The common agents could have explored other possible courses of action to discharge their obligations towards the Principal. They could have personally examined the textual instructions, or they could have looked at non-textual manifestations of the Divine Will such as intuition or history. However the common agents forgo such alternatives because they perceive the special agents as having special competence over understanding and analyzing the Principal's instructions.[159]

There are several contingencies to the authoritativeness of the special agents or the jurists. Each of these contingencies must be satisfied or discharged, otherwise it is reasonable to conclude that, as far as the common agents are concerned, the special agents have acted *ultra vires* and violated the trust placed in them. One can imagine a hypothetical in which *x* and *y* are agents whom the Principal has given a set of fairly complicated instructions commanding that they discharge certain tasks and that they discharge them in a particular way. *X* claims to *y* that she has thoroughly studied and reflected on the Principal's instructions and understands what the Principal wants. Let us further assume that part of the instructions permits one of the agents to follow the guidance of the other. Nonetheless, according to those instructions *x* and *y* will ultimately be held individually accountable to the Principal. Before trusting *x*, *y* takes some time to satisfy himself that *x* has in fact spent the time studying the instructions and is in fact sufficiently literate so as to be able to comprehend what she is studying. After forming a reasonable preponderance of belief that *x* is so qualified, *y*, who is not sufficiently literate or is simply too busy doing other things, decides to trust *x* and follow her lead. Mindful of his obligations towards the Principal, *y* does not trust *x* without qualifications – the terms of the agency simply do not permit *y* to pass all responsibility or accountability to *x*. Consequently, *y* will follow *x*'s lead, but with reservations. These reservations are the contingencies upon which the relationship of authoritativeness is founded.

There are five contingencies. These contingencies define a relationship of trusting authoritativeness: *y* will consider *x* an authority to be followed because *y* trusts *x*. However, this trust is founded on a reasonable assumption that the five contingencies have been fulfilled. *X* may provide an explanation or justification to *y* and, as argued earlier, providing such an explanation is not inconsistent with a relationship of authoritativeness. In fact, an explanation might be offered by *x* in order to assure *y* of the fulfillment of the five contingencies and to reaffirm *x*'s entitlement to *y*'s trust. The five contingencies that constitute a trusting authoritativeness are the following:

*Honesty: Y* can plausibly assume that in all matters, *x* is being truthful and honest in the representation of the Principal's instructions. This is not a question of interpretation but simply of presentation. *Y* assumes that *x* is not intentionally concealing a part of the instructions or intentionally, and for whatever reasons, replacing the Principal's instructions with another set of instructions. In other words, *x* is not censoring, concealing, lying or deceiving, and is presenting *all* the instructions that she did, in fact, find. Significantly, the contingency of honesty includes the expectation that *x* will not pretend to know what she does not know and will be forthright about the extent of her knowledge and abilities.

*Diligence: Y* can plausibly assume that *x* has exerted a reasonable amount of effort in finding and understanding the relevant set of instructions pertaining to a particular problem or set of problems. This presumption of diligence is not easily quantifiable, but at a minimum, it mandates that *x* has reflected on the problem at hand, and has expended a conscientious effort in investigating, studying and analyzing the instructions. The standard for diligence is not entirely subjective and is not based on community standards unless one can show that the instructions were to follow community standards. In Islamic reality, the Qur'ān persistently condemns those who blindly follow the standards of their community without conscientious individual reflection.[160] The standard should be what is reasonably necessary in order to comply with the other four contingencies. The Qur'ān consistently condemns those who make claims about God or on behalf of God without a basis in knowledge, but on the basis of wishfulness, arrogance, or self-interest.[161] The standard of diligence is what permits people to claim that they are being honest in claiming knowledge of

God's law. But that claim cannot be made unless they have been comprehensive, self-restrained, and reasonable in their approach. People must expend whatever energy is necessary to be able honestly to claim that they have done everything possible to discover and understand the indicators, and must be willing to defend this effort before God in the Hereafter. Importantly, in Islamic theology, the duty of diligence increases in direct proportion to the extent that the law affects the rights of others. A person is responsible for misleading or for transgressing upon the rights of others.[162] Hence, for the reasonable people, the more the rights of others are affected, the more they will exercise caution, and the harder they will work to discharge their duties towards other human beings. The more they violate the rights of others, the greater their liability before God.

*Comprehensiveness: Y* can plausibly assume that *x* has tried to be as thorough as possible in investigating the instructions of the Principal and will justifiably expect that *x* has thought about the range of relevant instructions, has made an assiduous effort to acquire all the pertinent instructions, and has not negligently decided not to investigate or pursue certain lines of evidence (instructions) for the sake of convenience or comfort.

*Reasonableness: Y* can plausibly assume that *x* has made an effort to interpret and analyze the instructions of the Principal in a sensible fashion. Of course, sensibleness is an indeterminate concept, however, it seems to me that, at a minimum, it means what would commonly be considered justifiable under a certain set of circumstances. For instance, suppose the Dean of my law school pats me on the back and says, "We are proud of you! You represent all of us." If I later blurt out in a faculty meeting, "We all represent each other! The Dean told me so," the statement might be silly or naive but it is justifiable under the circumstances and thus sensible. If, however, I send an e-mail to my friend and say, "Good news, I now represent the school and, hence, I am making you an offer of employment," one could hardly say that, under the circumstances, my behavior is justifiable or sensible. In other words, in choosing one's constructions, one ought to be cognizant of communities of interpretation and communities of meaning – one ought to think about whether a particular construction will make any sense to one's relevant community. One ought to keep in mind that inquiry into meaning is not an individual affair, but that reality and meaning are constructed within and by communities. I am not arguing that one should adhere to established communities of meaning and never attempt to deviate from them. I am arguing, however, that one should be respectful towards established communities of meaning and towards the integrity of the text itself. To use Umberto Eco's term, one should not "over-interpret" the text by forcing upon it an inconsistent fictitious text. Put differently, one should not read the instructions in such a fashion as to impose upon them the instructions that the reader would have liked to see, rather than the instructions that in fact exist. Over-interpreting the text could take the form of opening up the text to an endless array of meanings that the text cannot reasonably bear. On the other hand, one can take a text that is open to a range of meanings and insist that it can support but a single meaning. In doing so, one is arbitrarily closing the range of the text. Both, the limitless opening of the text and the arbitrary closing of the text, violate the contingency of reasonableness as well as other contingencies.[163]

*Self-restraint:* $Y$ can plausibly expect $x$ to exhibit a considerable degree of modesty and restraint in representing the will of the Principal. This contingency is well-represented by the Islamic phrase, "And, God knows best." As explained earlier, this phrase acts as an epistemological and moral disclaimer. Beyond the articulation of a certain phrase, the significant notion here is that the agent must exercise particular care to avoid usurping, or the appearance of usurping, the role of the Principal. Self-restraint means that the agent must be cognizant of the limits of his or her role. In order to exercise the necessary self-restraint, the agent would have to take to heart the Qur'ānic verse, "Remind them for you are nothing but a reminder. You do not control them."[164] Furthermore, the agent might have to issue the necessary disclaimers to remind himself or herself and others of the nature of his or her role. The agent might have to refrain from reaching positive or negative conclusions about certain matters if the evidence is insufficient. In other words, the agent might have to say, "I don't know." Consistent with the obligation of self-restraint are the large number of anecdotal reports stating that such-and-such jurist was asked about twenty issues but agreed to answer only one. To the rest, the jurist reportedly responded, "I don't know." Importantly, these reports are mentioned to extol the humility and knowledge of the jurist. The ability to refrain from talking about what one does not know is portrayed in these reports as a mark of true knowledge.[165] Self-restraint partly accounts for Abū Ḥāmid al-Ghazālī's (d. 505/1111) argument that to let a thousand *kāfirs* (unbelievers) go unharmed is better than to unjustly harm a single Muslim.[166] Pursuant to the obligation of self-restraint, the agent is bound to avoid over-reaching or exceeding the bounds of his or her delegation.

I am not arguing that what I called above the special group or agents will have to demonstrate to the common agents that they have fulfilled all five contingencies on every legal issue that may arise. Rather, these contingencies are the implied terms that define the relationship between the special agents and the common agents. These implied terms justify the reliance of the common agents on the special agents, and therefore, the common agents have every right to expect that the special agents have observed and will continue to observe these terms on every issue and at all times. If the common agents call upon the special agents to demonstrate a fulfillment of these terms, and if the special agents wish to continue to be authoritative, the special agents should provide an accounting and demonstrate compliance. As a matter of conscience, if the special agents refuse to provide such an accounting or fail to convince the common agent of their compliance, reasonable common agents should become alarmed and should, in fact, suspend the special agents' authoritative status. Common agents have reasonable grounds to believe that they are unjustifiably relying on special agents who are acting *ultra vires*, and that they (the common agents) might be held liable before the Principal for a dereliction of their own duties. Most significantly, as I will argue later, if the special agents are acting in breach of these implied terms, they are usurping the functions of the Principal and are acting in an authoritarian fashion.

Anticipating possible criticisms, one might ask, what are the origins of these contingencies? What is the authority for these particular contingencies, and not others? My response is that these are *ḍarūriyyāt ʿaqliyyah* (rational necessities) for the very logic of the relationship between agent, Principal, and instructions in Islam. If one rejects the logic of agency and Divine instructions, then these rational necessities would be inapposite. These rational necessities, I would argue, are the only way possible that an appropriate balance can be maintained between the notion of individual accountability, the reality of diverse and complex instructions, and the ultimate role of God as the reference point. It is logical to think that unless each and every common agent will dedicate himself or herself to the full-time and lifetime task of deciphering the instructions, there will have to be a division of functions, a delegation of tasks, and the practical necessity of trust.

Significantly, as noted above, while accountability is individual, the Qurʾān does impose a collective responsibility upon nations. The Qurʾān provides that if a nation collectively fails in discharging its obligations towards God, God will cause that nation to suffer and will ultimately replace it with another. The Qurʾān talks of offering the Trust to the heavens, earth, and mountains, yet none agreed to accept it. Ultimately, human beings carried it and with it, human beings accepted a weighty responsibility.[167] God delegated a Trust to humanity in general but the Qurʾān speaks of God giving a Covenant to nations. God grants this Covenant as a distinctive gift, but if the nation consistently breaches the Covenant, God entrusts the Covenant to another, and perhaps causes the destruction of the breaching nation.[168] This collective responsibility is consistent with the notion of individual accountability because in the Hereafter individuals are only made to answer for their own actions. Of course, the failures of the collective may impose additional duties upon the individual to affirmatively discharge particular obligations such as the obligation to enjoin the good and forbid the evil in society (*al-amr bi al-maʿrūf wa al-nahy ʿan al-munkar*).[169] The instructions of the Principal cover a variety of functions such as waging military *jihād*, feeding the poor, taking care of the orphans, etc. Even more, it should be recalled that according to juristic theory, the instructions cover every aspect of life. The existence of collective obligations and the expanse of the instructions mandate a division of labor. This is why, for instance, the jurists divided all legal obligations as *farḍ kifāyah* and *farḍ ʿayn*. *Farḍ ʿayn* is an obligation, such as prayer or fasting, which is mandatory upon every single Muslim in society. *Farḍ kifāyah* is an obligation that needs to be performed by a sufficient number of people in society, and not by every single individual. Such obligations would include the existence of people who can take care of the injured or sick, or the existence of people who may act as teachers, or the existence of a sufficient number of people that can defend the nation from military aggressors.[170] Effectively, in the *farḍ kifāyah* category certain tasks are entrusted to a particular group that will perform the task on behalf of the collectivity. Yet, the accountability in the Hereafter remains individual. The Qur'ān, however, provides that God does not hold people accountable as to the ultimate results, but only for their efforts. At the same time, the Qur'ān emphasizes that God holds individuals accountable only to the extent of their abilities and efforts.[171] Consequently, a reasonable person would entrust certain tasks to individuals only after expending a reasonable effort to ascertain that these individuals are capable and willing to perform the delegated task.[172] Furthermore, a reasonable person would not delegate such tasks without implied or express conditions upon the violation of which a person may clear himself or herself from responsibility before God (this is what the jurists called *tabri'at al-dhimmah ʿind Allāh*).

In the context of delegating the juristic task, the contingencies reviewed above seem to be the most logical. Importantly, these contingencies are the most consistent with the jurists' vision of their authority. As explained earlier, I have accepted the juristic vision of authority as a sociological presumption and normative value. To the extent that one invokes or relies on the juristic vision of authority, the contingencies above would apply. It is my contention that these contingencies articulate the presumptions of the juristic theory, and are, in fact, mandated by the theology articulated by the jurists. If a person debunks the juristic tradition and articulates a theory of authority that does not rely on the Qur'ān and *Sunnah*, or articulates a theory of authority that does not rely on Divine instructions or does not rely on the idea of agency, some or all of the contingencies explained above might be quite inapposite. But if one accepts, relies upon, or uses the juristic vision of authority, these contingencies are necessary for any systematic and respectful discharge of one's obligations towards God. The violation of these contingencies on the part of the special agents is a betrayal of the trust and delegation placed in them by the common agents. I believe that this form of betrayal, if persistent, intentional or reckless, falls under the type of betrayal of trust that the Qur'ān so vehemently condemns.[173]

At this point, one might ask if these are the only possible contingencies. Even if one accepts the juristic vision of authority, and that authority cannot be entrusted to the jurists without this authority being contingent on plausible assumptions, why not include other contingencies, such as a requirement of knowledge or a requirement of piety? It is important to respond to this point because knowledge and piety are two requirements that are consistently listed in classical juristic works as necessary for one to qualify as a jurist.[174] Classical sources have always required both proof of knowledge and piety before one may qualify as a jurist. In response, I would argue that both knowledge and piety do not relate to the dynamics of the inquiry and, therefore, do not relate to the issues of agency and trust. Knowledge and piety might enable a person to perfrom more effectively or more faithfully the task of deciphering the instructions but, in themselves, do not constitute a tool or methodology of inquiry. Consequently, they cannot be measures for evaluating an *ultra vires* act or for assessing whether the special agents exceeded the bounds of their authority. Assuming that a special agent has knowledge and is pious, what does that mean? Does that mean that all his or her acts are justified, authoritative, and defensible? It is quite possible for someone to possess piety and knowledge, and yet, fail to discharge his or her obligations towards the common agents and God because such a person has not done the requisite research on a particular issue, or was unreasonably idiosyncratic in his or her interpretations. In addition, an excess of piety may induce someone to exhibit undue zeal in defending what he or she believes to be the Will of God. Knowledge and piety are not sufficient conditions for discharging one's responsibilities before the Principal or the other agents. But are they necessary conditions? Must people be knowledgeable and pious in order to discharge their obligations? This question is largely inapposite because knowledge and piety may be qualifying requirements to engage in the process, but they are not related to the actual process of investigating on a case-by-case situation. Again, simply because one is knowledgeable and pious does not mean that one has applied this piety and knowledge to a specific problem at hand. Furthermore, one cannot perform the tasks of diligence, honesty, comprehensiveness, and reasonableness without being knowledgeable. In addition, I very much doubt that self-restraint can be exercised without piety. Self-restraint is based on being cognizant of the balance between the role of the Principal and agent; it is doubtful that one who is not concerned about his or her fate in the Hereafter is going to exercise self-restraint in this context. Nevertheless, as far as the common agent is concerned, if the special agent fulfills the five contingencies to the common agent's satisfaction, there is no reason for the common agent to be concerned about the special agent's piety. The special agent's piety or lack of piety will neither protect nor endanger the common agent's position before God. As the Prophet is reported to have said, "I have not been commanded [by God] to inquire about what people conceal in their hearts."[175] As long as the special agent has performed his job in a competent fashion and the common agent has cleared his or her conscience in that regard, what is in the heart of the special agent is for God to judge.

Another possible objection to the approach advocated here is that I am demanding that jurists engage in a process that is historically unfounded. In several books on the protocol or the mannerisms (*adab*) of the *muftī* and *mustaftī* (the person issuing the *responsa* and the person requesting one), classical jurists explicitly state that a juris-consul is under no obligation to disclose the evidentiary basis of his legal opinion to the laity. In fact, at times, it is affirmatively suggested that a juris-consul ought not to give complex and detailed responses to the laity because such responses are bound to confound them. Rather, juris-consuls ought to produce a concise response without going into the evidentiary and methodological basis. Some sources even state that a juris-consul owes a duty only to God, and does not owe a duty to the laity. Furthermore, most jurists hold that it is lawful for a lay person to imitate or follow the practice of a qualified jurist (this is known as the practice of *taqlīd*). *Taqlīd*, in this context, is defined as the following of a legal determination without understanding the reasoning behind it (*qubūl qawl bi-lā ḥujja*).

Notably, these classical positions are consistent with one of the conceptions of authoritativeness, which, as discussed above, endorses deference without an evaluation of the evidence. The argument that a juris-consul owes a duty of care and diligence only to God, and not to other human beings, I would contend is irreconcilable with the vision of Islamic theology espoused by this book, and is sadly misguided. This argument is similar to the contention that a ruler is responsible only to God, and does not have to answer to his constituency in any way. Ultimately, according to this vision, only God may hold such a person liable for breaching his trust, and the constituency will have to suspend judgment on the lawfulness of the ruler's conduct until the Final Day. This view does not seem supportable unless one is to assume that a ruler is appointed, sanctioned, and rendered immune from human accountability by God.[176] Even those jurists who argued that a ruler is a divine appointee did not go so far as to argue that such a ruler does not have to answer to his constituency. Even more, to my knowledge, no notable source in the classical tradition argued that jurists are divinely appointed or selected. Many jurists argued that jurists are the inheritors of the prophets, but that simply meant that in the absence of prophets, the jurists are charged with exploring and guarding the Divine law. The only elements that commended jurists were piety and knowledge – otherwise, jurists were considered normal human beings. Furthermore, this view seems to vitiate any sense of personal responsibility or accountability in Islam. A person would have to select a jurist to follow or imitate and regardless of how absurd or idiosyncratic the conclusions of that jurist are, a person would never have an opportunity to question the judgment of the jurist, and would, in turn, never be accountable for any legal determination adopted.

Fortunately, the view that the duty of care is owed only to God is not supported by the majority of classical scholars. For the majority, the interaction between the jurist and the laity was treated like any other relationship that induces reliance by one party and generates a duty of care by the other. Interestingly, the most common analogy invoked by the classical jurists in discussing the role of the juris-consul was that of a medical doctor treating patients. A medical doctor, like a jurist, was charged with a duty to use best efforts in advising and treating a patient, and a violation of this duty was considered a sin and might even lead to legal liability. For most classical scholars, the existence of duty towards the laity or petitioner, was not the issue. Rather, the issue was: does the duty of care include an obligation to disclose the evidentiary basis for a legal determination? Was it sufficient for a jurist to give a short and direct response to a legal inquiry or was a jurist obligated to explain the basis for his determination? It is important to note that the debate was not about whether a jurist had to be honest, diligent, or thorough; it was assumed that these obligations had to be fulfilled. It is possible for a jurist to give a "yes" or "no" response, and still be diligent and thorough. This ought not be confused with the separate issue of disclosure.[177] The problem, however, is at what point does the failure to disclose become dishonest, misleading, or fraudulent? Furthermore, at what point does the failure to disclose become a breach of duty towards the other? I would argue that in the context of the juris-consul and a petitioner, it depends on the question posed. If the question is what do you think is the proper Islamic ruling, then the juris-consul is only speaking for himself and no one else. If the question is what does the Ḥanbalī school hold as to *x*, this would elicit a very different response. If the question is what does God hold as to *x*, here the duty is to disclose the full array of the evidence and schools of thought that interpreted this evidence. The point is to provide whatever information necessary for the petitioner to make an informed decision considering the scope of authority delegated by the petitioner to the juris-consul.

Of course this is not the way that classical jurists understood the dynamic between the juris-consul and the laity. In the pre-modern era, there were recognizable indicia signifying the qualifications, position, rank, and school of thought of a jurist. Information as to the *madhhab* to which a jurist belonged and his rank within it was readily accessible. The *responsa* of juris-consuls played a significant social and legal role both in formal and informal settings.[178] Furthermore, the structured system of legal guilds exercised a strong supervisory role over the activities of the various legal scholars.[179] Therefore, it was consistently presumed that a petitioner would be dealing with an identifiable professional quality when dealing with a reputable jurist. Jurists often treated the practice of dealing with non-reputable pretenders as a highly immoral act. The failure to consult reputable jurists was a moral failure that either indicated a profound state of ignorance or reckless indifference to God's law. And, I think there is little doubt that the ethos of a specialized professional class, which was rightly authorized to speak for God's law, betrayed a pronounced sense of paternalism. Nevertheless, it is important to note that the primary concern of the classical jurists was not, so to speak, "to hide," or conceal the evidentiary basis of their determinations. Rather, they had a threefold concern. Firstly, not to popularize and denigrate a technical discourse. Secondly, to maintain the aura and dignity of the juristic culture. Thirdly, to avoid over-taxing the resources and energies of the jurists with redundant disputations with non-specialists. It is rather telling that the discussions about the disclosure requirements appear in the context of elaborating upon the proper mannerisms to be adopted towards juris-consuls. So, for instance, these elaborations often state that a petitioner should not interrupt or raise his voice to a juris-consul. In addition, a petitioner may or may not accept the *responsa* of a juris-consul, but in either case, the petitioner should not be argumentative, insulting, or offensive. Nonetheless, several sources state that if a petitioner wants to know the basis for a *responsa*, he or she should make an arrangement to meet with the jurist separately to go over the evidence.[180] The point is that although there is an element of paternalism in the discourses of the classical jurists, this paternalism is not all-encompassing. Understood in its appropriate historical context, it is the paternalism manifested by a guilded profession, such as doctors, who take pride in their literacy and disdain the illiteracy of the masses.

Despite the points mentioned above, a considerable number of jurists did, in fact, argue that it is improper for a layperson to defer to any legal determination without first evaluating its evidentiary basis. To this, however, the majority responded that this would be impractical because a jurist would be forced to explain the evidence to each and every petitioner. This would not be feasible because a jurist in issuing a *responsa* is ruling not just on a legal issue, but on a factual scenario as well. Each petition or request for a legal opinion presents a unique set of facts, and no two sets of facts are exactly the same. The jurist must apply legal principles to the particular set of facts presented in each case. Therefore, it is not possible to issue thoroughly reasoned but standardized legal opinions that would cover all the factual permutations relevant to a particular legal issue.[181] Each legal opinion must be tailored to the facts of a particular case. Importantly, however, the majority argued, if the facts of a particular case are relevant as a precedent or if a case raises contentious issues of law, then a fully reasoned and justified written, or dictated, *responsa* would be appropriate. In other words, if a jurist wishes to argue for a particular position in a contentious debate, or if a jurist is dealing with a legal issue of general significance for the public, then it is advisable to document the full reasoning behind such a determination, especially if a jurist is addressing other jurists.[182] Consequently, the *fatāwā* collections of jurists such as al-Wansharīsī, al-Subkī, Ibn Rushd I, al-Ramlī, Ibn Taymiyya, and Ibn ʿĀbidīn contain lengthy, well-reasoned *responsa* in which the legal evidence is fully analyzed.[183] In summary, it would be fair to say that the classical position on the issue of disclosure is the following: if a juris-consul is responding to a question involving a specific set of facts, and if the *responsa* does not carry precedential value and is tailored to those specific set of facts, and if there is no particular reason to disclose the evidentiary basis of a *responsa*, such as a request by the petitioner, the juris-consul need not disclose the evidentiary basis for his *responsa*.[184] On the other hand, if the *responsa* deals with a contentious, difficult or novel issue, and is expected to carry precedential value, and is also expected to be preserved in writing, then a detailed discussion of the evidence would be warranted. This position would be consistent with the approach advocated in this book, however, I would add that the juris-consul must truthfully represent the evidence. So, for instance, a jurist cannot say that such-and-such is "well-established" or such-and-such is "agreed upon," if these statements are not truthful and/or misleading. Furthermore, the juris-consul must disclose the evidence if disclosure is necessary so that the petitioner can make an informed decision about whether to defer to one position or another. Importantly, the duty to disclose the full range of the evidence is augmented if one is issuing a *responsa* to the public. It is one thing for a jurist to respond to an individual inquiry, and quite another to issue a *responsa* for public consumption. The possible liability in advising an individual is not as onerous as when one is possibly misleading a large number of people. This, however, is related to the measure or extent of the duty, and not as to whether there is a duty in the first place. The more public the *responsa*, the heavier the burden and the possible liability. Whether private or public, however, I believe that a failure to disclose, regardless of good intentions, is a sin and potentially authoritarian.[185]

Thus far, we have explained the dynamics of authoritativeness in Islamic law and attempted to set out the basic elements of these dynamics. But we have not addressed the question of where Islam draws the line between orthodoxy and heterodoxy. The dynamics, as explained, involve special agents who probe the instructions and common agents who accept the special agents' probing and follow it. But the common agents are ultimately only accountable to God, and they have full discretion to refuse the efforts of the special agents. This is all at the moral level. If the special agents violate one of the five contingencies, they are morally culpable, and if the common agent has reason to believe that the special agent has failed to comply with the five contingencies, a moral and rational common agent would no longer consider this special agent to be an authority. As alluded to earlier, structural authority and the implementation of a specific set of laws, as a matter of administration, is a different matter. Nevertheless, as a moral matter, is it possible to morally bind the special or common agents to a specific normative doctrine? Is it possible for special agents to inform common agents that over a set of determinations, they have no choice but to accept these determinations regardless of whether the five contingencies have been fulfilled or not? Can the special agents inform the common agents that, over certain issues, if the common agents refuse to accept the determinations of special agents, they cease to be Muslim? To put it differently, the notion of authoritativeness in Islam, as I set it out, leads to considerable moral indeterminacy. It appears from our exposition that the main determinacy is the morality of the process, and as is the case with process-oriented jurisprudence in general, it is never clear why the line of determinacy should be drawn at the point of the process.[186] To state it bluntly, why shouldn't we focus on the morality of the substantive results rather than the morality of the process?

As noted earlier, I do not exclude the possibility that the process would be based on certain substantive moral assumptions. These moral assumptions could be based or derived from one's understanding of the nature or function of God or the nature of existence, or could be the product of rational postulates. Many of the debates in classical Islam regarding whether justice or reason binds God or whether whatever God does defines justice or reason, arise from this same problem.[187] These debates often related to whether justice or reason exist independently of God and, hence, whether God follows their dictates because God is moral and rational, or whether God is the One that defines justice and reason, so that whatever He decides defines justice and defines reason. Obviously, these positions are epistemologically very different and are likely to produce very different results, but for the purposes of this study we do need to take a position in this debate. For one who accepts the methodology set out above, it would become necessary for the special agent to explicate the epistemological postulates that he or she is making so that the common agent can make an informed decision as to whether to consider this particular special agent as an authority on the Principal's instructions.

Classical Muslim jurists did try to create doctrines that would limit the indeterminacy inherent in the juristic concept of authority. There were two main such doctrines, the doctrine of consensus (*ijmāʿ*) and the doctrine of the foundations versus the branches (*uṣūl* and *furūʿ*).

With regard to the doctrine of consensus, certain matters, whether relating to ultimate determinations or methodological issues, are not subject to further inquiry or consideration. If a consensus is reached on an issue, that issue can be considered resolved once and for all. However, there are several methodological problems with the doctrine of consensus. There is some juristic disagreement on whether there is a consensus on accepting the authoritativeness of the doctrine of consensus. Although the majority of jurists accepted the doctrine of consensus in principle, they disagreed on whose consensus counts – the Companions of the Prophet's, the jurists', or the laity's? They also disagreed on whether the consensus of all jurists should be counted, the jurists of a specific locality, or only jurists with advanced degrees and qualifications. Jurists debated whether the opinion of an iniquitous (*fāsiq*) person or the opinion of jurists specialized only in positive laws can count towards the consensus. They also disagreed on how to verify a consensus, for instance, whether the silence of a jurist can count towards a consensus. In addition, they disagreed on whether the consensus of one generation binds another generation and whether a consensus established in one locality binds other localities. Most importantly, the majority of jurists agreed that whoever refuses or denies the existence of a consensus cannot be considered a *kāfir* (unbeliever) or even a *fāsiq* (iniquitous).[188] The ambiguities surrounding the doctrine of consensus effectively meant that the claim of *ijmāʿ* was often used as a rhetorical device in the polemics among the various schools. Jurists from a particular school would often claim the existence of a consensus among Muslims on a certain point in order to confound the arguments of his opponents. Furthermore, several jurists wrote books known as *kutub al-ijmāʿ* attempting to list all the issues that have been resolved by consensus in Islam.[189] But these books themselves did not achieve a level of prominence or widespread acceptance in Islamic juristic discourses. Rather, like the works on *taṣḥīḥ* (books that attempted to select the most correct position among the various opinions of the scholars), the books on "the established consensus" remained of ambiguous legitimacy and authoritativeness.

The second main doctrine to attempt to limit indeterminacy in the juristic discourse was the distinction between the fundamentals (*uṣūl*) and the branches (*furūʿ*) of the religion. According to this conceptual framework Muslims may legitimately disagree on the *furūʿ*, and not the *uṣūl*. Therefore, according to this view, Islamic legal schools, for instance, disagree only on the *furūʿ* of Islam and do not disagree on anything related to the fundamentals or basics of the religion. Conceptually, this is not a tremendously useful distinction. It could mean that Muslims may disagree on everything except the basics or it could mean that Muslims only disagree on marginal and peripheral issues. In other words, one may define the *uṣūl* so expansively as to allow disagreements only on marginal and insignificant issues. Alternatively, one may define the *uṣūl* so restrictively as to open the gates for debate and disagreements on all material issues.

There is no doubt that the trend in the contemporary age is to limit the span of the *furūʿ* and to incorporate more and more *aḥkām* (rules) within the scope of the *uṣūl*, thus limiting the possibility for diversity in discourse. However, the impact of this doctrine largely depends on how one defines *uṣūl* and *furūʿ*. Importantly, unlike contemporary Muslims who rarely bother with definitions, classical Muslim jurists debated this matter for centuries. The historical debate, unlike the contemporary debate, has not been about which specific positive laws are among the *uṣūl* and which are among the *furūʿ*. Rather, the debate has been about the use, authority and interpretation of different sources of knowledge. The majority of classical jurists argued that the *uṣūl* are what is clearly proven by human reason or by a *naṣṣ* (textual source). In the case of human reason, it must be something that is rationally apparent to any thinking person (*dhū ʿaql*), or that can be conclusively demonstrated or proven by reason (*dalālah ʿaqliyyah wāḍiḥah*). Any reasonable person, for instance, would agree that one plus one is two, and any reasonable person would realize that normal human beings do not fly. But beyond this, there are matters such as the Oneness of God or the attributes of God or the necessity of Divine Justice that, according to these jurists, can be conclusively demonstrated by rational proof. In the case of a textual source, it must be of definite authenticity, and clear and precise meaning (*dalālah samʿiyyah wāḍiḥah*). For something to count as among the *uṣūl*, it would need to be supported by a text upon the meaning of which reasonable minds could not disagree. Other jurists have adopted a rather circular definition: *uṣūl* are whatever Muslims cannot and do not disagree upon. This is another way of saying that whatever Muslims unanimously agree upon is part of the *uṣūl*.[190] The concept of *al-maʿlūm min al-dīn bi al-ḍarūrah* (what is known to be a part of religion as a matter of necessity) belongs to the same genre of arguments. According to this concept, there are laws and doctrines that have become so persistent and well-established, that they constitute part of the essential dogma of the religion, and no Muslim may disagree over these issues. Examples, of such matters would be prayer, fasting in the month of Ramadan, and believing that the Prophet Muḥammad was the final prophet of God. Especially in modern discourses, denying an issue that is so fundamental and well-established in religion takes a person out of the fold of Islam. Generally speaking, classical jurists were far more reserved in claiming that positive laws fall in this category. The focus tended to be on theological postulates related to the attributes of God, the createdness of the Qur'ān, and whether some Companions had become apostates or sinners after the death of the Prophet.[191]

In the Muslim historical experience, however, claiming unanimity on most issues remained problematic as long as there were learned challengers to an established dogma or doctrine. The continued existence of different theological schools of thought such as the Māturidīs, Ashʿarīs, Muʿtazilīs, Qādarīs, Murji'īs, and Khawārij made the reliance on self-evident or clearly proven reason problematic. In fact, Muslim theological schools never achieved consensus on issues such as God's attributes, predestination, the nature of evil and good, or the createdness or uncreatedness of the Qur'ān.[192] This often led to rather virulent sectarian polemics on the topics of *ahl al-bidaʿ* (the people of heterodoxy or innovations).[193] Often these polemics attempted to differentiate between people who commit a rebellion while adhering to a legitimate *ta'wīl* (interpretation or belief) and those who did not enjoy a legitimate *ta'wīl* and therefore counted as among *ahl al-bidaʿ*. Frequently, Ḥanbalī jurists, in particular, accused the Shiʿah and Khawārij of being among the *ahl al-bidaʿ* who are either *kuffār* (unbelievers) or *fussāq* (sinners and iniquitous). It is important to emphasize that these polemics were often used over theological disagreements, such as the status of the Companions of the Prophet who rebelled against ʿAlī b. Abī Ṭālib, and not used in issues related to the production of positive law.[194] Furthermore, systematic methodologies were never developed in the discourse on *ahl al-bidaʿ*, and the field often consisted of polemic name-calling. In addition, whatever the merits of the various positions, after concluding the discussion on the distinction between *furūʿ* and *uṣūl*, Muslim jurists would then discuss whether the principle "every *mujtahid* is correct" applies to *uṣūl* and *furūʿ* or only to *furūʿ*. If one argues that this principle applies to both then one admits the possibility of disagreements in *uṣūl*. If one applies this principle only to *furūʿ* then one is arguing that disagreements may occur only in the branches of law and not on the fundamentals of religion.[195]

I am not attempting to debunk the notion of essentials or fundamentals in religion. As I pointed out earlier, I do not entirely accept the idea of reader-determined meaning, but I think it is important to keep in mind that in the process of negotiating human agency, one confronts two extremes. On one extreme, one might argue that no evidence or text concerning authenticity or meaning is excluded from investigation and nothing is predetermined by the Divine. But the risk here is that one will have a religion that is entirely subjective, relative, and individual. One might risk undermining the very foundation of legitimacy and meaning, and the very logic of authority. A religion that does not have any established dogma might defy being defined as a religion. If all interpretations of a religious text, regardless of how idiosyncratic, unfounded or subjective, are admitted as orthodox, one runs the risk of diluting any authority a text might have. All texts are ultimately engaged, experienced, and understood by human beings. If one argues that all such experiences with texts, regardless of how subjective they might be, are equally valid, then one runs the risk of negating the value of the text as a source of authority. In doing so, one might invalidate the authoritativeness of religious textual sources.

On the other extreme, one might argue that all issues of competence and meaning are decisively resolvable and that the agent need only worry about faithful execution of the instructions. But the risk is a religion that is rigid, inflexible, and ultimately, impractical and irrelevant. Even more, we risk a religion that, as defined by its agents, is not only authoritative, but authoritarian. If one expands the realm of religious dogma and argues that the majority of religious texts have one possible meaning, then one might co-opt the authoritativeness of the religious text and transform it into human authoritarianism. Since the Islamic text is mediated through human agents, it would make little sense to speak of an authoritarian text. Rather, it is the human agent who would transform the authority of the Islamic text into human authoritarianism. The agent takes the authoritativeness of the instructions and produces himself or herself as authoritarian. Additionally, this authoritarianism might become institutionalized if one creates a defined body that represents and speaks for the text.

To a large extent, the challenge is to strike a balance between authoritativeness and authoritarianism while mediating the religious text through human agents. Ultimately, because religion, as doctrine and belief, must rely on human agency for its mundane existence, one runs the risk that those human agents will either render it subjectively determined, or rigid and inflexible. In either case, one risks that the Divine Will be made subservient to human comprehension and human will.

There is, however, another level to the challenge of agency and its encounters with the Divine Will. As noted earlier, some contemporary Muslims take great pride in the idea of Islam being "the simple religion." This often manifests itself in a rabid anti-intellectualism reminiscent of certain forms of evangelical Christianity.[196] Simplicity is seen as the key for unity and, therefore, there is a strong demand to limit the range of disagreements and to promote intellectual homogeneity. In order for Islam to be the simple religion, it is argued that Islam must have a clear and unambiguous position on the vast majority of issues that might confront human beings, and that to complicate matters is mere sophistry.[197] But this is a result-oriented argument that attempts to impose an artificial uniformity upon a tradition rich with diversity and upon an epistemology that does not promote such uniformity. Simplicity is antithetical to individual accountability, egalitarianism and diversity. In fact, simplicity is the antithesis to the very notion of culture and civilization. With diversity is born complexity and a pluralist reality, and civilization and culture are rarely simplistic or one-dimensional. The fact is that the more one emphasizes simplicity and uniformity, the more one must reject ambiguity, complexity and diversity. But in order for things to be clear and simple, there must exist a unitary authority that resolves most disputes and settles most issues that might result in disagreement, essentially vitiating the epistemology of individual accountability, egalitarianism and diversity inherent to Islam. The simplistic response often given to this dilemma is that the Qur'ān and *Sunnah* resolve most issues and disputes. Perhaps and perhaps not! But Islamic history is the greatest testament that the Qur'ān and *Sunnah* inspired the greatest complexity in Islamic history, namely the complexity of the juristic tradition in Islam.

In this chapter, I have addressed the problem of agency and the epistemology of authority in juristic Islam. At the heart of this epistemology is the idea of divine-based instructions that direct people towards the Way of God. But the complexity of the instructions mandates the creation of specialists who study and analyze these instructions. The authoritativeness of these specialists is derived from their presumed competence over those instructions. Muslims are expected to defer to the authority of these specialists only because of this presumed competence. The deferment of the laity to the specialists in Islamic law is founded on trust – a trust that the specialists are in fact acquiring, understanding, and interpreting the instructions of God. I have argued that this trust is contingent on five main elements: honesty, comprehensiveness, reasonableness, diligence, and self-restraint.

As explained earlier, other than the issue of agency, there are two more components to the dynamics of authority in Islamic discourses. The first component is what I called the problem of competence or authenticity. The second component relates to the limits of interpretation or what I called the problem of determination. After addressing the problems of competence and determination, I will elaborate upon the dynamics of the authoritarian in Islamic discourses. I will deal with these issues in some detail in Chapters Four and Five. However, I will undertake the unusual step of summarizing the findings of the fourth and fifth chapters in Chapter Three. Chapters Four and Five are somewhat abstract and, by the standards of Islamic discourses, quite unorthodox. In order to accommodate the reader (and acting upon the advice of friendly readers), I will spell out the findings of Chapters Four and Five in Chapter Three but without providing the theoretical justification for these findings. Readers who are restless to get to the *responsa* section of the book, and who might not be interested in the details of my argument may proceed to Chapter Six of the book directly after reading the third chapter. However, I feel obligated to note that Chapter Three is not an adequate replacement for Chapters Four and Five. Consequently for those who are not willing to defer to my findings in the third chapter, a full evaluation of my arguments is not possible without reading the fourth and fifth chapters.

I hesitate before writing a summary of Chapters Four and Five because I worry that unwittingly I might be contributing to the rampant anti-intellectualism prevalent among Muslims today, a phenomenon that was alluded to above. I am aware that the abstractions of Chapters Four and Five are unusual in Muslim discourses, and that a few readers might even feel at liberty to evaluate the faith and fate of the author. Nevertheless, leaving faith and fate to that Who is empowered to assess these matters, my main purpose is to provide a transition into a style of reasoning that I think is crucial for the proper handling of the burden of speaking in God's name. Without a proper and thorough understanding of the nature and parameters of this role, I fear that the burden will invariably be mishandled. One possible approach to the chapters that follow, is to inverse the order of chapters – i.e. to read Chapters Three, Six, and Seven before reading Chapters Four and Five.

*NOTES*

1 Narrated by al-Bukhārī, Muslim, Abū Dāwūd, al-Nasāʾī, Ibn Mājah, Aḥmad b. Ḥanbal and others. See, al-Shawkānī, *al-Qawl al-Mufīd fī Adillat*, pp. 89–91.

2 See, for instance, Qurʾān, 6:164, 17:15, 35:18, 39:7, 53:38, 52:21, 2:181, 2:186; 3:161; 40:17, 45:22.

3 Al-Juwaynī, *Kitāb al-Ijtihād min Kitāb al-Talkhīṣ*, pp. 43–44; Shāh Walī Allāh, *al-Inṣāf.*

4 Shāh Walī Allāh, *al-Inṣāf*, pp. 10–16; al-Juwaynī, *Kitāb al-Ijtihād*, pp. 37–39; Hammad, *Islamic Law*, pp. 27–41; al-ʿAlwānī, *Adab al-Ikhtilāf fī al-Islām.*

5 Al-Dimashqī, *Raḥmat al-Ummah fī Ikhtilāf al-Aʾimmah.*

6 Al-Jirāḥī, *Kashf al-Khafāʾ*, 1:66–68. There is disagreement in the sources on whether this statement is a Prophetic *ḥadīth* or simply an inherited wise tradition (*āthār*).

7 Shāh Walī Allāh, *al-Inṣāf*, p. 12; al-Suyūṭī, *Ikhtilāf al-Madhāhib*, pp. 22–23; Dutton, *The Origins of Islamic Law*, p. 29; Crone and Hinds, *God's Caliph*, p. 86. Incidentally, there is a disagreement over whether the caliph in question was al-Manṣūr or Hārūn al-Rashīd (d. 193/809).

8 I memorized this statement during my youth, but I have not been able to locate it in a source. However, I found the quote cited in Hammad, *Islamic Law*, p. 44, but the author does not indicate that it belongs to Abū Ḥanīfah. This statement has also been attributed to al-Shāfiʿī. Another version of this report states, Abū Ḥanīfah is reported to have said: "We know [that] this [position] is one opinion, and it is the best we can arrive at. [If] someone arrives at a different view, then he adopts what he believes [is best] and we adopt what we believe [is best]" (*ʿalimnā hādhā raʾy wa huwa aḥsan mā qadarnā ʿalayhi fa man qadara ʿalā ghayr dhālik fa lahu mā raʾā wa lanā mā raʾaynāhu*). Ibn Ḥazm al-Ẓāhirī, *Kitāb al-Faṣl*, 2:46; Maḥmaṣānī, *Falsafat al-Tashrīʿ*, p. 42.

9 Of course, this is a misuse of the tradition. "*Al-dīn al-samiḥ*" does not mean the simple religion but the religion of facility and ease. "*Al-Islām al-dīn al-samiḥ*" or "*al-Islāmu dinun samiḥ*" are based on *ḥadīths* reported in al-Bukhārī (Kitāb al-Īmān) and the *Musnad* of Aḥmad b. Ḥanbal. These *ḥadīths* state that the most beloved religion to God or

the most authentic religion is the tolerant *Ḥanīfiyyah*. The *Ḥanīfiyyah* was an early monotheistic faith in the Arabian Peninsula prior to the revelation of the Qur'ān in Mecca. Historically, the expression "*al-Islām al-dīn al-samiḥ*" meant Islam is the religion of ease, tolerance, or compassion. Co-opting the expression as an argument for a simple or simplistic religion seems to have taken place in the modern age, particularly by the Salafī school of thought.

10 Edward Said broke new ground in his study of the cultural and intellectual discursive dynamic between the colonial West and the Islamic world in his *Orientalism*. See also, Yeğenoğlu, *Colonial Fantasies*, for further analysis and adaptation of orientalism in light of a feminist paradigm. For more general studies, see Tibi, *The Crisis of Modern Islam*; Tibi, *Islam and the Cultural Accommodation of Social Change*, pp. 102–118; Haddad, *Contemporary Islam and the Challenge of History*; Ajami, *The Arab Predicament*, pp. 50–75, 138–200; Shayegan, *Cultural Schizophrenia*; Vol I, *Islam*, pp. 289–374.

11 Of course, it is not possible to compartmentalize one's intellect, and I realize that simply because I had an original method or thought that does not preclude the possibility of a Western intellectual influence.

12 Ahmed, *A Border Passage*; Said, *Out of Place*; Abou El Fadl, *The Conference of the Books*.

13 Gellner, *Muslim Society*; Brown, *Rethinking Tradition*; Roy, *The Failure of Political Islam*; Asad, *Islam at the Crossroads*; Akhtar, *A Faith for All Seasons*.

14 For instance, see Qur'ān, 9:31.

15 Kennedy, *The Prophet and the Age of the Caliphates*, pp. 50–81; Lapidus, *A History of Islamic Societies*, pp. 54–58; Hourani, *A History of the Arab Peoples*, pp. 22–25; Abou El Fadl, "The Islamic Law of Rebellion", pp. 44, 62.

16 Crone and Hinds, *God's Caliph*; al-Azmeh, *Muslim Kingship*; Madelung, *The Succession to Muhammad*; Dabashi, *Authority in Islam*; Modarressi, *Crisis and Consolidation*; Hodgson, *The Venture of Islam*, vol. 1, pp. 195–230; Ja'īṭ, *al-Fitnah*.

17 Mottahedeh, *Loyalty and Leadership*, pp. 135–150; Zaman, "The Caliphs, the 'Ulamā', and the Law"; Makdisi, "The Guilds of Law in Medieval Legal History"; 1:233–252, 236–242; Makdisi, *The Rise of Colleges*, pp. 2–9; Crone and Hinds, *God's Caliph*, pp. 1, 19, 48–49; Abou El Fadl, "Islamic Law of Rebellion," p. 377.

18 See generally, Makdisi, "The Guilds of Law in Medieval Legal History"; Makdisi, "La Corporation à l'époque classique de l'Islam," pp. 35–49. Bulliet in his, *The Patricians of Nishapur*, investigates how legal education, in particular of the Ḥanafī and Shāfi'ī schools, confirmed one's status and class in Nishapuri society. Urvoy, "The 'Ulamā' of al-Andalus," in *The Legacy of Muslim Spain*, pp. 849–877, writes about the interaction between the *'ulamā'* and the ruling class, and how each impacted the other.

19 Jackson, *Islamic Law and the State*, pp. 142–185; Jackson, "From Prophetic Actions to Constitutional Theory," pp. 71–90; Makdisi, *Rise of Colleges*, pp. 200–202; Gaudefroy-Demombynes, *Muslim Institutions*, pp. 148–154; Bulliet, *Patricians of Nishapur*; Rebstock, "A Qāḍī's Errors," pp. 1–37; Müller, "Judging with God's Law on Earth". For a general historical discussion of the institution of *qaḍā'*, see, al-'Ajilānī, *'Abqariyyat al-Islām*, pp. 405–442.

20 Makdisi, *Rise of Colleges*, p. 200. For instance, Sufyān al-Thawrī (d. 161/778) was appointed by the 'Abbāsid caliph al-Manṣūr (r. 754–775) as *qāḍī*, but refused and fled to Mecca. Later he was appointed to the position of *qāḍī* over Kufa by the caliph al-Mahdī (r. 775–785), and again rejected the position. Notably, each time he rejected the caliphal offer, Sufyān had to flee in order to escape persecution. Al-Dhahabī, *Siyar A'lām*, pp. 229–279; Ibn Khallikān, *Wafayāt al-A'yān*, 2:322–326. Also, the famous historian and jurist al-Ṭabarī (d. 310/932) was offered the lucrative positions of *qāḍī* and overseer of *awqāf*, but each time he refused. When his associates implored him to take one of the positions so that he could dedicate himself thereafter to his scholarship without economic hardship, al-Ṭabarī responded scoldingly: "I would have thought that if I wanted such positions, you would have forbidden me from doing so." Al-Dhahabī, *Siyar A'lām*, 14:275. Likewise, Abū Bakr al-Jaṣṣāṣ, perhaps because of his piety and asceticism, refused an offer to become a judge. Al-Dhahabī, *Siyar A'lām*, 16:340–341.

21 Of course, different jurists accepted or rejected any or all of these elements to various extents or degrees. For instance, Fakhr al-Dīn al-Rāzī (d. 606/1210), Sayf al-Dīn al-Āmidī (d. 631/1233), and Muḥammad b. Aḥmad b. Rushd (d. 595/1198) incorporated more reason and rationality. Fakhr al-Dīn Muḥammad b. ʿUmar b. al-Ḥusayn al-Rāzī, *al-Maḥṣūl fī ʿIlm Uṣūl al-Fiqh*, ed. Ṭāhā Jābir Fayyāḍ al-ʿAlwānī, 3rd ed.; Sayf al-Dīn Abū al-Ḥasan ʿAlī b. Abī ʿAlī b. Muḥammad al-Āmidī, *al-Iḥkām fī Uṣūl al-Aḥkām*, ed. ʿAbd al-Razzāq ʿAfīfī, 2nd ed.; Abū al-Walīd Muḥammad b. Aḥmad b. Muḥammad b. Aḥmad al-Qurṭubī b. Rushd, *Bidāyat al-Mujtahid wa Nihāyat al-Muqtaṣid*. Ibrāhim b. Mūsā al-Shāṭibī (d. 790/1388) and Shihāb al-Dīn al-Qarāfī (d. 684/1285) incorporated more social use and customary practices. Abū Isḥāq Ibrāhīm b. Mūsā al-Shāṭibī, *al-Muwāfaqāt fī Uṣūl al-Fiqh*, eds. ʿAbd Allāh Darāz and Muḥammad ʿAbd Allāh Darāz; Shihāb al-Dīn Abū al-ʿAbbās Aḥmad b. Idrīs al-Qarāfī, *al-Furūq*, ed. Muḥammad Rawwās Qalʿah Jī. Ibn Taymiyyah (d. 728/1328), al-Ṭūfī (d. 716/1316) and Ibn al-Qayyim (d. 751/1350) incorporated more public utility and welfare. Taqī al-Dīn Aḥmad b. ʿAbd al-Ḥalīm b. Taymiyyah, *al-Ḥisbah fī al-Islām aw Waẓīfat al-Ḥukūmah al-Islāmiyyah* (Beirut: Dār al-Kutub al-ʿIlmiyyah, 1992); *idem*, *al-Siyāsah al-Sharʿiyyah fī Iṣlāḥ al-Rāʿī wa al-Raʿiyyah* (Beirut: Dār al-Kutub al-ʿIlmiyyah, 1988); *idem*, *Majmūʿ al-Fatāwā*, ed. ʿAbd al-Raḥmān b. Muḥammad b. Qāsim (Cairo: Maktabat Ibn Taymiyyah, n.d.); Najm al-Dīn al-Ṭūfī, "al-Ḥadīth al-Thānī wa al-Thalāthūn," in *al-Maṣlaḥah fī al-Tashrīʿ al-Islāmī wa Najm al-Dīn al-Ṭūfī*, Muṣṭafā Zayd, 2nd ed.; Shams al-Dīn Abī ʿAbd Allāh Muḥammad b. Abī Bakr b. Qayyim al-Jawziyyah, *Iʿlām al-Muwaqqiʿīn ʿan Rabb al-ʿĀlamīn*, ed. ʿAbd al-Raḥmān al-Wakīl (Cairo: Maktabat Ibn Taymiyyah, n.d.). But the vast majority of jurists grounded their legal analysis in text and treated these various elements or factors as aids to the hermeneutic and interpretive activity.

22 Abū al-Ḥasan ʿAlī b. Muḥammad b. Ḥabīb al-Māwardī, *al-Aḥkām al-Sulṭāniyyah*, pp. 19–21; al-Qāḍī Abū Yaʿlā Muḥammad b. al-Ḥusayn al-Farrāʾ, *al-Aḥkām al-Sulṭāniyyah*, p. 28; Lambton, *State and Government in Medieval Islam*, p. 19; Watt, *Islamic Political Thought*, pp. 102–103; Mikhail, *Politics and Revelation*, pp. 20–21; Gibb, "Constitutional Organization," pp. 3–27, 9, 12; Abou El Fadl, "Islamic Law of Rebellion," p. 8; Muḥammad Jalāl Sharaf and ʿAlī ʿAbd al-Muʿṭī Muḥammad, *al-Fikr al-Siyāsī fī al-Islām: Shakhṣiyyāt wa Madhāhib*, p. 399; Yūsuf Aybash, *Nuṣūṣ al-Fikr al-Siyāsī al-Islāmī: al-Imāmah ʿind al-Sunnah*, p. 55.

23 Abū Bakr Muḥammad b. ʿAbd Allāh b. al-ʿArabī, *Aḥkām al-Qurʾān*, ed. ʿAlī Muḥammad al-Bajāwī (Beirut: Dār al-Maʿrifah, n.d.), 2:603, justifies this concept by stating, "the ruler (*al-imām*) is not empowered to act as the agent (*wakīl*) of a particular group of people in regards to any particular set of rights. The ruler is the peoples' agent only in their general, non-specific, and non-particulized rights." He concludes from this that the ruler is not empowered to act on behalf of his subjects as their agent over specified and identifiable rights, and, therefore, the ruler needs specific consent to dispense with a specific right or entitlement. See also, al-Qurṭūbī, *al-Jāmiʿ* (1993), 6:103; Ibn Taymiyyah, *al-Siyāsah al-Sharʿiyyah*, pp. 65–144; ʿAlī Ḥasab Allāh, *Uṣūl al-Tashrīʿ al-Islāmī*, 3rd ed. (Cairo: Dār al-Maʿārif, 1964), pp. 293–297; Aḥmad Farrāj Ḥusayn, *Uṣūl al-Fiqh al-Islāmī* (Lebanon: al-Dār al-Jāmiʿiyyah, 1986), pp. 405–415; Lambton, *State and Government*, pp. 19–20.

24 Abū Muḥammad Maḥmūd b. Aḥmad al-ʿAyīnī, *al-Bināyah fī Sharḥ al-Hidāyah*, 6:482.

25 Ibn Qayyim al-Jawziyyah, *Iʿlām al-Muwaqqiʿīn* (Cairo), 3:5–6. For more elaboration on this passage, see Abou El Fadl, "Muslim Minorities and Self-Restraint in Liberal Democracies," pp. 1525–1542, 1526.

26 Ibn Qayyim al-Jawziyyah, *Iʿlām al-Muwaqqiʿīn* (Cairo), 3:5. See also, al-Shāṭibī, *al-Muwāfaqāt*, vol. 2, in which al-Shāṭibī spends the entire volume addressing the interplay and relationship between *maṣāliḥ* (public welfare) and *maqāṣid* (purposes of the law); and, al-Ṭūfī, "al-Ḥadīth al-Thānī wa al-Thalāthūn," whose discussion of the importance of *maṣlaḥah* in legal inquiry is unique in breadth and scope.

27 Ibn al-Jawzī Jamāl al-Dīn, Abū al-Faraj ʿAbd al-Raḥmān b. ʿAlī b. Muḥammad, *al-Shifāʾ fī Mawāʿiẓ al-Mulūk wa al-Khulafāʾ*, ed. Fuʾād ʿAbd al-Munʿim Aḥmad (Alexandria: Dār al-Daʿwah, n.d.), p. 57.

28 Fakhr al-Dīn ʿUthmān b. ʿAlī al-Zaylaʿī, *Tabyīn al-Ḥaqāʾiq: Sharḥ Kanz al-Daqāʾiq* (Medina: Dār al-Kitāb al-Islāmiyyah, n.d.), 3:24; also reported in Muḥammad b. Muḥammad b. Shihāb al-Kurdarī b. al-Bazzāz, *al-Fatāwā al-Bazzāziyyah*, printed in the margins of *al-Fatāwā al-Hindiyyah*, 3rd ed. (Beirut: Dār al-Maʿrifah, 1973), 6:430. On the prohibition of the use of torture in obtaining a confession see, al-Māwardī, *al-Aḥkām al-Sulṭāniyyah*, p. 58.

29 Hallaq, *A History of Islamic Legal Theories*, pp. 162–206; Enayat, *Modern Islamic Political Thought*, p. 74; Mikhail, *Politics and Revelation*, pp. 48–49; Abou El Fadl, "Islamic Law of Rebellion," pp. 377–395.

30 Enayat, *Modern Islamic Political Thought*, pp. 1–68. Also see, for instance, M. Isabel Calero Secall, "Rulers and Qāḍīs," who writes of how the ruling regime, through the power of judicial appointment, could render a *qāḍī* subservient to the political regime.

31 This is inspired by Richard L. Abel, *Politics by other Means*, p. 523, which states "[Law] is 'relatively autonomous,' influenced by economic infrastructure, pressured by political forces, and shaped by the social system, but not fully determined by any of them."

32 Ibn Qayyim al-Jawziyyah, *Iʿlām al-Muwaqqiʿīn*, 1:10. Of course, there is vast literature on the creative art of reconciling seemingly contradictory *ḥadīth*. Among the better known works are: Abū Jaʿfar Aḥmad b. Muḥammad b. Salāmah al-Ṭaḥāwī, *Sharḥ Mushkil al-Ḥadīth*, ed. Shuʿayb al-Arnaʿūṭ, 16 vols.; Abū ʿAbd Allāh Muḥammad b. Idrīs al-Shāfiʿī, *Ikhtilāf al-Ḥadīth*, printed in the margins of *al-Umm*, vol. 7 (Cairo: Maṭbaʿat Būlāq, 1325 A.H.); Abū Muḥammad ʿAbd Allāh b. Muslim al-Daynūrī b. Qutaybah, *Kitāb Taʾwīl Mukhtalaf al-Ḥadīth*.

33 Weiss, *The Spirit of Islamic Law*, pp. 113–114; Coulson, *History*, p. 52; Makdisi, *Rise of Colleges*, p. 106. Hiroyuki Yanagihashi, "The Judicial Functions," relates how political officials could exercise a limited equity jurisdiction on a case-by-case basis where the prevailing law imposed significant hardship on litigants.

34 See, for example, Abū al-Walīd Muḥammad b. Aḥmad al-Qurṭubī b. Rushd, *al-Bayān wa al-Taḥṣīl wa al-Sharḥ wa al-Tawjīh wa al-Taʿlīl fī al-Masāʾil al-Mustakhrajah*, ed. Muḥammad Ḥajjī, 2nd ed.; Aḥmad b. Yaḥyā al-Wansharīsī, *al-Miʿyār al-Muʿrib wa al-Jāmiʿ al-Maghrib ʿan Fatāwā ʿUlamāʾ Ifrīqiyah wa al-Andalus wa al-Maghrib*, ed. Muḥammad Ḥajjī which do preserve and report on the adjudications of some jurists.

35 Very early juristic sources, however, tended to selectively incorporate the adjudications of some rulers. See, for example, Wakīʿ Muḥammad b. Khalaf b. Ḥayyān, *Akhbār al-Quḍāh*, 1:305, 2:267. See also, Crone and Hinds, *God's Caliph*, pp. 43–57.

36 Ibn Rushd, *Bidāyat al-Mujtahid*; Shams al-Dīn Muḥammad b. ʿAbd Allāh al-Zarkashī, *Sharḥ al-Zarkashī ʿalā Mukhtaṣar al-Khiraqī fī al-Fiqh ʿalā Madhhab al-Imām Aḥmad b. Ḥanbal*, ed. ʿAbd Allāh b. ʿAbd al-Raḥmān b. ʿAbd Allāh al-Jibrīn; Khalīl b. Isḥāq al-Jundī, *Mukhtaṣar Khalīl*; ʿUmar b. al-Ḥusayn al-Khiraqī, *Mukhtaṣar al-Khiraqī* (n.p.: n.p., 1964); Abū al-Qāsim Najm al-Dīn Jaʿfar b. al-Ḥasan al-Ḥillī, *al-Mukhtaṣar al-Nāfiʿ fī Fiqh al-Imāmiyyah*; Ṭāhā b. Aḥmad b. Muḥammad b. Qāsim al-Kūrānī, *Sharḥ Mukhtaṣar al-Manār fī Uṣūl al-Fiqh*, ed. Shaʿbān Ismāʿīl; Muḥammad b. Aḥmad b. ʿAbd al-ʿAzīz b. ʿAlī al-Fatūḥī b. al-Najjār, *Sharḥ al-Kawkab al-Munīr al-Musammā Mukhtaṣar al-Taḥrīr aw al-Mukhtabar al-Mubtakar Sharḥ al-Mukhtaṣar fī Uṣūl al-Fiqh*, eds. Muḥammad al-Zuḥaylī and Nazīr Ḥammād; Abū ʿAlī al-Ḥasan b. Aḥmad b. ʿAbd Allāh b. al-Bannā, *Kitāb al-Muqniʿ fī Sharḥ Mukhtaṣar al-Khiraqī*, ed. ʿAbd al-ʿAzīz b. Sulaymān b. Ibrāhīm al-Buʿaymī; Abū al-Ḥasan Aḥmad b. Muḥammad b. Aḥmad b. Jaʿfar al-Qaddūrī, *Mukhtaṣar al-Qaddūrī fī al-Fiqh al-Ḥanafī*; Manṣūr b. Yūnus al-Bahūtī, *al-Rawḍ al-Murbiʿ Sharḥ Zād al-Mustaqniʿ*; Tāj al-Dīn Abī Naṣr ʿAbd al-Wahhāb b. ʿAlī b. ʿAbd al-Kāfī al-Subkī, *Rafʿ al-Ḥājib ʿan Mukhtaṣar Ibn al-Ḥājib*, ed. ʿAlī Muḥammad Muʿawwaḍ and ʿĀdil Aḥmad ʿAbd al-Mawjūd; ʿAlī b. Hilāl al-Dabbāb, *al-Shuʿāb al-Fāʾiḍ Sharḥ Mukhtaṣar ʿIlm al-Farāʾiḍ*.

37 Mohammad Fadel, "The Social Logic"; Fadel, "Rules, Judicial Discretion".

38 Makdisi, *Rise of Colleges*, pp. 116–122, writes about the *taʿlīqah* that students of law would write in which they would elaborate on various issues and disputations, often building upon the works of their predecessors. Melchert, *The Formation*, pp. 60–67, indicates the

emergence of commentary-literature from the 10th century to the 13th century on foundational texts within the Ḥanafī school of law.

39 Christelow, *Muslim Law Courts*; Anderson, "Modern Trends in Islam; Cleveland, *A History*, pp. 61–98; Coulson, *History*, pp. 149–181; Brinton, *The Mixed Courts of Egypt*; Mitchell, "Family Law". Of course, at times, colonial powers took over the implementation of Islamic law as in the case of the Anglo-Muhammadan law experience in India. Ali S.A., *Muhammadan Law*, pp. 1–4; Schacht, *An Introduction to Islamic Law*, pp. 94–97; Coulson, *History*, pp. 164–172. On the impact of Colonialism on the institutions of Islamic law in India see, Singha, *A Despotism of Law*, pp. 52–3, 60–70, 294–6, 300.

40 Perlmutter, *Egypt*.

41 Zebiri, *Mahmud Shaltut*; Abyaḍ, *Rashīd Riḍā*; Haddad, *Rashid Rida*; Ra'ūf Sha'labī, *Shaykh al-Islām*; Aḥmad Ziyādah, *al-Imām 'Abd al-Ḥalīm Maḥmūd: Ākhir al-'Ulamā' al-Awliyā'*; Muḥammad 'Imārah, *al-Shaykh Muḥammad al-Ghazālī: al-Mawqif al-Fikrī wa al-Ma'ārik al-Fikriyyah*; J.M.S. Baljon, *Religion and Thought*; Brown, *Rethinking Tradition in Modern Islamic Thought*; Albert Hourani, *Arabic Thought in the Liberal Age, 1798–1939*, pp. 222–244; Hüseyn Hilmi Işik, *The Religion Reformers in Islam*, pp. 135–143.

42 Mohammed Arkoun, *Rethinking Islam: Common Questions, Uncommon Answers*, pp. 68–70; Hallaq, *Islamic Legal Theories*, pp. 259–260. For studies on the social, political, and economic roles played by the *'ulamā'* in modern Iran, see, Hamid Algar, "The Oppositional Role of the Ulama in Twentieth-Century Iran," pp. 231–255; Shaul Bakhash, *The Reign of the Ayatollahs: Iran and the Islamic Revolution.*

43 Wahhābism is the reform ideology whose theological foundations were set in place by the eighteenth-century reformer Muḥammad b. 'Abd al-Wahhāb (d. 1792), and which are articulated in his book, *Kitāb al-Tawḥīd alladhī huwa Ḥaqq Allāh 'alā al-'Abīd*. In the late eighteenth-century, the Wahhābī doctrine was merged with the political and military might of the Āl Sa'ūd in the Arabian Peninsula in an effort to challenge Ottoman hegemony in the region. This challenge to Ottoman power was quashed by Egyptian forces under the direction of Muḥammad 'Alī (r. 1221–1265/1805–1848). Nevertheless, the Wahhābī ideology would be resuscitated in the early twentieth-century under the leadership of 'Abd al-'Azīz b. Sa'ūd, who succeeded in merging the puritanical ideology with the political and military might of his and neighboring tribes, thereby establishing the beginnings of what would become Saudi Arabia. Cleveland, *A History*, pp. 116–117, 215–216; Işik, *Religion Reformers*, pp. 112–121, Muḥammad Khalīl Harrās, *al-Ḥarakah al-Wahhābiyyah*; Lansiné Kaba, *The Wahhabiyya*, p. 5; Lawrence Paul Goldrup, "Saudi Arabia: 1902–1932: The Development of a Wahhabi Society". More than just a nationalist ideology, the Wahhābī ideology has permeated the thought of Muslim communities worldwide. See, Abou El Fadl, *Conference*; Kaba, *The Wahhabiyya*. The nineteenth-century Wahhābī movement in India associated with Syed Ahmad (d. 1248/1832) shares the same name as the Arabian ideological movement, but is distinct in its origins. See, Fasihuddin Balkhi, *Wahabi Movement*; Qeyamuddin Ahmad, *The Wahabi Movement in India*. For a critique of the Wahhābī doctrine, see the work by Muḥammad b. 'Abd al-Wahhāb's brother, Sulaymān b. 'Abd al-Wahhāb, *al-Ṣawā'iq al-Ilāhiyyah fī al-Radd 'alā al-Wahhābiyyah*. See also, Hüseyn Hilmi Işik, *Advice for the Wahhabi*, and Muḥammad al-Ḥusayn Āl Kāshif al-Ghiṭā', *Naqḍ Fatāwā al-Wahhābiyya*.

44 For critiques of *Shaykh* Muḥammad al-Ghazālī, see, Abū 'Ubaydah b. Ḥasan Āl Salmān, *Kutub ḥadhdhara minhā al-'Ulamā'*, 1:214–228, 327–329; Jamāl Sulṭān, *Azmat al-Ḥiwār al-Dīnī*; Salmān b. Fahd 'Awdah, *Fī Ḥiwār Hādī ma'a Muḥammad al-Ghazālī*; Rabī' b. Hādī Madkhalī, *Kashf Mawqif al-Ghazālī min al-Sunnah wa Ahlihā wa Naqd Ba'ḍ Ārā'ihi*; Ashraf b. 'Abd al-Maqṣūd b. 'Abd al-Raḥīm, *Jināyat al-Shaykh Muḥammad al-Ghazālī 'alā al-Ḥadīth wa Ahlihi*. For a *fatwā* prohibiting the distribution of Muḥammad Asad's translation of the Qur'ān, see, *Fatāwā al-Lajnah al-Dā'imah li al-Buḥūth al-'Ilmiyyah wa al-Iftā'*, 3:213–215. For the claim that Shāh Walī Allāh al-Dahlawī and 'Abd al-Qādir al-Jīlānī were unbelievers (*kāfir, mushrik*), see, *Fatāwā al-Lajnah* (1991), 3:344.

45 Authority is difficult to define. See Richard Tuck, "Why is Authority Such a Problem?". My purpose here is not to develop a philosophically refined definition of authority, but to explore the possible meanings of authority, and to develop an understanding of authority that could help us understand the dynamics of authoritativeness in Islam.
46 Friedman, "On the Concept of Authority in Political Philosophy," pp. 56–91.
47 Friedman, "On the Concept," p. 80. Also see, Joseph Raz, *The Authority of Law*, pp. 21–5, who makes the same type of distinction.
48 Friedman, "On the Concept," p. 83.
49 Hannah Arendt, "What is Authority," pp. 91–141, 128, has quite correctly noted that tradition is at the heart of both religion and authority.
50 Friedman, "On the Concept," p. 67.
51 Friedman, "On the Concept," p. 69.
52 Arendt, "What is Authority," p. 93.
53 Arendt, "What is Authority," p. 103.
54 Arendt, "What is Authority," pp. 91, 128–141.
55 Qur'ān, 2:260.
56 For the role of influence in the notion of power see, Steven Lukes, *Power: A Radical View*, pp. 11–13, 17–18, 36, 42, 43. On the idea of normative power and its relation to authority see Raz, *Practical Reason and Norms*, pp. 98–104. In his *The Authority of Law: Essays on Law and Morality*, p. 18, n. 19, it appears that Raz adopts a more restrictive definition of normative powers. I find the analysis in his former work more convincing. At any case, although I was inspired by Raz, I do not use the expression "normative power" in the same way. By normative power I mean the ability to influence the beliefs or conduct of people by convincing them that compliance with a certain directive is in their best interest and is consistent with their sense of self-reponsibility.
57 See Raz, "Authority and Justification," pp. 115–139, on the notion of abdication of responsibility.
58 Raz, *Practical Reason and Norms*, pp. 35–48, 58–84; Raz, *The Authority of Law*, pp. 22–3, 26–7, 32–3.
59 Again, I am not adopting this language solely in the Razian sense. Raz's analysis is multi-layered and complex, but is too intricate for the purposes of this study.
60 Finnis, *Natural Law and Natural Rights*, pp. 233–4.
61 On the symbolic significance of *shūrā* in the anti-ʿUthmān rebellions see, Abū ʿUmar Khalīfah b. Khayyāṭ al-ʿAṣfarī, *Ta'rīkh Ibn Khayyāṭ*, 1:146; Abū Yaʿqūb Yūsuf b. Ibrāhīm al-Warjalānī, *al-ʿAdl wa al-Inṣāf fī Maʿrifat Uṣūl al-Fiqh wa al-Ikhtilāf*, 2:44–45; Muḥammad b. Ibrāhīm al-Yamānī al-Wazīr, *al-ʿAwāṣim wa al-Qawāṣim fī al-Dhabb ʿan Sunnat Abī al-Qāsim*, 8:82; Jaʿīṭ, *al-Fitnah* (1989), pp. 114, 210–213; Hodgson, *Venture of Islam*, 1:213; Kennedy, *The Prophet*, pp. 72–75.
62 Jaʿīṭ, *al-Fitnah* (n.d.), p. 207; Abū al-Ḥasan ʿAlī b. Ismāʿīl al-Ashʿarī, *Maqālāt al-Islāmiyyīn wa Ikhtilāf al-Muṣallīn*, 1:61–64; G. Levi Della Vida, "Khāridjites," 4:1074–1077, 1074; Majid Fakhry, *A History of Islamic Philosophy*, pp. 37–38; Hodgson, *Venture of Islam*, 1:215–216; W. Montgomery Watt, *The Formative Period*, pp. 12–15; Kennedy, *The Prophet*, p. 79.
63 Abou El Fadl, "Islamic Law of Rebellion," p. 45.
64 ʿIzz al-Dīn Abī Ḥāmid ʿAbd al-Ḥamīd b. Hibat Allāh b. Abī al-Ḥadīd al-Madā'inī, *Sharḥ Nahj al-Balāghah*, 1:488.
65 Shihāb al-Dīn Aḥmad b. ʿAlī b. Ḥajar al-ʿAsqalānī, *Fatḥ al-Bārī bi Sharḥ Ṣaḥīḥ al-Bukhārī*, 14:303; Muḥammad b. ʿAlī b. Muḥammad al-Shawkānī, *Nayl al-Awṭār Sharḥ Muntaqā al-Akhbār min Aḥādīth Sayyid al-Akhyār*, 7:166. Also see, Farid Esack, *Qur'an Liberation and Pluralism*, p. 50.
66 al-Dhahabī, *Siyar Aʿlām*, 18:190.
67 Qur'ān, 12:40. See also, Qur'ān, 6:57, 6:62, 12:40.
68 Qur'ān, 12:67.
69 Qur'ān 5:49, 38:26.

70 Qur'ān, 4:105. See also, Qur'ān, 2:213, 5:48.
71 Qur'ān, 3:23, 5:44–5, 5:47, 24:48, 4:65, 42:10.
72 Qur'ān, 33:36.
73 The Arabic words used are *ḥukm* and *qaḍā'*. *Ḥukm* can be literally translated into decree and *qaḍā'* into judgment. But, of course, the translations do not come close to capturing the subtleties invoked by the terms. On the other hand in al-ʿAjilānī, *ʿAbqariyyat al-Islām*, p. 405, the author argues that the two terms have the same meaning. Arguably, there is at least a semiotic difference between the words judgment, law and rule. There is also a historical context to each of the verses cited above. These factors will have a considerable impact upon the hermeneutics of these verses, but this is a matter I do not deal with in this study.
74 Later, I will explain more fully why I am referring to this issue as competence instead of authenticity.
75 Perhaps this is exactly why the Khawārij held that a Muslim who commits a major sin or fails to see the truth is a *kāfir* (infidel). Muḥammad b. ʿAbd al-Karīm Abī Bakr Aḥmad al-Shahrastānī, *al-Milal wa al-Niḥal*, 1:132–133, 141; Abū Muḥammad al-Yamanī, *ʿAqā'id al-Thalāth wa al-Sabʿīn Firqah*, 1:20; al-Ashʿarī, *Maqālāt al-Islāmiyyīn*, 1:168; Fakhry, *Islamic Philosophy*, p. 38; Watt, *Formative Period*, p. 15; *idem*, *Islamic Philosophy and Theology*, pp. 8–10; Binyamin Abrahamov, *Islamic Theology*, p. 42; Levi Della Vida, "Khāridjites," p. 1076.
76 On the seriousness of *shirk* see, Qur'ān, 4:48, 4:116, 5:72. On submission to God and the doctrine of associating partners with God see, Fazlur Rahman, *Major Themes of the Qur'ān*, pp. 11–12, 23–24, 26–28, 67.
77 See Qur'ān, 6:164, 14:51, 40:17, 45:22, 74:38, 24:11, 2:286
78 See Qur'ān, 6:164, 17:15, 35:18, 39:7, 53:37. See also, Qur'ān, 2:255, 74:48, 6:51, 6:70, 32:4, 30:13, 2:123.
79 See Qur'ān, 2:30, 6:165, 7:69, 7:74. See also, Rahman, *Major Themes*, pp. 54, 61–62.
80 Qur'ān, 35:39.
81 See Qur'ān, 5:42, 5:58, 4:58, 5:8, 6:152, 16:90. See also, Rahman, *Major Themes*, pp. 41–43.
82 On the concept of justice and equity in the Qur'ān, see, Rahman, *Major Themes*, pp. 38–43, 46–52; Essack, *Qur'an, Liberation and Pluralism*, pp. 103–106; Majid Khadduri, *The Islamic Conception of Justice*, pp. 8–11. On the difference between procedural and substantive justice in Islamic sources see, Khadduri, *Islamic Conception*, pp. 135–160.
83 Qur'ān, 3:55. See also Qur'ān, 16:92, 16:124, 22:69, 39:3, 39:46, 3:55, 5:48, 6:164, 10:93, 16:124, 32:25, 39:3, 45:17, 2:113, 4:141, 7:87.
84 Qur'ān, 2:213. See also, Qur'ān, 3:19.
85 Qur'ān 16:64.
86 Qur'ān, 5:43.
87 Qur'ān, 5:47.
88 Qur'ān, 11:118 (emphasis added).
89 Qur'ān, 10:19 (emphasis added).
90 Qur'ān, 49:13 (emphasis added).
91 Al-Ashʿarī, *Maqālāt al-Islāmiyyīn*, 1:213–234; al-Shahrastānī, *al-Milal wa al-Niḥal*, 1:161–169; al-Yamanī, *ʿAqā'id*, 1:271–295; W. Madelung, "Murdji'a," 7:605–607; Watt, *Islamic Philosophy*, pp. 21–24; *idem*, *Formative Period*, pp. 119–143; Fakhry, *Islamic Philosophy*, pp. 38–39; Khadduri, *Islamic Conception*, pp. 27–29.
92 On the impact of the idea of *irjā'* on Islamic thought, see the two volume work, Ṣafar b. ʿAbd al-Raḥmān al-Ḥawālī, *Ẓāhirat al-Irjā' fī al-Fikr al-Islāmī*.
93 On the Ashʿariyyah and Muʿtazilah, see, al-Shahrastānī, *al-Milal wa al-Niḥal*, 1:56–97, 106–118; al-Ashʿarī, *Maqālāt al-Islāmiyyīn*, 1:235–249; Watt, *Islamic Philosophy*, pp. 46–55, 64–68, 75–97, 106–109; *idem*, *Formative Period*, pp. 120–121, 209–250, 297–312; *idem*, Ashʿariyya," 1:696; D. Gimaret, "Muʿtazila," 7:783–793; Fakhry, *Islamic Philosophy*, pp. 44–65, 203–217; Khadduri, *Islamic Conception*, pp. 54–58; George Makdisi, "Ashʿari and the Ashʿarites in Islamic Religious History," 17 (1962): pp. 37–80, and 18 (1963):

pp. 19–39. According to Watt, the Murji'ah, in their opposition to the Shīʿah and Khawārij, were the forerunners of Sunnī Islam. Watt, *Formative Period*, p. 128. Al-Shahrastānī indicates that the Murji'ah were not simply a pure or exclusive theological movement, but were also represented within different theological movements. For instance, he indicates that there were those among the Khawārij, Qadariyyah, and the Jabriyyah who held Murji'ī views. Al-Shahrastānī, *al-Milal wa al-Niḥal*, 1:162; Madelung, "Murdji'a," 7:606. The eponym of the Ḥanafī school of law, Abū Ḥanīfah (d. 150/767), was reported to have held Murji'ī beliefs. Some have suggested that his association with this theological movement assisted in the later perpetuation of its thought within different theological movements, such as the Najjāriyyah and Māturīdiyyah. See Madelung, "Murdji'a," 7:606–607.

94 Maḥmaṣānī, *Falsafat al-Tashrīʿ*, pp. 21–24; Weiss, *The Spirit of Islamic Law*, pp. 119–121.

95 Maḥmaṣānī, *Falsafat al-Tashrīʿ*, pp. 199–200; Muḥammad Abū Zahrah, *Uṣūl al-Fiqh*, p. 291; Muṣṭafā Zayd, *al-Maṣlaḥah fī al-Tashrīʿ al-Islāmī wa Najm al-Dīn al-Ṭūfī*, p. 22; Yūsuf Ḥāmid al-ʿĀlim, *al-Maqāṣid al-ʿĀmmah li al-Sharīʿah al-Islāmiyyah*, p. 80; Muḥammad b. ʿAlī b. Muḥammad al-Shawkānī, *Ṭalab al-ʿIlm wa Ṭabaqāt al-Mutaʿallimīn*, pp. 145–151.

96 The Arabic is "*kull mujtahid muṣīb*" and "*lī kull mujtahid naṣīb*". I will discuss these traditions in greater detail later.

97 Abū ʿUmar Yūsuf b. ʿAbd al-Barr al-Namarī, *Jāmiʿ Bayān al-ʿIlm wa Faḍlihi wa mā yanbaghī fī Riwāyatihi wa Ḥamlihi*, 1:7–10; Abū ʿAbd Allāh Muḥammad b. Yazīd al-Qazwīnī b. Mājah, *Sunan al-Ḥāfiẓ Ibn Mājah*, 1:81. Importantly, most collections of Prophetic traditions start out with a chapter on the importance of seeking knowledge.

98 Ibn ʿAbd al-Barr, *Jāmiʿ Bayān*, 1:60–62; al-Shawkānī, *Ṭalab al-ʿIlm*, p. 15.

99 See al-Suyūṭī, *Ikhtilāf al-Madhāhib*, pp. 21–39.

100 See on these issues, ibid., pp. 47–64.

101 Badrān Abū al-ʿAynayn Badrān, *Uṣūl al-Fiqh*, p. 322; ʿAbd al-Karīm Zaydān, *al-Madkhal li Dirāsat al-Sharīʿah al-Islāmiyyah*, p. 141; Mannāʿ al-Qaṭṭān, *Ta'rīkh al-Tashrīʿ al-Islāmī: al-Tashrīʿ wa al-Fiqh*, p. 304; Ṣubḥī al-Ṣāliḥ, *Maʿālim al-Sharīʿah al-Islāmiyyah*, p. 46; Maḥmaṣānī, *Falsafat al-Tashrīʿ*, p. 59; Mohammad Hashim Kamali, *Principles of Islamic Jurisprudence*, p. 285.

102 Shāh Walī Allāh, *al-Inṣāf*, p. 12; al-Suyūṭī, *Ikhtilāf al-Madhāhib*, pp. 22–23; Dutton, *Origins of Islamic Law*, p. 29; Crone and Hinds, *God's Caliph*, pp. 86–87.

103 Muḥammad Ṣidqī b. Aḥmad al-Būrnū Abū al-Ḥārith al-Ghazzī, *Mawsūʿat al-Qawāʿid al-Fiqhiyyah*, 1:33; ʿAlī Aḥmad al-Nadhwī, *al-Qawāʿid al-Fiqhiyyah*, pp. 27, 65, 158; Aḥmad b. Muḥammad al-Zarqā, *Sharḥ al-Qawāʿid al-Fiqhiyyah*, pp. 227–229; Maḥmaṣānī, *Falsafat al-Tashrīʿ*, pp. 200–202. Tyser, C.R. (trans.), *The Mejelle*, p. 8.

104 The failure to take account of the distinction between *Sharīʿah* and *fiqh* has led some Western scholars to misleadingly claim that Islamic law is immutable and unchangeable. See, Schacht, *Introduction*, pp. 1–2, 5, 202–204; Coulson, *History*, pp. 1–4, 82–85; *idem*, *Conflicts and Tensions*, pp. 20–21; Patricia Crone, *Roman, Provincial and Islamic Law*, pp. 18–19. *Sharīʿah* as a moral abstract is immutable and unchangeable, but no Muslim jurist has ever claimed that *fiqh* enjoys the same revered status.

105 A more historical translation for text would be *matn* or *khiṭāb*.

106 Schacht, *Introduction*, pp. 37–48. See also, Crone and Hinds, *God's Caliph*, pp. 43–57; Norman Calder, *Studies in Early Muslim Jurisprudence*, pp. 198–222.

107 Schacht, *Introduction*, pp. 45–48. See also, Coulson, *History*, pp. 53–61, which considers al-Shāfiʿī to have been the "master architect" of Islamic jurisprudence. For a refutation of this view, see, Hallaq, *Islamic Legal Theories*, pp. 30–35; *idem*, "Was al-Shafiʿi the Master Architect of Islamic Jurisprudence?," pp. 587–605; Dutton, *Origins of Islamic Law*, pp. 4–5.

108 For instance, see Qur'ān, 2:120, 2:145, 4:135, 5:49, 6:119, 18:28, 23:71, 38:26, 47:14–16, 79:40.

109 Qur'ān, 45:23, 28:50.

110 Muslim jurists differentiated between pure reason and practical or applied reason. Principles of law such as *al-barā'ah al-aṣliyyah* and *istiṣḥāb al-ḥāl* (presumption of non-

liability, and presumption of continuity) are derived from pure reason. Interpretive tools, such as *qiyās* and *istiḥsān*, and hermeneutic categories (addressed below) are all instances of applied or practical reason. *Ijtihād* is performed through the use of applied reason in light of the dictates of pure reason. In each case, a jurist must determine if the evidence adequately supports the modification of the presumptions of pure reason through the use of applied reason. In other words, the issue is when does one abandon the dictates of pure reason in favor of applied reason. This partly depends on the evidence that would support the use of applied reason.

111 Muḥammad Amīn b. ʿUmar b. ʿĀbidīn, "Nashr al-ʿArf fī Bināʾ Baʿḍ al-Aḥkām ʿalā al-ʿUrf," pp. 112–163; Abū Zahrah, *Uṣūl al-Fiqh*, pp. 217–219; Muhammad Khalid Masud, *Islamic Legal Philosophy*, pp. 226, 293–299;

112 Muḥammad Saʿīd Ramaḍān al-Būṭī, *Ḍawābiṭ al-Maṣlaḥah fī al-Sharīʿah al-Islāmiyyah*, pp. 207–216, 285–357; ʿAllāl al-Fāsī, *Maqāṣid al-Sharīʿah al-Islāmiyyah wa Makārimuhā*, pp. 137–140; Maḥmaṣānī, *Falsafat al-Tashrīʿ*, pp. 172–175; John Makdisi, "Legal Logic and Equity in Islamic Law," pp. 63–92; Kamali, *Principles*, pp. 167–168; Hallaq, *Islamic Legal Theories*, pp. 107–113; Dutton, *Origins of Islamic Law*, p. 34.

113 For instance, Najm al-Dīn al-Ṭūfī (d. 716/1316) was widely criticized by his fellow jurists when he suggested that public interest could be an independent and sufficient source of law even with the existence of text that is on point on a particular issue. Muṣṭafā Zayd, *al-Maṣlaḥah fī al-Tashrīʿ al-Islāmī wa Najm al-Dīn al-Ṭūfī*, pp. 65–172; al-Būṭī, *Ḍawābiṭ al-Maṣlaḥah*, pp. 178–189; Masud, *Islamic Legal Philosophy*, pp. 165, 174–175; Hallaq, *Islamic Legal Theories*, p. 208; Ihsan Abdul Baghby, "Utility in Classical Islamic Law, pp. 166–170.

114 Maḥmaṣānī, *Falsafat al-Tashrīʿ*, p. 168; Kamali, *Principles*, p. 197; Hallaq, *Islamic Legal Theories*, pp. 83–84.

115 Maḥmaṣānī, *Falsafat al-Tashrīʿ*, pp. 172–175; Kamali, *Principles*, pp. 253–257.

116 Watson and Abou El Fadl, "Fox Hunting, Pheasant Shooting, and Comparative Law," pp. 1–37, 28–36; Abou El Fadl, "Islamic Law of Rebellion," pp. 377–401.

117 On the idea of linguistic practice in a juristic culture see, Conley and O'Barr, *Just Words*.

118 Muslim jurists often raised this point to justify the laity's adherence (*taqlīd*) to the opinions of *mujtahids* and *muftīs* in matters of *furūʿ*. See, for example, Abū Isḥāq Ibrāhīm b. ʿAlī b. Yūsuf al-Fayrūzābādī al-Shīrāzī, *al-Tabṣirah fī Uṣūl al-Fiqh*, p. 414; *idem*, *Sharḥ al-Lumʿah*, 2:1010–1011; Ibn al-Najjār, *Sharḥ al-Kawkab al-Munīr*, 4:540; Abū Bakr Aḥmad b. ʿAlī b. Thābit al-Khaṭīb al-Baghdādī, *Kitāb al-Faqīh wa al-Mutafaqqih wa Uṣūl al-Fiqh*, pp. 252–253; Abū ʿAlī al-Ḥasan b. Shihāb al-Ḥasan al-ʿUkbarī, *Risālah fī Uṣūl al-Fiqh*, p. 130; Maḥfūẓ b. Aḥmad b. al-Ḥasan Abū al-Khaṭṭāb al-Kalūzānī, *al-Tamhīd fī Uṣūl al-Fiqh*, 4:399–402.

119 Over certain issues and under particular circumstances, ignorance of the law is an excuse. For example, if someone is a recent convert to Islam who has not had an adequate opportunity to learn the law.

120 See generally, George Makdisi, *Ibn ʿAqil*, pp. 60–64; *idem*, *Rise of Colleges*; *idem*, "The Guilds of Law in Medieval Legal History"; *idem*, "La Corporation à l'époque classique de l'Islam"; Bulliet, *The Patricians of Nishapur*.

121 Makdisi, *Rise of Colleges*, pp. 82–84, 96–98; *idem*, *Ibn ʿAqil*, p. 25.

122 Jackson, *Islamic Law and the State*, pp. 76–112; *idem*, "*Taqlīd*", pp. 165–192; Fadel, "The Social Logic of *Taqlīd*".

123 Wael Hallaq, "Was the Gate of Ijtihād Closed?", pp. 3–41; Jackson, *Islamic Law and the State*, pp. 96–102; *idem*, "*Taqlīd*," pp. 167–173. For the thesis that the "door of *ijtihād*" is closed, see, Schacht, *Introduction*, pp. 69–72; Coulson, *History*, pp. 80–82. For a conceptual and historiographical overview of the debate on the "door of *ijtihād*", see Shaista P. Ali-Karamali and Fiona Dunne, "The Ijtihad Controversy," pp. 238–257.

124 Watson, *The Nature of Law*, pp. 94–95; *idem*, *Failures of the Legal Imagination*, pp. 97–101.

125 One can see this, for instance, in the fact that it took about four years to punish Ibn ʿAqīl for his defiance of the Ḥanbalī legal guild. Makdisi, *Ibn ʿAqil*, p. 28; Abou El Fadl, "The Scholar's

Road," pp. 325–338. Adherents of the Ḥanbalī school in the 4th/10th century were forced to rely on their own means to oppose, harrass, and even physically attack the jurist and historian al-Ṭabarī (d. 310/923), in part because he deemed Aḥmad b. Ḥanbal to be a *ḥadīth* collector and transmitter, and not a jurist. Al-Dhahabī, *Siyar Aʿlām*, 14:272, 277; Makdisi, *Rise of Colleges*, p. 146. For an example of government intervention in legal guild disputes, consider the efforts by the Saljuq wazīr, Niẓām al-Mulk (d. 485/1092), in favor of the Shāfiʿī *madhhab* in Nishapur. In an attempt to make the *ʿulamāʾ* dependent on the government, he distributed goverment largesse to the Shāfiʿī guild. In doing so, he shifted the balance of power in Nishapur against the adherents of the Ḥanafī *madhhab*, who had been favored by the prior Saljuq wazīr ʿAmīd al-Mulk al-Kundūrī (d. 456/1064). Bowen and Bosworth, "Niẓām al-Mulk," 8:69–73, 71–72; George Makdisi, "al-Kundūrī," 5:387–388, 388; Bulliet, *The Patricians of Nishapur*, pp. 72–75. Opponents of the Mālikī jurist and philosopher Ibn Rushd (Averroes) (d. 595/1198) allied themselves with the Almohad Caliph al-Manṣūr, who ultimately decreed that Ibn Rushd be exiled and that his books be burned. Khayr al-Dīn al-Ziriklī, *al-Aʿlām*, 5:318; Abou El Fadl, "A Homily for Ibn Rushd," pp. 141–146. When Ṭūmānbāy al-Ashrafī Qāytbāy assumed the office of Sultān in Egypt, he assisted the Ṣūfīs of the Baybarsiyyah *khānqāh* in their attempts to discredit their *Shaykh*, the famous Jalāl al-Dīn al-Suyūṭī (d. 911/1505). E.M. Sartain, *Jalāl al-Dīn al-Suyūṭī*, p. 98. Tāj al-Dīn al-Subkī (d. 771/1370), the famous Shāfiʿī jurist and historian, was subject to intense persecution by those jealous of his ability and judicial position. It is remarked that he was oppressed in a manner never before experienced by a jurist. He was imprisoned for eighty days and it is reported that he was physically tortured. However it is not clear whether his oppressors were supported by the ruling agents or not. Abū al-Falāḥ ʿAbd al-Ḥayy b. al-ʿImād, *Shadharāt al-Dhahab fī Akhbār man Dhahab*, 6:221–222; al-Ziriklī, *al-Aʿlām*, 4:184–185; Schacht and Bosworth, "al-Subkī," 9:743–745, 744.

126 To name a few, consider the examples of Ibn Taymiyyah (d. 728/1328), Ibn Qayyim al-Jawziyyah (d. 751/1350), Ibn ʿAqīl (d. 513/1119), Abū Bakr al-Sarakhsī (d. 483/1090), Fakhr al-Dīn al-Rāzī (d. 606/1210), Jalāl al-Dīn al-Suyūṭī (d. 911/1505), Abū Ḥāmid al-Ghazālī (d. 505/1111).

127 For instance, when Muwaffaq al-Dīn b. Qudāmah (d. 620/1223) died in Damascus, the turnout for his evening funeral was unprecedented at the time, such that the torches used to light the city made it appear as if all of Damascus were ablaze. Ibn al-ʿImād, *Shadharāt al-Dhahab*, 5:92. Nearly a century later when Ibn Taymiyyah (d. 728/1328) died in Damascus, it is reported that 200,000 people turned out for his funeral, 15,000 of whom were women. Ibn ʿImād, *Shadharāt al-Dhahab*, 6:86. Ibn ʿAqīl, likewise received a massive public turnout for his funeral; it is reported that nearly 300,000 people attended his funeral services. Al-Dhahabī, *Siyar Aʿlām*, 19:447; Ibn al-ʿImād, *Shadharāt al-Dhahab*, 4:38; Abou El Fadl, "The Scholar's Road," p. 337. Furthermore, the public lectures given by Abū Ḥāmid al-Ghazālī would regularly be attended by hundreds of people, many of whom were the local notables. Ibn al-ʿImād, *Shadharāt al-Dhahab*, 4:13. When al-Ghazālī's former teacher, *Imām al-Ḥaramayn* al-Juwaynī (d. 478/1085) would give his lessons, three hundred students regularly attended, many of whom included prominent scholars (*akābir al-ʿulamāʾ*). Ibn al-ʿImād, *Shadharāt al-Dhahab*, 3:359; al-Ziriklī, *al-Aʿlām*, 4:160. Trained jurists (*fuqahāʾ*) would travel from various regions to study under Ibrāhīm b. ʿAlī al-Shīrāzī (d. 476/1083), only to become significant jurists themselves (*tukhraju bihi aʾimmah akābir*). Ibn al-ʿImād, *Shadharāt al-Dhahab*, 3:349. Alternatively, a few local notables attended the inaugural lecture of the Shāfiʿī *ḥadīth* expert Jamāl al-Dīn al-Mizzī (d. 742/1341) upon his appointment to the professorship of the Dār al-Ḥadīth al-Ashrafiyyah in 718/1319 because of the displeasure among some local *ʿulamāʾ* at his appointment. Makdisi, *Rise of Colleges*, p. 158.

128 It is likely that asserting that a large number of laity attended a jurist's funeral became a topoi, of sorts, indicating the popularity of the jurist.

129 For instance, the famous Mālikī jurist Shihāb al-Dīn al-Qarāfī (d. 684/1285) conceptualized his constitutional theory of the *madhhab* in the face of judicial over-

reaching by the Shāfiʿī chief *qāḍī* of Cairo, Tāj al-Dīn b. bint al-Aʿazz (d. 665/1267), who subjected judicial decisions made by judges of the different legal guilds to his own views. While Ibn bint al-Aʿazz was chief *qāḍī* of Cairo, he seems to have achieved no other significant recognition as a jurist. Jackson, *Islamic Law and the State*; al-Ziriklī, *al-Aʿlām*, 3:315. Likewise, Sharīf Abū Jaʿfar (d. 470/1077) led an effort to persecute Ibn ʿAqīl when the latter was appointed to the leading chair of the Ḥanbalī school in Baghdad. However, Abū Jaʿfar himself does not seem to have been particularly talented as a jurist. Makdisi, *Ibn ʿAqil*; al-Ziriklī, *al-Aʿlām*, 3:292. Jalāl al-Dīn al-Suyūṭī held the post of *Shaykh* in the Baybarsiyyah Ṣūfī *khānqāh*. The opposition against him, which ultimately kindled an antagonism between al-Suyūṭī and the sulṭān, was orchestrated by ʿAbd al-Khāliq al-Mīqātī, whose biographical details are scant. His biographers describe him as a pious and virtuous scholar, but otherwise, he is negligible. Sartain, *Jalāl al-Dīn al-Suyūṭī*, pp. 97, 99. Likewise, as noted above, Tāj al-Dīn al-Subkī was persecuted by those who seemed jealous of his judicial posts and prestige. However those who persecuted him seem to have been forgotten over the course of time. Ibn al-ʿImād, *Shadharāt al-Dhahab*, 6:221–222.

130 In jurisprudential sources this field is known as *ʿilm al-tarjīḥ* or *ʿilm al-taʿāruḍ wa al-tarjīḥ* or *ʿilm al-taʿdīl wa al-tarjīḥ* – the field of conflict and preponderance or the field of balance and preponderance.

131 Weiss, *The Search for God's Law*, pp. 734–8. Other than Weiss, see sources listed in *infra*, n. 144.

132 This is the well-known problem of *al-taghannī bi al-Qurʾān* (singing the verses of the Qurʾān).

133 These lists have been compiled by consulting Weiss and the following sources: Sayf al-Dīn Abū al-Ḥasan ʿAlī b. Abī ʿAlī b. Muḥammad al-Āmidī, *al-Iḥkām fī Uṣūl al-Aḥkām*, 4:245–297; Abū Bakr Muḥammad b. Aḥmad b. Abī Sahl al-Sarakhsī, *Uṣūl al-Sarakhsī*, 2:249–265; Jamāl al-Dīn Abī Muḥammad ʿAbd al-Raḥīm b. al-Ḥasan al-Asnawī, *Nihāyat al-Sūl fī Sharḥ Minhāj al-Wuṣūl ilā ʿIlm al-Uṣūl*, 2:963–1023; al-Kalūzānī, *al-Tamhīd*, 4:226–251; al-Qāḍī Abū Yaʿlā Muḥammad b. al-Ḥusayn al-Farrāʾ, *al-ʿUddah fī Uṣūl al-Fiqh*, 5:1465–1539; Abū al-Muẓaffar Manṣūr b. Muḥammad b. ʿAbd al-Jabbār al-Simʿānī, *Qawāṭiʿ al-Adillah fī al-Uṣūl*, 2:235–258; Abū al-Ḥusayn Muḥammad b. ʿAlī b. al-Ṭayyib al-Baṣrī, *al-Muʿtamad fī Uṣūl al-Fiqh*, 2:457–459; al-Shīrāzī, *al-Tabṣirah*, pp. 472–491; Saʿd al-Dīn Masʿūd b. ʿUmar al-Taftazānī, *Ḥāshiyah ʿalā Mukhtaṣar al-Muntahā al-Uṣūlī li al-Imām Ibn Ḥājib*, 2:309–319; Shams al-Dīn Maḥmūd b. ʿAbd al-Raḥmān al-Iṣfahānī, *Sharḥ al-Minhāj li al-Bayḍāwī fī ʿIlm al-Uṣūl*, 2:781–818; Muwaffaq al-Dīn Abū Muḥammad ʿAbd Allāh b. Aḥmad b. Qudāmah al-Maqdisī, *Rawḍat al-Nāẓir wa Jannat al-Munāẓīr*, 2:456–474; Muḥammad b. ʿAbd al-Ḥamīd al-Asmandī, *Badhl al-Naẓar fī al-Uṣūl*, pp. 650–670; Saʿd al-Dīn Masʿūd b. ʿUmar al-Taftazānī, *Sharḥ al-Talwīḥ ʿalā al-Tawḍīḥ li Matn al-Tanqīḥ fī Uṣūl al-Fiqh*, 2:102–117; Ḥasan al-ʿAṭṭār, *Ḥāshiyat al-ʿAṭṭār ʿalā Jamʿ al-Jawāmiʿ*, 2:400–420; Tāj al-Dīn Abī Naṣr ʿAbd al-Wahhāb b. ʿAlī b. ʿAbd al-Kāfī al-Subkī and ʿAlī b. ʿAbd al-Kāfī al-Subkī, *al-Ibhāj fī Sharḥ al-Minhāj ʿalā Minhāj al-Wuṣūl ilā ʿIlm al-Uṣūl*, pp. 212–269; Sirāj al-Dīn Maḥmūd b. Abī Bakr al-Urmawī, *al-Taḥṣīl min al-Maḥṣūl*, 2:253–277; Abū al-Fatḥ Aḥmad b. ʿAlī b. Burhān al-Baghdādī, *al-Wuṣūl ilā al-Uṣūl*, 2:351–361; Muḥammad b. al-Ḥasan al-Badakhshī, *Sharḥ al-Badakhshī Manāhij al-ʿUqūl maʿa Sharḥ al-Asnawī Nihāyat al-Sūl*, 3:202–263; Abū Ḥāmid Muḥammad b. Muḥammad al-Ghazālī, *al-Mustaṣfā min ʿIlm al-Uṣūl*, 2:384–394, 560–565; ʿAlāʾ al-Dīn ʿAbd al-ʿAzīz b. Aḥmad al-Bukhārī, *Kashf al-Asrār ʿan Uṣūl Fakhr al-Islām al-Bazdāwī*, 4:131–173; Shams al-Dīn Muḥammad b. Mufliḥ al-Maqdisī, *Uṣūl al-Fiqh*, 4:1581–1630; Abū al-Walīd Sulaymān b. Khalaf al-Bājī, *Iḥkām al-Fuṣūl fī Aḥkām al-Uṣūl*, pp. 645–688; *Imām al-Ḥaramayn* Abū Maʿālī ʿAbd al-Malik b. ʿAbd Allāh b. Yūsuf al-Juwaynī, *al-Burhān fī Uṣūl al-Fiqh*, 2:175–257; Abū Isḥāq Ibrāhīm al-Shīrāzī, *Sharḥ al-Lumʿa*, 2:950–965; Fakhr al-Dīn Muḥammad b. ʿUmar b. al-Ḥusayn al-Rāzī, *al-Maḥṣūl fī ʿIlm Uṣūl al-Fiqh*, 2:434–488; ʿAbd al-Qādir b. Aḥmad b. Muṣṭafā Badran al-Dawmī al-Dimashqī, *Nuzhat al-Khāṭir al-ʿĀṭir*, 2:394–409.

134 See Tāj al-Dīn Abī Naṣr ʿAbd al-Wahhāb b. ʿAlī b. ʿAbd al-Kāfī al-Subkī, *Ṭabaqāt al-Shāfiʿiyyah al-Kubrā*, 6:186–199, where Tāj al-Dīn (d. 771/1370) presents a list of legal

problems upon which his father, Taqī al-Dīn ʿAlī b. ʿAbd al-Kāfī (d. 756/1355), purportedly performed a *taṣḥīḥ*.

135 For instance, Abū Ḥāmid al-Ghazālī, *al-Mustaṣfā*, 2:565–566; Ibn Mufliḥ al-Maqdisī, *Uṣūl al-Fiqh*, 3:1411–1429.

136 Al-Juwaynī, *al-Burhān*, 2:162. See also al-Samʿānī, *Qawāṭiʿ al-Adillah*, 2:259–260; al-Taftazānī, *Ḥāshiyah ʿalā Mukhtaṣar al-Muntahā*, 2:281.

137 For instance, see al-Shīrāzī, *Sharḥ al-Lumʿah*, 2:1043; Ibn Mufliḥ al-Maqdisī, *Uṣūl al-Fiqh*, 4:1469; al-Asnawī, *Nihāyat al-Sūl* (1999), 2:1025; Abū Ḥāmid al-Ghazālī, *al-Mustaṣfā*, 2:598; ʿAbd al-Majīd ʿAbd al-Ḥamīd al-Dībānī, *al-Minhāj al-Wāḍiḥ fī ʿIlm Uṣūl al-Fiqh wa Ṭuruq Istinbāṭ al-Aḥkām*, 2:345; al-ʿUkbarī, *Risālah fī Uṣūl al-Fiqh*, p. 124; al-Badakhshī, *Sharḥ al-Badakhshī*, 3:260–261; al-Āmidī, *al-Iḥkām* (1402 A.H.), 4:162; Fakhr al-Dīn al-Rāzī, *al-Maḥṣūl* (1997), 6:6; Muḥammad ʿUbayd Allāh al-Asʿadī, *al-Mūjaz fī Uṣūl al-Fiqh*, p. 262; Abū Zahrah, *Uṣūl al-Fiqh*, p. 301; al-Kalūzānī, *al-Tamhīd*, 4:394.

138 Al-Dībānī, *al-Minhāj al-Wāḍiḥ*, 2:355; Ibn al-Najjār, *Sharḥ al-Kawkab al-Munīr*, p. 492. Often Muslim jurists would inquire into the nature of the *mujtahid's* obligation (*taklīf*) when facing *de novo* issues of law. Whether or not they held that God specifies a particular ruling (*ḥukm muʿayyan*), they would often maintain that the *mujtahid's taklīf* in these circumstances was to engage in the search (*ṭalab*) itself. Impliedly, any negligence in the quality and scope of *ijtihād* would constitute a breach of the *mujtahid's* obligation before God. See, al-Kalūzānī, *al-Tamhīd*, 4:310–311; Fakhr al-Dīn al-Rāzī, *al-Maḥṣūl* (1997), 6:56; al-Shīrāzī, *Sharḥ al-Lumʿah*, 2:1049; al-Shīrāzī, *al-Tabṣirah*, p. 498.

139 For instance, a judge or jurist may be held liable for reckless or malicious judgments. See, Abū Bakr Aḥmad b. ʿAmr b. Muhīr al-Shaybānī al-Khaṣṣāṣ, *Kitāb Adab al-Qāḍī*, pp. 364–365; Abū al-Ḥasan ʿAlī b. Muḥammad b. Ḥabīb al-Māwardī, *Adab al-Qāḍī*, 1:233; Abū al-Qāsim ʿAlī b. Muḥammad al-Raḥbī al-Simnānī, *Rawḍat al-Quḍāh wa Ṭarīq al-Najāḥ*, 1:157–8. Some jurists have argued that a jurist can be held financially liable for negligence in discharging his or her duties in the issuance of *responsa*. Ibn Qayyin al-Jawziyyah, *Iʿlām al-Muwaqqiʿin* (Cario, n.d.), 4:225–7.

140 In his *al-Iḥkām fī Uṣūl al-Aḥkām*, Ibn Ḥazm (d. 456/1064), the Ẓāhirī jurist of Andalusia, opposes the use of analogical reasoning (*qiyās*) in the law. In doing so, he claims that those who support the use of *qiyās* lack sufficient understanding (*man lahu aqall fahm*), and that their arguments are ambiguous, corrupt, and fraudulent (*ishkāl wa ifsād wa tadlīs*). Abū Muḥammad ʿAlī b. Aḥmad b. Saʿīd b. Ḥazm, *al-Iḥkām fī Uṣūl al-Aḥkām*, 8:489. In another example, as related above, few local notables attended the inaugural lecture of Jamāl al-Dīn al-Mizzī, who was appointed to the professorship of the Dār al-Ḥadīth al-Ashrafiyyah in 718/1319. The poor turnout was attributed to the fact that the local *ʿulamāʾ* objected to his appointment. Makdisi, *Rise of Colleges*, p. 158. Shihāb al-Dīn al-Qarāfī assserts that the jurists of his age could not provide a logically consistent understanding of the technical interpretive categories of *ʿāmm* and *muṭlaq*. Jackson, "*Taqlīd*," pp. 165–192, 175.

141 See n. 121, 124.

142 *Al-Fatāwā al-Hindiyyah*, 6:346.

143 This tension in methodology, for instance, can be seen in the conflict between al-Ṭabarī and the students of the Ḥanbalī *madhhab* in 4$^{th}$/10$^{th}$ century Baghdad. For al-Ṭabarī, Aḥmad b. Ḥanbal's reliance on *ḥadīth* to resolve *de novo* issues of law rendered his legal methodology rigid and mechanical. Hence, al-Ṭabarī claimed that Aḥmad b. Ḥanbal was no more than a *muḥaddith* (collector of *ḥadīth*), as opposed to being a jurist capable of employing a technical and conceptual methodology of legal analysis. The Ḥanbalīs responded with outrage and disdain against al-Ṭabarī, to the point of effectively placing him under house arrest and physically attacking him. Al-Dhahabī, *Siyar Aʿlām*, 14:272, 277; Makdisi, *Rise of Colleges*, p. 146.

144 Ibn Aḥmad al-Makkī, *Manāqib Abī Ḥanīfah*, p. 350. The jurist al-Baṣrī notes that there are many individuals who memorize and study the *ḥadīth* but are not qualified to be jurists. Abū al-Ḥusayn al-Baṣrī, *al-Muʿtamad* (1983), 2:362.

145 Qurʾān, 9:122.

146 Qur'ān, 21:7.
147 Al-Qurṭubī, *al-Jāmiʿ* (1993), 8:186–188, 11:180–181; Ibn al-ʿArabī, *Aḥkām al-Qur'ān* (n.d.), 2:1030–1032.
148 Al-Māwardī, *Aḥkām al-Sulṭāniyyah*, p. 5; Lambton, *State and Government*, p. 1; Watt, *Islamic Political Thought*, p. 94.
149 Qur'ān, 88:21–22.
150 Typically, Muslim jurists argue that if everyone would dedicate himself to studying the Divine law society or law would collapse. Either there will be no doctors, scientists, merchants, and other professionals because everyone is too busy studying the law or the study of the law would have to be performed by non-specialists, which will lead to the disintegration of law. Society needs all kinds of professionals, and jurists specialize in the study of law on behalf of the whole nation. See Abū Ḥāmid Muḥammad b. Muḥammad al-Ghazālī, *al-Mustaṣfā min ʿIlm al-Uṣūl*, 2:389; Abū al-Ḥusayn al-Baṣrī, *al-Muʿtamad*, (1983), 2:361; al-Kalūzānī, *al-Tamhīd*, 4:400.
151 In this context, the sources often cite the tradition attributed to the Prophet, "Ask your heart even if (people) advise you, advise you again, and then advise you again." Aḥmad b. Ḥanbal, *Musnad al-Imām Aḥmad b. Ḥanbal*, 4:311–312.
152 See al-Suyūṭī, *Ikhtilāf al-Madhāhib*, pp. 41–52, for his discussion on changing legal schools. For a discussion on the laity's obligation to investigate the competence of the *muftī*, see, Shihāb al-Dīn Abū al-ʿAbbās Aḥmad b. Idrīs al-Qarāfī, *Sharḥ Tanqīḥ al-Fuṣūl fī Ikhtiṣār al-Maḥṣūl fī al-Uṣūl*, p. 442; al-Kalūzānī, *al-Tamhīd*, 4:403; al-Rāzī, *al-Maḥṣūl* (1997), 6:81–82; Ibn al-Najjār, *Sharḥ al-Kawkab al-Munīr*, 4:541–544; Abū al-Ḥasan ʿAlī b. ʿUmar b. al-Qaṣṣār, *al-Muqaddimah fī al-Uṣūl*, pp. 26–27; al-Āmidī, *al-Iḥkām* (1402 A.H.), 4:232; Jamāl al-Dīn Abī Muḥammad ʿAbd al-Raḥīm b. al-Ḥasan al-Asnawī, *al-Tamhīd fī Takhrīj al-Furūʿ ʿalā al-Uṣūl*, pp. 530–531; al-Shīrāzī, *Sharḥ al-Lumʿah*, 2:1037–1038; Muḥammad b. ʿAlī b. Muḥammad al-Shawkānī, *Irshād al-Fuḥūl ilā Taḥqīq al-Ḥaqq min ʿIlm al-Uṣūl*, pp. 399–401; Badrān, *Uṣūl al-Fiqh*, p. 497.
153 I am not at all excluding the possibility that the medium could also be non-textual or ultra textual evidence of the Divine Will. For example, signs revealed through God's various creations and creatures could also be relevant. The past or present course of conduct of poeple or the habits and intuitions of human beings (*ṭabīʿat al-khalq* or *sharʿ man qablana* or *ʿādat al-nās* or *sunnat al-khalq*) or the laws of nature (*sunnat al-kawn*) could all be relevant considerations in investigating the Divine Will.
154 This idea is explored to a greater detail in my *Conference of the Books*.
155 Finnis, for instance, argues that such basic values should be respected through an evaluation of every act. In other words, if it can be reasonably concluded that an act will negatively affect the realization of certain basic goods in society, then that act should be avoided. Effectively, the act itself becomes an indicator of its legal value, and hence of right conduct. Finnis, *Natural Law and Natural Rights*, pp. 118–125.
156 Elsewhere, I argue that the fundamental character of God's Way is beauty. Abou El Fadl, "The Search for Beauty," *Conference of the Books*, pp. 113–116. Beauty encompasses all lower order values such as justice, compassion, dignity and so forth.
157 I do not mean to say that human beings are God's agents in the sense that they undertake to perform acts on His behalf and for His benefit. I am using the word "agents" as the equivalent of *khulafā'* – i.e. individuals who act pursuant to God's instruction to accomplish goals set out by God. The benefits of the agency accrue solely to the benefit of the agent and not the Principal. In other words, the agency here refers to a delegation in which the delegating power does not expect to receive any benefit. I prefer to use the word agents instead of delegates because it might be more respectful towards Muslim sensitivities.
158 Muslim jurists argued that a jurist is entitled to deference only to the extent that his views are based on the evidence. If the jurist basis himself on whim or caprice (*hawā*), he is not entitled to deference. For instance, see Abū Ḥāmid al-Ghazālī, *al-Mustaṣfā*, 2:387–388 (argues that unless there is evidence supporting a determination then it is a ruling based

on ignorance); Abū ʿAmr ʿUthmān b. ʿAbd al-Raḥmān b. al-Ṣalāḥ al-Shahrazūrī, *Adab al-Muftī wa al-Mustaftī*, p. 162; Abū Bakr Aḥmad b. ʿAlī b. Thābit al-Khaṭīb al-Baghdādī, *Kitāb al-Faqīh wa al-Mutfaqqih*, pp. 319, 316; Shihāb al-Dīn Abū al-ʿAbbās al-Qarāfī, *al-Iḥkām fī Tamyīz al-Fatāwā ʿan al-Aḥkām wa Taṣarrufāt al-Qāḍī wa al-Imām*, pp. 120–121; al-Shīrāzī, *Sharḥ al-Lumʿa*, 2:1033–1035; al-Kalūzānī, *al-Tamhīd*, 4:394–397 (notes that the specialists and laity are equally capable of searching for and understanding the fundamentals. However, more technical issues require specialization and proficiency in the study of the evidence.)

159 Importantly, I do not understand the relationship between the special agents and common agents to be hierarchical; rather, it is a delegation of power by the common agents to the special agents.

160 For instance, see Qur'ān, 2:170, 5:104, 7:28, 26:74, 31:21, 43:22. Rahman, *Major Themes*, p. 24.

161 For instance, see Qur'ān, 2:80, 2:169, 7:28, 7:33, 10:68.

162 See Qur'ān, 16:25.

163 See Eco, *The Limits of Interpretation*, esp. pp. 23–42. See also, Dowling, *The Senses of the Text*, pp. 79–97; Juhl, *Interpretation*, pp. 196–238. I will address the concepts of open and closed texts more fully in the next chapter.

164 Qur'ān, 88:21–22.

165 See Ibn ʿAbd al-Barr, *Jāmiʿ Bayān al-ʿIlm wa Faḍlihi*, 2:52–55. Mālik b. Anas is reported to have responded "I do not know" to thirty-two out of forty-eight questions posed to him on a single day. In fact, one of Mālik's student is reported as saying that he could fill an entire page with questions that Mālik did not answer before Mālik would respond to even one question. Dutton, *Origins of Islamic Law*, p. 21. See also, ʿAbd al-ʿAzīz b. Aḥmad al-Bukhārī, *Kashf al-Asrār*, 4:30, who reports that of forty questions posed to Mālik b. Anas, he said "I do not know" (*lā adrī*) to thirty-six of them. Ibn Qayyim al-Jawziyyah, *Iʿlām al-Muwaqqiʿīn*, 1:57, reports that the jurist Saʿīd b. Manṣūr (d. 683/1284) said that saying "I don't know" is one-third of all knowledge. A report attributed to the jurist Nāfiʿ (d. 117/735) states that knowledge is based on three things: the Qur'an, the *Sunnah*, and the statement "I don't know." Ibn Qayyim al-Jawziyyah, *Iʿlām al-Muwaqqiʿīn* (Beirut), 1:59.

166 Al-Shawkānī, *Nayl al-Awṭār*, 7:168.

167 Qur'ān, 33:72.

168 See Qur'ān, 47:38, 9:39, 2:83, 13:20, 2:27, 13:25.

169 On the principle of enjoining the good and forbiding the evil, see, Qur'ān, 2:104, 3:110, 3:114, 7:157, 9:71, 9:112, 16:90, 22:41, 31:17. The duty to enjoin the good and forbid the evil presents a moral imperative to Muslims. How Muslims are to carry out this imperative is a matter of discussion among Muslim jurists and thelogians. For instance, ʿAbd al-Qādir b. Abī Ṣāliḥ al-Jīlānī (d. 561/1166) argues that the extent of one's obligation depends on the extent of his capacity (*qudrah*) and knowledge of good and evil. In this context, jurists and theologians refer to a *ḥadīth* in which the Prophet is reported to have said: "If one of you observes evil, he must take active steps to change it [lit. change it by his hand]. If he cannot do so, then he should speak against it. And if he cannot do that, then he should oppose it in his heart, and that is the weakest of faith." ʿAbd al-Qādir b. Abī Ṣāliḥ al-Jīlānī, *al-Ghunyah li Ṭālibī Ṭarīq al-Ḥaqq ʿAzza wa Jalla fī al-Akhlāq wa al-Taṣawwuf wa al-Ādāb al-Islāmiyyah*, 1:110–117. See also, Abū Ḥāmid Muḥammad b. Muḥammad al-Ghazālī, *Iḥyāʾ ʿUlūm al-Dīn*, 2:306–357; Corbin, *History of Islamic Philosophy*, pp. 111–112; Kamali, *Principles*, pp. 283–284; Watt, *Islamic Philosophy*, p. 52.

170 Muḥammad al-Amīn b. Muḥammad al-Mukhtār al-Shinqīṭī, *Mudhakkirah fī Uṣūl al-Fiqh*, p. 15; al-Rāzī, *al-Maḥṣūl* (1997), 1:96; Abū Zahrah, *Uṣūl al-Fiqh*, pp. 28–30; Abdur Rahim, *The Principles of Muhammadan Jurisprudence*, p. 197; Kamali, *Principles*, p. 325; Weiss, *Spirit of Islamic Law*, p. 150, who indicates that warfare is a communal duty.

171 See, for instance, Qur'ān, 2:286, 2:233, 4:84, 6:152, 7:42, 23:62, 65:7.

172 Muslim jurists asserted that a lay person carries the burden of ensuring that a purported jurist is knowledgeable. While the jurist is expected to exert reasonable efforts in studying

the law, the lay person must exert reasonable efforts in trying to find qualified jurists. Abū Ḥāmid al-Ghazālī, *al-Mustaṣfā*, 2:387, 390; Ibn al-Ṣalāḥ al-Shahrazūrī, *Adab al-Muftī wa al-Mustaftī*, pp. 133–134, 158–168 (reports on several schools of thought as to the extent of the effort that needs to be expended in the search for a qualified jurist).

173 See Qur'ān, 8:27; 33:72, 23:8, 70:32.

174 Al-Asnawī, *al-Tamhīd*, pp. 530–531; ʿAbd al-ʿAzīz b. Aḥmad al-Bukhārī, *Kashf al-Asrār*, 4:27–30; al-Khaṭīb al-Baghdādī, *Kitāb al-Faqīh wa al-Mutafaqqih*, pp. 300–301; al-ʿUkbarī, *Risālah fī Uṣūl al-Fiqh*, pp. 126–127; Badrān, *Uṣūl al-Fiqh*, pp. 474–477; Wahbah al-Zuḥaylī, *al-Wasīṭ fī Uṣūl al-Fiqh al-Islāmī*, pp. 596–604; Abū Zahrah, *Uṣūl al-Fiqh*, pp. 301–309; Murād Shukrī, *Taḥqīq al-Wuṣūl ilā ʿIlm al-Uṣūl*, p. 94; Ibrāhīm Muḥammad Salqīnī, *al-Muyassar fī Uṣūl al-Fiqh al-Islāmī*, pp. 376–380; Ḥāfiẓ Thanā' Allāh al-Zāhidī, *Taysīr al-Uṣūl*, pp. 324–325.

175 Abū Zakariyyā Muḥyī al-Dīn b. Sharaf al-Nawawī, *Sharḥ Ṣaḥīḥ Muslim*, 7–8:169; Ibn Ḥajar al-ʿAsqalānī, *Fatḥ al-Bārī*, 8:394.

176 On the conception of Divine appointment of rulers in early Islamic thought, see Crone and Hinds, *God's Caliph*. Also see Abou El Fadl, *Rebellion and Violence in Islamic Law*.

177 So, for instance, later I criticize *responsa* in for their lack of diligence and for their failure to disclose material elements of their analysis when it was necessary to do so.

178 For instance, individuals would often obtain a *responsa* to use as persuasive evidence in a court of law. Furthermore, it was common for a judge (*qāḍī*) to seek out the *responsa* of a *muftī* where the legal question before him was ambiguous. Masud, Messick, and Powers, "Muftis, Fatwas, and Islamic Legal Interpretation," pp. 3–32, 9, 11; Al-ʿAjilānī, *ʿAbqariyyat al-Islām*, pp. 425–426.

179 On the guild system, see generally, Makdisi, *Rise*, pp. 200–202; *idem*, "Guilds"; *idem*, "La Corporation"; Bulliet, *Patricians;* Urvoy, "ʿUlamā';" Jackson, *Islamic Law and the State*, pp. 142–185; *idem*, "Prophetic Actions"; Gaudefroy-Demombynes, *Muslim Institutions*, pp. 148–154; Rebstock, "Qāḍī's Errors"; Müller, "Judging".

180 For example, al-Khaṭīb al-Baghdādī suggests that the *muftī* must be conscious of the laity's limited ability to comprehend his *fatwā* (*siflat al-nās*), and therefore must make every effort to present simple and concise, but thorough, responses, see al-Khaṭīb al-Baghdādī, *Kitāb al-Faqīh wa al-Mutfaqqih*, pp. 319, 320. Furthermore, al-Baghdādī cautions the laity not to burden the *muftī* with questions about his proofs (*ḥujja*) or to ask why or how he arrives at his answer (*wa lā yaqūl limā wa lā kayf*). However, if the lay questioner wishes to learn the evidence the *muftī* relies upon, he should arrange for a separate opportunity after receiving the *fatwā* to sit with the *muftī* and ask him for the evidence. Id. at p. 313. Ibn al-Ṣalāḥ does not oppose the idea of the *muftī* presenting the evidence for his *fatwā* where such evidence is a clear, concise textual proof (*naṣṣ wāḍiḥ mukhtaṣar*). Where the evidence is based on a rational proof, though, the *muftī* is not subject to any disclosure requirements. However, Ibn al-Ṣalāḥ does suggest that where the issue is vague or ambiguous (*ghumūḍ*), it is better (*ḥasan*) if the *muftī* indicates his evidence. Ibn al-Ṣalāḥ al-Shahrazūrī, *Adab al-Muftī wa al-Mustaftī*, pp. 134, 151–152. On the other hand, if the lay questioner, after having received a *fatwā*, wishes to learn the evidence used by the *muftī*, Ibn al-Ṣalāḥ states that he should ask the *muftī* in a different sitting or in the same sitting without expressing defiance. Ibn al-Ṣalāḥ also reports that other jurists have argued that nothing ought to prevent the lay questioner, out of concern for his well-being, from asking the *muftī* for his evidence. In this case, the *muftī* is required to elucidate his evidence if the evidence is clear and unambiguious (*in kāna maqṭūʿan bih*). If the evidence is ambiguous, the jurist ought not elucidate upon such evidence because the laity does not have the ability to properly evaluate the matter Id. at p. 171.

181 Of course, these standardized *responsa* have become the standard practice in the contemporary age.

182 For instance, Shihāb al-Dīn al-Qarāfī argues that where the lay-questioner asks about a grave matter (*wāqiʿa ʿaẓīma*) involving important matters of faith or the welfare of Muslims, it is better if the *muftī* explains his position in great detail (*al-ishāb fī al-qawl*),

provides increased elucidation (*kathrat al-bayānāt*), and mentions the evidence which invokes the significant interests raised by the question (*al-adilla al-ḥāththa ʿalā tilka al-maṣāliḥ al-sharīfa*). However, where the question is not so grave, such measures need not be taken. Al-Qarāfī, *al-Iḥkām fī Tamyīz*, p. 124.

183 Abū al-Ḥusayn al-Baṣrī, addressing this issue in the context of *taqlīd*, indicates that the Muʿtazilah of Baghdād prohibited the laity from simply following the views of jurists in legal particulars (*furūʿ*) before the latter had fully disclosed the evidentiary basis for their rulings. However, the majority of theologians and jurists, al-Baṣrī argues, permitted *taqlīd* in *furūʿ* without requiring a full presentation of the evidence. Nevertheless, the jurist must exert his best efforts in reaching a determination, and if he does then, by definition, the result reached is correct. Abū al-Ḥusayn al-Baṣrī, *al-Muʿtamad*, (1983), 2:360–363. Al-Kalūzānī, *al-Tamhīd*, 4:397–399, argues that the laity can understand the fundamentals, and the broader issues, but not the technicalities of law. Abū Ḥāmid al-Ghazālī asserts that the very definition of *taqlīd* is to adopt another's view without assessing his evidence (*qabūl qawl bi lā ḥujja*). Al-Ghazālī contends that this type of imitation is reprehensible because an indivdual remains responsible for his decisions. In legal matters, while the layperson cannot dedicate himself to the evaluation and weighing of the legal evidence, the layperson must diligently select a knowledgeable jurist to follow. This is not considered a form of reprehensible imitation because legal opinions must be based on the evidence, otherwise they should not be followed. Abū Ḥāmid al-Ghazālī, *al-Mustaṣfā*, 2:387–389. Al-Shīrāzī, *Sharḥ al-Lumʿah*, 2:1035, argues that the jurist should explain and clarify his opinions (*yajibu an yubayyina al-jawāb*). He adds that if the matter is complex, the jurist should exhaustively address the possibilities and details.

184 The early juristic practice was to issue very short responses to questions without discussing the evidence. Frequently, Aḥmad b. Ḥanbal or Mālik would answer questions with expression such as, "I do not agree with this", "I would not prefer this", "I think this would be impermissible", and "I think he would be within his rights to do this". This style had much more to do with the under-developed nature of Islamic law at the time, than with any principled position. For instance, on performing *wuḍūʾ* (ritual ablutions) with water that was licked by a dog, Mālik b. Anas states: "*Wuḍūʾ* with the excess water [left by] a dog does not please me, where the water at issue is of a small amount... But it is not a problem if the water is of a large quantity." Saḥnūn b. Saʿīd, *al-Mudawwanah al-Kubrā* (Egypt: Maṭbaʿat al-Saʿāda, n.d.), 1:6. See also, Dutton, *Origins of Islamic Law*, pp. 46–50. Aḥmad b. Ḥanbal was asked about a man who pronounces the divorce of his wife, does not utter it audibly, yet intends the divorce to be valid. Aḥmad b. Ḥanbal responded: "I prefer (*arjū*) that it be of no legal consequence." Spectorsky, *Chapters on Marriage and Divorce*, p. 74.

185 Contemporary writers often include the discussion on the *muftī–mustaftī* relationship within a general discussion of *taqlīd*, and assert that *taqlīd* is simply following the opinion of another without knowing the evidences upon which he relied. However, contemporary jurists often condemn the practice of *taqlīd*. Al-Zuḥaylī, *al-Wasīṭ*, p. 666; al-Dībānī, *al-Minhāj al-Wāḍiḥ*, 2:363; al-Shawkānī, *al-Qawl al-Mufīd*.

186 In twentieth-century American jurisprudence, a school of thought emerged which, by emphasizing the importance of reason in judicial decisions, challenged the legal indeterminacy proferred by the American Realist school. Adherents of "process jurisprudence" suggested that the rational processes of the law are what provide a legal decision its justification and authority. For an intellectual history of process jurisprudence, see, Duxbury, *Patterns of American Jurisprudence*, pp. 205–299; idem, "Faith in Reason: The Process Tradition in American Jurisprudence," pp. 601–705. See also, White, "The Evolution of Reasoned Elaboration," pp. 279–302.

187 De Boer, *The History of Philosophy in Islam*, p. 52; Khadduri, *Islamic Conception*, pp. 41–77; Fakhry, *Islamic Philosophy*, pp. 204–205; Watt, *Formative Period*, pp. 238–242.

188 On the issue of *ijmāʿ* generally, see, Abū Bakr Aḥmad b. ʿAlī al-Rāzī al-Jaṣṣāṣ, *al-Ijmāʿ*, pp. 137–223; Maḥmaṣānī, *Falsafat al-Tashrīʿ*, pp. 159–162; Ahmad Hasan, *The Doctrine of Ijmaʿ in Islam*. Islamic legal history illustrates some diversity of opinion on this issue,

however most agree that one who challenges or violates an *ijmāʿ*-based ruling is not a *kāfir*. For instance, Abū Bakr al-Sarakhsī (d. 483/1090) argues that because *ijmāʿ*, as a source of law, is clear and certain (*qaṭʿī*) proof for a *ḥukm*, any violation of an *ijmāʿ*-based ruling is tantamount to *kufr*. Abū Bakr Muḥammad b. Aḥmad b. Abī Sahl al-Sarakhsī, *al-Muḥarrar fī Uṣūl al-Fiqh*, 1:238–240. Fakhr al-Dīn al-Rāzī, on the other hand, argues that the ontological authority of *ijmāʿ* is not certain, but rather probable (*ẓannī*), and that there is an *ijmāʿ*-based ruling which holds that one who opposes or violates a rule based on *ẓannī* proof is not a *kāfir*. Furthermore, he also argues that *ijmāʿ* is not essential or fundamental to religion. Fakhr al-Dīn Muḥammad b. ʿUmar b. al-Ḥusayn al-Rāzī, *al-Maḥṣūl fī ʿIlm Uṣūl al-Fiqh*, 2:98–99. See also, al-Urmawī, *al-Taḥṣīl*, 2:86. Others such as al-Zarkashī and al-Āmidī argue that failure to adopt an *ijmāʿ*-based ruling on a fundamental matter of faith constitutes *kufr*, whereas a violation of a lesser matter does not. Shams al-Dīn Muḥammad b. ʿAbd Allāh al-Zarkashī, *al-Baḥr al-Muḥīṭ*, 4:524–528; Sayf al-Dīn Abū al-Ḥasan ʿAlī b. Abī ʿAlī b. Muḥammad al-Āmidī, *al-Iḥkām fī Uṣūl al-Aḥkām*, 1:209. Other jurists held that denial of *ijmāʿ*, as a source of law, constitutes *kufr*, but that rejection of a specific *ijmāʿ*-based ruling does not. ʿAbd al-ʿAzīz b. Aḥmad al-Bukhārī, *Kashf al-Asrār*, 2:479–480. On the other hand, jurists like *Imām al-Ḥaramayn* al-Juwaynī disagreed with the claim that the rejection of *ijmā*ʿ as a source of law led to disbelief and *kufr*. Rather, al-Juwaynī argued that only if one accepts the ontological value of *ijmāʿ*, but subsequently rejects a particular *ijmāʿ*-based ruling, then he would be engaged in an act of *kufr*. Al-Juwaynī, *al-Burhān*, 1:280. Al-Juwaynī's student, Abū Ḥāmid al-Ghazālī, states that it is *ḥarām* (prohibited) to oppose an *ijmāʿ*-based ruling or to engage in what the *ummah* has prohibited. However he does not suggest that violating an *ijmāʿ*-based ruling is tantamount to *kufr*. Abū Ḥāmid al-Ghazālī, *al-Mustaṣfā*, 1:198.

189 See, for example, Yaḥyā b. Muḥammad b. Hubayrah, *al-Ijmāʿ ʿind Aʾimmat Ahl al-Sunnah al-Arbaʿah*; Abū Muḥammad ʿAlī b. Aḥmad b. Saʿīd b. Ḥazm, *Marātib al-Ijmāʿ fī al-ʿIbādāt wa al-Muʿāmalāt wa al-Iʿtiqādāt*; Muḥammad b. Ibrāhīm b. al-Mundhir, *al-Ijmāʿ*.

190 See, for instance, al-Juwaynī, *Kitāb al-Ijtihād*, pp. 23–27; al-Dībānī, *al-Minhāj al-Wāḍiḥ*, 2:353.

191 Al-Khaṭīb al-Baghdādī, *Kitāb al-Faqīh wa al-Mutafaqqih*, p. 252; Ḥasab Allāh, *Uṣūl al-Tashrīʿ*, p. 82; al-Dībānī, *al-Minhāj al-Wāḍiḥ*, 2:353; al-ʿUkbarī, *Risālah fī Uṣūl al-Fiqh*, p. 129; Badrān, *Uṣūl al-Fiqh*, p. 473; Zakī al-Dīn Shaʿbān, *Uṣūl al-Fiqh al-Islāmī*, p. 416; Kamali, *Principles*, p. 368.

192 Fakhry, *Islamic Philosophy*, pp. 205, 223. See generally, ʿAbd al-Qāhir b. Ṭāhir b. Muḥammad al-Baghdādī, *al-Farq bayn al-Firaq*; Abū Muḥammad ʿAlī b. Aḥmad b. Saʿīd b. Ḥazm, *al-Faṣl fī al-Milal wa al-Ahwāʾ wa al-Niḥal*; al-Ashʿarī, *Maqālāt al-Islāmiyyīn*; al-Shahrastānī, *al-Milal wa al-Niḥal*.

193 The phrases often used in classical discourses were *ahl al-ahwāʾ* and *ahl al-bidaʿ wa al-ahwāʾ*. See al-Shahrastānī, *al-Milal wa al-Niḥal*, 1:240.

194 Abou El Fadl, "Islamic Law of Rebellion," pp. 284, 292–293; al-Shawkānī, *Nayl al-Awṭār*, 7:168. For a discussion by a contemporary author on the limits of a plausible *taʾwīl* see, al-ʿAlwānī, *Adab al-Ikhtilāf*, pp. 36–43.

195 Al-Shīrāzī, *Sharḥ al-Lumʿah*, 2:1045–1046; al-Dībānī, *al-Minhāj al-Wāḍiḥ*, pp. 352–354; Ḥasab Allāh, *Uṣūl al-Tashrīʿ*, pp. 82–83.

196 See the fascinating study, Noll, *The Scandal of the Evangelical Mind*, esp. pp. 10–12, 123–126. See also, Wolfe, "The Opening of the Evangelical Mind," who writes about efforts within the Evangelical community to overcome its anti-intellectualism.

197 For instance, see ʿAbd al-Jalīl ʿĪsā, *Mā lā yajūz fīhi al-Khilāf bayn al-Muslimīn*.

# 3 A summary transition

*Competence*

As noted earlier, competence relates to the qualifications of the point of reference. In Islamic theology, ultimate authority for any determination resides in God. God is the ultimate authority in the sense that if God wants one thing and not another, any person who wants the contrary does so in defiance of God.[1] More concretely, God is the ultimate authority in the sense that God has the power to provide exclusionary reasons that warrant deference.[2] This is assumed as a matter of faith or conviction and, therefore, it is a starting point for the analysis. Having made this faith-based assumption, we still need to deal with understanding what God wants as well as the means for understanding what God wants. For a Muslim, the most obvious ways of knowing what God wants are the Qur'ān and *Sunnah*. There are other possible ways of knowing, such as reason, intuition, the study of history and nature, observable empirical facts, the consensus of the pious, prayer, and supplications. However, in the juristic culture of Islam, the Qur'ān and *Sunnah* occupy the paramount positions as the means for discovering the Divine Will.

The Qur'ān and *Sunnah* are texts in the sense that they are comprised of symbols (letters and words) that invoke meaning in a reader. These texts have an author and use linguistic symbols to signify meaning. One could consider the Qur'ān and *Sunnah* to be, in part, a set of instructions intended to address an audience. Their authoritativeness is derived from the fact that they either come from God or that they tell us something about what God is instructing us to do.

The first issue one must deal with when considering any text that purports to say something about the Divine Will is to assess the qualifications of this text. By qualifications I mean the authority of the text to speak for or about God. For instance, if a text is traced back to God (God is the author) or the Prophet then it is eminently qualified to speak for or about the Divine. If the text goes back to a Companion of the Prophet, then we have to ask to what extent does this Companion speak for the Prophet, and in turn, God. If the text goes back to a pious, intelligent, or knowledgeable person, we must pose the same question.[3] We are simply asking: What competence does a particular source have to speak for or about God? This question relates to the authenticity of the medium that transmitted the authoritative instructions of the Divine.

In evaluating the issue of competence, I made the faith-based assumption that the Qur'ān is the immutable and uncorrupted Word of God. This is tantamount to assuming that God is the author of the Qur'ān, and that the competence of the Qur'ān is not subject to reproach. As far as the Qur'ān is concerned, the only pertinent issue is to determine its meaning. The *Sunnah*, and other historically relevant material, however, pose a very different challenge.

What we know about the Prophet and his Companions, or their pronouncements, we know because someone has told us. Some information about the Prophet and his Companions is conveyed by the Qur'ān, but most of what we know was transmitted through human historical reports. These reports pose an the intriguing problem of the possibility of multiple authorship. According to the documented chains-of-transmission (pl. *asānīd*; sing. *isnād*) that preserved these reports, someone, typically a Companion, heard or witnessed the Prophet do or say something or other, and then a long list of people transmitted this information through several generations, until they reached the collectors of traditions who documented the whole process. For instance, a chain-of-transmission would say: *a* told *b* who told *c* who told *d* who told *e* who told *f* that *g* heard the Prophet say such-and-such, and a collector, such as al-Bukhārī or Muslim, would have documented the full chain of transmitters and the substance of the report.

In order to evaluate the authenticity of such reports, scholars of *ḥadīth* have developed a sophisticated process of scrutinizing the chain of transmitters. This is known as *'ilm al-rijāl*, a science in which the circumstances and credibility of each reporter is evaluated according to the best available information. Furthermore, within limited parameters, the substance is also assessed. The end product of this process is to categorize each particular report on a scale ranging from authentic to fabricated. Importantly, there is a difference between traditions that have been reported cumulatively by the early generations, and traditions that have been reported by a few individuals from or about the Prophet. The former because of the larger number of individuals who witnessed or heard the Prophet say or do something are considered more reliable and authentic. I do not reject the traditional methods of authentication (known as *'ilm al-ḥadīth*), but I do argue that these methods need to be more historically grounded. Branding a particular transmitter, in the chain of transmission, as reliable or unreliable is helpful but not conclusive. The life of each individual is complex and heavily contextual, and it is not possible to sum up such a life in a single judgment such as reliable or unreliable. Furthermore, claiming that a specific tradition is authentic or unauthentic, by itself, is not particularly probative. The issue is not whether the Prophet said or did not say something but what role did the Prophet play in a particular report.

We should remember that other than the possibility of fabrication, there is also the issue of creative selection and recollection. Those who experienced the life of the Prophet, interacted, and talked to him, did not experience the Prophet in some ideal objective medium. The Companions and others experienced the Prophet in a subjective fashion, and this subjectivity influenced what they saw or heard, how they saw or heard it, and what they ultimately remembered and conveyed to others. Therefore, the personality of the transmitter of a report is indelibly imprinted upon the report transmitted. In fact, each generation of transmitters has its own subjectivities that cause it to remember some reports and not others, and to authenticate some reports and not others. I argue in the fourth chapter that each tradition attributed to the Prophet is the end-product of an authorial enterprise. The primary member of the enterprise might be the Prophet, but the enterprise will also include those who selected, remembered, and transmitted the report. Concretely, upon examining the totality of historical circumstances, we might be able to conclude that a specific report tells us much about the Prophet, or we might conclude that a report tells us far more about the historical context of the transmitters than anything else. The concept of authorial enterprise forces us to understand the Prophetic reports not just as *Sunnah*, but as history as well. In addition, the notion of authorial enterprise plays a significant role in understanding the interpretations attached to any report. Even if we assume that the Prophet did, in fact, make a particular statement, the words and phrases of the statement do not reach us in a vacuum. The words and phrases often reach us with a meaning or set of meanings attached to them. For instance, if we find the word *firāsh* used in a Prophetic report, we could understand it to mean bed, spread, or sexual relations. A variety of interpretations proposed by a variety of literary agents give this word its particular meaning in a particular context. The determinations of these various interpreters or literary agents constitute a part of the authorial enterprise as well because they powerfully influence how we understand the traditions conveyed to us.

In terms of legal application, I argue that it is imperative to correlate between the reliability of a report and its legal effect. This is what I have described as a proportionality requirement.[4] I concede that the Prophet's authoritativeness is to be accepted as a faith-based assumption. Muslims, in my view, ought to defer to the judgments of the Prophet to the extent that such judgments are instructive as to the Divine Will. In Islamic theology, the Prophet's authoritativeness is entirely derived from God – from the fact that the Prophet's statements and behavior are probative as to what God demands of human beings. Arguably, not everything that the Prophet said or did was legislative in nature because not all Prophetic acts were intended to represent the Divine Will.[5] As to the reports conveying legislative acts, they carry authoritative weight to the extent that the Prophet played a role in these reports. Hence, as we assess the authorial enterprise as a whole, we strive to assess the role of the Prophet in these reports. As to some reports, we will have very strong doubts about the role of the Prophet – for instance, we will tend to think that the Prophet probably said such-and-such, but that there are historical reasons to suspect that many other collateral influences have also played a part in shaping this report. With other reports, we will be fairly confident that the external collateral influences were far more limited, and that the process of historical transmission preserved much of the Prophet's role. The idea of proportionality correlates between the role of the Prophet in the authorial enterprise and the normative effect of a report. Put simply, the more confident we are that a report is not apocryphal, and the more confident we are about the nature and extent of the Prophet's role in the authorial enterprise, the more we are justified in relying on a report when making normative determinations. Importantly, reports that have widespread moral, legal, or social implications must be of the highest rank of authority. In considering each report, we need to think about the effect or impact of applying this report in a normative fashion, and the greater the impact, the stricter the scrutiny. The greater the impact the heavier the burden of proof that a report will be required to meet.[6] This is simply a part of assessing the competence of a report. In a sense, we can phrase the issue in terms of authority – we need to ascertain the extent to which any report is authorized or empowered to effect change. The more dramatic or extensive the effect, the higher the evidence of authorization or empowerment that is demanded of a report.

## *Determination*

Determination refers to the act of deciding upon the meaning of a text. Who decides the meaning of a text? When I ask a jurist, what does this text mean, what do I mean by that question? Am I asking the jurist, what does God mean by this text? Am I asking what does the language mean? Am I asking what images and associations are invoked in the mind of the jurist by the text?

To the extent that the Divine instructions rely on texts, they also rely on the medium of language. Language, however, is a tricky artifact. Letters, words, phrases, and sentences are dependent on a system of symbols, and these symbols invoke particular associations, images, and emotions in an audience that may also change over time. In a sense, language has an objective reality because its meaning cannot be determined exclusively by the author or reader. When I use the medium of language, to an extent, I am submitting to its limitations and boundaries. These boundaries were constructed by many generations of language users. Instead of this system of bounded linguistic symbols, I might choose to draw a stick-man, a stick-woman, and something resembling a tree. But even then, what I convey by this image is still bounded by the social and cultural experiences of the audience. For instance, some people might think that my image is referring to the story of Adam and Eve, others might think I am referring to two people in love, others will think I am expressing boredom or that I am expressing loneliness, and crying for companionship. Similarly, language has agreed-upon usages and meanings, but they are constantly shifting and mutating. An author exercises considerable discretion in choosing the linguistic symbols that best communicate an image in his or her head, but cannot control the effect of the language upon readers. The meanings that a language acquires through generations of use impose limitations on its users. In a sense, once the author uses the medium of language with all its rules and limitations, the author surrenders his or her intent to the text. The author might want to express X, but the language utilized could possibly convey XY, XZ, XT, or even W. The text is at best an approximation of the author's intent, especially since language, itself, is not constant or stable.

The author uses language, most often intending to convey meaning, but cannot control the meaning actually conveyed. Language is semi-autonomous, it superimposes its own rules and limitations, and shapes and channels meaning as well. And the reader? The reader has the ability to impose whatever meaning he or she wishes upon the text. A reader could read this book and conclude that it is an exciting romp in the world of sensuality or that it is an encoded message to the terrorists of the world. But I, as the author, would think that the reader is insane. Furthermore, if one could personify the text, the text would probably protest that its integrity has not been respected or honoured. In addition, hopefully, other readers would think these interpretations bizarre and absurd. In short, normatively speaking the reader's handling of the text ought to be reasonable – unreasonable interpretations are unfair to the author and the text.

This raises the question: what defines reasonableness? In practice, the parameters of reasonableness are set by what can be called communities of interpretation. Various communities of readers develop ways of reading and understanding a text. These communities develop both conventions of reading, and a range of shared determinations that are considered accessible to others. An esoteric reading of a text, unless it develops its own community of meaning, is not shared and is inaccessible to others. I argue below that meaning should be the product of the interaction of author, text, and reader – that there should be a balancing and negotiating process between the three parties, and that one party ought not to dominate the determination of meaning.

In the Islamic context, especially in the case of the Qur'ān, language and the authorial intent acquire a special significance. Muslims believe that the Qur'ān is the literal Word of God, and therefore, neither the Author's intent nor the language of the text can be ignored. Muslims believe that God chose every word of the Qur'ān for a reason. However, the fact remains that God chose a medium of communication that is bounded by human usage, and that evolves through human dynamics. To a large extent, the legitimacy of a reader's determination depends on the extent to which a reader respects the integrity of the authorial intent and the text. Nevertheless, the power of determination has been delegated to the human agent. In this sense, God has used two mediums: the medium of the text and the medium of the human. The text is expected to shape the attitudes and conduct of the human agent, but there is little doubt that the human agent also shapes the meaning of the text.

This analysis brings into focus the question of what does God expect from the human process of determination? Does God expect the human agent to search for and find the correct textual determination as to all matters? Much of the debate on these questions has revolved around the tradition attributed to the Prophet that states: "Every *mujtahid* is correct." Here, there are two main schools of thought. The first school argues that as to every issue, there is a correct answer. However, in this mundane life, it is not possible to know what the correct answer is, especially as to issues that relate to the non-essentials of the religion. The most one can do is strive, work hard, and do one's very best in trying to discover the correct legal determination. If people do their very best, and find the correct determination, they will be rewarded with full credit in the Hereafter. On the other hand, if after exerting a diligent effort one does not find the correct answer, there will be less credit in the Hereafter. In either case, humans will not discover who was right or wrong until the Final Day, and even those who turned out to be wrong will receive some credit for their diligence and hard work.

The second school of thought argues that on issues not related to the essentials of religion, there is no correct determination. God's Will is the search – God wants human beings to live a conscientious, reflective, and diligent life. Therefore, whatever an individual honestly and sincerely believes is God's Will, as to this individual, this is in fact God's law. Provided that this individual was diligent in his or her search for God's law, and provided that all the relevant evidence was examined, God's law comes into accord with the sincerely held belief of that person. According to this school of thought, a person sins by failing to exercise due diligence in searching for the mandates of God's law, and in failing to abide by the call of his or her conscience.

Both the first and second school of thought demand an active role for the author, text, and reader. Both schools mandate that the integrity of each actor be respected and that the role of each actor be given considerable weight. Significantly, both schools require that the interpretive process remain open. Under the first school, we can never be sure which determination is correct, and under the second school, the search *is* the Divine Will. Therefore, the process or the possibility of a search must remain available and open. If the possibility of a search is closed, the idea that "every *mujtahid* is correct" becomes meaningless.

## *The authoritarian*

Closing the interpretive process is a despotic act. If the reader attempts to "lock" the text into a specific meaning, this act risks violating the integrity of the author and text. Effectively, the reader is saying: "I know what the author means, and I know what the text is saying; my knowledge ought to be conclusive and final." This type of assertion assumes that the reader is empowered or authorized to end the role of the author and the text. In fact, the reader's determination replaces the role of the author and the text. For example, the reader might say the meaning of the text is "*x*." If the reader succeeds in establishing *x*, and only *x*, as the meaning of the text, then there is no practical need to refer back to the author or the text any more. X, a determination, now fully and effectively represents the author and the text, and so we only need to refer back to *x*, and we can safely ignore the author and the text. This type of interpretive despotism by itself, however, is not the main focus of this study. As noted above, the primary concern of this study is the despotism of the special agent as he or she interacts with others.

It should be recalled that the authoritativeness of the special agent is asserted only through reliance on the instructions of the Principal. But the instructions are not the only possible relationship with God. For example, a person could develop an intimate and loving relationship with God. The challenge, however, is that this intimate and largely private relationship is not necessarily accessible to others. Other people can scrutinize the textual evidence, but they may not be able to share with me the results of any direct, personal, and non-textual encounter with God. For instance, I might spend a lot of time with God in supplications or the like. As a result of these encounters, I experience God's Will in a very personal and real (to me) fashion. I might become convinced that God wants all people to take up dancing. The textual evidence might or might not be consistent with this conviction, nevertheless I am convinced that this is what God wants me and others to do. To what extent can I present to other individuals this determination of God's Will as authoritative? I would argue that it is authoritative only if other individuals believe that this personal experience does in fact communicate the Divine Will. However, I would hasten to add that I and those who defer to me are duty bound to investigate the Divine textual instructions as a reality check. One cannot exclude the possibility that what I thought was direct and personal instructions commanding me to dance are no more than a self-serving delusion. As a special agent, the obligations of restraint, diligence, comprehensiveness, and reasonableness demand that I thoroughly investigate the possibilities before resting assured that I was the recipient of some special Divine message. Furthermore, I am obligated to be honest as to the basis of my determination so that the common agents can make an informed decision about their own duties and obligations.

Does the failure to discharge the five contingencies of authoritativeness constitute an act of authoritarianism? If the special agent is not honest, diligent, restrained, comprehensive, or reasonable, is that what is meant by authoritarianism? I would tend to think not. A violation of one of the contingencies would be a breach of duty, and an abuse of authority, but this is not sufficient for the construction of the authoritarian. Authoritarianism is the act of "locking" or captivating the Will of the Divine, or the will of the text, into a specific determination, and then presenting this determination as inevitable, final, and conclusive. I very much doubt that it is possible to do this without violating at least one of the five contingencies. The authoritarian is an act in which one exceeds one's authority or delegated powers to appropriate or usurp the powers of the delegator. It is difficult to imagine how one might accomplish this without violating at least one of the contingencies.

Does this mean that special agents are condemned to the realm of indeterminacy lest they tumble into the authoritatrian? Must they always be tentative about the Principal's Will and the meaning of the text for fear of usurping God's role? Is it impossible to authoritatively speak for God? I think that speaking for God and speaking in God's name are different things. The Prophet, through revelation, and the Qur'ān, through dictation, in a literal sense, speak for God. Everyone else claims to speak in God's name. Everyone else is functioning in the realm of the possible and probable while struggling with indicators (pl. *adillah*, sing. *dalīl*). To claim full or perfect knowledge of God's Will is to challenge the singularity and uniqueness of the Divine perfection.

However, if all determinations must take account of the indicators and evidence, what do we make of morality, or a basic sense of right and wrong? Is all right and wrong only derived from the Divine text and nothing but the text? Although I do not present a theory of Islamic morality in this study, I do not think that one can persuasively argue that notions of right and wrong are determined only through text. As I have repeatedly emphasized, the text is not the only possible representative of the Divine. Nevertheless, it would be irresponsible to present a vision of morality without considering and thoroughly evaluating the indicators of the text. In this context, I develop the idea of the conscientious-pause that might result in a faith-based objection to the textual evidence.

A person develops a knowledge of God, not through textual indicators alone, but through a complex matrix of relationships that are collateral to the text. A person develops a direct relationship perhaps through prayer and supplication, and might develop an understanding of the Creator by reflecting upon creation, or might observe the work of God and Satan through reflecting upon history. These various avenues to the knowledge of God exist apart from the indicators of the text, but they work in conjunction with the text to formulate a conviction about the nature and normativities of the Divine. Although the text plays a role in forming these convictions, one cannot exclude the possibility that the conviction which has been formulated might come into friction with certain determinations of the text. A person can read a text that seems to go against everything that he or she believes about God and will feel a sense of incredulous disbelief, and might even exclaim, "This cannot be from God, the God that I know!"

What does one do in such a case? The appropriate response is to exercise, what I have called, a conscientious-pause. Having experienced this fundamental conflict between a conscientious conviction and a textual determination, a responsible and reflective person ought to pause. The point of the pause is not to simply dismiss the text or the determination, but to reflect and investigate further. It is akin to flagging an issue for further study, and suspending judgment until such study is complete. After due reflection, a person might conclude that the conflict is more apparent than real, or that this determination does not do justice to the text, or might conclude that in good-conscience, he or she ought to yield and defer to the textual determination. All of these and other ways of resolving the conflict are possible. But it is also possible that an adequate resolution would not be found, and that the individual conscience and the textual determination continue to be pitted in an irresolvable conflict. I argue that as long as a person has exhausted all the possible avenues towards resolving the conflict, in the final analysis, Islamic theology requires that a person abide by the dictates of his or her conscience. A faith-based objection to the determination might be necessary. Faith-based objections are founded on one's sense of *īmān* (conviction and belief in and about God), and it seems to me that after all is said and done, it is this sense that ought to be given deference.[7] But a faith-based objection that is not preceded by a diligent and exhaustive investigation runs the serious risk of being a simple exercise of capricious whimsy.

*NOTES*

1 The Qur'ān makes this point clear, see for instance 4:64–65. This, of course, does not exclude the possibility that God might want human beings to use their intellect and will.
2 I am assuming the existence of coercive power – God is the ultimate authority in the sense that God could compel whatever action God wishes to compel.
3 I am not assuming that the pious, intelligent, or knowledgeable cannot say something about or from God. From a juristic paradigm, unlike the authoritativeness of God or the Prophet, the authoritativeness of such individuals is indirect or derivative.
4 Muhammad Fadel has alerted me to a useful conceptual distinction that is found in American law. American law distinguishes between the admissibility of evidence and the weight of the evidence. An evidence could be admissible, but that does not determine how much weight it ought to be given. In a sense, the authenticity of a tradition relates to its admissibility, but the weight to be given to a tradition is akin to an evaluation of proportionality. The difference between weight and admissibility is illustrated by an interesting report related by the Shāfiʿī jurist al-Suyūṭī. Al-Suyūṭī reports that a man claimed that the Prophet appeared in a dream and told him the location of a buried treasure. The Prophet instructed the man to dig out the treasure, and keep it without paying the 20% tax exacted on such finds. The judge al-ʿIzz b. ʿAbd al-Salām ruled that while he believed that the man was speaking the truth about seeing the Prophet in a dream, the man's report (i.e. the dream) is outweighed by other more reliable traditions, and so the

man was forced to pay the tax. In other words, al-ʿIzz̄ admitted the evidence but did not give it much weight. Al-Suyūṭī, *Tanwīr al-Ḥawālik Sharḥ Muwaṭṭaʾ Mālik*, 2:44.

5 In jurisprudence, Muslim jurists divided the Prophet's precedent into two categories. The first, known as *afʿāl jibilliyyah*, is comprised of acts that he did as a private human being. These acts are not probative as to the Divine Will and do not carry legislative weight. The second category, known as *afʿāl tashrīʿiyyah*, are acts that represent the Divine Will and, therefore, are legislative in nature. See Kamali, *Principles of Islamic Jurisprudence*, pp. 50–57.

6 This means that as the social circumstances change and evolve, the role of the various reports will change and evolve as well. A report that might have had a little impact in one age might have a huge impact in another age. A report that could be reasonably be relied upon in one age might become unreliable in another age.

7 In this context, I take note of the tradition attributed to the Prophet that states: "Defer to your heart even if others advise you, advise you, and advise you."

# 4 The text and authority

Mohammed Arkoun has argued that Islamic culture has always suffered from the problem of the "unthought" and "unthinkable."[1] There are certain issues in Islamic culture, Arkoun argues, that remain unthought while other issues remain unthinkable. In other words, there are certain mental sets that prevent Muslims from entertaining or exploring certain thoughts. In this book we are not dealing with such issues since authority, competence, and determination of sources have been debated frequently in Islamic history. But as far as contemporary Islamic discourses are concerned, we have a new category to contend with, namely the category of the "forgotten." While in the pre-modern age the authority of the *mujtahid*, the authoritativeness of the source and its agent, and the risk of intellectual despotism (*al-istibdād bi al-ra'y*) were debated vigorously, this discourse is now forgotten.[2] This book seeks to rekindle the debate and to remember an age-old discourse that has not outlived its usefulness.

The notion of *al-istibdād bi al-ra'y* was often used as part of a theological and legal linguistic practice connoting the imposition of opinions without proper authority. In its historical context, this phrase was used as part of the linguistic arsenal against perceived heterodoxy and sectarian groups. The language of *al-istibdād bi al-ra'y* was frequently used to describe the epistemology of sectarian groups that the jurists persistently accused of being motivated by caprice and whim. Consequently, the jurists often described these sectarian groups as *ahl al-ahwā'* (people of caprice). Regardless of the particular historical linguistic practice or use surrounding it, the phrase conveyed a significant ontological foundation in the juristic culture. Intellectual despotism is equated with the dismissal of textual evidence and a blatant disregard of the communities of meaning constructed around that textual evidence.[3] The refusal of groups or individuals to support their arguments by reference to the Qur'ān and *Sunnah*, or to defer to the structure of constraints produced by the juristic interpretive communities was often described as whimsical or capricious. Of course, intellectual dismissiveness is often a sign of despotic orientation, however, the mere act of rejecting the juristic interpretive communities and their authoritative sources can hardly be described as despotic or capricious. Whether the dismissal of any particular interpretive community can be described as despotic depends on the reasons and methodology of the dismissal. Despotism, or authoritarianism as used in this book, deals with a different issue altogether. The relevant authoritarianism, for this work, relates to the acts of those who invoke the symbolism of the juristic interpretive community in support of their arguments. It is irrelevant whether those persons actually believe in the juristic interpretive community or whether they consider themselves an outsider or insider to that community. What is of essence is that the actor is invoking a set of symbolisms that co-opt the authority of juristic culture to the actor's service. There is a distinctive culture of symbols that characterizes the juristic interpretive community and these symbols are primarily linguistic in nature. I would argue that in the contemporary age, the simple invocation of the categories of forbidden (*ḥarām* or *maḥẓūr*), permissible (*ḥalāl* or *mubāḥ*), reprehensible (*makrūh*), and recommended (*mustaḥabb* or *mandūb*) are sufficient to co-opt and yield the authority of the juristic community. In fact, the very idea of the *Sunnah* or *ḥadīth* is inseparable from the creative practice of the juristic community. If one speaks about the *Sunnah* or *ḥadīth* in the contemporary age, one is necessarily speaking about a symbolic construct that obtains its meaning and normative power from the juristic culture.

This is an important point and it deserves a bit of elaboration. Let us assume that *x* tells *y* that he should do such-and-such because she read traditions in the *Sunnah* that make it imperative upon *y* to do so. X's assertion rests on a host of assumptions that make sense only by implicit reference to the juristic interpretive community. X is making the implicit assumption that the Prophet, in fact, uttered the tradition found in the *Sunnah*. However, *x* has not heard the Prophet utter this tradition but is relying on the cumulative creative activity that remembered, selected, preserved, and defended that tradition as in fact attributable to the Prophet.[4] This cumulative creative activity decided that this tradition was worth saving, supported and defended it against competing traditions, and ultimately preserved it in a particular form in books. But the linguistic form of the tradition, itself, uses words and phrases that cannot be separated from the community of meaning that preserved or produced it. In addition, *x* is implying that the tradition is *ṣaḥīḥ* (authentic, not fabricated), and that a *ṣaḥīḥ* tradition should carry normative weight. Y will understand the idea of authenticity and normativity only in reference to the juristic community of meaning. As the history of Islamic jurisprudence demonstrates, the normative weight given to the traditions of the Prophet in the particular form in which they were preserved and transmitted was not inevitable. Rather, it was the cumulative efforts of generations of jurists that created a nexus between authenticity and normativity.[5] Moreover, *x* is communicating to *y* that assuming that the Prophet did, in fact, issue a command, that compliance becomes mandatory. Perhaps *x* is telling *y* that the context or the historical context of the command is irrelevant, or perhaps that the report should not be understood metaphorically, or that the report is not contradicted by other reports. All of this invokes a particular community of meaning and understanding that neither *x* nor *y* invented, but which forms the basis for their communication nonetheless. None of the implied premises that formed *x* and *y*'s basis for communication are inevitable. A particular community constructed those meanings, and without the constructions of this community *x*'s discourse will be incoherent to *y*. Of course, both are free to try to invent a completely new culture of meaning, and are free to issue disclaimers against the juristic culture. They are entirely free to try, but how effective they will be is a different matter.

Often the reliance on the inheritance of the juristic interpretive community is more pervasive than in the example given above. For instance, if one says, "A Muslim woman ought to wear the *ḥijāb* (cover her whole body except her face and hands)," or if one says it is immodest for a woman to reveal her hair, this assertion necessarily relies not just on some inevitable meaning of some text, but relies on the meaning constructed by the juristic interpretive community. This assertion about modesty relies on a reference to a set of Qur'ānic verses, Prophetic traditions, reports about the Companions and most importantly, the cumulative juristic efforts in selecting, preserving and giving meaning to these textual sources. Similarly, if one uses the words *quṭb* or *murīd*, they invoke the symbolic meanings produced by the interpretive community of Sufism.[6] These words have been successfully co-opted by the Sufi interpretive community. They might mean something to a jurist but the meaning is not embedded in the juristic culture, and the jurist will understand it by reference to the constructions of the Sufi community. This *does* mean that when one speaks about what is forbidden, allowed, recommended or reprehensible, one is invoking the criteria, symbolism and authority of the juristic interpretive culture. Unless one explicitly eschews the juristic tradition, and proceeds to set out an independent epistemology, which may or may not require an independent method of authentication and determination of meaning, one is necessarily relying on an already constructed community of meaning. In the present Islamic literary culture, this community is juristic.

There are two points raised by this issue. First, what are the dynamics between the text, the interpretive community, the determination of meaning, and authority? Second, in light of what we have said above, how is the authoritarian constructed in relation to the first issue?

## *The Qur'ān and* Sunnah

From the outset, I think it is important to be forthcoming about the ontogeny of my discourse on this issue. Western scholars, influenced by their own specific historical experience, have generated a complex discourse on literary theory, hermeneutics, theories of textuality, and deconstructionism. I have consistently talked about communities of meaning as relevant to the identification of text and construction of authority, but the very expression "communities of meaning" is a symbolic construct that originated from this Western tradition. The problem, as I see it, is that these largely Western discourses are alien to the Islamic tradition and its constructs of symbolism and meaning. Furthermore, Muslim culture is undergoing its own unique historical transformations and emerging with its own intellectual paradigms. As one Muslim scholar recently put it, "It is puzzling to see our intellectuals so keen on deconstructing an already thoroughly deconstructed culture."[7] Of course, the fact that the linguistic categories and symbols that originated with the West will not necessarily resonate with meaning for Muslims does not mean that these categories and symbols are not probative or useful. Nevertheless, it is somewhat problematic for a work on authority in Islam to employ a set of symbolisms that does not carry weight or authority with Muslims. This does not mean that Muslim intellectuals should sanctify tradition or that they should refrain from introducing useful conceptual constructs into contemporary Muslim culture, even if these constructs originated with the West. It does mean, however, that an author who is interested in talking to Muslims should exercise self-restraint and reasonableness when employing a discourse that runs the risk of imposing artificial categories upon Muslim historical and intellectual experience. By self-restraint and reasonableness I mean that an author should resist the temptation to use the Muslim experience as a text upon which to continue a debate about the Western historical experience.[8] An author should resist the temptation to co-opt and essentialize the Muslim experience in order to service a debate, for instance, between Gadamer and Habermas.[9] One should start with the Muslim experience and then carefully consider the ways that either Gadamer or Habermas, or both, might be utilized in the service of the Muslim experience. However, even in this process of utilization, reasonableness demands that one not pillage through the Muslim experience with categories that reconstruct and re-model that experience according to Western paradigms.

The methodological tension addressed above is well illustrated when one talks about textuality and determinations of meaning in the Islamic context. Western discourses have produced a prodigious amount of scholarship on the notion of text and textuality and the ontology, character, and identity of texts.[10] Some of the issues debated included whether texts are distinguishable from other categories such as language, signs, artifacts, art objects, and work. Are texts physical or non-physical (including mental states), are they aggregate productions, and are they substances or features? Furthermore, what is the relationship between texts and intention, texts and meaning, and texts and audiences? Does it make any sense to talk about a text without intention, meaning or an audience? For instance, is an "X" drawn on the sand to signal a landing zone for aliens a text? What if the X is drawn for no particular reason, does not have an audience, and there is no intention behind it? What if I draw an X in the sand simply because I am bored, but later it is taken by a group of my students as a secret message to them to re-establish the caliphate? Is this X a text even if the author did not intend it as such? Assuming it is, is the meaning of the X determined by me, my students, or the context of the X in the sand? These questions are fascinating, but it is important to remember that they arose from a specific cultural and historical context, primarily in Europe and later on in the United States. Perhaps the experience of modernity in Western countries created post-modernity and post-structuralism, and perhaps the *grand recits* of the Enlightenment and the colonial narrative generated Jean-Francois Lyotard's *The Postmodern Condition*;[11] but it is important not to superimpose an epistemology upon Muslims that might not faithfully reflect the Muslim experience. Importantly, as already noted above, the fact that certain epistemological approaches might enjoy limited legitimacy in the Islamic context is not a prescription for conservative approaches that legitimate existing power structures and notions of hierarchy. I am not suggesting that epistemological transplants from one culture to another are necessarily illegitimate but that such transplants must be executed with measured restraint and a degree of reasonableness so that the receiving body will not violently reject them.[12]

It will be useful to illustrate this issue by focusing on the example of the Qur'ān and *Sunnah* in the Islamic tradition. As mentioned earlier, the Qur'ān and *Sunnah* are considered the primary texts of Islam. The Qur'ān is considered to be the immutable and literal word of God, revealed, memorized, orally transmitted, and eventually collected and put into writing at the time of the Companions after the death of the Prophet (d. 10/632).[13] In terms of the authorial act, what does the orality of the Qur'ān mean? Are the transmitters and documenters of the Qur'ān part of the authorial enterprise? Does it make sense to talk about the authorial enterprise being partly or wholly responsible for the meaning generated by the Qur'ānic text? Does analyzing the Qur'ān from the perspective of the power dynamics that surrounded the remembering, transmitting, and preserving of it make sense? It does not make sense unless one wants to drastically re-shape Muslim notions of Divine authorship, and unless one is not particularly concerned with the reception of the ideas in a Muslim context.[14] Does this mean that there are dogma and venerated sanctities in religion? It would be intellectually dishonest to deny the existence of such sanctities, and it would be irresponsible and unreasonable to ignore them.

Now, let's take the example of the *Sunnah*. The established dogma in Islam does not award the *Sunnah* the same level of authenticity or immutability as the Qur'ān. The *Sunnah* is an amorphous corpus of reports about the Prophet's actions and history (*sīrah*) and his statements (*ḥadīth*), and also includes numerous reports about the Companions of the Prophet. It appears to have had primarily oral origins but was eventually documented in a variety of books known as the *sunan* or *masānīd*. In its oral form, the *Sunnah* documented the living traditions of the early Muslim community.[15] In its documented form, these traditions no longer mutated and developed but took a highly structured and organized format.[16] The way the *Sunnah* was documented was through a fairly long chain of narrators going back to the Prophet, the Companions (*ṣaḥābah*), and Successors of the Companions (*tābiʿīn*), and ending with the last narrator before the tradition was written down. A complex science known as *al-ʿadl wa al-tarjīḥ* was developed that aimed to document and evaluate the credibility of each of the narrators that transmitted traditions. So, for instance, X would say, I heard Y say I heard Z say I heard U say I heard C say I heard the Prophet say such and such. Using the science of *al-ʿadl wa al-tarjīḥ*, one would evaluate the credibility of X, Y, Z, U, and C, and on that basis, issue a judgment as to the authenticity of a tradition's *isnād* (chain of transmission).[17] Importantly, social, political, and theological judgments entered the process of evaluating the credibility of the transmitters of a tradition. So, for example, it is reported that Aḥmad b. Ḥanbal (d. 241/855) refused to narrate traditions from any scholar who succumbed to the theological inquisition (*miḥnah*) that was imposed by the Abbasid caliph al-Ma'mūn (r. 197/813–217/833) and lasted until the reign of al-Mutawakkil (r. 232/847–247/861).[18] Although scholars of traditions frequently claimed that the standards for authenticating transmissions were entirely objective these standards were, in fact, the subject of vibrant debates and were heavily contextual.

Scholars of tradition did distinguish between traditions narrated through singular chains of transmission (*āḥādī*) and traditions narrated through cumulative chains of transmission (*mutawātir*). The second category of traditions was considered more reliable and authentic than the first. The technical definition of *āḥādī* traditions was somewhat circular: it is that which has not reached the level of the *mutawātir*. The definition of *tawātur* (the *mutawātir* type traditions), in turn, depended on the school of thought defining the term. Generally, however, *mutawātir* meant that the tradition or narration was transmitted throughout the first three generations of Muslims by such a large number of transmitters that it is highly unlikely that the tradition was fabricated. Opinions differed as to the number of transmitters in each generation that is required for a tradition to attain the level of *tawātur*. Some scholars said seven, some forty, some seventy and some even more. *Āḥādī* traditions, according to the scholars, are those transmitted in the first three generations by a number less than that required for the *mutawātir* category. Generally speaking, as to the *mutawātir* category, the scholars of tradition concluded that it is fairly certain that the Prophet uttered the report attributed to him. In the *āḥādī* category, there remains the suspicion that the tradition is not authentic.[19]

Significantly, as part of the process of authentication, jurists and scholars of tradition would perform an analysis of the substantive content of the tradition (*matn* analysis). This field of inquiry was known as *ʿilm ʿilal al-matn* (the defects that relate to the substance). According to this type of analysis, a report with an impeccable chain of transmission may be rejected because the substance of the tradition is not sound. Such a tradition would be rejected either because it contained grammatical or historical errors, or because it contradicted the Qur'ān, or the text was contrary to the laws of nature, common experience, or the dictates of reason.[20] Scholars of tradition would declare a tradition suffering from these defects, or others, to have *ʿilal qādiḥah fī al-matn* (an effective defect in content).[21] This field of analysis, however, was fraught with ambiguities, and not much has been written about it. Scholars of tradition often stated that *ʿilal al-matn* is a mysterious science in which only the most learned scholar can delve. After studying the totality of issues surrounding the language, style and meaning of a particular tradition, a scholar would make a judgment about the existence of an effective defect in the tradition.[22] Effectively, that meant that the methodologies of the field were elusive, and the judgments reached were fairly subjective.

This is a short synopsis of the theory of the legitimating structure for the traditions of the Prophet and the Companions. Importantly, much of the corpus of Islamic law is built upon these traditions. According to the formal theory, scholars such as al-Bukhārī (d. 256/870), Muslim b. al-Ḥajjāj (d. 261/875), Ibn Mājah (d. 273/887), al-Nasā'ī (d. 303/915), al-Tirmidhī (d. 279/892), Ibn Ḥayyān (d. 469/1076), Ibn Khuzaymah (d. 311/924), and many others, applied the methodology of the science of traditions and collected what they determined to be authentic traditions. Reportedly, these scholars considered and rejected thousands of traditions that they deemed to be apocryphal. It is difficult to reconstruct the context of the selective processes that guided the efforts of these scholars, but there is no doubt that the process of authentication and documentation was both negotiative and creative. My point is that selecting, authenticating, and documenting the traditions was not the product of mathematical formulas or some highly structured process. Rather, these scholars understood and responded, negotiated and created, and were impacted by and in turn impacted their various contexts by deciding which traditions could be ascribed to the Prophet or the Companions and which could not. Therefore, it is hardly surprising that the scholars of tradition disagreed as to which particular traditions were authentic, hence, one finds considerable variations in their books. Some traditions were declared authentic and were documented by most scholars, and some traditions were documented by just one scholar, or none at all.[23]

My aim here is to focus on the issues of authorship and text. Jorge Gracia, a relatively conservative scholar of texts, has defined them as, "Groups of entities, used as signs, that are selected, arranged and intended by an author in a certain context to convey some specific meaning to an audience."[24] This definition actually emphasizes the complexity of the concept of texts. Texts are composed of signs, and signs are constituted of entities. Letters, words, and numbers could be signs if composed of entities that convey some meaning. Expressions, sentences, and paragraphs are texts that are contextual in nature. For instance, writing "666" on my forehead in a Christian country might be a text that alludes to Satan. Writing it on my forehead in a Muslim country, because I saw someone do it in an American movie, might not qualify as a text, if I intend nothing by it except blind imitation. If my son writes "666" on my forehead while I am asleep because he thinks it makes me as cool as movie stars, but I later inform people that this sign means I have sold my soul to the devil, we have a text with different types of authors – my son is an author, my proprietary claim to my forehead makes me an author, and my students who might think that this is simply a sign of insanity form a different type of author. Texts are formed of sub-texts because the signs often contain sub-signs and the entities contain sub-entities. Furthermore, the author of a text is inevitably part of the audience of the text, and to the extent the audience recognizes and understands the signs of a text, the audience partakes in the authorial enterprise. In this sense, a text could have a variety of authors: there is the historical author who once created the text, there is the production author who might typeset and print the text, there is the revisionist author who edits, alters, and recasts the text and there is the interpretive author who receives and creates meaning from the signs composing the text.[25] These various authors do not play equal roles or functions, in fact the roles and functions of the various authors will change according to specific contextual factors.

Even the relatively conservative conception of what constitutes a text, described above, is far more fluid and dynamic than the notion of *naṣṣ* in traditional Muslim discourses. The *naṣṣ*, whether Qur'ānic or *Sunnaic*, is treated as an integrated, symmetrical, and structured entity determined by a single author. Other than deciphering the meaning of the text, the role of the audience in dealing with the *naṣṣ* is to search for that unitary and integrated author who is the creator. Once a certain *naṣṣ* is matched with the specific author, whether God, the Prophet, a Companion or Successor, the author's proprietary claim over the *naṣṣ* is complete and total. Therefore, the specific wording of the *naṣṣ* becomes sacrosanct and non-negotiable. The transmitters, collectors, documenters, and audiences of the *naṣṣ* are not part of the authorial enterprise in any way.

As I noted above, the *naṣṣ*-type approach is consistent with the belief in the immutability and Divinity of the Qur'ān. The established doctrine in Muslim theology is that God intentionally and meticulously phrased every letter, word, and sentence in the Qur'ān. Muslims have long cited the Qur'ānic verse, "And, We have sent down the Remembrance and We vow to protect it" (Qur'ān 15:9), as proof that God will protect the Qur'ān from all human corruption. Furthermore, it is a central tenet of the Islamic religion that the Torah and Bible were redacted and corrupted by Jews and Christians, but the Qur'ān remained immune from any such attempts.

If one accepts these tenets as a matter of faith, does it make sense to speak of an authorial enterprise, that includes the oral transmitters and collectors of the Qur'ānic text, as the collective authors of the Qur'ān? Is the logic of authorial enterprise consistent with the idea of Divine authorship? Can we, for instance, argue that God is the historical author of the Qur'ān, but that the mediation of the Prophet, and the functions of the copyists, the editors, the collectors, and interpreters are all a part of the authorial enterprise? It is possible to make this type of argument only if one can argue persuasively that the authorial enterprise was part of the Divine intent or otherwise legitimated by the Divine. This is an argument that I do not wish to make for two main reasons. One, I do not believe that a persuasive argument can be made to that effect. The Qur'ān consistently speaks of itself as God's exclusive text. Two, the argument as to the authorial enterprise would be sufficiently offensive to Muslims and would be perceived as a form of pillaging through the Islamic tradition. Certainly, exercising a degree of self-restraint because of the fear of giving offense is a risky proposition. Where does one draw the line between empathetic consideration and complacency? Is self-censor in the face of sensitivities ever justifiable? Is it ever acceptable to sanction the "unthinkable" and "unthought"?

All arguments stand on the grounds of some tradition or another. The tradition is composed of a community of linguistic practices, historical assumptions, and shared beliefs. All such communities change, develop, and re-invent themselves often through the onslaught of an epistemological crisis, but as Alasdiar MacIntyre has argued, "Some core of shared belief, constitutive of allegiance to the tradition, has to survive every rupture."[26] In fact, the sense of historical reality that constitutes a tradition is often based on nothing more than some well-entrenched prejudices.[27] But as Hans-Georg Gadamer has pointed out, some are legitimate, helpful or true. Legitimate prejudices often sustain the structure of authority within a tradition.[28] Each epistemological crisis creates the possibility of change by putting into question some of those prejudices, and by raising the possibility of re-examination, re-construction, and re-invention. Importantly, however, to borrow MacIntyre's expression, each rupture in a tradition questions the tradition's claims to truth, and challenges its warrants.[29] At this point, we must distinguish between two authorial roles. If I assume the role of an outsider to a tradition, observing and documenting its structure and mechanics, in effect, I am assuming the role of a social scientist who observes and documents and tries to avoid, as much as possible, interfering or re-structuring the subject of study. If, however, I assume the role of an insider to the tradition who is undertaking a normative role, exercising both self-restraint and reasonableness, I will proceed to identify which parts of the tradition – which are a part of its communities of prejudice – warrant critical re-examination. I will consider which parts can no longer be defended or possibly justified either on rational, moral or theological grounds. In other words, I will try to identify which parts of the tradition have become incoherent or fundamentally inconsistent with the basic assumptions of the tradition, or with what I believe to be the basic moral positions of the tradition. Importantly, as an insider, if I am interested in sustaining the legitimacy of the tradition and sustaining my own legitimacy within the community of the tradition, I must make a Rawlsian-type decision as to what could form the basis for a reasonable overlapping consensus.[30] If I accept the Divinity of the Qur'ān, I see no inconsistency or rupture in accepting the idea of a text protected by the Divine from human alterations or redactions. The idea of authorial enterprise does not necessarily mean the mundaneness of the Qur'ān and does not necessarily mean that the Qur'ān was corrupted, however, in deference to the sensibilities of Muslims, I will not use the expression of authorial enterprise as far as the Qur'ān is concerned.

The *Sunnah*, however, is a different matter. There is already a substantial literature on *ḥadīth* criticism written by Muslim scholars. As discussed above, the history of the traditions of the Prophet and Companions as narrated by Muslim scholars is far more complex and contested than the history of the Qur'ān. Furthermore, Muslim dogma does not assert that the *ḥadīth* literature is immutable or Divinely protected from the possibility of corruption. In addition, as explained above, there is a considerable degree of creative subjectivity in the process of authenticating, documenting, organizing, and transmitting the reports attributed to the Prophet and the Companions. Yet, as noted earlier, what I called the *naṣṣ*-approach has persistently tended to ascribe a single authorial voice to each tradition. In addition, the text of the tradition would typically begin with the open-quotes of the particular report and end with the close-quotes. So, for example, a report would say, the Prophet said "such-and-such" – it is this and that constituted the full authoritative text. The objection that I have to this approach is that it is unabashedly ahistorical. This approach ignores that there are a number of authorial voices that contribute to any tradition attributed to the Prophet. Assuming that the Prophet is, in reality, the origin of a certain statement, there is the person or persons who heard this statement and engaged in a selective and constructive process of singling out this particular statement as worthy of remembering. The statement was uttered within a context that the reporter or reporters might or might not have deemed to be relevant, and so some Prophetic traditions are reported with some comment on the context and others are not. Each person or persons who transmitted Prophetic traditions from one generation to another, and from within one context to another, engaged in the same type of selective and constructive process. The scholars of traditions whether al-Bukhārī, Muslim, or any other, in turn selected from a wealth of traditions, organized the selected traditions and documented them in books. This process of selection and documentation reflected the context and subjective normative judgments of each scholar about the tradition of Islam.[31] Significantly, the same process was reproduced as some traditions, and not others, made their way into the negotiative and creative dynamics of the juristic culture. Some traditions developed a loyal community of interpreters while other traditions did not, and different traditions rose to levels of particular prominence within particular schools. So, for instance, the tradition attributed to the Prophet that provides that a divorce made in jest is to be treated seriously is of central importance in the Ḥanafī school, but not the other schools. The tradition that provides that the most important contractual conditions, and the most worthy to comply with, are the conditions set out in a marriage contract, had a considerable degree of influence in the Ḥanbalī school, but had lesser influence on the other schools. Other traditions had considerable influence on popular culture but had very little effect on the legal culture.[32]

I am not implying that the process of integrating certain Prophetic traditions within particular legal cultures was haphazard or whimsical. Traditions were integrated into legal cultures and acquired meaning through the dynamics of a variety of micro and macro processes that were relevant to an evolving set of contexts. The evolution of the process of transmitting, collecting, and documenting these traditions was both collective and contextual. But even after the process of documenting the traditions in canonical books was completed, communities of meaning and linguistic practice continued to develop around selected traditions, either in the juristic or the social context. All of this leads us to pose the question: when one cites, quotes, or otherwise refers to a tradition from the *Sunnah*, what is one referring to exactly? The notion that a person can directly refer to the authority of the Prophet is incoherent. As explained, each tradition is the product an authorial enterprise in which the Prophet occupies the role of the historical author. But we are not receiving the communication of the Prophet through an immutable or Divinely-warranted process. We are receiving the communication of the Prophet through a highly negotiative medium that had selected, retained and reproduced segments of the complex truth that was the Prophet. I do not intend to dilute or somehow deconstruct the authoritativeness of the Prophet's tradition in Islamic discourses. I am merely pointing out that authoritativeness is not one-dimensional. Authoritativeness is produced within a context, and this context forces the authoritative to speak in a communal, rather than an individual, voice. To state the point a bit more forcefully, it is unrealistic to assume that it is possible to refer to the singular and unmediated authority of the Prophet. The Prophet speaks to us today only through an enterprise that includes several authorial voices, and a diachronic process of development. Communities of interpretation have formed around this authorial enterprise, and aspects of these interpretive communities have become sufficiently entrenched that they now form a part of the authorial enterprise. Synchronic approaches to *ḥadīth* literature are ahistorical and quite misguided. For example, consider the word *mutʿah* that occurs in several traditions and in some Qurʾānic verses. As it developed in the juristic tradition, this became a technical and versatile word. *Mutʿah* means pleasure, delight or gratification. However, as used in the Prophetic traditions, it could mean sexual pleasure or consummation of a marriage, it could mean a temporary marriage, it could mean compensation paid to a divorced woman, and it could refer to ritual acts performed during pilgrimage.[33] When we encounter the words *mutʿah*, *istimtāʿ*, or *tamattuʿ* in reports attributed to the Prophet or the Companions, we understand these words to refer to one or another of these meanings. Each meaning, as it emerged from each tradition is the product of a cumulative and evolving process of interpretation. At present, the meanings produced by the interpretive communities have become firmly established to the point that they have become a part of the authorial enterprise. If, for instance, a student reads the word *mutʿah* in a particular tradition and asserts that it is referring to temporary marriages, I might feel justified in correcting him by saying, "No, here the word refers to ritual acts performed at pilgrimage," and I might even accuse my student of ignorance. But we need to ask, what am I accusing him ignorance of? I am accusing him of ignorance of the Prophet's linguistic usage or intent. But I only know of the Prophet's intent in an indirect fashion – I know it through the cumulative efforts of so many others who formed an authorial enterprise and an interpretive community. On the other hand, assume the same student does extensive research and persuasively argues that all the scholars who thought that this tradition was referring to pilgrimage were wrong. My student produces much evidence demonstrating that the Prophet was talking about temporary marriages. Depending on the quality of the research, my ignorant student suddenly becomes transformed into either a holy man or a brilliant person. If the Prophet appeared to the student in person and explained his authorial intent to him, the student is quite possibly a holy man. But I have no access to this spiritual experience; either I will believe him or not, and because of the premises of my theology and the interpretive communities that command my allegiance, I will not believe him. If, however, the student is relying on analytical evidence, he is quite possibly brilliant. I, however, might rely on a different interpretive community or on a set of interpretive communities, and, thus, I could argue that my particular interpretive community was closer to the intent of the reported historical author (the Prophet) than any other competing interpretive community.

The essential point that follows from this discussion is that the process of referring to the authoritative sources of the *Sunnah* invokes a complex dynamic. Any such reference necessarily brings into relevance a host of authorial voices and interpretive communities. In fact, what is made relevant is itself the product of an authorial and interpretive tradition. In other words, any reference to primary sources elicits a reference to the secondary dynamics – any reference to Islamic sources is a reference to the continuing Islamic tradition. Importantly, I have rejected the notion of referring to an authorial enterprise as far as the Qurʾān is concerned. I did so not to exclude the interpretive community that has formed around the text of the Qurʾān but, partly, in deference to this interpretive community. As noted above, speaking about the Qurʾānic tradition in terms of an authorial enterprise would be perceived as illegitimate and a form of *qillat adab* (inappropriate way of speaking or inappropriate behavior). Nevertheless, aside from the issue of authorial enterprise, there is no doubt that interpretive communities have formed around various Qur'ānic verses and chapters. To an extent, these linguistic and interpretive communities have become firmly integrated within the text of the Qur'ān. So for instance, when the Qur'ān states that women should take a *khimār* and strike with it their *jayb*, the vast majority of Muslims read this to mean that Muslim women should wear a veil and cover their necks or bosom with such a veil.[34] Furthermore, the majority of Muslims understand this as a normative command and not as simply advisory or contingent on a specific group of women in a particular time and place. Nonetheless, our understanding of the words *khimār* and *jayb* is thoroughly dependent on a tradition of interpretive communities. Linguistically, *khimār* could be a scarf, a partition, a turban, a piece of cloth, a flowing garb, a garb without stitches and, metaphorically, it could refer to spiritual and mental states. *Jayb* could mean folds of skin, the beginning of the chest area, a woman's cleavage area, pockets, and the areas subject to concealment on a human body, as well as other things. But the specific, and particular signification given to the text and the acquired contexts of the Qur'ānic discourse were the product and continue to be the product of communities of interpretation. Importantly, however, since the sole and exclusive Author of the Qur'ān is God, no community of interpretation can possibly become a part of the Authorial enterprise. This means that one must conceptually distinguish, as far as the Qur'ān is concerned, between the Authorial voice and the communities of interpretation that formed around the Authorial voice. What logically follows from the theological premises of Islam and from the belief in the Divine sanctity of the Qur'ān is that no interpretive community can partake in the Authorial voice of the Divine text. To state it rather bluntly, this leads to the sanctification of the Qur'ān and the de-sanctification of the *Sunnah* – the Qur'ān is exclusively from God but the *Sunnah* is not. This, of course, is consistent with the already established dogma of Islamic theology. But the important point is that as far as the *Sunnah* is concerned, the authorial voice is entitled to less deference than the Authorial voice of the Qur'ān. But to the extent that the author's intended meaning behind a text is determinative of the meaning of the text, interpretive communities that form around the text are entitled to less deference. Put differently, to the extent that the author is identifiable in a text, the jurisdiction of the author, especially a living author such as God, must be acknowledged. This, in turn, means that the interpretive community must undertake its activities in light of this jurisdiction and this necessarily means the interpretive community's claim over the meaning of the text can never be decisive or complete. So, for instance, as far as the Qur'ān is concerned, I will defer to the interpretive community, but my allegiance is to the authorial voice of the text. If, as a matter of conscience, I believe the interpretive community has violated or contravened the authorial intent of the Qur'ān, I will feel that I have a right to dissent and reject the product of any Qur'ānically-based interpretive community. The *Sunnah*, however, demands a different type of analysis.

As explained earlier, the Qur'ān commands obedience to the Prophet, and Muslim dogma has long held that the Qur'ānic obligation to obey the Prophet is binding during and after his lifetime. The *Sunnah* tradition had become the repository of the Prophet's commands. As argued above, there is an authorial enterprise responsible for the *Sunnah* tradition. For a Muslim who accepts the authoritativeness of the Prophet's commands, the issue becomes distilling the authorial core that, in fact, can relate back to the Prophet. Assuming that one can do so – assuming that the Prophetic core is recognizable and reachable – then the same analysis that applies to the Qur'ān will be pertinent for the *Sunnah*. If I sincerely believe that the interpretive community was in error in understanding the Prophet's injunctions, as a matter of conscience, I am obliged to dissent. Nevertheless, I believe that in the vast majority of traditions, this Prophetic core is unreachable. In the vast majority of traditions, the different forms of authorship are thoroughly intermingled with the Prophetic authorship, and it is practically impossible to differentiate between the various authorial voices. It must be emphasized that I am not talking about authenticity of the traditions – I am not claiming that the vast majority of Prophetic traditions are apocryphal. I am arguing that since the Prophet was a human being who, unlike God, is subject to mundane historical processes, his legacy cannot exist outside the context of human mediation and the human authorial process. The authenticity and genuineness of the Prophet, from the point of view of Islamic theology, is exactly his humanness. The Prophet does not interact with history as a God, but as a part of the normal human dynamics.[35] This necessarily means that the Prophet's moral and normative presence exists within a historical context. This normative presence is represented and contested by the historical context, but the historical context cannot and does not embody the full truth or reality of the moral experience. Consequently, in terms of evaluating the activities of the interpretive communities formed around the text of the *Sunnah*, the pertinent issue is the extent to which the interpretive communities reflect, understand or incorporate the historical context of the authorial enterprise. The interpretive community is bound to take account of the authorial enterprise with all its historical permutations in order to understand the appropriate balance between the historical author (the Prophet) and the various authorial voices that provided the context for the historical author.

The scholars of tradition in Islamic history have largely ignored the issue of the context of the Prophet's voice. Several contemporary scholars, the most notable of which is Fazlur Rahman, have already pointed out this problem.[36] But even in the pre-modern age, Ibn Khaldūn (d. 784/1382) had criticized the tendency of Muslim scholars to ignore the historical context in the process of identifying the authorial voice of the Prophet. He states in his famous *al-Muqaddimah* the following:

> When it comes to reports, if one relies only on the [method] of transmission without evaluating [these reports] in light of the principles of human conduct, the

> fundamentals of politics, the nature of civilization, and the conditions for social associations, and without comparing ancient sources to contemporary sources and the present to the past, he [or she] could fall into errors and mistakes and could deviate from the path of truth. Historians, [Qur'ānic] interpreters and leading transmitters have often fallen into error by accepting [the authenticity of certain] reports and incidents. This is because they relied only on the transmission, whether of value or worthless. They did not [carefully] inspect [these reports] in light of [fundamental] principles [of historical analysis] or compare the reports to each other or examine them according to the standards of wisdom or investigate the nature of beings. Furthermore, they did not decide on the authenticity of these reports according to the standards of reason and discernment. Consequently, they were led astray from the truth and became lost in the wilderness of error and delusion.[37]

Although Ibn Khaldūn focuses on the problem of authenticity and the necessity of historicism in the process of authentication, what he articulates applies on a much broader scale. The issue is not simply the authenticity of any particular tradition. It is possible to come to the conviction that the Prophet had no role whatsoever in the production of a particular tradition and, therefore, we might determine that this tradition is inauthentic. But this determination is of limited utility. The much more pertinent issue is to evaluate the historical context that generated the authorial enterprise and to analyze the cumulative and evolving process that led to the development of communities of interpretation around that enterprise. In terms of analyzing the work product of communities of interpretation, we must inquire into the extent to which such communities constructed or were constructed by their respective historical contexts, and we must inquire into the nature of a community's understanding of the authorial enterprise and its historical context. In addition, we must analyze the interpretive community's understanding of the role of the Prophet in that enterprise. Often the issue in this process is not subject to the reductionism of the authenticity inquiry but should be evaluated in terms of what I have called the competence of a tradition.

Competence refers not just to the ultimate decision of authenticity of a tradition but to the totality of circumstances that affect the authoritativeness of the tradition. Authenticity is a part of this inquiry, but much more important is to evaluate the totality of the authorial enterprise and reach some determination as to the way and the extent to which the various authorial voices constructed and re-constructed the voice of the reported historical author (in most cases the Prophet or a Companion). A competence inquiry does not seek simply to reach a judicial-type decision declaring a tradition to be *ṣaḥīḥ* (authentic) or *mawḍūʿ* (fabricated). It is a comprehensive inquiry into the full historical context in order to evaluate the role of the Prophet in a particular tradition. This inquiry will not end up with a decisive determination as to authenticity versus the lack of authenticity. Rather, the focus is on degrees of responsibility and roles played by the various actors.

I will demonstrate this point with some examples later in the book after we have had an opportunity to analyze the mechanics of *responsa* issued in the contemporary age. Nevertheless, it would be helpful to give a concrete form to the abstractions of the argument by analyzing one example at this point. Various juristic communities of interpretation have long held that women are not qualified to hold either a judicial position or a political leadership position such as caliph. However, there have been some disagreements among these interpretive communities.[38] For instance, Ibn Ḥazm (d. 456/1064) and many Mālikī jurists argued that a woman may serve as a judge without restrictions, but Abū Ḥanīfah (d. 150/767) asserted that a woman may act as a judge in all commercial and civil cases, but not in criminal and personal injury cases. Al-Ṭabarī (d. 310/923), the jurist who held that women may lead men in prayer, also held that women may serve as judges in all cases without restrictions.[39] Importantly, most of the juristic debates revolved around a tradition attributed to the Prophet in which the Prophet reportedly says, "No people will succeed who entrust their affairs to a woman." Although this is the most common version of this report, there are variations in other reports.[40] The overwhelming majority of the reports go back to the Companion Nufayʿ b. al-Ḥārith, known as Abū Bakrah al-Thaqafī (d. 52/672). A late convert to Islam, Abū Bakrah reported that he was in the Prophet's presence when the Prophet heard that a woman had taken power in Persia, and that upon receiving the news the Prophet made the statement quoted above.[41] This version of the report has been declared authentic (*ṣaḥīḥ*) by a large number of *ḥadīth* documenters, including the famous al-Bukhārī.[42] In a version with more dramatic flair, Abū Bakrah reports that the Prophet was lying down with his head in his wife ʿĀʾishah's lap (d. 58/678) when an unidentified man came to the Prophet and informed him that the Persians had lost a battle. The Prophet became alert and declared three consecutive times, "Verily, men are doomed when they obey women!"[43]

Reportedly, Abū Bakrah narrated over one hundred and thirty traditions attributed to the Prophet.[44] Scholars of tradition have accepted the credibility of Abū Bakrah, and some have described him as one of the best Companions.[45] Nonetheless, there are various relevant points to consider surrounding the life of Abū Bakrah, most notably was that he was punished for slander, and the caliph ʿUmar b. al-Khaṭṭāb refused to treat him as a credible witness in legal cases. The story begins when al-Mughīrah b. Shuʿbah (d. 48–51/668–671), the governor of Baṣra at the time of the caliph ʿUmar (r. 12/634–23/644) used to visit a married woman by the name of Umm Jamīl bint ʿAmr. Reportedly, Abū Bakrah, and his half-brothers Nāfiʿ, Ziyād, and Shubal b. Maʿbad, witnessed al-Mughīrah and Umm Jamīl unclothed and engaging in some type of sexual activity. After witnessing the act, Abū Bakrah refused to pray behind al-Mughīrah, accusing him of adultery. Eventually, the matter reached the caliph ʿUmar who called for and presided over a trial. Abū Bakrah, Nāfiʿ, and Shubal testified that they witnessed the legally material act of actual intercourse. Ziyād, however, testified that the actual act of intercourse was not observable, rather, Ziyād asserted they saw naked bodies with one body on top of the other, saw motions consistent with the act of intercourse, and heard heavy breathing. This testimony, however, fell short of the evidentiary standard required to prove adultery. ʿUmar ruled that Abū Bakrah, Nāfiʿ, and Shubal should be flogged for slander against al-Mughīrah. After carrying out the flogging Nāfiʿ and Shubal repented and withdrew their accusations, and so their credibility as witnesses in legal acts was rehabilitated. Abū Bakrah refused to withdraw the accusation and, reportedly, ʿUmar thought of repeating the punishment against him, but never did. As a result of these events, ʿUmar refused to accept Abū Bakrah as a credible witness concerning any legal case or act. Interestingly, Abū Bakrah never forgave Ziyād for his testimony and he refused to talk to Ziyād until he died.[46]

This series of events raises a variety of questions on which the sources on tradition are silent. Al-Mughīrah, the person accused of adultery, was a Companion and was entrusted by the prominent ʿUmar to be the governor of Baṣra. Apparently even after the event, al-Mughīrah continued to enjoy ʿUmar's confidence.[47] One can pose a variety of speculative questions such as whether the testimony against al-Mughīrah was politically motivated? Is it relevant that the witnesses were brothers? What were the witnesses doing at the location of the incident? What accounts for the inconsistency in testimony among the witnesses? The normal course and practice of juristic communities of interpretation is to refuse to accept reports narrated by individuals who were convicted of moral crimes such as slander or false accusation. What accounts for the fact that Abū Bakrah's reports, and especially the one about the leadership of women, were accepted as reliably going back to the Prophet, despite ʿUmar's refusal to count Abū Bakrah as a credible witness?

There are other elements to the Abū Bakrah character that are not directly related to the slander incident. Reportedly, when ʿĀʾishah, joined by Ṭalḥah and Zubayr, rebelled against ʿAlī, she wrote to Abū Bakrah asking him to join her forces, but he refused her invitation narrating that he heard the Prophet say the tradition quoted above.[48] In other reports, upon hearing that ʿĀʾishah was defeated in the Battle of the Camel (36/656), Abū Bakrah comments that he knew this would happen because the Prophet had told him that a people led by a women cannot succeed. In yet other reports, Abū Bakrah counsels people not to join a rebellion led by a woman. Interestingly, these reports are somewhat balanced by other reports that Abū Bakrah refused to support ʿAlī, ʿĀʾishah, *and* Muʿāwiyah. In fact, he, reportedly, was extremely unhappy with his own sons because they accepted political appointments during Muʿāwiyah's rule. To Abū Bakrah's great dismay, his brother Ziyād also accepted a political appointment at the time of Muʿāwiyah. Abū Bakrah reportedly refused to reconcile with his brother Ziyād despite Mālik b. Anas' (d. 179/796) intercessions, and even requested that his brother Ziyād not be allowed to perform funeral prayers on his corpse after his death. It is asserted in some reports that Abū Bakrah also boycotted his sons for accepting the political appointments – appointments that incidentally allowed them to die as wealthy individuals in Baṣra.[49] At the same time, Abū Bakrah is reported to have narrated from the Prophet traditions strongly condemning anyone who cuts off his family ties.[50]

In a set of reports, Abū Bakrah is quoted as the source for several traditions calling for political pacifism. According to some of these reports, Abū Bakrah narrates that the Prophet told him that he (Abū Bakrah) is one of the best Companions and that the caliphate will change to *mulk* (dynastic rule) and that when that occurs, Muslims should not rebel or resist. In yet other reports, Abū Bakrah states that the Prophet told him that Muʿāwiyah will come to power and he should not be opposed, and that honoring whoever is in power is part of honoring God.[51] Importantly, there are reports in which Abū Bakrah is cast as a rabid women hater. For instance, when he is asked about the worst hardships in life, he reportedly responds, "The death of a father breaks the back, the death of a son splits the heart, the death of a brother severs the wings and the death of a woman deserves no more than one hour of grief."[52]

This is just a part of the relevant data on Abū Bakrah, the person reportedly responsible for transmitting the Prophet's opinion regarding the leadership of women. But the information reviewed above is sufficient to permit us to raise questions about the authorial voice of Abū Bakrah in relation to the authorial voice of the Prophet. What is striking about the legacy of Abū Bakrah is that he is a late convert to Islam yet his impact upon the Islamic tradition is disproportionate to his status as a Companion of the Prophet. His background before his conversion to Islam is largely untraceable but he is consistently cast into the role of the conservative legitimist who defends the traditional role of men, eschews involvement in politics and is stubborn in adhering to whatever he believes is right. Ironically, however, many of the traditions coming through him are highly politicized. His tradition about the leadership of women can be taken as a condemnation of ʿĀʾishah's political role and his traditions about politics espouse obedience to power. His resistance to power is largely passive such as his refusal to obey ʿUmar in retracting his accusations against al-Mughīrah. From the point of view of the Abū Bakrah narrations, politics is always corrupting – it corrupts al-Mughīrah, it induces Ziyād to recant his testimony, it upsets the scales of justice, and, most of all, it incites women to rebel and men to follow in their follies. Abū Bakrah could have become a symbol for gender tensions, and so the tradition quoted above about grieving over women could have been put into circulation to discredit Abū Bakrah. On the other hand, it is possible that Abū Bakrah was, in fact, someone who saw little value in women. If that is the case, is it possible that the Prophet had commented on the developing situation in Persia by saying, "A people who are led by *this* woman will not succeed?"[53] Is it possible that Abū Bakrah misheard the statement because he was receiving it through his own subjectivities? But if the Prophet did make a statement such as the one reported by Abū Bakrah, why was he the only one who seems to have heard it? If, as in some versions, the Prophet made this statement in the presence of ʿĀʾishah, why did she not report it? If ʿĀʾishah, in fact, asked Abū Bakrah to join her rebellion, and Abū Bakrah wrote her back with the Prophet's quote, what was ʿĀʾishah's reaction?

All of these questions lead to speculation but they also raise serious questions about the authorial enterprise behind this one tradition. We focused on the figure of Abū Bakrah, but it is important to remember that there are further processes to this tradition. What was the context of the transmitters who narrated this report from Abū Bakrah? Among which communities did this report become popular, and why was it so readily accepted as authentic by tradition collectors such as al-Bukhārī? Was the patriarchical message of this tradition responsible for its wide dissemination and acceptance in various interpretive communities? Was the evidentiary burden lowered by the jurists and scholars of tradition because Abū Bakrah's report seemed to make sense in terms of their context and communities of practice? In other words, did the juristic communities, and others communities, treat this tradition with uncritical favoritism because it struck a chord with their contextual subjectivities? Did this lead them not to evaluate the authorial enterprise with the requisite degree of diligence and scrutiny?

In light of these various issues, the question of authenticity seems to be not particularly interesting. The issue is the extent to which we can assert that we understand or have a good sense of the Prophet's involvement in the total authorial enterprise. If, because of all the questions raised above, we conclude that the picture is too complex and that we are unable to ascertain with any degree of confidence the role, if any, of the Prophet, this raises a further question. What is the competence of this tradition? To what extent, if any, should it have normative power? To what extent should we defer to the interpretive communities if these communities did not do a thorough job in analyzing the tradition? Does the fact that the literalist jurist Ibn Ḥazm, and al-Ṭabarī, the jurist who led notorious battles with *ahl al-ḥadīth* (the people of traditions), refused to consider this tradition dispositive on the issue of the legality of a woman's leadership make a difference in the analysis?

My response is that all the questions raised above do make a difference. It seems mistaken to acknowledge much competence in this tradition. The fact that a prominent scholar such as al-Bukhārī declared the tradition authentic is not probative as to the larger issue of the legal or theological effect that this tradition should have in our present context. The inquiry into the authorial enterprise leads to numerous queries, challenges, and puzzlements. Most importantly, the communities of interpretation that have dealt with this tradition have performed an inadequate or negligent job in analyzing the authorial enterprise. As a result, I would argue that this tradition has very limited competence and that the work of the interpretive communities has limited precedent-value to our contemporary interpretive communities.

Thus far we have focused on the competence of the authorial voice but we have not identified the exact role of the authorial voice. Much of the analysis has proceeded on the assumption that the authorial voice determines the meaning of the text and that the role of the interpretive community is to figure out that meaning. However, we need to examine this issue in greater detail because the dynamics between the author, the interpreter and the meaning is fundamental to any notion of authoritativeness. As explained earlier, authority in Islam is derived from the Principal, and the Principal issues instructions to His agents to regulate their activities and goals. The authoritativeness of what I called the special agents (the jurists) is legitimated only by their avowed mastery over the instructions issued by the Principal. Determining whether the instructions truly came from the Principal is an issue of competence. The competence of the Qur'ān is beyond dispute. The competence of other avenues for Divine instructions is a more complex matter. As noted earlier, the juristic culture had always assumed that the vehicle for the Divine instructions is primarily textual. But texts are complex entities. Human texts subject to normal historical and contextual processes are often formed of authorial enterprises and of a multitude of subtexts. Although I rejected the idea of authorial enterprise as far as the Qur'ānic text is concerned, this does not address issues related to determinations of meaning or interpretation. One can believe that every letter, word, and sentence in the Qur'ān is intended to be where it is by the All-Knowing and Infallible Author, but this does not resolve the issue of who determines the meaning of the Qur'ān or how it is determined. Therefore, I turn to the issue of the text and the determination of meaning next.

## *Text, determination, and authority*

Before getting into the fairly knotty issues related to hermeneutics, it is appropriate to examine Qur'ānic verses that many have understood to address the issue of interpretation. In a text that has acquired considerable power in contemporary Islamic discourses, the Qur'ān states:

> It is God who sent the Book down to you. In [the Book] are verses that are of established and clear meaning, and these [verses] are the foundation of the Book. Other verses in the Book are not of established and clear meaning. Those in whose hearts is perversity follow the part [of the Book] that is not of established and clear meaning seeking discord and searching for its concealed meanings. In truth, only God knows its true meaning, and those who are firmly grounded in knowledge say, "We believe in the Book; the whole of it is from our Lord." None will grasp the true message except men of understanding.[54]

This verse is fascinating because it appears to challenge the whole notion of human determination of meaning. The text concedes the existence of ambiguities in the text but goes on describe those who focus on the ambiguities as perverse. The Qur'ānic verses that have a clear and established meaning are described as the foundation of the Book, but the treatment of ambiguities appears to enjoy an illegitimate status – ambiguities are utilized and exploited by people whose credibility is suspect. This raises questions as to the role of interpretation in engaging the Qur'ān: is interpretation an illegitimate activity and what is the role of ambiguity if it is not to be engaged?

Interestingly, this verse has been cited to condemn everything from metaphorical interpretations and juristic deductions to the interpretive practices of *kalām* (scholastic theology) and Sufism. In the contemporary age, it has been used to condemn intellectualism and reformist re-interpretations of the Qur'ān. This verse has been taken to mean that there are verses that are clear and precise in the Qur'ān and that the attempt to use interpretation to obfuscate the meaning of these verses is reprehensible. Furthermore, people with perversity in their hearts dwell over the ambiguous verses to manipulate and corrupt God's Will.[55] Before engaging this argument, we should examine another Qur'ānic passage that also has played a powerful symbolic role in this field.

The following passage deals with the well-known Biblical story of the red heifer and the Israelites, but the narrative takes very different dimensions in the Qur'ānic discourse. In the Qur'ān, God commands the Israelites to slaughter a cow – any cow. But instead of prompt compliance, the Israelites responded with a set of questions that displeased God. The Qur'ānic text provides:

> And remember when Moses said to his people, "God commands that you sacrifice a heifer." They said: "Do you mock us Moses?" Moses said: "May God protect me from being among the ignorant!" They said: "Beseech on our behalf your Lord to make clear to us which heifer is it." Moses said: "God says, the heifer should be neither too old nor too young but of middling age. Now, do what you are commanded." They said: "Beseech on our behalf your Lord to make plain to us her color." He said: "God says it is a fawn-colored heifer, pure and rich in tone, the admiration of beholders." They said: "Beseech on our behalf your Lord to make plain to us what she is, to us all heifers look alike. God willing, we will be guided." He said: "God says, it is a heifer not trained to till the soil or water the fields; sound and without blemish." They said: "Now hast you brought the truth." Then they offered the heifer in sacrifice, and they were reluctant to do so.[56]

The symbolic connotation of this Qur'ānic discourse is that the Israelites were condemned for this encounter. But the question is: what is the reason for this condemnation? One obvious response is that the Israelites are condemned for their reluctance to carry out God's commands, but this only prompts the question, why are the Israelites reluctant? The Israelites initially react to Moses' command to sacrifice a heifer with a certain degree of surprise; in fact, they think that he is jesting or ridiculing them. After Moses assures them that he is conveying God's Will, the Israelites proceed to ask a series of questions but, eventually, do comply. Importantly, the nature of the questions is either clarifying, obstructionist or ridiculing. The Israelites might have understood God's command but asked questions in order to ridicule or resist what might have seemed to be a pointless or illogical command. Alternatively, the Israelites reacted to what appeared to be a senseless command by demanding further clarification, perhaps in order to make sense of, or rationalize, God's Will. Most Qur'ān commentators agreed that the Israelites were condemned for their reluctance and pedantic obstructionism (*mumāṭalah* and *tanaṭṭuʿ*), but the story of the heifer raised a more complicated issue.[57] By the time this verse was revealed, the Talmud had already been collected and the Kararite and Rabbinic traditions established.[58] The Kararites, who had established some communities in Arabia, rejected the interpretive practices of Rabbinic Judaism.[59] Could the Qur'ānic discourse be taken as an implicit condemnation of the Rabbinic tradition? For instance, some commentators concluded that the Qur'ānic passage intends to condemn the over-intellectualization of issues – that the proper response to God's commands is to comply without seeking to over-complicate things that God has made straightforward and clear. From this, the connection between the heifer story and the verse concerning the perversity of exploiting ambiguities becomes clear. Arguably, God issued what should have been understood as a straightforward and clear command, and the Israelites responded with perverse efforts rendering what is clear, ambiguous.[60] Therefore, Yusuf Ali, the well-known translator of the Qur'ān, notes that the moral of the story is to condemn the Israelites for playing "fast and loose with their own rites and traditions."[61]

The use of these Qur'ānic discourses to condemn intellectual or interpretive approaches to the Islamic tradition, itself, underscores the significance of the role of the reader in engaging the text. Understanding these discourses in this particular fashion is not determined by the text but by the ideological orientation of the reader. For instance, the first verse could be read as applying to the specific context of the existence of the hypocrites (*al-munāfiqūn*) in Medina who misused particular verses as part of a propaganda campaign against the Prophet and his followers. That verse could also be read to refer to the motive of the reader who engages the Divine text. If the motive of the reader is sinister, then the reader will be liable before God and God only. Furthermore, one should note that the Qur'ān does not deny the existence of ambiguities in the text. In fact, the verse could be read as asserting that there is a core or kernel to the Qur'ān and that this core is clear and unambiguous. But the verse does not say anything about the extent of the ambiguities in the Qur'ān or the reason for the existence of such ambiguities. The Qur'ān simply warns against an improper animus in dealing with these ambiguities. Similarly, the second Qur'ānic passage does not explicitly, or in direct fashion, condemn the interpretive act or limit the role of the reader. Arguably, reading the heifer story as teaching an anti-intellectual lesson or as constraining the role of the reader is, itself, a highly interpretive act. In the verses following those quoted, the Qur'ān invokes the familiar Biblical story of the murdered man who is touched by the flesh of the heifer and comes back to life to reveal the name of his murderer. The reluctance to slaughter the heifer could have been an attempt to avoid responsibility for the crime.[62] My point, quite simply, is that if there is a condemnation of the process of interpretation, it can be extracted from the Qur'ān only through an interpretive act. The verses above, which are often used to stem and restrain the interpretive activities of the reader, are not determinative one way or the other.

Muslim scholars have generated a prodigious tradition of Qur'ānic exegesis known as *ʿilm al-tafsīr*, which tends to focus on developing rules for deciphering the meaning of the text in its original time and place. The exegetical efforts of pre-modern scholars explored God's intentions and meanings through the text.[63] Since God is infallible and immutable, it was assumed that every letter, word, and sentence was in the Qur'ān for a reason. Furthermore, there was no possibility of the Author expressing Himself in an imperfect or incomplete manner. As far as the Qur'ān was concerned, the intentionality of the Author pervaded and controlled the text. The context of the text was investigated primarily through the science of the occasions for revelations (*ʿilm asbāb al-nuzūl*), but this contextual inquiry was primarily concerned with deciphering the original intent of the Author.[64]

Other than exegesis, contrary to the assumption of some Western scholars, there was also a lively interpretive process revolving around the text of the Qur'ān. By interpretation, I mean the process of exploring the contemporaneous significance of the original meaning. While exegesis focused on deciphering the meaning of the Author, interpretation dealt with the implications and significance of the original meaning. This interpretive process took place primarily in the field of jurisprudence. The jurisprudential inquiry did not focus on the original intent in order to service the text, but in order to service the socio-political reality through the use of the text.[65]

Of course, in the contemporary age, the relationship between exegesis and interpretation is addressed through the discipline of hermeneutics. I am not going to attempt a definition of hermeneutics, and I am not even sure that a definition is possible. I do think, however, that one can describe the study of hermeneutics as involving both the understanding of the rules for exegesis and the epistemology of understanding – the study of the constructions of meaning in the past and their relationship to the constructions of meaning in the present.[66] Particularly after the work of Heidegger and Gadamer, hermeneutics became the study of what Heidegger called the "ontological event" between the text and its interpreter, and the way these ontological events shape the history of understanding. Hermeneutics, as a discipline, tended to focus on understanding the subjectivities of the experience of meaning and the process by which the act of understanding meaning inevitably transforms it. Hermeneutics became interested in analyzing the conditions for the possibility of knowledge and the conditions for the transformation of such knowledge.[67]

The discipline of hermeneutics evolved from the discourses of biblical criticism, and even the founder of modern hermeneutics, the theologian

Friedrich Schleiermacher, situated his seminal work *Hermeneutics and Criticism* as a work on the methodologies of textual criticism of the New Testament.[68] The Christian origin of the discipline has without doubt formed a barrier against its adoption into Islamic discourses. Contemporary Muslim intellectuals have been suspicious not only of Western notions of relativism and indeterminacy, but also of what Muslim scholars considered to be the non-reverential methodologies by which biblical criticism dealt with the religious text. Nevertheless, recently, a few Muslim scholars have started utilizing the post-Schleiermacher hermeneutic discourse in attempting to understand the subjectivities and transformations of the interpretive process.[69] In fact, the field of hermeneutics as it developed in the West does provide useful conceptual frameworks or categories for analyzing the interpretive process and its impact on the notion of authority. The important consideration is that one ought to apply these categories with the requisite degree of sensitivity to the specificity of the Islamic context and also with a certain amount of deference to established Muslim systems of belief.

Pre-modern and modern Muslim scholars have written a large number of works on what they named the sciences of the Qur'ān (*'ulūm al-Qur'ān*) and the interpretation of *ḥadīth* (*ta'wīl al-ḥadīth*).[70] These works laid out rules for deciphering the meaning of the Qur'ānic verses and *ḥadīth* reports with the predominant emphasis being on the authorial intent behind the text. Particularly in the legal field, the rules of interpretation were based on logical and linguistic premises of expression – an informed author who abides by the rules of Arabic grammar and syntax, ideally, would express himself according to these premises. Since the author of the Qur'ān is God and the author of the *ḥadīth* is the Prophet, it was assumed that the authors have perfect knowledge of Arabic linguistic usage, and that the authors intended to abide by this usage. Of course, this assumption was justified partly by the fact that the Qur'ān describes itself as an eloquent Arabic book not open to the possibility of error.[71] Assuming the authors' perfect knowledge of Arabic and an intent to abide by such usage, Muslim jurists focused their efforts on deducing rules that they believed were mandated by the structure and nature of the Arabic language in order to understand the authorial intent behind the linguistic usage. Some of the categorical analytical concepts developed by Muslim jurists are the following: the *ẓāhir* and the *khafiyy* – what is the apparent external meaning versus the subtle and hidden meaning; the *wāḍiḥ* and the *mubham* – whether the words used are of clear meaning or unclear meaning; the *mufassar* and the *mujmal* – whether the words taken in their context are unequivocal and specific, or ambivalent and non-specific; the *muḥkam* – whether the words or sentences used are inherently clear, beyond doubt, and not open to abrogation; the *mushkil* – whether the words and sentences used are inherently ambiguous or rendered ambiguous by their context; the *mutashābih* – words whose meaning is not known at all because of the lack of precedent in usage; the *'āmm* and *khāṣṣ* – whether the words and sentences used are general or specific in scope; the *muṭlaq* and the *muqayyad* – whether the words and sentences used are absolute and unqualified, or limited and qualified; the *mashrūṭ* – whether the words or sentences are dependent or contingent upon others; the *ḥaqīqī* and *majāzī* – whether the words or sentences used are literal or metaphorical; and the *mushtarak* – whether the words or sentences used involve homonyms or have more than one meaning.[72] There was no consensus among Muslim jurists about which particular words or sentences fall under which category but that was largely irrelevant to the rationale behind the conceptual framework of this field. These various categories were methodological tools intended to restrain and limit the interpretive subjectivities of the reader of the text. As we already observed in the context of discussing the conditions for authority in the Islamic legal tradition, Muslim jurists set out methodological tools aimed at promoting restraint and accountability in dealing with the text. Similarly, the linguistic categories identified above, and others, were not designed to produce canonical results but to promote restraint against the subjectivities of the reader and to render such subjectivities accountable. There was a substantial amount of overlap and indeterminacy in the application of these categories, and, in fact, they were not designed or expected to produce precise and uniform interpretive results. Rather, categories such as the *wāḍiḥ* versus the *muḥkam* connoted levels or degrees of precision that are susceptible to various evaluations.

Instead of presenting a full-length survey of the traditional categories and rules of interpretation, it would be much more fruitful to take a conceptual approach to the field. These rules of interpretation were the result of a historical moment that produced linguistic labels that were appropriate for their time. Rather than adhere to linguistic labels that might or might not resonate with meaning in the contemporary age, it is more important to analyze the epistemological issues that inspired the creation of these labels in the first place. At the core of the analysis is the role of the author, text, and reader in determining meaning, and the relationship of this process to the establishment of authority in Islamic law.

In the past twenty years or so, there have been extensive debates on the nature of the dynamics between the author, the text, and the reader. Although some of these debates tended to confuse socio-empirical inquiries with normative arguments, the point of departure for the analysis is to ask: what is meaning and how do we acquire it? As to the issue of meaning, debates tended to focus on the relationship between linguistic meaning and mental representations, and on the possibility of logical versus psychologically-based interpretations of language. Advancements in the fields of semiotics and psychology have allowed us to better understand the ways that people formulate meaning, and the role of reference, association, signs and symbols in the construction of such meaning.[73] In light of our understanding of the complexities of the concept of meaning, the question becomes, stated somewhat vulgarly: what should determine meaning in interpretation? At least at a simplified level, there are three possibilities. The first possibility is that meaning should be determined by the author or, at least, by the attempt to understand the author's intent. Arguably, the author of a text formulates an intention when constructing a text, and the reader either tries to understand the authorial intent or should attempt to do so. E. D. Hirsch states, for example, "Verbal meaning is whatever someone has willed to convey by a particular sequence of linguistic signs and which can be conveyed (shared) by means of those linguistic signs."[74] Concretely, in writing this book I intend to convey certain meanings to readers. If someone writes a review arguing that the meaning of this book is to legitimate the rule of despotic governments, I might protest by saying, "the reader misread my book." But in making this argument, I am wedding the meaning of the text to my intent as an author. Understandably, the reader might then retort by saying, "regardless of your intent, that is the natural meaning of the concepts, categories, and language you employed," and "if you wanted to say something different, you should have employed different concepts, categories, and language. I, as the reader, cannot be expected to know the subtleties of your inner-self." In fact, since the author's intent does not in fact determine the meaning of the text, there is no valid justification for demanding that the reader be limited by it. Furthermore, as some scholars have argued recently, the very notion of intent in the formulation of meaning is very complex and problematic.[75] Intents are often compound realities, quickly evolving, unstable and transferable. Even more, intents are primarily attributed and projected rather than understood. Nevertheless, even if the authorial intent is not and should not be the only discriminating norm in the interpretive process, that does not necessarily mean that the authorial intent is or should be entirely irrelevant in the determination of meaning.[76]

The second possibility is to focus on the role of the text in determining meaning, and to recognize a degree of autonomy to the text in such determinations. One can argue that the text, which possesses an intricate system of linguistic significations, is the only instrument that is capable of laying claim to any validity in the determination of meaning. To carry forward the example used above, if I argue with a reader over the meaning of the text, I will invariably have to resort to the details of the language used in the text. If I, as the author, claim that the reader misunderstood the book, the only common referential point between the reader and me is the text itself. The subjectivities and contextual contingencies of the authorial intent and the reader's understanding will not yield determinacy. Careful and close readings of the text could serve as the basis for a degree of objective commonality and determinacy. This has led a number of commentators to argue that the text does have a reality and integrity and that it is entitled to a certain amount of deference.[77] As already discussed, even Umberto Eco has argued that texts have a basic integrity that ought to be respected, and that the reader should not be free to use texts without limits. In other words, there is such a thing as the abuse of a text.[78] The objections to this position are many. Most notably, texts are complex entities whose meanings are historically and contextually contingent. Furthermore, from a pragmatic point of view, as Richard Rorty has argued, there is no reason to concede a reverential status to texts. Arguably, the value of the text is determined by the use to which the reader may put it, and, therefore, any use of the text is legitimate as long it serves some utilitarian purpose.[79]

The third possibility is to deposit the determination of meaning in the reader. All readers bring their own subjectivities to the process of reading. These subjectivities are projected onto the authorial intent and the text. What readers will understand from this book, for instance, largely depends on their own experiences, which could mean that meaning is subjectively determined or entirely indeterminate. Context and historical reality is everything in the formulation of meaning. All interpretations are historically, socially, and politically embedded in contextual subjectivities. From a normative point of view, one should openly acknowledge the subjectivities of understanding and seek to critically evaluate the power dynamics that shape our constructions of meaning.[80] Texts cannot provide a stabilizing force for any argument for objectivity.[81] This type of argument has been criticized as unequivocally relativistic and nihilistic.[82] Furthermore, it has been argued that the focus on the response of the reader has ignored the important role that language and text play as a bridge between the various subjectivities. The fact that texts are complex entities containing ambiguities and uncertainties does not mean that their meaning is endlessly subjective.[83]

The three possibilities described above are a gross simplification of the discourses regarding the determinacy of meaning, but they serve a useful role as building blocks for our discussion. To my knowledge, very few scholars have argued that meaning is either determined or ought to be determined exclusively either by the author, text, or reader. Frequently, the argument is that there is a complex, interactive, dynamic, and dialectical process between these three elements. However, authors disagree about which element plays a major role or minor role, and the extent or degree of influence each has in the interpretive process.[84] In fact, regardless of normative intentionalities, meaning is often the product of complex engagements between author, text, and readers in which meaning is contested and negotiated, and continuously evolved.[85] Importantly, a large number of commentators have argued that meaning is formed within the context of interpretive communities that share certain epistemological assumptions, concerns and basic values.[86] These interpretive communities form around a sufficient level of commonalities that permit the sharing and objectification of the subjective experiences of their members. Interpretive communities are historical, sociological, and textual. They form around a text or set of texts within a historical period and a set of sociological forces. Interpretive communities do not necessarily agree on a whole host of determinations of meaning, but they share particular epistemological assumptions, a common linguistic practice, or an overlapping way of talking about meaning.[87]

Gadamer, in particular, has argued that these communities of interpretation are historically dependent, founded on historical prejudices, and are constantly changing and evolving.[88] This has led many critics, most notably Habermas, to accuse Gadamer of relativism and of espousing the indeterminacy of meaning.[89] Regardless of the merits of this debate, the significant point for our purposes is that interpretive communities do form around texts and that they form common methods of discourse in the process of generating meaning. Importantly, however, interpretive communities do not simply invent the meaning of text – they negotiate it and are negotiated by it. As James Boyd White has argued, texts create and shape their own communities.[90] Texts are not passive receptacles of meaning but actively engage, shape and revise their communities of meaning. The negotiative process takes place within a specific historical context, but it also continuously evolves in response to motivating historical factors or factors determined by the interpretive culture itself. The interpretive community and its text, or set of texts, forms a tradition of interpretation and meaning that become the vehicle for authority within such a community. However, the tradition also forms restraints on the indeterminacy and the development of the interpretive community.[91] The interpretive traditions increasingly become linguistically, culturally, and methodologically bounded. The formative tradition of the interpretive community might become its source of stability, but it also becomes the burden restricting its evolution.

Importantly, an overriding interpretive community and a unifying tradition could contain various communities of interpretation. Although the various communities may contain sufficient differences from one another to warrant identifying them as separate and distinct communities, they may also share sufficient commonality to form a larger overriding community. The overriding community is constituted of the overlap between different communities. So, for instance, the Shāfiʿī school is an interpretive community in itself but what defines it as an interpretive community is the degree of overlap between the various sub-communities that accept the basic methodology of the eponym of the school, the jurist Muḥammad b. Idrīs al-Shāfiʿī. Yet, the Shāfiʿī, Ḥanafī, Ḥanbalī, and Mālikī schools have sufficient overlap to constitute a larger interpretive community known as the Sunnī schools of legal thought, and in turn the Sunnī and Shīʿī schools have sufficient overlap to constitute a broader category that could be called Islamic schools of legal thought. The overlap of which I speak partly relates to the methods of discourse but is also a matter of presuppositions of understanding or, in Rudolph Bultmann's expression, "a prior relationship to the subject matter."[92] For instance, even if Sunnīs and Shīʿīs share many of the same symbolisms, linguistic practices, and methodologies of discourse, they cannot belong to the same interpretive community or tradition unless they agree on some basic presuppositions. The most basic presupposition that the Sunnīs and Shīʿīs need to accept is the recognition of each other as belonging to the same Islamic tradition. If distinct and separate interpretive communities do not mutually recognize each other as legitimate, it makes little sense to speak of an overlapping community that unites them in an overriding tradition. The essential point here is that traditions are not simply the product of language or interpretations, but are the product of normativities, commitments, and presuppositions that are mediated by texts. This does not mean that these presuppositions are constant and stable. Rather, they are challenged and reconstructed by a variety of factors including the texts themselves. As noted earlier, texts do not enjoy a passive existence nor do readers approach texts with a clean slate. Readers approach texts with presuppositions and normativities that they bring to bear on the interpretive process. The interactive dynamic creates interpretive communities, but a constant reading and re-reading, interpreting and re-interpreting of texts can reformulate the suppositions of the members of the community, and their conceptions of meaning. I will return to this point in a moment.

All discussions emerge from a tradition, or in due course, create their own tradition. Even when a specific tradition, or the very idea of tradition, is contested or challenged, a new interpretive tradition is created, and in due time that tradition forms the basis for new presuppositions. For example, anyone who has debated one of the Michel Foucault or Jacques Derrida faithfuls quickly realizes that these icons have generated their own interpretive communities, that these communities have evolved and coalesced into a tradition, and that the tradition now serves as the basis of a set of new presuppositions. As Alasdair MacIntyre has argued, "There is no standing ground, no place of enquiry, no way to engage in the practices of advancing, evaluating, accepting, and rejecting reasoned argument apart from that which is provided by some particular tradition or other."[93] Interestingly, MacIntyre seems to believe that traditions need to be based on texts that serve as authoritative reference points in the evolution of the tradition. In explaining the idea of an evolving tradition he states:

> For . . . a tradition, if it is to flourish at all has to be embodied in a set of texts which function as the authoritative point of departure for tradition-constituted enquiry and which remain as essential points of reference for enquiry and activity, for argument, debate, and conflict within that tradition. Those texts to which this canonical status is assigned are treated both as having a fixed meaning embodied in them and also as always open to rereading, so that every tradition becomes to some degree a tradition of critical reinterpretation in which one and the same body of texts, with of course some addition and subtraction, is put to the question, and to successively different sets of questions, as a tradition unfolds.
>
> Thus at any particular stage in the development of a tradition the beliefs which characterize that stage of that particular tradition carry with them a history in which the successive rational justification of their predecessors and themselves are embodied, and the language in which they are expressed is itself inseparable from a history of linguistic and conceptual transformations and translations.[94]

MacIntyre's description of the role of the text and authority in tradition is particularly fitting for the Islamic context. I am not sure whether MacIntyre's discourse on tradition is normative, but my argument is not. Rather, I am arguing that interpretive communities inevitably form interpretive traditions, and such interpretive traditions form a considerable degree of restraint on the determination of meaning. But these traditions are also capable of evolving, and this evolution often takes place, not in spite of the text, but because of the text. The text has the ability to play both a restraining and negative role in the determination of meaning, and an active and positive role in the evolution of interpretive communities. I argue later that the authoritarian interpretive process usurps the autonomy of the text, and attempts to prevent the evolution of the tradition in response to social instigators or interpretive pressures.

Before moving on to address the authoritarian we must ask: what does the discourse on the determination of meaning mean for the Islamic context? Does it make sense to leave the determination of meaning to the reader, or does it make sense to speak of a text with an indeterminate meaning? As noted earlier, addressing the problem of meaning in Islam through the application of Western categories is epistemologically problematic. However, as I hope to demonstrate, these categories are no more than methodological tools that enable us to bring appropriate critical insight to Islamic categories.

At a symbolic level, the interpretive inquiry in Islam should begin and end with the authorial intent because the Divine intent is determinative of all meaning. By symbolic level, I mean the level of emotions that are invoked by comfortable and familiar associations. The whole point of *Sharīʿah* is to search for the Divine Way, which entails that a moral life must be lived by the guidance of the Divine Will. The Qurʾān consistently speaks of *ḥukm Allāh* (God's ruling) as decisive and binding in all circumstances. As explained earlier, the function of the *dalīl* (indicator) is to point towards the Divine Will. The repository of indicators is primarily the text, and so, arguably, the only task before a reader is to search for the original intent of the author of the text. As the debates between the Khawārij and ʿAlī regarding God's Sovereignty demonstrate, there is a strong symbolic power to the idea of the law being a Divine instrumentality directly guiding and guarding people. Furthermore, the idea of the original (Divine) intent as being the object of all interpretation and all legitimacy has a strong hold on the Muslim imagination.

I do not wish to contest the idea of original intent as determinative of meaning, but I must confess that the meaning of this assertion is not apparent to me. The first issue that we would have to deal with is whether the Divine intent is expressed within a context and a historical setting or not. Islamic history witnessed the well-known controversy of the Muʿtazilah who claimed that the Qurʾān was created and their opponents who claimed that the Qurʾān was uncreated. If the Qurʾān was created, this meant that God created it in response to a specific historical context, which in turn meant that it was a historical and contextual text. But, if the Qur'ān was uncreated, that meant that it was primordial, non-contextual and not contingent on historical incidents.[95] The controversy over the createdness and uncreatedness of the Qur'ān died out shortly after the end of the inquisition in 234/849 although Mu'tazilī thought continues to exercise some influence on contemporary Muslim thinkers.[96] Aside from the issue of the createdness versus the uncreatedness of the Qur'ān, as noted earlier, the very fact that early and late Muslim scholars have always insisted that particular incidents occasioned the revelation of the Qur'ānic verses, points to the historicity of the Qur'ānic text.[97] Furthermore, it is not contested that the Qur'ān was revealed in a language that had its own historically-bounded nature. The Qur'ānic language is the language that was predominant in specific localities and specific eras. But even if the Qur'ānic text was occasioned by historical incidents or employed a historically bounded language, that does not mean that the textual meaning is incapable of transcending its context. Any historical text can be read in order to extract its implications or connotations for a contemporaneous setting. In fact, if the text is being read for the sole purpose of aesthetic enjoyment, I am not sure that a historical reading is necessary. However, if we are reading the text for the purpose of examining its indicators and for the purpose of drawing normative implications from it, a historical reading is necessary. In order to study the dynamics between the text and its historical context, it must be read with a precise understanding of the connection between the text and its historicity. To borrow E. D. Hirsch's phrase, it is useful to employ counterfactuals in this type of interpretative process. This means that an interpreter would try to imagine what a text from the past would mean if it were re-authored in the present.[98] Meaning can and should transcend its context but a conscientious reader would be mindful of the fact that a text exists in the past and also exists in the present. A text from the past conveys a meaning or set of meanings within the context of that past. Understanding the meaning of the text in the past helps avoid the type of anachronisms that are opportunistic projections of the readers' subjectivities upon the text. This is not a matter of antiquarianism or slavish worship of the past, but the insightfulness and usefulness of historical inquiry and interpretive integrity. Furthermore, as we discussed earlier, the Qur'ān is demonstrably hostile to whimsical and idiosyncratic determinations of meaning.

We need to understand the linguistic practice of the text within its past context, not in order to understand the true or real meaning of the text, but to understand the dynamics between the text and its initial recipients. In particular, if we are considering a text with a Divine element to it, studying the text in its historical moment is part of recognizing its integrity. However, part of acknowledging the integrity of the text is to recognize that it has a continuing and persistent life. If God is truly speaking to all ages and generations, the text of the Qur'ān cannot be understood to be limited to a historical context. Therefore, having examined the relationship between the text and meaning in the past, the question becomes, what should the relationship between the text and meaning be in the present? Put differently, if this text would have been written today, what would it mean? Are there any compelling reasons that require that we transplant the dynamics of the text from the past to the present? For example, the Qur'ān consistently speaks about the cunning and conspiracies of the hypocrites (*munāfiqūn*) against God and His Prophet. If we understand this discourse solely within the paradigms of our contemporary understanding of hypocrisy, we might end with the conclusion that any person who pretends to like his boss at work is an enemy of God and His Prophet. However, understanding that the Qur'ān, at the time of its revelation, was addressing the specific problem of a particular group led by ʿAbd Allāh b. Ubayy b. Salūl will produce a different set of connotations for the text in the present age.

To take another example, the Qur'ān consistently praises those who "guard what is between their thighs" (*al-ḥāfiẓīn li furūjihim*). If we consider this expression solely within its present context, we will have to speculate as to its meaning. Does it mean those who keep what is between their thighs clean? Does it mean those who wear some added protection between their thighs in order to protect their reproductive organs? Does it mean those who refuse to castrate themselves or those who avoid birth control? Why just what is between the thighs? What about a person's buttocks or chest or mouth? The expression functioned within a particular dynamic in the past, and upon examining this dynamic, we realize that the expression in fact referred to illicit sexual activity. We will also realize that the dynamics between the text and its audience in the past has resulted in the conclusion that masturbation is prohibited. Masturbation was considered to be a form of violating "what is between the thighs."[99] Having understood this past context, we can now analyze whether the dynamic of the past is fundamental and essential to the integrity of the expression or not. If someone argues, for instance, that the expression in its present dynamic should mean the wearing of extra protection in the groin area, we can examine this argument (and hopefully reject it) in light of the dynamics of the past.

Assuming that the historical context is important, does this necessarily mean that all determinations must focus on the authorial intent? My response is that a text does not contain an authorial intent – a text contains an *attempt* at an authorial intent or a *partial* view of the authorial intent. In other words, the text only tells us what the author thought necessary to reveal about himself in response to the specific historical dynamic that confronted him. The authorial intent, as expressed in the text, is bounded by its audience, historical context, and language. For instance, as I write this book I have a complex set of motivations, associations, mental images, goals, assumptions, and a variety of audiences that I am hoping to reach. Unless someone can download my psychology and mind into some entirely objective and limitless medium, it is impossible for any text to become the repository of my full intent. To take a different example, Gabrielle Spiegel has argued that Derrida's concept of grammatology reflects a psychology that is deeply marked by the Holocaust. She argues that Derrida's attitude towards language as intransitive, self-reflective, indeterminable, and incapable of signifying anything beyond itself is a product of a traumatized post-Holocaust second-generation that has lost its trust in the efficacy of language.[100] This type of subtlety that might have influenced Derrida's sense of reality or meaning, or might have formed a part of his assumptions and emotive associations is not explicitly spelled out in his writings. Yet, it might be a significant part of his understandings, motivations, normativities, and a significant component of understanding the dynamics between his text and its context.

In the Islamic context, the legal text is the repository of indicators that point towards the Divine Will, but the text does not contain the Divine Will. As to the Qur'ān, there is no doubt that God expresses God's Self perfectly and completely. Nonetheless, language is an imperfect human medium, and although God uses this medium perfectly, the medium itself is not perfect. I believe that it would be inconsistent with God's Majesty and Immutability to claim that any language can fully encompass the magnanimity of the Divine intent. Even if language was a perfect medium for the Divine Will, as explained before, Muslims have not limited the search for the Divine Will to the text of the Qur'ān. The very fact that Muslim jurists searched the *Sunnah* for evidence of the Divine Will is an indication that God has not chosen to reveal His full intent in the text of the Qur'ān. But as I argued earlier, the *Sunnah* is the product of an authorial enterprise and this fact only complicates the search for a cohesive and comprehensive authorial intent.

I am not arguing that the search for the Divine Will should be abandoned; I am arguing that the text does not embody the full Divine Will and does not embody the full authorial intent either. The text embodies indicators to the Divine Will and indicators to authorial intent as well. I am not prepared to make an argument as to the full range of sources through which the Divine Will may be investigated, but it is sufficient for our purposes to establish that as far as the legal inquiry is concerned, we investigate the text for the textual indicators. As argued earlier, the Principal has issued textual instructions to His agents, and it is justifiable and reasonable for the agent to execute them. But it is not justifiable or reasonable for the agent either to assume that the textual instructions fully embody the Principal's intent and wisdom, or to ignore the textual instructions on the wishful belief that these instructions do not represent the real Will of the Principal. The Qur'ān emphasizes that declaring anything permitted or prohibited is legitimate only if God authorizes the declaration.[101] The textual evidence is an indication of such an authorization, but it does not exclude other indicators. However, as discussed earlier, the agent must argue the competence of the specific textual indicator, and, similarly, would have to argue the competence of the non-textual indicator. In all circumstances, the agent is able to explore the dynamics between the indicators and their past or present, and the agent may argue that the examined indicators seem to point to the Divine Will in this or that direction. But the agent is not capable of encompassing or embodying the Divine Will. In short, no agent may assert to his or her fellow agents, that she or he is representing the Divine Will.

The Divine, or any author for that matter, only initiates the process of meaning by placing the text into the stream of interpretation. But neither the Divine nor the author determine the meaning. At the sociological level it is impossible for the author to determine the meaning unless the author can and will despotically control the development of the interpretive process, and unless the author possesses the means to do so. But even the author will have to deal with the text as a text – the author will have to stand vis-à-vis the text as an outsider arguing that the text is intended to mean such-and-such. If the author becomes the exclusive reference point for the text then the integrity of the text is not respected. Effectively, the author becomes the authoritative reference point and the text becomes irrelevant and entirely unnecessary. If the author does not respect the value or authority of the text and constantly references his intentions as an author regardless of what is scripted in the text, this raises a serious question as to the value of the text. Arguably, one should not reference the text at all, but should go directly to the source of meaning – i.e. the author. In order to give the text any authority, weight or value, even the author will have to deal with the text as an outsider and even the author will have to honor the independence of the word.

This does not mean that the author is irrelevant to the process of understanding or interpreting. The reader could form a separate and independent relationship with the author, and this relationship could influence the interpretation of the text. For instance, assume that after reading a book on slavery in Islam, I reach the conclusion that slavery was not racially based and that slaves were treated well in Islamic history. However, later on I meet the author who tells me that it is her firm conviction that slavery was racially based and that slaves were not treated well in Islamic history. The conversation I have with the author is not part of the text of the book that the author wrote and that I read. It is a separate relationship altogether. This relationship with the author may consciously or unconsciously affect my understanding of the text, but the understanding of the text remains my own and not the author's. To clarify this point let us assume that the author did not have a conversation with me about her book but wrote me a letter instead. In the letter she explained that she had noticed that many African-Americans were converting to Islam, and wrote the book to discourage this tide. This letter is a separate text that has an authorial nexus with the book. My understanding of the letter might influence my understanding of the book not because my understanding is focused on the authorial intent but because it is influenced by my relationship with another text that is collateral, but relevant, to the book. The meaning of the book is still the product of the interaction between my psychology and the text of the book.

Similarly, my relationship to God or the Prophet will, without a doubt, influence my interpretation of the text. Importantly, however, this relationship is collateral to the text, although it is an inseparable part of my interpretive apparatus. Any interpreter of the Divine Word will be informed by a set of relationships with the Author, with other texts and other authors, and a range of experiences that will form an inseparable part of the psychology of the interpreter.

Now, an important issue that needs to be addressed is: can a collateral relationship ever be absolutely determinative of the result in a process that involves a text? For example, let us assume that through a series of spiritual experiences I have developed the firm conviction that God is just and that God only desires what is just. Assume that I read a text and become convinced that what the text appears to demand is unjust. Can I, based on this collateral relationship, refuse to believe that the unjust result is the genuine instruction of God? If I read the Principal's instructions and realize that they seem to demand of me what I consider to be fundamentally inconsistent with my knowledge of the Principal, what should be my reaction? I will deal with this issue in greater detail when I address the issue of moral exceptions to the law. For the moment, it is important to note that the relationship with the Principal is a part of *īmān* (faith in God), and *īmān* cannot be considered irrelevant to the determination of the obligations of the agent. The relationship of *īmān* is part of the relevant indicators towards the ultimate question of the Will of the Principal, and this type of indicator might in fact outweigh the textual evidence. A person's faith and conviction might very well militate against the acceptance of a textual instruction from the Principal.[102] Nonetheless, *īmān* is not readily accessible, accountable or transferable to others. It is based on a conviction that is not restrained by external evidence such as a text. Therefore, the agent should be cognizant of the fact that a non-accessible, non-accountable, and non-transferable conviction could be considered by the Principal as a whimsical or capricious determination. Consequently, a conscientious agent would adhere to the requirements of honesty, diligence, self-restraint, comprehensiveness, and reasonableness in weighing the evidence between his or her *īmān* or personal relationship with the Principal and other pieces of evidence contained in the textual instructions. These requirements would call upon the agent to give the textual evidence its due weight and to exercise self-restraint in dismissing evidence that contradicts his or her own convictions. Furthermore, before deciding not to follow the textual instructions, the agent would exercise diligence and comprehensiveness in examining whether there is any way his or her conscience and the text could be reconciled. Before dismissing any part of the written instructions, the agent would first investigate all possible reasonable interpretations of the text that might resolve the conflict between conscience and written instructions. Ultimately, the agent might have to say, "I have exerted every effort on this matter, but based on what I know about the Principal, I cannot reconcile myself with the textual instructions on this particular matter.

Therefore, I am going to have to act according to my conscience, and I will anxiously wait to ask the Principal about this matter when I see Him (in the Hereafter). In the meanwhile, I have exerted my best efforts, and God knows best."

The existence of collateral relationships that are brought to bear upon the text through the reader only serve to emphasize the complexity of the relationship between the text and the reader. The reader's relationship with the legal text is rich with tension. The legal text is entitled to its integrity and independence, but so is the reader. From the Islamic perspective, the integrity of the legal text is derived from the possibility that it contains the indicators to the Divine. The integrity of the reader is derived from the fact that the reader is the Divine's agent. The text and the reader are in a constant state of negotiation and construction. This negotiative process is ultimately what determines the meaning. Similarly, the negotiative dynamics between the instructions and the agents' of the Principal is what produces the attempt at compliance. But the determination or the attempt at compliance is not God's – it belongs to the text and the reader. A reader, for example, may approach the Qur'ānic verse stating "There is no compulsion in religion."[103] The reader must negotiate the meaning with the text. The text uses the words compulsion (*ikrāh*) and religion (*dīn*), but the reader will have to ask the text what these words mean. Arguably, this verse means that no one should be forced to become a Muslim. Alternatively, this verse could mean that while one may be forced to become Muslim, one could not be compelled to believe. The verse could also mean that one may not be forced to pray, fast or wear the *ḥijāb* (the veil for women). Possibly, the verse also means that one may not be punished for apostasy. Furthermore, one might argue that since there is no compulsion in religion there should be no compulsion as to anything else. Therefore, one may conclude that contracts entered into under compulsion are invalid. One may further argue that free consent is necessary for a marriage contract. Arguably, one may extend this logic to invalidate contracts of adhesion.

In each of these steps the reader is negotiating and constructing the meaning of the text. The text only states that there is no compulsion in religion. It may or may not have intended to address prayer, *ḥijāb*, apostasy, marriage or contracts of adhesion. A state of tension exists between the reader and the text because the text stands steadfast, constantly challenging any and all constructions the reader may give it. In effect, the text is anchored in words while the reader attempts to pull it towards one determination or another. The further the reader attempts to pull the text, the more the text challenges the reader. This does not mean that the reader is mistaken; it only means that the reader might be over-interpreting and stretching the text beyond its limits. If stretched beyond reasonable bounds, the text may not only de-legitimate the interpretation of the reader but may challenge the ability of the reader to interpret. So, for instance, if I, as an interpreter, argue that no compulsion in religion means that all criminal penalties including the penalty for consumption of alcohol or fornication are unenforceable because they constitute a form of compulsion in religion, or if I argue that there is no punishment in the Hereafter because punishment is inconsistent with freedom of religion, this determination is likely to challenge my legitimacy as an interpreter.[104]

### *Unreasonable interpretations and the authoritative*

The fact that an interpretation is unreasonable or speculative does not mean that it is authoritarian or despotic. The unreasonableness of an interpretation is partly a function of its lack of persuasiveness within the interpretive community that the text has helped to form. Reasonableness or unreasonableness, however, is not determined solely by the interpretive community but by the interaction between the reader or readers and the text. This means that an individual from within the interpretive community can rightfully argue that the interpretive community has not respected the integrity of the text or has adopted an unreasonable interpretation of the text. Meaning does not reside either comfortably or permanently in the text, reader, or interpretive community. Determinations of meaning can never be immutable or infallible. The fact that the interpretive community might have reached a point of consensus over the meaning of the text should be given considerable weight by a reasonable reader, but it can never be decisively determinative of any issue. A reasonable reader endowed with the humility of self-restraint would take very seriously the fact that so many other readers chose a particular interpretation of the text. The duty of comprehensiveness and diligence would require the reader who is considering disagreeing with the interpretive community to seriously study and reflect upon the conclusion of that community. But deferring absolutely and without thought to any interpretive community violates the requirement of honesty. An unmitigated deference to an interpretive community effectively means that, as far as the dissenting reader is concerned, the interpretive community becomes the permanent and exclusive representative of the text and perhaps the Divine Will. Respecting the integrity and independence of the text and respecting the absolute autonomy of the Divine means that no interpretive community or individual can forever foreclose the possibility of re-engaging and re-examining the text or the Divine Will.

Perhaps it is clear from what I have said thus far that I consider authoritativeness to be a multidimensional problem. The Divine Will is the ultimate source of all authority and the authoritative is whatever the reader (or agent) is willing to defer to and is willing to treat as an exclusionary factor in all relevant determinations. Accordingly, for a believer in the juristic paradigms, the instructions containing the indicators of God's Will are authoritative (i.e. the Qurʾān and *Sunnah*). Furthermore, any interpretive community or individual that bases itself on the deciphering and understanding of the Divine instructions is authoritative as long as the believer is willing to trust that such a community or individual has discharged its obligations of honesty, self-restraint, diligence, comprehensiveness, and reasonableness. As discussed earlier, authoritativeness is a function of deferment of judgment based on the conditions of trust. This, in my view, is the normative process of authoritativeness in Islam.

What now remains is to clearly identify epistemologically the authoritarian in Islamic discourses, and to this we turn next.

*NOTES*

1 Arkoun, *Rethinking Islam.*

2 On the idea of *al-istibdād bi al-ra'y* see Kamali, *Freedom of Expression*, p. 146.

3 See, Taqī al-Dīn Aḥmad b. ʿAbd al-Ḥalīm b. Taymiyyah, *Iqtiḍā' al-Ṣirāṭ al-Mustaqīm Mukhālafat Aṣḥāb al-Jaḥīm*, pp. 35–36; Ibn Qayyim al-Jawziyyah, *Iʿlām al-Muwaqqiʿīn*, 1:47–85.

4 When I say creative activity I do not mean to imply that the tradition is necessarily apocryphal. I only mean that memory, selection and reproduction is a creative activity where choices are made.

5 Fazlur Rahman, *Islamic Methodology in History*, pp. 15, 18–19; Ahmed Hasan, *The Early Development of Islamic Jurisprudence*, pp. 85–109; Schacht, *Introduction*, pp. 29–33; Dutton, *Origins of Islamic Law*, pp. 161–167.

6 *Quṭb* literally means pole or axis, but in the Ṣūfī tradition it refers to the spiritual leader within the Ṣūfī hierarchy of the spiritual world. The *quṭb* is understood to be the most saintly or perfect person (*al-insān al-kāmil*) and thereby the leader of the hierarchy of mystics. Within the Shīʿī tradition, the terms *quṭb* and *imām* are deemed to be synonomous, and refer to the same person. Notably, the conceptualization of *quṭb* within Sunnī Ṣūfism has been understood by some to be a Sunnī cooptation of an essentially Shīʿī idea. F. de Jong, "al-Ḳuṭb," 5:542–543. Schimmel, *Mystical Dimensions of Islam*, pp. 57, 200; Ernst, *Sufism*, pp. 60, 61. *Murīd*, on the other hand, literally means one who desires. As a technical term in the Ṣūfī tradition, it invokes the student–teacher relationship. The Ṣūfī disciple (*murīd*) is expected to follow the guidance of his teacher in the process of spiritual development with God being the ultimate aspiration (*murād*). "Murīd," 7:608–609; Schimmel, *Mystical Dimensions*, pp. 100–104; Ernst, *Sufism*, pp. 30, 124.

7 Unfortunately, my friend has asked not to be identified. He asserts that he made this statement at an emotional moment, but I think that his point is still well taken.

8 For instance, Mohammed Arkoun, in his *Rethinking Islam*, employs the categories of post-modernity to call for a rethinking of the whole Islamic tradition. In doing so, he seems to be using the Islamic tradition as a text upon which to continue a debate about Western epistemology. He pays little attention to the specificity of the Islamic condition or tradition, as if the Islamic tradition is expected to serve as a yielding raw material for constructing the epistemological edifice of the West. Consequently, the book finds little resonance in the Islamic context.

9 See, Palmer, "Habermas versus Gadamer?", pp. 487–499; Couzens Hoy, "Interpreting the Law, pp. 319–329.

10 See, for instance, Barthes, "Theorie du texte"; Cohen, ed., *Text and Textualities*; Gracia, *A Theory of Textuality*; Greetham, *Theories of the Text*; Joseph Grigely, *Textualterity*; Kristeva, "Theory of the Text," pp. 31–47; McGann, *The Textual Condition*; Tolhurst, "On What a Text Is and How it Means," pp. 3–14.

11 Lyotard, *The Postmodern Condition*. For a critique of the epistemology of post-modernity see, Rorty, *Contingency, Irony and Solidarity.*

12 For an insightful and spirited critique of the colonial epistemological legacy see, Spivak, *A Critique of Postcolonial Reason*, esp. pp. 312–421. For a very good survey of Spivak, Said and Homi Bhabha, and post-colonial theory see, Moore-Gilbert, *Postcolonial Theory.*

13 Abū Bakr ʿAbd Allāh b. Abī Dāwūd Sulaymān b. al-Ashʿath al-Sijistānī, *Kitāb al-Maṣāḥif*; Sulaymān b. Ṣāliḥ al-Qarʿāwī and Muḥammad b. ʿAlī al-Ḥasan, *al-Bayān fī ʿUlūm al-Qurʾān maʿa Madkhal fī Uṣūl al-Tafsīr wa Maṣādirihi*, pp. 191–219; Abū Mūsā al-Ḥarīrī, *ʿĀlam al-Muʿjizāt*, pp. 131–176; Amīr ʿAbd al-ʿAzīz, *Dirāsāt fī ʿUlūm al-Qurʾān*, pp. 102–108; Mannāʿ al-Qaṭṭān, *Mabāḥith fī ʿUlūm al-Qurʾān*, pp. 118–156; Muḥammad Ḥusayn ʿAlī al-Ṣaghīr, *Taʾrīkh al-Qurʾān*, pp. 69–97; Abū ʿAbd Allāh al-Zanjānī, *Taʾrīkh al-Qurʾān*, pp. 35–86; Muḥammad Reza Jalālī, *Taʾrīkh Jamʿ al-Qurʾān al-Karīm*, pp. 24–135; Muḥammad ʿAlī al-Ushayqir, *Lamaḥāt min Taʾrīkh al-Qurʾān*, pp. 58–119; Abū al-Faḍl Mīr Muḥammadī, *Buḥūth fī Taʾrīkh al-Qurʾān wa ʿUlūmihi*, pp. 82–179; Modarressi, "Early Debates on the Integrity of the Qurʾān," pp. 5–39; von Denffer, *ʿUlūm al-Qurʾān*, pp. 31–56.

14 Orientalist scholarship on the Qurʾān reflects this very tendency. See, for example, Watt and Bell, *Introduction to the Qurʾan*; Wansbrough, *Qurʾānic Studies*. Crone and Cook, in *Hagarism*, adopt a similar approach to understanding the early formative period of Islam and the Muslim identity. Relying on non-Muslim pre-modern sources, they argue that the Muslim community arose from a group of Arabs inspired by messianic Judaism who used the idea of *hijrah* to gradually create a new identity for themselves and establish an independent power-base in the Ḥijāz. Importantly, Crone and Cook admit that no Muslim could accept their account. In the preface to *Hagarism*, they write: "[T]he account we have given of the origins of Islam is not one which any believing Muslim can accept... This is a book written by infidels for infidels, and it is based on what from any Muslim perspective must appear an inordinate regard for the testimony of infidel sources. Our account is not merely unacceptable; it is also one which any Muslim whose faith is as a grain of mustard seed should find no difficulty in rejecting." Crone and Cook, *Hagarism*, pp. vii–viii.

15 Coulson, *History*, p. 39; Schacht, *Introduction*, pp. 17, 29–31; Dutton, *Origins of Islamic Law*, pp. 164–166; Rahman, *Islamic Methodology*, pp. 27–31.

16 Zaman, "The Evolution of a Hadith; Dutton, *Origins of Islamic Law*, pp. 168–173; Rahman, *Islamic Methodology*, p. 33.

17 Siddīqī, *Hadīth Literature*, pp. 129–137, 165–168, 189–193; Azmi, *Studies in Early Ḥadīth Literature*, pp. 212–213; al-Khaṭīb, *al-Mukhtaṣar al-Wajīz fī ʿUlūm al-Ḥadīth*, pp. 103–114; Abū ʿUmar b. al-Ṣalāḥ, *ʿUlūm al-Ḥadīth*, pp. 107–111, 126–138.

18 Zaman, *Religion and Politics*, p. 109 n. 147.

19 Maḥmaṣānī, *Falsafat al-Tashrīʿ*, pp. 155–156; Ibn al-Ṣalāḥ, *ʿUlūm al-Ḥadīth*, pp. 146–151; al-Khaṭīb, *ʿUlūm al-Ḥadīth*, pp. 125–127; Kamali, *Principles*, pp. 68–77; Ṣiddīqī, *Hadīth Literature*, pp. 193–194.

20 Ṣiddīqī, *Hadīth Literature*, pp. 196, 201; ʿIzz al-Dīn Balīq, *Minhāj al-Ṣāliḥīn*, pp. 36–39. In the contemporary age, *Shaykh* Muḥammad al-Ghazālī was an advocate of *matn* analysis. Many of his writings focus on the need to evaluate the substantive plausibility of *āḥādī ḥadīth* regardless of the structure of the chain of transmission. See, *Shaykh* Muḥammad al-Ghazālī, *al-Sunnah al-Nabawiyyah bayn Ahl al-Fiqh wa Ahl al-Ḥadīth*. Al-Ghazālī was severely attacked by Wahhābī scholars for his views. On the controversy on the publication of the above cited book, see Yūsuf al-Qaraḍāwī, *al-Imām al-Ghazālī bayn Mādiḥīh wa Nāqidīh*; Kishk, *al-Shaykh Muḥammad al-Ghazālī bayn al-Naqd al-ʿĀtib wa al-Madḥ al-Shāmit*.

21 Ibn al-Ṣalāḥ, *ʿUlūm al-Ḥadīth*, pp. 91–92. See also, Abū Muḥammad ʿAbd al-Raḥmān al-Rāzī, *ʿIlal al-Ḥadīth*.

22 Al-Ṣāliḥ, *ʿUlūm al-Ḥadīth*, pp. 179–187; Nūr al-Dīn ʿItr, *Manhaj al-Naqd fī ʿUlūm al-Ḥadīth*, pp. 447–454.

23 Eventually, a social and legal consensus emerged in the Sunnī world around the 3rd–4th/9th–10th centuries that recognized the collections of al-Bukhārī and Muslim as the most reliable sources on traditions. In fact, among Sunnī Muslims, a consensus emerged over the authoritativeness of six *ḥadīth* collections which achieved a near canonical status, and are collectively called *al-Kutub al-Sittah* (the six books). Aside from the collections of al-Bukhārī (d. 256/870) and Muslim b. al-Ḥajjāj (d. 261/875), the four remaining sources are the *sunan* of al-Tirmidhī (d. 279/892), al-Nasāʾī (d. 303/915), Abū Dāwūd (d. 275/889),

and Ibn Mājah (d. 273/887). Coulson, *History*, p. 64; al-Khaṭīb, *'Ulūm al-Ḥadīth*, pp. 132–139; Maḥmaṣānī, *Falsafat al-Tashrī'*, pp. 152–153; Ibn al-Ṣalāḥ, *'Ulūm al-Ḥadīth*, p. 48. Incidentally, there is some disagreement as to whether the sixth book in this consensus is Ibn Mājah's *Sunan*, or whether it should be *al-Muwaṭṭa'* by the Medinese jurist Mālik b. Anas (d. 179/796). Al-Khaṭīb, *'Ulūm al-Ḥadīth*, p. 139. The Shī'īs also have their own set of authentic sources for *ḥadīth* and narrative traditions. The four most significant Shī'ī sources are as follows: (1) Muḥammad b. Ya'qūb al-Kulaynī (d. 329/941), *al-Kāfī*; (2) Muḥammad b. 'Alī b. Bābawayh (d. 381/991), *Man lā yaḥḍuruhu al-Faqīh*; (3) Abū Ja'far Muḥammad b. al-Ḥasan b. 'Alī al-Ṭūsī (d. 460/1067), *al-Istibṣār fī mā ikhtalaf min al-Akhbār*; and (4) Abū Ja'far Muḥammad b. al-Ḥasan b. 'Alī al-Ṭūsī, *Tahdhīb al-Aḥkām*. Maḥmaṣānī, *Falsafat al-Tashrī'*, p. 153.

24 Gracia, *Texts*, p. 3. By calling him conservative, I do not mean to deprecate Gracia. I am simply pointing out that Gracia does not accept as text more non-intuitive forms such as artifacts or art objects.

25 See ibid., pp. 91–140, for a discussion on the different type of authors that form a text. Gracia identifies a historical author, a pseudo-historical author, a composite author and interpretive author.

26 MacIntyre, *Whose Justice? Which Rationality?*, p. 356.

27 On the idea of prejudices as conditions of understanding see, Gadamer, *Truth and Method*, pp. 265–307.

28 Gadamer, *Truth and Method*, pp. 277–285.

29 MacIntyre, *Whose Justice*, p. 363.

30 See Rawls, *A Theory of Justice*, p. 340; Rawls, *Political Liberalism*, pp. 164–168. Of course, I am not co-opting Rawls' theory of political liberalism. I am simply arguing that responsible dissent might have to consider the limits of the achievable.

31 For instance, al-Bukhārī is reported to have selected the *aḥādīth* in his collection from approximately 600,000 *aḥādīth*, while Abū Dāwūd selected from nearly 500,000. Al-Khaṭīb, *'Ulūm al-Ḥadīth*, pp. 133, 136; Robson, "al-Bukhārī, Muḥammad b. Ismā'īl," 1:296–297; J. Robson, "Abū Dā'ūd al-Sidjistānī," 1:114.

32 Notably, Muslim jurists created a genre of legal literature that addressed the authenticity of such popular *ḥadīth*, or what they would call *aḥādīth mashhūrah* or *aḥādīth mushtahirah*. The following is a sample of texts from this genre: Muḥammad 'Abd al-Raḥmān al-Sakhāwī, *al-Maqāṣid al-Ḥasanah fī Bayān Kathīr min al-Aḥādīth al-Mushtahirah 'alā al-Alsinah*; Jalāl al-Dīn 'Abd al-Raḥmān b. Abī Bakr al-Suyūṭī, *al-Durar al-Muntathirah fī al-Aḥādīth al-Mushtahirah*; Muḥammad b. Aḥmad b. Jār Allāh al-Ṣaghrī al-Yamānī, *al-Nawāfiḥ al-'Aṭirah fī al-Aḥādīth al-Mushtahirah*; 'Abd al-Raḥmān b. 'Alī b. Muḥammad b. 'Umar al-Shaybānī, *Kitāb Tamyīz al-Ṭayyib min al-Khabīth fī mā yadūr 'alā Alsinat al-Nās min al-Ḥadīth*; 'Abd al-Muta'āl Muḥammad al-Jabrī, *al-Mushtahir min al-Ḥadīth*; al-Jirāḥī, *Kashf al-Khafā'*.

33 Abū al-Ḥusayn Muslim b. al-Ḥajjāj b. Muslim, *al-Jāmi' al-Ṣaḥīḥ* (Beirut: Dār al-Ma'rifah, n.d.), 4:132–135. See, Shams al-Dīn Muḥammad b. Jamāl al-Dīn al-Makkī al-'Āmilī, *al-Lum'ah al-Dimashqiyyah*, ed. al-Sayyid Muḥammad Kalantar (Beirut: Maṭba'at al-Ādāb, n.d.), 5:245–284; Abū 'Abd Allāh 'Abd al-Raḥmān Aḥmad b. Shu'ayb b. 'Alī al-Nasā'ī, *Sunan* (Beirut: Dār al-Qalam, n.d.), 3:151–155.

34 Abou El Fadl, "Corrupting God's Book," *Conference of the Books*, pp. 289–302.

35 Various verses in the Qur'ān emphasize the Prophet's humanity. See, for instance, Qur'ān, 3:79: "It is not (possible) that a man, to whom is given the Book, and Wisdom and the Prophetic office, should say to people 'Be my worshippers rather than God's.' On the contrary (he would say): 'Be worshippers of Him who is truly the Cherisher of all'"; Qur'ān, 3:144: "Muhammad is no more than a messenger; many were the messengers who passed away before him. If he died or were slain, will you then turn back on your heels"; Qur'ān, 25:20: "And the messengers whom We sent before you were all [men] who ate food and walked through the streets."

36 Rahman, *Islamic Methodology*, pp. 1–31; Jackson, "Prophetic Actions."

37 Abū Zayd ʿAbd al-Raḥmān b. Muḥammad b. Khaldūn, *al-Muqaddimah*, pp. 9–10.
38 Mohammad Fadel, "Two Women, One Man, pp. 185–204, 196.
39 See Shihāb al-Dīn Ibrāhīm b. ʿAbd Allāh b. Abī al-Damm, *Kitāb Adab al-Quḍāʾ aw al-Durar al-Manẓūmāt fī al-Aqḍiyyah wa al-Ḥukūmāt*, 1:202; See, Ibn Ḥajar al-ʿAsqalānī, *Fatḥ al-Bārī*, 14:559; Abū Muḥammad al-Ḥusayn b. Masʿūd b. Muḥammad al-Farrāʾ al-Baghawī, *Sharḥ al-Sunnah*, 6:60; al-Shawkānī, *Nayl al-Awṭār*, 7:265, 8:508; Ibn Rushd, *Bidāyat al-Mujtahid*, 6:205.
40 See, for example, Shihāb al-Dīn Aḥmad b. ʿAlī b. Ḥajar al-ʿAsqalānī, *Fatḥ al-Bārī*, 8:126–129, 13:53–59; Jalāl al-Dīn ʿAbd al-Raḥmān b. Abī Bakr al-Suyūṭī, *Sharḥ Sunan al-Nasāʾī*, 8:227; Muḥammad ʿAbd al-Raḥmān b. ʿAbd al-Raḥīm al-Mubārakfūrī, *Tuḥfat al-Aḥwadhī bi Sharḥ Jāmiʿ al-Tirmidhī*, 6:446–450.
41 See, Abū Muḥammad al-Ḥusayn b. Masʿūd b. Muḥammad al-Farrāʾ al-Baghawī, *Maṣābiḥ al-Sunnah*, 3:13; al-Sakhāwī, *al-Maqāṣid al-Ḥasanah*, p. 540; Ibn Ḥajar al-ʿAsqalānī, *Fatḥ al-Bārī* (1993), 14:558. The woman referred to in the report is Būrān bint Kisrā Abrawīz b. Hurmuz b. Kisrā Anūsharwān. Her short reign over the Sassanid Empire is reported to have lasted only one year and four months (r. 8/630–9/631). Abū Jaʿfar Muḥammad b. Jarīr al-Ṭabarī, *Taʾrīkh al-Ṭabarī*, 1:493; Bosworth, *The Sāsānids, the Byzantines, the Lakmids, and Yemen*, vol. 5, *The History of al-Ṭabarī*, pp. 403–405; Abū al-Ḥasan ʿAlī b. al-Ḥusayn b. ʿAlī al-Masʿūdī, *Murūj al-Dhahab wa Maʿādin al-Jawhar*, 1:322.
42 Ibn Ḥanbal, *Musnad*, 5:58, 63; al-Baghawī, *Sharḥ al-Sunnah*, 6:60; Ibn Ḥajar al-ʿAsqalānī, *Fatḥ al-Bārī* (1993), 14:558; ʿAlī b. Sulṭān Muḥammad al-Qārī, *Marqāt al-Mafātīḥ Sharḥ Mishkāt al-Maṣābīḥ*, 7:270; Ibn Jār Allāh al-Yamānī, *al-Nawāfiḥ al-ʿAṭirah*, p. 273.
43 Ibn Ḥanbal, *Musnad*, 5:61; al-Jirāḥī, *Kashf al-Khafāʾ* (1983), 2:197.
44 Abū Muḥammad ʿAlī b. Ḥazm al-Ẓāhirī, *Asmāʾ al-Ṣaḥābah al-Ruwāḥ*, p. 59.
45 See Jamāl al-Dīn Abī al-Ḥajjāj Yūsuf al-Mazzī, *Tahdhīb al-Kamāl fī Asmāʾ al-Rijāl*, 30:6; Abū al-Faraj ʿAbd al-Raḥmān b. ʿAlī b. Muḥammad b. al-Jawzī, *al-Muntaẓam fī Taʾrīkh al-Umam wa al-Mulūk*, 5:248; Abū ʿAbd Allāh Muḥammad b. Saʿd, *al-Ṭabaqāt al-Kubrā*, 7:15–16; al-Dhahabī, *Siyar Aʿlām*, 3:8. Abū al-Ḥasan ʿAlī b. Abī al-Karam b. ʿAbd al-Waḥīd b. al-Athīr, *Usud al-Ghābah fī Maʿrifat al-Ṣaḥābah*, 5:151; Abū ʿAbd Allāh Ismāʿīl b. Ibrāhīm al-Jaʿafī al-Bukhārī, *Kitāb al-Taʾrīkh al-Kabīr*, 4(2):112–3.
46 Abū al-ʿAbbās Shams al-Dīn Aḥmad b. Muḥammad b. Abī Bakr b. Khallikān, *Wafayāt al-Aʿyān wa Anbāʾ al-Zamān*, 6:364–365; Ibn al-Jawzī, *al-Muntaẓam*, 5:248; al-Mazzī, *Tahdhīb al-Kamāl*, 30:7; al-Dhahabī, *Siyar Aʿlām* (1986), 3:6–8.
47 At least in one report, ʿUmar tells al-Mughīrah that he actually believed Abū Bakrah's testimony and that everytime he (ʿUmar) sees al-Mughīrah, he has to resist the temptation to pick up a rock and throw it at al-Mughīrah. Picking up the stone is symbolic of the act of stoning. See, Ibn Khallikān, *Wafayāt al-Aʿyān* (n.d.), 6:366.
48 Ibn Ḥajar al-ʿAsqalānī, *Fatḥ al-Bārī* (1993), 14:557–558; al-Sakhāwī, *al-Maqāṣid al-Ḥasanah*, p. 540.
49 Al-Mazzī, *Tahdhīb al-Kamāl*, 30:7; Ibn Saʿd, *al-Ṭabaqāt al-Kubrā* (1985), 7:16; Ibn al-Jawzī, *al-Muntaẓam*, 5:248.
50 Ibn Ḥanbal, *Musnad*, 5:50.
51 Ibn Ḥanbal, *Musnad*, 5:54, 57, 59, 65, 67.
52 Al-Mazzī, *Tahdhīb al-Kamāl*, 30:8.
53 The version narrated in Bukhārī leaves open the possibility that the Prophet was simply predicting the downfall of Persia, i.e. the Prophet was saying, "With this woman in power, Persia will fall." Interestingly, not all *ḥadīth*-collectors placed this tradition in the chapter on governorship (*wilāya*), which means that they did not believe the tradition was setting out the qualifications of a ruler.
54 Qurʾān, 3:7.
55 Modern exegetes of the Qurʾān have understood this verse as a warning against interpreting ambiguous verses (*mutashābih*). Generally the concern is that such interpretive efforts will only take one further away from religous truth. For instance, Sayyid Abū al-Aʿlā al-Mawdūdī (d. 1979) writes that the proliferation of interpretations on ambiguous verses will only

"alienate one progressively further away from the Truth instead of bring one closer to to it." Sayyid Abū al-A'lā al-Mawdūdī, *Towards Understanding the Qur'ān*, 1:237 n. 6. Sayyid Quṭb (d. 1387/1966) writes that those with an erring heart (*zaygh*) investigate ambiguous verses because the existence of unsettling interpretations (*al-ta'wīlāt al-muzalzalah*) allows for discord (*fitnah*) in matters of belief. Sayyid Quṭb, *Fī Ẓilāl al-Qur'ān*, 1:369–370. See also, Ḥijāzī, *al-Tafsīr al-Wāḍiḥ*, 1:94. Pre-modern Muslim jurists, on the other hand, understood this verse differently. For instance, al-Nasafī (d. 710/1310) regarded the distinction between ambiguous and non-ambiguous (*muḥkam*) verses to involve the ability to know (*muḥtamal*) their respective meanings. The ambiguous verses are to be understood in light of the non-ambiguous verses (*tuḥmal al-mutashābihāt ʿalayhā* [*al-muḥkamāt*] *wa turadd ilayhā*). Al-Nasafī's concern for *fitnah* seems to focus on the fact that one may have a corrupted heart, but not on the fact of textual ambiguity itself. Al-Nasafī, *Tafsīr al-Nasafī* (ʿĪsā al-Bābī al-Ḥalabī), 1:146. See also, Jalāl al-Dīn ʿAbd al-Raḥmān b. Abī Bakr al-Suyūṭī and Jalāl al-Dīn Muḥammad b. Aḥmad al-Maḥallī, *Tafsīr al-Jalālayn*, p. 67, who suggest that those whose interpretations of the *mutashābih* verses lead to *fitnah* are those who are immersed in an ignorance resulting from their own doubts and confusions (*li jahlihim bi wuqūʿihim fī al-shubuhāt wa al-labs*). For al-Bayḍāwī (d. 685/1286), the issue posed by *mutashābih* verses relates to the interpretive competence of the jurist (*faḍl al-ʿulamā'*) and the extent of his diligence in examining (*faḥṣ*) and investigating (*naẓar*) the meaning of the verse. Al-Bayḍāwī, *Anwār al-Tanzīl*, 2:4. Notably, the meaning of *mutashābih* is subject to dispute, as indicated by Muḥammad b. Jarīr al-Ṭabarī (d. 310/923). Some have understood it to refer to those verses which have been abrogated; to those verses which are subject to multiple interpretations; to facts which only God knows; or to the ambiguous letters (*al-ḥurūf al-muqaṭṭaʿah*) which begin many Qur'ānic chapters. Al-Ṭabarī seems to adopt a narrow view of *mutashābih* as referring to those issues which only God can know (e.g. the time of the Final Day or the meaning of the *ḥurūf muqaṭṭaʿah*). With such a narrow definition, he effectively avoids the need to limit interpretive activity. Al-Ṭabarī, *Tafsīr al-Ṭabarī*, 2:213–14. See also, al-Qurṭubī, *al-Jāmiʿ* (1993), 4:8. Fakhr al-Dīn al-Rāzī (d. 606/1210) lists five reasons why the *mutashābih* verses play an important role in the interpretive process: (1) Understanding the meaning of an ambiguous verse is difficult, but with greater difficulty comes greater reward (*mazīd al-thawāb*); (2) If the Qur'ān only had *muḥkam* verses, there would be only one understanding of the Qur'ān, which is not the case. Furthermore, jurists can utilize the *muḥkam* verses to understand the *mutashābih* ones, and hence reach the true meaning of the latter; (3) The *mutashābih* verses provide an opportunity to utilize rationally based proofs (*dalīl al-ʿaql*). Without them Muslims would be subject to the oppresiveness of *taqlīd* (*ẓulmat al-taqlīd*); (4) Without the *mutashābih* verses, the interpretive sciences such as grammar and *uṣūl al-fiqh* would be unnecessary; (5) Most importantly, the *muḥkam* and *mutashābih* verses are used together to arrive at a resolution on a matter. The generality of the *mutashābih* verses combines with the specificity of the *muḥkam* verses, thereby allowing one to reach a clear and unequivocal conclusion (*al-ḥaqq al-ṣarīḥ*) on a specific matter. Fakhr al-Dīn Muḥammad b. ʿUmar b. al-Ḥusayn al-Rāzī, *al-Tafsīr al-Kabīr li al-Imām Fakhr al-Dīn al-Rāzī*, 8:141–142. For a modern exegetical work that accounts for the premodern diversity of opinions, see Abū al-Faḍl Shihāb al-Dīn al-Sayyid Maḥmūd al-Alūsī (d. 1270/1853), *Rūḥ al-Maʿānī fī Tafsīr al-Qur'ān al-ʿAẓīm wa al-Sabʿ al-Mathānī*, 3:80–83.

56 Qur'ān, 2:67–71.

57 For a discussion by premodern jurists on these verses, see, Ibn Kathīr, *Mukhtaṣar Tafsīr Ibn Kathīr*, 1:75–78; al-Zamakhsharī, *al-Kashshāf*, 1:286–289; al-Hawwāriyy, *Tafsīr Kitāb Allāh al-ʿAzīz*, 1:115–117; al-Shawkānī, *Fatḥ al-Qadīr*, 1:125–128; al-Ṭabarī, *Tafsīr al-Ṭabarī*, 1:240–248; al-Qurṭubī, *al-Jāmiʿ* (1993), 1:301–309; Ibn al-ʿArabī, *Aḥkām al-Qur'ān* (n.d.), 1:22–26.

58 Rabbinic Judaism developed gradually, first through the efforts of scholars of the Tanna'im (70–220 C.E.) and later under the Amora'im scholars (220–500 C.E.). Thereafter it became normative. The Amora'im are responsible for having produced the Talmud. Both the Babylonian Talmud and the Jerusalem Talmud were compiled by 600 C.E. Dorff and Rosett,

*A Living Tree*, pp. 133, 143; Rakover, *A Guide to the Sources of Jewish Law*, p. 43; Neusner, *The Talmud*, ix; Horowitz, *The Spirit of Jewish Law*, pp. 36–37.

59 Originating in eighth century Persia, the Karaites adopted a puritan approach to the Pentateuch, and thereby rejected the oral tradition and rabbinic authority. Dorff and Rosett, *A Living Tree*, p. 243.

60 Saʿīd Ḥawwā, *al-Asās fī al-Tafsīr*, 1:158–159; Sayyid Quṭb, *Fī Ẓilāl al-Qurʾān*, 1:77–79; al-Alūsī, *Rūḥ al-Maʿānī*, 1:285–293; Milgrom, *The JPS Torah Commentary*, pp. 283–285, 438–443.

61 Qurʾān, p. 36 n. 81.

62 Yūsuf ʿAlī alludes to this interpretation of the verse. See Qurʾān, p. 36 n. 81.

63 See Gatje, *The Qur'an*, pp. 30–44.

64 Al-Ṣāliḥ, *Mabāḥith fī ʿUlūm al-Qurʾān*, pp. 127–163; Maḥmaṣānī, *Falsafat al-Tashrīʿ*, pp. 144–145; ʿAllāmah Sayyid M.H. Ṭabaʾṭabāʾī, *The Qur'an in Islam*, pp. 88–97; Kamali, *Principles*, pp. 39–41.

65 Al-Jaṣṣāṣ, *Aḥkām al-Qurʾān*; Ibn al-ʿArabī, *Aḥkām al-Qurʾān* (n.d.); al-Qurṭubī, *al-Jāmiʿ* (1993).

66 Ferguson, *Biblical Hermeneutics*, p. 5.

67 For an overview of the history and theories of hermeneutics see, Abrams, *Doing Things with Texts*; Stone, "Christian Praxis as Reflective Action," pp. 103–121; Burns, *Hermeneutics*. The best concise overview of the field as it applies to legal analysis is, Binder and Weisberg, *Literary Criticisms of Law*, pp. 112–200.

68 Schleiermacher, *Hermeneutics and Criticism*. On the contributions of Schleiermacher and Wilhelm Dilthey, see, Gadamer, "Hermeneutics as a Theoretical and Practical Task," pp. 113–137.

69 Ebrahim Moosa, introduction to Rahman, *Revival and Reform in Islam*; Esack, *Qur'an, Liberation & Pluralism*.

70 Al-Suyūṭī, *al-Itqān fī ʿUlūm al-Qurʾān*; al-Ṣāliḥ, *Mabāḥith*; Muḥammad Sayyid Ṭanṭāwī, *Mabāḥith fī ʿUlūm al-Qurʾān*; Muṣṭafā Qaṣr ʿĀmilī, *al-Wajīz fī ʿUlūm al-Qurʾān wa Taʾrīkhihi*; von Denffer, *ʿUlūm al-Qurʾān*; Ibn Qutaybah, *Kitāb Taʾwīl*; Ḥammād, *Mukhtalaf al-Ḥadīth bayn al-Fuqahāʾ wa al-Muḥaddithīn*; ʿSusāwah, *Manhaj al-Tawfīq wa al-Tarjīḥ bayn Mukhtalaf al-Ḥadīth wa Āthārihi fī al-Fiqh al-Islāmī*.

71 See Qurʾān, 16:37, 16:103, 26:195, 41:44, 12:2, 13:37, 20:113, 39:28, 41:3, 42:7, 43:3, 46:12.

72 See generally, Kamali, *Principles*, pp. 86–137; al-Ṣāliḥ, *Mabāḥith*, pp. 281–286. 299–312.

73 See Barwise, "On the Circumstantial Relation Between Meaning and Content," pp. 23–38; Eco, "On Truth. A Fiction," pp. 41–59, Johnson-Laird, "How is Meaning Mentally Represented," pp. 99–116.

74 Hirsch, *Validity in Interpretation*, p. 31. In "Counterfactuals in Interpretation," pp. 55–68, Hirsch calls for a greater interest in a text's original historical intention arguing that this would lead to a more vigorous and literary culture.

75 See the valuable study by Raymond W. Gibbs, *Intentions in the Experience of Meaning*, pp. 205–233, 273–292.

76 For this argument, see Juhl, *Interpretation*, pp. 45–65.

77 See, Dowling, *The Senses of the Text*, pp. 79–112; Fried, "Sonnet LXV, pp. 45–51; Graff, "*Keep Off the Grass*," pp. 175–18; Prince, "Introduction to the Study of the Narratee," pp. 7–24; Poulet, "Criticism and the Experience of Interiority," pp. 41–49; Donoghue, *The Practice of Reading*, pp. 80–108.

78 Notably, Eco made this argument in the context of a response to Richard Rorty. See, Eco, *Interpretation and Overinterpretation*, pp. 45–88, 139–151. On the notion of giving the text "breathing space," and maintaining a balance vis-à-vis the text, see Frei, "Conflicts in Interpretation," pp. 344–356, 353; Babuts, "Text: Origins and Reference," pp. 65–77.

79 Rorty, "The Pragmatist's Progress," pp. 89–108; Culler, "In Defence of Overinterpretation," pp. 109–123.

80 Fish, "Literature in the Reader, pp. 70–99; Culler, "Literary Competence," pp. 101–117; Tompkins, "The Reader in History, pp. 201–226.

81 Fish, "Fish v. Fiss," "Wrong Again," "Still Wrong After All These Years," pp. 120–140, 103–119, 356–371. In the first article Fish critiques Fiss's notion of a text as a stabilizing force. In the last two articles Fish criticizes Dworkin's idea of "integrity" in law and interpretation. See also, Fish, *The Trouble With Principle*, pp. 293–308.
82 Fiss, "Objectivity and Interpretation," pp. 229–249. For a critique of deconstructionism and a defense of intentionalism see, Abrams, *Doing Things with Texts*, pp. 237–332.
83 See James Boyd White, *Heracles' Bow*, pp. 80–90.
84 See Gibson, "Authors, Speakers, Readers and Mock Readers," pp. 1–6; Iser, "The Reading Process," pp. 50–68; Holland, "Unity, Identity, Text, Self," pp. 118–132.
85 Lyon, *Intentions*, pp. 27–80.
86 Fish, "Interpreting the Variorium," pp. 147–173; *idem*, "Interpreting 'Interpreting the Variorum'," pp. 174–180; *idem*, "Is There a Text in This Class?", pp. 303–321.
87 Bleich, "Epistemological Assumptions," pp. 134–159; Stock, *Listening for the Text*, pp. 140–158; Dallmayr, "Hermeneutics and the Rule of Law," pp. 3–20; Burns, "Law and Language, pp. 23–34; Binder and Weisberg, *Literary Criticisms of Law*, pp. 123–145.
88 Gadamer, *Truth and Method*, pp. 265–307; Gadamer, *Philosophical Hermeneutics*, pp. 3–42, 130–177. See also Page, "Historicistic Finitude and Philosophical Hermeneutics," pp. 369–382.
89 See Palmer, "Habermas versus Gadamer?" pp. 487–499, who argues that the disagreements between the two are artificial; Theunissen, "Society and History, p. 255. See also, Hoy, "Interpreting the Law," pp. 319–338, who argues for moving beyond Gadamer's relativism to Habermas's transcendental element in hermeneutics. See the insightful review of the debates between Habermas and Gadamer in Jean Grondin, *Introduction to Philosophical Hermeneutics*, pp. 124–139.
90 James Boyd White, *Heracles' Bow*, p. 80.
91 Gadamer, *Truth and Method*, pp. 293, 300–307, 335–341, 389–405; Grondin, *Sources of Hermeneutics*, p. 121; Eco, *Interpretation and Overinterpretation*, p. 150; Stone, "Christian Praxis as Reflective Action," pp. 111–118; Grondin, *Introduction to Philosophical Hermeneutics*, pp. 130–131.
92 Bultmann, "The Problem of Hermeneutics," pp. 86–87.
93 MacIntyre, *Whose Justice?*, p. 350. See also, MacIntyre, *After Virtue*, p. 223.
94 MacIntyre, *Whose Justice?*, p. 383.
95 Wolfson, *The Philosophy of the Kalam*, pp. 235–303; Nagel, *History of Islamic Theology*, pp. 130–131; Corbin, *History of Islamic Philosophy*, p. 116; Watt, *Islamic Philosophy*, pp. 34–35; De Boer, *History of Philosophy in Islam*, pp. 48–49; Watt, *Formative Period*, pp. 242–245.
96 Martin, Woodward, and Atmaja, *Defenders of Reason in Islam*, pp. 199–230.
97 Both the Ashʿarīs and Muʿtazalīs – the opponents and proponents of the createdness doctrine – interpreted the Qur'ān without attempting to historicize it. The doctrine of createdness was not utilized by its proponents to generate historicized interpretations.
98 Hirsch, "Counterfactuals in Interpretation," pp. 55–68. Unlike Hirsch, I do not mean by this that the focus of interpretation should be the search for the authorial intent.
99 All-Shīrāzī, *al-Muhadhdhab fī Fiqh al-Imām al-Shāfiʿī*, 3:341; al-Sayyid Sābiq, *Fiqh al-Sunnah*, 2:422–423; Musallam, *Sex and Society in Islam*, pp. 33–34.
100 Spiegel, *The Past as Text*, pp. 36–40.
101 See Qur'ān, 10:59, 42:21.
102 The incident, mentioned earlier, of the man who dreamt of the Prophet telling him to excavate a treasure is relevant here. The man had a personal, and rather self-serving, encounter with the Prophet that took the form of a dream. In the dream, the Prophet reportedly told the man that he does not have to pay the 20% tax on *al-rikāz* (the found treasure). The judge al-ʿIzz b. ʿAbd al-Salām reportedly believed the man's testimony, but considered that the evidence produced by this individual and idiosyncratic experience to be inferior to competing textual evidence. Jalāl al-Dīn al-Suyūṭī, *Tanwīr al-Ḥawālik*, 2:44.
103 Qur'ān, 2:256.

104 Wolfgang Iser had argued that there is an active dialectical process between the text and the reader. In dealing with the text, the reader learns from the text rather than simply re-experience his pre-existing expectations. See, Iser, "The Reading Process," pp. 274–94.

# 5 The construction of the authoritarian

The issue of authoritarianism in the determination of meaning has received modest scholarly attention. Some scholars have tended to equate speculative or unreasonable interpretations of the text and epistemological authoritarianism, while some have branded the attempt to limit the instabilities of textual meaning or the dependence on authorial intent as the source of meaning, as authoritarian. Others have argued that the rejection of the possibility of allocratic (other governed) interpretations and the insistence on self-governed interpretations are autocratic or despotic.[1] In addition, Joseph Vining wrote a whole book on the distinction between the authoritative and authoritarian. In his book, he argues that although there needs to be a shared belief in a system prior to any interpretive act, the authoritarian is a norm of blind obedience while the authoritative is the practice of "rationally determined excellence."[2]

In the Islamic context, I believe that authoritarianism is an act of ultimate lack of self-restraint that involves a fraudulent claim whose natural effect is to usurp the Divine Will. Authoritarianism, then, is the marginalization of the ontological reality of the Divine and the depositing of this Divine Will in the agent so that the agent effectively becomes self-referential. In the authoritarian dynamic, the distinction between the agent and the Principal becomes indistinct and blurred. The Will of the Principal and the speech of the agent become one and the same, as the agent superimposes his or her own determination upon the instructions of the Principal. Since the Principal is represented by textual and non-textual indicators, in the authoritarian process, the agent, for all practical purposes, negates the autonomy of the indicators and makes the voice of the indicators absolutely and irrevocably contingent on his or her determination. The authoritarian dynamic denies the integrity of the indicators by foreclosing the possibility of self-expression of the indicators, and prevents the development and evolution of meaning in the interpretive community. In the remainder of this chapter, I will elaborate upon this concept, but I will limit my comments to the indicators found in the text.

I will not elaborate upon the notion of self-authoritarianism. An agent may be negligent, reckless, dishonest or moronic with himself or herself, and may read the instructions of the Principal and unreasonably and whimsically determine that they mean *x* or *y*. The agent may then conclude that as far as his or her affairs are concerned, he or she will follow this determination regardless of any evidence to the contrary or competing determinations. Can it be argued that the agent is acting despotically towards himself or herself? I doubt whether this treatment of the self can be described as authoritarian unless the agent adopts a normative role vis-à-vis others. It seems to me that the agent's negligence or megalomania is an affair between the agent and God as long as there is no representation of authoritativeness by that agent to others. The authoritarianism with which I deal is contingent on a claim of authoritativeness made by the agent who is interpreting the instructions of the Principal.

## *The iron law of authoritarianism*

Robert Michels in his classic treatise on democracies persuasively argues that all political systems, including democracies, are under the grip of what he named the Iron Law of Oligarchy. Michels argued that political systems suffer very powerful pressures towards centralization and oligarchy, and that these pressures are a natural tendency within all human organizations.[3] Similarly, there is an undeniable tendency in all interpretive processes towards authoritarianism that manifests itself in the emergence of stable and unchangeable determinations. The authoritative will invariably gravitate towards the authoritarian unless there is a conscientious and active effort to resist this tendency by the interpreting and by the receiving agent. When the reader engages the text and derives from it a rule of law, the ever-present risk is that the reader will become unified with the text, or the determination of the reader will become the exclusive embodiment of the text. The risk is that the text and the construction of the reader will become one and the same. In this process, the text is rendered subservient to the reader and, effectively, the reader is substituted for the text. If the reader chooses a particular reading of the text and claims that no other readings are possible, the text is diluted in the character of the reader. If the reader overcomes and usurps the text, the danger is that the reader stands suspended, untouchable, transcendent, and authoritarian.

The authoritarian tendency is resisted through the implementation of the five contingencies discussed earlier – honesty, self-restraint, diligence, comprehensiveness, and reasonableness. In fact, authoritarianism invariably involves the violation of one or more of the five contingencies. Since authoritarianism primarily manifests itself in the act of representation to others, the authoritarian act will involve either the active misrepresentation or the nondisclosure of the failure to comply with the five contingencies. But disclosure or truthful representation is not a separate requirement because the failure to disclose or the act of misrepresentation is itself a violation of the five contingencies. The failure of agents to disclose their limitations in the search for the Divine Will, or to distinguish themselves from the Divine Will, is a violation of the duties of honesty and self-restraint vis-à-vis other agents and the Principal. Every act of authoritarianism will involve the violation of one or more of the five contingencies, but the violation of one or more of the contingencies is not necessarily authoritarian. I think this point is best demonstrated through some examples.

For the first example, we will deal with the issue of the veiling of women in Islamic law. This is not intended to be a full exposition on this matter; I am simply selecting some issues in order to clarify the argument. Let us assume that I read the following Qur'ānic verse: "O' Prophet tell your wives, daughters and the women of the believers to draw upon themselves their garments. This is better so that they will be known and not molested. And, God is forgiving and merciful."[4] Assume that I also read the following Qur'ānic verses: "And say to the believing women to lower their gaze, and guard their private parts, and that they should not display their adornments except what would ordinarily appear. And, that they should draw their veils over their bosoms and that they should not display their beauty except to their husbands."[5] After reading these verses, I assert to my friend that these verses require women to cover their entire bodies except the face and hands, and that they should do so in all circumstances except in front of certain men such as their husbands, fathers, and brothers. Somewhat confused, my friend inquires how I reached this conclusion since the verses do not seem to explicitly dictate the law as I see it. Puzzled, my friend adds that the first verse seems to incorporate an element of signaling and differentiation. The verse mandates that the "garments" be drawn so that Muslim women may be recognized, differentiated from others, and not molested. Furthermore, my friend inquires whether the crux of the matter is the fear of molestation or harm so that a woman need cover only if there is a risk of molestation or harm. In addition, my friend asks if the statement that women may show the "adornments that may ordinarily appear" is an indication that the laws of modesty might partly depend upon customary practices within a society. My response to this is that various juristic interpretive communities throughout the ages have decided that the whole body of a woman is a *'awrah* (private part that must be covered) except for the hands and face, and that this matter is not open to discussion or reconsideration. Let us assume that in responding to this question, I concealed the fact that these same juristic interpretive communities have held that a slave-girl should not cover other than what is between the knees and navel. This is material because if the issue is the natural immodesty of a woman's body, why is it acceptable that a slave-girl does not have to cover her hair or chest? Let us also assume that I concealed that some jurists have held that it is desirable for women to cover their hair, but it is not mandated.[6]

Of course, I could have disclosed these material issues, and then proceeded to argue that they are irrelevant or distinguishable. I may argue that the slave-girl rule was an unfortunate exception to the law that is now irrelevant. Regardless of the persuasiveness of my argument, the important point is that the obligation of honesty demands full disclosure of the evidence, the duty of comprehensiveness requires that I take account and deal with the full scope of the evidence, and the duty of self-restraint would militate against the claim that I know God's Will and that my knowledge is unchallengeable and not subject to reconsideration.

Now, let us assume that I have positioned myself as a person knowledgeable in Islamic law; in other words, I have positioned myself as a special agent in Islamic law. Let us also assume that there are agents who have granted me their trust and have come to treat my opinions as an exclusionary reason and, hence, defer to my judgment. One of those agents asks me whether in Islamic law, a woman has the power to divorce her husband. I respond by saying, according to Islamic law a woman always has the power to divorce her husband for cause or no cause. This response is misleading and dishonest because by asking about Islamic law, and not simply my personal opinion, the agent is implicitly asking about the determination of the system that produced Islamic law. Therefore, an honest response would explain that the vast majority of jurists have given men the power of divorce for cause or no cause and denied it to women. I may go further and explain that I have studied the evidence of the jurists, and I disagree with those reasons and, therefore, I respectfully dissent. The failure to give a full response, when a reasonable person would be aware of the need for full disclosure, is fraudulent and an abuse of authority. An abuse of authority is authoritarian if its natural effect is to equate the will of the agent and the Will of the Principal. Therefore, authoritarianism is not just a matter of its effect on the audience, it also relates to the dynamics of the agent with the Principal as well. Authoritarianism is generated when the open Will of God is artificially closed, so, for instance, the alleged closing of the doors of *ijtihād* would be a prime example of an authoritarian dynamic because it lacks self-restraint, comprehensiveness, diligence, and honesty.[7] This issue mandates further elaboration.

Assume that there is a special agent who is held in high regard by a group of people, and those people tend to follow all his opinions. We will call that special agent the master. The master, however, is honest and forthcoming about his limitations and refuses to misrepresent the evidence. In fact, the master never claims to represent God's truth, but only claims to do his best with the evidence available and leaves the judgment up to his followers. The problem, however, is that the master's followers tend to obey blindly all his legal determinations and, therefore, completely assign judgment to him. If, in fact, the master abides by the five contingencies, one can hardly claim that he is acting in an authoritarian fashion although the followers violate their own obligations towards the

Principal by failing to distinguish between the Will of God and the determinations of the master. Of course, the fact that the followers tend to follow the master so blindly makes one suspect that he is doing something that is not consistent with the five contingencies. It is rare, if not impossible, to find someone who is obeyed blindly without that person being responsible for this situation in one fashion or another.

On the other hand, assume that the master is dismissive of all evidence that is not consistent with his own opinion. He does not necessarily assert that his opinions are the truth, but he presents the evidence in such a fashion that it creates the mistaken impression that the evidence is uniform, cohesive and that all the evidence leads to one possible conclusion. The master accomplishes this by failing to note differences of opinions or conflicting evidence, or even by simply issuing disclaimers stating that other interpretations are possible. We can say that this is an authoritarian practice if the master is representing himself as authoritative to others. The authoritarian dynamic is created when the master generates the dishonest and arrogant impression that he is, in fact, privy to the Divine Will, and that this entitles him to dismiss evidence that might challenge his opinions. The master can create this impression by selectively misrepresenting the evidence or by deciding issues without regard to the instructions of the Principal, while representing himself to others as someone who is, in fact, an authority on the instructions of the Principal. Even if his claims persuade no one, the mere fact that he represented his claims to others is sufficient to earn him the label of authoritarian.

## *Islamic law as a work in movement*

I do not wish to slip into a sociological analysis of the authoritarian; this is an entirely different field of inquiry. The essential point is that in researching *Sharīʿah* issues, there is a duty of intellectual integrity and investigative diligence (*badhl al-naẓar wa jahd al-qarīḥah*) in analyzing and presenting the full array of relevant texts on a specific issue. Furthermore, the reader must exercise self-restraint by realizing that although the text might embody the Divine Will, the reader does not. Although the reader negotiates the meaning of the text, the reader must maintain a distance between himself or herself and the text. The material point is not whether the reader accurately represents the true intention of the author of the text, but whether the reader sufficiently respects the text by trying to understand but not replace it. In this sense, the highest morality is the morality of the discourse and not necessarily correctness.

This point is well illustrated in a quote by *Imām al-Ḥaramayn* al-Juwaynī (d. 478/1085). He states: "If the *mujtahid* is not negligent in his research and is diligent in his search for sources and does not find them, then the law of God, as to him, is according to his *ijtihād*."[8] In fact, every time a reader develops the conviction that he or she has discovered the true meaning of the text or has located the Divine Will, the reader is running the risk of exceeding his authority and falling into the authoritarian.

The idea of the open text is particularly helpful here. The Qur'ān and *Sunnah*, to borrow Umberto Eco's expression, are "works in movement" – they are works that leave themselves open to multiple interpretive strategies.[9] This does not mean that they are open to any interpretation, but that they are capable of supporting a dynamic interpretive movement.[10] If the *Sharī'ah* is going to have a continued relevance through a variety of contexts and ages, Islamic law must embrace the idea of an active movement in the construction of meaning. In fact, as we discussed earlier, the juristic culture has insisted that the Divine Will is discoverable through a cumulative and evolving search, and that Islamic sources are subject to multiple interpretations. The open text, however, does not only support multiple interpretations, but instigates a process of engagement in which the text occupies a central role. The text speaks with a renewed voice to successive generations of readers because its meaning is unfixed and actively evolving. The text remains relevant and central because its openness enables it to continue having a voice. As long as the text is open it can speak, and as long as it speaks it remains relevant and pertinent. Readers will constantly return to it because it can yield new insights and interpretations. If the text is no longer capable of speaking or if the text is denied its voice, there is no reason for engaging the text, after all, the text is frozen in the state that it had at the last time it was engaged. Hence, the text is closed when it is frozen upon the meaning it possessed when it was last engaged. The closing of the text takes place when the reader insists that the text has a determined, stable, constant and unchangeable meaning. A source becomes a closed text when a reader is able to shut down the interpretive process and is able to merge the text with a particular determination. So for instance, if the meaning of a particular *ḥadīth* becomes forever settled, the text is effectively declared closed.

The risk in closing a text is that it could be rendered irrelevant. The last determination given to the text becomes the final word on its meaning, and the text becomes irrelevant in that readers do not have a reason to return to it and engage it. The readers only need to return to the last determination and debate *its* meaning, or simply follow it. From a sociological point of view, in some cases this might be inevitable, but it is also morally suspect. Closing the text is intellectually arrogant; the reader is claiming a knowledge that is identical to God's knowledge. By claiming to know what the text really means, the reader is saying, "My interpretation can be rightly equated with the true meaning of the text." This claim, in effect, merges the determination of the reader with the original text. If the reader's determination is thoroughly and irreversibly merged and equated with the original text, what emerges from this dynamic is a new text. The original text only speaks through this new text – a new text that is comprised of the original text plus the irreversible determination. In effect, the original text loses its autonomy – it becomes a text dependent on another.

The theological difficulty with this is that it conflicts with the idea of God's supreme knowledge. The Qur'ān insists that God's knowledge is supreme and that it is not equaled by anyone.[11] More concretely, the Qur'ān states: "The Word of your Lord has been completed in truth and justice. None can replace your Lord's Words for your Lord is the All-Hearing and All-Knowing."[12] Elsewhere, the Qur'ān points to the fact that all knowing exists on a scale, and so the Qur'ān simply states, "We raise to degrees of knowledge whom We please. Over everyone endued with knowledge is one more knowing."[13] These verses, and others, raise the question, to what extent is God's knowledge attainable? This, of course, is an incredibly complex issue, but the concrete problem that confronts us is: at what point does a subjective determination of meaning constitute a replacement of God's Words?" If God says X, and I say X means XY, a what point does XY, for all practical purposes, replace X?

I am not claiming that closing the text is never justified. Perhaps in some circumstances, X can mean XY, and only XY but this kind of claim is rarely justified. The readers or the interpretive community must be willing to claim that human knowledge and God's knowledge have become one and the same on this particular point, and that the human determination cannot possibly threaten to replace the Divine Word. This, for me, is theologically problematic.[14] The possibility that one can make this type of claim while discharging the obligations of honesty and self-restraint is not very high. Even more, it is doubtful that one can be diligent, comprehensive and reasonable in evaluating the totality of the evidence, and yet, be able to claim that the text is closed because its meaning is definitively determinable. In all likelihood, this claim will be an act of usurpation of the Divine authority, and will be a constructed authoritarianism.

The issue of the extent to which the Divine Will is accessible or attainable, either through the text or some other means, takes us back to a debate that we touched upon in the previous chapter. As noted earlier, pre-modern Muslim jurists frequently debated the meaning of the phrase "Every *mujtahid* is correct."[15] The question that troubled the Muslim jurists was, how could there be several correct answers to the same exact question? Naturally, this would depend on how one defines "correctness," but at a more fundamental level, the question raises the issue of the purpose or the motivation behind the existence of the textual evidence. What is the Divine Purpose behind setting out texts that contain indicators and then requiring that human beings engage in a search? If the Divine wants human beings to reach *the* correct understanding then how could every reader or jurist be correct?

The juristic discourses focused on whether or not Islamic law had a determinable result, in all cases, and if there is such a determinable result are Muslims obligated to find it? Put differently, is there a correct legal response to all legal problems, and are Muslims charged with the legal obligation of finding that response? Nearly all Muslim jurists agreed that good faith and diligence protect one from liability before God. As long as the reader exercises due diligence in searching for the Divine intent, the reader will not be held liable nor incur a sin regardless of the result. Beyond this, the jurists were divided into two main camps. The first school, known as the *mukhaṭṭiʾah*, argued that ultimately, there is a correct answer to every textual or legal problem. However, only God knows what the correct response is and the truth will not be revealed until the Final Day. In this sense, on every legal issue and in every textual encounter, God has predetermined a correct answer that exists in the repository of Divine Knowledge. But human beings, for the most part, cannot conclusively know whether they have found that correct response. In this sense, every *mujtahid* is correct in trying to find the answer, however, one reader might reach the truth while others might mistake it. God, on the Final Day, will inform all readers who was right and who was wrong. Correctness here means that the *mujtahid* is to be commended for putting in the effort, but it does not mean that all responses are equally valid. Often, the *mukhaṭṭiʾah* argued that any one thing cannot have two realities; something is either good or bad, ugly or beautiful. The reality of something does not depend on the recognition or acknowledgement of an observer, rather the reality of something is inherent to it. Likewise, a legal act cannot be valid and invalid at the same time or permissible and impermissible at the same time – it is one or the other. God knows the truth, and in the Hereafter, will reward everyone who struggled to find the correct answer; those who actually found it will receive a double-reward. Interestingly, the *mukhaṭṭiʾah* would add that if responses could be equally correct, and if people could not aspire to find the correct answer, then what would be the point of legal debates and discussions (*munāẓarah*)? Debates and discussions are useful exactly because they have the potential of bringing us closer to the truth.[16]

The second school, known as the *muṣawwibah*, included prominent jurists such as al-Juwaynī, al-Suyūṭī (d. 911/1505), al-Ghazālī (d. 505/1111) and al-Rāzī (d. 606/1210), and it is reported that the Muʿtazilah were followers of this school as well.[17] The *muṣawwibah* argued that there is no specific and correct answer (*ḥukm muʿayyan*) that God wants human beings to discover, in part, because if there were a correct answer, God would have made the textual evidence conclusive and clear. God cannot charge human beings with the duty to find the correct answer when there is no objective means of discovering the correctness of a textual or legal problem. If there were an objective truth to everything, God would have made such a truth ascertainable in this life. Legal truth or correctness, in most circumstances, depends on belief and evidence, and, in fact, the nature of legal acts often does depend on recognition. In this context, the *muṣawwibah* jurists invoked an example that was first cited by the master jurist al-Shāfiʿī. A man may purchase a slave-girl and proceed to have conjugal relations with her, but later it is discovered that that woman is the man's sister. At the point that the man and woman become aware that they are siblings, they may not continue conjugal relations, although before that point, it was permissible for them to do so. Here, whether the conjugal relations were permissible or not depended on the knowledge of the parties involved. The same act was permissible and became impermissible because of a fact that was collateral to the intrinsic nature of the act. The act may have an inherent moral quality (*qabīḥah* or *ḥasanah bi dhātihā*), but its legal quality is contingent on things unrelated to its inherent nature.[18] Human beings are charged with the duty diligently to investigate a problem and then follow the results of their own *ijtihād*. Human beings are not charged with the obligation of finding some abstract or inaccessible legally correct result. Rather, they are charged with the duty to search and honestly and diligently ascertain what they believe to be true and correct. Al-Juwaynī explains this point by asserting, "The most a *mujtahid* would claim is a preponderance of belief (*ghalabat al-ẓann*) and the balancing of the evidence. However, certainty was never claimed by any of [the early jurists]... If we were charged with finding [the truth] we would not have been forgiven for failing to find it."[19] According to al-Juwaynī, what God wants or intends is for human beings to search – to live a life fully and thoroughly engaged with the Divine. He explains that it is as if God has said: "My command to My servants is in accordance with the preponderance of their beliefs. So whoever preponderantly believes that they are obligated to do something, acting upon it becomes My command."[20] God's command to human beings is to diligently search, and God's law is suspended until a human being forms a preponderance of belief about the law. At the point that a preponderance of belief is formed, God's law becomes in accordance with the preponderance of belief formed by that particular individual. It is not that the individual has a good-faith excuse vis-à-vis the law, rather the legal obligation does not form or exist until the person forms a preponderance of belief as to the law. In summary, if a person honestly and sincerely believes that such and such is the law of God, then, as to that person "that" is in fact God's law.[21]

What if two individuals, each with their own preponderance of belief, have a conflict of interest? What if it is impossible to accommodate each preponderance of belief at the same time and over the same issue? What is the law of God then? Al-Juwaynī and other *muṣawwibah* jurists argue that in this situation the law of God for each individual remains the preponderance of his or her belief. However, in relation to each other, the law of God is suspended until there is a formal legal adjudication between the competing interests. In contemporary language, one might say that the private law of God for each individual is the individual's preponderance of belief, but the public law is suspended pending a formal adjudication.

Al-Juwaynī demonstrates this argument through two interesting examples. Assume there is a Shāfiʿī husband who in a moment of anger yells at his Ḥanafī wife "You are divorced." Since the husband is Shāfiʿī he might believe that since the pronouncement of divorce was uttered in anger it is ineffective and his wife is still his wife. However, since the wife is Ḥanafī she might believe that a divorce pronounced in a moment of anger is effective. According to the husband's preponderance of belief, they are still married but according to the wife's preponderance of belief they are no longer married. In another example, al-Juwaynī discusses a Ḥanafī wife who marries without the permission of her guardian. Since she is Ḥanafī, she might believe that it is her right to marry whomever she wants. Meanwhile, the woman's guardian (presumably her father), who happens to be a Shāfiʿī, marries her off to a second husband. Since the guardian is a Shāfiʿī he might believe that it is his right to marry his daughter to whomever he wants, with or without her permission. Al-Juwaynī poses the question: what is the law of God in these situations? He argues that the command of God as to both of them accords with their sincere beliefs. However, since there is a conflict of interest among the different parties, the law of God becomes one of suspension until a judge decides the matter. In other words, since the different parties have conflicting interests, the law of God is suspended until the matter is referred to a judge. The judge's verdict will then be the law of God. However, that verdict is not the law of God because it is more correct than any other ruling, it is the law of God as a matter of procedural justice.[22]

Al-Juwaynī's approach effectively distinguishes sin from legal liability. Sin is only incurred for failure to investigate diligently the evidence and not for any result reached. Legal adjudication arises from the necessity to resolve conflicting interests. But at the same time, no one may claim to have reached the only possible right answer. In the absence of legal adjudication, one is bound to follow the result of his or her own *ijtihād*.

The effect of al-Juwaynī's approach is to preserve the integrity and authoritativeness of the text. Discourse is a moral value in itself, and final determinations imposed upon the text are inconsistent with the morality of the process of discourse. Even in the case of a legal adjudication, one may continue to believe and argue that the positive law has misconstrued the Divine text. Even a judge must be cognizant of the fact that he or she represents only an opinion about the Divine law and not the Divine law itself. Importantly, both the *mukhaṭṭi'ah* and *muṣawwibah* do not adopt positions that mandate the closing of the text. The *mukhaṭṭi'ah* endorses the theoretical possibility of closing the text upon locating the truth, but as a practical matter, that might not be possible as long as there is juristic disagreement upon the meaning of the text. As long as there is disagreement, God will have to resolve the dispute in the Hereafter. However, the *muṣawwibah* adopts a position that normatively would refuse closing the text. The possibility of individual conviction and commitment must remain open, and this is not possible unless the text, itself, remains open. The text's determinacy is hinged on the encounters of the reader, and the subjective determinacy of that reader. Effectively, the meaning of the text remains indeterminate.

## *The fundamentals of religion and burdens of proof*

We mentioned earlier that the debates regarding legal determinacy were invariably accompanied by discussions on the fundamentals and branches of religion. Each religion espouses certain basic values or fundamentals, and this is what Muslim jurists described as the *uṣūl* or certain truths. Both the *mukhaṭṭiʾah* and *muṣawwibah* were not willing to extend the notion of indeterminacy to all matters, and both excepted from the idea that "every *mujtahid* is correct" all matters that fall within the purview of the fundamentals. Even the *muṣawwibah* argued that as to these fundamentals, the ultimate value is not the discourse but the fundamental or certain truth itself. Interestingly, the *mukhaṭṭiʾah* often criticized the *muṣawwibah* for what they considered a logical inconsistency. They contended that if the *muṣawwibah* wish to be consistent and coherent, they would have to extend the idea of indeterminacy even to the fundamentals. If, in fact, they argued, the law and "correctness" are contingent on a person's sincere belief, then how can one except the fundamentals from this doctrine? To be consistent, the *muṣawwibah* would have to concede that a sincere and honest belief is a full defense even as to anything related to the fundamentals of religion. Typically, the *muṣawwibah* responded to this criticism by reminding their opponents that people do commit a sin if they are negligent, whimsical or capricious in their search. The *muṣawwibah* then added that it is not possible for a conscientious, diligent and honest person to develop a preponderance of belief that would contradict the fundamentals of religion.[23]

We alluded earlier to the fact that the distinction between a fundamental and non-fundamental matter of religion is elusive. Most jurists argued that indeterminacy or performing *ijtihād* in matters of *uṣūl* is a sin because in these types of issues there is an unwavering duty to realize the truth.[24] However, defining the fundamentals remained a rather challenging problem. As discussed earlier, some argued that the fundamentals are those things that are *ʿaqliyyāt* (things that are clearly apparent through the dictates of reason). Others argued that all legal matters that have been established to the point of conclusive certainty are not susceptible to indeterminacy, and therefore, for instance, if a text's meaning is clear, precise and unambiguous, any attempt to re-interpret the text is sinful. Other jurists simply argued that anything that is a certain truth (*masāʾil qaṭʿiyyah*) is to be considered among the fundamentals of religion. Yet, all these descriptions of the fundamentals of religion are not particularly helpful or coherent. What Muslim jurists intended to do was to remove certain matters from the realm of discussion or debate. Such matters included the status of Muḥammad as the last prophet to humanity, the immutability and Divinity of the Qurʾān, the position of the *Sunnah* as a source of legislation, the merit and justness of all the Prophet's Companions and the necessity of enforcing the law of *Sharīʿah*.[25] However, the inability to articulate a systematic and coherent definition of those fundamentals raises several issues that require the delineating of some careful distinctions. It is one thing to argue that there are matters so clear and obvious in the pertinent Islamic texts that it is sinful to attempt to re-interpret them, and it is quite another to argue that it is appropriate to censor someone who wishes to re-interpret the matters. In other words, perhaps there are certain issues that are so clear that in all likelihood anyone who attempts to re-interpret them will do so only by being idiosyncratic, whimsical or negligent. As to these issues, we might suspect that anyone attempting to re-open the interpretive process, most probably, will do so only by violating one of the five contingencies. And, hence, we may strongly suspect that such a person will incur serious sins, and we may even refuse to recognize the authoritativeness of such as far as the juristic interpretive community is concerned. But all of this does not mean that we have the right to censor the discourse of such a person or to claim that he or she is no longer a Muslim. The most one can do is to say to such a person, "I believe that you are probably incurring sin because, in my opinion, it is not possible to reach the conclusions that you have reached without being negligent and without failing to be reasonable, comprehensive and self-restrained. Furthermore, as far as the juristic interpretive community is concerned, your interpretations are so off the charts that the presumption of authoritativeness is not in your favor." In my view, there is no Islamic justification for censoring discourses on any purported fundamentals, but one is justified in believing in the sinfulness of such discourses. But sin, or the lack of it, is ultimately only a matter for God to resolve.

Another issue raised in this context is related to burdens of proof. If one claims that a certain matter is a certain truth or fundamental matter in Islam, this is a formidable claim. The essence of such a claim is that a certain matter is so important that its absence is an undermining of the affirmative Will of God. In effect, one is making the implicit claim that this matter deserves to be a point of inclusion or exclusion, for the juristic interpretive community as a whole. Therefore, the burden of proof is on the person who is making this claim, and the claimant must meet a heightened duty of diligent scrutiny and self-restraint. The burden of proof is much higher and the duty of exertion in research is much more demanding than on any other issue. At the same time, if the parameters of a particular determination have become firmly established in the juristic community, it is entitled to a presumption of soundness. What this presumption means is that since this determination has been consistently and cumulatively accepted as supported by evidence, one can presume that it is a legitimate and sound determination. It is reasonable then to assume that anyone who claims to be part of the juristic interpretive community, and who wishes to challenge the legitimacy or soundness of this well-established determination, bears the burden of proof. For instance, let us assume that the juristic interpretive community has consistently and cumulatively maintained that Muslim women should cover their entire body and hair (i.e. wear the *ḥijāb*). Let us further assume that the juristic community has consistently and persistently held this to be a legal obligation upon every Muslim woman to the point that it believes this matter to be resolved and closed. Furthermore, the juristic community has come to suspect that it is not possible to challenge this determination without violating the five contingencies and committing the sin of negligence. Now, let us assume that I claim to be a part of the juristic interpretive community and, yet, I wish to challenge the *ḥijāb* determination. I am cognizant of the fact that the juristic community is advising me that I am at risk of committing the sin of negligence by producing an alternative determination. I am the one claiming the error of the juristic community, therefore, I bear the burden of proof – I must produce enough evidence to support my claim that the established determination of the juristic community is erroneous. As the Islamic legal maxim dictates, "The burden of proof is invariably against the claimant" (*al-bayyinah ʿalā man iddaʿā*). The question at this point is: is the juristic interpretive community obligated to consider and evaluate my evidence or can it simply ignore my claims? The answer is that this depends on the evidence produced. I might produce a sufficient amount of evidence to the point that it would not be feasible for the juristic community to discharge its obligation of diligence, comprehensiveness, and honesty without considering my evidence. In other words, with the existence of evidence, a blind dismissal of the alternative point of view, itself, becomes a sin.

The final, and the most important, issue raised by the problem of fundamentals in the juristic community is the nature of those fundamentals themselves. It is important to remember that, as an epistemological matter, all arguments commence from certain premises and assumptions, and these assumptions provide the basis for the formation of particular interpretive communities. As we noted earlier, shared normative assumptions are central for the formation of interpretive communities. Furthermore, religion, and ideology in general, relies on dogma that serves as the foundation for a distinctive system of thought. For instance, the belief that the Qurʾān is the literal uncorrupted word of God is a matter of dogma; it serves as an irrebuttable presumption in the juristic interpretive community so that any attempt to challenge this presumption is very likely to exclude the claimant from the interpretive community. The question then becomes, is it appropriate to consider these basic assumptions to be immune from critical re-examination? And, is not the existence of these basic assumptions itself authoritarian?

My response is that we ought to differentiate between the various types of what may be termed "basic assumptions" of the interpretive community. As an initial step to the analysis it is important to note that not all basic assumptions that might be relevant to a theological school of thought are necessarily relevant to a legal school of thought. Many of the legal schools that agreed on the same theological assumptions disagreed on issues of legal methodology such as the permissibility of utilizing analogy or the scope of equity. Furthermore, theological schools that disagreed on predestination or the return of the Mahdī (Messiah) shared the same juristic methodological assumptions. There is no necessary correlation between the theological and legal schools of pre-modern Muslim jurists. Consequently, members of the Ashʿarī or Māturīdī theological schools tended to cross juristic schools boundaries, so for instance, an Ashʿarī could be a Ḥanafī, Mālikī or Shāfiʿī.[26] Furthermore, some Ḥanbalī jurists such as Najm al-Dīn al-Ṭūfī or Ibn ʿAqīl, as far as their theological approaches were concerned, were rationalists.[27] Pre-modern Muslim jurists, themselves, were aware of the difference between the basic juristic assumptions and the theological assumptions. This awareness is underscored in the juristic argument that, as a matter of principle, Muslim jurists do not engage in *takfīr* (declaring that someone is not a Muslim). The type of assumptions adopted by theologians might lead to discourses on heresies and sectarianism, but these discourses are not relevant for the juristic practice. Therefore, several jurists, somewhat condescendingly, pointed out that while the theologians engage in *takfīr*, the jurists do not (*al-fuqahāʾ lā yukaffirūn*).[28]

I am not claiming that theological assumptions have no effect on juristic methods, I am only pointing out that not all theological assumptions are relevant or material as far as juristic communities are concerned. For instance, despite the significant theological differences between Shīʿī and Sunnī Muslims, we notice that Shīʿī and Sunnī law are remarkably similar both in terms of their methodologies and positive determinations. In fact, Shīʿī Jaʿfarī law is very similar to Sunnī Shāfiʿī law, and Shīʿī Zaydī law is very similar to Sunnī Ḥanafī law. Many of the legal differences between Sunnīs and Shīʿīs, such as the permissibility of temporary marriages, are only indirectly influenced by theological differences, and other differences, such as the law of wills, are not at all influenced by theology.

As far as the basic assumptions of the juristic communities are concerned, one can differentiate between four types. This is not an exhaustive survey of all the pertinent assumptions, but I have sought to take account of the major unspoken assumptions in the Islamic juristic culture. These assumptions serve as the basis upon which the legal analysis is built, and at times, serve as the outer limits for legal determinations. There are four main types of assumptions: value-based; methodological; faith-based; and reason-based.

Value-based assumptions are founded on normative values that the legal system considers necessary or basic. They are the fundamental values of a juristic culture, or what a particular juristic community considers normatively desirable. For instance, the preservation of life, the protection of private property, the necessity of modesty, the freedom of speech, or the furtherance of forms of self-expression could all be basic normative values of a legal system. Muslim juristic theory often differentiated between what it called *ḍarūriyyāt* (basic necessities), *ḥājiyyāt* (basic needs) and *taḥsīniyyāt* (also known as *kamāliyyāt* – luxuries or embellishments).[29] Muslim jurists often asserted that the basic necessities are five essential values (*al-ḍarūriyyāt al-khamsah*): religion, life, intellect, lineage, and property.[30] These were the basic values or objects that the *Sharīʿah* is supposed to satisfy or guard. However, this field remained underdeveloped, and the asserted values were not necessarily those actually served or protected by the juristic culture. Muslim jurists argued that the five basic values were derived solely through textual analysis, and this might explain the largely mechanical way that they asserted or defended them. For instance, they contended that the prohibition of murder served the basic value of life, the law of apostasy protected religion, the prohibition of intoxicants protected the intellect, the prohibition of fornication and adultery protected lineage, and the right of compensation protected the right to property.[31] Nevertheless, if one wants to analyze and identify the actual basic values and the resulting assumptions of a juristic community, one will find that such values are a product of sociological and textual dynamics. For instance, one suspects that in some Muslim juristic cultures, order, stability and obedience, the exclusion of women from public life, and the protection of the financial interests of the elite are the actual primary values of the legal systems. These basic values lead to normative and analytical assumptions that, in turn, affect the development of the law. For instance, it could be factually and normatively presumed by the juristic culture that the increased mobility or visibility of women is generally undesirable.

Methodological assumptions differ from value-based assumptions in certain respects, and in other respects they tend to overlap with value assumptions of the legal system. For instance, whether the consensus of the jurists of Medina is probative, or whether a law deduced through analogy can serve as the basis for a further extension of the law through a compounded analogy is a methodological matter. Methodological assumptions relate to the means or requisite steps for achieving the normative goals of the law. Such assumptions purport to be enabling devices that facilitate the fulfillment of legal objectives. Methodological assumptions might emerge from systematic theoretical approaches to the law, but they tend to persist and evolve through the force of habit. They become the way that a juristic culture has always done things as far as the production of law is concerned. Significantly, the differences between the various Islamic schools of law purport to be largely methodological. The extent to which the methodological differences between the legal schools are co-mingled with normative values is debatable. Nevertheless, it is not always possible to distinguish between methodological assumptions and value-based assumptions. For instance, whether a public interest can override or suspend a textual proof, or the exact role of necessity (*ḍarūrah*) in creating exceptions of the law, or the proper role of equity or custom, are methodological issues that are intimately intertwined with basic normative assumptions such as the importance of public interest, or the necessity of private justice, or the significance of social habits.

Unlike value-based assumption or methodological assumption, a reason-based assumption defends its existence by an appeal to logic or legal evidence on a substantive legal determination. It is not the product of a direct dynamic between Muslims and God, but is based on a relationship between Muslims and the available evidence or instructions of the Principal. A reason-based assumption purports to rely on cumulative pieces of evidence and proofs. Such an assumption claims to be the product of an objective process of a rational weighing of the evidence, and not the product of personalized ethical, existential, or metaphysical experiences. A reason-based assumption does not admit that it is influenced by normative values, but claims detachment and objectivity. The determinative issue for this type of assumption is that, similar to literal readings of the law, it claims to be value-neutral, and to be based solely on the weight of the evidence. I refer to "reason-based assumptions," rather than "reason-based determinations," because I am addressing legal determinations that have been persistently upheld in a juristic culture through the force of long established precedents, to the point that such determinations are presumed to be firmly grounded in persuasive evidence. The juristic culture will assume a particular determination to be supported by evidence because of the persistence of such a determination in the juristic culture.

Faith-based assumptions find their genesis in a collateral relationship between the agent and the Divine. These assumptions do not claim to be derived directly from the instructions of the Principal, but from a dynamic between the agent and the Principal. Faith-based assumptions are founded on what one can call core or fundamental understandings of the very nature of the Divine message and its purposes. As such, these assumptions constitute a matter of conscience or basic belief that is neither accessible nor accountable to others. For instance, *x*, after developing what *x* believes is an intimate relationship with God, might become convinced that God is Beautiful and wants beauty to exist in all of creation. Or, *x* might become convinced that God is Just and God loves justice. If *x* finds enough jurists who had similar experiences with God, and share these normative values with him, *x* could commence the process of forming an interpretive community. This interpretive community might then assert that the law of God must comply with the requirement of beauty or justice – all interpretations of the law will seek to fulfill this basic relational understanding of God. All interpretations will attempt to promote these core moral values because they are fundamental for the interpretive community's faith in God. To put it bluntly, *x*'s interpretive community might not be willing to believe in a God who affirmatively wills ugliness or injustice, and all of the community's legal interpretations will reflect these basic moral assumptions. These assumptions are faith-based because although aided by particular textual evidence and rational proofs, they primarily rely on an irrational, largely unverifiable element of conviction. For example, whether I love Egypt or not could be based on some verifiable pieces of evidence – I love the Pyramids, I like the Sphinx, my family lives in Egypt, and so on. I might argue and present evidence in order to convince a friend to love Egypt as well, but what I am asking for is not a rational position based on cumulative evidence, I am asking for an emotional commitment to a value.

As the reader will surely notice, faith-based assumptions will often overlap or emerge from theological assumptions, and as we noted, some theological positions do materially affect legal determinations. In fact, one can argue that faith-based assumptions are nothing more than theological convictions that have a direct impact on legal determinations. But theological convictions are often based on textual evidence while faith-based assumptions are the product of something less tangible. They are like believing that God will always take care of you, or that your mother, despite her faults, is the best woman in the world, or that your wife only cares about herself. Similarly, there is overlap between value-based assumptions and faith-based assumptions. However, value-based assumptions claim to be derived solely from textual analysis, or an analysis of the larger goals of the Principal's instructions while faith-based assumptions relate to understanding the Principal, Himself. In a sense, faith-based assumptions are about the normativities of the Principal, and value-based assumptions are about the normativities of the instructions. Faith-based assumptions are often founded on convictions regarding the inherent character of the Principal.

It is imperative that an interpretive community be conscientious about identifying the exact nature of its basic assumptions – is it normative, is it methodological, is it evidentiary, or is it a matter of faith and pietistic conviction? Is one making an argument related to the most logical or effective method to deduce the law, is one making an argument based on the normative functions of the law, or is it integral to the moral message of Islam? Clarifying and critically examining the nature of the assumptions of the juristic community, for one, aids the coherence of the discourse itself. For instance, assume that a particular juristic community asserts that the testimony of two women is equal to the testimony of one man. Assume further that the juristic community asserts that this position is a firmly established presumption to the point that anyone who denies it is committing a grave sin. I might ask the interpretive community, "What is the basis for this presumption?" The interpretive community responds, "Have you not read the Qur'ānic verse that mandates that debts be documented in writing, and that two men, or one man and two women witness the document, so, as the Qur'ān states, 'if one [of the women] errs, the other can remind her'?" (Qur'ān 2:282) I might reply, "But a literal reading of the Qur'ānic verse would mandate that the rule of two women for one man be in the field of debts and nothing else." The interpretive community responds, "If this rule applies in debts, it is reasonable to assume that it applies in all commercial matters, and if it applies in commercial matters, it is reasonable to assume that it applies in all other important matters. Furthermore, all the jurists that examined this matter concluded that in most cases, the testimony of two women is equal to one man." I then respond, "This does not necessarily follow; this is based on a methodological assumption that permits the extension of a specific rule, regarding a particular matter, to collateral situations and collateral matters. Your methodological assumption permits the generalizing from the specific to the non-specific, and I do not share this methodological assumption. Furthermore, the verse you cited is the product of a specific context in which women were under-educated and did not normally engage in business. Consequently, if we no longer believe that a woman, or all women, will 'forget,' there is no justification for the two women for one man rule, in debts or otherwise." The interpretive community could respond, "Your methodology looks to the underlying factual and normative basis of the law, and we do not accept this methodological approach. We say that God determined that women are forgetful, and we are going to assume this factual matter in all our legal determinations." I in turn respond, "God is not a sexist! God does not decide that all women are forgetful – God acted on a factual assumption that existed at a particular time and place. The law should not commit the injustice of branding women as deficient or incapable." Of course, the interpretive community can retort, "As to your claim that God is not a sexist, this arises from faith-based assumptions about the immorality of sexism and the nature of God that we do not share. Furthermore, as to your argument that the law should not brand women as deficient or incapable, that is a value-based assumption that we do not share." In turn, I might respond, "Your acceptance of the idea that the law may exclude women or burden women in matters of legal testimony is, itself, based on value-based assumptions, and your willingness to assume that God would brand women as inferior to men is, itself, faith-based."

Although the example above is highly condensed, it hopefully, illustrates the basic fact that legal arguments often make various kinds of assumptions that need to be unpacked and analyzed. In the following chapters, I will further demonstrate this point in the context of contemporary discourses on Islamic legal issues. But other than the issue of coherence, faith-based, reason-based, value-based and methodological assumptions might draw the lines of demarcation between one juristic community and another. The assumptions that might characterize a particular juristic community could differ in material respects from the assumptions of another community. Importantly, the adoption of particular assumptions, in itself, cannot be characterized as authoritarian. Assumptions are often adopted as a matter of efficient discourse – instead of re-arguing and re-demonstrating the same exact points again and again, a juristic community will take certain determinations for granted and proceed onwards with the analysis from the point that was assumed to be settled. In effect, at least in theory, juristic assumptions are often adopted for the sake of efficiency or as discursive short cuts, and if used reasonably, might facilitate, not hamper the discourse. There is a difference between assuming a certain starting point for the analysis so that the analysis may proceed further, and the closing of the interpretive process by the adoption of non-negotiable convictions about matters of ultimate truth. It is the closing of the interpretive process and the violation of the conditions of agency that can be described as authoritarian. In other words, the adoption of assumptions is not per se authoritarian, but to the extent that these assumptions threaten to become the object of loyalty and, eventually, displace the authoritativeness of the Principal or the instructions, the assumptions could become problematic. As to value, reason, and methodological assumptions, the highest morality remains the morality of the process and not the results.

Faith-based assumptions demand a different analysis. These are assumptions that act as moral values serving as the foundation for the legal discourse. This does not mean that they are necessarily closed to discussion or analysis. It does mean that they might provide the effective boundary lines between one interpretive community and another, and that these boundary lines are not resolvable by textually-based arguments. Ultimately, the merits or worthiness of faith-based assumptions are reduced to being a matter of conscience that God will judge in the Hereafter. As to these assumptions, the highest morality might not be the morality of the process, but the morality of conscience. While in all matters, the results of the search are secondary to the process of searching, faith-based assumptions precede, direct and judge the process itself. They are convictional moral judgments about what are the determinative values of the religion that guide, and are not guided by, the process. There is no doubt, however, that these assumptions tend to close the process of determination of meaning or, at least, remove certain realms from the purview of such a process. They do so because they often act as exclusionary factors in the process of investigating the instructions of the Principal. So for instance, there is a report attributed to the Prophet stating that looking at a pretty face improves one's eyesight. Regardless of the authenticity of the chain of transmission supporting this report, Muslim jurists refused to accept it because, they argued, it is contrary to the moral character of the Prophet.[32] Similarly, many Muslim scholars rejected offhand the Satanic Verses reports because they contended that the whole incident is inconsistent with the Prophet's moral character.[33] Furthermore, most jurists considered the story of ʿUraynah or the reports asserting that ʿAlī's family tortured and mutilated ʿAlī's assassinator as inherently unbelievable.[34] I am not interested in the theological assumptions that led to the rejection of these reports, but I am concerned with the fact that these reports were denied the possibility of playing a role in the process of legal determinations.

As we discussed above, Muslim jurists often claimed that the Islamic legal system is founded on unwavering fundamentals called the *uṣūl*. However, what was often claimed as part of the *uṣūl* were positive legal determinations or reason-based assumptions. But as argued above, assumptions that are derived or extracted from the text should ultimately be refereed by the text. Assumptions derived from rational or deductive arguments, except for the purpose of discoursive efficiency, are open to re-determination. Importantly, the very act of claiming any determination or doctrine to be presumptively settled runs the very serious risk of being authoritarian. Consequently, someone proposing such a premise must be aware that he or she is flirting with the possibility of usurping the Divine Will and marginalizing the text. In short, it would be prudent for a judicious person to exercise self-restraint in asserting the status of *uṣūl* for any normative claim or determination.

In my view, any attempt to claim that a determination is part of the *uṣūl* if such a claim is based on textual evidence or the instructions of the Principal, and not a collateral relationship with the Principal, in all probability sets the stage for an authoritarian dynamic. Anything that is based on an objective understanding of the written instructions of the Principal should be accessible and challengeable by others, and any attempt to limit this accessibility will violate the terms of the authoritative agency, and, hence, will be authoritarian. However, if a presumption is primarily based on a collateral relationship with the Principal, it is doubtful whether it can be described as authoritarian. Rather, it stands outside the juristic interpretive process.

Since the determination that results from the collateral relationship is not subservient to the instructions of the Principal, its formation is not subject to the dynamics of the juristic culture. Of course, I am fully aware of the fact that suggesting that there could be a fundamental determination that is not based on God's text is controversial in the contemporary setting. But the reality is that our understanding of God and the moral values that follow from that understanding are not based on text alone. In fact, the Qur'ān assumes the existence of a prior relationship between God and a believer that guides and navigates the interaction between the text and the reader. That is why we find the Qur'ān emphasizing that its meaning and power unfold only to those who have a genuine relationship with God.[35] Furthermore, the Qur'ān often refers to terms such as *ʿadl* (equitable, just), *iḥsān* (beneficent), *maʿrūf* (a generally accepted good) without defining them as if the Qur'ān assumes a pre-existing relationship to justice, equity, and morality – a relationship that precedes the text. In fact, the Qur'ān assumes a pre-existing sense of morality in human beings to which it consistently appeals.[36] In any case, the relationship between morality, faith, and the text is too complicated to be appropriately dealt with here. It is important, however, to take note of the fact that pre-modern jurists extensively debated this issue under the heading of *ḥusn* (what is by its very nature good or beautiful) and *qubḥ* (what is by its very nature bad or ugly), but this whole discourse has been dogmatically ignored in the contemporary age.[37] The pre-modern juristic discourses focused on whether the notions of right and wrong, good and bad, emerge from the text or exist independent of the text.[38] I do not deny the fact that notions of morality can emerge from the text, but one cannot deny that they could emerge from faith-based, non-textual sources. Simply put, my contention is that when such determinations emerge from non-textual sources and are faith-based, the determination, itself, takes place outside the juristic process, and is not accountable to the normal juristic criteria. Nonetheless, although the determination is not subject to the juristic process, if the interpreter claims that his or her faith-based determinations are authoritative, as far as other agents are concerned, the five contingencies must be fulfilled. Therefore, if the interpreter claims that his or her faith-based determinations are authoritative and should serve as exclusionary reasons for other agents, those agents will expect the interpreter to discharge his or her obligations towards the Principal. Such agents will expect that the interpreter is being honest in disclosing the nature of the assumption or determination that he or she is making and will also expect that the interpreter has diligently and comprehensively investigated all the relevant evidence that might challenge these faith-based assertions. Furthermore, the agents will expect that the interpreter has exercised self-restraint and reasonableness in not taking liberties in shaping God in the image that would fit his or her whim. At a minimum, the interpreter would have to restrain and limit himself or herself to the faith-based assumptions that he or she is confident reasonably represent the Divine. If the interpreter is negligent or dismissive about these duties then he or she has no right to claim authoritativeness.

## *Moral objections and authoritarianism*

I will demonstrate the argument thus far with two cases that will also help summarize the arguments of this chapter. Consider al-Juwaynī's example of the Ḥanafī woman who married herself to a man without her father's knowledge or consent. Meanwhile, her Shāfiʿī father married her to someone else, without her knowledge or consent. The woman, pursuant to her Ḥanafī convictions, thinks that she is married to her chosen husband while her father, pursuant to his Shāfiʿī convictions, believes her to be married to the husband he chose. Al-Juwaynī argues that between the two, the law of God is suspended until a judge renders a decision in the matter. Assuming that the judge decides that, according to the positive law of the land, judgment should be rendered in favor of the father, the Ḥanafī woman in question might be forced to adopt the position of a conscientious objector to the law. The wife might argue that regardless of the decision of the judge, she will not live with the husband her father selected because she cannot live with someone that she believes is not her husband. Furthermore, the woman adds that she believes that her right to choose her husband is fundamental to her understanding of Islam. She contends that as a matter of conviction and belief she cannot imagine that a compassionate, merciful, and just God would require her to live with someone she does not believe to be her husband. Even more, she is willing to take full responsibility for that belief in the Hereafter when she stands before God. In essence, the Ḥanafī woman is making a moral argument that might have developed from a reason-based analysis, but has now become faith-based. As far as the legal system is concerned, to the extent to which the Ḥanafī woman's moral argument is not challengeable, accessible, or accountable to others, it stands outside the legal system. Her assumptions, however, are effective if the legal culture in which the case is adjudicated happens to share the woman's faith-based convictions, but if the legal culture does not share these convictions, effectively, there is an irresolvable conflict between her morality and the morality of the system. Consequently, if the woman insists on not complying with the decision of the judge, she would be treated as a *bāghiyah* under the Islamic law of rebellion. This means that she cannot be harshly punished because she is a *muta'awwilah* (a rebel with a principled cause).[39] Nonetheless, in my opinion, if her conviction is truly faith-based, she is morally and religiously obligated not to obey the judge's decision. Her refusal to obey the judge's opinion and her insistence on following her conscience cannot be described as authoritarian; one can only call it principled.

To examine this problem from a different perspective, we should consider the scenario from the point of view of an outsider to the case who claims to be a part of the juristic interpretive community. This outsider has held himself out as a special agent interpreting the instructions of the Principal. As a jurist, he is asked about the legal basis for the woman's stand and after discharging the five obligations, gives the following response: "I have examined the evidence, and while the Ḥanafī jurists do hold that a previously unmarried woman may marry without the approval of her guardian, they consider that to be reprehensible. Furthermore, they have given the guardian the standing to challenge the woman's decision on the grounds of non-suitability in court. Jurists from the other schools did not concede to women an unequivocal right to live with the partner that she wishes to live with. This is the work product of various interpretive sub-communities that belong to the general interpretive community of Muslim jurists. The evidence that these jurists relied on is the following ... However, I believe that consistent with Islamic morality, all the evidence should be re-read and re-interpreted in order to concede to women full autonomy in living with the partner that they choose. I am fully prepared to share with you how these re-interpretations and re-determinations can be executed without abusing the integrity of the text. The bottom line for me is that I do not believe it possible for God to be unjust or ugly, and to force a woman to live with someone that she feels she is not married to is not consistent with my knowledge of God, or my Islamic moral obligations."[40] This response does not invoke an authoritarian dynamic; it clearly delineates the authoritative, the principled, and the aspirational. It discloses to the common agents the indicators found in the instructions of the Principal, and the determinations of previous interpretive communities, and the potential for re-determination. But it also puts the common agents on notice that there is a fundamental faith-based issue that needs to be considered. The common agents need to reflect on whether they want to share or reject this faith-based assumption."[41]

Now, assume that instead of the above response, the jurist responds in the following fashion: "Islamic law liberated women, and Islamic law has always guaranteed the right of this woman, and all women, to choose their partners. Clearly, the decision of the judge in favor of the husband is against Islamic law. In fact, anyone that supports the decision of the judge is either ignorant or not a Muslim because God said, 'There is no compulsion in religion' and so the matter is very clear."

This response is authoritarian – it ignores the evidence, misrepresents the tradition, and usurps the integrity and autonomy of the Principal's instructions. The jurist invokes the authoritativeness of the juristic tradition by referring to "Islamic law," but then proceeds to ignore its determinations as simply misguided or non-existent. There is no attempt to be comprehensive, diligent or honest in the presentation of the evidence. Furthermore, he does not distinguish between his faith-based assumptions and the reality of the instructions, and there is no attempt to disclose the faith-based assumptions that informed his determinations. The end result is that there is a conjoining of the will of the interpreter, the text and the Principal so that there is no hope of knowing where one ends and the other begins. In short, the checks and balances of the interpretive process, which requires three distinct participants – the reader, the text, and the author (or authorial enterprise) – has been diluted into a unified dictatorship.

I will summarize the arguments of this chapter by working through a second example. Consider the Qur'ānic verse that states: "Do not take a life which God has sanctified unless for just cause."[42] Arguably, we can conclude from this verse that the preservation of human life is a value, and that the legal system should seek to preserve and protect life. The boundaries of this value are not clear – for instance, does it include all life or just human life. Furthermore, the verse creates a just cause exception, the exact definition of which is debatable. Importantly, the text or the Principal's instructions remain central to the process of determining meaning. There is no question that sociological contexts will bias an interpreter's understanding of the value of life and the meaning of this value. Moreover, the sociological context will orient the understanding of just cause in a variety of ways. But the determination of meaning will depend on an interactive and negotiative process between the reader, text and the Author. An interpreter steps forward and claims to be a special agent who will put in the time and effort in understanding the instructions of the Principal. The person claiming this special status does not propose a new epistemology for understanding the instructions, but only refers to Islamic law. The special agent, explicitly or implicitly, sets himself or herself up as authoritative. Common agents will treat the special agent's determinations as providing exclusionary rules, and will defer to these determinations to the extent that the special agent is constructing the instructions of the Principal. In order for the special agent not to abuse or violate the trust placed in her or him, she or he will have to satisfy the five contingencies discussed earlier. Importantly, by invoking Islamic law, and by not proposing an alternative epistemology, the special agent is claiming to be a part of the juristic tradition that collected, organized, and preserved the instructions in the first place. The common agents will expect, at a minimum, that the special agent will consider and evaluate the determinations of the juristic interpretive community, and that the five contingencies will be executed as to the original instructions and the determinations of the juristic community as well. The special agent might adopt value-based, reason-based or methodological assumptions that will affiliate her or him with a particular sub-interpretive community. Common agents who share these assumptions might find the determinations of that sub-community particularly authoritative. Again, at a minimum, the special agent will need to be honest in disclosing whatever assumptions he or she is making so that the common agents can evaluate whether they wish to share these assumptions. If the special agent violates the five contingencies and, thus, renders the text or the Author or authors marginal by usurping or freezing (closing) their role, the special agent has become authoritarian and not authoritative.

Now, assume that the special agent studies the "just cause" exception to the sanctity of life in the Qur'ānic verse quoted above. The special agent confronts the issue of apostasy in Islam and is aware of the Qur'ānic verse that states that there is no compulsion in religion. She or he is also aware of the Qur'ānic verse that states: "Say, the truth is from your Lord so let who wills believe and let who wills not believe, for the wrongdoers We have prepared Hellfire."[43] The special agent is also aware of other Qur'ānic verses that affirm that belief or the lack of it is a matter of choice.[44] After studying the issue of apostasy further, the agent realizes that there is a tradition attributed to the Prophet that states, "Whoever changes his religion, kill him,"[45] and that the vast majority of scholars declared the tradition to be authentic. Furthermore, the vast majority of jurists held that a Muslim who converts to another religion must be executed.[46] Some contemporary jurists have objected to this rule, but they remain in the minority.[47] The special agent examines the arguments of the minority view but does not find them persuasive. Furthermore, it would have been possible for the special agent to adopt a methodological assumption that dictates that if the Qur'ān conflicts with any Prophetic tradition, the Qur'ān prevails. Nevertheless, the special agent does not adhere to this methodology and, therefore, in his or her view, the evidence is conflicting. The special agent, dealing with the Qur'ān as the literal word of God, reflects on the meaning of the verses, not as a part of the instructions of the Principal, but as a part of his or her personal relationship with God. Pondering the normativities of God and his or her own conscience, he or she develops the conviction that, quite apart from the evidence pointing to one determination or another, the morality that guides the relationship with God would be seriously challenged if an apostate is to be executed. At this point, the special agent has two options: either to conceal his or her thought process and assumptions, and present the conclusions as the determination of Islamic law, or to disclose his or her analysis, explain the faith-based assumptions and hope that some or all of the common agents will share these convictions. Of course, the latter runs the risk of a loss of authoritativeness and influence because the common agents might conclude that the special agent is no longer entitled to their trust. Nonetheless, this is the nature of a dynamic that eschews authoritarianism. The authoritarian special agent will want to remain in power, and to remain authoritative even at the cost of misrepresenting the textual evidence or at the cost of impersonating the Principal. The early jurist Wakīʿ is reported to have said: "The people of knowledge (the scholars) document all the evidence [on a matter], whether pro or con. The people of whim, however, document only the evidence that supports their position [and ignore the rest]."[48] I think that this statement nicely captures the notion of the authoritarian.

*NOTES*

1 See Eco, *Interpretation and Overinterpretation*, p. 7; Binder and Weisberg, *Literary Criticisms of Law*, p. 119; Stone, "Christian Praxis," p. 114.

2 Vining, *The Authoritative and the Authoritarian*. Vining's book is a bit esoteric and difficult to follow in parts, but interestingly he notes the similarity between the types of assumptions and premises theologians and lawyers make when addressing a point of theology or law.

3 Michels, *Political Parties*, esp. pp. 342–356.

4 Qur'ān, 33:59.

5 Qur'ān, 24:31.

6 Ibn Rushd, *Bidāyat al-Mujtahid*, 1:156–158; Abū Muḥammad ʿAbd Allāh b. Aḥmad b. Muḥammad b. Qudāmah, *al-Mughnī*, 1:601–602; Abū ʿAbd Allāh Muḥammad b. Muḥammad b. ʿAbd al-Raḥmān al-Maghribī al-Ḥaṭṭāb al-Raʿīnī, *Mawāhib al-Jalīl li Sharḥ Mukhtaṣar Khalīl*, 2:177–194; Shams al-Dīn Muḥammad b. Abī al-ʿAbbās Aḥmad b. Ḥamzah b. Shihāb al-Dīn al-Anṣārī al-Ramlī, *Nihāyat al-Muḥtāj ilā Sharḥ al-Minhāj fi al-Fiqh ʿalā Madhhab al-Imām al-Shāfiʿī*, 2:5–8; Abū Bakr Muḥammad b. Aḥmad al-Shāshī al-Qaffāl, *Ḥulyat al-ʿUlamāʾ fī Maʿrifat Madhāhib al-Fuqahāʾ*, 2:61–68; Abū Jaʿfar Muḥammad b. al-Ḥasan b. ʿAlī al-Ṭūsī, *al-Mabsūṭ fī Fiqh al-Imāmiyyah*, 1:87–89; Abou El Fadl, "Corrupting God's Book," in *Conference of the Books*, pp. 289–302.

7 According to Orientalist scholars such as Schacht, Muslim jurists of the 4th/10th century considered all questions of law to have been resolved, and thereby forestalled any further use of independent reasoning in matters of law. Rather, according to Schacht, Muslim jurists were to adhere (*taqlīd*) to the precedent established by their predecessors. Schacht, *Introduction*, pp. 69–72. See also, Coulson, *History*, pp. 80–82. This view held considerable sway throughout the twentieth century, even among Muslim writers on Islamic law. See, for example, Kamali, *Principles*, pp. 5, 171, 386; Maḥmaṣānī, *Falsafat al-Tashrīʿ*, p. 183. However, Hallaq has convincingly refuted the idea that the capacity to engage in *ijthād* was ever curtailed. Rather, he argues that the closing of *ijthād* involved debates concerning whether a *mujtahid* must be in existence at all times. Hallaq, "Was the Gate of Ijtihād Closed?"; Ali-Karamali and Dunne, "The Ijtihad Controversy," pp. 247–248.

8 Al-Juwaynī, *Kitāb al-Ijtihād*, p. 64.

9 Eco, *The Open Work*, pp. 1–23.

10 Eco, *The Limits of Interpretation*, pp. 13, 41.

11 See Qur'ān, 2:255, 24:35, 24:58–9, 46:23, 67:26.

12 Qur'ān, 6:115. Qur'ān commentators have assumed that this verse means that no one will be able to physically corrupt the Book of God. See, al-Zamakhsharī, *al-Kashshāf*, 2:46; al-Qurṭubī, *al-Jāmiʿ* (1993), 7:47; al-Ṭabarī, *Tafsīr al-Ṭabarī*, 3:334–335; Ibn Kathīr, *Mukhtaṣar Tafsīr Ibn Kathīr*, 1:610–611; al-Suyūṭī and al-Maḥalī, *Tafsīr al-Jalālayn*, p. 188; Ḥijāzī, *al-Tafsīr al-Wāḍiḥ*, 1:288.

13 Qur'ān, 12:76. This verse can also be read to say that everyone endowed with knowledge is the One more knowing.

14 Interestingly, Ibn Nujaym (d. 970/1562) contends that non-prophets cannot understand or attain the Divine Will, but properly qualified jurists do have that ability. Zayn al-ʿĀbidīn b. Ibrāhīm b. Nujaym, *al-Ashbāh wa al-Naẓāʾir*, p. 389.

15 See al-Baṣrī, *al-Muʿtamad* (1983), 2:370–372; ʿAbd al-ʿAzīz b. Aḥmad al-Bukhārī, *Kashf al-Asrār*, 4:30–55; Abū Ḥāmid al-Ghazālī, *al-Mustaṣfā*, 2:363–367; al-Juwaynī, *Kitāb al-Ijtihād*, pp. 26–32; Ibn Ḥazm, *al-Iḥkām*, 5:68–81, 8:589–592; Ibn al-Najjār, *Sharḥ al-Kawkab al-Munīr*, 4:488–492; al-Khaṭīb al-Baghdādī, *Kitāb al-Faqīh*, pp. 245–250; Abū al-Thanāʾ Maḥmūd b. Zayd al-Lāmishī, *Kitāb fī Uṣūl al-Fiqh*, pp. 201–202; al-Qarāfī, *Sharḥ Tanqīḥ al-Fuṣūl*, pp. 438–441; Fakhr al-Dīn al-Rāzī, *al-Maḥṣūl* (1997), 6:29–36; al-Shawkānī, *Irshād al-Fuḥūl*, pp. 383–389; al-Shīrāzī, *Sharḥ al-Lumʿah*, 2:1043–1071; *idem*, *al-Tabṣirah*, pp. 496–508. In this context, Muslim jurists also debated a report attributed to the Prophet in which he says, "whoever performs *ijtihād* and is correct will be rewarded twice and whoever is wrong will be rewarded once." See, al-Suyūṭī, *Ikhtilāf al-Madhāhib*, p. 38. Ibn Ḥazm, *al-Iḥkām*, 5:73–74, 8:591; *idem*, *al-Nubadh fī Uṣūl al-Fiqh al-Ẓāhirī*, pp. 119–120; Ibn al-Qaṣṣār, *al-Muqaddimah fī al-Uṣūl*, pp. 114–115; al-Kalūzānī, *al-Tamhīd*, 4:317–318; al-Qarāfī, *Sharḥ Tanqīḥ al-Fuṣūl*, p. 440; Abū ʿAbd Allāh Muḥammad b. Idrīs al-Shāfiʿī, *al-Risālah*, p. 494; al-Shīrāzī, *al-Tabṣirah*, p. 499; al-Asmandī, *Badhl al-Naẓar*, pp. 702–703.

16 See, for example, al-Khaṭīb al-Baghdādī, *Kitāb al-Faqīh wa al-Mutafaqqih*, p. 248; al-Asmandī, *Badhl al-Naẓar*, pp. 703–704; al-Baṣrī, *al-Muʿtamad* (1983), 2:383–384; Abū Ḥāmid al-Ghazālī, *al-Mustaṣfā*, 2:371–372; al-Kalūzānī, *al-Tamhīd*, 4:325–326; al-Juwaynī, *Kitāb al-Ijtihād*, p. 42.

17 For discussions of the two schools, see, ʿAbd al-ʿAzīz b. Aḥmad al-Bukhārī, *Kashf al-Asrār*, 4:18; Abū Ḥāmid Muḥammad b. Muḥammad al-Ghazālī, *al-Mankhūl min Taʿlīqāt al-Uṣūl*, p. 455; *idem*, *al-Mustaṣfā*, 2:550–551; Fakhr al-Dīn al-Rāzī, *al-Maḥṣūl* (1988), 2:500–508; al-Qarāfī, *Sharḥ Tanqīḥ al-Fuṣūl*, p. 438; al-Zuḥaylī, *al-Wasīṭ*, pp. 638–655; Ḥasab Allāh, *Uṣūl al-Tashrīʿ*, pp. 82–83; Badrān, *Uṣūl al-Fiqh*, p. 474.

18 Al-Shāfiʿī, *al-Risālah*, pp. 499–500; al-Asnawī, *al-Tamhīd*, pp. 533–534.

19 Al-Juwaynī, *Kitāb al-Ijtihād*, pp. 50–51.

20 Al-Juwaynī, *Kitāb al-Ijtihād*, p. 61.

21 Al-Āmidī, *al-Iḥkām* (1402 A.H.), 4:183; al-Asnawī, *al-Tamhīd*, pp. 531–534; al-Badakhshī, *Sharḥ al-Badakhshī*, 3:275–281; Abū Ḥāmid al-Ghazālī, *al-Mustaṣfā*, 2:375–378; al-Juwaynī, *Kitāb al-Ijtihād*, p. 41; al-Lāmishī, *Kitāb fī Uṣūl al-Fiqh*, pp. 202–203; al-Qarāfī, *Sharḥ Tanqīḥ al-Fuṣūl*, p. 440; Fakhr al-Dīn al-Rāzī, *al-Maḥṣūl* (1997), 6:34–35, 6:43–50; Shaʿbān, *Uṣūl al-Fiqh al-Islāmī*, pp. 418–419; Badrān, *Uṣūl al-Fiqh*, p. 474; al-Zuḥaylī, *al-Wasīṭ*, p. 643.

22 Al-Juwaynī, *Kitāb al-Ijtihād*, pp. 36–38. Al-Juwaynī is not arguing that the only morality is the morality of the process or that there are no ultimate truths. It should be recalled that he argues that as to the fundamentals or *uṣūl*, there are ultimate truths. As to the *furūʿ*, the ultimate morality is that of the process. I disagree with al-Juwaynī's definition of *uṣūl* and *furūʿ*. See also al-Badakhshī, *Sharḥ al-Badakhshī*, 3:274–5 who discusses similar examples.

23 See al-Baṣrī, *al-Muʿtamad* (1983), 2:375; al-Kalūzānī, *al-Tamhīd*, 4:309; al-Lāmishī, *Kitāb fī Uṣūl al-Fiqh*, p. 202; Fakhr al-Dīn al-Rāzī, *al-Maḥṣūl* (1997), 6:53; Abū Ḥāmid al-Ghazālī, *al-Mustaṣfā*, 2:359; al-Dībānī, *al-Minhāj al-Wāḍiḥ*, p. 355.

24 Al-Āmidī, *al-Iḥkām* (1402 A.H.), 4:180–182; al-Dībānī, *al-Minhāj al-Wāḍiḥ*, p. 355; Abū Ḥāmid al-Ghazālī, *al-Mustaṣfā*, 2:63; Ibn al-Najjār, *Sharḥ al-Kawkab al-Munīr*, 4:488; Ibn al-Qaṣṣār, *al-Muqaddimah*, p. 114.

25 Al-Juwaynī, *Kitāb al-Ijtihād*, p. 25, al-Khaṭīb al-Baghdādī, *Kitāb al-Faqīh wa al-Mutafaqqih*, pp. 250–251; al-Shahrastānī, *al-Milal wa al-Niḥal*, 1:238; al-Shīrāzī, *al-Tabṣirah*, pp. 401–402; *idem*, *Sharḥ al-Lumʿah*, 2:1043–1044; al-ʿUkbarī, *Risālah fī Uṣūl al-Fiqh*, pp. 128–129; al-Āmidī, *al-Iḥkām* (1402 A.H.), 4:178; al-Asmandī, *Badhl al-Naẓar*, pp. 694–695; Abū Ḥāmid al-Ghazālī, *al-Mustaṣfā*, 2:359–363; Ibn al-Najjār, *Sharḥ al-Kawkab al-Munīr*, 4:488, 490; al-Shawkānī, *Irshād al-Fuḥūl*, pp. 383–385; al-Zuḥaylī, *al-Wasīṭ*, pp. 638–641.

26 The Ashʿarī school of theology is attributed to Abū al-Ḥasan ʿAlī b. Ismāʿīl al-Ashʿarī (d. 324/935–6). Originally a student of Muʿtazilī rationalism, al-Ashʿarī broke from its teachings, and formulated a theological view that effectively steered a middle course between the rationalism of Muʿtazilism and the anti-rationalism of the Traditionists.

However, he used rational argument to uphold the orthodox doctrine espoused by the Traditionists and argue against Muʿtazilī positions, such as the createdness of the Qur'ān. Al-Shahrastānī, *al-Milal wa al-Niḥal*, 1:106–118; Fakhry, *Islamic Philosophy*, pp. 204–209; Watt, *Formative Period*, pp. 303–312; *idem*, "al-Ashʿariyya," in *Encyclopaedia of Islam*, 1:694–695. Another theological school, the Māturīdī school, critiqued many Ashʿarī and Muʿtazilī theological positions, although its rationalism brought it closer to Muʿtazilī thought than Ashʿarī doctrine. Little is known about the early history of this school. Importantly, though, its eponymn, Abū Manṣūr al-Māturīdī (d. 333/944), is reported to have studied Ḥanafī law. Not suprisingly, many Ḥanafīs adhered to this school of theology. Furthermore, with the Seljuq and Ottoman patronage of the Ḥanafī *madhhab* in the eleventh and twelfth centuries, the Māturīdī theological school gained greater prominence, and during the Mamlūk period became widely recognized as the second orthodox school of *kalām* besides the Ashʿariyyah. Weiss, *Spirit of Islamic Law*, pp. 35–37; Watt, *Formative Period*, pp. 312–316; W. Madelung, "al-Māturīdī," 6:846–847; *idem*, "Māturīdiyya," 6:847–848.

27 Furthermore, some Shīʿī scholars became certified as Ḥanafī or Shāfiʿī jurists. Some scholars argued that Rationalist scholars became Ḥanafī jurists and Shīʿī scholars became Shāfiʿī or Ḥanafī as a matter of dissimulation (*taqiyyah*). Arguably, by becoming members of orthodox Sunnī juristic schools of thought, these scholars could conceal their theological positions. Stewart, *Islamic Legal Orthodoxy*, pp. 61–109; Makdisi, *Rise of Colleges*, p. 8.

28 Abou El Fadl, "Islamic Law of Rebellion," p. 327.

29 Zakariyyā al-Birrī, *Uṣūl al-Fiqh al-Islāmī*, 1:144–146; al-Zuḥaylī, *al-Wasīṭ*, pp. 500–501; Badrān, *Uṣūl al-Fiqh*, pp. 434–435; Ḥasab Allāh, *Uṣūl al-Tashrīʿ*, pp. 260–263; Shaʿbān, *Uṣūl al-Fiqh al-Islāmī*, pp. 381–385; Kamali, *Principles*, pp. 271–272; Hallaq, *Islamic Legal Theories*, pp. 168–169. A rule of basic necessity (*ḍarūrī*) upholds the five basic values of the law (*maqāṣid al-sharīʿah*), namely life, religion, rational capacity, lineage, and property. So for example, a rule of necessity would include the prohibition against consumption of alcohol, by which one's rational capacity (*ʿaql*) is preserved. A rule of basic need (*ḥājī*), which generally removes significant hardship, would include rules such as allowing a traveler to shorten his prayer when away from his home. The final category involves those rules which enhance one's aesthetic sensibilities, such as rules of etiquette concerning hygiene and table manners. Importantly, my use of the phrase "normative value" is distinct from this taxonomy of legal values found in Islamic legal theory. Rather this taxonomy is specific to certain aspects of Islamic jurisprudence, and is itself a product of historical development. My use of "normative value" is meant to capture in a historically unspecific sense legally recognized values by which normative inquiries are propelled.

30 Abū Ḥāmid al-Ghazālī, *al-Mustaṣfā*, 1:286–287; Fakhr al-Dīn al-Rāzī, *al-Maḥṣūl* (1997), 5:159–160; al-Shāṭibī, *al-Muwāfaqāt*, 2:7–8; al-Qarāfī, *Sharḥ Tanqīḥ al-Fuṣūl*, p. 391; Abū Zahrah, *Uṣūl al-Fiqh*, pp. 291–293; Shaʿbān, *Uṣūl al-Fiqh al-Islāmī*, p. 382; al-Zuḥaylī, *al-Wasīṭ*, pp. 500–501; Kamali, *Principles*, pp. 271–273.

31 Al-Asʿadī, *al-Mūjaz fī Uṣūl al-Fiqh*, p. 247; Badrān, *Uṣūl al-Fiqh*, pp. 430–431; al-Birrī, *Uṣūl al-Fiqh al-Islāmī*, pp. 144–145; al-Zuḥaylī, *al-Wasīṭ*, pp. 498–499; Abū Zahrah, *Uṣūl al-Fiqh*, pp. 291–293; Ḥasab Allāh, *Uṣūl al-Tashrīʿ*, p. 260; Shaʿbān, *Uṣūl al-Fiqh al-Islāmī*, pp. 382–384; Kamali, *Principles*, pp. 271–272.

32 See Balīq, *Minhāj al-Ṣāliḥīn*, p. 38.

33 On the Satanic Verses incident, see al-Ṭabarī, *Tafsīr al-Ṭabarī*, 5:331–332; al-Qurṭubī, *al-Jāmiʿ* (1993), 12:53–57; al-Zamakhsharī, *al-Kashshāf*, 3:18–19; Sayyid Quṭb, *Fī Ẓilāl al-Qur'ān*, 4:2431–2433; Ḥijāzī, *al-Tafsīr al-Wāḍiḥ*, 2:74–75; Shahab Ahmed, "Ibn Taymiyyah and the Satanic Verses," *Studia Islamica* 2 (1998): pp. 67–124.

34 On those who contested the ʿUraynah incident, see al-Suyūṭī, *al-Durr al-Manthūr fī al-Tafsīr bi al-Maʾthūr*, 2:305–306; ʿImād al-Dīn Abū al-Fidā' b. ʿUmar b. Kathīr, *Tafsīr al-Qur'ān al-ʿAẓīm*, 2:56–58; al-Jaṣṣāṣ, *Aḥkām al-Qur'ān*, 2:407–408; Aḥmad b. Muḥammad al-Ṣāwī, *Ḥāshiyat al-ʿAllāmah al-Ṣāwī ʿalā Tafsīr al-Jalālayn*, 1:208; al-Alūsī, *Rūḥ al-Maʿānī fī Tafsīr al-Qur'ān al-ʿAẓīm wa al-Sabʿ al-Mathānī*, 6:121–122; Abū Jaʿfar Muḥammad b. Jarīr

al-Ṭabarī, *Jāmiʿ al-Bayān fī Tafsīr al-Qurʾān*, 5:134–135; ʿImād al-Dīn b. Muḥammad al-Ṭibāʾī al-Kiyā al-Harrāsī, *Aḥkām al-Qurʾān*, 3:65; Abū Bakr Muḥammad b. ʿAbd Allāh b. al-ʿArabī, *Aḥkām al-Qurʾān*, 2:594; Abū ʿAbd Allāh Muḥammad b. Aḥmad al-Anṣārī al-Qurṭubī, *al-Jāmiʿ li Aḥkām al-Qurʾān*, 6:149–150; ʿAbd al-Raḥmān b. Muḥammad b. Makhlūf al-Thaʿālibī, *al-Jawāhir al-Ḥisān fī Tafsīr al-Qurʾān*, 1:459; Quṭb al-Dīn Saʿīd b. Hibbat Allāh al-Rāwandī, *Fiqh al-Qurʾān*, 1:366. Notably, al-Zaylaʿī and Ibn al-Humām assert that the Prophet never crucified anyone. al-Zaylaʿī, *Tabyīn al-Ḥaqāʾiq*, 3:237; Kamāl al-Dīn Muḥammad b. ʿAbd al-Wāḥid b. al-Humām, *Fatḥ al-Qadīr*, 5:407–409. See also, Abū al-Ḥasan ʿAlī b. Muḥammad b. Ḥabīb al-Māwardī, *al-Nukat wa al-ʿUyūn*, 2:33; al-Sayyid Muḥammad Ḥusayn al-Ṭabaʾṭabāʾī, *al-Mīzān fī Tafsīr al-Qurʾān*, 5:333. Regarding the treatment afforded to ʿAlī b. Abī Ṭālib's assassin, Ibn Muljim, see, Abū al-Ḥasan ʿAlī b. al-Ḥusayn b. ʿAlī al-Masʿūdī, *Murūj al-Dhahab wa Maʿādin al-Jawhar*, 1:609; Abū al-Ḥasan ʿAlī b. Abī al-Karam b. ʿAbd al-Waḥīd b. al-Athīr, *al-Kāmil fī al-Taʾrīkh*, 3:258; Ibn al-Jawzī, *al-Muntaẓam*, 5:175; Jamāl al-Dīn Abū al-Faraj ʿAbd al-Raḥmān b. ʿAlī b. al-Jawzī, *Tablīs Iblīs*, p. 130; Zayn al-Dīn ʿUmar b. Muẓaffar b. al-Wardī, *Taʾrīkh Ibn al-Wardī*, 1:155; Abū Muḥammad Aḥmad b. Aʿtham, *al-Futūḥ*, 2:281, 284.

35 See Qurʾān, 16:89, 17:9, 17:41, 17:82, 29:47, 41:2–3, 47:24

36 See Izutsu, *Ethico-Religious Concepts*, pp. 184–202. Izutsu also argues that aside from the Qurʾānic context, one can adopt a conceptualization of God that is distinguished by the approach he adopts, whether theological, mystical, or philosophical. Izutsu, *God and Man*, pp. 45–52.

37 See, for example, al-Lāmishī, *Kitāb fī Uṣūl al-Fiqh*, pp. 66–68; Al-Juwaynī, *al-Burhān*, pp. 8–14; Abū Ḥāmid al-Ghazālī, *al-Mustaṣfā*, 1:55–61; Fakhr al-Dīn al-Rāzī, *al-Maḥṣūl* (1997), 1:105–109; ʿAbd al-ʿAzīz b. Aḥmad al-Bukhārī, *Kashf al-Asrār*, 1:389–446; Abū al-Ḥusayn Muḥammad b. ʿAlī b. al-Ṭayyib al-Baṣrī, *Kitāb al-Muʿtamad fī Uṣūl al-Fiqh*, 1:177–180; Badrān, *Uṣūl al-Fiqh*, pp. 15–16; Muḥammad Maʿrūf al-Dawālībī, *Madkhal ilā ʿIlm Uṣūl al-Fiqh*, pp. 166–173.

38 The theological dispute over *ḥusn* and *qubḥ* concerns whether good and evil are subject to rational inquiry or are determined only by text. The rationalist Muʿtazilīs adhered to the view that through the use of reason, one can arrive at an understanding of good and evil. On the other hand, their opponents, such as the Ashʿarīs and traditionist Ḥanbalīs, argued that good and evil are determined by revelation. God alone determines good and evil, and to hold otherwise would deny God's authority. The implications of this theological dispute extend to conceptions of law and justice. For instance, the Muʿtazilīs, who called themselves the Partisans of Justice and Oneness (*ahl al-ʿadl wa al-tawḥīd*), argued that God only upholds that which is just. Further, they argued that justice on earth is known through reason. Therefore, if one asserts that performing a particular act is just as a matter of reason, it thereby becomes the law of God, albeit an approximation of Divine justice. The Ashʿarīs and traditionists, however, would argue that the law of God is established by revelation. The fact that a particular act is commanded or prohibited by revelation is what makes the legal outcome just. See, Khadduri, *Islamic Conception*, pp. 39–77; Leaman, *An Introduction to Medieval Islamic Philosophy*, pp. 123–165; Hourani, "Divine Justice and Human Reason," pp. 73–83. See also Reinhart, *Before Revelation*.

39 The Islamic law of rebellion is very complex and it is debatable whether she would fall under the purview of the law of rebellion, but, in my opinion, she should be covered by the protections of the Islamic law of rebellion. In my view, conscientious objection should be treated with great leniency under Islamic law. See, Abou El Fadl, "Islamic Law of Rebellion"; *idem*, "Political Crime," pp. 1–28.

40 Arguably, under the classical law, this woman would be declared a *nāshiz* (disobedient or defiant). If one rejects the Shāfiʿī doctrine of *ṭāʿah*, which could compel this woman to return to her husband's household, this woman might be entitled to a *khulʿ* (a form of divorce according to which she returns her dowry or pays a sum of money in return for divorce). However, classical jurists disagree on whether the consent of the husband is necessary in order to obtain a *khulʿ*. Furthermore, the husband, according to some schools,

may demand a higher amount than the amount of the dowry. For the sake of argument, I am assuming that this woman would not be entitled to *khulʿ*, which is the result that I believe would be supported by most classical schools of thought.

41 For another example, see my treatment of the Qurʾānic verse on the beating of women. Abou El Fadl, "On the Beating of Wives" *Conference of the Books*, pp. 167–176; *idem*, "The Beating of Wives Revisited," *Conference of the Books*, pp. 177–188.

42 Qurʾān, 6:151.

43 Qurʾān, 18:29.

44 Other Qurʾānic verses emphasize that if God would have willed God would have made all human beings believe or made all humans a single nation, but God had given human beings the choice to believe or not believe. See Qurʾān, 5:48, 6:35, 6:107, 10:99, 11:118, 16:93, 18:29, 42:8, 74:55, 76:29, 80:12, 81:28, 88:22.

45 See, for instance, Ibn Ḥajar al-ʿAsqalānī, *Fatḥ al-Bārī* (n.d.), 6:149–151; 12:267–275, 13:339–344; al-Mubārakfūrī, *Tuḥfat al-Aḥwadhī*, 5:20–21; al-Suyūṭī, *Sharḥ Sunan al-Nasāʾī*, 7:103–106; Shams al-Dīn Abī ʿAbd Allāh Muḥammad b. Abī Bakr b. Qayyim al-Jawziyyah, *ʿAwn al-Maʿbūd Sharḥ Sunan Abī Dāwūd*, 12:3–14.

46 On the law of apostasy, see Ibrāhīm b. Muḥammad b. Sālim b. Ḍawayyān, *Manār al-Sabīl fī Sharḥ al-Dalīl*, 3:285–291; Abū al-Ḥasan ʿAlī b. Abī Bakr b. ʿAbd al-Jalīl al-Marghīnānī, *al-Hidāyah Sharḥ Bidāyat al-Mubtadī*, 2:164–170; al-Bahūtī, *al-Rawḍ al-Murbiʿ*, pp. 681–684; Abū ʿAbd Allāh Muḥammad b. Idrīs al-Shāfiʿī, *Kitāb al-Umm*, 6:168–184; Abū Ḥāmid Muḥammad b. Muḥammad al-Ghazālī, *al-Wajīz fī Fiqh al-Imām al-Shāfiʿī*, 2:165–166; al-Shīrāzī, *al-Muhadhdhab*, 3:255–261; Abū al-Walīd Muḥammad b. Aḥmad al-Qurṭubī b. Rushd, *al-Muqaddimāt al-Mumahhidāt*, 3:227–238; al-Ṭūsī, *al-Mabsūṭ*, 7:281–290, 8:71–74.

47 See, for example, Muḥammad Rashīd Riḍā, *Tafsīr al-Qurʾān al-Ḥakīm al-Shahīr bi Tafsīr al-Manār*, 5:324–325; Shaltūt, *al-Islām*, pp. 280–281; Abdullahi Ahmad An-Naʿim, *Toward an Islamic Reformation*, pp. 108–109; Majid Khadduri, *Islamic Conception*, p. 238; Mohamed S. El-Awa, *Punishment in Islamic Law*, pp. 49–56, 61–64.

48 "*Ahl al-ʿilm yaktubūn mā lahum wa mā ʿalayhim wa ahl al-ahwāʾ lā yaktubūn illā mā lahum.*" ʿAlī b. ʿUmar al-Dārquṭnī, *Sunan al-Dārquṭnī*, 1:19.

# 6 The anatomy of authoritarian discourses

## *The demise of the juristic tradition*

Islamic law has staunchly resisted codification or uniformity, at least until the contemporary age. The earmark of traditional Islamic methodology has been its open-ended and anti-authoritarian character. Fundamental to this character was an evolutionary process of exploration, investigation, and adjudication that, according to its own inner logic, resisted settlement or inertia. The law of God was fully embodied in the search for God's law. Islamic law consisted of a set of methodological approaches, normative principles, and positive commandments that were in a constant state of evolvement. As such, traditional Islamic law resembled, somewhat, the common law legal system. However, jurists and not judges developed the positive commandments of Islamic law. Jurists systematically incorporated and integrated the adjudications of judges into the normative legal system. Of course, many jurists served as judges, but not all judges performed the role of jurists. In all cases, it is those who performed the role of scholarly or academic jurists who undertook the systematic and comprehensive development of the law. Importantly, the jurists treated the positive legal commandments as default rules that were developed from factual scenarios that were stated as hypotheticals. Default rules meant that hypothetically, everything being equal, rule *y* would apply in situation *x*. But the jurists were not articulating these rules as positive commandments that were ready-made for implementation. The hypothetical situation would rarely exist in actuality. Rather, the judge and the *muftī* (jurist issuing a *responsum* or *fatwā*) would evaluate the particulars of a certain case or situation in light of the jurisprudential and methodological principles, and scholarly hypotheticals, and a fact-specific adjudication or *fatwā* would be issued. Whether the *fatwā* would serve as a normative precedent would depend on its scholarly usefulness, uniqueness, and educative quality. A single notable case or set of cases would be transformed, through juristic efforts, into a hypothetical yielding a positive rule in an ongoing process of development. Most significantly, this process, and its supporting epistemology, is now largely defunct.

As a set of positive commandments (*aḥkām*), Islamic law is alive and well in the contemporary age. In other words, if Islamic law consists of a set of rules then, by that measure, Islamic law is thriving in the present age. The annals of modern Islamic law are full of rules and there are plenty of Muslims willing to implement them faithfully. But as an epistemology, process, and methodology of understanding and searching, as a *fiqh*, Islamic law, for the most part, is dead.[1] Contemporary applications of Islamic law tend to treat the law as a settled, constant, and closed set of rules (*aḥkām*), which are to be implemented without much possibility for development or variation. Put differently, Islamic law exists in the present age as a set of *aḥkām*, and not as a process of *fiqh*. Although there have been consistent calls for the re-kindling of *ijtihād* (legal innovations) since the beginning of this century, such calls have missed the point.[2] Typically, calls for the re-kindling of *ijtihād* have focused on the need for the production of new rules or *aḥkām*. Without the reinvigoration of the necessary epistemological foundations, such calls yielded very little other than some new positive commands that lacked the necessary conceptual justifications.[3] Rules, by themselves, do not form a legal system, and they do not form a critical process capable of supporting a creative intellectual discourse. In effect, the contemporary *ijtihād* process arbitrarily and despotically replaced old rules with new ones without setting out a methodology for further development and even without the expectation of an evolving discourse. The product of the new *ijtihād* efforts often read like a codified set of rules that had little to do with the traditional methodological processes of Islamic jurisprudence. Essentially, contemporary *ijtihād* efforts often were the product of an authoritarian process that yielded closed determinations, which effectively signaled the death of the same legal system that the *ijtihād* efforts hoped to reinvigorate. The usual process, if one can call it a process, of this code-like new *ijtihād* largely consisted of citing some anecdotal evidence or selective reports attributed to the Prophet, and then declaring the law of God to be such-or-such.[4] So for instance, if a new *ijtihādist* wanted to argue that women have a right to engage in the political process, he or she would cite the report of the woman who argued with the caliph ʿUmar b. al-Khaṭṭāb regarding placing a cap on the price of dowries. After noting that the woman won the debate and ʿUmar admitted that he was at fault, the new *ijtihādist* would declare whatever rule he or she was seeking to support.[5] If the new *ijtihādist* wanted to argue that women have a right to divorce their husbands without restrictions, he or she would cite the report of the woman who complained to the Prophet that her father forced her to marry a particular man, and that the Prophet gave her the right to revoke the marriage.[6] Interestingly, it is rare to find a new *ijtihādist* who would be bothered by contrary or conflicting evidence. So, for instance, the persuasive authority of the two traditions mentioned above is challenged by contrary evidence, but the deductions of new *ijtihādists* were unabashedly result-oriented and disingenuously selective. The proponents of this style of *ijtihād* often consisted of modern apologists or reformers anxious to prove that Islamic law is capable of addressing all contemporary challenges.[7] However, the modern *ijtihāds* shared little with the traditional methodologies of Islamic jurisprudence, and, in my opinion, were most certainly not an improvement upon these traditional methodologies either. If anything, they denied Islamic law any sense of integrity, seriousness, or viability in the modern age. In many ways, Islamic law became the playing field for shabby scholarship, political sloganism, and ideological demagogues. Often the advocates of the new *ijtihād* were political and social Islamic activists who enjoyed a minimal degree of training in the Islamic scholastic tradition, and who reconstructed Islamic law into a set of highly simplified and dogmatic commands. Pursuant to these, so-called, reformative formulations, Islamic law became a poorly justified and non-persuasive set of rules, and not a methodology for an open process of discourse and determination.

There is little doubt that part of the reason for the breakdown of the methodologies of traditional Islamic law was the dissipation of the traditional institutional and sociological structures that supported classical Islamic jurists. The process of institutional deterioration included a variety of elements such as colonialism and the reception of the Civil Law system into Muslim territories, the nationalization of Islamic *awqāf* (charitable trusts), and the spread and prevalence of secular schools of law. A full study of the reasons for what I called the death of traditional Islamic law would have to analyze a variety of other socio-historical and economic reasons. Nonetheless, documenting the transformations in the practice of Islamic law in the contemporary age requires a separate study.[8] In the context of the present study, I will demonstrate only a part of the story of modern Islamic law, but I will not focus on the dynamics of the *ijtihāds* of the modernists or reformers. As I noted in the beginning of this book, the influence of the modernists or reformers has been receding in the present age. The, at times, justified suspicion that such reformers are apologists or Westernizers, and their profoundly superficial intellectual product contributed to the erosion of their influence. More importantly, it is not clear whether these reformers are claiming to be an extension or natural growth of the Islamic legal tradition or whether they are advocating a sharp break with this tradition. In the case of some such as Rashīd Riḍā, Maḥmūd Shaltūt, *Shaykh* Muḥammad al-Ghazālī, or ʿAbd al-Ḥalīm Maḥmūd, it is clear that they claim allegiance to the inherited jurisprudential heritage while being critical of many of the conclusions of that heritage. But at the same time, these particular individuals represent the best of the reformative effort and can hardly be described as apologists, Westernizers, or demagogues. As to the majority, it is not clear whether they claim to represent an alternative to the methodologies of classical juristic tradition, and if they are, what is the alternative methodology? From the point of view of this book, the ambiguous foundations of the new *ijtihādists* make them poor candidates for study. While the likes of Rashīd Riḍā can be described as intellectually formidable, the overwhelming majority can be studied as a sociological phenomenon, but do not merit engagement at a doctrinal level.

In this chapter, I will attempt to demonstrate the conceptual framework developed thus far by analyzing what, I believe, has become the predominant approach to Islamic law in the present time. Nevertheless, whether I am correct in thinking that the approaches discussed below have become predominant is not the main point of this chapter, which is to present case studies or examples of authoritarianism that further explore the conceptual thesis presented thus far.[9] The examples below all involve a fundamental violation of the logic of special agency, and the contingencies of honesty, diligence, comprehensiveness, self-restraint, and reasonableness. In addition, the examples all result in a closed dynamic and the usurpation of the integrity and independence of the text and the Principal. Importantly, the examples involve individuals or institutions that unmistakably invoke the *Sharīʿah* to legitimate and justify their roles.

The case studies discussed below are focused on *responsa* issued by jurists who claim to represent the law of God. Most of the *responsa* are taken from The Permanent Council For Scientific Research and Legal Opinions (hereinafter, C.R.L.O), the official institution in Saudi Arabia entrusted with issuing Islamic legal opinions.[10] Other *responsa* are taken from jurists issuing legal opinions in a private capacity. All the jurists discussed are well-known in the Arabic-speaking world both at the juristic and popular level. The questions presented to these jurists arrive from different parts of the Muslim world including Egypt, Saudi Arabia, Syria, Lebanon, Jordan, the United Arab Emirates, the Sudan, Algeria, Morocco, Tunisia, Mauritania, Nigeria, Pakistan, and Indonesia. Typically, a person submits a written question, and either a council of jurists or individual jurists issue a written response. The topics addressed in the *responsa* compilations of these jurists cover all aspects of jurisprudence but the ones discussed in this chapter and that which follows are primarily focused on legal issues related to women. The legal *responsa* issued by the *Saudi Permanent Council* often serve as the basis for official state law – the Saudi government often adopts the legal opinions of the Council as the law of the land. Otherwise, the *responsa* of the jurists have persuasive authority for those who consider the opinions authoritative. Most of the legal issues dealt with here relate to women. I have focused on these issues because of their wide impact in Muslim societies. Furthermore, the *responsa* on women provide powerful demonstrative case studies in the construction of authoritarian discourses.

Nearly all the *responsa* analyzed in this chapter are by jurists who adhere in one form or another to the Wahhābī school of thought. Of course, this is not coincidental – I selected *responsa* by jurists from this particular school of thought for two distinct reasons. The first, and more important, reason is that the intellectual product of the jurists from this school epitomizes the interpretive authoritarianism that this book aims to analyze. The second reason is the one already alluded to – it is my impression that, other than Sufism, this has become the predominate school in contemporary Islam. In fact, I would go as far as to claim that the Wahhābī methodology has been transplanted to schools ideologically at odds with Wahhābism, such as Sufi schools of thought. For instance, if one examines the works of Sufis such as Nuh Ha Mim Keller or Hisham al-Kabbani, one notices that while the positive determinations are different, the methodology is substantially the same.[11] In the methodology of individuals not affiliated with the Wahhābī school one finds that all legal problems yield a definitive, singular determination in which the law of God is searched, discovered and clearly asserted for all times to come. Put differently, one notices that the earmark of contemporary approaches to Islamic law, whether Wahhābī or anti-Wahhābī, is the certainty of results, incontrovertibility of conclusions, and the unequivocalness of the asserted determinations.[12] The end result is that the subtlety and richness of the Islamic legal heritage is largely absent in the contemporary age.

A difficulty raised by the *responsa* of the Wahhābī jurists is that, like the reformers mentioned above, the Wahhābīs are ambiguous towards the classical juristic tradition. Like the reformers, the Wahhābīs championed the idea of *ijtihād* and rejected the notion of blind obedience (*taqlīd*) to any particular juristic tradition. The Wahhābīs, and the Salafī movement,[13] insisted on the right to return to the original sources of the Qur'ān and *Sunnah* and to re-interpret the traditions without being bound by the "mistakes" of the past. The Wahhābīs, Salafīs, and reformers rejected the notion of fidelity to specific legal schools and argued that there is no reason why a Muslim should be obligated to limit himself to a particular set of determinations.[14] In fact, it is appropriate, they argued, to choose and mix between the various schools in order to reach the most prudent and useful results.[15] This practice is known as *talfīq*. Importantly, the basic idea was one of liberation and flexibility – by liberating oneself from the shackles of tradition, one can better confront the challenges of modernity and return to the pure and pristine Islam unburdened by all the failures of the past.[16] Of course, this approach relied on a rather arrogant premise: since the age of the rightly guided caliphs,[17] Muslims, for the most part, have miserably failed in fulfilling God's Will, and we, in the present age, can get it right if only we go back to the true and authentic Islam. This idea was well exemplified in the Wahhābī, Salafī, and reformist statement, "they were men and we are men" (*hum rijāl wa naḥnu rijāl*) which meant that if the ancestors could interpret the original sources, we could as well.[18] Naturally, as a slogan one can hardly disagree with its sagacity, but to the extent that it connoted a return to a pristine, original, and uncorrupted Islam, it proved to be entirely incoherent. This approach, besides being ahistorical, proved to be hopelessly simplistic and naive – it was impossible to return to the Qur'ān and *Sunnah* in a vacuum. For instance, a return to the

Qurʾān necessarily meant a return to classical sources that commented on the context and meaning of the verses and that explained the collection and documentation of the Qurʾānic text. Furthermore, a return to the *Sunnah* necessarily meant a return to the classical sources that compiled, authenticated, contextualized, and interpreted the traditions of the Prophet and his Companions. Furthermore, it was soon discovered that Islamic law simply does not exist without the cumulative classical tradition with its many and varied sources. For instance, Muslims know how to perform the five daily prayers, how to fast in the month of Ramadan, the meaning and connotations of the prohibition against usury, the details of criminal punishments, and many other issues, largely from the classical sources. The juristic tradition of Islam and the main sources of Islam (the Qurʾān and *Sunnah*) had become irrevocably interwoven and interlinked so that the negation of one would necessarily deconstruct the other. The material result of the purist system of thought of the Wahhābīs and Salafīs was a return to the classical tradition, but in a highly selective, unsystematic, and opportunistic fashion. The return to the classical tradition, however, was not deliberate, purposeful or perspicuous – the role of the classical tradition was not overtly and plainly dealt with, rather, the role of that tradition remained circuitous and oblique in the modern age. Effectively, this meant that the various factions within contemporary Islam would hurl opportunistically selected pieces of the tradition against each other. As a result, to date, coherent and systematic ways of talking or even thinking about the tradition have not developed. Some of the symptoms of this incoherence are manifested in the type of contradictions discussed earlier in the book. On the one hand, for instance, one finds that there is great pride taken in the idea that Islam endorses and even promotes diversity of opinions, but, on the other, one finds an insistence that disagreements are only permitted as to relatively unimportant issues relating to the branches (*furūʿ*). This is significant in light of the fact that contemporary Muslims have included more and more legal determinations under the rubric of the fundamentals of religion (*uṣūl*). On the one hand, it is often argued that Muslims should not be shackled by the juristic tradition, but on the other, that legal issues such as the veil for women are not open to discussion because the juristic tradition has reached a binding consensus on the matters. Similarly, the Islamic intellectual tradition is often treated as an aberration or corruption of the true Islam, while also being cited as an example of the civilizational promise of Islam. There is great pride taken in the idea that Islam is the religion of reason and rationality but rationalistic schools, such as the Muʿtazilah, are condemned as a corruption of the real Islam. On the one hand, it is often asserted that Islam is the religion of human intuition (*fiṭrah*), but on the other, there is a pronounced suspicion and hostility towards intuitive notions of natural rights. Also, there is an insistence on the notion that the *Sharīʿah* is capable of effectively responding to all historical circumstances, while there is at the same time, a tenacious insistence on the idea that all historical circumstances should yield and adapt themselves to the rules of *Sharīʿah*. On the one hand, Muslim scholars consistently assert that the Islamic legal system is as sophisticated and rich as any of the major legal systems of the world, but on the other, there is an unmistakable tendency to empty this legal system of all its doctrinal richness or sophistication.

The contradictions are many, but perhaps nothing sums up and exemplifies the escape from the confusions of this ambiguity better than the widespread statement in contemporary Islam that, "anyone who understands the real Islam would become a Muslim." In this fashion, the ambiguities are shifted away and distanced from Islam, itself. The real Islam is out there, and regardless of the confusions of practice, a truly intuitive, rational, and knowledgeable person would see through the confusions, and discover the pristine, unburdened, and real Islam. Thus, the conversion of the non-Muslim to Islam becomes the assurance, in fact, the extrication from the dilemmas that confront Muslims today.[19]

The contradictions and dilemmas are clearly discernable in the *responsa* discussed in this chapter. The jurists writing these *responsa*, for example, will favor one or two classical jurists over all others, but the criteria for inclusion or exclusion are never clearly articulated. Furthermore, the writers of the *responsa* repeatedly assert that they are representing the true and real Islam. As will be seen, they do not claim to represent a process or even the best interpretive efforts, but the actual law of God. In this sense, they provide good case studies in our effort to distinguish between the authoritative and authoritarian.

The jurists' claim to authoritativeness is derived from the fact that they are acting as special agents deciphering the instructions of the Principal. Their claim to authenticity is largely dependent on the assertion that they are not innovators in religion (*mubtadiʿūn fī al-dīn*), and that their opinions are representative of the *jamāʿah* (the critical mass of God-fearing Muslims or orthodoxy).[20] This dual notion of avoidance of *bidʿah* (unlawful innovations in religion) and representing the *jamāʿah* (orthodoxy) is critical to the legitimacy and authoritativeness of the legal opinions of these jurists. Significantly, both concepts are heavily dependent on the classical juristic tradition for their symbolic value. In other words, both derive their symbolic power from Islamic juristic history. To the extent that the authors of the *responsa* may be constructing a *bidʿah* or deviating from the *jamāʿah*, they are no longer representing the true or real Islam, and, therefore, are keen to position themselves as the articulators of the authentic Islamic tradition. This, of course, begs the question of what is authentic and how we define it. The dogmatic and typical response is that whatever is in accord with the Qur'ān and *Sunnah* is authentic. Nevertheless, this conceals a considerable degree of ambiguity towards the interpretive communities of the past. Furthermore, it raises the question as to whether or not the only relevant authenticity is that which is represented by the interpretive community of the authors. Put differently, the Qur'ān and *Sunnah* do not interpret themselves – they require interpretive agents that will inevitably form interpretive communities.

Hence, are the authors intimating that the only relevant, authentic and orthodox interpretive community is their own?[21] If that is, in fact, the claim of the authors, and I doubt that they would confess as much, then it is a violation of their responsibilities as special agents to fail to disclose this claim.

One final point before delving into the *responsa*. I am not as interested in the specific conclusions reached by these jurists, as I am in why they reached the conclusions they did. I cannot deny that I have chosen the *responsa* that best demonstrate the authoritarian process of construction, and that I often find the determinations of this process, to say the least, distasteful. But my point in this chapter is not to argue that the determinations of these jurists are qualitatively wrong, but to explore the dividing line between the authoritative and the authoritarian.

There are a large number of legal issues that warrant comment, but due to the limitations of time and space, I am obliged to be selective, and am not able to analyze all the legal evidence that is relevant to any specific issue. Rather, I will note only the evidence relevant to the point being argued. A reader interested in a full exposition on a particular legal topic should pursue the matter in the sources cited in this book. We will start with a discussion on some of the less legally demanding topics and progress to more complex issues.

## *Consistency*

### THE CHALLENGE OF BRASSIERES, HIGH HEELS, AND MARITAL VOWS

In a straightforward fashion, Shaykh Ibn Jibrīn[22] is asked whether the wearing of brassieres is permissible under Islamic law. Ibn Jibrīn's response is equally straightforward[23] – he asserts that some women have adopted the habit of wearing support in order to create the impression that they are either young or virgins, and if that is the case then this is a prohibited form of fraud. However, if a woman wears a brassiere for health or medical reasons, then it is permissible.[24] Apparently, if the brassiere lifts the breasts, and the intent behind wearing it is to defraud, then it is prohibited. Of course, one is left wondering if the legal principle being established here is a matter of truthful physiological disclosure then how far is the jurist willing to take this principle? But we will overlook this point. The more material issue is: who is prohibiting exactly what? Put differently, is Ibn Jibrīn contending that the instructions of the Principal include a specific intent as to brassieres? To what extent is this law derived from the instructions, the Principal or the reader? There is little doubt that fraud is illegal in Islamic law, but who is the owner of the brassiere determination?

Notably, Ibn Jibrīn does not cite any particular instructions of the Principal on brassieres or other items of clothing. There is no mention of instructions regarding turbans that make a man look taller, undergarments that make a man look well-endowed, shirts that make a man appear more muscular, or clothing that makes a man look thinner. While fraud, as a principle, is outlawed, the most honest physiological disclosure would be nudity. I do not mean to be facetious, but it is important for a jurist to explore the full implications of his argument.

Islamic sources are replete with proscriptions against fraud and misrepresentation, but none of them are on point. The most notable textual proscription, and perhaps the one Ibn Jibrīn has in mind, is the *ḥadīth* attributed to the Prophet stating, "Whoever defrauds us is not one of us." However, the context of that report has little to do with brassieres. Reportedly, the Prophet catches a merchant misrepresenting food items, and disapprovingly announces that misrepresentation of commercial items is not acceptable conduct.[25] Ibn Jibrīn does not disclose if he makes a value-based, or perhaps a faith-based, assumption that women are somehow analogous to commercial products.

Ibn Jibrīn relies on factual assumptions about the social roles of brassieres – a factual determination that is beyond his competence as a special agent. More importantly, the *responsum* is founded on value-based assumptions about the role and orientation of women – assumptions that are not disclosed, or explored. It appears that Ibn Jibrīn assumes a general intent on the part of women that is not presented to him in the inquiry posed in the question. This raises the question, what social-based values inform Ibn Jibrīn's response? The answer is that women are a constant source of *fitnah* (sexual enticement), and so everything related to the functionality of women is seen from that perspective.[26]

We observe this point more explicitly in another group of *responsa* that deal with the permissibility of women wearing high heels. These *responsa* were issued by a C.R.L.O panel, and Shaykh Ibn Bāz, Shaykh Ibn Jibrīn, and Shaykh al-ʿUthaymīn, both as members of C.R.L.O and in their individual capacity.[27] The jurists, again, hold that high heels are not permissible in Islam.[28] Among the reasons offered for the prohibition are that high heels might be unhealthy, they might be dangerous because they may cause a woman to trip and fall, high heels are fraudulent because they make a woman appear taller than her true height, and high heels cause *fitnah* because they emphasize a woman's thighs. Again, the legal methodology or instructional evidence used to reach this determination is not cited. Naturally, this raises the question of the capacity of the special agents – if these determinations are offered in a purely personal capacity and purely as a personal opinion, that fact needs to be disclosed. Put differently, we hardly need special agents to tell us whether women will trip on high heels or whether high heels will damage their spinal cords. The legally material issue is, assuming the factual determination as to the health or safety determination is established or assumed, what is the legal standard extracted from the instructions of the Principal? Are the jurists arguing that every possible source of tripping is unlawful? Are they arguing that everything that could damage the spinal cord is unlawful? Does the illegality cover bad shoes, bad posture, unhealthy seats, and some forms of slouched sitting? More importantly, the factual circumstances surrounding the incidents of high-heel wearing are, once again, tied to the issue of misrepresentation. The most troubling aspect about the normative assumptions of the jurists is the connection between the misrepresentation of a commodity, and the misrepresentation of the physical attributes of women. For instance, are the jurists assuming that women who are taller, and have larger chests, are more desirable, so that the legal cause for the prohibition is the incorrect positioning of the product?

Perhaps the jurists have reached a faith-based conclusion that the Principal does not tolerate any form of misrepresentation, whomever commits it and wherever it is committed and, therefore, our suspicions regarding their motives and assumptions are unwarranted. Perhaps this faith-based conviction has led the jurists to attempt to close all the possible means to all forms of misrepresentation. Unfortunately, our suspicions are merely confirmed when we examine how the same jurists dealt with another form of misrepresentation – this one far more serious. C.R.L.O is asked about the legality of what is known in Saudi Arabia as the *misyār* marriage, pursuant to which a man marries a woman with the intent of divorcing her after a particular period of time, but without disclosing to her his latent intent. A typical scenario would be that a man would go overseas to study. While abroad he would marry a woman with the undisclosed intent to divorce her upon the completion of his studies. Both C.R.L.O and, in separate *responsa*, Ibn Bāz determine that this marriage is lawful and does not in anyway reproach the male partner for his fraudulent behavior.[29] In fact, C.R.L.O and Ibn Bāz do not even comment on the misrepresentations that are invariably involved in this type of marriage. Rather, they note two points: one, most classical jurists agreed that this marriage is lawful, and, two, that this marriage is distinguishable from a temporary marriage (*zawāj al-mutʿah*). Temporary marriages, they contend, involve a marriage contracted for a specified and disclosed time period – two people would marry for a period of time which upon expiration, the marriage would automatically dissolve unless renewed. So, we end with an interesting result; if the temporariness of the marriage is disclosed and agreed upon, the marriage is unlawful. But if the intent to terminate is deceptively concealed at the time of marriage, the marriage is lawful. Furthermore, the C.R.L.O and Ibn Bāz misunderstand the holding of some classical Ḥanbalī jurists on this issue. Some Ḥanbalī jurists held that if only one of the parties had an intent to enter into a permanent marriage while the second party had an unlawful undisclosed intent to enter into a temporary marriage, the marriage is still valid. These Ḥanbalī jurists held that an improper motive by one of the parties does not necessarily invalidate the marriage. They did not hold that it is lawful or acceptable for one of the parties to hold a deceptive intent.[30] Interestingly, the majority of Mālikī and Ḥanbalī jurists held that an intent to enter into a temporary marriage, disclosed or undisclosed, by one or both of the parties invalidates the marriage. The majority of Ḥanafī and Shāfiʿī jurists held that an intent to enter into a temporary marriage by one of the parties, if undisclosed, is sinful but does not invalidate the marriage. These Ḥanafī and Shāfiʿī jurists argued that the legal system does not have the competence to investigate the subjective intents of the parties to a marriage, and even if the legal system did have that ability, it would be bad policy.[31]

At the very least, one can conclude that the jurists of the C.R.L.O have not adopted a general unwavering principle against misrepresentation. Some misrepresentations are unproblematic. The crucial point is that the common agents are left guessing as to how or why these determinations relate to the instructions of the Principal, and what are the methodologies and assumptions of the special agents. In fact, it is difficult to discern much of a role for the text or the author in these determinations. These *responsa* exhibit a considerable degree of lack of self-restraint, diligence, and reasonableness, and when examined in a comparative perspective one is left suspecting that there is a measure of conscious selectivity in the presentation of the evidence. As a result, the only voice that emerges in the *responsa* is the voice of the interpreter who has despotically controlled the process of determination.

## *Selectivity of evidence*

We will return below to the notion of women as a source of enticement, but for now it is necessary to explore further the practice of selectivity in the use of evidence as it relates to the role of the special agent. Selectivity in the use of evidence could violate the obligation of honesty or the obligations of diligence and comprehensiveness. If the special agent is selective in scrutinizing the evidence so that the special agent does not search the instructions, but searches for support in the instructions, that is a clear violation of the obligations of diligence and comprehensiveness. The quintessential form of selectivity in investigation is when a special agent reaches a particular determination that is in accord with his value-based assumptions, and then proceeds to bolster his determination through a selective reading of the sources. If for instance, I feel that *x* ought to be the case, and I proceed to sift through the instructions to prove that *x* is, in fact, the case, I am fulfilling the role of an advocate, not a special agent. While no special agent is capable of overcoming his subjectivities, it is important for the special agent to make a good-faith attempt to give the text and the author their due weight by restraining, to the extent possible, those subjectivities. If the special agent has a faith-based belief that she wishes to advocate, the duty of honesty requires full disclosure of the altered role of the special agent. In other words, there is nothing wrong with faith-based advocacy as long as the advocate does not misrepresent the role. Of course, as argued earlier, if faith-based convictions lead to selectivity in the investigation of evidence, such convictions run the risk of being whimsical, which, as we saw, is quite problematic in Islamic theology. Nevertheless, this is a matter that is between God and the interpreter – as far as the common agents are concerned, truthful disclosure of the faith-based conviction, and the consequent selectivity in accepting or rejecting the evidence, will discharge one's duties towards the common agents. If, however, the special agent claims not to have a faith-based conviction, and claims to discharge the role of interpreter of the instructions as he or she finds them, selective investigation of the evidence is a clear violation of the interpreter's obligations towards the common agents. As repeatedly emphasized, the earmark of the matter is the claim of authoritativeness – to the extent that one claims to be authoritative over the instructions of the Principal, one is obligated to balance his role as an interpreter against the independence of the text and the author.

Other than the problem of selective investigation, there is the separate problem of selective disclosure. If we assume that the special agent has been comprehensive and diligent in investigating the instructions of the Principal, to what extent is the special agent obligated to disclose the full range of the evidence to the common agents? Again, the response to this question largely depends on the nature of the authoritativeness claimed by the special agent. If the special agent purports to represent Islamic law or the law of God at large, then, as we argued earlier, Islamic law is inseparable from the juristic tradition. The duties of diligence, comprehensiveness, self-restraint, and honesty demand that the agent investigate the interpretive efforts of the communities that formulated the tradition of Islamic law, and truthfully to represent the conclusions of these communities. On the other hand, if the special agent does not claim to speak for the law of God in general, but claims to speak for a specific interpretive community and not any other, then the special agent is obligated to disclose the exact scope of his or her competence and representation. For instance, if the special agent claims to represent the Wahhābī or Ḥanbalī schools of thought, and only these schools of thought, then this defines the extent of his or her duty of disclosure. However, if a petitioner asks about the rule of *Sharī'ah*, and the special agent responds by disclosing only the Ḥanbalī point of view, this is a form of misrepresentation, especially if the special agent generates the impression that the Ḥanbalī point of view represents Islamic law at large.[32]

## THE ENTICEMENTS OF VISITING THE DEAD

With this background in mind, we can analyze a group of *responsa* dealing with the legality of women visiting graves. Several jurists, 'Abd Allāh b. Qa'ūd, 'Abd Allāh b. Ghidyān, 'Abd al-Razzāq 'Afīfī, 'Abd al-'Azīz b. 'Abd Allāh b. Bāz, Muḥammad al-Ṣāliḥ al-'Uthaymīn, and Ṣāliḥ b. Fawzān,[33] are asked if it is lawful for Muslims to visit the graves of deceased relatives or non-relatives, including the grave of the Prophet. Among the *responsa*, a woman states that out of love and respect for her deceased husband, she visits his grave every Thursday and performs certain religious supplications. She insists that she does not perform any of the prohibited acts such as wailing or the ripping of cloth. Again, the virtue of the jurists' response is its straightforwardness and clarity. They determine that visiting graves for men is lawful, and, in fact, encouraged. In this context, they cite a *ḥadīth* attributed to the Prophet that states, "Visit the graves for it will remind you of the Hereafter." However, the same rule does not apply to women. The Prophet, they assert, stated, "May God curse women who visit the graves." Regardless of the reason or motive, women are not allowed to visit the graves of relatives or non-relatives. The jurists then offer speculations as to the reason for this prohibition: they argue that women are intellectually meek and emotionally weak; if they visit the graves they are prone to commit reprehensible acts such as screaming, wailing, and beating their chests in grief. Furthermore, due to their fragile state, the visitation of graves is bound to damage and endanger their psychology. Importantly, the jurists contend, if women are allowed to visit graves, increasing numbers will do so until cemeteries become points for female congregation. This is only bound to attract immoral men who will head to the cemeteries to look at women or, worse, to molest them. In summary, the visitation of graves by women is bound to be a source of *fitnah*.[34]

Importantly, the determination of the jurists mentioned above is the minority view in the Islamic legal tradition, including in the Ḥanbalī school of thought. Nevertheless, the jurists do not mention any disagreements on this matter although some of their language indicates that they are well aware of its existence.[35] To summarize the juristic tradition on this matter, there are three distinct points of view. A minority view held that the visitation of graves by women is always prohibited. The majority, however, held that the visitation of graves was initially prohibited for men and women, and then was permitted both for men and women. They relied on several traditions, one in which ʿĀʾisha, the Prophet's wife, confirms that the abrogation of the prohibition against visiting graves included men and women. ʿĀʾishah, herself, is reported to have visited the graves of her relatives. Furthermore, various traditions report that the Prophet encountered women visiting the cemeteries, and did not advise them against doing so. Another minority view, argued that whether it is unlawful for men or women to visit graves depends entirely on the conduct and customary practices of the time and place in question. If individuals, within a particular society, tend to commit prohibited acts such as wailing or self-beating while visiting graveyards, then it is unlawful for those individuals to do so. But if a man or woman adheres to proper Islamic conduct in graveyards, their visitations are lawful, and, in fact, recommended.[36] Some jurists, for instance, argued that the prevailing practice of women in Egypt is to engage in un-Islamic conduct, and therefore, it is unlawful for women in that country to visit graveyards unless they can exercise the requisite degree of self-control.[37]

There is another issue that warrants a comment. The tradition relied on by the modern jurists which states, "May God curse women who visit graves," is problematic at several levels. In numerous traditions, the Prophet is reported to have said that he is not a curser (*laʿʿān*) or that it is not consistent with proper

Islamic character to curse even one's enemies (*al-laʿn*).[38] This blanket curse hurled at women who visit graves is not consistent with reports in which the Prophet affirmatively refuses to curse individuals or groups.[39] A comprehensive response would evaluate and assess the impact of this inconsistency. This is important in light of the fact of the doubts raised about the authenticity of the cursing tradition. In addition, there are different versions of the cursing *ḥadīth*. One version, which is mentioned above, condemns women who visit graves (*zā'irāt al-qubūr*), but another, condemns women who frequent the graveyards or those who repeatedly visit cemeteries (*zawwārāt al-qubūr*). This is significant because it raises the issue of the socio-historical context of the tradition. As is the practice in some countries today, there were women who mourned the dead for a living. As such, the mourning of the dead and the visitation of graveyards becomes a professional activity. The common practice of these women was to wail, beat their chests, and rip their cloth in return for compensation. This was done because of the belief that the louder and more vigorous the mourning, the higher the social position of the deceased. Many jurists condemned this practice, and argued that the cursing tradition is directed at those individuals, and not directed at women in general.[40] In other words, the term *zawwārāt* referred to a specific social practice by a particular guild of professional mourners.[41]

None of these subtleties emerge in the *responsa* of the modern jurists, but as stated above, it is unlikely that this is the result of a lack of knowledge or sloppy investigation. Rather, what is more likely is that the authors of the *responsa*, because of their value-based assumptions about the role of women, selectively disclosed the evidence to their audience. The net result was to misrepresent the efforts of the interpretive communities of Islamic law, and to create the impression that the determination is far more closed than the evidence, itself, admits. Accordingly, the roles of the author and the text become far more limited and diminished while the reader (special agent) stands supreme and uncontested in the determinative process. Most importantly, unless the common agents have a faith-based belief that those particular special agents are divinely guided or inspired, the trust that the common agents have placed in the special agents has been violated.

## THE PERILS OF THE TRAVELING WOMAN

I will discuss two more examples in order to demonstrate that the practice of selectivity in presentation, if not in investigation, seems to be quite widespread. In another set of *responsa*, several individuals inquire whether it is lawful for a woman to travel without a male relative (*maḥram*) either for personal reasons or in order to perform the duty of *ḥajj*. In one such inquiry, a woman asks, if her husband is injured in an accident and she is asked to go see him in the place of injury, is it permissible for her to travel alone if she cannot find a male relative to accompany her on her trip? In another inquiry, a male from Egypt states that he works in Saudi Arabia and wishes to see his wife and young child. However, he cannot afford to travel to Egypt to see them and so purchases them a non-stop flight from Egypt to Saudi Arabia. The question is whether this practice is lawful? The response by members of C.R.L.O is that in all circumstances it is unlawful for a woman to travel without a *maḥram* for more than eighty kilometers. The jurists cite a tradition attributed to the Prophet that states, "It is not permissible for a woman who believes in God and His Prophet to travel beyond the distance of a day's travel (and in a different version of the report, three days) without a *maḥram*." Ibn Fawzān, in particular, states that this is necessary because the plane, car or train may break down and leave the woman stranded without a protector. Even if the means of transportation involves a non-stop flight, the plane might be forced to change its route in an emergency. The jurists of C.R.L.O then argue that because of the risk of *fitnah*, it is better that women do not travel any distance without a *maḥram*. Significantly, the C.R.L.O jurists present their determinations as the rule of Islamic law without giving any sense of any further complexity.[42]

Most of the reports upon which C.R.L.O relies have been related by Abū Hurayrah (d. 59/679) or Abū Saʿīd al-Khudrī (d. 74/693),[43] but, in my opinion, there are some serious questions about the authenticity of these reports.[44] However, for now I will defer analyzing the problems of authenticity, and focus on the problem of selectivity. A large number of classical jurists, including Saʿīd b. Jubayr (d. 95/714), Mālik b. Anas (d. 179/796), al-Awzāʿī (d. 157/774), and al-Shāfiʿī (d. 204/820), argued that the issue is not the availability or unavailability of a *maḥram*, rather, the crux of the matter is safety (*amn*). Women will need to travel for business reasons, such as trade, to visit family, or for religious reasons, such as to perform *ḥajj*. The operative cause (*ʿillah*) for the necessity of a *maḥram* is the lack of safety. Therefore, if safety is assured through whatever means, a woman may travel alone or in the company of other women. Other jurists made the factual determination that the risk inherent in travel is worthwhile only in order to perform *ḥājj*. As a result, they argued that the rule of safety applies if a woman wishes to perform *ḥājj* but not otherwise. Yet, another group of jurists assessed the risks on different grounds. They argued that if the women in question are older, so that they would not fear captivity by bandits, they may travel alone. But if they are young women, then the risk is too high, and a *maḥram* is needed.[45]

In summary, assessing the totality of evidence including the fact that women traveled alone in the time of the Prophet when it was safe to do so, Muslim jurists separated into two camps – a camp that considered the *maḥram* rule to be a religious or ethical rule that applies regardless of the social interests involved, and a camp that considered the rule to be hinged on public interest considerations. The latter camp then disagreed as to how to assess the factual circumstances before them. Some argued that older women are safe while young women are not, some that the risk has to be justifiable in light of the interest in

*made on*
*a case to case*
*basis*

question, and some that factual determinations as to safety need to be made on a case by case basis. The basic point is that it is inaccurate to state that Islamic law requires a *mahram* for a traveling woman in all circumstances. If we ask either the woman who wanted to visit her injured husband, or the man who wanted to see his wife and child, if they feel betrayed by the special agents' concealment of the counter-determinations of the legal tradition, the response most certainly would be in the affirmative. However, other than the reaction of the common agents, there is little doubt that the special agents have exceeded the bounds of their delegated authority.

TO CLAP OR NOT TO CLAP AND THE SEDUCTIONS OF SOUND

The final example involves a rather peculiar use of evidence by the C.R.L.O jurists. The issue in this example is not just the selectivity of disclosure, but what appears to be a result-oriented selection of evidence that is not related to the immediate issue at hand. The petitioners ask in two sets of *responsa* whether clapping is lawful for men or women, and whether the voice of a woman is an *'awrah* (a private part of the body that must be concealed). If the voice of women is considered an *'awrah*, then women should not speak or raise their voices in the presence of foreign men (i.e. not a husband, father or brother).[46] As might be expected, the C.R.L.O answers both questions in the affirmative – the voice of women is *'awrah*, and clapping by men or women is unlawful. What is most interesting is the evidence cited on both occasions. The C.R.L.O jurists cite a tradition in which the following is reported to have taken place. Abū Bakr al-Ṣiddīq (d. 13/634), the Prophet's Companion, was leading prayer during the Prophet's illness shortly before the Prophet died. While Abū Bakr led prayer, the Prophet arose from his bed and went to join the praying congregation. When the congregation noticed that the Prophet arrived, they started clapping in order to indicate to Abū Bakr to step back and allow the Prophet to lead the prayer. After the prayer was completed the Prophet informed the congregation that instead of clapping, they should have done *tasbīḥ* (a supplication in which a Muslim calls out "*subḥān Allāh*"). Importantly, the Prophet reportedly announced, "While in prayer, men should call out a *tasbīḥ* and women should clap (in order to attract the attention of the *imām* leading the prayer to a mistake or a problem)." Quoting this tradition, the C.R.L.O jurists conclude two things: One, the voice of women is *'awrah*, otherwise the Prophet would not have told women to clap, and two, Muslims, in general, should not indicate approval, happiness, or praise by clapping. Clapping, the C.R.L.O argues, is prohibited because it is the practice of *kuffār* (non-believers) and women, and Muslims in general should not imitate either. The C.R.L.O also quotes the Qur'ānic verse, "Their [the unbelievers'] prayer at the House was nothing but whistling and clapping of hands. Taste you the punishment for your blasphemy."[47] From this Qur'ānic verse, and the tradition cited above, the C.R.L.O concludes several things: a woman's voice is *ʿawrah* because women are supposed to clap in prayer; women are supposed to clap in prayer because if they raise their voices in saying amen, or anything else, this is bound to create a *fitnah*; and, since women and *kuffār* clap, Muslims, in general, should not (*ʿadam al-tashābuh bi al-nisāʾ wa al-kuffār*).

It seems that the C.R.L.O jurists are not aware that their response is entirely incoherent.[48] The most that can be extracted from the Qurʾānic verse quoted above is that it is unlawful to worship God by whistling and clapping. Furthermore, the C.R.L.O ignores the historical and normative specificity of the verse. It explicitly addresses only the impropriety of the forms of worship adopted by the Meccans in the vicinity of the Kaʿbah.[49] More importantly, if Muslim women are allowed to clap in prayer, it cannot follow that the act of clapping is an imitation of the *kuffār*, unless we are willing to argue that Muslim women are unbelievers. In addition, the C.R.L.O's approach rests on an assumption that Muslim women do not set or do not count in setting Islamic normativities. If Muslim women do something then Muslims, in general, should not do it – if Muslim women clap in prayer, Muslims, in general, should not clap in any other circumstance. Of course, some jurists from the classical tradition did discuss whether it is lawful for Muslim *men* to clap. These jurists would discuss if the act of clapping is socially specific to women or unbelievers. If it is, they would conclude, men should not imitate the customs of women, and Muslims, in general, should not imitate the customs of unbelievers. Most of these jurists would then conclude that if the *purpose* of clapping is for men to imitate women, or for Muslims to imitate unbelievers, it is reprehensible (*makrūh*).[50]

I must confess that I find this clapping analysis inadequate and ahistorical. The traditions prohibiting imitating the unbelievers or one gender imitating the other arose from an authorial enterprise that was responding to problems of social consolidation and hierarchy. The type of mechanical treatment that some classical jurists afforded this issue is remarkably myopic. Nevertheless, C.R.L.O does not seem to rely on this limited juristic tradition, but builds its whole anti-clapping discourse on a gender-based assumption (clapping is what women do), and a historical assumption (clapping is what unbelievers do). Interestingly, there are no specific or on-point instructions by the Principal on clapping. Furthermore, it is notable that the tradition attributed to the Prophet on clapping is supposed to have taken place in the final episode of his life. If the tradition is historical, the fact that Muslims were clapping in prayer would indicate that clapping was socially acceptable behavior. Yet, prior to this tradition we do not find the Prophet condemning clapping in any form, and even as to this tradition, it only addresses the act of clapping in prayer. Even then, it does not ban it completely, but limits it to women.

All this relates to the lawfulness of clapping, and does not relate to whether or not the voice of women is a *ʿawrah*. The C.R.L.O, however, finds a nexus between the two in dealing with the outsider, the other, the undesirable – i.e. women and unbelievers. To reinforce the idea of the exclusion and silencing of women, the C.R.L.O cites the Qur'ānic verse, "Oh women of the Prophet, you are not like other women. If you fear God, be not too complaisant (soft, subdued) in speech, lest one in whose heart is a disease should be moved by greed (desire), but speak you with a speech that is just."[51] The C.R.L.O contends that this verse complements the Prophet's tradition as to clapping by emphasizing that a woman's voice is a *'awrah*. The least one can say about this verse is that it is inapposite to the legal issue at hand. By its own terms, the verse addresses the Prophet's wives and explicitly states that they are not like other women. The reverse implication is that what might be lawful to other women might not be lawful to the wives of the Prophet. Furthermore, by its own terms, the verse distinguishes between forms of speech – the *khuḍū'* speech (soft, seductive, kind, enticing, submissive) and normal speech. At most, one can argue that it advises against submissive speech, and commends principled and just speech. If anything, the verse advises the Prophet's wives to not be submissive or meek, but to speak in a firm and principled fashion. Finally, obviously, there is a historical context to this verse. Historical reports indicate that vagabonds who converted to Islam in order to achieve some degree of financial security were reluctant to pressure the Prophet with demands. Instead, they approached his wives with numerous demands. While the Prophet's wives were kind and gentle, reportedly, the demands exceeded the bounds of reasonableness, and reached a point in which some of the flimsy converts were taking advantage of their kindness. The verse was revealed to instruct the Prophet's wives to speak out of principle, and not simple emotion. Therefore, the verse addresses the Prophet's wives by emphasizing that they have a special social position unlike other Muslim women.[52] In short, there is nothing in this verse that decrees that the voice of women is *'awrah*. Furthermore, it is indeed an unreasonable proposition to suggest that a women's pronouncement of *tasbīḥ* or the saying of "*āmīn*" in prayer is the type of *khuḍū'* that the Qur'ān is talking about.

Nonetheless, one can justifiably ask, doesn't "the clapping is for women and *tasbīḥ* is for men," dictate the logic of feminine alienation – the positing of women as silenced, muted, and censored, even in prayer? I believe that the answer would have to be in the affirmative. There are numerous historical reports detailing the public role of women, which included speaking in public, at the time of the Prophet and afterwards, so what justifies the silence of women in prayer? There are several points to consider here. The authenticity of the tradition is questionable for three reasons: first, it is not likely that the Companions were ignorant of such a basic rule of prayer until near the end of the Prophet's life; second, this is among the *āḥādī* (singular transmissions), and it is not likely that such a public Prophetic injunction would be recalled and transmitted by a small number of Companions; and, third, the prevalence of the role of Abū Hurayrah in several of the transmissions is problematic, as discussed later. Importantly, Ibn al-Qāsim (d. 191/806) reported that Mālik b. Anas did not accept the authenticity of the report, and ruled that both men and women should perform *tasbīḥ* in prayer and, in fact, prohibited the act of clapping in prayer.[53] Other jurists, for a variety of reasons related to the probative value of the tradition, argued that it is recommended that women clap in prayer if they wish to attract the attention of the *imām* to an error or mistake, and men should perform *tasbīḥ*. However, it is *not* unlawful for women to perform *tasbīḥ* as well, and most certainly, it does not invalidate their prayer. The essential element in this determination is that confronted by the apparent irrationality of the tradition, most jurists downgraded the clapping ruling to a recommendation. Other jurists argued that rules for prayer cannot be generalized outside prayer – so whatever the reason, the fact that women should clap in prayer has no implications for women outside prayer. Most significantly, the vast majority of jurists held that a woman's voice is not a *ʿawrah*. Seductive speech, however, whether by men or women, is unlawful if done with improper motives. For instance, a wife or husband may speak seductively to his or her spouse, but not to a neighbor. The vast majority of jurists were sufficiently discerning not to brand the voice of women as invariably seductive, and as worthy of being muted under all circumstances. If these jurists did not have the courage to challenge the authenticity of the tradition, at least they had the sense to mitigate its impact. In addition, a large number of jurists from a variety of schools did not deal directly with the issue – they only mention that the way to correct the *imām* in prayer is to call out a *tasbīḥ*, but do not mention a special rule for women.[54]

On the evidence, the least one can say is that the determination of C.R.L.O is negligent, if not deceitful. But I feel obligated to confess that I find that the assertion that if women raise their voices in prayer this could be a source of seduction or *fitnah*, to be bewildering. It would have been more fitting for C.R.L.O to chastise the men, if such exist, who cannot keep their minds on their prayers instead of becoming aroused by the voice of women in worship. At a value-based level, I find those men, if they exist, to be rather misguided. At a faith-based level, I cannot believe that God would accommodate those men in this way.

## *Balancing of interests and the use of discretion*

Legal analysis is founded on a bed of discretion. Extracting a general rule or principle is not nearly as demanding as applying that principle or rule to a set of facts. Determining whether a particular factual situation is governed by rule *x* or rule *y* is a matter of judgment that might be guided by rules or a methodology of application, but involves a considerable amount of discretion nonetheless. For instance, if I articulate a rule that demands modesty and dictates that situations of sexual enticement or seduction be avoided, determining the empirical question of what is a sexually enticing situation that violates the rule of modesty involves considerable discretion. Furthermore, it raises a serious issue of competence. Assuming that the special agents are qualified to articulate the rule of modesty, how and according to what standards do they determine the empirical questions surrounding seduction? To what extent are they qualified to determine that one situation x as opposed to another is, as an empirical matter, contrary to the rule of modesty? I believe that the answer would have to be, not at all. A judge makes this determination not necessarily because he or she is the best qualified to understand reality or even to understand reality as it relates to law, but because of his or her institutional position. This position might permit the judge to acquire a concentrated set of experiences in performing the job of judging. This only means that the judge acquires competence in the institutional practice as it relates to the assessment of facts, not that he or she has a greater sense of reality than a social scientist or the casual observer of human affairs.

A jurist's, as opposed to a judge's, assessment of factual situations does not have institutional authority, and must resort to processes of common persuasion. A judge may decide that something, according to community standards, is obscene, a jurist simply has to argue it.[55] We should add another element to this analysis. The special agent's analysis of factual circumstances might rely on factual determinations made by the Principal. So, for instance, whether wearing a particular item of clothing is contrary to modesty might be a determination made by the Principal. The reference point here is to the instructions of the Principal, which means that the special agent is not claiming to make the factual determination as an empirical matter, but is making the determination as an interpretive matter. In other words, the special agent is claiming authoritativeness by depending on a purported empirical determination by the Principal. The five contingencies obligate the special agent to carefully distinguish between an empirical determination that is made as a matter of judgment, and an empirical determination that was purportedly made by the Principal. In addition, the special agent is obligated to fully disclose the extent to which individual discretion played a role in the determination.

In a series of *responsa* issued by C.R.L.O, as an official organization, or by jurists affiliated with that organization, we notice a broad use of undisclosed discretion. The discretion used is not necessarily authorized by a specific set of instructions, but is incidental to the nature of the question posed. The problematic aspect, however, is that the determination is presented as if it is God's unwavering decree. Consequently, whatever discretionary element is inherent in the problem, it is monopolized by the jurist and denied to all others. This often arises in the context of a determination that requires the balancing of competing interests or conflicting rules. Importantly, however, C.R.L.O jurists do not disclose the very act of balancing, and whatever the result reached by the jurists is presented as if the balancing and decision were made by the Principal or text (instructions), and simply reported by the special agents.

## THE DEVIL IN THE CAR

In *responsa* issued by Ibn Bāz and Ibn Fawzān, and adopted as state law in Saudi Arabia, Islamic law prohibits women from driving cars.[56] Apparently, God has not forbidden women to ride in cars, but has forbidden the act of driving. The prohibition would cover a woman who would drive her blind husband or elderly father. In fact, in a *responsum* in which a woman explains that she might be forced to drive in emergencies, Ibn Fawzān decides that driving would remain unlawful.[57] Importantly, it is unlawful, according to the C.R.L.O, for women to ride in a car alone with a foreign man, including the driver. Therefore, a woman either needs to take advantage of car pools or be driven by a *maḥram* (male close family relation).[58] Presumably, God forbade the stepping on the gas, the turning of the wheel, and the changing of the clutch if undertaken by a woman. As long as a man is in control of the car, God is satisfied. Of course, this raises an issue not dealt with in the *responsa*, and that is the problem of a backseat driver who intrusively regulates the speed and direction of the car. There are no instructions from the Principal on women driving anything, but there were many women who rode camels and horses in the time of the Prophet and afterwards. The fact that Ibn Bāz and the others do not bother to account for these historical precedents will not detain us. If there is no textual material on point and the historical precedent is contrary to the Ibn Bāz determination, what, then, explains the *responsa*? Ibn Bāz's opinion rests on a factual determination as to the dangers involved if women drive. He makes the contradictory argument that if women drive, this would lead to *ikhtilāṭ* (mixing between men and women) and *khalwah* (illicit privacy between man and woman). Assuming that both are unlawful, he argues that it is better for women to stay home and not venture into public life.[59] The crux of Ibn Bāz's *responsa* is that the independence and mobility driving might give women *leads* to moral and social harms. Ibn Fawzān adds another factual determination: cars break down and have accidents, and therefore, this poses dangers to the safety of women. For good measure, Ibn Fawzān seems to doubt a woman's ability to drive – he elaborates that women are emotional and of a limited intellectual ability, and this could endanger their own safety and the safety of others. The juristic "hook" that serves as an enabling device for these factual determinations is the idea that what leads to something unlawful is, in turn, unlawful. In the parlance of Islamic jurisprudence, this is known as *sadd al-dharīʿah*, which literally means the blocking of the means, or the prevention of harm. The concept of *sadd al-dharīʿah* is derived from some doctrinal sources that suggest that it is appropriate to prevent harm before it actually materializes.[60] For instance, digging a hole is lawful, but if people are likely to fall in it, the digging of holes might be outlawed. Likewise, I am free to do whatever I wish with my land, but I cannot lay traps in my backyard if I know that children tend to trespass on my land. Importantly, the idea of prevention of harm is the other side of the coin of the concept of *al-maṣāliḥ al-mursalah* (public interests or good) in Islamic jurisprudence. According to the concept of public interest, whatever might be necessary to achieve a good might become lawful or obligatory.[61] Ironically, an observer can identify the political and social inclinations of a modern jurist by how they use the two concepts – a liberal or reformer would normally talk of *al-maṣāliḥ al-mursalah*, and a conservative would normally talk of *sadd al-dharīʿah*. In what has become juristic opportunism, liberals invoke the idea of public interest whenever they wish to advocate the legality of any policy determination that they find desirable, and prevention of harm is invoked by conservatives when resisting social or political changes that they find undesirable.

The essential point is that both concepts are based on empirical policy determinations – for instance, is the digging of the hole likely to cause injury, and are speed limits necessary to avoid accidents? Furthermore, both concepts necessarily require a balancing of interests since every interest promoted will implicate the rights of different parties in various ways. There is hardly a public interest that can be promoted or a harm that can be avoided which will not have a social cost attached to it. Ultimately, each harm avoided will entail a cost to a particular group who will have to forego a right or interest in order to promote the interests of others. So, for instance, I might have to forego my interest in digging holes in my backyard in order to promote the interests of those who might fall in the hole. Obviously, the distinct risk in all these public interest or prevention of harm determinations is that the interests of some groups will be considered as less worthy than others, and that these groups will tend to be the powerless, oppressed or those excluded from the institutions of power. For those reasons, most Ḥanafī and Shāfiʿī jurists rejected the concept of *sadd al-dharīʿah* as a principle of jurisprudence. They argued that as a methodological tool, it was dangerously unprincipled. Mālikī and Ḥanbalī jurists endorsed the principle, but with limitations.[62] In summary, the act that will be made unlawful by the enforcement of the principle of prevention of harm, must be the type of act that will definitely lead to the evil feared. There must be a nexus between the prohibited act and the feared evil, which must be established to a degree of certainty or, at least, a degree of high likelihood (*al-ẓann al-ghālib*). In addition, the prohibited act cannot be the means to more good than harm, or, put differently, the harm from the feared evil must exceed the actual good achieved by the act that we intend to prohibit. Furthermore, the least restrictive means must be pursued so as to safeguard the most rights possible. For example, before a jurist may prevent me from digging holes in my backyard, a strong nexus must be established between the digging of holes and the concern that people might fall in the hole. If in the past fifty years in which I have been digging holes, no one other than myself has fallen in one of these holes, arguably this is insufficient to outlaw the digging of holes. Furthermore, let us assume that I am digging holes to supply a full town with water while those who fall in the holes are people who sneak in my backyard at night to rob me. Under these circumstances, arguably, a jurist has no right to deny the townspeople their water in order to protect a few thieves who have no business coming on my land anyway. Even more, if placing fences or warning signs around every hole I dig could solve the problem, then banning me from digging holes would be unlawful overreaching. A jurist should choose the least restrictive or intrusive means possible to avoid the most evil possible.[63]

The difference between this rather careful and self-restrained methodology and the C.R.L.O jurists' approach I think is self-evident.[64] The C.R.L.O jurists seem to assume that anything that might possibly lead to any degree of evil is to be prohibited. Regardless of the amount of good that driving women could achieve, and regardless of how speculative our fears of possible evils, they believe that women should bear the burden of the sacrifice.

If applied fairly, a methodology guided by the fear of speculative evils would lead to what are plainly absurd results. If we fear that many men from the Arabian Gulf area who travel to Europe and the United States will visit nightclubs, then we should ban men from traveling outside Arabia. If a large number of people sniff glue, then we should ban the use of glue, and if people tend to talk about nonsense, backbite and malign others, then we should ban talking. Why not castrate all impious men since they are likely to use their sexual organs improperly? Nevertheless what is most despotic about the determinations discussed above is not only the failure to rely on a sound methodology, but even more, is that they are founded upon value-based determinations without being forthright about the policy assessments made. In fact, the authors of these *responsa* are often explicit about claiming the solemnity of God's law to their side. They are also quite dismissive of arguments pointing out the obvious subjectivities inherent in their approach. Their *responsa* often conclude with attacks on those who question the wisdom of the law of God, and by calling upon Muslims to be sufficiently pious in closing the doors to evil. I must confess that I believe that the *responsa* discussed above are based on impressionistic, and even idiosyncratic, empirical claims, and that they exhibit an extreme tendency to undervaluing the suffering and harm inflicted upon women. In my view, women should not suffer exclusion and restrictions lest men suffer a fleeting moment of temptation.

## SUCKLING HUSBANDS, SKIN DISEASE, AND OTHER TOLERABLES

Perhaps it does not come as a surprise that in most determinations, if the rights of women must be balanced against the rights of others, the C.R.L.O consistently demands that women bear the burden of the loss of rights. These determinations, however, are presented as the dictates of God without any reference to the empirical and policy assumptions made in each case. The claim or appearance of divinity empowers these determinations with a persuasiveness that reaches well beyond their specific social context. A casual observer, for instance, will notice the pronounced impact of these *responsa*, even upon

Muslims living in the West.[65] Since my point is largely methodological, I have selected some *responsa* that have achieved a level of widespread popularity, and others that are lesser known but that serve as good demonstrative examples.

The first set of *responsa* were by women who presented substantially similar fact situations. Apparently, the petitioners are young women who are being pressured, in one form or another, by their families to marry. The person they are asked to marry varies, some are relatives such as cousins, and some appear to be a person that the parents consider to be well-qualified. In each circumstance, the woman in question is opposing the marriage. Some women desire to marry someone else, some state that they are not prepared to marry at the present time, and some state that they wish to continue their schooling before marriage. The questions presented are the following: are parents allowed to force their daughters to marry? Is it lawful for the daughter in question to refuse to marry the person her parents have selected? Is it unlawful for a woman to defer marriage so that she may complete her studies? Is a woman religiously obligated to marry?

In legal opinions issued by Ibn Bāz, al-ʿUthaymīn, and others, it is asserted that it is unlawful to force a woman to marry; consent is a necessary element in the marriage contract and so coercion is impermissible. This holding is unremarkable, except for the fact that some classical jurists had held that the consent of a young and immature girl, or in the opinion of some, a virgin, is unnecessary. Ibn Bāz and al-ʿUthaymīn do not refer to this opinion although it might be inferred that they find it unpersuasive. Next, they state that even though a father may not coerce his daughter into marriage, it is unlawful for a daughter to disobey her father by rejecting a suitor without good cause. Ibn Bāz and al-ʿUthaymīn contend that fathers know what is in the best interest of their child, especially in the case of women because women are overcome by irrational emotions. If a father selects or approves of a suitor, then it is obligatory upon the daughter to accept that person unless the suitor is not religious – for example, he does not pray or drinks alcohol. Furthermore, it is religiously incumbent upon all women to marry, and deferring marriage in order to study is unlawful. Al-ʿUthaymīn offers the advice that if the woman wishes, she may set a condition in the marriage contract that would obligate her husband to allow her to complete her education. However, he adds that he does not believe that it is necessary for a woman to attain an education beyond the elementary level. It is sufficient for a woman to learn to read and write, and a pious Muslim woman should not aspire to more than that.[66] In a separate *responsum*, Ibn Fawzān asserts that a woman may not neglect her housework or her obligation to take care of her husband in order to pursue Islamic studies. While religious knowledge is important, it is sufficient that a wife achieve a minimal degree of religious education.[67]

It is difficult to extract from the *responsa* what might be considered a legal determination as opposed to social counseling. Whether fathers know best, or whether an elementary level education is sufficient for women, implicates value-based social assumptions that I will not engage at this point. At least al-ʿUthaymīn indicates that the idea that an elementary education for women is sufficient for them is an opinion, and not a legal determination. As to the remaining issues, the jurists use the word "unlawful" to describe the behavior of a woman who refuses to obey her father, prefers study to marriage, prefers celibacy to marriage, and gives more attention to her studies than her husband. The use of the word "unlawful" invokes the authoritativeness of God, and indicates a legal determination. This, of course, raises the question: what is the basis of this determination? At the most basic level, the jurists were engaged in an undisclosed balancing process between different legal obligations, and the different interests attached to these legal obligations. Assuming that a daughter does have an obligation to obey her father, is weighed against the fact that a daughter has the right to choose her marital partner. The right to choose is affirmed by the prohibition of coercion in marriage. Furthermore, there is a clear Islamic obligation upon men and women to become educated, and to seek knowledge (*ṭalab al-ʿilm*). Assuming that marriage is a legal obligation, the woman's interest in discharging the obligation of seeking knowledge must be weighed against the obligation to marry. Again, coming from particular value-based orientations, these jurists have no difficulty in ruling against the mobility and autonomy of women. Importantly, however, the outcomes of the balancing process are presented as clear Divine determinations not open to questioning.

The outcomes of the balancing process should be analyzed in light of the reason-based assumptions that informed the determinations of the authors of the *responsa*. Put differently, what are the doctrinal foundations for the determinations of these jurists? The jurists, themselves, do not cite or reference many instructions from the Principal or from particular interpretive communities formed around the instructions. This is significant when we consider the fact that, at least in my opinion, as far as decisions of marriage are concerned, there is no evidence that requires a woman to obey her parents. The Qurʾān and *Sunnah* do demand respect and reverence, by both men and women, for parents.[68] However, conceptually, there is a difference between respect and obedience. Furthermore, the Islamic legal principle, "obedience is due (to anyone) only in what is good (*innamā al-ṭāʿah fī al-maʿrūf*),"[69] raises the question, how do we define the good? For instance, assume that the husband picked by the parents is a pious person, but boring, short-tempered, bad-smelling or stupid. The fact that these traits might not bother the parents, or that they might not have noticed them, do not affect the parents but do affect the spiritual and intellectual balance of the spouse who has to live with them. Nothing in the sources dictates that the preferences, tastes or repose of the person who will do the actual marrying ought to be ignored or ought to be outweighed by the preferences, tastes or repose of the parents.[70] The sources do set out principles such as respect your parents, marry a pious and good person, seek knowledge, and live a life of tranquility etc., but they do not necessarily create a hierarchy for these principles. Importantly, the Qurʾān emphasizes that marriage ought to be a source of tranquility and repose for the spouses, and, arguably, this weighs the balance in favor of full autonomy for children in choosing their spouses.[71]

Another element to consider here is the determination of the jurists that women ought to marry, even if it means cutting their studies short. The Qur'ān does recommend marriage to those who are able to carry its burdens, and traditions attributed to the Prophet emphasize the same point.[72] Importantly, however, the classical interpretive communities had determined that marriage is recommended, and is part of the Prophet's *Sunnah*, but it is not a legal obligation (*al-zawāj nadb wa lā yalzam*).[73] In fact, well-known jurists such as Ibn Taymiyyah and al-Nawawī never married.[74] According to the classical jurists, a sin is not incurred for failing to marry unless a man or woman fears that they will be unable to abstain from illicit sexual relations. In addition, a person does incur a sin if they marry when they are unable to carry the burdens of marriage. Even more, the seeking of knowledge (*ṭalab al-ʿilm*) is considered a *farīḍah* (religious obligation) or, at least, a *wājib* (religious duty).[75] Meanwhile, according to classical jurists, marriage is a *Sunnah* (recommended or favored act), and not a mandatory obligation. Yet, Ibn Bāz, al-ʿUthaymīn, and their colleagues, do not explain how they reached the determination that marriage takes precedence over the pursuit of knowledge. In their *responsa*, they invoke the categories of lawful or unlawful, but it is not clear to what extent are they relying on the authoritativeness of the classical juristic tradition, and if they are performing a *de novo* determination (*ijtihād*), what forms the basis for it. Furthermore, whether it is possible to marry and pursue knowledge at the same time hardly needs the determination of a special agent. This type of personal decision is very fact specific, and there is no indication that jurists are particularly qualified to make a general determination as to the appropriate balance to be struck in all cases.

We observe the same process in a host of other *responsa* issued by the same jurists identified above and other C.R.L.O members. A group of women ask whether their husbands may lawfully prohibit them from visiting or communicating with their parents. It is notable that severing one's ties with parents or blood-relatives is called *qaṭʿ al-raḥim*, and is considered a major sin in Islamic law (*kabīrah*).[76] The C.R.L.O jurists concede that severing family ties is a major sin, and under normal circumstances, it is impermissible. However, they argue, a woman must also trust and obey her husband. The *responsa* explain that between parents and husbands, one should obey the parents. Nonetheless, if the husband perceives some harm from allowing his wife to visit or be visited by her family, including her parents, he may lawfully prohibit the visits. For instance, if the husband fears that his wife's relatives are turning her against him, he can rightfully limit their contact to an exchange of cards on special occasions. If the husband has abused his discretion, he is incurring a sin that he will have to answer to before God, but his wife must abide by his decision.[77] Again, figuring out the basis for this juristic determination is rather mystifying. Even if we assume that a husband is owed an obligation of obedience, which is an assumption I do not concede, that would still not resolve the issue. The C.R.L.O jurists recognize the fact that one of the foundational principles in Islamic law is that "no obedience is owed to any person if it entails disobeying God" (*lā ṭāʿah li makhlūq fī maʿṣiyyat al-Khāliq*), and God commanded that parents, or family members, not be abandoned, alienated, boycotted, or even treated unkindly.[78] There are historical reports of a fight that ensued at the time of the Prophet when a man attempted to prevent his wife from visiting her parents. The rather vague reports state that the Prophet intervened and reconciled between the fighting parties, but there are no reliable reports that the Prophet supported the husband's right to ban dealing with his in-laws.[79] In another report, the Prophet supported the right of a woman to be visited by her father who was an unbeliever and to offer him protection despite the opposition of the Medina community.[80] This anecdotal evidence is not dispositive of the issue at hand, but it should be incorporated into a systematic analysis of the issue.[81] Fundamentally, once again, we have a conflict between a presumed duty to obey a husband, and a well-established duty to maintain a relationship with one's parents. Balancing the two, the C.R.L.O apparently decided that the possibility of a speculative concern on the part of a husband takes precedence over the interest of a wife in maintaining a meaningful relationship with her family. Social presumptions about the sagacity of women, the role of in-laws, the authority of husbands, the meaning of family and even the understanding of legal priorities, are not disclosed. The determination, which as explained later I consider immoral, is presented as the rule of Islamic law.

We find the same tendency to undervalue the interests and rights of women in *responsa* in which women complain of mistreatment by their husbands, and, as might be expected, the C.R.L.O jurists proclaim that the law of God requires the women to be patient and persevere.[82] The C.R.L.O jurists expend no effort in trying to set out fair or equitable principles for a dignified life even though the Qurʾān explicitly dictates that either a married couple live together in kindness or separate in kindness.[83] At the very least, it would have been judicious for the C.R.L.O to inquire about the nature or extent of mistreatment before advising perseverance.

The C.R.L.O jurists are also asked about a woman who suffers from a skin disease afflicting her head and face. Despite the fact that her doctor advised her not to wear a head or face cover, the C.R.L.O jurists respond that she may remove her covers in front of her husband only! Otherwise, she should not remove her covers – instead, she should be patient and persevere.[84] This *responsum* clearly contradicts the well-known legal principle that provides that, "all unlawful matters become lawful in cases of necessity (*al-ḍarūriyyāt tubīḥ al-maḥẓūrāt*)," and the Qurʾānic verses stating that God does not wish people to endure hardship.[85] Furthermore, in two *responsa*, wives complain that their husbands like to be suckled like babies, a behavior that they apparently find objectionable. The response of the jurists is remarkably dogmatic, and in fact, offensive – they state that a husband has a right to enjoy his wife in any lawful way. They emphasize that sodomy or intercourse during the menstrual cycle is unlawful, but there is no prohibition against breastfeeding or suckling.[86] The C.R.L.O jurists do not inquire, and do not seem to think it is relevant whether the wives in these cases find breastfeeding their husbands annoying, distasteful, or unpleasurable. Again, the C.R.L.O jurists ignore prior determinations by classical jurists that women have an equal right to sexual fulfillment, as do their spouses. For instance, some jurists argued that it is reprehensible for a man to climax sexually before his wife, if that denies his wife her pleasure. Even if he does, he must continue to stimulate his wife until she climaxes if that is what she wants.[87] Furthermore, classical jurists also argued that a husband should refrain from sexual acts that a wife finds unpleasurable, lewd, or offensive.[88]

### DISSECTIONS, CADAVERS, AND WALLET PICTURES

The tendency to act upon undisclosed value-based assumptions that clearly prejudice the process of balancing between competing interests is not limited to judgments concerning women. It is fair to say that the C.R.L.O, like many juristic works in contemporary Islam, is not sensitive to the need to balance the subjectivities of the interpreter with the roles of the instructions (text) and Principal (author). This tendency is only exasperated by the entirely whimsical way that many modern commentators, including the C.R.L.O, deal with the juristic tradition in Islam. In most situations, it is not clear whether the writer is adopting the juristic tradition as a whole or in part or not at all, and according to what principles. In order to demonstrate the unsystematic balancing of interests in issues unrelated to women, I will discuss two more examples, one regarding the taking of face photographs of human beings, and the other regarding the dissecting of cadavers.

The jurists ʿAbd Allāh b. Qaʿūd, ʿAbd Allāh b. Ghidyān, ʿAbd al-Razzāq ʿAfīfī, and ʿAbd Allāh b. Bāz are presented with the cases of individuals who are expatriates working in a country away from their families. One person inquires whether it is lawful to send photographs of himself to his family, while the other inquires whether it is lawful to keep pictures of his children in his wallet. Once again, the response is an unequivocal, no. Photographs, as well as all pictures of beings with souls, are unlawful because of the traditions that curse the *muṣawwirūn* (those who produce images or statues). All images of beings, including photographs and statues, are unlawful in Islam – there are no exceptions, and this matter is not open to reconsideration. Asked about the use of photographs in passports, driver licenses, and other forms of identification, the same jurists respond that it is, in fact, lawful. The jurists cite the principle of necessity (*ḍarūrah*) as justification explaining that these matters are essential in order to maintain order, capture criminals, and other socially significant purposes. In a rather peculiar determination, the same jurists held that television broadcasts are not unlawful, per se, but are unlawful only if used for promiscuous or lecherous purposes. Therefore, the moving image or picture of a person reciting the Qur'ān is lawful. But the still picture of a person reading the Qur'ān, or of a face staring at the camera, is unlawful.[89] Apparently, an expatriate may see his family on a television screen from a videocassette, but not in still photographs. Regardless of the consistency of the logic, what is noticeable is the type of social interests that the jurists consider material. Social non-institutional interests are not as weighty or significant as institutional and governmental interests. The expatriate experience with its particular pains is not a part of their sensitivities or consciousness. Consequently, it is fairly easy to dismiss the role of photographs for expatriates who, quite often, cannot afford to visit their families, as a non-necessity. Meanwhile, the photographs of the King of Saudi Arabia, which decorate the C.R.L.O building itself and most other public places, is a necessity. This, what may be called, "institutional sensitivity"[90] is also noticeable in the numerous *responsa* that have decided it is unlawful for a Muslim to socialize with or befriend a non-Muslim, but that it is lawful for the Saudi government to ally itself with the United States against Iraq.[91]

The insensitivity to the expatriate social experience is underscored by the fact that the legal basis for the prohibition against photographs is far from clear. There are several traditions attributed to the Prophet that condemn or prohibit the act of *taṣwīr* and *ṣuwar* (the production of images or statues) but the only similarity between the images and statues of the traditions and photographs is linguistic. Of course, photographs were unknown at the time of the Prophet. In the contemporary age, Arabic speakers co-opted the pre-modern word, *taṣwīr*, to describe the act of taking photographs, so that the word that referred to a particular historical practice is now used to describe a modern practice. The question then becomes: is the historical act of *taṣwīr* sufficiently similar to modern acts of *taṣwīr* for us to extend the old precedent to the new case? In Islamic jurisprudential jargon, the question becomes: is there sufficient unity between the operative causes of the old case and the new case to justify the application of the same rule (*ittiḥād al-ʿilal bayn al-aṣl wa al-farʿ*)? Naturally, this depends on the nature of the historical practice of *taṣwīr*, and the character of the operative cause for the precedent. It should be remembered that Islam was revealed among idol worshipers, and that linguistically speaking, the pre-Islamic Arabs worshipped *ṣuwar* (images and statues). It is significant, for example, that the creating of images and statues was called *taṣwīr* and also *taṣlīb*. The word *taṣlīb* is the verb form of the word *ṣalīb*, which means a worshiped image or statue. Therefore, Christianity was known among pre-modern Muslims as *Ṣalībiyyah*, or those who worship images and statues (i.e. the cross, and the images of Jesus and the Virgin Mary). Some early reports indicate that Muslims were aware of Christian practices in which tombstones were decorated with images or statues, which would become revered religious symbols.[92] The obvious point here is that the intended *ṣuwar* or *ṣulab* (images and statues) at the time of the Prophet were those that posed a very real risk of becoming objects of worship. So for instance, there is a tradition in which the Prophet saw ʿĀʾishah playing with a doll in the shape of a human being and did not reproach her.[93] Furthermore, there are reports that ʿĀʾishah had images of beings in her home that disturbed the Prophet during prayer. The Prophet reportedly asked her to remove the image from before him, but did not, in this context, condemn the existence of images. Other reports contend that the Prophet pronounced blanket condemnations against all images and statues.

Importantly, the interpretive activity of classical jurists reflected the contextual particularity of the prohibition against images. Early juristic interpretations tended to focus on the dangers that images or statues posed to the Islamic message, and their determinations aimed at alleviating these very practical concerns. For example, some jurists argued that the prohibition does not apply to items that do not have a shadow. The significance of this is that paintings, unlike statues, do not have shadows, and so were less likely to be revered as idols. Most jurists, however, disagreed with the materiality of the shadow factor, and held that if images or statues are degraded or mutilated in some form, then they are not covered by the prohibition. For example, if the image is on the floor so that it is stepped on, or if it is on the shoes, or if the image or statue was missing a head or mutilated in some other way, then it is lawful to make and own such images and statues. Essentially, if due to degradation or mutilation, the image or statue is unlikely to become an object of worship, it is not covered by the prohibition.[94] Other jurists adopted a much more direct and straightforward approach and argued that whatever can be taken as an idol to be worshipped (*mā yuttakhadh ka wathan*) is prohibited, otherwise, it is allowed.[95]

In light of the above, we can re-ask the question: to what extent do the words *ṣuwar*, *taṣwīr*, or *muṣawwirūn* of fourteen-hundred years ago, refer to the same conceptual, physical, and social category or experience that exists today? In fact, it is likely that the Prophet was worried about the possible social and religious role images might have upon his people – considering that Islam was a fairly new religion, it was quite reasonable to assume that people could easily revert to the worship of idols. It is also likely that the Prophet said something to warn his followers against these dangers. However, it is very likely that various people remembered his warnings in a variety of ways, and exaggerated and embellished what he originally said. To what extent was the authorial enterprise that produced the traditions on images talking about family photos, or to what extent were the participants in the authorial enterprise thinking about items that play the functional equivalent of the role that family photos play today? Furthermore, if C.R.L.O claims that it is not interested in the opinions of the early juristic communities on how or why images are prohibited, the question becomes: to what extent is it possible to differentiate between the authorial enterprise that produced the anti-images tradition, and the dynamics of the interpretive communities that accompanied the formation of these authorial enterprises?

My final example on this issue is embarrassingly simple. A medical student inquires from Ibn Fawzān if it is lawful to dissect the body of a Muslim for the purposes of education and research. Ibn Fawzān responds that a dead person should be buried. If dissections are necessary to benefit the living, then the bodies of unbelievers may be used for the purpose – under no circumstance may a Muslim be dissected, for educational purposes or otherwise. The only evidence that Ibn Fawzān cites in support of his *responsa* are Qur'ānic verses that state that human beings came from soil of the earth and will be returned to the earth, and a tradition that he attributes to the Prophet stating, "The sanctity of a dead Muslim is the same as his sanctity when alive."[96]

First of all, I have not been able to locate this so-called tradition in any book. Ibn Fawzān could have cited some traditions in which the Prophet prohibits the mutilation of cadavers (*lā tumaththilū*), but he did not. In any case, the Qur'ānic verses cited in the *responsa*, and the prohibition against mutilation, are all inapposite. Ibn Fawzān's determination is based on the assumption that dissections desecrate the sanctity of the body. If that is true, there is no basis whatsoever for differentiating between the body of a Muslim and a non-Muslim. But why does Ibn Fawzān assume that a dissection is the equivalent of desecration? Can't one argue that far from being a desecration, it honors the body of a Muslim to be used for the good of medical research, which in turn benefits all human beings? What is the basis for the assumption that dissections are so offensive that even the necessity of medical education and research cannot justify the offense? As is well-known, Muslim civilization excelled in the field of medicine, and especially in the field of anatomy. I have not been able to find a single classical jurist who has held that dissections performed for medical reasons count as mutilations and, thus, can be considered a desecration of the body.[97]

I think that it is fair to say that Ibn Fawzān is relying on certain value-based assumptions about the role of medicine, the value of empirical research and experience, the importance of medical doctors in society, an understanding of the physicality of the body, and a particular understanding of dignity that is perhaps consistent with certain social values. Balancing the interests of society in medicine and his own notions of dignity for himself and other Muslims, the balance is weighed in a particular direction. But as we have found so often, the values and the balancing are not disclosed. In fact, the values of the interpreter are equated, completely, to the values of the Principal. There is a perfect unity between the will of the interpreter, and the Will of the Principal – whatever the interpreter feels, thinks, desires, or values is imputed to the Principal. Unless the common agents are willing to give their loyalty, commitment, and submission to the special agent, this is a blatant violation of the relation based on diligence and deference between the special agent and those who placed their trust in him.

*NOTES*

1 Recently, Wael Hallaq seems to have reached the same conclusion. See Hallaq, *Authority, Continuity and Change*, p. 126.
2 On the necessity of having a *mujtahid* in every age, see, al-Shawkānī, *Irshād al-Fuḥūl*, pp. 374–377. For Muḥammad ʿAbduh's call for *ijithād* and a sensitivity to the exigencies of the age, see, Muḥammad ʿAbduh, "Ikhtilāf al-Qawānīn bi Ikhtilāf Aḥwāl al-Umam," pp. 309–315; Albert Hourani, *Arabic Thought*, pp. 145–149. For ambiguous, undefined demands for reform and change, see, Hamdi, *The Making of an Islamic Leader*, pp. 36–38; al-Hibri,"Marriage Laws in Muslim Countries," pp. 227–244, 241–242; *idem*, "Family Planning and Islamic Jurisprudence," pp. 2–11, 2–3. For general treatments of *ijtihād* as an instrument of Islamic revivalism in recent decades, see Shahin, *Political Ascent*, pp. 220–229; Ghadbian, *Democratization and the Islamic Challenge in the Arab World*, pp. 26, 76; Enayat, *Modern Islamic Political Thought*, pp. 82–101.
3 See, for example, al-Turābī, *Tajdīd al-Fikr al-Islāmī*, pp. 33–53, who writes on the need for new *uṣūl al-fiqh*, but does not analyze the need for an open ended process of legal exploration.
4 See, for example, Doi, *Sharīʿah*: *The Islamic Law*, whose broad treatment of Islamic law generally utilizes this methodology. See also al-Hibri et al., who cites a handful of Qurʾānic verses and *ḥadīth* to enunciate the Islamic legal approach to family relations and a child's duty to her parents. "Symposium on Religious Law, pp. 9–95, 25–27. Additionally, Muslim apologists will utilize this methodology by simply citing Qurʾānic verses and *ḥadīth* to support their contention that Islamic law incorporates and protects human rights, without critically investigating what that position entails. See, Osman, *Sharia in Contemporary Society*, pp. 9–17; *Shaikh* Shaukat Hussain, *Human Rights in Islam*, pp. 37–72. For an example of this methodology being used to justify the legal principle against *ex post facto* criminal prosecution, see, Sanad, *The Theory of Crime*, pp. 41–42. Apologists may refer to juristic sources, in addition to Qurʾānic verses and *ḥadīth* reports. However, their treatment of these sources often lacks critical evaluation and is generally used to bolster their conclusions established at the outset.
5 For an example of such an *ijthādist*, see, al-Hibri, "Islamic Constitutionalism and the Concept of Democracy," pp. 1–27, 24–25. In this incident, the second caliph, ʿUmar b. al-Khaṭṭāb, is reported to have decreed a maximum amount for dowries (*mahr*) to be paid to brides. A woman protested his decree, citing the Prophet's Sunnah. In response ʿUmar admitted his error. See, al-Shawkānī, *Fatḥ al-Qadīr*, 1:563; al-Zamakhsharī, *al-Kashshāf*, 1:514; Ibn Kathīr, *Mukhtaṣar Tafsīr Ibn Kathīr*, 1:369.
6 Ibn Mājah, *Sunan Ibn Mājah*, 1:602–603; Abou El Fadl, "The State Between Two States," *Conference of the Books*, pp. 253–263, 258.
7 See Smith, *Islam in Modern History*, pp. 85–89, who argues that modern Muslim apologetics are intended to defend and bolster Islam in the face of the challenges posed by modernity. However, this approach suffers from a lack of critical investigation and understanding. Smith rightly notes that apologists win the hearts of Muslims, but lose their minds. See, also, Roy, *Failure of Political Islam*, pp. 94–106, who describes these "Islamic new intellectuals" as "tinkerers" in knowledge, and contends that their claims for renewed *ijtihād* provide them legitimacy, and at the same time, diminish the significance of the corpus of the Islamic tradition, to the extent that mastering it and commenting upon it is no longer the task of the new Islamic intellectual.
8 For a discussion of modernizing Islamic legal reform efforts, see Anderson, *Islamic Law in the Modern World*; *idem*, *Law Reform in the Muslim World*. Hallaq presents a brief history of legal modernization in the Middle East, during which wholesale adoption of European codes led to the diminished significance of Islamic law for adjudicatory purposes. Furthermore, through the process of *talfiq*, reformers constructed an Islamized legal code by selecting rules (*aḥkām*) from different *madhāhib* without concern for the epistemological integrity of each school. Consequently, the historical and normative legacy of Islamic law

was gradually corroded. Hallaq, *Islamic Legal Theories*, pp. 207–211. Afaf Marsot notes that Muḥammad ʿAlī's (r. 1805–1848) efforts to centralize power in nineteenth-century Egypt led to the disintegration of *awqāf* endowments, which had supported the *ʿulamāʾ*, and allowed them to remain independent from the government. Furthermore, the *ʿulamāʾ's* role in society was drastically reduced with the diminished jurisdiction of *Sharīʿah* courts to adjudicate legal issues. Marsot, *Women and Men in Late Eighteenth-Century Egypt*, pp. 136, 141–142. See, also, Hourani, *Arabic Thought*, p. 52. For a further discussion of the diminished jurisdiction of Islamic courts under colonial domination, see, Christelow, *Muslim Law Courts and the French Colonial State in Algeria*; Brinton, *The Mixed Courts of Egypt*; Hoyle, *Mixed Courts of Egypt*. Brinkley Messick argues that nationalist and bureaucratic centralizing forces in nineteenth- and twentieth-century Yemen contributed to the disintegration of Islamic legal institutions. Messick, *The Caligraphic State*. In his novel, Nabil Saleh presents the life of a nineteenth-century *qāḍī* in Ottoman Beirut who must contend with a society changing in a period of increasing European colonialism and Ottoman reform. Saleh, *The Qadi and the Fortune Teller*.

9 In recent Islamic conferences Egyptian academics have challenged my contention that authoritarian approaches to Islamic law have become predominant. I remain uninfected by their optimism.

10 *Al-Lajnah al-Dāʾimah lī al-Buḥūth al-ʿIlmiyyah wa al-Iftāʾ*.

11 For instance, in his translation of the Islamic legal manual *ʿUmdat al-Sālik*, Nuh Ha Mim Keller methodologically approaches matters concerning women much as the Wahhābīs do. Keller, *Reliance of the Traveller*, p. 122. See below. Kabbani generally presents a series of anecdotal and juristic statements for most issues he addresses. However his treatment lacks a critical analysis of the material. Rather his conclusions, whether on the legality of wiping over one's socks for ritual ablutions or the permissibility of juristic difference, are simplistic and unequivocal. Kabbani, *Forgotten Aspects of Islamic Worship*, pp. 7–16, 131–146.

12 For example, the following contemporary texts are not considered Wahhābī sources; nevertheless they adopt a similar approach in that all their conclusions are unilateral and unequivocal. See Zaydān, *Aḥkām al-Dhimmiyīn wa al-Mustaʾminīn fī Dār al-Islām*; *idem*, *al-Mufaṣṣal fī Aḥkām al-Marʾah*; Ḥassān, *Naẓariyyat al-Maṣlaḥah*; al-ʿĀlim, *al-Maqāṣid al-ʿĀmmah*; Zayd, *al-Maṣlaḥah fī al-Tashrīʿ*. These texts lie in sharp contrast to premodern texts in which a jurist not only addresses opposing opinions of law, but also the ambiguities in the relevant evidence that allow for such differences of opinion to exist. See Ibn Rushd, *Bidāyat al-Mujtahid*. For a contemporary example, see, Abū Zahrah, *Uṣūl al-Fiqh*.

13 Originating in the mid-nineteenth century, the Salafī movement attempted to reform Islamic thought as Muslim sovereignty yielded to increasing European colonial domination. The term "salaf" is meant to indicate a return to the righteous ancestors or the earliest generation of Muslims (*al-salaf al-ṣāliḥ*). The Salafīs urgently called for renewed *ijithād* in order to reform Islamic law in light of changed circumstances. Notably, the Salafī paradigm included a rejection of the premodern interpretive communities that focused their attention on understanding and elaborating upon the Qurʾān and *Sunnah*. Rather, the Salafīs sought to interpret these foundational sources without reliance on what they considered outdated or misdirected expositions from previous generations of Muslims. Khadduri, *Political Trends in the Arab World*, pp. 67–68; Shahin, *Political Ascent*, pp. 32–33; Enayat, *Modern Islamic Political Thought*, p. 69; Roy, *Failure of Political Islam*, pp. 31–34.

14 Ibn al-Fawzān, *al-Muntaqā min Fatāwā Faḍīlat al-Shaykh Ṣāliḥ b. Fawzān b. ʿAbd Allāh al-Fawzān*, 2:213.

15 *Idem*.

16 As indicated above, this attitude is the hallmark of the Salafī movement. Roy, *Failure of Political Islam*, pp. 31–34; Enayat, *Modern Islamic Political Thought*, p. 69; Shahin, *Political Ascent*, pp. 32–33; Khadduri, *Political Trends*, p. 67. Importantly, *talfīq* was a reformist technique by which modern codes of Islamic law were constructed. This process involved combining parts of the legal doctrine of one school with parts from another. This process

effectively undermined the integrity of the schools by ignoring each school's epistemological coherence. See, Hallaq, *Islamic Legal Theories*, p. 210; Coulson, *History*, pp. 192–201; Hourani, *Arabic Thought*, pp. 152–153.

17 The phrase "rightly guided caliphs" (*al-khulafāʾ al-rāshidūn*) refers to the first four caliphs to rule over the nascent Islamic polity after the Prophet's death. They were, in order of their reign, Abū Bakr al-Ṣiddīq (r. 11/632–13/634), ʿUmar b. al-Khaṭṭāb (r. 13/634–23/644), ʿUthmān b. ʿAffān (r. 23/644–35/656), and ʿAlī b. Abī Ṭālib (r. 35/656–40/661). The phrase *al-khulafāʾ al-rāshidūn* is principally a Sunnī designation.

18 ʿAbd al-ʿAzīz b. ʿAbd Allāh b. ʿAbd al-Raḥmān b. Bāz, *Majmūʿ Fatāwā*, ed. al Tayyar, 2:1270–1272.

19 This is clearly demonstrated in the apologetic literature that became very widespread in the 1960s and onwards recounting the stories of conversion of prominent Westerners to Islam and documenting the testimonials of non-Muslims as to the greatness of the Islamic Civilization. See, for example, Muḥammad Quṭb, *Shubuhāt ḥawl al-Islām*; Kishk, *al-Ghazw al-Fikrī*; *idem*, *Ḥaqq al-Murr*; Hofmann, *Islam: The Alternative*; Lang, *Even Angels Ask*; *idem*, *Struggling to Surrender*; Barboza, *American Jihad*.

20 In their *fatāwā*, the jurists address a *ḥadīth* in which the Prophet is reported to have said that his nation will divide into seventy-three different groups, only one of which will attain paradise. Consequently, the questions in these *fatāwā* concern how one knows which group is the favored one. The jurists explain, by reference to the *ḥadīth*, that this favored group follows the practice of the Prophet and his Companions (*mā kāna ʿalā mithl mā anā ʿalayhi al-yawm wa aṣḥābī*). Effectively, this group represents orthodox doctrine, and is labelled as the *ahl al-sunnah wa al-jamāʿah*. *Fatāwā al-Lajnah* (1991), 2:150–164, 3:174–178. Further, they identify the founder of the Wahhābī doctrine, Muḥammad b. ʿAbd al-Wahhāb, with the *ahl al-sunnah wa al-jamāʿah*. Consequently, they assert that in its attempt to adhere to the teachings of Muḥammad b. ʿAbd al-Wahhāb, the state of Saudi Arabia also adheres to the *ahl al-sunnah wa al-jamāʿah*. *Fatāwā al-Lajnah* (1991), 2:155–156. Some versions of these traditions state that there will be seventy-one groups. All of these traditions are of dubious authenticity. See al-Jurjānī, *al-Kāmil fī Ḍuʿafāʾ al-Rijāl*, 3:516, 4:497–498.

21 Interestingly, when these jurists are asked which books Muslims should read in order to learn the true religion, the jurists do not hesitate to name specific books mostly by Wahhābī authors. These books include, but are not limited to, the following: Muḥammad b. ʿAbd al-Wahhāb, *al-Tawḥīd*, *Ādāb al-Mashy li al-Ṣalāh*, and *al-Uṣūl al-Thalāthah*; Ibn Taymiyyah, *al-ʿAqīdah al-Wāsiṭiyyah*, *al-Ḥamawiyyah*, *al-Tadmiriyyah*, and *Majmūʿ Fatāwā*; *Shaykh* Muḥammad b. Ibrāhīm, *Majmūʿ Fatāwā*; *Shaykh* ʿAbd al-ʿAzīz b. Bāz, *Majmūʿ Fatāwā*; *Shaykh* ʿAbd al-Raḥmān al-Saʿdī, *Majmūʿ Fatāwā*; ʿAbd al-Raḥmān b. Ḥasan, *Fatḥ al-Majīd Sharḥ Kitāb al-Tawḥīd*; *Shaykh* Sulaymān b. ʿAbd Allāh, *Taysīr al-ʿAzīz al-Ḥamīd*. For a more complete listing, see *Fatāwā al-Lajnah* (1991), 2:177; Ibn Fawzān, *al-Muntaqā*, 2:212–213, 214–215.

22 ʿAbd Allāh b. Jibrīn was born outside of Riyāḍ in 1349/1930. After serving as director of legal education at the Institute of Imām al-Daʿwah, he taught at the College of Islamic law in the department of theology and contemporary thought. Thereafter, he was appointed a director of the Bureau for Scientific Research, Legal Responsa, Prosyletization, and Guidance (*idārāt al-buḥūth al-ʿilmiyyah wa al-iftāʾ wa al-daʿwah wa al-irshād*). In his graduate studies, he submitted a thesis on the significance of *āḥādī ḥadīth*. He has written at least thirty books. *Fatāwā al-Marʾah al-Muslimah*, ed. Abū Muḥammad Ashraf b. ʿAbd al-Maqṣūd, 1:6.

23 The *responsa* is translated in the appendix, p. 272.

24 ʿAbd al-ʿAzīz b. Bāz, Muḥammad b. al-ʿUthaymīn, and ʿAbd Allāh b. Jibrīn, *Fatāwā Islāmiyyah*, 3:205.

25 For this and similar reports, see al-Sakhāwī, *al-Maqāṣid al-Ḥasanah*, p. 494; al-Jirāḥī, *Kashf al-Khafāʾ wa Muzīl al-Ilbās ʿan mā ishtahar min al-Aḥādīth ʿalā Alsinat al-Nās*, pp. 266–267; ʿal-Shaybānī, *Kitāb Tamyīz al-Ṭayyib*, pp. 140, 171; Ibn Jār Allāh al-Yamānī, *al-Nawāfiḥ al-ʿAṭirah*, pp. 293–294.

26 For a concentrated dosage of this misogyny, see the following collections of juristic *responsa* on legal issues related to women: *Fatāwā al-Mar'ah al-Muslimah*; Ibn Baz et al, *Islamic Fatawa Regarding Women.*

27 ʿAbd al-ʿAzīz b. ʿAbd Allāh b. ʿAbd a-Raḥmān b. Bāz (1911–1999) was the grand *muftī* of Saudi Arabia until his death. Prior to holding this office, he worked as a justice in the Saudi judiciary and later taught at the Riyāḍ Islamic law college. Although he adhered to the Ḥanbalī school of law, he claimed that he performed *de novo* investigations of law and did not simply hold to (*taqlīd*) the school's positive rulings. Muḥammad b. Ṣāliḥ b. Muḥammad b. ʿUthaymīn (1927–) is a highly respected jurist in the Muslim world. He has taught law and religion at the university level, and is the author of numerous books. See, *Fatāwā al-Mar'ah* (1995), 1:4–5; *Islamic Fatawa*, p. 8.

28 Interestingly, Ibn Jibrīn in particular, adopts a more nuanced approach. He maintains that high heels, if not forbidden, are disfavored or reprehensible. He mentions without elaboration that the legality might depend on the intent behind wearing them. Ibn Bāz, *Fatāwā Islāmiyyah*, 3:190–191.

29 ʿAbd al-ʿAzīz b. ʿAbd Allāh b. ʿAbd al-Raḥmān b. Bāz, *Majmūʿ Fatāwā wa Maqālāt Mutanawwiʿah*, 4:29–31. Interestingly, al-ʿUthaymīn issued a *fatwā* in which he argues that this marriage is unlawful because it involves deception. Al-ʿUthaymīn contends that Ḥanbalī jurists have agreed that such a marriage is invalid. Muḥammad al-Ṣāliḥ al-ʿUthaymīn, *Fatāwā al-Shaykh Muḥammad al-Ṣāliḥ al-ʿUthaymīn*, 2:789–790. On the uses and abuses of this form of marriage by Saudi men in Egypt see, ʿAbd Allāh Kamāl, *al-Dā'irah al-Ḥalāl*, pp. 66–73.

30 Al-Bahūtī, *Kashshāf al-Qinā'*, 5:106; Abū Isḥāq Burhān al-Dīn Ibrāhīm b. Muḥammad b. ʿAbd Allāh b. Muḥammad b. Mufliḥ, *al-Mubdiʿ fī Sharḥ al-Muqniʿ*, 7:88. Ibn Qudāmah, *al-Mughnī* (Dār Iḥyā' al-Turāth al-ʿArabī), 6:645–646; al-Ḥaṭṭāb al-Raʿīnī, *Mawāhib al-Jalīl*, 5:85; Abū Bakr b. Masʿūd al-Kāsānī, *Badā'iʿ al-Ṣanā'iʿ fī Tartīb al-Sharā'iʿ*, 3:479–480. Some jurists have held, however, that where one party has an unstated intent to divorce, the marriage is equivalent to a *mutʿah* marriage. See, Ibn Mufliḥ, *al-Mubdiʿ fī Sharḥ al-Muqniʿ*, 7:88; Ibn Qudāmah, *al-Mughnī* (Dār Iḥyā' al-Turāth al-ʿArabī), 6:646; al-Bahūtī, *Kashshāf al-Qinā'*, 5:106. Others have suggested that such conduct is contrary to good manners (*laysa min akhlāq al-nās*). Al-Ḥaṭṭāb al-Raʿīnī, *Mawāhib al-Jalīl*, 5:85.

31 ʿAbd al-Ḥamīd Abū al-Makārim Ismāʿīl, *al-Adillah al-Mukhtalaf.*

32 Notably, the muftis of C.R.L.O insist that they do not represent a specific school of thought and that it is inappropriate to use the term *Wahhābī* to describe them. Rather, they contend that they represent Islamic law in general. See *Fatāwā al-Lajnah* (1991), 2:156, 173–174.

33 Ṣāliḥ b. Fawzān was one of the most notable jurists in Saudi Arabia. He was a member of C.R.L.O and was the director of the Supreme Judicial Council (*al-Maʿhad al-ʿĀlī li al-Quḍā'*). Ibn Fawzān was appointed as the spiritual director of the central mosque in Riyāḍ and has authored numerous books on religious doctrine and thought. *Fatāwā al-Mar'ah* (1995), 1:7.

34 *Fatāwā al-Lajnah al-Dā'imah lī al-Buḥūth al-ʿIlmiyyah wa al-Iftā'*, pp. 100–107; al-ʿUthaymīn, *Fatāwā al-Shaykh*, 1:170–171; ʿAbd al-ʿAzīz b. ʿAbd Allāh b. ʿAbd al-Raḥmān b. Bāz, *Majmūʿ Fatāwā*, 2:753–757; Ibn Fawzān, *al-Muntaqā*, 1:226–227, 2:168–170; Ibn Bāz, *Majmūʿ Fatāwā wa Maqālāt Mutanawwiʿah*, (1992) 5:332–335.

35 Interestingly, in a *responsum* by Ibn Fawzān, he admits that there is "some" juristic disagreement on this matter, but he only does so when the questioner informs him that another Wahhābī jurist, al-Albānī, had held that women may visit graves. Ibn Fawzān confesses that there are other points of view, but insists, nonetheless, that the correct rule is to prohibit such visits because women are weak. Ibn Fawzān, *al-Muntaqā*, 1:226–227.

36 Al-Suyūṭī, *Sharḥ Sunan al-Nasā'ī*, 4:89–90; Ibn Ḥajar al-ʿAsqalānī, *Fatḥ al-Bārī* (n.d.), 3:148–150; al-Nawawī, *Sharḥ Ṣaḥīḥ Muslim al-Musammā al-Minhāj Sharḥ Ṣaḥīḥ Muslim b. Ḥajjāj*, 7/8:49; Muḥammad Amīn b. ʿUmar b. ʿĀbidīn, *Ḥāshiyat Radd al-Muḥtār*, 3:150–1; al-Ramlī, *Nihāyat al-Muḥtāj* (1967), 3:36–7. Al-Māwardī, *al-Ḥāwī al-Kabīr*, 3:70, does not even mention the distinction between men and women.

37 Ibn Qayyim al-Jawziyyah, *'Awn al-Ma'būd*, 9:57.
38 Ibn Ḥajar al-'Asqalānī, *Fatḥ al-Bārī* (n.d.), 9:295.
39 Al-Nawawi, *Sharḥ Saḥiḥ Muslim* (n.d.), 16:387. See Abou El Fadl, "Dreaming of the Prophet," *Conference of the Books*, pp. 233–241, 238. Interestingly, Ibn Bāz is asked if it is permissible to curse Saddam Hussein. He responds that Saddam Hussein is a *kāfir* (unbeliever), but does not specifically state whether it is permissible to curse him. Ibn Bāz, *Majmū' Fatāwā*, (1416 A.H.), 2:536–537.
40 For many of the early traditions on visiting graves and specifically on wailing, self-beating and tearing the cloth, see al-Qayrawānī, *al-Nawādir wa al-Ziyādāt*, 1:574–578; Ibn Qayyim al-Jawziyyah, *'Awn al-Ma'būd*, 8:399; Ibn Ḥajar al-'Asqalānī, *Fatḥ al-Bārī* (n.d.), 3:163–164.
41 al-Mubārakfūrī, *Tuḥfat al-Aḥwadhī*, 4:136–139; Ibn Qayyim al-Jawziyyah, *'Awn al-Ma'būd*, 9:58–59.
42 Al-'Uthaymīn, *Fatāwā al-Shaykh*, 2:898; Ibn Bāz, *al-Fatāwā*, p. 199; Ibn Fawzān, *al-Muntaqā*, 3:63, 295, 5:187–188, 386–387.
43 Abū Hurayrah was a late convert to Islām. He is said to have converted when the Prophet led the seige of Khaybar in 7/629. Notably, despite the fact that he spent considerably less time with the Prophet than other notable Companions such as Abū Bakr, 'Umar, 'Alī, and his wife 'Ā'ishah, Abū Hurayrah transmitted more *ḥadīth* than any other Companion. Because of this, the authenticity of Abū Hurayrah's transmissions has been the subject of debate among Muslims for centuries. Al-Dhahabī, *Siyar A'lām*, 2:578–632; Ibn Sa'd, *al-Ṭabaqāt al-Kubrā* (n.d.), 2:362–364, 4:325–341; al-Ziriklī, *al-A'lām*, 3:308. Abū Sa'īd al-Khudrī was also a Companion of the Prophet who fought alongside the Muslims at the Battle of the Trench (5/627). Al-Dhahabī, *Siyar A'lām*, 3:168–172; al-Ziriklī, *al-A'lām*, 3:87.
44 Other than the reasons explained below, the chains of transmission of these reports contain unreliable transmitters, and so the authenticity of the traditions are suspect, see al-Jurjānī, *al-Kāmil fī al-Ḍu'afā'*, 3:256, 6:362.
45 Al-Nawawī, *Sharḥ Ṣaḥīḥ Muslim* (1996), 9:108–114; Ibn Qayyim al-Jawziyyah, *'Awn al-Ma'būd*, 5:151–154; al-Mubārakfūrī, *Tuḥfat al-Aḥwadhī*, 4:280–282; Ibn Ḥajar al-'Asqalānī, *Fatḥ al-Bārī* (n.d.), 4:240–242.
46 By foreign men, I mean an *ajnabī*. *Ajnabī* means any man that a woman may potentially marry – i.e., a man not excluded by blood or other familial relationship (such as suckling).
47 Ibn Bāz, *Fatāwā Islāmiyyah*, 3:183–184, 204; Ibn Fawzān, *al-Muntaqā*, 3:301–302; *Fatāwā al-Lajnah* (1991), 4:126; Ibn Bāz, *al-Fatāwā*, pp. 227–228; Ibn Bāz, *Majmū' Fatāwā*, 2:928; Ibn Bāz, *Majmū' Fatāwā wa Maqālāt Mutanawwi'ah*, 4:151. The cited verse is Qur'ān, 8:35.
48 The C.R.L.O does not seem troubled by the fact that many classical scholars contended that the clapping traditions are unreliable and are probably fabricated. See al-Jurjānī, *al-Kāmil fī al-Ḍu'afā'*, 3:17, 5:422, 494.
49 According to pre-modern commentators on the Qur'ān, this verse was directed against the Quraysh of Mecca whose religious practices included encircling the Ka'bah naked, as they clapped and whistled. Others have said that when the Prophet was praying, the Quraysh would clap and whistle in order to disturb him. See, al-Qurṭubī, *al-Jāmi'* (1993), 7:254; al-Ṭabarī, *Tafsīr al-Ṭabarī*, 4:35; al-Zamakhsharī, *al-Kashshāf*, 2:156; al-Rāzī, *al-Tafsīr al-Kabīr* (1999), 5:480–481; Ibn Kathīr, *Mukhtaṣar Tafsīr Ibn Kathīr*, 2:102–103.
50 For instance, see al-Ramlī, *Nihāyat al-Muḥtāj* (1967), 2:47–48.
51 Qur'ān, 33:32.
52 Al-Qurṭubī, *al-Jāmi'* (1993), 14:115; Ibn Kathīr, *Mukhtaṣar Tafsīr Ibn Kathīr*, 3:93; al-Ṭabarī, *Tafsīr al-Ṭabarī*, 6:176; al-Rāzī, *al-Tafsīr al-Kabīr* (1999), 9:167.
53 Saḥnūn b. Sa'īd al-Tanūkhī, *al-Mudawwanah al-Kubrā*, 1:190.
54 Ibn Ḥajar al-'Asqalānī, *Fatḥ al-Bārī* (n.d.), 13:204; al-Nawawī, *Sharḥ Ṣaḥīḥ Muslim* (1996), 13/14:14; Ibn Qayyim al-Jawziyyah, *'Awn al-Ma'būd*, 8:159; Ibn Qudāmah, *al-Mughnī* (Beirut: Dār al-Kutub al-'Ilmiyyah, n.d.), 1:670–671; Abū Zakariyyā Muḥyī al-Dīn b. Sharaf al-Nawawī, *Majmū' Sharḥ al-Muhadhdhab*, 4:82, 85, 88, 114; Ibn 'Ābidīn, *Ḥāshiyat Radd al-Muḥtār* (1994), 2:403; al-Ramlī, *Nihāyat al-Muḥtāj* (1967), 2:47–48; Ibn Nujaym, *al-Baḥr al-Rā'iq Sharḥ Kanz al-Daqā'iq*, 1:471.

55 With his typical keen insight, Shihāb al-Dīn al-Qarāfī (d. 684/1285) distinguished between the roles and functions of a judge and a jurist. Al-Qarāfī, *al-Iḥkām fī Tamyīz al-Fatāwā* (1995).

56 One of the *responsa* is translated in the appendix p. 272–273.

57 Ibn Bāz, *Islamic Fatawa*, pp. 309–313; Ibn Bāz, *Majmūʿ Fatāwā wa Maqālāt Mutanawwiʿah* (Cairo: Maktabat Ibn Taymiyyah, 1990), 3:351–353; Ibn Fawzān, *al-Muntaqā*, 5:383.

58 It is not clear whether a woman utilizing public transportation is prohibited. Al-ʿUthaymīn, *Fatāwā al-Shaykh*, 2:898; Ibn Bāz, *al-Fatāwā*, p. 199; Ibn Fawzān, *al-Muntaqā*, 3:295.

59 C.R.L.O and Ibn Bāz make the same point when holding that it is unlawful for women to work outside their homes. Ibn Bāz, *Majmūʿ Fatāwā wa Maqālāt*, (1987), 1:422–431; Al-ʿUthaymīn, *Fatāwā al-Shaykh*, 2:837–838; Ibn Bāz, *Islamic Fatawa*, pp. 313–317.

60 Pre-modern Muslim jurists extracted the concept of *sadd al-dharīʿah* from precedents and textual prescriptions in the Qur'ān and Sunnah. See, for example, al-Qarāfī, *al-Furūq*, (n.d.), 3:266; al-Bājī, *Iḥkām al-Fuṣūl fī Aḥkām al-Uṣūl* (1995), 2:696–697; al-Zuḥaylī, *al-Wasīṭ*, pp. 572–573; Abū Zahrah, *Uṣūl al-Fiqh*, pp. 228–229; al-Dībānī, *al-Minhāj al-Wāḍiḥ*, 2:252–253.

61 Pre-modern Muslim jurists recognized this fact when they contrasted *sadd al-dharīʿah* with *fatḥ al-dharīʿah* (opening the means). See, Abū Muḥammad Ibn ʿAbd al-Salām, *Qawāʿid al-Aḥkām fī Maṣāliḥ al-Anām*, pp. 91–93; al-Qarāfī, *al-Furūq*, 2:33; Abū Zahrah, *Uṣūl al-Fiqh*, p. 229; al-Zuḥaylī, *al-Wasīṭ*, p. 566.

62 Al-Qarāfī, *al-Furūq*, 2:32; Abū Zahrah, *Uṣūl al-Fiqh*, pp. 227–228; al-Zuḥaylī, *al-Wasīṭ*, pp. 571–572; Kamali, *Principles*, p. 314.

63 Ibn Qayyim al-Jawziyyah, *Iʿlām al-Muwaqqiʿīn* (Cairo), 3:180–181; al-Dībānī, *al-Minhāj al-Wāḍiḥ*, p. 251; Abū Zahrah, *Uṣūl al-Fiqh*, pp. 230–232; Kamali, *Principles*, pp. 314–317.

64 See, for example, the *responsum* in which Ibn Fawzān explains the concept of *sadd al-dharīʿah*. Ibn Fawzān, *al-Muntaqā*, 2:287. Ibn Fawzān's treatment is remarkably simplistic, and consists of saying that whatever leads to something prohibited is also prohibited. For instance, contrast his treatment with: Ibn al-Najjār, *Sharḥ al-Kawkab al-Munīr*, pp. 434–437; Ibn ʿAbd al-Salām, *Qawāʿid al-Aḥkām*, pp. 43–50, 91–95, 199–204; al-Qarāfī, *Sharḥ Tanqīḥ al-Fuṣūl*, pp. 160–162; *idem*, *al-Furūq*, 2:29–34, 3:266–269; al-Shāṭibī, *al-Muwāfaqāt*, 4:140–152, see esp. pp. 143–145; Ibn al-Laḥḥām, *al-Qawāʿid wa al-Fawā'id*, pp. 130–142; Ibn Ḥazm, *al-Iḥkām*, 6:179–191; al-Bājī, *Iḥkām al-Fuṣūl* (1995), 2:695–700; al-Dībānī, *al-Minhāj al-Wāḍiḥ*, 2:251–253.

65 Zarabozo's translation into English of many of these *responsa* (*Islamic Fatawa*), I am informed by Muslim book merchants, is one of the best sellers in the field. I was recently informed by a book merchant in Austin, Texas that he sells more copies of that book than all the other books on Islamic law put together.

66 Al-ʿUthaymīn, *Fatāwā al-Shaykh*, 2:754; Ibn Fawzān, *al-Muntaqā*, 5:243, 245.

67 Ibn Fawzān, *al-Muntaqā*, 4:179.

68 Qur'ān, 17:23; al-Mubārakfūrī, *Tuḥfat al-Aḥwadhī*, 4:333–334, 6:23–25; Ibn Qayyim al-Jawziyyah, *ʿAwn al-Maʿbūd*, 8:77–78; al-Nawawī, *Sharḥ Ṣaḥīḥ Muslim* (1996), 2:268–274; Ibn Ḥajar al-ʿAsqalānī, *Fatḥ al-Bārī* (n.d.), 5:261–263, 10:405–413, 11:66–67, 11:555–557, 12:191–197, 12:264–267; al-Dhahabī, *Kitāb al-Kabā'ir*, pp. 39–46.

69 Al-Jirāḥī, *Kashf al-Khafā'* (1968), pp. 365–366; ʿAbd al-Raḥmān al-Shaybānī, *Kitāb Tamyīz al-Ṭayyib*, p. 194; Ibn Jār Allāh al-Yamānī, *al-Nawāfiḥ al-ʿAṭirah*, p. 463.

70 I have already dealt with this issue in, Abou El Fadl, "On Obedience," *Conference of the Books*, pp. 57–59.

71 Qur'ān, 2:187, 30:21.

72 Qur'ān, 2:187, 4:4, 4:19–21; 4:25, 4:34, 16:72, 30:21. In support of marriage, the Prophet is reported to have said: "O young men! Whoever among you has the ability should marry, for [marriage] restrains the eyes and protects [one's] chastity...." Ibn Ḥajar al-ʿAsqalānī, *Fatḥ al-Bārī* (n.d.), 4:119–9:112–115; al-Nawawī, *Sharḥ Ṣaḥīḥ Muslim* (1996), 9/10:175–180.

73 Al-Nawawī, *Sharḥ Ṣaḥīḥ Muslim* (1996), 9/10:175–180, see esp. p. 177.

74 Abou El Fadl, "State Between Two States," *Conference of the Books*, p. 261.

75 Ibn Ḥajar al-ʿAsqalānī, *Fatḥ al-Bārī* (n.d.), 1:505; al-Nawawī, *Sharḥ Ṣaḥīḥ Muslim* (1996), 5/6:420; Ibn ʿAbd al-Barr, *Jāmiʿ Bayān al-ʿIlm*, 1:7–10; Ibn Mājah, *Sunan* (1972), 1:81.

76 Al-Dhahabī, *Kitāb al-Kabāʾir*, pp. 47–49; Ibn Ḥanbal, *Musnad*, 2:639, 3:19, 3:104; al-Nawawī, *Sharḥ Ṣaḥīḥ Muslim* (1996), 15–16:328–331; al-Mubārakfūrī, *Tuḥfat al-Aḥwadhī*, 6:28–30.

77 Ibn Fawzān, *al-Muntaqā*, 3:246–247, 3:329, 5:263.

78 Al-Jirāḥī, *Kashf al-Khafāʾ* (1968), pp. 365–366; ʿAbd al-Raḥmān al-Shaybānī, *Kitāb Tamyīz al-Ṭayyib*, p. 194; Ibn Jār Allāh al-Yamānī, *al-Nawāfiḥ al-ʿAṭirah*, p. 463; Ibn Qayyim al-Jawziyyah, *ʿAwn al-Maʿbūd*, 7:288–292; al-Nawawī, *Sharḥ Ṣaḥīḥ Muslim* (1996), 11/12:426–433; Ibn Ḥanbal, *Musnad*, 1:512.

79 Al-Suyūṭī, *al-Durr al-Manthūr*, 6:99; al-Alūsī, *Rūḥ al-Maʿānī* (1985), 5:330, 26:151; al-Kabīr, *Tafsīr al-Suddī al-Kabīr*, p. 442; Ibn Kathīr, *Tafsīr al-Qurʾān al-ʿAẓīm*, 4:222; al-Thaʿālibī, *al-Jawāhir al-Ḥisān*, 4:188; al-Andalūsī, *Tafsīr al-Nahr al-Mādd*, 2(2):979; al-Nasafī, *Tafsīr al-Nasafī* (1996), 3:1678; al-Ṣanʿānī, *Tafsīr al-Qurʾān*, 2:188; al-Rāwandī, *Fiqh al-Qurʾān*, 1:372; al-Kāshānī, *Tafsīr al-Ṣāfī*, 5:50; al-Bayḍāwī, *Anwār al-Tanzīl wa Asrār al-Taʾwīl*, 5:88; al-Qurṭubī, *al-Jāmiʿ li Aḥkām al-Qurʾān* (1952), 16:316–317; al-Ṭabrīsī, *Majmaʿ al-Bayān*, 6:88; al-Ṭabarī, *Jāmiʿ al-Bayān*, 25:81–82; al-Jaṣṣāṣ, *Aḥkām al-Qurʾān*, 3:399–400; al-Ṣāwī, *Ḥāshiyat al-ʿAllāmah*, 4:110–111; al-Māwardī, *al-Nukat wa al-ʿUyūn*, 5:330; Abou El Fadl, "Islamic Law of Rebellion," pp. 40–53.

80 Ibn Hishām, *al-Sīrah al-Nabawiyyah* (Beirut: Dār al-Maʿrifah, n.d.), 3/4:411; Martin Lings, *Muḥammad: His Life Based on the Earliest Sources* (United Kingdom: George Allen & Unwin, 1983), p. 299.

81 In an absurdly formalistic, and immoral, tradition, a husband, before leaving on a business trip, orders his wife not to leave the second floor of her two-story home. Pursuant to the husband's instructions, the woman could not visit her father who lived on the first floor of the same house. After the husband left, the wife's father fell gravely ill, and the wife wanted to see her father before he died, but she did not wish to disobey her husband. Consequently, she sent to the Prophet asking him if she may visit her father. The Prophet told her that she may not do so because she must obey her husband's commands. The father soon died, and the woman again sent to the Prophet to ask if she may visit him before burial. She received the same response commanding her to obey her husband. After the father was buried, without the presence of his daughter, the Prophet sent to the woman informing her that God has forgiven her father's sins because she obeyed her husband. This report has a defective chain of transmission. See Abū Ḥāmid al-Ghazālī, *Iḥyāʾ*, 2:57; al-Tirmidhī, *Nawādir al-Uṣūl*, p. 176. Although most classical jurists seem to have dismissed this tradition as unreliable, it exemplifies the immoral logic and absurd situations that such determinations promote.

82 Ibn Bāz, *al-Fatāwā*, pp. 193–195; Ibn Fawzān, *al-Muntaqā*, 4:177. In a tradition, not cited by the C.R.L.O, it is reported that the Prophet stated that even if a husband is unjust or unfair, his wife ought to try to appease him. Even if he rebuffs her efforts, she has done her duty, and she will be rewarded. This tradition is considered weak. See al-Bayhaqī, *Kitāb al-Sunan al-Kubrā*, 7:293.

83 Qurʾān, 65:2.

84 Al-ʿUthaymīn, *Fatāwā al-Shaykh*, 2:871–872

85 Qurʾān, 2:173, 6:145, 16:115. The law of *ḍarūrah* (necessity) alters, as a matter of law and on a case-by-case basis, a prohibited act into a permissible one in exceptional circumstances. For example, under a *ḍarūrah* analysis, a starving person may consume the flesh of a dead animal to avoid his own death, despite the general legal prohibition against eating carrion. The challenge posed by the *ḍarūrah* inquiry is in determining whether the circumstances warrant the legal exception and the extent to which one may engage in the exceptional act. So for instance, if one is starving, he may eat carrion. However, he may do so only to the extent he can avoid death by starvation. Thereafter, the rule of law in his case reverts to the general prohibition. Zaydān, *al-Madkhal*, p. 84; al-Zuḥaylī, *Naẓariyyat al-Ḍarūrah*; Schacht, *Introduction*, p. 84.

86 ʿAbbāsī, *Fatāwā wa Rasāʾil*, 1/2:478; al-ʿUthaymīn, *Fatāwā al-Shaykh*, 2:757.

87 This position has been attributed to the Prophet in the form of traditions. According to these reports the Prophet said, "If a man has intercourse with his wife, he should not climax until she does, and if he climaxes [before his wife] he should lie with her until she climaxes [as well]." See al-Hindī, *Kanz al-ʿUmmāl,* 16:344. Some versions of this report have problematic chains of transmission, see al-Jurjānī, *al-Kāmil fī Ḍuʿafāʾ,* 7:333.

88 Al-Tijānī, *Tuḥfat al-ʿArūs*; Ibn Qayyim al-Jawziyyah, *Rawḍat al-Muḥibbīn*; al-Iṣbahānī, *al-Qiyān*; al-Suyūṭī, *Rashf al-Zulāl*; Maḥmūd, *Jughrāfiyā al-Maladhdhāt*; al-Nīfāsh, *Nuzhat al-Albāb.*

89 *Fatāwā al-Lajnah* (1991), 1:457–465, 469–471, 494–495, 496–497.

90 Interestingly, however, there are short C.R.L.O *responsa* holding that hanging photographs of kings and notables is not permissible, and that photographing women in prison is unlawful as well. *Fatāwā al-Lajnah* (1991), 1:484–87. The C.R.L.O does not elaborate upon these rulings, and does not explain if this prohibition applies to public buildings or to photographing men in prison.

91 The *responsa* deciding that it is lawful to wage war with the United States and Britain against Iraq rest on three main justifications: (1) Saddam Hussein has become an unbeliever, and so Saudi Arabia is fighting unbelievers and not Muslims; (2) Seeking the assistance of the United States and Britain is a necessity; and (3) The American forces are similar to hired labor. The American forces are not proper allies, but hired hands to fight on behalf of Muslims against unbelievers (i.e. Saddam Hussein). Ibn Bāz, *Majmūʿ Fatāwā,* 2:536–537, 1056–1065, 1237–1239.

92 Ibn Ḥajar al-ʿAsqalānī, *Fatḥ al-Bārī* (n.d.), 10:382–386.

93 Interestingly, in some *responsa* C.R.L.O jurists assert that it is unlawful for children to play with toy dolls or figures. Ibn Bāz, *Majmūʿ Fatāwā,* 2:828.

94 Al-Nawawī, *Sharḥ Ṣaḥīḥ Muslim* (1996), 13/14:306–321; al-Mubārakfūrī, *Tuḥfat al-Aḥwadhī,* 5:349–353; al-Suyūṭī, *Sharḥ Sunan al-Nasāʾī,* 8:212–217; Ibn Ḥajar al-ʿAsqalānī, *Fatḥ al-Bārī* (n.d.), 4:314–315, 4:416–417, 10:382–390, 10:516–518, 12:427–430.

95 Al-Mubārakfūrī, *Tuḥfat al-Aḥwadhī,* 5:350.

96 Ibn Fawzān, *al-Muntaqā,* 4:11–13.

97 Pre-modern Muslim juristic discussion on human corpses generally extended to a discussion on the obligation to bury (*dafn*) the dead. See, for instance, Ibn Rushd, *al-Muqaddimāt al-Mumahhidāt,* 1:236; al-Nawawī, *Rawḍat al-Ṭālibīn,* 2:131–137; al-Marghīnānī, *al-Hidāyah,* 1:90–94; al-Shīrāzī, *al-Muhadhdhab,* 1:253; Ibn Qudāmah, *al-Mughnī* (Dār Iḥyāʾ al-Turāth al-ʿArabī), 2:496–499; Ibn Rushd, *Bidāyat al-Mujtahid,* 1:362–363. For instance, al-Shīrāzī specifically states that it is not permissible to simply neglect the body without burial (*lā yajūz isqāṭuhu*). Notably, a contemporary scholar has interpreted Ibn Ḥajar al-Haytamī's (d. 974/1567) prohibition against breaking the bones of the dead (*kasr ʿaẓm al-mayyit*) as a prohibition against autopsies. Keller, *Reliance,* p. 973. In either case, one cannot ignore the prodigious development in medical science in Islamic history, particularly by the celebrated doctor and philosopher, Ibn Sīnā (Avicenna). See, for instance, Ibn Sīnā, *al-Qānūn fī al-Ṭibb*; Siraisi, *Avicenna in Renaissance Italy,* pp. 19–40. On the history of science and medicine in Islam generally, see, Nasr, *Science and Civilization in Islam*; al-Andalusī, *Science in the Medieval World*; Rosenthal, *Science and Medicine in Islam*; Conrad, "The Social Structure of Medicine in Medieval Islam," pp. 11–15.

# 7 Faith-based assumptions and determinations demeaning to women

The juristic determinations analyzed thus far can be described as negligent or reckless with regard to the trust of special agency. At the heart of this negligence or recklessness is a violation that involves a degree of lack of honesty, self-restraint, diligence, comprehensiveness, or reasonableness. In each determination, the special agent failed to disclose a critical balancing act of competing interests, or failed to show reasonable concern and respect for one set of interests as opposed to others. Alternatively, the special agent failed to adequately analyze or take account of the critical material upon which his or her authoritativeness is based, whether this critical material is the instructions of the Principal or the activities of the relevant interpretive communities that formed around the instructions of the Principal. In each determination, we could point to a serious analytical flaw, the effect of which is to make the special agent self-referential and authoritarian. This type of analysis, however, is not adequate in addressing determinations that involve fundamental points of departure over the moral or ethical foundations that define our relationship to the Principal, Himself.

In a particular genre of determinations, the problem cannot be ascribed to a failure to investigate the evidence adequately or simply to an abuse of discretion. Here, the problem is not solely a sociologically based insensitivity to the interests of a particular group of people, or a failure to take account of the weight of the evidence. Rather, the issue is the basic moral commitments or understandings of the special agents, and the way they impact the dynamics of their relationship to the common agents. From a certain perspective, in this genre of determinations, the quantitative weight of the textual (instructional) evidence might point to a particular determination, nevertheless the moral convictions of the agents might pose a serious challenge to the acceptance of these determinations. This problem is well-illustrated in a whole set of traditions that can be described as demeaning to women. As discussed below, these traditions relate to a variety of issues including the nature of women, the role of women, or even the fate of women. I am not arguing that textual evidence plays no role in this analysis for in fact, as we will see, the evidence is often conflicting and complex. The evidence in these cases tells a complex and contradictory story, and the question boils down to what and whom do you believe? In these cases, the dispositive reference often becomes the conscience or the moral understanding that defines one's relationship to the Principal. This argument is better demonstrated through the analysis of a group of determinations and the traditions cited in them. Most of the traditions that I will discuss are cited by C.R.L.O in the context of determinations that prohibit the mixing of the sexes (*ikhtilāṭ*), the employment of women outside the home, the veiling of women, or determinations maintaining that the spiritual status of a woman depends on the extent of her obedience to her husband.[1]

## *Prostrating to husbands, licking their ulcers while struggling with* Ḥadīth *methodology*

The C.R.L.O jurists, and in fact many others in the modern age, assert that wives are commanded to obey their husbands as long as the husband's command is lawful. Usually, this means that a wife must obey her husband if he orders her not to leave the home, not to work, not to visit friends, not to cook Indian food, or not to wear her grandmother's nightgown or curlers to bed. In other words, a wife should obey her husband in all mundane matters. She should also obey in other matters that, perhaps, are not so mundane. If the husband wants to have sex, she should promptly submit. If she wishes to fast, other than in the month of Ramadan, she must obtain his permission.[2] Furthermore, according to some traditions, discussed below, women must obey their husbands even if these husbands are wrong or unjust.[3] Typically, these jurists cite the Qur'ānic verse stating: "Men are the maintainers (*qawwāmūn*) of women by what God has given some over the others, and by what they spend."[4] The word used in the Qur'ānic verse, *qawwāmūn*, could mean the "protectors," "maintainers," "guardians," or even "servants." That same word is used in the Qur'ān in one other context, and that is when Muslims are commanded to be the *qawwāmūn* of justice. Typically, those who agree with the C.R.L.O assert that this verse is added proof that husbands have the right to command and discipline their wives. I have dealt with the issue of obedience to husbands and the so-called "beating-verse"[5] elsewhere, and it is not fruitful to repeat the analysis here.[6] In this context, it is sufficient to note that this verse is not dispositive. For one, the word *qawwāmūn* is ambiguous, and more importantly, the verse seems to hinge the status of being a maintainer, guardian or protector on objective capacities, such as the ability to provide financial support. Arguably, if a woman is the one providing financial support, or stability, she becomes the one entrusted with the burden of guardianship. Furthermore, arguably, if financial responsibility is shared between the partners, then they become each other's guardians. Furthermore, at no point does the Qur'ān use the word *ṭā'ah* (obedience) in characterizing the marital relationship. Rather, marriage is characterized as a relationship of companionship and compassion (*mawaddah wa raḥmah*), not a relationship between a superior and inferior.[7]

Nevertheless, the Qur'ānic discourse does not play the primary role in determinations of spousal obedience. The primary role is played by traditions attributed to the Prophet, the most notable of these being the one in which the Prophet reportedly says, "It is not lawful for anyone to prostrate to anyone. But if I would have ordered any person to prostrate to another, I would have commanded wives to prostrate to their husbands because of the enormity of the rights of husbands over their wives."[8] This tradition is narrated in a variety of forms and through a variety of transmissions by Abū Dāwūd, al-Tirmidhī, Ibn Mājah, Aḥmad b. Ḥanbal in his *Musnad*, al-Nasā'ī, and Ibn Ḥibbān.[9]

In one version, Maḥmūd b. Ghaylān reports that Abū Hurayrah said that the Prophet asserted: "If I would have ordered anyone to prostrate to anyone I would have ordered a wife to prostrate to her husband."[10] This version also occurs by the way of Faḍl b. Jubayr from Abū Umāmah al-Bahlī.

In another version, Abū Bakr b. Abī Shaybah reports that 'Ā'ishah said that the Prophet said: "If I would have ordered anyone to prostrate to anyone I would have ordered a wife to prostrate to her husband. If a man orders his wife to move from a red mountain to a black mountain and [again] from a black mountain to a red mountain it is incumbent upon her to obey."[11]

In a related version, 'Ā'ishah is reported to have said that the Prophet was standing among a group of *Muhājirūn* (Muslim migrants from Mecca to Medina) and *Anṣār* (native converts of Medina) when a camel came and prostrated to the Prophet. The Companions said, "O Prophet the cattle and trees prostrate before you; are we not more deserving [of such an honor]?" (meaning: Shouldn't we prostrate to you?). The Prophet said: "Worship your God and honor your brothers ..." but the balance of the report is the same as above.[12]

Another version comes from Azhar b. Marwān. He reports that when Mu'ādh returned from Shām, he prostrated to the Prophet. The Prophet said, "What are you doing Mu'ādh?" Mu'ādh said, "I was in Shām and I saw that the people there prostrated to their priests and clergy and I wished we could do the same for you." The Prophet said, "If I would have ordered anyone to prostrate before anyone but God, I would have ordered a woman to prostrate to her husband. By God, a woman cannot fulfill her obligations to God until she fulfills her obligations to her husband and if he asks for her [i.e. for sex] while she is on a camel's back, she cannot deny him [his pleasure]."[13]

Another version has Mu'ādh returning from Yemen, not Shām, and asking the Prophet if Muslims should prostrate to him. The Prophet's reply is the same as above but without the addition about having sex on a camel's back. In yet another version, it is Qays b. Sa'd b. 'Ubādah who is returning from Ḥīrah. The same scenario then takes place as above.[14] Still another version has the Prophet adding that, "a woman cannot fulfill her obligations towards God unless she fulfills her obligations towards her husband. [In fact,] if he desires her while she sits on a saddle (or an upright seat used for birthing), she should submit."[15]

In a final version, Anas b. Mālik reports that the Prophet said, "No human may prostrate to another, and if it were permissible for a human to prostrate to another I would have ordered a wife to prostrate to her husband because of the enormity of his rights over her. By God, if there is an ulcer excreting puss from his feet to the top of his head, and she licked it for him she would not fulfill his rights."[16]

According to scholars of *ḥadīth*, the authenticity of these traditions ranges from *ḍaʿīf* (weak) to *ḥasan gharīb* (good).[17] All of them are *āḥādī ḥadīth* (reports of singular transmissions) not reaching the level of *tawātur* (reports of several transmissions).[18] Importantly, these reports reach beyond other traditions that specify a narrow legal obligation; these reports explicate a fundamental principle that is supposed to impact upon all marriages and all gender relations. While the physical act of prostration to the husband is not permitted, the moral substance of prostration does apply through such traditions. The clear implication of the reports is that a wife owes her husband, by virtue of him being a husband, a heavy debt. The husband is owed the utmost degree of respect and even servitude.[19] It is not an exaggeration to say that according to these traditions, the wife lives as the husband's humble servant; she is to submit sexually on the back of a camel and lick his puss-filled ulcers if need be. A similar message is affirmed by another tradition also reported by Abū Hurayrah asserting that the Prophet said: "If a man calls his woman to bed, and she refuses to come, the angels will continue to curse her until the morning." There are several other versions of this report, which assert that if the man becomes upset because his wife will not have sex with him, the angels will continue cursing the woman until the husband is no longer angry.[20]

There is no question that these traditions, and others discussed below, have grave theological, moral, and social consequences. They do not only support C.R.L.O's determinations mandating obedience to husbands, but they also contribute to the general denigration of the moral status of women. After all, even the angels in the heavens are moved to the point of cursing women if they do not surrender their will and body to their husbands. Regardless of the jargon generated by apologists about how Islam liberated and honored women, these traditions subjugate a woman's honor to the will of men.[21] It is significant, for example, that after citing the prostration and submission traditions, the jurist Ibn al-Jawzī (d. 521/1201) makes the immoral claim that a wife should consider herself, for all practical purposes, the husband's slave. He states in part:

> It is incumbent upon a woman to know that it is as if she is owned (*ka al-mamlūkah*) by her husband, therefore she may not act upon her own affairs or

> her husband's money except with his permission. She must prefer his rights over her own and over the rights of her relatives, and she must be ready to let him enjoy her through all clean means. She must not brag about her beauty and must not taunt him about his shortcomings ... It is incumbent upon a woman to endure her husband's mistreatment as a slave should. We have seen that the virtues of a slave woman were described to Mālik b. Marwān. When she was presented to him, he asked her about her affairs. She said, "I cannot forget who I am. I am your slave." So [Mālik] said, ""This covered [woman] is worth her price."[22]

Although this quote is not representative of the predominant view in classical juristic tradition, the point remains that the prostration and submission traditions legitimate, if not induce, this type of discourse.[23] Because of the drastic normative consequences of traditions such as this, they require a conscientious pause. If by the standards of age and place, or the standards of human moral development, traditions lead to *wakhdh al-ḍamīr* (the unsettling or disturbing of the conscience), the least a Muslim can do is to pause to reflect about the place and implications of these traditions. If we assume that the human *fiṭrah* (intuition) is socially and historically limited, it will necessarily be changing and evolving. Consequently, what will disturb the conscience in one context will not necessarily do the same in another. Nevertheless, if a Muslim's conscience is disturbed, the least that would be theologically expected from thinking beings who carry the burden of free will, accountability and God's trust, is to take a reflective pause, and ask: to what extent did the Prophet really play a role in the authorial enterprise that produced this tradition? Can I, consistently with my faith and understanding of God and God's message, believe that God's Prophet is primarily responsible for this tradition?

This is not an invitation to the exercise of whimsy and feel-good determinations. The duties of honesty, self-restraint, diligence, comprehensiveness, and reasonableness demand that a Muslim make a serious inquiry into the origin, structure, and symbolism of the authorial enterprise that produced the tradition before simply waiving it away and proceeding on his merry way. The conscientious-pause would obligate the Principal's agent to apply thorough critical thought to the tradition in question, in search for the role of the Prophet in it. To demonstrate this point, I will examine the prostration tradition, and similar reports, in some detail.

Perhaps the most notable thing about the prostration traditions is that they are structurally peculiar. In most reports, the Prophet is asked whether it is permissible to prostrate to him, the Prophet. To this he is supposed to have answered, "No! But actually if a human could prostrate to a human it would be the wife to a husband." Such a fundamentally revolutionary view is expressed out of context and in a rather casual way. Basically, according to these reports, the Prophet volunteers this injunction although that is not what is being asked. In most versions, the one doing the asking is a man and the response is given to a man or men. Although the traditions have a profound impact upon women, this advice is supposed to be enunciated before an audience of men. This is quite a casual way of delivering advice that will have profound social and theological implications upon women in particular. Furthermore, as a matter of symbolic discourse, an unjustifiable nexus is created between the Prophet and husbands. The question posed to the Prophet is about the respect that is owed the Prophet. The response addresses the respect that is owed husbands. A powerful symbolic association is created between the status of the Prophet and the status of husbands. We observe a similar association between husbands and the symbols of Divinity in the submission tradition. A whole host of angels in the Heavens are aggrieved by the frustration of a man's libido. This only raises the question: what is it about a man's sexual urges that make them so fundamental to the pleasure of the Heavens? Does this include all forms of pleasure by men or only sexual? What if a man's pleasure consists of being breastfed by his wife or of being tied up and whipped by his wife? Do the Heavens maintain their enthusiasm for the male libido regardless of its many forms and regardless of the emotional consequences upon the wife?

The context and structure of the traditions makes them suspect. It is highly unlikely that the Prophet, in such an unsystematic or haphazard fashion, would address Islamic theological questions. Furthermore, the Qur'ān is rather vigilant in asserting the unshared, undivided, and non-contingent supremacy of God. This assertion formed the basis for the Islamic dogma maintaining that submission to God necessarily means non-submission to anyone else. Consequently, any tradition that draws an association between the status of the Prophet, or the pleasure of God, and the status or pleasure of a human being is inherently suspect. Under all circumstances, it is reasonable to claim that if a tradition has serious theological, moral, and social implications, it should meet a heavy burden of proof before it can be relied upon. But even more, if a tradition is suspect because of a contextual or structural defect, among other reasons, then there should be a presumption against its authenticity, and the evidence supporting the authenticity of the tradition should be conclusive.

In the case of the prostration and submission traditions, the evidence suggests that they cannot be relied upon because we cannot conclusively assert that the Prophet played the primary role in the authorial enterprise that produced them. For one, they contradict the theological notion of the undivided supremacy of God and God's Will. In addition, they are inconsistent with the Qur'ānic discourse on marriage. The Qur'ān states: "From God's signs is that God created mates for you among yourselves so that you may find repose and tranquility with them, and God has created love and compassion between you" (Qur'ān 30:21). The Qur'ān also describes spouses as garments for each other (Qur'ān 2:187). In addition, these traditions are not consistent with the cumulative reports describing the conduct of the Prophet with his own wives. For example, al-Bukhārī narrated that 'Umar's wife while arguing with 'Umar told him, "You reproach me for answering you! Well, by God, the wives of the

Prophet answer him, and one of them might even desert him from morning until night."[24] In Tayalīsī's report, one of the Prophet's wives might argue with him until she angers him.[25] Furthermore, there are numerous reports by the Prophet's wives asserting that the Prophet never struck or insulted any one of them, and that his demeanor with his wives was gentle and playful, and that he would frequently seek their counsel.[26] These reports cast an image of the Prophet, as a husband, that is very different from the image advocated by the prostrating and submission tradition. The point, again, is not whether these reports, even if in *Ṣaḥīḥ al-Bukhārī*, have legal imperative value. The point is that the Prophet, as the most elementary reading of the *sīrah* (traditions of the Prophet's life) would reveal, was not a dictator within his family.

A person suffering the conscientious-pause would have to consider the above-mentioned considerations as part of the totality of evidence that must be sifted through in order to ascertain whether the suspect traditions meet the onerous burden of proof placed upon them. In addition, one might ask, considering the patriarchical society in which Islam was revealed, what are the chances that the Prophet did, in fact, prohibit the act of prostrating to him, but that the authorial enterprise added the part about the prostration of wives? As some commentators have noted, the tradition seems to be highly exaggerated (*fīhi ghāyat al-mubālaghah*) with what appears to be later editorial additions about mountains, saddles, backs of camels, and puss-filled ulcers.[27] Is it possible that the prostration part of the tradition was added as a, so-to-speak, rider-bill on an otherwise unrelated historical incident? To what extent should we probe the circumstances of the individuals engaged in the authorial enterprise? For instance, many of the versions of both the prostration and submission traditions go back to Abū Hurayrah, which is a problematic fact.[28] As we will see below, many of the traditions demeaning to women are reported, in one version or another, by Abū Hurayrah who has been a rather controversial figure in early Islamic history. In fact, criticism directed at his credibility is not novel, and, in fact, has induced some writers to compose books in his defense.[29] The basic criticism directed at him is that he was a late convert to Islam who became a Muslim only three years before the Prophet's death. Nevertheless, Abū Hurayrah transmitted more traditions attributed to the Prophet than most of the Companions who lived with the Prophet for as much as twenty years. Furthermore, compared to some Companions such as Abū Bakr, ʿUmar, ʿAlī, or Abū Dharr al-Ghifārī, he does not seem to have been particularly close to the Prophet. As a result, there are a large number of reports asserting that several Companions such as ʿĀʾishah, ʿUmar, and ʿAlī severely criticized Abū Hurayrah for transmitting so many reports. Abū Hurayrah's contemporaneous detractors objected to the fact that Abū Hurayrah was a late convert, and transmitted many traditions that contradicted the transmissions of more notable Companions. To these criticisms, Abū Hurayrah responded, that it was not his fault that other Companions forgot what they heard and saw while he cared to remember.

He also added that while other Companions were busy pursuing their commercial interests, he piously stayed with the Prophet, learning at his feet. Of course, this, in itself, implicitly detracted from the virtue of the other Companions, which only made Abū Hurayrah's credibility more problematic. For instance, in one such report, ʿĀʾishah called upon Abū Hurayrah to come see her, and she told him, "Abū Hurayrah! What are these reports from the Prophet that we keep hearing that you transmit to the people! Tell me, did you hear anything other than what we heard, did you see anything other than what we observed?" Abū Hurayrah responded, "O mother, you were busy with your kohl and with beautifying yourself for the Prophet, but I – nothing kept me away from him."[30] In a similar report, Abū Hurayrah would consistently say, "My close companion (*khalīlī* – i.e. the Prophet) told me such-and-such, and my close companion did such-and-such." ʿAli confronted Abū Hurayrah and said, "Abū Hurayrah, since when was the Prophet your close companion!"[31]

Other reports asserted that Abū Hurayrah would contradict himself, or that he was corrected by other Companions such as Zubayr and ʿUmar. In fact, ʿUmar reportedly threatened to punish him if he did not refrain from transmitting traditions. In one report, ʿUmar told Abū Hurayrah, "If you don't stop transmitting *ḥadīth* from the Prophet, I will exile you."[32] Interestingly though, after ʿUmar's death, Abū Hurayrah only accelerated his transmission activities, and would reportedly comment that if ʿUmar was alive he would have had him beaten for his narratory zeal. On several occasions, as discussed below, ʿĀʾishah, the Prophet's wife, specifically objected to transmissions by Abū Hurayrah that demeaned women. In one report unrelated to women, Abū Hurayrah was addressing some legal issue when ʿĀʾishah was praying, but she overheard him nevertheless. By the time she finished her prayers, Abū Hurayrah had left the mosque upon which ʿĀʾishah reportedly said, "Did you see this man (*Abū fulān*), he came and sat next to my room as I was praying, saying such-and-such. If I would have caught up with him after finishing my prayers, verily, I would have corrected him."[33] Some reports even allege that the narration of reports became a means by which Abū Hurayrah earned a living. Other reports mention that Abū Hurayrah was knowledgeable in the Talmud and that many of his transmissions correlated with Jewish mythology and lore. Importantly, Abū Hurayrah seemed to claim esoteric knowledge of the Prophet. Reportedly, he would comment that he transmitted some things from the Prophet, but that he conceals so much more. If he would transmit everything he heard or knows from or about the Prophet, people would have had him pelted with shoes and garbage, and said Abū Hurayrah must be insane.[34] To this, al-Ḥasan (d. 50/670), the Prophet's grandson, responded, "By God, he is right! If he would tell us that the Kaʿbah is burning or crumbling no one would believe him!"[35]

These various issues led some early jurists to refuse to rely on the transmissions or legal opinions of Abū Hurayrah. Some later jurists such as al-Sarakhsī (d. 483/1090) accepted his transmissions only if they did not contradict analogical analysis.[36] Importantly, however, Abū Hurayrah's reputation, primarily for sectarian reasons, has been substantially rehabilitated. In response to Shīʿī criticisms, Sunnīs insisted on the credibility and justness of character of all the Companions including ʿAlī's foe, Muʿāwiyah, and Abū Hurayrah, who reportedly supported Muʿāwiyah.[37] Some circulated traditions explained Abū Hurayrah's role as being the result of exceptional or super-natural circumstances. One such report, asserts that the reason Abū Hurayrah transmitted so much is that the Prophet made a special prayer asking God to allow Abū Hurayrah to forget nothing. Other reports assert that Abū Hurayrah was uniquely inspired so that he was able to ask the Prophet questions that the Prophet had hoped to be asked for twenty years.[38] Basically, through the persuasive powers of Sunnī apologetics most Sunnī collections of *ḥadīth* accepted the reports of Abū Hurayrah. In fact, it is likely that in order to defend Abū Hurayrah's credibility, some of the reports that originated with him were also circulated in the name of other Companions. So, for instance, in one report, the prostration tradition is transmitted in the name of ʿĀ'ishah thus, giving the impression that even ʿĀ'ishah accepted Abū Hurayrah's transmissions.

My point is not to impeach Abū Hurayrah, but these various pieces of information are relevant to determining whether traditions in which he figures prominently should be relied upon when the consequences of this reliance are so grave. If there is no reason for a conscientious-pause, the interpreter might be willing to be less critical or to give the report the benefit of the doubt. If, however, the theological, moral, and social implications are profound, an interpreter cannot treat the report with the same degree of tolerance. The approach I am advocating requires that the totality of circumstances be considered in evaluating reliance on a tradition. There should be a *proportional relationship* between the theological and social implications of a tradition and the burden of proof it should satisfy. If a tradition is suspect because it induces a conscientious-pause, then it should not be relied upon unless its authenticity can be conclusively established.

The suggested approach would evaluate issues related to the substance (*matn*), chain of transmission (*isnād*), historical circumstances (*ẓarf al-riwāyah*), and the moral and social consequences.[39] As we noted earlier, *matn* or substantive analysis, which relies on an analysis of a variety of intangible factors, is not a novelty in Islamic history.[40] According to the classical scholarship on the *ʿilal al-ḥadīth* (analysis of defects in tradition), a report with an impeccable chain of transmission may be rejected because the text of the tradition is not sound. As mentioned earlier, such a tradition would be rejected either because it contains grammatical or historical errors, or it clearly contradicts the Qur'ān, or the text is contrary to the laws of nature, common human experience or the dictates of reason.[41] After evaluating the totality of the evidence, classical scholars would declare a tradition suffering from these defects, or others, to have *ʿilal qādiḥah fī al-matn* (an effective defect in the substance of the tradition that renders it unreliable).[42] But as noted earlier, this field remained under-developed and under-utilized by Muslim scholars, and its ambiguities led some scholars to describe it as the "mysterious science."[43]

My point, of course, is to make the self-serving plea of orthodoxy, but, admittedly, classical and modern scholars have not attempted to correlate the authenticity of a tradition with its theological and social ramifications. The scholars of *ḥadīth* did not demand a higher standard of authenticity for a tradition that could have sweeping theological and social consequences. Additionally, as the passage from Ibn Khaldūn, quoted earlier implies, *ḥadīth* scholars did not engage in historical evaluation of traditions or examine their logical coherence or social impact, and as a result, they often accepted the authenticity of traditions with problematic theological and social implications.

If one adopts the proportionality inquiry advocated here, the conscientious-pause would lead one, at a minimum, to refuse to rely on traditions such as the prostration and submission tradition in legal or theological matters. This does not necessarily mean that one is conclusively deciding that the tradition is not authentic. Rather, one is only deciding that the tradition cannot be conclusively said to originate primarily from the Prophet. Since one suspends, perhaps indefinitely, reliance on such traditions, one does not need to affirmatively decide whether they are authentic or not. All one needs to decide is that they are not good enough to rely on, and, therefore, we do not even reach a faith-based determination. Now, let us assume that after discharging the five obligations by thoroughly evaluating everything I can discover about these traditions, my conscience remains troubled. My conscience remains troubled either because my evaluation of the evidence leads me to think that to the best of my knowledge this tradition appears authentic, or I find the tradition so fundamentally offensive to my understanding and relationship with God. In other words, assume that I evaluate everything related to the prostration tradition, and my conscience is not satisfied with a simple decision not to rely on the tradition because my conscience is satisfied only if I affirmatively believe the tradition is not authentic. I very much want to believe that the Prophet did not say this. Alternatively, assume that I find that the evidence points to the actual authenticity of the tradition, and yet, my conscience remains troubled because as a believer, I cannot believe that the Prophet said such things. What do I do then? I take the stand of a faith-based objector, and refuse to accept the authenticity of the traditions. If I am wrong, the fact that I discharged the five obligations would vindicate me, hopefully, before God, from the onerous charge of being whimsical. But if I am right in arguing that God looks to the effort and not the results, the simple fact that I discharged the five obligations would free me from liability.

## *Keeping husbands and God happy, and making it to heaven*

Being fully conscious of the fact that the approach advocated above, particularly in the contemporary age, is at the very least quite controversial, the balance of this chapter will attempt to demonstrate the necessity of this approach by addressing several more examples. This will require that I provide some more detail as to the classical methodology of traditions, and why I think it is inadequate. I will continue to focus primarily on the traditions cited by the C.R.L.O in reaching its determinations. This is not because I wish to discredit the C.R.L.O or its long list of affiliated jurists, but because it is my belief that the methodology utilized by the C.R.L.O has become very widespread in the Muslim world today.

In order to bolster its determination mandating obedience of wives to husbands, the C.R.L.O and the jurists who agree with this position frequently cite traditions that go beyond the submission and prostration reports. These traditions make a wife's religious salvation explicitly contingent on her husband's pleasure. For example, a tradition narrated by Abū Dāwūd, al-Tirmidhī, Ibn Mājah, Ibn Ḥibbān, and al-Ḥākim claims that Umm Salamah, the Prophet's wife, reported that the Prophet said, "Any woman who dies while her husband is pleased with her enters Heaven." This tradition is of the same degree of authenticity as the reports on prostration.[44] The commentators on the well-known classical source *Riyāḍ al-Ṣāliḥīn* say that this means only if the woman is pious and her husband is pleased with her, will she enter Heaven.[45] This is, of course, read by implication (*mafhūm al-naṣṣ*, *mīthāq al-naṣṣ*, or *maḍmūn al-naṣṣ*). The literal text does not say a pious woman, it says any woman who dies with her husband pleased with her will enter Heaven. This is problematic because it makes God's pleasure contingent on the husband's pleasure. But even if we say the tradition only applies to pious women, it is still problematic because God's pleasure is still contingent on the husband's pleasure regardless of how impious the husband might be. The wife might be pious and the husband impious, and yet, the husband's pleasure matters. Then, we are forced to read a further implication; this tradition applies only if the husband is pious and the wife is pious. But even then, it is still problematic because what happens if the wife is more pious than the husband? What if the husband is spend-thrifty or ill-mannered or ill-tempered or violent or cowardly or stupid or lazy? Despite any possible occasionality, God's pleasure would be contingent on the husband's pleasure. This is a revolutionary concept with profound theological and social implications. Before it can be recognized as setting a theological foundational principle, it must be of the highest degree of authenticity, which it is not.

Another version of this tradition has Anas b. Mālik reporting that the Prophet said: "If a woman prays five [times a day], fasts Ramadan, obeys her husband, and guards her chastity, she will enter Heaven."[46] Arguably, this version explains or specifies (*takhṣīṣ*) the earlier version. So it is not simply any woman that obeys her husband who will enter Heaven; rather, only a woman who obeys, prays, fasts and guards her chastity. However, there are several problems with this logic as well.[47] First, this version is accepted by a fewer number of narrators than the first. Second, one of the individuals in the chain of transmission of this version is Ibn Luhayʿah, who is not trustworthy.[48] Third, this version does not at all avoid the ambiguities of the first version. For example, what happened to the *farḍ* (religious obligation) of paying *zakāh* (almsgiving), or performing *ḥajj* (pilgrimage to Mecca)? Perhaps this is relegated to the financial abilities of the husband. But what if the wife is rich and the husband is poor? Additionally, what if the wife prays, fasts, protects her chastity, and obeys her husband, but is despicable otherwise? What if she backbites, slanders people, beats her children, steals from the neighbors, tortures her cat, and mocks the poor? Is she still entitled to enter Heaven? The only way we can give a negative response to this question is by imputing different meanings to the tradition than the apparent meaning of the words.

Other traditions relied upon for the same obedience determination include one that claims that the Prophet stated, "A woman's prayers or good deeds will not be accepted [by God] as long as her husband is upset with her."[49] Another tradition reportedly transmitted by ʿAbd Allāh b. ʿUmar claims that the Prophet proclaimed, "God will not look at a woman who is not grateful to her husband despite her reliance on him" (i.e., despite the fact that she depends on her husband).[50] And yet another report claims that the Prophet said, "If a woman upsets her husband, his angelic wife in Heaven (*ḥūr al-ʿayn* – his wife among the angels waiting for him in the Hereafter) will say, 'May God confound you! Do not upset him (the husband)! He is but a visitor with you who is about to leave you and join us.'"[51]

The analysis presented above, applies to these traditions as well. These traditions invoke a conscientious-pause – they trouble the conscience, contradict other portrayals of the Prophet's character, and conflict with the Qur'ānic spirit. With a minimal amount of reflection, one can see a conflict between the foundational principles set by the Qur'ān and the traditions of subservience and obedience. The Qur'ān talks of love, compassion, friendship, and virtuous women who are obedient to God – not to husbands.[52] Arguably, compelling your wife to have intercourse on the back of an animal, demanding unquestioning reverence, or blind obedience is not conducive to love, compassion, friendship, virtue, or obedience to God. In my view, the Qur'ānic conception of marriage is not based on servitude, but on compassion and cooperation; and the Qur'ānic conception of virtue is not conditioned on the pleasure of another human being, but on piety and obedience to God.

Classical and modern jurists argue that if there is a conflict between the sources, one must reconcile them – not use one source to trump the other. This is a well-established principle in Islamic jurisprudence. Pursuant to this principle, the obedience traditions would serve to specify or particularize the broader discourses in the Qur'ān and *Sunnah* about friendship and companionship. This is the logic that the C.R.L.O uses in arguing that the obedience traditions add a further detail to the broader Qur'ānic discourses. According to this reasoning, Islam requires the establishment of friendship and companionship, but through obedience. But one should ask the following methodological question: should traditions of divergent versions, of singular (*āḥādī*) transmissions, which do not reach the highest level of authenticity, and which have suspect theological logic and profound social implications, be allowed to conflict with the Qur'ān in the first place? In fact, and more importantly, should traditions with the qualities described above, be recognized as establishing laws, let alone foundational principles, for something as essential as marriage? I propose that a rationale of proportionality must be adopted, which would necessarily require only those traditions of the highest degree of authenticity to be recognized as foundational in matters of crucial religious or social implications.

The *ahl al-ḥadīth*[53] have argued that traditions of singular transmission (*āḥādī* reports) create certain knowledge (*yaqīn qaṭʿī*) and hence, could support a binding rule not only in *ʿibādāt* (laws relating to worship) and *muʿāmalāt* (laws relating to social and commercial interactions), but also in *ʿaqā'id* (matters of faith). The other schools of thought disagreed – some arguing that *āḥādī* traditions do not yield knowledge at all and may not be used to support legal imperatives. The majority, however, held that such traditions, while not leading to certain knowledge, do produce a likelihood that the transmission is valid (*ẓann*). Furthermore, the majority of jurists argued that *āḥādī* traditions can support legal imperatives in the field of *furūʿ* (branches of religion) but not *uṣūl* (fundamentals of religion). The majority then disagreed within itself: some argued that *āḥādī* traditions can establish a legal imperative in the branches of religion as long as it does not contradict the Qur'ān or *mutawātir* traditions; others argued that *āḥādī* traditions cannot contradict the practice of the people of Medina; others that *āḥādī* traditions cannot contradict a *qiyās* (rule by analogy); and others asserted that *āḥādī* traditions cannot support independent legal imperatives, but only support an exception or a specification to a general rule.[54]

The C.R.L.O, and those who follow their school of thought, agree with the *ahl al-ḥadīth* in allowing *āḥādī* traditions to be dispositive in all fields of law as well as in matters of faith and conviction.[55] To a large extent, this position justifies the majority of their determinations, especially on issues related to women. Furthermore, this position seems to have gained widespread currency in the contemporary age.[56] However, it is important to note that, other than *ahl al-ḥadīth*, it is clear that the vast majority of classical Muslim jurists wanted to limit the scope of *āḥādī* traditions. Since *āḥādī* traditions cannot lead to certain knowledge of the Prophet's utterances, they cannot be relied upon to the same extent as *mutawātir* traditions. *Āḥādī* traditions, the majority argued, could be used to establish branches of the religion, but not the fundamentals. Although the majority of jurists struggled with the distinction between fundamentals and branches, the fact remains that they did not consider *āḥādī* traditions of sufficient probative value to establish matters that are essential to religion. Therefore, it makes perfect sense to argue for a proportional relationship between the authenticity of traditions and their effective scope. I cannot claim that the logic of proportionality is explicitly endorsed by the discourses of the classical jurists, but I believe that proportionality is the clear import of their debates on *āḥādī* traditions. However, to limit the logic of proportionality to the dichotomy between *uṣūl* and *furūʿ* is not plausible. As noted earlier in this book, the distinction between *uṣūl* and *furūʿ* is itself problematic.[57] It is not at all clear how one defines *uṣūl* or *furūʿ*. More importantly, the issue is not whether a problem could be technically classified as part of *uṣūl* or *furūʿ*. Rather, the issue is the existence of proportionality between our knowledge of the source of a text, and the impact of the text. The greater the potential impact of a textual source, the more one should insist on its authenticity. *Mutawātir* traditions lead to greater certainty as to the role of the Prophet in the authorial enterprise and, therefore, could possibly be relied upon to establish legal imperatives with far reaching theological, social or political implications. Nevertheless, the analysis should not simply be limited to whether a tradition is *mutawātir* or *āḥādī*. Especially in cases of the conscientious-pause, whether a tradition is *mutawātir* or *āḥādī* is only the beginning of the inquiry. Relying solely on the counting of the number of early transmitters will yield little benefit. The point is not only how many people from the first generations of Muslims transmitted a particular tradition. Rather, when a tradition has serious social, theological or political implications, the inquiry should be whether the totality of the evidence could provide us with a clear sense of the role of the Prophet in what is attributed to him. The totality of evidence would include the authenticity and trustworthiness of the transmitters, the number of transmitters from the early generations, the number of versions of the traditions, the factual contradictions between the different versions, the substance of the tradition, the relation between this tradition and more authentic or less authentic reports from the *Sunnah*, the Qur'ānic evidence (in terms of contradictions or consistencies), the historical context of the tradition, and the practices of the Prophet and Companions in related contexts. By their very nature, *mutawātir* traditions will be able to withstand greater scrutiny than their *āḥādī* counterparts. Ultimately, however, even after evaluating the totality of the evidence, one might have to take a faith-based stand in rejecting a particular position. Importantly, if this stand is taken by a special agent who had fulfilled the five contingencies including disclosing his or her conscientious objection, one cannot describe the special agent's behavior as authoritarian. After all, the special agent had showed humility, self-restraint, and diligence in exploring all the possibilities, and after disclosure, the common agents are free to affirm or withdraw their trust and deference.

## *Bargaining with crooked-ribs, defective intellects, bad omens, dogs and women*

I noted above that especially as to traditions that cause a conscientious-pause, the totality of circumstances must be carefully scrutinized. This has particular relevance to reports that demean women because of the stubborn institutions of patriarchy that are likely to have played a predominant role in the authorial enterprise that generated many traditions. For instance, in a remarkable tradition expressing this reality, Ibn ʿUmar (d. 73/692) reportedly commented, "When the Prophet was alive we were cautious when speaking and dealing with our women in fear that a revelation would come [from God] concerning our behavior. But when the Prophet died we were able to speak and deal with them [more freely]."[58] This tradition reflects a rather rare admission that there was social resistance to the early Islamic reforms regarding women.[59] Ibn ʿUmar's report is consistent with the many traditions that recount the widespread resistance, especially by Meccan men, to the presence of women in public forums, which compelled the Prophet to explicitly command men not to prevent women from attending prayers in mosques.[60] Nevertheless, despite the explicit command, men allowed women to attend prayers in the morning but not the night, which in turn, led the Prophet to specify that his command covered attending prayers at night as well.[61] The early traditions reflect a virtual war of reports on this and other issues, some of which are discussed below. It is sufficient, at this point, to note that one of the circulating reports even claimed that menstrual periods originated as a form of Divine punishment for the public role played by women. According to this report, the women of the Israelites would insist on attending temples of worship, but they inevitably misbehaved by unleashing their womanly charms upon the unsuspecting men. As a result, God forbade Jewish women from attending temples of worship, and inflicted the menstrual cycle upon all women as punishment, apparently to keep women from places of worship for a period of time each month.[62] Of course, I am not implying that the majority of classical scholars, or even a sizable number of them, accepted the validity of this report. Nonetheless, it is symptomatic of a socio-historical context that left its clear imprint on the raw materials that Muslim jurists are forced to work with. So, for instance, there are a considerable number of reports, one of which is quoted below, that the Meccan Muslims found the culture of the native Medinese too liberal for their taste. Medinese women played a very public role, and so, for example, formed part of the Medinese delegation that negotiated with the Prophet before his migration to Medina.[63]

As demonstrated below, understanding this context is important not only for evaluating the authorial enterprise behind several traditions, but also for understanding the role of several traditions that attempt to exclude women from public life. I will discuss several of what might be called the public function traditions in a section below. But as a foundation, I will analyze a set of traditions that relate to the construction of the symbolic nature of women. Again, I have focused on the traditions cited in juristic determinations by the C.R.L.O. These traditions create symbolic associations between women and some unflattering construct. Ultimately, these traditions lay the foundation for legal determinations affirming the position of patriarchy, the submission of women, and their exclusion from public life.

Among the conscientious-pause inducing determinations of the C.R.L.O are ones that deal with women and the negation of prayer, bad omens, and divorce. The C.R.L.O jurists are asked about the effect of a woman passing in front of a man in prayer. The C.R.L.O responds that if a man is praying and a woman passes in front of him without a screen separating the man and woman, the man's prayer is invalidated and must be repeated. In support, the C.R.L.O cites a transmission by Abū Hurayrah attributing to the Prophet the statement, "The passage of a woman, donkey, and black dog in front of a man, invalidates his prayer."[64] In another *responsum*, Ibn Bāz asserts that some women are bad omens and, therefore, divorcing them is justifiable. In support, he cites a Prophetic tradition stating, "If bad omens exist in anything, they exist in [some] houses, women, and mounts."[65]

These traditions and the C.R.L.O determinations hardly warrant a comment – the association drawn between women and animals is clear. In fact, other traditions, cited in the context of mandating the veil or in prohibiting the mixing of sexes, draw an association between women and the devil. For example, a tradition attributed to the Prophet, proclaims, "A woman comes in the image of a devil, and leaves in the image of a devil." The rest of the tradition goes on to say that if a man is aroused by a foreign woman, he should satisfy his desire lawfully with his wife.[66] It is important to note that the C.R.L.O does not use these reports in order to explicitly defile or demean women. In fact, according to the C.R.L.O, their determinations honor and protect women from all forms of degradation. Of course, the way the C.R.L.O makes this point is by asserting that Islam, apparently which they represent, fully honors and protects women.[67] The reports quoted above are utilized in making technical decisions on particular legal issues. However, having employed reports that draw a connection between women and unflattering symbolisms, the C.R.L.O is able to draw upon social constructs or typologies of womanhood with devastating results. These constructs or typologies enable the C.R.L.O to maintain that women should be excluded from public life, and all activities that are part of partaking in public life such as driving. Significantly, this is done with an air of condescending benevolence, and not confessed malignity. This is well illustrated in the C.R.L.O's utilization of what can be called the crooked rib and deficient intellect traditions. In the first, Abū Hurayrah reported that the Prophet said, "Take good care of women, for they have been created from a crooked rib, and the most crooked part of a rib is its upper part. If you try to straighten out a rib, you will break it and if you leave it [alone] it will remain crooked. So, take good care of women."[68] In another version of the same report, again transmitted by Abū Hurayrah, the Prophet reportedly said, "A woman is like a rib. If you try to straighten her, you will break her. If you accept her the way she is, you will enjoy [your life with] her, but she will remain crooked."[69] The C.R.L.O uses this tradition in ruling that women require understanding and care-taking by men – men ought to be tolerant of women's defects and so, in the existence of marital problems, husbands should not to rush to divorce their wives.[70]

Like the crooked rib reports, the deficient intellect traditions are easily co-opted into paternalistic and condescending discourses. This tradition in its most well-known version provides:

> Abū Hurayrah[71] reported that the Prophet passed by a group of women when he addressed them. The Prophet proclaimed, "O women! Increase your prayers, and then give more alms for I have seen that women are the majority of the inhabitants of Hell." A wise woman asked, "Why are we [women] the majority of the inhabitants of Hell, O Prophet of God?" The Prophet responded, "Because you frequently slander and curse, and you are ungrateful to your companions. I have not seen anyone more deficient in intellect and religion, who is able to prevail (mislead) the wise, than you." So, they (the women) asked, "And, what is [our] deficiency in intellect and religion?" The Prophet said, "[Your] deficiency in intellect is in the fact that the testimony of a man is worth [the testimony] of two women, and your deficiency in religion is that you spend days without fasting or praying (because of the menstrual cycle)."[72]

The C.R.L.O, as in the case of most apologists, insists that there is nothing demeaning in this tradition to women because the tradition clearly states that the deficiency is not substantive, but rather technical. The deficiency means legal incapacity, and not natural inability.[73] It is significant, however, that in a large number of determinations excluding women from public life and imposing the veil, the C.R.L.O frequently asserts that women are the majority of the inhabitants of Hell, and that they are of a limited emotional and intellectual capacity. According to the C.R.L.O, because women are not in control of their emotions and are not as sagacious as men, they should not work outside the home, occupy positions of leadership, drive cars, pursue higher education, visit graves, travel without a male companion, or even attend mosques other than the one closest to their homes.[74] Despite its assurances to the contrary, the C.R.L.O employs these traditions in the affirmation of certain typologies – perceptions or social constructs – of the capacities and function of women. This lays the foundation for most of the patriarchal and condescendingly paternalistic determinations of Islamic law.

Considering the nature of the traditions mentioned above, admittedly, one feels rather silly in saying that these traditions require a conscientious-pause, and perhaps, a faith-based protest. These traditions seem self-evidently immoral and shocking. Nevertheless, considering that the C.R.L.O and many other contemporary authors have given these reports determinative weight, we are forced to address them.[75] Attempting to evaluate these traditions by simply scrutinizing the chains of transmission is pedantic and non-probative. I am not dismissing the chain of transmission analysis as entirely irrelevant, but it simply constitutes one of the elements that needs to be evaluated.[76] The issues that confront us in addressing these traditions consist of evaluating the authorial enterprise supporting these reports, and exploring the extent that they can form part of the instructions that the special agent is charged with interpreting and implementing. I confess that, at a personal level, I am willing to be a conscientious faith-based objector to this genre of traditions. They are fundamentally inconsistent with my understanding of God and the Islamic message. This disclosure is consistent with the methodology advocated here. However, aside from any faith-based claims, it is my contention that contemporary jurists who rely on these traditions are violating the contingencies upon which their authoritativeness is founded. The failure largely consists in the fact that these contemporary jurists have not diligently investigated the authorial enterprise that retained, transmitted, and constructed these traditions. It is impossible to be sufficiently diligent in analyzing the authorial enterprise behind these reports without seriously considering the highly patriarchal context that these traditions reflect.

The tradition by Abū Hurayrah asserting that mounts, black dogs, and women invalidate the prayer of men is a good starting point for illustrating this issue, and so I will examine some of the circumstances surrounding this report. Interestingly, there are many existing versions of this report; the various versions are ascribed to transmissions by Abū Hurayrah, as well as Ibn ʿAbbās and Abū Dharr al-Ghifārī. The one element common to all versions is the inclusion of social undesirables in the possible list of things that could invalidate a prayer. For instance, one version, reportedly narrated by Ibn ʿAbbās, asserts that it is pigs, black dogs, donkeys, and women that invalidate a man's prayer. Some versions claim that all dogs, not just black, and only menstruating women, not all women, invalidate prayers. Other versions add Manicheans, unbelievers, and Jews, for good measure, to the list of invalidators. Clearly, this was a tradition that served as a receptacle for social condemnation, and the hurling of bigoted insults. Importantly, various historical reports assert that this tradition faced considerable opposition in early Islam. A large number of reports state that ʿĀʾishah, in particular, took offense – when informed that Abū Hurayrah was circulating this report, she exclaimed, "God confound you! You have made women the same as dogs and donkeys!" In another transmission, ʿĀʾishah reportedly responded, "You have made women like the worst animals! By God, I used to lie down in front of the Prophet, while on my menstrual cycle, as he continued to pray." Umm Salamah, the Prophet's wife, confirmed ʿĀʾishah's report, and recounted that they would be on their menstrual period and they would either pass or lay down in front of the Prophet as he prayed, and the Prophet never made mention of any such rule. Furthermore, ʿAlī and Ibn ʿUmar rejected the various versions of the tradition and contended that none of the categories mentioned above could invalidate a Muslim's prayers. Other reports add that Ibn ʿAbbās, the same person to whom one of the above versions is attributed, and other Companions, narrated that on several occasions, donkeys passed in front of the Prophet, and a dog played around the Prophet as he continued to pray. Ibn ʿAbbās adds that no one thought that donkeys or dogs affected the validity of prayers, and the Prophet never stated that they did either. Importantly, as far as the activities of the early interpretive communities are concerned, they reflect a general lack of confidence in all the versions of this tradition. For instance, early scholars disagreed on the authenticity of Abū Hurayrah's tradition, and its alternative versions.[77] Some argued that the tradition is weak, others said it was fabricated, and still others claimed that it is authentic, but that it was later abrogated by the Prophet. The jurists al-Shāfiʿī, al-Thawrī, Abū Ḥanīfah, and Mālik b. Anas did not rely on the tradition, and held that nothing that could pass in front of a praying person invalidates his or her prayers.[78] Even Aḥmad b. Ḥanbal, the founder of the Ḥanbalī school of legal thought, argued that while he is sure that black dogs do invalidate prayers, he very much doubted that the same rule applies to donkeys and women.[79]

From the point of view of the accumulation and evaluation of evidence, we cannot conclusively and with absolute certainty decide that the dog, donkey, and women tradition is authentic or inauthentic. More importantly, authenticity is not even the relevant issue. The relevant issue is how to assess the authorial enterprise. We have enough circumstantial evidence to indicate a strong bias in the early social dynamics of Islam to shape the tradition one way or another. There was a sufficient degree of vested interest in degrading women by associating them with dogs, donkeys or unbelievers, and there was a strong enough interest to add Jews to the list of undesirables as well. There was also a vested interest in defending women against this charge. In the midst of these social interests and lively dynamics, there was a strong incentive to embellish, exaggerate, construct, and re-construct.[80] The appearance of Abū Hurayrah in the reports, considering his background, adds another level of indeterminacy about the authorial enterprise. It is very likely, if not very probable, that this was a social debate in which the memory of the Prophet was co-opted, redacted, and at times, invented. Once again, we must refer to the doctrine of proportionality in considering the legal effect to give to a tradition. Considering the many ambiguities, suspicions, and doubts surrounding the authorial enterprise, it is irresponsible, and perhaps dishonest, to use the dog, donkey, and women tradition in the fashion in which the C.R.L.O uses it. Furthermore, considering the egregious moral implications of these traditions upon the normative status of women in society, it is outrageous that the C.R.L.O relies on them in such a perfunctory manner.

Substantially the same analysis applies to the traditions on crooked ribs, deficient intellects, and women as devils or bad omens. If we take, for example, the tradition on the bad omen of women, we observe very similar dynamics. The various versions of this tradition include some that omit any mention of women – only horses and homes are mentioned as possible sources of bad omens. Interestingly, one version states the exact converse of the bad omen tradition.

In this version it is reported that the Prophet said, "Bad omens do not exist, but if good omens exist in anything (*al-yumn* and, in another version, *al-fa'l al-ṭayyib*) then it would be in women, homes, and horses."[81] In addition, several reports assert that ʿĀʾishah strenuously opposed the bad omen tradition. In one such report, two men informed ʿĀʾishah that Abū Hurayrah was saying that the Prophet said that women and mounts could be bad omens. ʿĀʾishah was outraged and declared, "By God Who revealed the Qurʾān to Abū al-Qāsim (Muḥammad), whoever attributes this to the Prophet, has lied."[82] Again, because of the contextual ambiguities surrounding this issue, early jurists were reluctant in accepting or relying on the bad omen tradition in legal determinations. But as can be expected, this tradition served as the grazing ground for some of the most virulent anti-women rhetoric in Islamic history. Some commentators claimed that the intended meaning of "women who are a bad omen," is women who are unable to bear children. A report attributed to ʿUmar even proclaimed that "a straw rug on the floor is better than a barren woman." Yet, many of the early and late classical jurists, such as Taqī al-Dīn al-Subkī (d. 756/1355), asserted that men who consider some women to be bad omens, or who ascribe unfortunate events to women, are ignorant. Other classical jurists simply interpreted the tradition away. For example, Ibn al-ʿArabī (d. 543/1148) argued that the tradition was simply describing an unfortunate and reprehensible social practice in early Arabia. The Prophet was only saying that Arab customs used to ascribe disasters to horses, homes or women because it was believed that some houses, animals or women were cursed. The Prophet, Ibn al-ʿArabī contended, was advising Muslims to abandon such reprehensible superstitions.[83] In support of this argument, Ibn al-ʿArabī and others cite reports such as the following: Abū Hurayrah states that the Prophet said, "A believing man should not hate a believing woman, for if there is something that he dislikes about her, [surely] there will be something that he likes about her."[84] Arguably, believing that a Muslim woman is a bad omen, and that she is the herald of misery is inconsistent with the more nuanced and rationally based approach of the tradition above. Of course, for the conscientious jurist, this only raises many questions, among them: is this report Abū Hurayrah's way of rehabilitating himself with the women of Medina? Was this report attributed to Abū Hurayrah by others as a way of rehabilitating his reputation? Is this a counter-tradition intended to resist the bad omen tradition? Does the above quoted tradition betray a condescending attitude towards women similar to the crooked rib tradition, which also counsels tolerance and patience with women? Most importantly, to what extent can we discern the role of the Prophet in the authorial enterprise supporting the tradition?[85]

Limitations of time and space prevent me from providing a detailed analysis of every one of the traditions demeaning to women cited at the beginning of this section. Nevertheless, I think it is sufficient to note that all of them deserve a serious conscientious-pause, and are candidates for a faith-based objection. In addition, all arise from singular transmissions, and reflect the same troubled social context noted above. For instance, a careful reading of the deficient intellect and religion tradition would leave one with the distinct suspicion that this report had been redacted and constructed in stages, probably in response to socio-political dynamics. The first part of the tradition consists of a clear and unambiguous blanket condemnation of women – women constitute most of the inhabitants of Hell, they are slanderous and ungrateful beings, they are deficient in intellect and religion, and they lead sagacious men into error. There is no question that from these reports the fact that women do such terrible things is symptomatic of their religious and intellectual deficiencies, which in turn, will make women most of Hell's population. Interestingly, however, the second part of the tradition attempts to neutralize or rehabilitate the first – the deficiency is not substantive; it is merely technical. It is the law that creates this deficiency – the deficiency is born out of legal technicalities, and not out of anything inherent to womanhood. But if that is true and women are not morally responsible for the technicalities that the law imposes on them, why are they going to make up most of Hell's fodder? The incongruence between the first part and the second part of the tradition have led some commentators to adopt the rather implausible position that the Prophet was teasing or joking with the women present in the incident, and that the expression "deficient in intellect and religion" was intended as a pun (*fa kāna al-rasūl yatalaṭṭaf maʿahum*).[86]

The attempts to rehabilitate the first part with a redacted second part, or to orient the tradition into a narrow technicality, or perhaps make it all a joke, point to the fact that the authorial enterprise behind this report, and the others, was complex and multi-layered. One can cite an endless array of evidence demonstrating the tensions in the dynamic and hyperactive culture of early Islam. We have traditions that are at times attributed to either ʿUmar, Abū Hurayrah, or the Prophet, stating that men should consult with women and then do the exact opposite. In one such tradition, ʿUmar reportedly said, "do the opposite of what women advise you to do, for in doing the opposite is a [great] blessing."[87] In another report, as part of a long tradition, Abū Hurayrah claims that the Prophet said, "If the day comes when ... your affairs are controlled by women, then being below the earth will be better than being on its surface (i.e., it is better to be dead)."[88]

Furthermore, we already encountered the Abū Bakrah tradition asserting that people who are led by women will surely fail. Yet, we find the same evidence of protests by various women, and traditions insisting that the Prophet consulted with his wives on many affairs. For instance, the Prophet reportedly consulted with Umm Salamah regarding the Treaty of Ḥudaybiyyah, and consulted and deferred to Khadījah on numerous occasions.[89] In addition, we find numerous reports of women leading a very active social and political life at the time of the Prophet, and afterwards. Notably, ʿĀʾishah led, or was at least one of the leaders, of a rebellion after the death of the Caliph ʿUthmān – a role which people such as Abū Bakrah and Abū Hurayrah strenuously opposed. In fact, ʿĀʾishah was not the only woman to have been involved in an armed uprising. For instance, the rather famous Khārijiyyah, Ghazālah, and her husband sacked Kūfah in an anti-Umayyad rebellion and she reportedly led her male fighters in prayers in the Kūfah mosque.[90] Thus, we confront the very real possibility that most or all of the anti-women traditions were produced as a form of male resistance to the active public role played by women in early Islam.[91] We already saw this phenomenon in the case of the Abū Bakrah tradition about the leadership of women – a phenomenon that did not entirely escape the attention of the classical sources.[92]

It is likely that the new ideological revolution in Arabia, caused by the Islamic message, energized various segments and factions in society who explored and bargained for new positions, roles, and functions. As often happens in situations of rapid or revolutionary change, social structures, mores, and bonds are reconstructed and redrawn pursuant to a dynamic negotiative process. Various segments try to reposition and redefine themselves according to the newly emerging set of affiliations and symbolisms. Particularly if there is great enthusiasm and excitement about a potential new way of life, various segments in society jostle for positions of inclusion and worth in the new structure. There is no reason to believe that women, or various sub-groups of women, were an exception to this dynamic. In fact, there is considerable evidence that women in Medina demanded inclusion in the Islamic revolution. For instance, there are reports that women, as a group, demanded to meet with the Prophet in weekly sessions especially designated for them. In addition, reports record several incidents in which women met individually and privately with the Prophet, or one of his wives, to discuss their problems or seek advice.[93] Women also demanded that the Qurʾān address them specifically, and not simply refer to them in the generic linguistic male form.[94] We also encounter reports of the Qurʾān engaging women. For instance, "God has indeed heard the statement of the woman who argues with you (i.e., the Prophet) and complains to God, and God hears the arguments between you for God hears and sees all."[95] The Qurʾān goes on to address the concerns of the woman in question.[96] The Qurʾān also vindicated ʿĀʾishah by supporting her, and by criticizing the behavior of some male Companions who accused her of unchaste behavior.[97] Reportedly, after her vindication, ʿĀʾishah, apparently still upset, refused to thank the Prophet, and said, "I express my gratitude only to God," and the Prophet smiled in response.[98] Furthermore, women insisted on having the right to go out on military campaigns, to attend prayers in the mosque, and to grant assurances of safe conduct to the enemy.[99] After the Prophet died, energized by the sweeping social changes taking place, women played a major role in attempting to define and construct the Islamic tradition. Therefore, we find that roughly a third of the early transmissions or legal opinions are by women or attributed to women. Last, but not least, we also observe ʿĀʾishah's venture into the world of politics and armed rebellion, both during the reign of ʿUthmān and ʿAlī, and the indisputable shock waves this had created in early Islamic society.[100] It is reasonable to think that this legacy was bound to generate opposition, and that the opposition would take the form of traditions warning against a public role for women and speaking of crooked ribs, prostrating to husbands, bad omens, and deficient intellects. These traditions and their counter-traditions are indicative of the vibrant negotiative process that took place in early Islam – a process that most certainly included the re-definition of gender relations.

One area where this negotiative process is powerfully displayed is the field of marriage and the restrictions placed on wives. In this negotiative process, one observes a virtual battle of rhetorical devices, all utilizing traditions attributed to the Prophet. A simple change in the wording of a particular report would produce meaning and counter-meaning in an effective and powerful fashion. Understanding the negotiative processes of such traditions often involves a careful studying of the different versions of a core transmission. One such tradition is attributed variously to ʿĀʾishah, Ibn ʿUmar, Abū Saʿīd al-Khudrī, through his son, Abū Hurayrah, and Muʿādh b. Jabal. The core element to all the versions of this report is the story of a woman who is not thrilled about getting married, and who approaches the Prophet to ask him about the obligations of a wife towards her husband. In response to the woman's queries, the Prophet advises her that a husband has numerous rights over his wife: a wife must fulfill her husband's sexual desires, even if on top of a camel's saddle (*ẓahr qatab*); she should not fast, other than in Ramadan, without his permission; she should not spend any of his money without his permission; and she may not leave her home without his permission, and if she does, the angels will curse her until she returns home.[101] In another version, as mentioned earlier, the Prophet also informs her that even if a husband suffers from a puss-filled ulcer and she licks it, she cannot do him justice. In different versions of these same reports, the rights of the husband are further emphasized and sanctified. The female interlocutor inquires: "What if the husband is unjust (*ẓālim lahā*)?" Reportedly, the Prophet responds that a wife must obey her husband even if he is unjust. The patriarchical power of these traditions seem unchallengeable; a woman who, in the first place, is reluctant to get married receives a somber and uncompromising set of responses to her questions. There is very little room to negotiate the power of husbands. However, in several versions, we find an interesting variation. In one, a woman informs the Prophet that she dislikes marriage and that she has turned down many suitors. Furthermore, she has resolved not to marry until she first finds out what obligations she will owe to her husband. Upon receiving the responses mentioned above, the woman declares, "By God, if that is so, I resolve never to get married (in a different version, 'I will never be under a man's control as long as I live)'!" And, she leaves. In another version, we find the Prophet supporting the woman's decision. In this version, a father brings his daughter to the Prophet complaining that she refuses to marry anyone. The Prophet tells the daughter to obey her father. To this, the daughter responds, "No, not until you first tell me what rights a husband has over his wife." The Prophet reportedly gives her the answers mentioned above, and in response, she declares, "By the God who has sent you with the Truth, I will never get married as long as I live!" The Prophet then declares that women cannot be married without their full consent.[102] These reports battle over the contested territory of the role of woman in general, and wives in particular. But the duties of wife symbolize the role of women in society at large. The responses of the women who refuse the institution of marriage altogether can be read as a protest against the patriarchical religious dogma that places women in a submissive and degrading position. The symbolism of these reports conveys a compelling message: if need be, women will just have to do without men.

In order to emphasize the point about gender negotiations, and perhaps put it into perspective, I will close this section with a long quote by ʿUmar b. al-Khaṭṭāb. In response to a period of tension between the Prophet and his wives, ʿUmar shared his worries and concerns with the Prophet in the following passage:

> God is Great! O Prophet, you have seen us, the people of Quraysh, we were a people who controlled our women. Then, we came to Medina, and we found a people who are controlled by their women. Our women (the women of Mecca) started learning and imitating their women. One day, I became mad with my wife, and she started arguing with me. When I chided her for talking back to me, she said, "Why do you think I cannot argue with you! By God, the wives of the Prophet argue with him, and one of them even abandons him from morning until night." I told her, "Whoever does this is truly shameless!" How do they know that God might not become angered because of the hurt caused to the Prophet, and then they would be truly ruined!

In response, ʿUmar reports, the Prophet smiled.[103]

## *Praying in closets, hugging the wall, and the dangers of seduction*

Thus far, we have been skirting around the issue at the core of most juristic determinations mandating the exclusion of women from public places, and that is the issue of *fitnah* (seduction or seductive acts). But our exploration of the authoritarian would not be complete without, at least, addressing some of the main issues raised by this concept. I am not speaking here simply of the concept of the veil (*al-ḥijāb*), which mandates the covering of a woman's entire body except for the face and hands, or, in a minority school of thought, the covering of everything except for the eyes or one eye. Well-established interpretive communities have generated both points of view, although the first was and remains the predominant one. In the modern age, the minority school is espoused primarily by Saudi jurists. There is a sizable body of secondary literature on the veil, both as a legal imperative in Islam and as a sociological practice, and doing this issue justice would require a separate book.[104] The problem of *fitnah*, which I will address here, overlaps in important respects with the issue of the veil, but conceptually it remains a separate field of inquiry. *Fitnah* in Islamic discourses is often associated with turbulence, disorder, enticement, and the opening of the doors to evil. The issue addressed here focuses on determinations that utilize or rely on the doctrine of *fitnah* as an essential legal element justifying a particular ruling. Of course, the concept of *fitnah* is often at the core of the discourses on the necessity of the veil. However, my aim here is not to debunk the notion of *fitnah* as seduction or enticement, but to examine methodologies of determination as they relate to the authoritative and authoritarian.

At the outset, we need to keep in mind several considerations about the idea of *fitnah*, as seduction. *Fitnah* connotes the notion that certain things or acts produce the type of sexual arousal that is conducive to the commission of sin. Certain acts, such as *khalwah* (privacy and seclusion between a foreign man and woman) are presumed to be inherently dangerous because they produce the type of *fitnah* that is conducive to the commission of unlawful sexual acts – since the man and woman are enjoying their privacy, they may be tempted to engage in some form of sexual activity or another. The Qur'ān, does use the word *fitnah*, but not to refer to sexual arousal or seduction. The Qur'ān uses the word to refer to non-sexual temptations such as money, and to severe trials and tribulations. As to sexuality, other than the prohibition against engaging in illicit sex, the Qur'ān does command Muslim men and women to lower their gaze, be modest, and not to flash their adornments (*zīnah*) except when appropriate, such as with husbands or wives.[105] Significantly, early Islamic reports do not tie the issue of what eventually becomes known as the *ḥijāb* to the problem of *fitnah*. In other words, the technical issue of the proper form of *ḥijāb* is not directly related to the possibilities of *fitnah*, but to social status and physical safety. Interestingly, what becomes known in modern discourses as the *ḥijāb* is discussed in classical juristic sources in the chapter on prayer. In that chapter, among other things, the jurists discuss what needs to covered by men and women in prayer, and from that, the issue of *ʿawrah* (private parts that ought to be covered by clothing) is discussed as well.[106] In prayer, a Muslim man or woman must cover their full *ʿawrah*, or what the law considers to be the private parts of a human being. Presumably, what is considered to be the *ʿawrah* while in prayer is also the *ʿawrah* outside of prayer – what needs to be covered in prayer, also needs to be covered outside of prayer. This is at the heart of the debates on *ḥijāb* – the *ḥijāb*, in that sense, is whatever covers the private parts (*mā yastur al-ʿawrah*).[107]

*Fitnah* is a collateral matter. The *ʿawrah* is covered, presumably, because there is an affirmative independent command to do so, and not simply because it causes a *fitnah*. Arguably, the *ʿawrah* is to be covered even if it does not cause a *fitnah*, and not everything that causes a *fitnah* is necessarily a *ʿawrah*. As a juristic matter, we need to ask two separate questions: what is the evidence necessary to establish the *ʿawrah*? And what is the evidence necessary to ascertain a *fitnah*? As noted above, the evidentiary basis for the *ḥijāb*, which covers the *ʿawrah*, requires a separate study, but I will analyze some of the evidence that is relevant for *fitnah* determinations. In thinking about this matter, we need to first ask: how do we know that something causes a prohibited *fitnah*? Is a *fitnah* determination an empirical or doctrinal issue? In other words, if a friend is a good-looking fellow who wears a good-looking tie every morning before going to teach his classes, and my friend asks me if wearing such remarkably attractive ties everyday is an unlawful *fitnah*, do I undertake an empirical inquiry into the seduction of his ties, or do I search the doctrinal sources for determinations on tie-like items of clothing? Assume that my friend has a warm and loving voice; many of the students who hear the enchantments of his lectures are promptly seduced. Assuming I search the doctrinal sources and find nothing on male lecturers with seductive voices, based on the empirical evidence, may I advise my friend to find a non-lecturing job or, better yet, find a job that does not require human communication?

The response to these questions depends on whether empirical evidence is relevant to *fitnah* determinations or not, and depends on how broad the prohibition is against *fitnah*. Do the instructions of the Principal mandate that all sources of *fitnah* be snuffed out in society? If the answer is yes, this poses an insurmountable challenge. Assume that in order to put an end to all sources of *fitnah*, we lock up all women in society in fortified homes, has *fitnah* come to an end? There is also homosexual *fitnah* that presumably could result from the interaction of men with men and women with women. There is also the *fitnah* that comes through television stations, computer images, publications, poetry, and a vivid imagination. Do we prohibit these as well? But if we do, this assumes that eradicating the sources of *fitnah* is the only relevant interest under *Sharīʿah*. So, assume that human beings need to be exposed to some degree of *fitnah* in order to receive an education, medical attention, engage in trade and politics, and in order not to be painfully dull and boring. Why should *fitnah* take precedence over any other *Sharīʿah* value – what is the evidence that *fitnah* is the core value in Islam, and not knowledge, justice, utility or beauty?

There is another serious conceptual and moral difficulty with the idea of *fitnah*. The principle that no one can be called to answer for the sins of another is a core *Sharīʿah* value. In Qurʾānic discourses, one person or set of people cannot be made to suffer because of the indiscretions, sins, or faults of others – each individual is responsible and accountable only for his or her own behavior.[108] In fact, when addressing issues of modesty, the Qurʾān is quite careful to place the blame on those it labels the hypocrites, who harass or molest the innocent.[109] The jurisprudence of *fitnah*, however, runs the risk of violating this principle. For example, assuming that the reason we are confronted with a *fitnah* situation is because of men with an overactive libido or who are impious or ill-mannered. Demanding that women should suffer exclusion or limitations would violate the principle that the innocent should not pay for the indiscretions of the culpable. As we already explained, *ʿawrah* and *fitnah* are separate categories – a person covers the *ʿawrah* not because of *fitnah*, but because the covering of *ʿawrah* is a separate imperative based on a set of specific instructions. Whether revealing the *ʿawrah* leads or does not lead to *fitnah* is irrelevant. But from that perspective, the whole logic of *fitnah* as seduction becomes quite suspect. Whether a person covers his or her *ʿawrah* or not, he or she should not be made to suffer for the indiscretions or impiety of others. Put bluntly, whether a person is sexually aroused or not is entirely irrelevant as to what the object of arousal must or must not do. The laws and imperatives of modesty ought to be set by God and not by immoral individuals who are violating the law of God.

As we will see, most *fitnah* determinations rely on the dubious logic that women should pay the price for the impious failures of men. Furthermore, in these determinations, as far as women are concerned, *fitnah* emerges as the core value of Islam. Therefore, women's education, mobility, safety, and even religious liberty should be restricted in order to avoid *fitnah*. Hence, we observe that women can be banned from driving, working, serving in the military, or appearing in public life under the guise of *fitnah*. As far as the relationship between the special agent and the common agents is concerned, we find ourselves reverting back to the notion of fundamental disagreements about the Divine Will, Divine Justice, and the purpose and role of *Sharīʿah*. Nevertheless, one does not necessarily need to resort to faith-based objections to *fitnah* determinations that unjustly treat women if one can demonstrate that such determinations are based on an abusive treatment of the evidence. The suspected abuse relates to a lack of reasonableness or balance in weighing the evidence on a particular matter. Furthermore, the abuse could consist of an extreme lack of willingness to implement critical insight to evidence that could have dire consequences in perpetuating intolerable injustice upon half of the Muslim population.

The most pronounced feature of the legal determinations that exclude women from public life is the obsessive reliance on the idea of *fitnah*. In these determinations, women are persistently seen as a walking, breathing bundle of *fitnah*. One can hardly find a *responsa* that deals with women without the insertion of some language about the seductions of womanhood. So, for instance, according to the C.R.L.O, women may attend mosques only if it does not lead to *fitnah*; women may listen to a man reciting the Qurʾān or give a lecture, only if it does not lead to *fitnah*; women may go to the marketplace only if it does not lead to *fitnah*; women may not visit graveyards because of the fear of *fitnah*; women may not do *tasbīḥ* or say amen aloud in prayer because of the fear of *fitnah*; a woman praying by herself may not raise her voice in prayer if it leads to *fitnah*; a woman may not even greet a man if it leads to *fitnah*; and every item and color of clothing is analyzed under the doctrine of *fitnah*.[110] It does not seem to occur to the jurists who make these determinations that this presumed *fitnah* that accompanies women in whatever they do or wherever they go is not an inherent quality of womanhood, but is a projection of male promiscuities. By artificially constructing womanhood into the embodiment of seductions, these jurists do not promote a norm of modesty, but, in reality, promote a norm of immodesty. Instead of turning the gaze away from the physical attributes of women, they obsessively turn the gaze of attention to women as a mere physicality. In essence, these jurists objectify women into items for male consumption, and in that, is the height of immodesty.

The challenge, however, is that the jurists who make these determinations find support in a range of traditions that position women as an indefatigable source of seduction and temptation for men. The C.R.L.O jurists unfailingly cite and quote these traditions in arguing for the seclusion of women and in prohibiting the mixing of the sexes in public forums (*ikhtilāṭ*). There is a plethora of traditions that convey the same basic message: women are an unadulterated *fitnah.*[111] In some of the most common versions of this genre of traditions, we encounter the following: Abū Saʿīd al-Khudrī reports that the Prophet said, "This earth is lush and pretty, and God has entrusted you [in this earth] to see what you will do. When it comes to [the temptations of] this world be cautious, and as to women be cautious [as well] for the first *fitnah* that befell the Israelites was [the *fitnah* of] women."[112] In another oft-quoted version, the Prophet reportedly said, "I have not left in my people a *fitnah* more harmful to men than women."[113] In a report from a related genre of traditions, a version of which we encountered earlier, the Prophet reportedly said, "Women are the snares of the devil."[114] In a tradition that draws a connection between *ʿawrah* and *fitnah*, it is transmitted that ʿAbd Allāh b. ʿUmar narrated that the Prophet said, "[The whole of] a woman is a *ʿawrah* and so if she goes out, the devil makes her the source of seduction."[115] A particular genre of reports takes the message of these traditions to its logical extreme. This genre effectively declares that women ought to be either married or dead. In a version transmitted through Ibn al-ʿAbbās, the Prophet reportedly said, "A woman has ten *ʿawras*; when she marries, her husband covers one of her *ʿawras*, and when she dies, the grave covers the rest."[116] The logical conclusion to be drawn from this tradition is that for a woman to be thoroughly modest, she ought to be dead and buried.

Not surprisingly, these traditions lay the foundations for most of the determinations regulating a woman's appearance and conduct, regardless of whether a particular woman has covered her private parts. Therefore, even if a woman has covered her private parts, she may still not mix with men in all public forums and some private forums. Importantly, these traditions become the vehicle for symbolisms placing women in the role of the distrusted or treacherous, and for associating them with the construct of a menace that must be restrained. Consequently, in classical commentaries on these traditions, it is not unusual to find the following language:

> Since God has made men desire women, and desire looking at them, and enjoying them, women are like the devil in that they seduce men towards the commission of evil, while making evil look attractive [to men]. We deduct from this that women should not go out in the midst of men except for a necessity, and that men should not look at their cloth and should stay away from women all together.[117]

In a separate source, also commenting on the same traditions, we find the following passage:

> Some sages said women are pure evil, and the worst thing about them is that men cannot do without them. Women are deficient in intellect and religion, and they impel men to commit acts that lack reason or piety, such as becoming pre-occupied with worldly affairs and ignoring religious affairs, and this is the worst type of corruption.[118]

The first point of inquiry is to ask, do the *fitnah* traditions make an empirical claim or a normative claim? Are these traditions saying that as an empirical matter women will always have this affect on men? If the answer is yes, then the question is, what if the empirical reality contradicts the claim of the tradition? In the science of *ḥadīth*, any tradition that contravenes human experience cannot be accepted as valid. So, for instance, if a tradition says that the people of Yemen walk on three legs, since the tradition is empirically incorrect it cannot be relied upon in legal determinations. Therefore, if human experience reveals that men are the source of as much evil as women, how do we then deal with these traditions? Arguably, the *fitnah* traditions are not describing an empirical state of affairs, but are setting a normative principle. The normative principle is that women are dangerous, and whether you can empirically verify this or not, you must accept it, believe it, and act on it. This, of course, takes us to the full circle of construction of reality – by prophesying that women are dangerous and treating them are dangerous, we are never able to realize any reality other than that women are dangerous.

Perhaps I can demonstrate this point by dealing with the example that became a subject of virulent debate between the modern scholar *Shaykh* Muḥammad al-Ghazālī and his opponents. There is a tradition that says, in effect, if a fly falls in your cup, dunk the fly in the liquid before drinking the liquid. Why? Because, according to the tradition, the disease is on one wing and the cure is on the other – by submerging the fly in the drink, we neutralize any potential harmful effects of diseases carried by the fly.[119] If this tradition is making an empirical claim, then it could be accepted or rejected on empirical grounds. If, however, the tradition is making a normative claim, effectively it is as if the tradition is saying, "regardless of any empirical evidence, trust in what I say because I know best." As a result, every time someone dunks the fly in the drink and gets ill, we must refuse to consider any empirical evidence that would debunk the claim of the tradition. We must tell ourselves, "the sick person got sick, not because of the fly, but because of any other reason." The same analysis applies to Abū Hurayrah's tradition claiming that there is no such thing as contagious disease.[120]

This points to a serious problem related to our proportionality analysis. As argued earlier, traditions of singular transmissions should not support determinations of faith. Matters of faith and conviction are too serious and grave to be determined by traditions that arose from tumultuous social contexts, in which the role of the Prophet cannot be ascertained with absolute reliability. The requirement of proportionality would demand that the greater the theological, social, and political impact of a tradition, the stricter the scrutiny that the tradition must pass. Because of this, it is important to ask, if these traditions cannot establish points of conviction or faith, then what claims do remain? Once we disqualify these traditions from establishing points of faith (*'aqīdah*), what remains of the tradition? What remains is the empirical claim – what remains is sociology.

The implications of my argument are clear; since these traditions only qualify under a proportionality analysis to make empirical claims then they become empirically verifiable. Human experience can either confirm or completely refute their credibility. This, of course, relates to the believability of the tradition; it, however, is not conclusive as to its enforceability. If the tradition is empirically unbelievable, then it cannot be relied on and cannot be enforced either. Nonetheless, if it is empirically verifiable that is not the end of the process. If we discover that, in fact, women are dangerous, that flies have the disease on one wing and the cure on another, or that there is no such thing as contagious disease, that only means that the tradition is *potentially* enforceable. Whether the tradition is enforceable depends on whether it is consistent with higher doctrinal, legal, or moral considerations. Therefore, assuming that we are able to empirically verify that women are the source of *fitnah*, as I noted above, that is not the only consideration. The ending of seduction must be weighed against the principles of Islamic justice. Consequently, if the core of the problem is in the promiscuities of men, then women should not be made to suffer for the faults of men. Furthermore, in all cases higher values, such as education or health, cannot be sacrificed in order to guard against the dangers of *fitnah*.

One can imagine that a fair-minded person reading this text might pause before saying, "This just does not feel right. The Prophet tells us that women are a *fitnah*, and you rationalize the Prophet's statement away!" But that is exactly the point; we are unable to ascertain that the Prophet played the primary role in the authorial enterprise that generated these traditions. Since we are unable to ascertain the Prophet's role, and considering the impact of these traditions, there is no possible justification for taking the traditions at their word. Rather, one can conscientiously require the traditions to be empirically believable and not to trump values that have been established through more reliable means. If we could establish the role of the Prophet in the authorial enterprise, then and only then, we might have to resort to a faith-based protest against these traditions because they seem to contravene higher moral values such as justice and fairness.

Now, we should assess the issue of the authorial enterprise as it relates to the *fitnah* traditions. I start the analysis with the following speculation: is it possible that the Prophet in one or more contexts warned against sexual promiscuities and immodesty, and that this warning was remembered and reconstructed into a warning against women? This speculation is warranted because it is entirely plausible that the Prophet would counsel modesty and virtue, and it is also plausible that the patriarchal society receiving the Prophet's counsel redirected this counsel into a statement against women. Importantly, one of the most problematic aspects about the *fitnah* traditions and their determinations is that they render a good part of the Islamic historical experience in Medina a corruption. It is difficult to reconcile the traditions of *fitnah* and exclusion with the numerous reports about the active participation of women in public life during the life of the Prophet and after his death as well. In fact, the reports that document incidents of seclusion of women are few in comparison with the reports documenting the opposite. The reports of public participation are too numerous to recount here, but they include the Prophet racing his wife in public, 'Ā'ishah and other women watching sports in Medina, women asking and complaining to the Prophet about a variety of problems, and women participating in Islamic battles in a variety of capacities. One of the widely reported incidents is one in which a group of women were meeting with the Prophet. Apparently, their voices had become quite loud; when 'Umar entered upon the rowdy group, the Prophet laughed at how quickly everyone quieted down. Furthermore, men and women visited each other and exchanged gifts. Several reports state that women would come to the Prophet in the street take him by the hand, sit with him, and discuss their problems.[121] In none of these reports about the historical practice is there a hint of obsession about *fitnah* or the affect of *fitnah*. Importantly, the overwhelming majority of the traditions of the *fitnah* genre do not purport to describe a historical practice. Rather, they present declarations, aspirations, claims, or normative prescriptions. If these traditions are to be believed, then there was an enormous disparity between the normative declarations of the Prophet, and the actual historical practice in Medina. Seen differently, either the reports that describe the historical practice are exaggerated or the traditions of *fitnah* are exaggerated. It is implausible that the Companions and the Prophet, himself, consistently chose to ignore the Prophet's normative injunctions about *fitnah* in actual practice. The typical C.R.L.O response to this type of argument is to claim that all of the incidents mentioned above took place before the imposition of the *ḥijāb*. Once the *ḥijāb* was imposed, all of the above mentioned incidents became irrelevant. However, considering that the *ḥijāb* was introduced in the very last years before the death of the Prophet, we end up with the peculiar result that most of the Islamic historical experience, as far as gender relations are concerned, becomes an utter nullity. In addition, most Qur'ānic commentaries explicitly state that the *ḥijāb* was imposed only upon the Prophet's wives. In fact, the verse explicitly addresses itself to the wives of the Prophet and comments that the wives of the Prophet are unlike other women in the Muslim community.[122] Furthermore, many of the reports about the historical practice describe numerous incidents of public participation by women in the last years of the Prophet's life and after his death. For instance, a good portion of the reports describe incidents that took place during the reign of ʿUmar, ʿUthmān, and ʿAlī. Moreover, even assuming that the law of *ʿawrah* was revealed in the last year or two of the Prophet's life, as argued above, the issue of *ʿawrah* is separate from the issue of *fitnah*. Although the issue of *ʿawrah* needs a separate treatment, it is significant that according to the authorial enterprise that conveyed the laws of *ʿawrah*, the *ʿawrah* of female slaves are different from the *ʿawrah* of free women. As noted earlier in the book, a female slave does not require the covering of the hair, the arms, or part of the legs. If the discourse of *ʿawrah* was related to the discourse of the *fitnah*, there would be no grounds for distinguishing the two.[123] Most certainly, slave women are as capable of creating *fitnah* as free women, and, yet, what is required of each category is different. In my view, the mere fact that the authorial enterprise distinguished between the *ʿawrah* of free and non-free women is sufficient in itself to warrant a complete re-examination of the *ʿawrah* laws.

There are several material elements that are often ignored when discussing the issue of *ḥijāb* or the *ʿawrah* of women. These elements suggest that the issue of *fitnah* might have dominated and shaped the discourse on the *ʿawrah* of women, but they are also informative as to the possible authorial enterprise behind the *fitnah* traditions. There are six main elements that, I believe, warrant careful examination in trying to analyze the laws of *ʿawrah*, and that invite us to re-examine the relationship between *ʿawrah* and *fitnah*. Firstly, early jurists disagreed on the meaning of *zīnah* (adornments) that women are commanded to cover. Some jurists argued that it is all of the body including the hair and face except for one eye. The majority argued that women must cover their full body except for the face and hands. Some jurists held that women may expose their feet and their arms up to the elbow. Importantly, someone such as Saʿīd b. Jubayr asserted that revealing the hair is reprehensible, but also stated that the Qurʾānic verses did not explicitly say anything about women's hair.[124] Secondly, the jurists frequently repeated that the veiling verse was revealed in response to a very specific situation. As explained above, corrupt young men would harrass and, at times, assault women at night as these women headed to the wild to relieve themselves. Apparently, when confronted, these men would claim that they did not realize that these women were Muslim but thought them non-Muslim slave-girls, and, therefore, not under the protection of the Muslim community. In Medina society any individual was under the protection of either a clan or, if the individual was Muslim, under the protection of Muslims. Therefore, these verses seem to address a very specific, and even peculiar, historical social dynamic. The interaction between the text and the text's social context is not easily transferable or projectable to other contexts.[125] Thirdly, as noted above, Muslim jurists consistently argued that the laws mandating the covering of the full body did not apply to slave-girls.[126] In fact, it is reported that ʿUmar b. al-Khaṭṭāb prohibited slave-girls from imitating free women by covering their hair. Apparently, Muslim jurists channelled the historical context of the verses into legal determinations that promulgated a particular social stratification. However, it is not clear whether the social stratification addressed by the Qur'ān is the same as that endorsed by the jurists. Fourthly, the jurists often argued that what could be lawfully exposed in a woman's body was what would ordinarily appear according to custom (*ʿādah*), nature (*jibillah*), and necessity (*ḍarūrah*). Relying on this, they argued that slave-girls do not have to cover their hair, face, or arms because they live an active economic life that requires mobility, and because by nature and custom slave-girls do not ordinarily cover these parts of their bodies. This makes the focal point of the law custom and functionality. Arguably, however, women in the modern age live an economically active life that requires mobility and, arguably, custom varies with time and place.[127] In other words, if the rules prescribing veiling were mandated to deal with a specific type of harm, and slave-girls were exempted because of the nature of their social role and function, arguably, this means that the rules of veiling are contingent and contextual in nature. Fifthly, several reports state that women, Muslim or non-Muslim, in Medina, normally would wear long head-covers – the cloth usually would be thrown behind ears and shoulders. They would also wear vests open in the front, leaving their chests exposed. Reportedly, the practice of exposing the breasts was common until late into Islam. Several early authorities state that the Qur'ānic verse primarily sought to have women cover their chests up to the beginning of the cleavage area. Sixthly, there is a sharp disjunction between the veiling verses and the notion of seduction. Seduction could be caused by slave-girls, or could be between woman and man, woman and woman, or man and man.[128] A man could be seduced by a slave-girl, and a woman could be seduced by a good looking man, yet neither slave-girls nor men are required to cover their hair or faces. Does the fact that a particular man might be sexually enticing to women affect the obligations of concealment as to this man?[129]

These six points are not exhaustive nor thorough, and they are not intended to be a full discussion of the issue of *ʿawrah* or *ḥijāb*. Nevertheless, they do indicate that the legal determinations as to the *ʿawrah* of women were the product of a complex authorial enterprise replete with competing social trends. The story behind the *ḥijāb* verses is not as simple and straightforward as the C.R.L.O seems to believe. Furthermore, the connection between the *ḥijāb* verses and the *fitnah* determinations is not as clear as the C.R.L.O alleges. In fact, these points invite us to re-evaluate the interaction between the idea of *fitnah* and the notion of *ʿawrah*. They also invite us to ponder the extent to which the *fitnah* traditions are indicative of a dynamic according to which there was a largely successful attempt to co-opt and appropriate the *ḥijāb* verses in the service of an effort to limit the public role of women. Furthermore, the historical context of these *ʿawrah* and *fitnah* determinations suggests that contemporary debates on these issues are somewhat anachronistic.

In order to evaluate the authorial enterprise behind the *fitnah* traditions, we need to examine the totality of the evidence including the rhetorical dynamics of these traditions along with their functions and potentialities. For instance, among the traditions that the C.R.L.O jurists frequently cite in support of their argument for the exclusion of women is one which was reportedly transmitted by Ibn ʿUmar. In this report, Ibn ʿUmar narrates that the Prophet said, "Do not forbid your women from going to the mosque, but praying at home is better for them." A version of this report purportedly transmitted from the Prophet by ʿAbd Allāh b. ʿUmar, becomes more extreme. It states: "The prayer of a woman in her room is better than her prayer house and her prayer in a dark closet is better than her prayer in her room."[130] The same message is then conveyed but this time through the involvement of a woman who reportedly goes to the Prophet to tell him that she loves to pray in the mosque with him. To this the Prophet responds that he knows that she loves to pray with him but gives her the same advice as above. As a result, the woman went home and prayed in the most isolated and the darkest area of her house until she died.[131] The least one can observe about these traditions are their remarkable vindictiveness – the more removed and inaccessible a woman is, the better, and even the love of the Prophet cannot change that fact. These reports coexist with other traditions that assert that the mosque of the Prophet was full of rows of women lining up for prayers. At times, men arriving late for prayer would pray behind women – men would be in the front rows followed by women, followed by rows of men who arrived late. Yet, the prayers of the men who prayed behind the women were considered valid.[132] These traditions also note that after completing his prayers the Prophet would delay a bit, presumably, to give the last rows an opportunity to leave the mosque.[133] Furthermore, there are reports that some women would stay for long periods and even sleep in the mosque.[134] Importantly, a large number of reports state that the Prophet wanted all women to join the community in ʿĪd prayers, and that he urged even menstruating women to listen to the sermon and join in the celebrations. When some women complained that they might not have a garb to wear, the Prophet advised those women who have two garbs to lend one to a woman without.[135] Interestingly, the early jurist Mālik b. Anas (d. 179/796) held that it is preferable for a woman to perform *iʿtikāf* prayers[136] in the mosque and not in her home.[137] In addition, several reports stated that women attended *iʿtikāf* prayer with the Prophet in the mosque, and did so during menstruation.[138]

Of course, reports of widespread attendance of prayers by women in mosques create a rather untenable situation. One would have to conclude that all these women ignored the Prophet's advice to pray in dark closets. In response to this tension, we find reports that try to rehabilitate the situation, somewhat. For instance, a report attributed to ʿĀʾishah asserts that ʿĀʾishah said, "If the Prophet would have seen what women are doing in mosques today, he would have prohibited them [from attending the mosque] as the women of Israel were prohibited [presumably, by Jewish law]."[139] The importance of this tradition is in the fact that it is attributed to ʿĀʾishah, who led an active political life and continued to pray and teach in the mosque in Medina after the Prophet's death. We are not told what it is that women did in mosques after the death of the Prophet and why the law of the Israelites is relevant. Naturally, the mention of the Israelites creates a connection with and validates the traditions regarding *fitnah*, since according to these traditions, women were the first cause of trials and tribulations for the Israelites. Importantly, in the historical context of the Islamic traditions, the Israelites were seen as the prime example of a people who violated God's covenant, and who were banished and exiled in the earth as punishment. Therefore, the symbolism drawn is quite compelling; women might bring the same unfortunate fate to the Muslim nation unless adequately restrained.

Another example of a rehabilitation tradition is one in which Abū Hurayrah narrates that the Prophet said, "As for men, the best rows [in prayer] are the front rows, and the worst rows are the last rows. As for women, the best rows [in prayer] are the last rows, and the worst rows are the front rows."[140] Interestingly, the classical jurists attempt to rationalize this tradition by arguing that it means that there should be a sufficient distance between the last row of men and the first row of women.[141] Nonetheless, this rationalization is not successful in concealing the basic incoherence of the report. In order for the report to make sense, we must read it to mean that men who come to congregational prayers early are the best because they will form the front rows. The worst women, however, are those who come early to congregational prayer, since they will form the front rows, and the best women are those who come late because they will form the last rows. Therefore, if a woman wants to be among the best, she will have to delay as long as possible before going to pray in the mosque – after all, she wants to make sure that she does not end up in the front rows. Assume that all women think in a similar fashion, what happens then? All women make a mad rush to the mosque in the last minute possible, and then fight it out for who ends up in the last rows?

The tradition is logically absurd, and, yet the C.R.L.O, and many other jurists, rely on it in arguing in support of the doctrine of *fitnah*. The best female rows are the last rows because they are the furthest away from men, and the least capable of causing *fitnah*. Confronted with the logical absurdity of the tradition, the C.R.L.O responds, that that is exactly why women should pray at home.[142] But then we come full circle, why did so many women at the time of the Prophet not understand this simple and straightforward point, which invites them all to pray in dark closets instead of bothering with going to the mosque!

Nevertheless, the stratagems of rehabilitation do not end here. Again, in the context of *fitnah* determinations, one finds a rather ambiguous tradition cited by the jurists. In this tradition, Abū Hurayrah reports that the Prophet said, "Do not forbid women from going to mosques, however, they should go out while they are *tafilāt*."[143] *Tafilāt* comes from the word *tafl*, which means bad smelling. Does this mean that women should go to mosques while protected from *fitnah* by a healthy bad stench? This sharply contrasts with the Qur'ānic injunction that states: "O children of Adam! Take your [full] adornments at every mosque, eat and drink but do not go to excess for God does not like those who go to extremes."[144] Moreover, there are other traditions attributed to the Prophet that advise Muslims, men and women, against undertaking certain behavior, like eating raw onions, before attending congregational prayers because the odor might be offensive to others.[145] Reports coming by the way of Zaynab al-Thaqafiyyah maintained that the Prophet advised women not to put perfume on if they wish to attend congregational prayers. However, this advice was transmitted by Abū Hurayrah as a prohibition conveying a degree of hostility towards perfuming women – he reports that the Prophet said, "Any woman who puts on perfume, let her not attend the *'Ishā'* prayers [last prayers in the evening] with us."[146] Based on these various traditions, the classical jurists concluded that the word *tafilāt*, mentioned in the tradition above, was used by the tradition to mean that women should not attend congregational prayers while perfumed, but should smell ordinary.[147] Nevertheless, this is hardly the point – the point is that these various traditions allow us to observe a vibrant historical dynamic in which a social issue is being negotiated through the subtleties of language. Observing this social dynamic allows us to assess the authorial enterprise behind the *fitnah* traditions in a more reasonable, comprehensive, diligent and honest assessment.

Part of the historical negotiative process was the co-option and redirecting of reports that described a historical practice into reports of normative warnings against the *fitnah* of women. In several traditions, 'Ā'ishah reports that women at the time of the Prophet would attend morning prayers wearing their cloaks. The women would attend and leave without being recognized because of the darkness (*min al-ghalas*). 'Ā'ishah reportedly says this in the context of arguing that morning congregational prayers should be performed early, at dawn, when it is still dark. Her point is technical and related to the proper timing of prayer.[148] Remarkably, however, this tradition becomes co-opted by some early and modern authorities into a statement against *fitnah*. According to these sources, and according to the C.R.L.O, the lesson of these traditions is that women should not be seen going to and coming from the mosque, or that if they go to the mosque, they should thoroughly wrap themselves in clothing so that no one will recognize them.[149] The rich social context of this debate is best demonstrated in a tradition documented by Muslim: 'Abd Allāh b. 'Umar heard that one of his sons (either Bilāl or Waqīd) had forbidden his wife from going to the mosque at night. 'Abd Allāh told his son, "The Prophet has told us not to ban women from going to the mosque at night." The son said, "Nevertheless, I will not allow them [his wife or other women] to go out to the mosque so that they can use [going out] as an excuse [to do improper things.]" ʿAbd Allāh was offended by the response, and said, "I tell you what the Prophet said, and you tell me, nevertheless I will not allow them!" Upset, reportedly ʿAbd Allāh refused to talk to his son until he retracted his decision.[150]

In a tradition that is particularly telling and resentful of public participation by women, it is claimed that during the Prophet's lifetime, after finishing prayer, men and women mixed with each other while exiting the mosque. The Prophet reportedly declared the following: "[O women,] fall back for you have no right to be on the road. You should walk on the outer fringes of the road." The narrator of the tradition then comments, "After that, women would walk [to the sides] so close to the walls that their robes would scratch against the walls."[151] Presumably, this testimony is inconsistent with traditions noted above about women taking the Prophet by the hand in the street, and by others describing the mixing of men and women in the market and in the mosque. Nevertheless, that is not the material issue here; what is important is that the tradition conveys a rather powerful message: the roads belong to men, and if women are on the road, they should submissively cower next to walls. The power of these types of traditions is exemplified in the fact that despite the fact that even the scholars of *ḥadīth* declared this report to be of doubtful authenticity, we find the C.R.L.O relying on it in order to prohibit the mixing of the sexes. The C.R.L.O cites the report in arguing that women should be on the public roads only out of necessity and should stay clear of men.[152] But this report and the fact that it is co-optable and usable in the modern age, serves to emphasize the importance of a diligent search into the authorial enterprise. Earlier on, I called this an issue of the legal competence of the instructions by the Principal. In all situations, by presenting a determination to the common agents, the special agent is not only making representations about meaning, but also about the qualifications of the instructions. The issue is not simply who said what, or who said what about whom, the relevant issue is to thoroughly, comprehensively and diligently investigate the totality of contextual evidence that might enlighten us about the motives, dynamics, values, memory and the construction of reality. For example, noticing that many of the reports that demean, and sometimes honor, women are consistently attributed to Abū Hurayrah, ʿAbd Allāh b. ʿUmar, and Abū Saʿīd al-Khudrī, a diligent agent must ask why? Is it possible that these traditions were the legal opinions of these Companions, and that these individual legal opinions were misremembered by later generations, and attributed to the Prophet? Is it possible that these Companions were collectively remembered as conservative men and, thus, they became a center for anti-women attributions? In other words, is it possible that people tended to attribute opinions that expressed a conservative view about women to these particular Companions who were collectively remembered as conservative men? Someone like Abū Saʿīd al-Khudrī was an honored and revered Companion of the Prophet, and we find that 1,170 traditions were attributed to him. Out of these, al-Bukhārī accepted only sixteen traditions as authentic, and Muslim accepted fifty-two.[153] For someone to come in the contemporary age, and argue that perhaps al-Bukhārī and Muslim should have included some or excluded others of the traditions attributed to al-Khudrī, is not heresy – it is simply a diligent discharging of the burdens of special agency.

The duty of diligence is only underscored by the very dynamics of the traditions that demean women. In my view, these traditions are not only demeaning to women, but are also demeaning to men. The often graphic and repulsive nature of these reports is evidence of the fact that they were produced in the context of highly contentious social dynamics. Their wording and style seem intended to shock, challenge, and frustrate a particular social strata or set of interests. By invoking sexually sadistic images, they appear to proclaim the futility of resisting patriarchy. There is a certain deviant eroticism in the image of a woman submissively licking a man's ulcers or promptly submitting to male desires even in the most inopportune moments. In short, these traditions might appear, in our modern age, to be a rather crimped erotic male projection satisfying the fancies of immodest men. Moreover, interestingly enough, some of these reports draw a connection between the empowerment of men and the disempowerment of insular groups such as women and slaves. In these reports, the Prophet is quoted as saying, "The prayers of three kinds of people will not be accepted [by God]: a woman who leaves her home without her husband's permission, a slave who escapes from his master (*al-ʿabd al-ābiq*), and a man who leads unwilling men in prayer." Variants on this transmission state that a woman whose husband is upset with her, a fugitive slave, and a man who leads prayer despite being hated by his congregation will not have their prayers accepted.[154] The point about leading prayer is a not so subtle reference to early despotic and unpopular caliphs and governors who, as a symbol of legitimacy and hegemony, would forceably lead prayer in the major cities of the Islamic empire.[155] In other words, a segment of these traditions express opposition to the disempowerment and dominance over free men – men ought to be able to choose the person who leads them in prayer, and, by implication, the person who rules over them, in general.

While these traditions affirm the autonomy of free men, they also deny women and slaves their autonomy. A slave who escapes from his master, and a wife who disobeys or displeases her master (husband), are equally reprehensible. By rebelling against their status in life, they lose favor with God. Meanwhile, a despot who denies free men their autonomy and rightful status confronts the same fate. Quite aside from the issue of the technical, chain-of-transmission-focused, authenticity of these traditions, they are indicative of a dynamic and highly negotiative historical process. In fact, I believe that as to the overwhelming majority of the traditions dealing with the role of women in society, the role of the Prophet in the authorial enterprise is minimal. If one adopts the faith-based conviction that the Prophet was not sent by God to affirm and legitimate conservative and oppressive power structures, traditions that affirm the hegemony of patriarchy would have to pass the strictest level of scrutiny. However, applying this level of scrutiny to these traditions would reveal that there were too many patriarchal vested interests circulating, advocating, and embellishing these types of reports. Consequently, one would have to conclude that the voice of the Prophet in the authorial enterprise behind these traditions is hopelessly drowned and muted.

## *Racism, sexism, and a sense of beauty*

As mentioned earlier, classical Muslim jurists have long debated the nature of beauty (*ḥusn*) and ugliness (*qubḥ*). As part of this debate, Muslim jurists explored whether the essence of beauty was created by God, whether beauty is recognizable by revelation alone or pure reason and intuition as well, and which manifestations of beauty are inherent and which are derivative. These discourses are remarkably abstract and complex; nonetheless, they need to be rekindled in the modern age. This book cannot do justice to this rich tradition, but one aspect of the discourse needs to mentioned here. Among the issues debated by Muslim jurists was the extent to which principles of pure reason,[156] observable natural phenomenon, or intuition can be utilized in the verification of the authenticity of traditions. The core-logic of the debate focused on a hierarchy of normativities according to which lower-order values are evaluated in light of higher-order values. These higher-order/lower-order values did not just refer to the five values of *Sharīʿah*, but also to moral imperatives. For instance, the Qur'ān mandates that justice be established. Classical jurists would proceed to break down the constituent elements of justice, organizing them into necessary elements, lesser order elements, and variables (elements that are dependent on the context). So, for example, the discourse would commence with asking what is necessary for justice? Different responses are possible – justice is equality of treatment, equality of value, equality of opportunity, a strict correlation between rights and duties, or that a person should not suffer for the sins of another. Assume that a jurist encounters a report that states that a deceased person will suffer if his relatives weep at his grave. The lesser-order value conveyed here is that weeping at a gravesight is unacceptable. But the higher-order values mandating justice and that a person should not suffer for the sins of another might create a conflict with this report because the deceased is suffering for the weeping, an act for which he is not responsible. Because of the tension created by the higher- and lower-order values, the question becomes whether the report could be interpreted to resolve the conflict. But before one may get to the issue of interpretation, the very existence of the tension impacts upon the evaluation of the authenticity of the report. The presence of a conflict between a higher order value might be an indication that the report, itself, is unreliable.

This type of analysis was typically undertaken when evaluating the *matn* (substance) of a tradition. This was not a means of preferring reason over revelation, but a means of insuring that revelation is in fact what it purports to be.[157] This discourse, with its sophisticated distinctions and conscientious explorations is dead and long forgotten in contemporary Islam. Nevertheless, as argued above, the puritan approaches of modern Islam incorporate a variety of normative value assumptions, while sheltering themselves behind screens of objectivity and literalism. These assumptions, however, are neither systematic nor conscientious. I want to illustrate this point with a final example correlating between traditions that are demeaning to a race and traditions that are demeaning to a gender.

A variety of reports have been attributed to the Prophet that explicitly demean Abyssinians, Sudanese, or blacks in general. Typically, these reports claim that ʿĀʾisha, Ibn ʿAbbās, Ibn ʿUmar, Abū Hurayrah, or Anas heard the Prophet say something derogatory towards blacks. One such report claims that the Prophet said, "Choose suitable [marriage partners] for your children, but avoid [marrying] blacks for they are a deformed race (*fa innahu lawnun mushawwah*)."[158] Other reports claim that the Prophet said, "Blacks live guided by their private parts and stomachs" (i.e., they fornicate and eat).[159] Furthermore, Ibn Ḥanbal narrated a report that, in effect, states, God created the white race (*dhurriyyah bayḍāʾ*) from Adam's right shoulder, and created the black race (*dhurriyyah sawdāʾ*) from Adam's left shoulder, then decreed that those on the right (Adam's right shoulder) will enter Heaven, and those on the left will enter Hell.[160] There is no question that these reports are racist – they brand and deprecate a whole race. As such, they share an unfortunate quality with the traditions that degrade women in general – these traditions brand and deprecate a whole gender. And, like the traditions demeaning of women, the racist traditions do not go unopposed. These traditions are contradicted by many reports asserting that the Prophet said all people are equal regardless of their skin color, or that condemn behavior that is deprecating to black Africans.[161] Both the sexist and racist reports are contradicted by traditions that either empower women or black Africans against demeaning attitudes that were prevalent in Arab society. Importantly, numerous jurists and *ḥadīth* scholars rejected the authenticity of the racist traditions and declared them pure fabrications. Despite the fact that the authenticity of these reports were accepted by some, the overwhelming majority of the classical authorities rejected the racist traditions, declaring them to be contrary to Islamic norms (*mughāyira li khuluq al-Islām*). These authorities also objectified the rejection of these reports by deciding that one or more of the narrators involved in transmitting these reports were liars and fabricators. The majority of the scholars of *ḥadīth* found serious defects in the chains of transmission of these reports. However, my contention is that the aversion that the overwhelming majority of the classical scholars felt towards the racist traditions guided their evaluation of the chains of transmission. Put differently, these scholars were prone to disbelieve the transmitters of these reports because, in essence, they felt that the message conveyed was simply ugly. Additionally, it is likely that these scholars scrutinized the chains of transmission more aggressively and meticulously than if dealing with non-problematic traditions. Furthermore, although notable *ḥadīth* scholars such Abū ʿAbd Allāh Muḥammad b. ʿAbd Allāh al-Ḥākim (d. 405/1014), Ibn Ḥibbān, and Aḥmad Ibn Ḥanbal considered some of the racist traditions authentic, the overwhelming majority refused to defer to their judgment.[162] Ibn al-Qayyim summed up the attitude of the vast majority of classical scholars in saying, "All the traditions deprecating the Abyssinians and Sudanese are pure fabrications." Importantly, Ibn al-Qayyim argued that a *matn* analysis by itself would be sufficient to reject these reports.[163]

The late Wahhābī scholar Nāṣir al-Dīn al-Albānī (d. 1999),[164] dealing with these traditions, reaches the same result. He quotes extensively from a variety of classical sources in an effort to impeach the transmitters of the traditions. Most importantly, in the context of commenting on one of the classical authorities who accepted the authenticity of some of the racist reports, al-Albānī states:

> This is because [the classical scholar who authenticated the report] stubbornly focused on the chain of transmission (*al-sanad*) without carefully scrutinizing the substance (*matn*). This substance (*matn*) conveys a message that can never be endorsed by the *Sharīʿah.* How could a rational person say that this fair and just *Sharīʿah* would condemn all of the Sudanese nation, with all its people, while there are pious and pure people in it, as is the case with all other nations. By God, how would a non-Muslim from Sudan react if he learns that all of his people have been condemned by the Islamic *Sharīʿah*![165]

I think it is fair to say that al-Albānī is revolted by the ugliness of these traditions, and is not willing to accept them as a matter of principle. He justifiably believes that the *Sharīʿah* cannot endorse this genre of traditions because they violate the ethical principles of the Islamic message. Of course, the analogies to the traditions demeaning to women are apparent. In the same fashion that one could be shocked by reports conveying a deprecating message towards black Africans, one can, just as reasonably, be shocked by traditions that mandate that women walk next to a wall, pray in dark spots in their homes, lick the puss-filled ulcers of their husbands, sexually submit to their husbands on the back of camels, liken women to crooked ribs and black dogs, or cast women as unbridled seducers who are defective in intellect and religion. I suspect that it all depends on the vision of morality and beauty that Islam has instilled in one's heart.

*NOTES*

1 Examples of the *responsa* prohibiting the mixing of the sexes, the prohibition against public employment and the necessity of veiling are translated in the appendix. Many other relevant *responsa* can be found in, Al-ʿUthaymīn, *Fatāwā al-Shaykh,* 1:420–421, 2:757, 2:770, 2:837–838, 2:863–872, 2:873–877, 2:892–899; Ibn Bāz, *Fatāwā Islāmiyyah,* 3:178; *idem, al-Fatāwā,* pp. 183–195, 199; *idem, Majmūʿ Fatāwā,* 1:349–350; *idem, Majmūʿ Fatāwā wa*

*Maqālāt Mutanawwiʿah* (1987), 1:422–431; *idem, Majmūʿ Fatāwā wa Maqālāt Mutanawwiʿah* (1990), 3:354–356; *idem, Majmūʿ Fatāwā wa Maqālāt Mutanawwiʿah* (1990), 4:242–258; *idem, Majmūʿ Fatāwā wa Maqālāt Mutanawwiʿah* (1992), 5:224–240; Ibn Fawzān, *al-Muntaqā*, 3:174–177, 3:242–243, 3:246–247, 3:292–312, 3:329, 4:69–70, 4:176–177, 5:13–14, 5:187–188, 5:263, 5:331–334, 5:385–387; *Fatāwā al-Lajnah* (1991), 1:360–361, 2:14–15; *Fatāwā al-Lajnah* (1996), pp. 339–341; ʿAfīfī, *Fatāwā wa Rasāʾil*, 1/2:478; Ibn Bāz, *Islamic Fatawa*, 313–317.

2 Ibn Bāz, *Fatāwā Islāmiyyah*, 3:178; Ibn Fawzān, *al-Muntaqā*, 3:242–243, 3:329, 4:69–70.

3 Al-Hindī, *Kanz al-ʿUmmāl*, 16:339.

4 Qurʾān, 4:34.

5 Qurʾān, 4:34 states: "Men are the protectors and maintainers of women because Allah has given the one [men] more than the other, and because they [men] support them [women] from their wealth. Therefore the righteous women are devoutly obedient, and guard in [the husband's] absence what Allah would have them guard. As to those women on whose part you fear disloyalty and ill-conduct, admonish them, refuse to share their beds, and beat them. But if they return to obedience, do not seek against them any means [of annoyance], for Allah is most high and great." Premodern Muslim jurists have generally understood the reference to beating in this verse restrictively. They usually held that beatings cannot be to the face and cannot cause pain or harm. See, Abou El Fadl, "On the Beating of Wives," *Conference of the Books*, pp. 167–176; *idem*, "The Beating of Wives Revisited," *Conference of the Books*, pp. 177–188.

6 See Abou El Fadl, "On the Beating of Wives," *Conference of the Books*, pp. 167–176; *idem*, "The Beating of Wives Revisited," *Conference of the Books*, pp. 177–188.

7 See Qurʾān, 30:21.

8 For instance, this tradition is cited in Ibn Fawzān, *al-Muntaqā*, 3:243; *Fatāwā al-Marʾah al-Muslimah* (1996), 2:678.

9 See generally, Ibn al-Jawzī, *Kitāb Aḥkām al-Nisāʾ*, pp. 136–139; al-Shawkānī, *Nayl al-Awṭār*, 6:207–208; al-Mubārakfūrī, *Tuḥfat al-Aḥwadhī*, 4:271–273; Ibn Qayyim al-Jawziyyah, *ʿAwn al-Maʿbūd*, 6:178; Ibn Ḥanbal, *Musnad*, 4:515, 6:89; Ibn Mājah, *Sunan* (1972), 1:595; al-Būṣayrī, *Zawāʾid Ibn Mājah*, p. 263. Most of the version are reported in al-Hindī, *Kanz al-ʿUmmāl* , 16:332–341.

10 Al-Mubārakfūrī, *Tuḥfat al-Aḥwadhī*, 4:271.

11 Ibn Mājah, *Sunan* (1972), 1:595.

12 Ibn Ḥanbal, *Musnad*, 6:89.

13 Ibn Mājah, *Sunan* (1972), 1:595.

14 Ibn al-Jawzī, *Kitāb Aḥkām al-Nisāʾ*, p. 137; al-Hindī, *Kanz al-ʿUmmāl*, 16:333.

15 Ibn Ḥanbal, *Musnad*, 4:515; Ibn Qayyim al-Jawziyyah, *ʿAwn al-Maʿbūd*, 6:179. The significance of the word *qatab* (saddle) employed in some traditions, was debated by jurists. Some stated that the use of saddle refers to submission while mounting an animal. Others argued that it is referring to a type of seat used to facilitate birthing. The second use is intended to signify the importance of sexual compliance; even if a woman is in the process of birthing she ought not refrain from fulfilling her husband's sexual desires. This, of course, is an exaggeration, but the point of the exaggeration is to emphasize that even if a woman is preoccupied with some immediate task or is in pain, she must fulfill her husband's sexual desires. See Ibn al-Athīr al-Jazrī, *al-Nihāyah fī Gharīb al-Ḥadīth*, 4:10; al-Harawī, *Gharīb al-Ḥadīth*, 2:361; al-Tirmidhī, *Nawādir*, 176; al-Ṭabarānī, *al-Muʿjam al-Kabīr*, 5:200, 208; 8:334.

16 Ibn Ḥanbal, *Musnad*, 3:200. Some versions of this genre of reports state that even if the husband's nose is oozing with puss and blood, and his wife licks it, she will not do him justice. Al-Hindī, *Kanz al-ʿUmmāl*, 16:338; Ibn Abī Shaybah, *al-Muṣannaf*, 3:399.

17 All the prostration traditions and the traditions mentioning sexual submission, even on the back of a camel, contain individuals, such as Ayyūb b. ʿUtbah, Muḥammad b. Jābir, and Ṣadaqa b. ʿAbd Allāh, whose credibility is suspect. This has led many scholars to question the authenticity of these reports. Al-Jurjānī, *al-Kāmil fī Ḍuʿafāʾ*, 2:13, 3:139, 4:332, 5:117.

18 As explained earlier, *mutawātir* traditions are those transmitted throughout the first three generations of Muslims by such a large number of transmitters that it is highly unlikely that the traditions are fabricated.

19 Other traditions attributed to the Prophet provide that for a woman, the one most entitled to her caretaking is her husband, and for a man, the one most entitled to his caretaking is his mother. Another tradition provides: "If a wife would truly acknowledge the rights of husband over her, she would remain standing [in his service] as he eats his lunch or supper until he is finished [eating]." Al-Hindī, *Kanz al-ʿUmmāl*, 16:331–332.

20 Ibn Qayyim al-Jawziyyah, *ʿAwn al-Maʿbūd*, 6:179–180; Ibn Ḥajar al-ʿAsqalānī, *Fatḥ al-Bārī* (n.d.), 6:314–316, 9:293–294; al-Nawawī, *Sharḥ Ṣaḥīḥ Muslim* (1996), 9/10:248–249. Relying on these types of traditions, al-Ḥakīm al-Tirmidhī asserts that a woman must submit to her husband's sexual desires whether she feels like it or not, even if doing so would cause her hardship. See al-Tirmidhī, *Nawādir*, p. 176.

21 Even the C.R.L.O reproduces this apologetic rhetoric by maintaining that Islam gave women their full rights. See Ibn Bāz, *Majmūʿ Fatāwā wa Maqālāt Mutanawwiʿah*, 3:348–350. For this apologetic argument, see also, Doi, *Women in Shariʿah*, pp. 4–10; Rahman, *Role of Women in Society*, pp. 9–45, 92–118; al-Farüqi, *Women, Muslim Society, and Islam*, pp. 6–10; al-Hibri, "A study of Islamic herstory," pp. 207–219.

22 Ibn al-Jawzī, *Kitāb Aḥkām al-Nisāʾ*,pp. 139–140.

23 In the juristic discourses, women are not normally seen as the social equivalent of slaves to their husbands. Nevertheless, influential pre-modern scholars such as Abū Ḥāmid al-Ghazālī have asserted that a wife is a "sort of" slave to her husband, and therefore, she must obey all his commands as long as he does not command her to perform a sinful act. See al-Ghazālī, *Iḥyāʾ*, 2:56.

24 Ibn Ḥajar al-ʿAsqalānī, *Fatḥ al-Bārī* (1993), 10:347.

25 Ibn Ḥajar al-ʿAsqalānī, *Fatḥ al-Bārī* (1993), 10:352.

26 Many of these traditions are in al-Nasāʾī, *Ishārat al-Nisāʾ*, pp. 151–2, 156–7, 157–60, 163–4. See also, Abū Shuqqah, *Taḥrīr al-Marʾah*, for a collection of these reports in four volumes.

27 However, some of these commentators go on to say this exaggeration is justified because of the seriousness of the husband's rights. Al-Mubārakfūrī, *Tuḥfat al-Aḥwadhī*, 4:271.

28 For Abū Hurayrah's role in this tradition, see, al-Jirāḥī, *Kashf al-Khafāʾ* (1983), p. 162; Ibn Jār Allāh al-Yamānī, *al-Nawāfiḥ al-ʿAṭirah*, p. 277.

29 For example, see, al-ʿAzzī, *Difāʿ ʿan Abī Hurayrah*; al-Zarʿī, *Abū Hurayrah*. The late jurist Rashīd Riḍā issued a *responsum* in 1928 in which he defended Abū Hurayrah's credibility. Nevertheless, noted that Abū Hurayrah did transmit Israelite reports through Kaʿb al-Aḥbār, a Jewish Rabbi and a close friend of Abū Hurayrah. See Riḍā, *Fatāwā al-Imām*, 5:2034–2035.

30 Al-Nīsābūrī, *al-Mustadrak*, 3:509.

31 Ibn Qutaybah, *Kitāb Taʾwīl*, p. 31; al-Mūsawī, *Abū Hurayrah*, pp. 196.

32 Ibn Kathīr, *al-Bidāyah wa al-Nihāyah*, 8:106.

33 Al-Dhahabī, *Siyar Aʿlām*, 2:607 n. 3.

34 For these reports and others see, al-Dhahabī, *Siyar Aʿlām*, 2:589, 594–609, 615; Ibn Saʿd, *al-Ṭabaqāt al-Kubrā* (n.d.), 2:362–364, 4:330–335. See also, Ibn Kathīr, *al-Bidāyah wa al-Nihāyah*, 8:109; For instance, it is reported that on separate occasions, ʿĀʾishah and ʿAlī openly declared that they disagreed with what Abū Hurayrah reported and would act contrary to his report (*la ukhālifanna Abā Hurayrah*). Ibn Qutaybah, *Kitāb Taʾwīl*, p. 19. Reportedly, al-Ḥasan al-Baṣrī said that Abū Hurayrah was not reliable, see al-Dhahabī, *Siyar Aʿlām*, 4:571.

35 Ibn Saʿd, *al-Ṭabaqāt al-Kubrā* (n.d.), 2:364, 4:331; al-Dhahabī, *Siyar Aʿlām*, 2:615–616.

36 See al-Dhahabī, *Siyar Aʿlām*, 2:608–609, 618–619; al-Sarakhsī, *Uṣūl al-Sarakhsī*, 1:341.

37 For an example of such an apologetic Sunnī work see, Ibn Saʿīd, *Naqd al-Marīsī*, 2:617–631. See also, al-Dhahabī, *Siyar Aʿlām*, 2:615.

38 These and similar reports are in Ibn Saʿīd, *Naqd al-Marīsī*, 1:617–631. See also, al-Dhahabī, *Siyar Aʿlām*, 2:600.

39 The idea of social effect or impact, as a methodological tool, is conceptually similar to the classical notion of *ʿumūm al-balwā* (the widespread affliction) used to evaluate the necessity for exceptional laws.
40 As noted earlier, in the contemporary age, *Shaykh* Muḥammad al-Ghazālī was one of the main advocates of *matn* analysis. See, *Shaykh* Muḥammad al-Ghazālī, *al-Sunnah al-Nabawiyyah*; *idem*, *Dustūr al-Wiḥdah.*
41 Siddiqi, *Ḥadīth Literature*, p. 114; Balīq, *Minhāj al-Ṣāliḥīn*, pp. 36–39.
42 Ibn al-Ṣalāḥ, *ʿUlūm al-Ḥadīth*, pp. 91–92; see also, ʿAbd al-Raḥmān al-Rāzī, *ʿIlal al-Ḥadīth*; Ṣubḥī al-Ṣāliḥ, *ʿUlūm al-Ḥadīth*, pp. 179–187; ʿIṭr, *Manhaj al-Naqd*, pp. 447–454.
43 Rahman, *Islam*, pp. 64–67; see also, *idem*, *Islamic Methodology in History*, pp. 27–82. Ironically, the C.R.L.O jurists, themselves, state that *isnād* analysis is insufficient, and that *matn* analysis is imperative. Al-ʿUthaymīn, *Fatāwā al-Shaykh*, 1:269–270. Inconsistently, the C.R.L.O maintains that all traditions documented in *Ṣaḥīḥ al-Bukhārī* are authentic. *Fatāwā al-Lajnah* (1991), 3:345.
44 Ibn Qayyim al-Jawziyyah, *ʿAwn al-Maʿbūd*, 6:177–178.
45 Khān, et al., *Nuzhat al-Muttaqīn*, 1:289. See generally on this *ḥadīth*, Zaydān, *al-Mufaṣṣal fī Aḥkām* (1994); al-Shawkānī, *Nayl al-Awṭār*, 6:207–210; al-Mubārakfūrī, *Tuḥfat al-Aḥwadhī*, 4:271–272.
46 Reported by Aḥmad, Ibn Ḥibbān and al-Ṭabarī. See Ibn Ḥanbal, *Musnad*, 1:236–7.
47 There are several *ḥadīth* attributed to the Prophet that assert that a woman's prayer or worship will not be accepted by God if she upsets or disobeys her husband. Other *ḥadīth* assert that the angels will curse any woman who upsets her husband by refusing him conjugal relations. See, al-Shawkānī, *Nayl al-Awṭār*, 6:209–210.
48 Ibn Ḥajar al-ʿAsqalānī claims that he is *ṣadūq* (truthful). Ibn Ḥajar al-ʿAsqalānī, *Taqrīb al-Tahdhīb*, 1:444. However, Ibn Luhayʿah's reliability was contested. It is reported that he became mentally unstable after his books burned in 170/787. Some considered him unreliable after that event. Others refused to transmit or accept *ḥadīth* from him before or after that event. See, Ibn Ḥibbān, *al-Majrūḥīn*, 2:11–16.
49 Ibn Ḥajar al-ʿAsqalānī, *Fatḥ al-Bārī* (n.d.), 9:294. Another report of this genre asserts that every Friday there is a particular hour when all prayers will be answered except the prayers of a woman who had upset her husband. Ibn al-Jawzī, *Kitāb al-Mawḍūʿāt*, 2:177. Ibn al-Jawzī asserts that this tradition is not authentic.
50 Ibn Qayyim al-Jawziyyah, *ʿAwn al-Maʿbūd*, 6:179.
51 Al-Mubārakfūrī, *Tuḥfat al-Aḥwadhī*, 4:283–284.
52 Qurʾān, 33:35; 4:34.
53 In matters of both law and theology, the *ahl al-ḥadīth* approached their subject matter by relying on transmitted knowledge (i.e. *ḥadīth*) and rejecting rationalist methods of inquiry. This is not to say they were simply *ḥadīth* collectors, or *muḥaddiths. Muḥaddiths* could be rationally inclined, since memorizing and collecting *ḥadīth* was a fundamental aspect of legal education, and was not exclusive to the *ahl al-ḥadīth.* Rather, the *ahl al-ḥadīth* rejected the rationalist tendencies among the Muʿtazilah, and the utilization of rationalist methods into legal inquiry. Consequently, their methodology was characterized by an often rigid reliance on tradition. The jurist and school of law most closely associated with the *ahl al-ḥadīth* is Aḥmad b. Ḥanbal and his adherents. George Makdisi, "Ashʿarī and the Ashʿarites, Part I," pp. 37–80, 38, 48–52; Fazlur Rahman, *Islam*, pp. 115, 146, 231, 239; Goldziher, *The Ẓāhirīs*, pp. 3–5; Melchert, *Formation*, pp. 2–3; Watt, *Formative Period*, pp. 66–67; Weiss, *Spirit of Islamic Law*, pp. 12–14.
54 See al-Āmidī, *al-Iḥkām* (1984), 2:48, 62–66; Fakhr al-Dīn al-Rāzī, *al-Maḥṣūl* (1988), 2:184, 215; al-Sarakhsī, *Uṣūl al-Sarakhsī*, 1:321, 333; al-Juwaynī, *al-Burhān*, 1:606. See also the useful discussion in Weiss, *Search for God's Law*, pp. 293–294, 299–300.
55 Al-ʿUthaymīn, *Fatāwā al-Shaykh*, 1:188–189; *Fatāwā al-Lajnah* (1991), 3:239–240, 4:289–290.
56 This manifested in a rather notorious controversy when the late *Shaykh* Muḥammad al-Ghazālī wrote *al-Sunnah al-Nabawiyyah.* Several conferences were held in Saudi Arabia to respond to him, and a large number of books refuted his arguments or attacked him

personally. See, for example, Sulṭān, *Azmat al-Ḥiwār*; ʿAwdah, *Fī Ḥiwār Hādī*; Madkhalī, *Kashf Mawqif al-Ghazālī*; Ibn ʿAbd al-Raḥīm, *Jināyat al-Shaykh Muḥammad al-Ghazālī.*

57 The confusion surrounding *uṣūl* and *furūʿ* is aptly demonstrated in the debate over the *ḥijāb* (veil) of the Muslim woman. The majority of Muslim writers argue that the issue of *ḥijāb* is not open to debate or discussion. According to them, a Muslim woman must cover all her body and hair except her face and hands. See al-Albānī, *Ḥijāb al-Marʾah*; al-Mawdūdī, *al-Ḥijāb.* Effectively, these writers are arguing that the *ḥijāb* is among the *uṣūl* of religion and, therefore, no disagreement may be tolerated. Other writers have argued that the *ḥijāb* is an appropriate subject for debate. See, Sharīf, *al-Marʾah al-Muslimah*; Mernissi, *The Veil and the Male Elite.* I would argue that it is not possible to systematically distinguish between *uṣūl* or *furūʿ*. The focus of the inquiry should be on burdens of proof in relation to the law claimed. If one wishes to maintain that *ḥijāb* is a mandatory and fundamental part of religion, in light of the widespread impact of the law, she/he bears a heavy burden of proof especially if he or she is arguing for a mandatory enforcement of the law. At any case, I don't see how it could be possible to prohibit discussions on the matter of the *ḥijāb.*

58 Ibn Ḥajar al-ʿAsqalānī, *Fatḥ al-Bārī* (n.d.), 9:253–254.

59 For a systematic argument on this point, see Mernissi, *The Veil and the Male Elite,* although I disagree with the author's conclusions.

60 Al-ʿĪd, *Iḥkām al-Aḥkām,* 1:157; Ibn Ḥazm al-Ẓāhirī, *al-Muḥallā bi al-Āthār,* 2:170; Ibn Ḥajar al-ʿAsqalānī, *Fatḥ al-Bārī* (n.d.), 2:350, 382–384; Ibn Qayyim al-Jawziyyah, *ʿAwn al-Maʿbūd,* 2:273–275; al-Nawawī, *Sharḥ Ṣaḥīḥ Muslim* (1996), 3/4:382–385.

61 Ibn Ḥajar al-ʿAsqalānī, *Fatḥ al-Bārī* (n.d.), 2:55–56; Ibn Ḥazm, *al-Muḥallā,* 2:170; al-Nawawī, *Sharḥ Ṣaḥīḥ Muslim* (1996), 3/4:383.

62 Muḥammad Aḥmad Ismāʿīl al-Muqaddim, *ʿAwdat al-Ḥijāb* (Riyāḍ: Dār Ṭaybah, 1996), 3:22; Ibn Ḥajar al-ʿAsqalānī, *Fatḥ al-Bārī* (n.d.), 2:350.

63 On the Medinese delegation to the Prophet, see, Lings, *Muhammad,* pp. 108–112. For a discussion on the more liberal culture of Medina, see, Mernissi, *Veil and the Male Elite,* pp. 142–145.

64 Al-ʿUthaymīn, *Fatāwā al-Shaykh,* 1:363.

65 Ibn Bāz, *Majmūʿ Fatāwā,* 1:282–284.

66 Ibn Qayyim al-Jawziyyah, *ʿAwn al-Maʿbūd,* 6:187–188; al-Mubārakfūrī, *Tuḥfat al-Aḥwadhī,* 4:280–281.

67 Ibn Bāz, *Majmūʿ Fatāwā wa Maqālāt Mutanawwiʿah* (1990), 3:348–350.

68 For the text of the report, see Ibn Ḥajar al-ʿAsqalānī, *Fatḥ al-Bārī* (n.d.), 6:363.

69 Al-Nawawī, *Sharḥ Ṣaḥīḥ Muslim* (1996), 9/10:298–299.

70 Ibn Ḥajar al-ʿAsqalānī, *Fatḥ al-Bārī* (n.d.), 6:363–364.

71 The narration of this report is also attributed to Abū Saʿīd al-Khudrī and ʿAbd Allāh b. ʿUmar.

72 Ibn Ḥajar al-ʿAsqalānī, *Fatḥ al-Bārī* (n.d.), 1:483; al-Nawawī, *Sharḥ Ṣaḥīḥ Muslim* (1996), 1/2:253–256; al-Mubārakfūrī, *Tuḥfat al-Aḥwadhī,* 7:300–301; Ibn Qayyim al-Jawziyyah, *ʿAwn al-Maʿbūd,* 12:438–439. In an alternative version of this report the Prophet does not address women at all. Rather, the Prophet was praying with his congregation when the sun eclipsed. Shortly afterwards, the Prophet was overtaken by tremors and nearly collapsed. The Prophet then informs the congregation that he just saw Hell and that women formed most of its population. When asked about the reason for this, the Prophet responds that it is because women are ungrateful beings. Ibn Ḥajar al-ʿAsqalānī, *Fatḥ al-Bārī* (n.d.), 9:298.

73 Ibn Bāz, *Majmūʿ Fatāwā wa Maqālāt Mutanawwiʿah* (1990), 4:292–294.

74 Ibn Ḥajar al-ʿAsqalānī, *Fatḥ al-Bārī* (n.d.), 4:220, 6:218, 10:215; Ibn Bāz, *Majmūʿ Fatāwā wa Maqālāt Mutanawwiʿah* (1987), 1:422–431; al-ʿUthaymīn, *Fatāwā al-Shaykh,* 1:382, 2:837–838, 2:856–857; Ibn Bāz, *Islamic Fatawa,* pp. 309–317; *Fatāwā al-Lajnah* (1996), p. 392; Ibn Bāz, *Majmūʿ Fatāwā wa Maqālāt Mutanawwiʿah* (1990), 3:351–353; Ibn Fawzān, *al-Muntaqā,* 3:300, 5:383.

75 For examples of other writers who rely on these traditions and more, see al-Barazī, *Ḥijāb al-Muslimah*; al-Muqaddim, *ʿAwdāt al-Ḥijāb.*

76 As noted earlier, C.R.L.O jurists agree that the analysis of the chain of transmission is insufficient and that the substance of the tradition must be evaluated as well. The C.R.L.O jurists, however, seem to evaluate the substance of traditions according to a very patriarchal set of values. Al-ʿUthaymīn, *Fatāwā al-Shaykh*, 1:269–270.
77 See al-Jurjānī, *al-Kāmil fī Ḍuʿafāʾ*, 2:397, 7:104.
78 Al-Kāndahlawī, *Awjaz al-Masālik*, 3:156–159; al-Suyūṭī, *Sharḥ Sunan al-Nasāʾī*, 2:62–66; al-Mubārakfūrī, *Tuḥfat al-Aḥwadhī*, 2:256–261; Ibn Ḥajar al-ʿAsqalānī, *Fatḥ al-Bārī* (n.d.), 1:698–703; al-Nawawī, *Sharḥ Ṣaḥīḥ Muslim* (1996), 3/4:450–454; Ibn Qayyim al-Jawziyyah, *ʿAwn al-Maʿbūd*, 2:394–402, 405–406.
79 Al-Mubārakfūrī, *Tuḥfat al-Aḥwadhī*, 2:260.
80 The same holds true for traditions attributed to the Prophet that seem to take sides in sectarian conflicts that took place years after the Prophet's death. These reports will often praise Muʿāwiyah or condemn the Khawārij.
81 Ibn Qayyim al-Jawziyyah, *ʿAwn al-Maʿbūd*, 10:420.
82 Al-Zarʿī, *Abū Hurayrah*, p. 65; Ibn Ḥajar al-ʿAsqalānī, *Fatḥ al-Bārī* (n.d.), 10:159.
83 On the bad omen tradition and the related debates see, Ibn Ḥanbal, *Musnad*, 2:381; Ibn Ḥajar al-ʿAsqalānī, *Fatḥ al-Bārī* (n.d.), 9:137–138; 10:158–163, 212–215, 243–244; al-Nawawī, *Sharḥ Ṣaḥīḥ Muslim* (1996), 13/14:440–442; Ibn Qayyim al-Jawziyyah, *ʿAwn al-Maʿbūd*, 10:405–421; al-Nasāʾī, *Ishārat al-Nisāʾ*, pp. 218–222.
84 Al-Nawawī, *Sharḥ Ṣaḥīḥ Muslim* (1996), 9/10:300–301.
85 A large number of classical authorities rejected the authenticity of these traditions. Again, this fact does not seem to bother the C.R.L.O. See al-Jurjānī, *al-Kāmil fī Ḍuʿafāʾ*, 4:286, 5:357.
86 Ibn Ḥajar al-ʿAsqalānī, *Fatḥ al-Bārī* (n.d.), 1:484; al-Mubārakfūrī, *Tuḥfat al-Aḥwadhī*, 7:300–301; Ibn Qayyim al-Jawziyyah, *ʿAwn al-Maʿbūd*, 12:438–439.
87 Al-Mubārakfūrī, *Tuḥfat al-Aḥwadhī*, 6:449–450.
88 Al-Mubārakfūrī, *Tuḥfat al-Aḥwadhī*, 6:449. Another report attributed to the Prophet asserts that obeying women will only earn a man much sorrow and regret. See al-Jurjānī, *al-Kāmil fī Ḍuʿafāʾ*, 4:249, 6:462; Ibn al-Jawzī, *Kitāb al-Mawḍūʿāt*, 2:177.
89 Al-Mubārakfūrī, *Tuḥfat al-Aḥwadhī*, 6:449. In 6/628 the Prophet led an expedition to Mecca in order to make a pilgrimage to the Kaʿbah. This pilgrimage took place prior to the surrender of Mecca to the Muslims. The Meccans, after having fought three unsuccessful battles against the Muslims, were not inclined to let them into the city. Instead, a settlement was reached which established peace between the Muslims and the Meccans for ten years. This settlement is called the Treaty of Ḥudaybiyyah. It provided in part that the Muslims would not enter the city, but could return one year later when the Meccans would abandon their city for three days. The Muslims were unhappy that they could not perform the pilgrimage, and refused to perform the rituals the Prophet later commanded. After consultation with his wife, Umm Salamah, the Prophet performed the rituals himself, and the Muslims followed suit. See, Ibn Hishām, *al-Sīrah al-Nabawiyyah*, 3/4:308–320; Watt, *Muhammad*, pp. 182–188; Salahi, *Muḥammad*, pp. 458–478; Kennedy, *The Prophet*, pp. 41–42; Lings, *Muhammad*, pp. 252–256.
90 Ibn Khallikān, *Wafayāt al-Aʿyān* (1998), 2:377–378; al-Dhahabī, *Siyar Aʿlām*, 4:148.
91 Evidence of this process can be seen in the virulently hateful reports of women that were invented and circulated in early Islam. For instance, some reports that were attributed to the Prophet and circulated early on stated that women should not be taught to read or write, and that they should not be housed in luxury. Other reports asserted that women should be kept hungry and needy because once they eat their fill and obtain their needs, they start aspiring to go out of their homes and venture in the streets, and there is nothing worse for women than leaving their homes. On the other hand, if they are kept hungry and needy, they will keep to their homes. Some versions add that instead of writing and reading women should be taught knitting. Some versions add that women should be starved but not to the point of physical harm (*ajīʿū al-nisāʾ jawʿan ghayr muḍirr*). Interestingly, these traditions were put in the mouth of ʿĀʾishah and Ibn ʿAbbās. However, the various versions

of these reports were rejected as fabrications by a large number of jurists. See al-Jurjānī, *al-Kāmil fī Ḍuʿafāʾ*, 1:507, 2:395, 5:537; Ibn Jawzī, *al-Ḍuʿafāʾ*, 2:173–174. Importantly, these traditions are not of a higher level of authenticity than the traditions cited and relied upon by the C.R.L.O for its various determinations.

92 This also produced a considerable amount of apologetics by Sunni conservative jurists who argued that ʿĀʾishah did not *really* rebel, and Abū Bakrah did not *really* oppose her rebellion, and that ʿĀʾishah did not *really* lead anything. See Ibn Ḥajar al-ʿAsqalānī, *Fatḥ al-Bārī* (n.d.), 8:128–129, 13:53.

93 Ibn Ḥajar al-ʿAsqalānī, *Fatḥ al-Bārī* (n.d.), 9:323.

94 Reportedly, this is the reason for the revelation of Qurʾān, 33:35. See, also, Ibn Kathīr, *Mukhtaṣar Tafsīr Ibn Kathīr*, 3:95–96; al-Qurṭubī, *al-Jāmiʿ* (1993), 14:120–121.

95 Qurʾān, 58:1.

96 See al-Zamakhsharī, *al-Kashshāf*, 4:69–70; al-Rāzī, *al-Tafsīr al-Kabīr* (1999), 10:477–478; al-Ṭabarī, *Tafsīr al-Ṭabarī*, 7:237–238; al-Qurṭubī, *al-Jāmiʿ* (1993), 17:175–177.

97 Qurʾān, 24:11. See, also, al-Rāzī, *al-Tafsīr al-Kabīr* (1999), 8:337–340; al-Zamakhsharī, *al-Kashshāf*, 3:52–53; al-Qurṭubī, *al-Jāmiʿ* (1993), 12:131–134; al-Ṭabarī, *Tafsīr al-Ṭabarī*, 5:400–406.

98 Al-Nasāʾī, *Ishārat al-Nisāʾ*, p. 54. The incident involving ʿĀʾishah is reported to have occurred in 6/628. She accompanied the Prophet on an expedition against the Banū Muṣṭaliq when she lost her necklace. She left her encampment to retrieve it, and by the time she returned, the army had left. She waited in the encampment hoping someone would return for her. Instead, she was found by Ṣafwān b. al-Muʿaṭṭal, who escorted her to the army's new encampment. When people saw her come into the camp with another man, rumors spread falsely accusing her of infidelity. See, Ibn Hishām, *al-Sīrah al-Nabawiyyah*, 3/4:297–307; Spellberg, *Politics, Gender, and the Islamic Past*, pp. 61–99; Mernissi, *Veil and the Male Elite*, pp. 177–179; Lings, *Muhammad*, pp. 240–246.

99 Abū Shuqqah, *Taḥrīr al-Marʾah*, 2:29–456, has collected and annotated the reports on these incidents and others. See also, Ibn Ḥajar al-ʿAsqalānī, *Fatḥ al-Bārī* (n.d.), 2:469; Ibn Hishām, *al-Sīrah al-Nabawiyyah*, 3/4:411.

100 Jaʿīṭ, *al-Fitnah* (1989), pp. 145–168; Kennedy, *The Prophet*, p. 76; Mernissi, *Veil and the Male Elite*, pp. 5–7; Spellberg, *Politics, Gender, and the Islamic Past*, pp. 101–149; Hodgson, *Venture of Islam*, 1:214.

101 See Abū Ḥāmid al-Ghazālī, *Iḥyāʾ*, 2:57.

102 For the different versions, see Ibn Abī Shaybah, *al-Muṣannaf fī al-Aḥādīth*, 3:396–397; Ibn ʿAbd al-Barr, *al-Tamhīd li-mā fī al-Muwaṭṭaʾ*, 1:229–231; al-Bayhaqī, *Kitāb al-Sunan*, 7:291–293; al-Suyūṭī, *al-Jāmiʿ al-Ṣaghīr*, 1:507–508; al-Hindī, *Kanz al-ʿUmmā*, 16:339.

103 Al-Nasāʾī, *Ishārat al-Nisāʾ*, pp. 159–160.

104 Many studies on the veil address it in the larger context of women's rights and social status in Islamic history and the modern Middle East. See, Mutahhari, *Masʾala-i Hijāb*; Minces, *Veiled Women in Islam*; Ahmed, *Women and Gender in Islam*; Mir-Hosseini, *Islam and Gender*; El Guindi, *Veil: Modesty, Privacy and Resistance*; Mernissi, *Veil and the Male Elite*; Macleod, *Accomodating Protest*.

105 Qurʾān, 24:30–1; 24:60.

106 The term *ʿawrah* is defined by referring to those parts of the body that must be covered during prayer and that are prohibited from being seen. Ibn Mufliḥ, *al-Mubdiʿ*, 1:359. Linguistically, it refers to something faulty (*nuqṣān* or *ʿayb*) or repulsive (*mustaqbaḥ* or *qubḥ*). Al-Bahūtī, *Kashshāf al-Qināʿ*, 1:312; Ibn Nujaym, *al-Baḥr al-Rāʾiq*, 1:467. Generally, jurists provide a definition of the *ʿawrah* when addressing how a Muslim should dress when making obligatory prayers (*ṣalāt*). Interestingly, the earliest traditions on the subject do not reflect a specific discussion on *ʿawrah*. Rather they address different dress styles and, at least in the case of women, draw distinctions between certain classes of women. For instance, early works relate traditions of the Prophet praying while wrapped in a single *thawb* or garment that draped over his shoulders and covered his front and back (*layukhālifu bayna ṭarafayhi ʿalā ʿātiqihi*). ʿAbd al-Razzāq, *al-Muṣannaf*, 1:350, 353. See

also, Ibn Abī Shayba, *al-Kitāb al-Muṣannaf,* 1:275–277. Others suggest that it is better to pray with two garments, namely one wrapped around the waist (*izār*) and another draped around the shoulders (*ridāʾ*). Al-Ṣanʿānī, *al-Muṣannaf,* 1:349, 353–354, 356; Ibn Abī Shayba, *al-Kitāb al-Muṣannaf,* 1:275–276. See also, al-Ramlī, *Nihāyat al-Muḥtāj* (1992), 2:13; al-Bahūtī, *Kashshāf al-Qināʿ,* 1:316–317. However, the conflict over men's proper attire arises when one's garment is too small. One set of traditions holds that if a man's garment is large enough, he should drape it over himself (*mutawashshiḥ*), but if it is small, he should pray with the garment wrapped around his waist (*muttazir* or *yukhālifu bayna ṭarafayhi*). Al-Ṣanʿānī, *al-Muṣannaf,* 1:352, 353; Ibn Abī Shayba, *Kitāb al-Muṣannaf,* 1:275, 276, 277. See also, al-Qarāfī, *al-Dhakhīrah,* 2:112; Ibn Mufliḥ, *al-Mubdi,ʿ* 1:64. Others argued that he can pray with a single garment as long as part of it can be draped over his shoulder. Al-Ṣanʿānī, *al-Muṣannaf,* 1:353; Ibn Abī Shayba, *Kitāb al-Muṣannaf,* 1:278. See also, al-Bahūtī, *Kashshāf al-Qināʿ,* 1:318; Muḥammad Amīn Ibn ʿĀbidīn, *Ḥāshiyat Radd al-Muḥtār,* (1966), 1:404. According to the Companion Ibn Masʿūd, if one cannot find sufficient material, then it is permissible to pray with only one garment. However if sufficient material is available, then he should pray with two. However, others such as ʿUmar b. al-Khaṭṭāb disagreed, and held that only one garment wrapped around the waist was sufficient for prayers. Al-Ṣanʿānī, *al-Muṣannaf,* 1:356; Ibn Abī Shayba, *Kitāb al-Muṣannaf,* 1:278–279. See also, Ibn Rushd, *Bidāyat al-Mujtahid.* 1:159. Incidentally, one report suggests that wearing a garment around the waist was endorsed partly to distinguish the Muslims from the Jews. Al-Ṣanʿānī, *al-Muṣannaf,* 1:352; Ibn Abī Shayba, *Kitāb al-Muṣannaf,* 1:278. Notably, the term *ʿawrah* does not appear in this discussion. Likewise, it is not used in the early discussion on women's attire in prayer. The traditions instead address the kinds of clothing a woman must wear in prayer, and distinguishes between the appropriate attire for free and slave women. Specifically, al-Ṣanʿānī relates traditions on two issues. The first issue concerns what a free woman must wear when praying. Generally, the items for consideration are a *khimār, jilbāb, dirʿ sābigh,* and *milḥaf.* Al-Ṣanʿānī, *al-Muṣannaf,* 3:128–129, 131, 135; Ibn Abī Shayba, *al-Muṣannaf,* 2:36–37. See also, al-Māwardī, *al-Ḥāwī al-Kabīr,* 2:169; Ibn Mufliḥ, *al-Mubdiʿ,* 1:366; al-Ramlī, *Nihāyat al-Muḥtāj* (1992), 2:13–14; al-Bahūtī, *Kashshāf al-Qināʿ,* 1:318; Ibn Ḥazm, *al-Muḥallā,* 2:2:249–250. The second issues concerns whether a slave woman must also wear a *khimār* for prayer? The *khimār* is generally a garment that covers a woman's head. Ibn Manẓūr, *Lisān al-ʿArab,* 4:257; Ibn Mufliḥ, *al-Mubdiʿ,* 1:366; al-Bahūtī, *Kashshāf al-Qināʿ,* 1:318. The meaning of *dirʿ sābigh* generally suggests some type of loose-fitting garment that extends to one's feet. The relevant distinction is that a *dirʿ* does not necessarily cover a woman's head. Ibn Manẓūr, *Lisān al-ʿArab,* 8:81–82; Ibn Mufliḥ, *al-Mubdiʿ,* 1:366; Lane, *Arabic-English Lexicon,* 1:871–872. *Jilbāb* refers to a garment that is larger than a *khimār* and generally covers a woman's head and chest area, but may also cover her entire body. In some cases it is used as a synonym for *khimār,* and in others for an *izār.* Ibn Manẓūr, *Lisān al-ʿArab,* 1:272–273. And a *milḥaf* is a blanket (*dithār*) or cover which is wrapped over other clothes. Ibn Manẓūr, *Lisān al-ʿArab,* 9:314. Al-Ṣanʿānī reports that the Prophet said that menstruating free women must wear a *khimār,* otherwise their prayer will not be accepted. Al-Ṣanʿānī, *al-Muṣannaf,* 3:130, 131; Ibn Abī Shayba, *Kitāb al-Muṣannaf,* 2:39–40. The reference to menstruation is generally regarded as a reference to adulthood or the age of majority. Al-Marghīnānī, *al-Hidāya,* 1:43. Women who are not adults are not necessarily subject to this requirement. Al-Ṣanʿānī, *al-Muṣannaf,* 3:132. In another tradition, a woman is supposed to wear a *khimār,* a *dirʿ,* and an *izār,* although there is some countervailing traditions against this position. Ibn Mufliḥ, *al-Mubdiʿ,* 1:366. Some traditions suggest that an acceptable *dirʿ* must be long and loose enough to cover the appearance of a woman's feet, although without a *khimār,* it is insufficient. Al-Ṣanʿānī, *al-Muṣannaf,* 3:128; Ibn Abī Shayba, *Kitāb al-Muṣannaf,* 2:36. One tradition relates that ʿĀʾisha was seen wearing during prayer a garment around her waist (*muʾtazirah*), a *dirʿ,* and a thick *khimār.* Al-Ṣanʿānī, *al-Muṣannaf,* p. 129. On the other hand, Umm Ḥabībah, a wife of the Prophet, is reported to have worn a *dirʿ,* and an *izār* that was large enough to drape around her and reach the ground. Notably, she did not wear a *khimār*. Id. Yet another tradition relates that the Prophet's wives Maymūna and Umm Salamah would wear a *khimār* and a *dir*ʿ *sābigh*. Ibn Abī Shayba, *Kitāb al-Muṣannaf*, 2:36.

107 The issue of *ʿawrah* is complex partly because it is extremely difficult to retrace and reclaim the historical process that produced the determinations as to *ʿawrah*. The conventional wisdom maintains that early on, Muslim jurists held that what should be covered in prayer should be covered outside of prayer. This, however, is not entirely true. The dominant juristic schools of thought argued that the *ʿawrah* of men is what is between the knee and navel. A man ought to cover what is between the knee and navel inside and outside of prayer. A minority view, however, argued that the *ʿawrah* of men is limited to the groin and buttocks only; the thighs are not *ʿawrah*. The *ʿawrah* of women was a more complex matter. As noted below, the majority argued that all of a woman's body except the hands and face is *ʿawrah*. Abū Ḥanifa held that the feet are not *ʿawrah*, and some argued that half the arm up to the elbow, or the full arm, is not a *ʿawrah*. A minority view held that even the face and hands are *ʿawrah* and therefore, must be covered as well. An early minority view held that the hair and calves are not *ʿawrah*. In addition, some argued that women must cover their hair at prayer, but not outside of prayer. Importantly, the jurists disgreed on whether the covering of the *ʿawrah* is a condition precedent for the validity of prayer. The majority held that covering the *ʿawrah* is a *farḍ* (basic and necessary requirement) so that the failure to cover the *ʿawrah* would invalidate a person's prayers. The minority view (mostly but not exclusively Mālikī jurists) held that covering the *ʿawrah* is not a condition precedent for prayer – accordingly, this school argued that covering the *ʿawrah* is among the *sunan* of prayer (the recommended acts in prayer), and the failure to cover the *ʿawrah* would not void a person's prayers. A large number of Ḥanafī jurists argued that as long as three-fourth of the body is covered the prayer is valid. Interestingly, Mālik reportedly allowed people to pray naked (*ʿurāh*), if they were unable to procure dressing garments. However he suggested that such people should pray alone so as not to see each other's *ʿawrah*, and remain standing throughout. However if they are praying in the dark of night (*layl muẓlim*), they may pray in congregation with an *imām* leading them. Saḥnūn b. Saʿīd, *al-Mudawwana al-Kubrā* (Beirut: Dār Ṣadr, n.d.), 1:95–96. See also, al-Qarāfī, *al-Dhakhīrah*, 2:106–107; Ibn Mufliḥ, *al-Mubdi*ʿ, 1:370–374. The Shiʿī al-Ṭūsī adopts the same view and also allows them to pray in congregation during daylight hours, as long as they pray in only one line and in a sitting position. al-Ṭūsī, *al-Mabsūṭ*, 1:87. Al-Bahūtī goes so far as to say that even in this case, congregational prayer remains obligatory. Al-Bahūtī, *Kashshāf al-Qinā*ʿ, 1:324. See also, Ibn Ḥazm, *al-Muḥallā*, 2:255–257. Being unclothed for prayers does not allow one to steal clothes out of necessity, according to al-Ramlī. Since one can pray naked, there is no necessity as in the case of stealing clothes to protect oneself from heat or freezing temperatures, or stealing food to prevent death by starvation. Al-Ramlī, *Nihāyat al-Muḥtāj* (1992), 2:12. See also, al-Bahūtī, *Kashshāf al-Qinā*ʿ, 1:322–324, who addresses the various means by which those without sufficient clothes can pray. The overwhelming majority of jurists held that the *ʿawrah* of a slave-girl, or even a female servant girl, is different. Some jurists argued that the *ʿawrah* of such a woman is between the knee and navel – the same as a man. The other jurists held that the *ʿawrah* of such a woman is from the beginning of the chest area to the knees and down to the elbows. Therefore, the majority agreed that a slave-girl or servant-girl may pray with her hair exposed. A minority view argued that slave-girls should cover their hair in prayer, but do not have to do so outside of prayer. In short, it seems to me that the conventional wisdom is not exactly correct; there seems to be sufficient grounds for differentiating between the *ʿawrah* in prayer and outside of prayer. Furthermore, as noted below, the *ʿawrah* of slave-girls or servant-girls, inside and outside of prayer, raise serious questions about the basis for the historical juristic determinations regarding the *ʿawrah* of women. See, on the law of *ʿawrah*: al-Ṣanʿānī, *al-Muṣannaf*, 3:128–136 (documents some of the early opinions). *For Mālikī school*, see: Ibn Rushd (II), *Bidāyat al-Mujtahid*, 1:156–158; Ibn Rushd (I), *al-Muqaddimāt al-Mumahhidāt*, 1:183–185; Saḥnūn, *al-Mudawwana* (Dār

Ṣadr), 1:94; al-Ḥaṭṭāb al-Raʿīnī, *Mawāhib al-Jalīl,* 2:177–187; al-Qarāfī, *al-Dhakhīrah,* 2:101–105. For *Shāfiʿī* school, see: al-Shāfiʿī, *al-Umm* (Beirut: Dār al-Fikr, n.d.), 1:109; al-Ramlī, *Nihāyat al-Muḥtāj* (1992), 2:7–8, 13; al-Māwardī, *al-Ḥāwī al-Kabīr,* 2:165–171. *For Ḥanafī school,* see Ibn Nujaym, *al-Baḥr al-Rā'iq,* 1:467, 469–476; Ibn ʿĀbidīn, *Ḥāshiyat Radd* (1966), 1:405; al-Kāsānī, *Badā'iʿ al-Ṣanā'iʿ,* pp. 543–546. *For Ḥanbalī school,* see Ibn Qudāmah, *al-Mughnī* (Dār Iḥyā' al-Turāth al-ʿArabī), 1:601; Ibn Mufliḥ, *al-Mubdiʿ,* 1:361–367; al-Bahūtī, *Kashshāf al-Qināʿ,* 1:315–317. For *Jaʿfarī* school, see al-Ṭūsī, *al-Mabsūṭ,* 1:87–88.

108 Qur'ān, 6:164; 17:15; 35:18; 39:7; 53:38; 24:11; 2:286; 4:32; 33:58.

109 Qur'ān, 33:58–60. Reportedly these verses were revealed in response to several incidents in which the hypocrites of Medina harassed and molested Muslim women. Al-Rāzī, *al-Tafsīr al-Kabīr* (1999), 9:183–184; al-Ṭabarī, *Tafsīr al-Ṭabarī,* 6:199–200; al-Qurṭubī, *al-Jāmiʿ* (1993), 14:157–158; Ibn Kathīr, *Mukhtaṣar Tafsīr Ibn Kathīr,* 3:114–115.

110 Ibn Fawzān, *al-Muntaqā,* 3:14–15, 3:40, 3:56, 3:294, 3;300, 3:307, 3:308, 3:309–310, 5:134–135; Al-ʿUthaymīn, *Fatāwā al-Shaykh,* 1:352–353, 1:362–363, 2:825–828; Ibn Bāz, *Fatāwā Islāmiyyah,* 3:182, 3:183–184, 3:189, 3:204–205; Ibn Bāz, *Majmūʿ Fatāwā,* 2:84–85, 2:173, 2:189–191; *Fatāwā al-Lajnah* (1991), 4:126–127; Ibn Bāz, *Majmūʿ Fatāwā wa Maqālāt Mutanawwiʿah* (1990), 4:242–244, 4:254–258.

111 In an extreme example of these seduction obsessed traditions, the Prophet is reported to have commanded that a man not sit in a spot where a woman was sitting until her body heat dissipates. If a man sits in the woman's spot without allowing sufficient time to pass, he is bound to feel her body heat and become aroused. This tradition is considered unreliable by scholars of *ḥadīth.* See Ibn al-Jawzī, *al-Mawḍūʿāt,* 2:162. See al-Makkī, *Manāqib Abī Ḥanīfah,* p. 351, where this position appears not as a *ḥadīth,* but as the pietistic habit of Abū Ḥanīfah. Regardless of the reliability of the chain of transmission, it seems to me that a man who is aroused by a warm seat where a woman once rested is in need of some serious medical attention. Of course, it is quite possible that as a matter of cultural practice, it was once considered impolite to take a seat that was recently occupied by a woman. Such a cultural practice, if it existed, would not necessarily have anything to do with sexual arousal.

112 Al-Nawawī, *Sharḥ Ṣaḥīḥ Muslim* (1996), 17/18:57–58; al-Mubārakfūrī, *Tuḥfat al-Aḥwadhī,* 6:356–359; al-Jirāḥī, *Kashf al-Khafā'* (1968), p. 39.

113 Ibn Ḥajar al-ʿAsqalānī, *Fatḥ al-Bārī* (n.d.), 9:137; al-Mubārakfūrī, *Tuḥfat al-Aḥwadhī,* 8:53; al-Nawawī, *Sharḥ Ṣaḥīḥ Muslim* (1996), 17/18:57; Ibn Jār Allāh al-Yamānī, *al-Nawāfiḥ al-ʿAṭirah,* p. 306; al-Jirāḥī, *Kashf al-Khafā'* (1968), p. 183; al-Sakhāwī, *al-Maqāṣid al-Ḥasanah,* p. 428; al-Shaybānī, *Kitāb Taymīz al-Ṭayyib,* p. 144.

114 Al-Jirāḥī, *Kashf al-Khafā'* (1968), pp. 315–316; ʿAbd al-Raḥmān al-Shaybānī, *Kitāb Tamyīz al-Ṭayyib,* p. 183. Another tradition asserts: "If not for women, God would have been [faithfully] served on this earth." Although this version has been declared unauthentic by many jurists, it is proof of an atmosphere in which anti-women circulations were common. See al-Jurjānī, *al-Kāmil fī al-Ḍuʿafā',* 6:495; Ibn al-Jawzī, *al-Mawḍūʿāt,* 2:162.

115 Al-Mubārakfūrī, *Tuḥfat al-Aḥwadhī,* 4:283.

116 This version is considered to be of weak transmission. Another version asserts that women have two sources of effective protection, a husband and the grave. See Abū Ḥāmid al-Ghazālī, *Iḥyā',* 2:58. At the symbolic level, this tradition is consistent with reports that assert that a woman, in total, is a *ʿawrah.* See Ibn al-Athīr al-Jazrī, *al-Nihāyah fī Gharīb al-Ḥadith wa al-Athar,* 3:288.

117 Al-Nawawī, *Sharḥ Ṣaḥīḥ Muslim* (1996), 9/10:181.

118 Al-Mubārakfūrī, *Tuḥfat al-Aḥwadhī,* 8:53.

119 For al-Ghazālī's discussion of this tradition, see *Shaykh* Muḥammad al-Ghazālī, *al-Sunnah al-Nabawiyyah; idem, Dustūr al-Wiḥdah.* The late al-Ghazālī was criticized for doubting the fly-tradition in the 1980's. In the 1920's a Muslim scholar named Muḥammad Tawfīq Ṣidqī was accused of being an infidel for doubting the authenticity of the fly-tradition. Those who attacked Ṣidqī asserted that since the tradition was narrated by Abū Hurayrah

and was accepted by Bukhārī, anyone who doubts its authenticity is an infidel. Rashīd Riḍā issued a *responsum* defending Ṣidqī, and calling into question the authenticity of the tradition. Riḍā argued that the fact that the report is in Bukhārī is not conclusive in evaluating the authenticity of any tradition. See Rashīd Riḍā, *Fatāwā*, 5:2043–2045. In a separate *responsum*, Riḍā also held that not all the traditions in Bukhārī are necessarily authentic. Riḍā argued that in general Bukhārī is the most reliable collection of traditions, but Bukhārī was fallible, and it is possible to reject a tradition accepted by Bukhārī if there is evidence challenging its authenticity. Rashīd Riḍā, *Fatāwā*, 5:2049–2051. For premodern juristic discussions on the fly-tradition, see, Ibn Qayyim al-Jawziyyah, *ʿAwn al-Maʿbūd*, 10:324–325; Ibn Ḥajar al-ʿAsqalānī, *Fatḥ al-Bārī* (n.d.), 6:359–360, 10:249–252.

120 Ibn Ḥajar al-ʿAsqalānī, *Fatḥ al-Bārī* (n.d.), 10:158–163, 10:212–215, 10:243–244; al-Nawawī, *Sharḥ Ṣaḥīḥ Muslim* (1996), 13/14:433–442; Ibn Qayyim al-Jawziyyah, *ʿAwn al-Maʿbūd*, 10:405–426; al-Jirāḥī, *Kashf al-Khafāʾ* (1968), p. 366.

121 See for these reports and others Abū Shuqqah, *Taḥrīr al-Marʾah*, 2:174–348.

122 Qurʾān, 33:32, 33:53. Ibn Kathīr, *Mukhtaṣar Tafsīr Ibn Kathīr*, 3:108–109; al-Qurṭubī, *al-Jāmiʿ* (1993), 14:143–148; al-Ṭabarī, *Tafsīr al-Ṭabarī*, 6:195–196; al-Rāzī, *al-Tafsīr al-Kabīr* (1999), 9:178–180.

123 Some of the late jurists argued that if a slave-girl will cause a *fitnah* she must cover her breasts or hair. Al-Ḥaṭṭāb relates that although a slave woman's *ʿawrah* is the same as a man's, some have said that it is reprehensible for someone who is not her owner to view what is under her garments, or to view her breasts, chest, or whatever else "leads to *fitnah*" (*wa mā yadʿū al-fitnah minhā*). Consequently, despite having the same *ʿawrah* as men, it is preferred that she bare her head but cover her body. Al-Ḥattāb, *Mawāhib al-Jalīl*, 2:180, 184. See also, al-Qarāfī, *al-Dhakhīrah*, 2:103–104. Al-Bahūtī relates views suggesting that as a matter of caution (*iḥtiyāṭ*), it is preferrable that the slave-girl cover herself in the same fashion as an adult free woman, including covering her head during prayer. Al-Bahūtī, *Kashshāf al-Qināʿ*, 1:316. Ibn ʿĀbidīn also argues that most of the scholars of the Ḥanafī school do not permit a slave woman to have her breasts, chest, or back exposed; however it is said that a slave woman's chest is part of her *ʿawrah* only in prayer but not otherwise. Nevertheless, Ibn ʿĀbidīn finds this latter view unconvincing. Ibn ʿĀbidīn, *Hūshiya Radd* (1966), 1:405. See also, Ibn Nujaym, *al-Baḥr al-Rāʾiq*, 1:474; al-Marghīnāī, *al-Hidāya*, 1:44.

124 Al-Jaṣṣāṣ, *Aḥkām al-Qurʾān* (1994), 3:410.

125 The Ẓahirī jurist Ibn Ḥazm is adamant in rejecting the authenticity of the reports about the occasion for revelation. Ibn Ḥazm calls these reports outright lies. His proffered reasons for rejecting the authenticity of the reports are morally based. He argues that it is entirely unbelievable that God would seek to protect the Muslim free women of Medina from molestation while leaving slave-girls to suffer. According to Ibn Ḥazm this would be simply wrong. Consequently, Ibn Ḥazm denies that there could be any distinction between the *ʿawrah* of slave-girls and free women. All women, slaves or not, have the same *ʿawrah*. Ibn Ḥazm, *al-Muḥallā*, 2:239.

126 Reportedly, the early jurists Dāwūd b. ʿAlī and Jarīr al-Ṭabarī, the founder of a now extinct school of jurisprudence, held that the *ʿawrah* of men and women, slave or otherwise, is the same. See al-Māwardī, *al-Ḥāwī al-Kabīr*, 2:167.

127 For instance, al-Rustāqī, *Manhaj al-Ṭālibīn*, 8:21, 26, argues that every place and time have their own laws. He states that in some places it is acceptable for women to reveal their hair while in Oman it is considered ugly (*qabīḥ*). He concludes by stating that whatever Muslims see as ugly is, in fact, ugly. Al-Marghīnānī, *al-Hidāya*, 1:44, mentions that slave-girls were not required to wear the veil because they need to work and requiring the veil would cause hardship (*dafʿan li al-ḥaraj*). Al-Qarāfī relates a tradition in which ʿUmar b. al-Khaṭṭāb asks his son why he was silent about the fact that the latter's slave woman walked about wearing an *izār* like a free woman. Reportedly, ʿUmar then adds that if he were to see her, he would hit her for doing so. Al-Qarāfī explains ʿUmar's position was relevant only to a very specific historical situation in Medina, in which crazed men would harass slave women but not free women. See al-Qarāfī, *al-Dhakhīrah*,

2:103. See also, Ibn Nujaym, *al-Baḥr al-Rā'iq,* 1:474; al-Ḥaṭṭāb al-Raʿīnī, *Mawāhib al-Jalīl,* 2:184.

128 Ibn Taymiyyah seems to be one of the few jurists who addressed the issue of homosexual attractions in the context of veiling. See the discussion in Taqī al-Dīn Ibn Taymiyya, *al-Tafsīr al-Kabīr,* ed. ʿAbd al-Raḥmān ʿAmīra (Beirut: Dār al-Kutub al-ʿIlmiyya, n.d.), 5:346–353.

129 For the six points above see, al-Ṭabarī, *Jāmiʿ al-Bayān,* 18:93–95, 22:33–34 (mentions a variety of early opinions including the up to the elbow and the beginning of cleavage area determinations; also mentions the distinction between free and slave girls; mentions the historical practice); al-Nasafī, *Tafsīr al-Nasafī* (Cairo: Dār Iḥyā' al-Kutub al-ʿArabiyya, n.d.), 3:140, 313, (mentions *ʿādah, jibillah,* and *ḥājah*; women need to reveal their faces, hands, and feet by custom, nature, and need; mentions the distinction applicable to slave-girls; mentions the historical practice); al-Jaṣṣāṣ, *Aḥkām,* 3:409–410, 486, mentions that slave-girls do not have to cover their hair; mentions the historical practice); al-Kiyyā al-Harrāsī, *Aḥkām al-Qur'ān* (1974), 4:288, 354 (notes slave-girls do not have to cover their faces or hair); Ibn al-ʿArabī', *Aḥkām al-Qur'ān* (n.d.), 3:1368–78, 1586–87 (mentions a variety of details to adornments; discusses the rule as to slave-girls); al-Qurṭubī, *al-Jāmiʿ*(1993), 12:152–153, 157; 14:156–157 (mentions that the verse was revealed to address the harassment of women, and to differentiate slave-girls from Muslim women; notes the opinion that held that the verse called for the covering of the bosom area); Ibn Kathīr, *Mukhtaṣar Tafsīr Ibn Kathīr,* 2:600; 3:114–115, (mentions determinations as to the bosom; also notes that free Muslim women must cover their faces); Abū Ḥayyān al-Andalusī, *Tafsīr al-Baḥr al-Muḥīṭ,* 6:412; 7:240–241 (mentions custom, nature, necessity; mentions the historical practice as to revealing the bosom; mentions the distinction as to slave-girls); al-Zamakhsharī, *al-Kashshāf,* 3:60–62, 274 (mentions the historical practice, distinction as to slave-girls, the rules as to functionality and custom, mentions that covering ought not cause hardship); Ibn al-Jawzī, *Zād al-Masīr fī ʿIlm al-Tafsīr,* 5:377–378; 6:224 (mentions *mashaqqah* – hardship); al-Māwardī, *al-Nukat wa al-ʿUyūn,* 4:90–93, 424–425, (notes the opinion that the purpose of revelation was to instruct women to cover their bosoms; mentions the differentiation as to slave-girls); al-Shinqīṭī, *Aḍwā' al-Bayān,* 6:192–203, 586–600 (mentions a variety of positions; mentions determinations as to revealing the arm up to the elbow and the view that the point is to cover the bosom; mentions the historical practice and differentiation as to slave-girls; author supports covering the face); Ibn Taymiyya, *al-Tafsīr,* 6:23, (notes that the law of veiling does not apply to slave-girls); Fakhr al-Dīn Muḥammad al-Rāzī, *al-Tafsīr al-Kabīr (a.k.a Mafātīḥ al-Ghayb),* 23:176–179; 25:198–199, (mentions *al-ʿādah al-jāriyah* (the habitual custom) and functionality as the focal issues in determining what women ought to cover; mentions the historical practice and the distinction as to slave-girls); Ibn ʿAṭiyya, *al-Muḥarrar al-Wajīz,* 4:178, 399 (mentions the determinations as to the bosom and arm up to the elbow; mentions the rule of functionality and custom; mentions the historical practice and the distinction as to slave-girls); al-Suyūṭī, *al-Durr al-Manthūr,* 5:45–46, 239–241 (mentions the determinations as to the arm up to the elbow and the bosom; notes the discussion regarding the beginning of the cleavage area; mentions the historical practice and the distinction as to slave-girls); al-Burūsī, *Tanwīr al-Adhhān,* 3:57–59, 254–255, (mentions the determinations as to the arm up to the elbow and the bosom; mentions the historical practice and distinction as to slave-girls); Abū Ḥafṣ ʿUmar b. ʿAlī Ibn ʿĀdil al-Dimashqī, *al-Lubāb fī ʿUlūm al-Kitāb,* 14:355–358; 15:588–590 (mentions that according to some reports the verse was revealed to vindicate ʿAlī's family. Also mentions that other reports contend that hypocrites of Medina would solicit women at night. Girls who practiced prostitution would respond to their solicitation. The verse was revealed partly to end this practice. Mentions the rule of practice and custom (*mā uʿtīda kashfuh*), and functionality and rule of necessity; mentions the distinction as to slave-girls); al-Alūsī, *Rūḥ al-Maʿānī* (1985), 18:140–142; 22:89, (mentions the issue of functionality and that slave-girls lead an active economic life; mentions custom, habit, and

nature; mentions the historical practice); al-Ṣāwī, *Ḥāshiyat al-ʿAllāmah,* 3:136–137, 288–289 (mentions various positions).

130 Ibn Qayyim al-Jawziyyah, *ʿAwn al-Maʿbūd,* 2:277; Ibn Ḥajar al-ʿAsqalānī, *Fatḥ al-Bārī* (n.d.), 2:350; al-Hindī, *Kanz al-ʿUmmāl,* 16:413–414.

131 Ibn Ḥanbal, *Musnad,* 6:417. Another version attributed to the Prophet states that the best prayer for women is that which is performed in the darkest spot of her household, see al-Hindī, *Kanz al-ʿUmmāl,* 16:415. Abū Ḥāmid al-Ghazālī, *Iḥyāʾ*, 2:57–59 cites a variant of this tradition as support for arguing that women should obey their husbands, and refrain from leaving their homes without a valid cause. The authenticity of these traditions have been called into question by some classical scholars, see al-Jurjānī, *al-Kāmil fī al-Ḍuʿafāʾ*, 5:297.

132 This is why the classical jurists held that if a woman prays in the midst of men it is undesirable but her prayers are valid, and if men pray behind the rows of women, the prayers of the men and women are valid. Saḥnūn, *al-Mudawwanah* (Dār al-Kutub al-ʿIlmiyya), 1:195; al-Qayrawānī, *al-Nawādir wa al-Ziyādāt,* 1:296; Ibn Qud–mah, *al-Mughnī* (Dār al-Kutub al-ʿIlmiyyah), 2:44; Abū Shuqqah, *Taḥrīr al-Marʾah,* 2:195–202.

133 Ibn Ḥajar al-ʿAsqalānī, *Fatḥ al-Bārī* (n.d.), 2:350–351.

134 Ibn Ḥajar al-ʿAsqalānī, *Fatḥ al-Bārī* (n.d.), 2:101–102; Abū Shuqqah, *Taḥrīr al-Marʾah,* 2:181–194.

135 Ibn Ḥajar al-ʿAsqalānī, *Fatḥ al-Bārī* (n.d.), 2:469–470, 3:504; al-Nawawī, *Sharḥ Ṣaḥīḥ Muslim* (1996), 5/6:418–420. Remarkably, the C.R.L.O attempts to use these traditions to argue for the seclusion of women. The C.R.L.O advances the bizarre logic that since all the women had to wear garbs that must mean that no woman was allowed to attend the ceremonies without being entirely veiled! Ibn Bāz, *Majmūʿ Fatāwā wa Maqālāt Mutanawwiʿah* (1990), 4:255; Ibn Bāz, *Majmūʿ Fatāwā wa Maqālāt Mutanawwiʿah* (1992), 5:231.

136 Prayers, usually performed in the last ten days of the month of Ramaḍān, that involve spending the night in the mosque.

137 Saḥnūn, *al-Mudawwanah* (Dār al-Kutub al-ʿIlmiyya), 1:295.

138 Ibn Qayyim al-Jawziyyah, *Iʿlām al-Muwaqqiʿīn* (Beirut), 3:26; Ibn Ḥajar al-ʿAsqalānī, *Fatḥ al-Bārī* (n.d.), 4:810, 818.

139 Ibn Ḥajar al-ʿAsqalānī, *Fatḥ al-Bārī* (n.d.), 2:623; Ibn Qayyim al-Jawziyyah, *ʿAwn al-Maʿbūd,* 2:276–277.

140 Al-Suyūṭī, *Sharḥ Sunan al-Nasāʾī,* 2:94; al-Mubārakfūrī, *Tuḥfat al-Aḥwadhī,* 2:13–14; Ibn Qayyim al-Jawziyyah, *ʿAwn al-Maʿbūd,* 2:374–375; al-Nawawī, *Sharḥ Ṣaḥīḥ Muslim* (1996), 3/4:380; Ibn Jār Allāh al-Yamānī, *al-Nawāfiḥ al-ʿAṭirah,* p. 137; al-Jirāḥī, *Kashf al-Khafāʾ* (1968), p. 394; al-Sakhāwī, *al-Maqāṣid al-Ḥasanah,* p. 248; al-Shaybānī, *Kitāb Taymīz al-Ṭayyib,* p. 77. Some versions of this tradition were transmitted by al-Khalīl b. Zakariyyā who is not reliable, see al-Jurjānī, *al-Kāmil fī Ḍuʿafāʾ,* 3:511.

141 Al-Suyūṭī, *Sharḥ Sunan al-Nasāʾī,* 2:94; al-Mubārakfūrī, *Tuḥfat al-Aḥwadhī,* 2:13–14; Ibn Qayyim al-Jawziyyah, *ʿAwn al-Maʿbūd,* 2:374–375; al-Nawawī, *Sharḥ Ṣaḥīḥ Muslim* (1996), 3/4:380.

142 Ibn Bāz, *Majmūʿ Fatāwā wa Maqālāt Mutanawwiʿah* (1990), 4:251; Ibn Fawzān, *al-Muntaqā,* 3:57. Arguably, the meaning of this tradition is figurative. In other words, this is a very awkward way of instructing women to stay as far away as possible from men.

143 Ibn Qayyim al-Jawziyyah, *ʿAwn al-Maʿbūd,* 2:273. Some versions of this report have been considered unreliable because al-Khalīl b. Zakariyyā is one of the transmitters. See al-Jurjānī, *al-Kāmil fī Ḍuʿafāʾ,* 3:511.

144 Qurʾān, 7:31.

145 Ibn Ḥajar al-ʿAsqalānī, *Fatḥ al-Bārī* (1993), 2:609–616.

146 Ḥajjāj, *Ṣaḥīḥ Muslim,* 2:33–34.

147 Ibn Qayyim al-Jawziyyah, *ʿAwn al-Maʿbūd,* 2:273–275.

148 Al-Mubārakfūrī, *Tuḥfat al-Aḥwadhī,* 1:402; al-Nawawī, *Sharḥ Ṣaḥīḥ Muslim* (1996), 5/6:145–146; Ibn Ḥajar al-ʿAsqalānī, *Fatḥ al-Bārī* (n.d.), 2:54, 55, 351.

149 Ibn Ḥajar al-ʿAsqalānī, *Fatḥ al-Bārī* (n.d.), 1:575, 2:349–350. Al-Nawawī and other jurists respond to this point by saying that the women were not recognizable because of the dark and not because they were wrapped up in clothing. Ibn Ḥajar al-ʿAsqalānī, *Fatḥ al-Bārī* (n.d.), 2:55.

150 *Ṣaḥīḥ Muslim*, 2:33. See, also, al-Nawawī, *Sharḥ Ṣaḥīḥ Muslim* (1996), 3/4:383–384; Ibn Qayyim al-Jawziyyah, *ʿAwn al-Maʿbūd*, 2:275.

151 Ibn Qayyim al-Jawziyyah, *ʿAwn al-Maʿbūd*, 14:190.

152 Ibn Qayyim al-Jawziyyah, *ʿAwn al-Maʿbūd*, 14:190; Ibn Bāz, *Majmūʿ Fatāwā wa Maqālāt Mutanawwiʿa* (1992), 5:238.

153 Al-Dhahabī, *Siyar Aʿlām*, 3:172.

154 Ibn Abī Shaybah, *al-Muṣannaf*, 3:399.

155 See Abou El Fadl, *Rebellion and Violence in Islamic Law.*

156 Pure reason is the method pursuant to which general principles of law are deduced, such as the presumption of innocence or the presumption of continuity.

157 Typically, *ahl al-ḥadīth* resolved most conflicts between competing values by resorting to highly contorted interpretations (called *al-tawfīq bayn mukhtalaf al-ḥadīth*). If all else failed, they often utilized the concept of abrogation (*naskh*) according to which a tradition of singular transmission could abrogate a whole set of Qurʾānic verses. Trying to avoid bruising encounters with *ahl al-ḥadīth*, Uṣūlī jurists would often declare a problematic tradition authentic, but give it very little weight in legal determinations.

158 Al-Hindī, *Kanz al-ʿUmmāl*, 16:295. Some versions of this report do not have the reference to blacks. They simply say choose suitable partners. See al-Jurjānī, *al-Kāmil fī Ḍuʿafāʾ*, 2:467; 4:286, 423; al-Mināwī, *Fayḍ al-Qadīr*, 3:237; 4:66.

159 There are a variety of versions of this central theme. Some reports state that the Abyssinians, Sudanese, and blacks if they eat well, they fornicate, and if they are hungry, they steal. Other reports state that the worse slaves are those who are black. Some versions state that blacks are deformed creatures, and others proclaim that a black person is a donkey. Some traditions say the exact opposite; these traditions praise blacks as honest, brave, and trustworthy. See al-Hindī, *Kanz al-ʿUmmāl*, 9:86–87; al-Ṭabarānī, *al-Muʿjam al-Kabīr*, 11:153, 338; al-Khaṭīb al-Baghdādī, *Taʾrīkh Baghdād*, 14:113. On the unreliability of all of these traditions see al-Jurjānī, *al-Kāmil fī Ḍuʿafāʾ*, 3:328; 6:155, 466–467, 7:103.

160 Ibn Ḥanbal, *Musnad*, 6:492.

161 In some traditions, the Prophet emphasizes the equality of all races. For instance, the Prophet is reported to have said: "Each prophet [before me] was sent specifically to his people, [but] I was sent to every [nation, whether] red or black (*wa buʿithtu ilā kulli aḥmara wa aswada*)." Al-Nawawī, *Sharḥ Ṣaḥīḥ Muslim* (1996), 5/6:6–7. See also, Ibn Ḥanbal, *Musnad*, 1:311, 374, 4:559. In another tradition, the Prophet is reported to have said, "Praise to God, there is only one book of God, and among you [the believers] are nations red, white, and black (*wa fīkum al-aḥmar wa fīkum al-abyaḍ wa fīkum al-aswad*)." Ibn Qayyim al-Jawziyyah, *ʿAwn al-Maʿbūd*, 3:59–60. The following tradition emphasizes that piety and not race is what distinguishes a Muslim. The Prophet is reported to have said to Abū Dharr, "Take note that you are not better than the red or black nations except to the extent you exceed [them] in piety (*taqwā*)." Ibn Ḥanbal, *Musnad*, 5:206. Another report illustrates the concern the Prophet had for people of all races. It states that one day, a black man or woman, who used to sweep the mosque, died. On the day of this person's death, the Prophet asked about his or her whereabouts. He was told that the person died. After asking why he was not informed, he was taken to the person's grave and subsequently prayed. Furthermore, the Prophet reportedly said, "People are as equal as the teeth of a comb; they are differentiated only by piety." Ibn Ḥajar al-ʿAsqalānī, *Fatḥ al-Bārī* (n.d.), 1:658–659, 3:204–205.

162 Al-Jirāḥī, *Kashf al-Khafāʾ* (1968), pp. 301–302; al-Suyūṭī, *al-Laʾālī al-Maṣnūʿa*, 1:443–447; al-Khaṭib al-Baghdādī, *Taʾrīkh Baghdād*, 14:113; al-Albānī, *Silsilat*, 2:155–161.

163 Al-Albānī, *Silsilat*, 2:158.

164 A Syrian scholar of *ḥadīth* (*muḥaddith*), al-Albānī was formerly a professor of *ḥadīth* at the Islamic University in Medina, Saudi Arabia from 1963–1965 and was the 1999 recipient of the King Faisal International Prize for Islamic Studies. Born in Albania, he moved to Syria with his family at a young age and therafter began his studies, including the sciences of *ḥadīth* (*ʿulūm al-ḥadīth*). During his life, he became prominent throughout the Middle East as an authority on the authentication of *ḥadīth*, and prepared for publication numerous collections of Prophetic traditions.

165 Al-Albānī, *Silsilat,* 2:158.

# Conclusion: Resisting the authoritarian while searching for the moral

Writing is a never-ending act of negotiation. The author negotiates with the anticipated audience and the language, and also with himself. The author struggles endlessly with meaning, language, aspirational goals, achievable goals, and conscience. As ʿImād al-Dīn al-Iṣfahānī (d. 598/1201) stated:

> I have yet to complete a book and to re-open it the next day without finding that I might have included this, or deleted that, or considered a different thought, or I might have polished my words or modified some others or transposed yet others. In short, a human being's work, his thinking, his revisions, and changes are never perfect or complete. Such is the unwavering fact about the nature of humankind.[1]

The author considers whether to stay within particular conventions or to go beyond them and, ultimately, to suffer the consequences. Yet, once the text is born, it acquires its own life, rights and integrity. Texts that are unable to become liberated from their authors, or unable to challenge the reader with levels of subtlety, or tease with nuances of meaning have a nasty of habit of becoming predictable, dull, and closed. Texts that remain open stay alive, relevant, and vibrant. But texts need another form of liberation. They need not only to become independent of the domineering paternalism of their authors, but also of the suffocating authoritarianism of their readers. If there is going to be a dynamic and vigorous process of determination in which the text plays a central role, there must be a continuing state of indeterminacy. A continuous balance of power is needed between the author, reader, and text. The dominance of one over the others leads to intellectual stagnation of the type that is well-exemplified in the determinations of the C.R.L.O.

As to Islamic law, it has become common in the modern age to use the authority of the Author (God) to justify the despotism of the reader. In effect, by claiming that the only relevant consideration is the Will of the Author, the reader is able to displace the Author and set himself as the sole voice of authority. In essence, the reader becomes God. I have argued that the displacement of God's authority with that of the reader is an act of despotism, and a corruption of the logic of Islamic law. Islamic law is founded on the logic of a Principal Who guides through instructions. Those instructions are issued to the agents who have inherited the earth and who are bound to the Principal by a covenant. I have argued that the point of the covenant is not to live according to the instructions, but to attempt to do so. Searching the instructions is a core value in itself – regardless of the results, searching the instructions is a moral virtue. This is not because the instructions are pointless, but because the instructions must remain vibrant, dynamic, open, and relevant. I have also argued that it is impossible for a human being to represent God's Truth – a human being can only represent his or her own efforts in search of this truth. The ultimate and unwavering value in the relationship between human beings and God is summarized in the Islamic statement, "And, God knows best."

Deferring to God and honoring the text (instructions), requires a human being to exercise self-restraint in speaking for God and the text. But discharging the obligations of human agency mandates that the reader (agent) take his or her role very seriously by aggressively and vigorously investigating both God and God's instructions. "God knows best" is not an invitation to intellectual complacency and smugness, but, as the Qur'ān states, to realize that "over every knowledgeable person is a One more knowledgeable."[2] Submission to God is at the core of the Islamic creed, but it does not mean blind submission to those who claim to represent God's law, and it does not mean submitting to the contentment and comfort of arrogant self-reference. Submission to God means the will and act of engaging the intellect and body in the pursuit of God, but also the humility of knowing that no intellect or body can ever fully represent God. The Qur'ān sums up this point by reminding the Prophet that even he has not been sent to control or dominate people, but to admonish and teach.[3]

This reminder is particularly pertinent to those who place themselves in the position of the devoted sages of the Divine instructions. Those special agents accept the responsibility of doing what is not feasible for everyone to do, and that is devote a lifetime to the study of the instructions. As the Qur'ān states, the task of these special agents is to study the instructions and to share the results of their search with the common agents who ultimately bear the responsibility of acting according to the dictates of their conscience.[4] The authority of these special agents is not inherent or institutional – it is persuasive. The common agents will and should defer to the determinations of those special agents, but only to the extent that the special agents are honestly and diligently representing what the special agents believe to be the Will of the instructions. I have argued that there are implied contingencies that define the authoritativeness of the special agents. These contingencies serve as the basis for the deferential relationship between the special agents and common agents. As argued, these contingencies are: honesty, diligence, self-restraint, comprehensiveness, and reasonableness. Violating these contingencies is a breach of responsibility and a betrayal of the trust that the common agents had placed in the special agents. These contingencies act as constraints on the special agents, and as controls against possible abuses of authority and, ultimately, despotism. A violation of one of the enumerated contingencies is most definitely an abuse that threatens to become a usurpation of the Principal's authority. Authoritarianism of the special agent takes place when such an agent speaks for God without being authorized by the instructions to do so. This is well-represented by the Qur'ānic concept of *idhn* according to which it is a grave violation to speak for the God's law without proper authorization.[5] At least when it comes to law, the primary form of authorization is the instructions contained in texts. This necessarily means that the five contingencies do not only apply to determining the meaning of the text, but also to verifying that the text has legal competency, which means verifying that the text is qualified to act as part of God's instructions.

I have argued that although every violation of one of the five contingencies is a breach or an abuse, not every abuse or breach will necessarily be a usurpation of God's authority. Each usurpation of God's authority, however, will involve one or more breach or abuse. Usurpation of God's authority or authoritarianism is invariably a matter of degree – a matter of assessing the extent of the violations, and the point at which we can say that the special agent's claim of representing God's instructions is nothing more than a shameful pretense. Importantly, special agents, like all readers, work within the context of interpretive communities that develop conventions of meaning and process. This does not mean that a special agent who refuses to work within an interpretive community lacks legitimacy. It only means that the special agent, and common agents must be cognizant of the fact that interpretations often rely on enabling assumptions – assumptions that work as efficiency tools so that the interpreter does not have to re-invent the wheel every time an argument is proposed. The special agent must be aware of these assumptions and must honestly disclose them if need be. The common agents have a right to be aware of the fact that although assumptions act as efficiency conventions, they also run the risk of replacing or violating the integrity of the instructions. In this context, I identified some of the possible assumptions that work in an interpretive community, which include reason-based, value-based, faith-based, and methodological assumptions.

Interpretive communities develop habits, and these habits could be a line of precedents that are considered dispositive of an issue, or factual beliefs about social practices or propensities, or the method by which an interpretive community analyzes an issue. The existence of assumptions within an interpretive community, in itself, is not authoritarian. However, these assumptions could lead to a breach of the conditions of authority pursuant to which the common agent defers to the determination of the special agent. If the special agent dogmatically treats these assumptions as part of the Principal's instructions, or considers such assumptions to be indisputable or immutable, this is likely to lead to the corruption of the process and to authoritarianism. This is especially the case when the special agent refuses to acknowledge that assumptions are merely enabling or efficiency tools and treats them as sacrosanct, or when the special agent fails to disclose the existence and the nature of these assumptions to the common agents.

Faith-based assumptions are always the most challenging and the most dangerous. By nature they are not accessible or sufficiently accountable to others. Faith-based assumptions are like saying, "I love God", "God is most merciful", or "God loves all people." Such statements must be believed and felt to mean anything. They could be engaged and debated, and one can attempt to refute them, but fundamentally, they rely on what I called a collateral relationship with God. If, for example, I believe that God cannot and will not command anything that is immoral or ugly, there is no doubt that this will affect all my interpretive activities and legal determinations. I am not arguing that it is inappropriate or futile to argue about faith-based matters – far from it. Faith-based assumptions are influenced by a variety of human experiences including textual evidence, sociological experience, human temper, and individual dialectics, but they are not determined by any of them. As such, faith-based assumptions do run the very high risk of becoming authoritarian. We witness this particularly in sectarian debates. Historically, Sunni scholars have rejected the determinations of Shīʿī narrators of *ḥadīth* and vice versa. In addition, *ahl al-ḥadīth* dismissed the transmissions of the Muʿtazilah, Khawārij, and Shīʿah as palpably false. Yet, faith-based assumptions are a matter of conscience and conviction, and so they cannot be dismissed as irrelevant.

The question becomes: what does a special agent do with faith-based assumptions? At a minimum, they must be honestly disclosed so that common agents may decide whether they share these assumptions or not. Moreover, it is important to remember that faith-based assumptions have a rather limited scope. If something is established in an interpretive community through rational analysis, factual determination, or methodological choices, in most circumstances, it is impeachable on the same grounds. Since faith-based assumptions are always at risk of being whimsical, they should be utilized sparingly. As will be recalled, the reliance on whimsical beliefs or determinations is treated in the Qurʾān as an abomination and a sin. Therefore, a cautious and wise agent will not hastily claim a faith-based determination, but will first pause and then honestly, diligently, comprehensively, reasonably, and humbly scrutinize the evidence before deciding to reach an opinion. If the evidence reasonably supports his or her claim, then there is no issue, but if it does not, the agent may be forced to revise his or her beliefs or decide to become a conscientious objector. As we saw, this becomes the case especially when deciding the competence of instructions that warrant a conscientious-pause. I have argued that the *ḥadīth* literature should properly be seen as the product of an authorial enterprise. It is an authorial enterprise because of the widespread participation of so many individuals from a variety of socio-historical contexts, with their own sense of values, levels of consciousness, and memories, who engage in the process of selecting, remembering, and transmitting the memory of the Prophet and the Companions. As a means of being conscientious about our reliance and presentation of the instructions of the Principal, I argued for a relationship of proportionality between our assessment of the competence of the instructions (mostly *Sunnah* and *ḥadīth*) and their theological, legal, and sociological impact. The greater the anticipated impact of a tradition, the more assured and confident should we be of its competence.

The above is a summary of the conceptual framework of this book, but as to the motivations and aspirations of the author, whatever they are worth, they invite the adoption of a different discourse and a different tone. As I have emphasized on several occasions in this book, I fear that Islamic jurisprudence as an epistemology and as a methodology of inquiry has become dominated by authoritarian discourses. Furthermore, I fear that this authoritarianism has not only denied Islamic jurisprudence any level of integrity and respectability, but that it has virtually obliterated the viability and dynamism of Islamic law in the modern world. Between the apologetics of the activists and the paralyzing dogmatism of today's special agents, nothing remains of the rich and complex intellectual legacy of Islamic jurisprudence. When one speaks about Islamic jurisprudence in the modern age, one often feels as if he is taking part in a collective and tragic fiction. There is little doubt in my mind that the Islamic juristic system was one of the most formidable and intellectually impressive legal systems that human history has seen. I also suspect that the Islamic juristic system heavily influenced and restructured the Common Law system in specific but important ways.[6] But that in no way alters or improves the state or status of Islamic law in the modern age. As noted earlier, if Islamic jurisprudence basically consists of rules (*aḥkām*), then one must conclude that Islamic law is thriving in the modern age. I do not believe there is a shortage of individuals, organizations, or countries willing to enter into mass production of *aḥkām*, and even live by them. However, if Islamic jurisprudence is about a methodology for a reflective life that searches for the Divine, and about a process of weighing and balancing the core values of *Sharīʿah* in pursuit of a moral life, then I think one would have to concede that it has disintegrated and disappeared in the last three centuries, but particularly in the second half of the twentieth century. I think that the results can be clearly observed when one considers the impact of contemporary Islamic rules on women.

I have used the C.R.L.O and its jurists to demonstrate the impoverishments of contemporary Islamic law. If the reader believes that the C.R.L.O is the exception to the rule and that its determinations represent a marginal reality in contemporary Islam, then what remains for the reader's consideration is the conceptual framework of this book that distinguishes between the authoritative and authoritarian. The reader may consider that framework as a normative argument that seeks to keep the instructions of the Principal open, dynamic, and relevant. Furthermore, such a reader may consider the C.R.L.O determinations as a case study, even if extreme, of possible abuses of authority and of whimsical authoritarianism by special agents. If, however, I am correct in my suspicion that the C.R.L.O represents a widespread and growing trend within contemporary Islam, then *Sharīʿah* is confronting a very serious challenge in the contemporary age.

What is problematic about the determinations analyzed in this book is not only that they are often blatantly result-oriented, or that they are remarkably careless and uncritical in handling the evidence, or that they are not clear or forthright about their sociological and factual assumptions, but also, and even more importantly, that they fail to integrate or give due weight to moral assessments. I realize that in the contemporary age, it is not fashionable to speak about morality when discussing Islamic law except to adopt a vulgar form of legal positivism by declaring that whatever the rule of law, therein lies the moral imperative. It is also not fashionable to speak of intuitive morality, or the application of reason to God's law. Very few contemporary Muslim authors attempt to rekindle and develop the classical discourses on the role of *ʿaql* (intellect), *fiṭrah* (intuition), or *ḥusn* and *qubḥ* (the moral and immoral) in the process of developing God's law.[7] I am not claiming that this book is the exception to this contemporary trend – obviously, I have not attempted to develop a theory of morality in this book. Nonetheless, even rudimentary notions of moral awareness, such as being aware of the value of fairness, dignity, and truthfulness, are hardly given any weight by the C.R.L.O, especially in determinations that deal with women. As I attempted to show, an application of even some of the most basic steps of critical analysis would challenge the C.R.L.O determinations. But there is a larger and more fundamental problem that confronts us here. Since no legal system functions in a moral vacuum, serious thought, by Muslims, needs to be applied to the visions of morality that might guide Islamic law in the contemporary age.

Finally, and in the spirit of truthful disclosure, I recognize that the C.R.L.O is a powerful organization in contemporary Islam, and, frankly, I am not jumping with joy at the idea of upsetting it. Furthermore, I am painfully aware that the reaction of some fellow Muslims to the ideas expressed in this book are going to be somewhat unpleasant. However, I feel that Muslims in the present age are going through their intellectual dark ages, and this creates an added burden on Muslim intellectuals. In the same way that Muslims of previous generations reached the awareness that slavery is immoral and unlawful, as a matter of conscience, I confess that I find the virtual slavery imposed on women by the C.R.L.O and like-minded special agents to be painfully offensive and unworthy of *Sharīʿah*. To claim that a woman visiting her husband's grave, a woman raising her voice in prayer, a woman driving a car, or a woman traveling unaccompanied by a male is bound to create intolerable seductions, strikes me as morally problematic. If men are so morally weak, why should women suffer? And, doesn't this assumed moral weakness run contrary to the assumption that men should be the heads of the family and the leaders of society because they are of a stronger and more enduring constitution? Doesn't this also contradict the C.R.L.O's persistent assumption that men are more rational and less emotional than women? Furthermore, arguing that women should pray in the most inaccessible area in a home, or should walk next to a wall to the point of rubbing against it, or should physically submit whenever it fits the husband's whimsy, or that women's salvation is contingent on the pleasure of their husbands, or that women will form most of Hell's population, or that women are a walking, talking, bundle of seduction, again, strikes me as morally offensive. If the analysis presented in this book is correct, the evidence, itself, does not warrant these misogynistic determinations. But the question remains: what solicits or generates these types of determinations? If one apologetically says that culture is the culprit – that these determinations have nothing do with the religion, but are the product of highly patriarchal cultural settings – I would politely have to say, I agree. However, I agree in a different way, and with a different claim. It would be dishonest to claim that these determinations find no support in Islamic sources for, as discussed in the book, they clearly find support in a variety of traditions and precedents. However, one can justifiably argue that these determinations are inconsistent with Qur'ānic morality, and that other Islamic sources challenge these determinations, at least as much as they lend them support.

In my view, herein is the true Divine test and challenge. One of the most fascinating, and understudied, aspects of the Qur'ānic text is its discourse on the idea of justice.[8] The Qur'ān connects the idea of bearing witness upon humanity with the idea of balance. For instance, the Qur'ān states in part: "Thus, We have made you [Muslims] a nation [that must be] justly balanced, so that you may bear witness over humanity."[9] Elsewhere, the Qur'ān interchanges the obligations towards justice with the obligations towards God. For instance, it states, "O you who believe, *stand firmly for God as witnesses for justice*, and let not the hatred of others to you make you swerve to wrong and depart from justice,"[10]and then, "O you who believe, *stand firmly for justice as witnesses for God*, even as against yourselves, or your parents, or your kin, and whether it be [against] rich or poor,"[11] It seems to me that standing firmly for God or standing firmly for justice are one and the same, or, at least, coexist in the same moral plane. Furthermore, without being themselves morally balanced, Muslims cannot discharge their obligation to bear witness upon humanity, let alone to bear witness upon themselves. It strikes me as unjust to bear witness upon others according to a balance that is neither accessible, nor understandable, nor accountable to those others. If Islam is a universal message, its language of morality and justice ought to make sense beyond the limited confines of a particular juristic culture in a particular cultural setting. I am not advocating a universal law, and I am not advocating the abolition of all cultural particularism. But, at a minimum, it seems that serving God means serving justice, and serving justice necessarily means engaging in the search for the just, moral and humane. The test and the challenge to our sense of balance and equanimity is, regardless of the socio-historical circumstances, or textual and doctrinal indicators, to try always to pose the questions: is it fair? Is it just? And, at the end of every conscientious and diligent process, to close with, "And, God knows best."

*NOTES*

1 This is a statement I memorized in my youth. Unfortunately, I am unable to remember or find the specific source.
2 Qur'ān, 12:76.
3 Qur'ān, 88:21–2.
4 Qur'ān, 9:122.
5 Qur'ān, 10:59; 42:21.
6 John Makdisi, "The Islamic Origins of the Common Law," pp. 1635–1739; *idem*, "An Inquiry into Islamic Influences," pp. 135–146; George Makdisi, *Rise of Colleges*, pp. 224–291; Avini, "The Origins of the Modern English Trust Revisited," pp. 1139–1163; Gaudiosi, "The Influence of the Islamic Law,"pp. 1231–1261; Boisard, "On the Probable Influence of Islam," pp. 429–450; Burnett, *Introduction of Arabic Learning*; Nakosteen, *History of Islamic Origins*; Metlitzki, *The Matter of Araby*; Wahba and Abousenna, eds., *Averroes and the Enlightenment*; Butterworth and Kessel, *Introduction of Arabic Philosophy.*
7 For a review of such authors, see, Hallaq, *Islamic Legal Theories*, pp. 207–254. Fazlur Rahman arguably relies on similar processes in his book on the Qur'ān. However, he does not address law, and in fact considers the positive legal tradition and its institutions partly to blame for moral stagnancy. Rahman, *Concepts*, pp. 47–48. Soroush, *Reason, Freedom, & Democracy.*
8 Rahman, *Concepts*, pp. 42–43, 46–51; Izutsu, *Ethico-Religious Concepts*, pp. 209–211
9 Qur'ān, 2:143. See, also, Qur'ān, 22:78.
10 Qur'ān, 5:8.
11 Qur'ān, 4:135 (emphasis added).

# Appendix: Translated legal opinions by C.R.L.O jurists

Below is a selection of translated *responsa* and legal opinions by C.R.L.O jurists. I have tried to retain the flavor and tone of the originals. Therefore, the translations are as literal as possible. Where the originals were ambiguous or unclear, I have not attempted improvement. I have indicated the author/authors of each legal opinion in the reference notes.

ON THE LEGALITY OF WOMEN WEARING BRASSIERES

*Question*: What is the ruling concerning women wearing brassieres on their breasts?
*Fatwā*: Some women have grown accustomed to lifting their breasts or supporting them with a piece of cloth, using them [i.e., the support] as a way of appearing younger or like virgins or something like that. If it is done for that purpose, then it [i.e., wearing brassieres] constitutes unlawful deception. But if it is done in order to avoid a particular injury or ward off pain or anything of a similar nature, then it is permissible in proportion to the need [for wearing the brassiere], and God knows best.[1]

ON WOMEN DRIVING

*Question*: Under circumstances of necessity, is it permissible for a woman to drive an automobile by herself, without the presence of a legal guardian, instead of riding in a car with a non-*maḥram* man, [*e.g.* as in riding a taxi or with a chauffeur]?[2] May God reward and bless you.
*Fatwā*: It is impermissible for a woman to drive an automobile, for that would entail unveiling her face or a part of it. Additionally, if her automobile were to break down on the road, if she were in an accident, or if she were issued a traffic violation, she would be forced to co-mingle with men. Furthermore, driving

would enable a woman to travel far from her home and away from the supervision of her legal guardian. Women are weak and prone to succumb to their emotions and to immoral inclinations. If they are allowed to drive, then they will be freed from appropriate oversight, supervision, and from the authority of the men of their households. Also, to receive driving privileges, they would have to apply for a license and get their picture taken. Photographing women, even in this situation, is prohibited because it entails *fitnah* and great perils.[3]

### ON SUCKLING HUSBANDS

*Question*: The *shaykh* was asked if a husband drinks the milk of his wife, does she become forbidden to him?
*Fatwā*: The *shaykh* responded: It is permitted for him to do so because her milk is *ḥalāl* and he can get nutrients from it until he dies. And, no prohibition results from this suckling because it did not take place in the first two years of life.[4]
*Question*: A young woman sent a letter saying, "I married my paternal cousin. I love him, and he loves me, but after only six months after our marriage, he would suckle at my breast like an infant every time I came to sleep. I told him this was shameful, but he did not desist and I did not try to stop him."
*Fatwā*: There is no problem with this because it is appropriate for spouses to enjoy each other in ways other than those prohibited by God, such as anal intercourse or intercourse during menstruation, postnatal bleeding, or during worship. Intercourse in these circumstances is prohibited as in the case of *ẓihār*[5] until the husband expiates for his sin. There are other acts of intercourse, well known to the scholars, which are prohibited because they result in harm to the spouses.[6]

### ON WOMEN INVALIDATING THE PRAYERS OF MEN

*Question*: What is the ruling, with supporting evidence, of the uttering of *āmīn*? Also, does a woman invalidate a man's prayer if she passes in front of him while he is praying either individually, or following the *imām* in the Grand Mosque in Mecca?
*Fatwā*: Uttering *āmīn* after the *imām* recites *al-Fātiḥah* in prayer is established by [clear] text. Textual evidence has established the practice of uttering aloud after. The Prophet (S)[7] said, "If the *imām* says *āmīn*, say *āmīn*." Another version states, "When the [*imām*] recites *wa lā al-ḍāllīn* [in prayer], say *āmīn*."... [The jurist cites more evidence in support of his conclusion].

As for the woman invalidating a man's prayer, it is established in *Ṣaḥīḥ Muslim*, in a *ḥadīth* narrated by Abū Dharr that the Prophet (S) said, "The prayer of a Muslim male is broken if a woman, a donkey, or a black dog crosses in front of him within the span of a camel's saddle."

So, if a woman passes between a worshiper and his *sutrah*,[8] or between him and the place where he prostrates if he has no *sutrah*, his prayer is voided and must be redone, even if he is almost finished. He must restart his prayer from the beginning. The texts are general and do not distinguish one location over another. He has to make it up whether he is praying in the Grand Mosque in Mecca or anywhere else. This is the stronger position.

For this reason, Bukhārī commented on this issue by titling a chapter of his book, "Chapter on the *sutrah* in Mecca and other Places." Thus, Bukhārī generalized [between Mecca and other places].

Accordingly, if a woman passes between a man and his *sutrah* or between him and the place where he prostrates, he must repeat the prayer. However, if a man is praying behind an *imām*, the *sutrah* of the *imām* is the *sutrah* of those behind him, and so it is permissible for people to pass in front of worshipers who are praying behind an *imām* without incurring sin. However, it is *ḥarām* [forbidden] for someone to pass in front of one who is not being led in prayer. The Prophet (S) said, "If the one who passes in front of those who are praying knows what sins he is accruing, he would have preferred to have waited for forty rather than passing in front of him." Al-Bazzār narrated that what is intended by forty here is forty *kharīf*, i.e., 40 years.[9]

## ON THE IMPORTANCE OF MARRIAGE VERSUS EDUCATION FOR WOMEN

*Question*: There is a widespread practice among women and their fathers to refuse to marry someone who proposes to her so that she may finish her high school or college education, or until she studies for a few years. What is the ruling on this issue and what is your advice for one who refuses marriage? Some women reach thirty years of age or more without marrying.

*Fatwā*: The ruling on this is that it is contrary to the command of the Prophet (S). The Prophet (S) said, "If a man's religion and character please you, marry him." And the Prophet (S) also said, "O youth, whoever amongst you is able to provide financial support, let him marry as it helps one lower his gaze and protect his private parts." Abstaining from marriage deprives one of its benefits. I counsel my Muslim brethren who are guardians over women to let women finish their education or teaching. Women have the option of including a condition in the marriage contract stating that she may stay in school until she completes it, or that she remains a teacher for one or two years after marriage as long as she is not busy with her children. There is nothing wrong with this. However, for a woman to progress through university education, which is something we have no need for, is an issue that needs examination. What I see [to be correct] is that if a woman finishes elementary school and is able to read and write, and so she is able to benefit by reading the Book of God, its commentaries, and Prophetic *ḥadīth*, that is sufficient for her. This is so unless she excels in a field that people need, such as medicine or its like, and as long as this study involves nothing prohibited, such as the mixing of the sexes and other things.[10]

ON MARRIAGE WITH THE INTENT OF DIVORCE

*Question*: I heard one of your *fatāwā* on audiocassette in which you permitted marriages in foreign countries where the man marries with the intent of divorcing his wife after the termination of his employment or student visa. What, then, is the difference between this type of marriage and an invalid temporary marriage? What should he do if his wife bears him a daughter? Should he abandon her in a foreign country with her divorced mother? I am in need of clarification.

*Fatwā*: Yes, the Permanent Committee for Scholarly Research and the Issuing of *Fatāwā*, over which I preside, has issued a *fatwā* permitting a marriage entered into with the intent of divorce as long as this intention remains concealed between the groom and his Lord. If he married in a foreign country with the undisclosed intent of divorcing his wife upon the completion of his studies or employment, he is not liable according to the majority of scholars. Furthermore, such an intention is not a pre-condition in marriage [as in the case of temporary marriages], and should remain between him and his Lord.

As for the distinction between this type of marriage and temporary marriages, which are unlawful, the latter stipulates an agreed upon period of time, like a month or two, or a year or two. When this period elapses, the marriage becomes nullified. This is an invalid temporary marriage. There is no liability on one who gets married according to the *Sunnah* of God and His Messenger while harboring the intention of divorcing upon the lapse of his stay in a foreign country. In the same vein, his intention might change as it was never publicized, nor is it a condition for marriage. Rather, it is between him and God and, therefore, he is not at fault. This type of marriage is a means of preserving him from fornication and lasciviousness. The majority of scholars maintain this position, as related by the author of *al-Mughnī*, Muwaffiq al-Dīn b. Qudāmah, may God bless him.[11]

ON WOMEN COMPRISING THE MAJORITY OF THOSE IN HELL

*Question*: Is it correct that women comprise the majority of the people of Hell? And why?

*Fatwā*: This is correct. The Prophet (S) said to a group of women, "O women, give charity, for you are the majority of the people of Hell-fire." The difficulty related by the questioner has also been asked of the Prophet (S). [It is reported that the women] asked, "Why, O' Messenger of God? He said, "Because all of you curse excessively and are ungrateful to your companions (husbands)." Thus, the Prophet (S) clarified the reasons for which so many women are in the Hell-fire as the following: because women curse excessively, insult and swear, and are ungrateful to their companions – companions means husbands. For these reasons, they will become the majority of the people of Hell.[12]

### ON REMOVING THE VEIL FOR MEDICAL REASONS

*Question*: I have been afflicted by an illness on my scalp. The doctor instructed me to remove the veil that I wear on my head which causes me a lot of pain. Am I allowed to do this? What should I do?
*Fatwā*: Yes, it is permitted for you to remove the veil from your head as long as you are not in the presence of foreign men; for instance, [it is permissible] if you are with your husband. It is also permissible to remove the veil if you are in the presence only of other *maḥram* relatives,[13] or in the company of other women, but not when their husbands are with them. However, if you were to go into the marketplace, where there are non-*maḥram* men, it is incumbent upon you to cover your head, your face, and other parts of your body.[14]

### ON WOMEN BEING CREATED FROM A CROOKED RIB

*Question*: What is the meaning of the Prophet's (S) *ḥadīth* which states that the women were created from a crooked rib? What is intended meaning of the rib being "crooked"?
*Fatwā*: The meaning is that a woman will not be free of [a certain degree of] crookedness in her moral character, exactly like a rib. Hence, it is not possible to straighten her without divorcing her. Therefore, patience is prescribed for men along with overlooking aspects of her crookedness while continuing to advise and direct her.[15]

### ABOUT OMENS AND PORTENTS

*Question*: How does one reconcile the following two traditions of the Prophet (S): "There are no bad omens," and "If bad omens exist then they exist in a house, a woman, and a horse?" I beseech you for an answer. May God reward you.
*Fatwā*: Omens are divided into two categories. The first is a prohibited form of polytheism. This is to perceive an evil omen in visible or perceptible things in the world. This is known as *ṭīrah*, and it is a form of *shirk*, and is unlawful.

The second type of omens are called a portents or *tashā'um*. They are exceptions, and are not considered to be forbidden. This is evidenced in the authentic *ḥadīth*, "Bad omens exist in three things: women, homes, and mounts." These are exceptions and are not considered to be a part of the omens that are forbidden. It is said that some women and animals are bad omens and are the harbingers of evil, by God's permission. This is a fated and eternal form of evil. Therefore, there is no blame on one who leaves a house that is not fitting, nor is there blame on one who divorces a woman, or abandons a mount that is not becoming. This is not the prohibited belief in omens (*ṭīrah*)."[16]

ON WOMEN BEING DEFICIENT IN REASON AND RELIGION

*Question*: We often hear the *ḥadīth*, "Women are deficient in reason and religion." Some men cite it to insult women, so we would like you to explain to us the meaning of that *ḥadīth*.
*Fatwā*: The Prophet's (S) *ḥadīth* is the following: "I have seen none more deficient in reason and religion and, at the same time, more capable of robbing the wisdom of the wisest men than you." They said, "O Messenger of God, what is their deficiency in reason?" He said, "Is it not the case that the testimony of two women is equivalent to that of one man?" They said, "O Messenger of God, what is their deficiency in religion?" He said, "Is it not the case that when they are on their menstrual period they neither pray nor fast?"

Thus, the Prophet (S) explained that their intellectual deficiency is in the fact that their memory is weak, and that their testimony needs the corroboration of another woman. This [requirement of corroboration] is necessary to achieve accuracy in testimony because she may add something to or subtract something from her testimony. As God said, "And get two witnesses out of your own men, and if there are not two men, then a man and two women, such as ye choose for witnesses so that if one of them errs, the other can remind her"(Qur'ān 2:282)[17]. As to her deficiency in religion, it is attributed to the fact that while menstruating, or having postpartum bleeding, women neither pray nor fast, and they do not make up their prayers. However, they (women) are not to be blamed for this deficiency; it is a deficiency imposed by the Law of God. It is what God decreed as a form of compassion because if she were to fast while menstruating, or during postpartum bleeding, that would harm her. It is God's mercy that she is permitted not to fast during menstruation, but she must make up the missed days [of fasting].

As for prayer, she is in a situation that keeps her from being purified during menses. It is again God's mercy that He decreed that she should not pray while menstruating, or during postpartum bleeding. God has also decreed that she need not make up her prayers because making up the prayers would constitute a hardship upon her. Prayer is offered five times each day. Menses may last for seven or eight days or more. Postpartum bleeding could last for forty days. It is the mercy and compassion of God toward women that they are not obliged to perform or make up the prayers under such conditions. This does not mean that women are deficient in reason in everything or that they are deficient in religion in every matter. The Prophet (S) made it clear that their deficiency in reason is with respect to her possible lack of ability to give accurate testimony, and in religion, with respect to her not being able to pray or fast during menstruation, or postpartum bleeding. This also does not mean that women are less than men in every matter, or that men are superior to them in every respect. Yes, for many reasons, men as a sex are generally superior to women. As God has stated: "Men are the protectors and maintainers of women, because Allah has given the one more (strength) than the other, and because they support them from their means" (Qur'ān 4:34). However, a woman, under certain circumstances, may excel a man in many matters. How many women are greater than many men with respect to their intelligence, religion, and proficiency? It has been narrated from the Prophet (S) that women are less than men in reason and religion as to the two matters explained by the Prophet (S). It is possible for a woman to perform many good deeds, and to exceed many men in virtue, piety, and to attain a higher place in Heaven. It is possible for her to develop a competence over certain issues that exceeds the competence of men over matters that she sought to learn and master. So, it is possible for her to become an authority over Islamic history and other topics. This is clear to those who study the situation of women at the time of the Prophet (S) and afterwards. From this, one knows that her shortcoming does not mean that she cannot be relied upon for narrations. Similarly, if another woman supports her testimony, it is accepted. There is nothing that prevents her, if she is steadfast in her religion, from becoming pious, and becoming one of the best of the servants of God and one of the best women-servants of God. She is not obliged to fast or pray while menstruating, or having postpartum bleeding. The fact that she does not have to pray or make up her prayers does not mean that she is deficient in every matter related to piety or in every matter related to her religious duties. With respect to her ability to testify, she has a specific deficiency, as the Prophet (S) explained, and that does not mean that this deficiency can be generalized. Therefore, a believer may not accuse her of having a shortcoming in everything or a weakness in her faith in every matter. It is a particular shortcoming in her religion and a particular shortcoming in her reasoning that is related to the reliability of her testimony and so forth. One must understand the words of the Prophet (S) properly and in the best and most appropriate manner. And God knows best.[18]

### ON THE PROHIBITION OF PHOTOGRAPHS

*Question*: If I were in a foreign country and wished to send a photograph of myself to my family, friends, and especially my wife, would this be permissible for or not?

*Fatwā*: Authentic traditions from the Prophet (S) have established the prohibition of depicting any being that possesses a soul, whether human or not. Thus, you may not send a picture of yourself either to your family or to your wife.[19]

### THE RULING ABOUT WOMEN DRIVING AUTOMOBILES

Thanks be to God and peace and blessing be upon His Prophet (S), and to the point at hand:

Much has been said in the *Jazīrah Newspaper* about women driving automobiles even though it is well-known that their driving would introduce vices that are in no way unfamiliar to those who propagate its permissibility. Among these vices are a man's seclusion with a woman, unveiling, uninhibited mixing with men, and the violating of those restrictions by which these vices came to be forbidden. The pristine *Sharīʿah* blocks the means that lead to that which is forbidden and thereby prohibits the means altogether. God Almighty commanded the wives of the Prophet (S) and those of the rest of the believers to remain in their homes, to veil themselves, and to avoid showing their apparels in front of non-*maḥram* men because all of this leads to promiscuities that undermine all of society. God Almighty said: "And stay quietly in your houses and make not a dazzling display, like that of the former Times of Ignorance, and establish regular prayer, and give regular charity, and obey Allah and His Messenger" (Qurʾān 33:33). The Almighty also said: "O Prophet, tell thy wives and daughters and the believing women that they should cast their outer garments over their persons (when abroad). That is most convenient that they should be known (as such) and not molested. And Allah is Oft-Forgiving, Most Merciful." (Qurʾān 33:59). God Almighty also said: "And say to the believing women that they should lower their gaze and guard their modesty: that they should not display their beauty and ornaments except what (must ordinarily) appear thereof; that they should draw their veils over their bosoms and not display their beauty except to their husbands, their fathers, their husbands' fathers, their sons, their husbands' sons, their brothers or their brothers' sons, or their sisters' sons, or their women, or the slaves whom their right hands possess, or male servants free of physical needs, or small children who have no sense of the shame of sex; and that they should not strike their feet in order to draw attention to their hidden ornaments. And O ye Believers! Turn ye all together towards Allah, that ye may attain bliss" (Qurʾān 24:31). The Prophet (S) said, "A man does not seclude himself with a woman except that the Devil becomes their third." The pristine *Sharīʿah* blocks all avenues that lead to immoralities, including the slander of chaste women. The *Sharīʿah* made the punishment for slander among the most severe in order to protect society from the proliferation of the causes of corruption. Women driving automobiles is among the causes of corruption that ought to be conceded. But the ignorance of people of Islamic laws and of the negative consequences of easing the means that lead to vice is among the calamities that afflict those people with diseased hearts, who revel in promiscuity, and enjoy gazing at women. All of this leads people to delve into these discussions in this and similar matters without knowledge and without regard for the dangers that result from these positions. God, the Exalted, said: "Say: the things that my Lord hath indeed forbidden are: shameful deeds, whether open or secret, sins and trespasses against truth or reason; assigning of partners to Allah, for which He hath given no authority; and saying things about Allah of which ye have no knowledge" (Qurʾān 7:33). God, the Glorified, also said: "and do not follow the footsteps of the Evil One, for he is an avowed enemy. For he commands you what is evil and shameful. And that ye should say of Allah that of which ye have no knowledge" (Qur'ān 2:168–9). The Prophet(S) said: "I have not left behind me a *fitnah* more harmful for men than women." Ḥudhayfah b. al-Yamānī (R)[20] said: "People used to ask God's Messenger about goodness while I asked him about evil, lest it should broach me. Once I inquired, 'O God's Messenger, we were entrenched in ignorance and evil, then God bestowed upon us this goodness [i.e., Islam]; so will this goodness be followed by any evil?' He answered, 'Yes.' I asked, 'Will this evil be followed by any goodness?' He responded, 'Yes, but it will be obscure,' to which I probed: 'What is the nature of its obscurity?' He answered, 'A people will guide by other than my guidance, but you will recognize them and will therefore reject them.' Then, I repeated, 'So will this goodness be followed by any evil?' He replied, 'Yes, callers at the gates of Hell. Whoever responds to their call shall enter it.' I asked, 'O Messenger of God, please describe them to me.' He answered, 'They share our complexion and dialect.' I asked, 'So what shall I do if I live to see all of this?' He responded, 'Adhere to the true Muslims and their leader.' I, then, asked, 'And suppose the Muslims have neither a political leader nor a recognizable majority?' He cautioned, 'Then eschew all factions even if you had to bite into the roots of a tree until death visits you and finds you doing so.'" Related by Bukhārī and Muslim.

I, veritably, call upon every Muslim to be conscious of God in his speech and actions and to guard himself from enticements and from people who incite them to pursue these enticements. I beseech every Muslim to distance himself from every endeavor deserving of or leading to that which deserves God Almighty's anger, and to be especially cautious not to be included among those callers whom the Prophet (S) described in the time-honored *ḥadīth* above. May God protect us from these tribulations and from its proponents, preserve for this community its religion, and save it from the evil of those who invite to corruption. May God direct our writers and the rest of the Muslims towards that which pleases God and benefits the affairs of the Muslims, and may God grant them prosperity in this world and the next. Indeed, God is the One in control of this and able to bring it to fruition.[21]

## ON ENDURING A HUSBAND'S MISTREATMENT

*Question*: My husband, may God forgive him, despite his overall good character and piety, takes absolutely no interest in me or in our house, he always has a frown on his face, and is impatient [with me]. You might suspect that I am the cause, but God knows that I fulfill all his rights, I try to provide him with comfort and tranquility, and I try to keep everything that displeases him away from him, and to be patient despite his mistreatment.

Whenever I ask him about something or speak to him about any matter, he gets angry, becomes furious, and says that what I am saying is insignificant and silly, although he is cheerful with his friends and colleagues. As for me, my share in living with him is blame and mistreatment. All of this has caused me pain and has tormented me considerably, and I have thought several times about leaving the home.

I am, praise God, a woman of average education, and I fulfill God's obligations upon me.

Your eminence the Shaykh: If I left the house, raised the children, and took on the responsibilities of life alone, would I be committing a sin? Or should I remain with my husband under these conditions and refrain from speaking and not try to share his feelings and problems? Please tell me what to do, may God reward you.

*Fatwā*: There is no doubt that the obligation upon spouses is to establish mutual companionship through kindness, a mutual exchange of love and praiseworthy characteristics, as well as good character and a kind disposition. God Almighty has said: "Live with them on a footing of kindness and equity," (Qur'ān 4:19) and in another verse God says: "and women shall have rights similar to the rights against them, according to what is equitable; but men have a degree (of advantage) over them" (Qur'ān 2:228). The Prophet (S) said, "Goodness (and kindness) is perfection of character," and in another statement, he said, "Do not underestimate the importance of every kind act even if it is meeting your brother with a cheerful face." Both of these reports were taken from Muslim in his authentic collection of *ḥadīth*. In another statement, the Prophet (S) said, "The best in the perfection of faith amongst the believers is the one who is the best of them in character, and best of you, are the ones that are the best to their wives, and I am the best of you towards my family." Other than these, there are numerous *aḥādīth* which emphasize good manners, kindness in dealing, and goodness in all exchanges between Muslims in general. Now, if this what is necessary towards all Muslims, then what does this tell us about the appropriate behavior towards one's own spouses and family members?

Your patience and endurance of your husband's unkindness and mistreatment is praiseworthy. I thus counsel you to increase your patience without leaving the house. In that, God Willing, will be much good and a praise-worthy reward, for the Almighty, has said: "And be patient and persevering: for Allah is with those who patiently persevere" 8:46. In another verse, the Almighty states: "Behold, he that is righteous and patient, never will God suffer the reward to be lost, of those who do right" 12:90. In another verse God states: "Those who patiently persevere will truly receive a reward without measure!" 39:10. The Almighty also says: "So persevere patiently: For the end is for those who are righteous" 11:49.

You should joke with him and talk to him in such a way as to soften his heart. This might open his heart to you and might cause him to recognize your rights. Do not make worldly claims of him as long as he is discharging his important obligations. It may be that his heart will open up to your important demands and that you will find the results to be pleasing, God-willing. May God grant you an increase in everything good, may God reform the condition of your husband, inspire him, guide him, and grant him a good character, a good nature, and the ability to discharge his obligations towards others. Indeed, God is the best of those who are beseeched and God is the Guide to the Straight Path.[22]

### ON OBEYING ONE'S HUSBAND

*Question*: What is your opinion about a woman who does not listen to her husband, does not obey him, and defies him in a number of matters. For example, she leaves without his permission and sometimes even does so stealthily, without his knowing.
*Fatwā*: A women must obey her husband in what is good. It is *ḥarām* for her to disobey him and it is not permissible for her to leave his house without his permission.

The Prophet (S) said, "If a man calls his wife to his bed and she refuses and he spends the night angry at her, the angels curse her until the morning." This is agreed upon by Muslim and Bukhārī.

The Prophet (S) also said, "If I were to command anyone to prostrate to another, I would have ordered a woman to prostrate to her husband because of the enormity of his rights over her." This is related by Abū Dāwūd in his *Sunan*.

God Almighty said: "Men are the protectors and maintainers of women, because Allah has given the one more (strength) than the other, and because they support them from their means. Therefore the righteous women are devoutly obedient, and guard in (the husband's) absence what God would have them guard. As to those women on whose part ye fear disloyalty and ill-conduct, admonish them (first), (next), refuse to share their beds, (and last) beat them (lightly)" (Qur'ān 4:34).

God Almighty has clarified that the man is the guardian of the woman, so if a woman treats her husband with hostility, he should take decisive measures that teach her of her duty to obey him and the prohibition against defying him without a just cause.[23]

*Question*: A woman lives with her husband in the same city where her parents reside, yet her husband prevents her from contacting or visiting them more than once a month. As for her other relatives, such as her brothers, uncles, and grandparents, visiting them is out of the question. So is she expected to obey him in severing familial ties? Can she seek a divorce on these grounds alone? This situation has driven her to the edge. He has even refused to allow anyone to visit her in his house to the point that he has isolated her from everyone. Is his behavior permissible?
*Fatwā*: Maintaining familial ties by visiting and dealing in kindness with one's relatives is obligatory. Relatives have certain rights as part of the general rights that God Almighty has prescribed. This is especially so when it comes to the parents. But a wife's obedience to her husband is also an obligation, and she is not allowed to leave his house without his permission, whether to visit a relative

or otherwise. She is obligated to obey her husband and not to leave the house except with his permission. On the other hand, the husband is not allowed to misuse his rights or to prevent his wife from visiting her parents and relatives unless visiting her family results in harm. If such visits result in harm to the husband, he has the right to forbid his wife from visiting her family.[24]

### ON THE PROHIBITION AGAINST WOMEN VISITING GRAVES

*Question*: What is the ruling regarding women visiting the tomb of the Prophet (S)? And, what is the ruling regarding women visiting graves in general and what is the evidence?

*Fatwā*: The visiting of women to graves is forbidden; in fact, it is among the grave sins because the Prophet (S) said: "My God curses the women who visit graves or those who build mosques or tombs [upon graves]. This is because women are deficient in intellect and are emotional beings who are easily affected. If women visit graves, several vices will result. If women visit graves, because of her emotionalism and weakness, such visits will become frequent and the graveyards will become full of women. If this happens, graveyards will become the playground of the corrupt and iniquitous who will stakeout graveyards. Graveyards are often located far away from inhabited areas and, therefore, grave evils will inevitably result. This is why [we must realize that] the Prophet's (S) curse, directed at women who visit graves, is founded on great interests. However, if a woman passes by a graveyard, by coincidence and without intending a visit, she may pause to utter the calling of peace (*al-salām*), which is: "Peace be upon you, O' believers and Muslims, God willing we will [soon] join you." This is because 'Ā'ishah asked the Prophet (S) what should a Muslim say when they pass by the graveyards, and he advised her to say the supplication mentioned above. But for a woman to visit the graveyards purposely, that is prohibited and is one of the biggest sins.

As to women visiting the grave of the Prophet (S), it is probably included in the prohibition. Thus, a woman should not visit the Prophet's (S) grave but some jurists said that a woman may visit the Prophet's (S) grave because it is not like other graves. The Prophet's (S) grave is surrounded by three walls so if a woman visits his grave, in reality, she has not visited it. However, the preferred view is that since as a matter of customary practice, this is known as visiting graves, a woman should refrain from doing so. It is sufficient for a woman to say in her prayers: "Peace be upon you, O' Prophet, and may the mercy and blessings of God [be upon you]." This blessing will reach the Prophet (S) and she will be rewarded for it.[25]

### ON THE MIXING BETWEEN MEN AND WOMEN

It is my duty to remind and advise people, and to bring their attention to an issue that cannot be ignored. In fact, people should be warned about this matter and people should be cautioned against it. This matter is the mixing between men and women without the presence of any *maḥram*, a circumstance that is occurring amongst some of the ignorant people in some places and towns. They do not deem intermixing as objectionable. They cite, as evidence, the fact that this was the practice of their fathers and grandfathers, and that they have pure intentions. You will find, for example, a woman sitting with her brother-in-law, male cousin, or other non-*maḥram* male relatives without wearing the veil and without any care.

It is known that wearing the veil, and covering the face in the presence of *ajānib* (foreign) men, is an obligatory matter. The Qur'ān, the *Sunnah*, and the consensus of the early pious Muslims have established this as a duty. God Almighty says, "And say to the believing women that they should lower their gaze and guard their modesty; that they should not display their beauty and ornaments except what (must ordinarily) appear thereof; that they should draw their veils over their bosoms (Qur'ān 24:31), and "And when ye ask (his [the Prophet's] ladies) for anything ye want ask them from before a screen: that makes for greater purity for your hearts and for theirs" (Qur'ān 33:53), and "O Prophet! Tell thy wives and daughters and the believing women, that they should cast their outer garments over their persons (when abroad): that is most convenient, that they should be known (as such) and not molested. And God is Oft-Forgiving, Most Merciful" (Qur'ān 33:59). The loose garment (*jilbāb*) is worn over the veil (*khimār*) in the place of a cloak-like woolen wrap (*'abā'ah*). Umm Salamah said, "When this verse was revealed, 'they should cast their outer garments over their persons (when abroad),' the women of the Helpers (*Anṣār*) came out, as if crows had nested on their head because of their subdued and quiet demeanor, and because they had worn black outer garments."

These venerable verses are clear evidence obligating women to cover their heads, hair, necks, and the upper portion of their chests when in the presence of any non-*maḥram* man. The Prophet (S) also indicated this obligation when he ordered the women to go out to the place of *'īd* prayer. The women complained that they do not have any garments, so the Prophet (S) replied, "Let their sisters loan them one of theirs." This has been recorded by Bukhārī and Muslim. This *ḥadīth* is proof that the established practice amongst the women of the Companions was to not go out without wearing the *jilbāb*. The Prophet (S) did not permit them from going out without wearing an outer garment *jilbāb*.

The books of authentic *ḥadīth* have recorded some reports from 'Ā'ishah. She said, "The Messenger of God used to pray Morning Prayer and I used to see, with him, the believing women wrapped up in pieces of cloth. Afterward they would return to their houses, and no one would recognize any one of them because of the darkness." In another narration, she said, "If the Prophet could see what we have seen some women do, he would have prohibited them from going to mosques, just as the Israelites have prohibited their women [from visiting places of worship]." This *ḥadīth* is evidence that the veil and seclusion (*tasattur*) were some of the established practices of the women of the Companions. The Companions were the best generation, the most honored in the sight of God, the Tremendous, the Powerful, the most excellent in character and etiquette, the most perfect in faith, the most righteous in action, and as a result, were the best example for others. In another narration, 'Ā'ishah said, "Riders used to pass by us, the Prophet's wives, while we were on our way to performing pilgrimage in the company of the Prophet. Whenever they rode parallel to us, we would bring our veils down from our heads to cover our faces, and when they passed us by, we would unveil our faces again." This *ḥadīth* is an indicator of the obligation to cover the face.

When we examine the issue of unveiling women's faces in the presence of foreign (*ajānib*), non-*maḥram* men, we find that this practice contains many potential causes of corruption. Among these are that it causes sexual enticement which occurs when women openly show their faces, and this is the greatest cause leading to evil and corruption, the disappearance of shame in women, and the corresponding sexual enticement stirred in men. For these reasons, it is forbidden for women to uncover their faces, upper part of her chest, neck, arms, and calves, in the presence of non-*maḥram* men, or to mix with such men without the presence of *maḥram* men and without wearing a face veil. When the woman looks at herself as equal to the man in regards to being able to uncover her face and travel without a face-veil, she will lose her sense of modesty and shame, while competing with men in this right. In this, there is great danger of sexual enticement and tremendous corruption. One day, the Prophet (S) went out of the mosque where the men and the women were mixing in the street, and the Prophet (S) said, "Delay in leaving the mosque, for you have no right of way." The women used to walk in such close proximity to the wall that their garments would cling to it. In his commentary on the verse: "And say to the believing women that they should lower their gaze" (Qur'ān 24:31). Ibn Kathīr mentions, "It is forbidden for the woman to uncover her face in the presence of non-*maḥram* men, rather, it is obligatory for her to cover it, just as it is forbidden for her to be alone with them, mix with them, or extend her hand to them in greetings. God Almighty has clarified which individuals are permitted to glance at the beauty of a woman in the following verse: "that they should not display their beauty and ornaments except what (must ordinarily) appear thereof; that they should draw their veils over their bosoms and not display their beauty except to their husbands, their fathers, their husbands' fathers, their sons, their husbands' sons, their brothers or their brothers' sons, or their sisters' sons, or their women, or the slaves whom their right hands possess, or male servants free of physical needs, or small children who have no sense of the shame of sex; and that they should not strike their feet in order to draw attention to their hidden ornaments. And O ye Believers! Turn ye all together towards Allah that ye may attain bliss" (Qur'ān 24:31).

The brother of the husband, or the husband of the sister, or sons of the uncles and aunts, and others (as such), are not considered to be *maḥram*, therefore, they cannot look at the face of such a woman, nor is it permitted for her to remove her *jilbāb* in their presence. If she did so, it would only cause them to be enticed by her. For in a *ḥadīth* narrated by ʿUqbah b. ʿĀmir (R) in which the Prophet (S) said, "Woe to those who unexpectedly enter in upon non-*maḥram* women," and a man from amongst the Helpers (*Anṣār*) asked, "Have you considered the in-laws?" To this, the Prophet (S) replied, "Be cautious with your in-laws [literally, your in-laws are death]." Both Muslim and Bukhārī have recorded this. What is meant by the word *ḥamū* is the brother of the husband, or his uncle, or the like. This is because the Companions used to enter the house without any misgivings even though they weren't *maḥram* for her, with nothing more than their kinship with her husband. For this reason, it was not permitted for her to uncover her beauty, even though they were righteous, and trustworthy with them. Because, in the previously cited verse, God restricted the categories of people to whom a woman is allowed to reveal her beauty, and the husband's brothers, uncles, or nephews are not included in this category. The Prophet (S) in a *ḥadīth* recorded by both Bukhārī and Muslim, said, "The men may not be alone with a woman who is not his *maḥram*." A *maḥram* is any man whom a woman is forbidden from marrying because of a relationship either through kinship, marriage, or the sharing of a foster milk mother. Examples of this would be the father, son, brother, uncle, and anyone analogous to them.

The Prophet (S) forbade women from this in order to prevent Satan from causing women to corrupt others, give free rein to sin, walk amongst them causing corruption, entice them, and make disobedience seem attractive to them. It has been established that the Prophet (S) said, "No man will be in seclusion with a women without the devil being their third." This was authentically related by Aḥmad from ʿUmar b. al-Khaṭṭāb.

Whoever continues the cultural practices of their respective countries while contradicting the above principles and justifies this by citing the cultural practice of their families or the people of their countries as normative evidence, must struggle against themselves to discontinue doing so. They must mutually assist each other in ending mixing, and in becoming purified from its evil effects. They must assist each other in achieving goodness and piety, and in executing the command of God Almighty and His messenger (S). They must turn in repentance to God Almighty for what they have done in this respect, work hard in enjoining the good and forbidding the evil, and must persevere in this. They must not let the censure of the critic overtake them in their struggle to establish the truth and invalidate falsehood. They must not let the derision or mockery of some people repel them from this, for it is obligatory for the Muslim to follow the legislation of God with pleasure, obedience, and desire in what is with God, while fearing His punishment. This is because Islam is the religion of truth, the guidance, and the standard of justice in everything. Islam calls for the perfection of the noble qualities of human character, the perfection of good deeds, and a prohibition of anything that contradicts it.

We ask God to give to us and all of the Muslims as much success as He pleases, and to protect all of us from the evil of ourselves and our bad deeds. He is the Generous, the Honorable. May God bless and give peace to our Prophet, his family, and his Companions.[26]

### THE RULING REGARDING THE WORK OF WOMEN

*Question*: What is the Islamic ruling with respect to a woman's working and leaving her home with such attire as we often see in the streets, at school, and at home? Additionally, what about a peasant woman who works with her husband in the fields?

*Fatwā*: There is no doubt that Islam came to ennoble and protect women, guarantee their rights, exalt their stature, and preserve them from the wolves of humanity. Islam deemed them partners with men in inheritance, forbade the burial of infant daughters, stipulated their permission in marriage, and granted them full discretion in spending their wealth as long as they are of a mature age. Islam prescribed many rights for them over their husbands. It mandated their fathers and male relatives to support them in circumstances of need, and required veiling for them to prevent non-*maḥram* men from lusting after them. Thus, women would not be reduced to being cheap commodities consumed by everyone. God Almighty said: "and when you ask (his [the Prophet's] ladies) for anything ye want ask them from before a screen. That makes for greater purity for your hearts and for theirs" (Qur'ān 33:53). God, the Glorified, said in the same chapter: "O Prophet! Tell thy wives and daughters and the believing women, that they should cast their outer garments over their persons (when abroad): that is most convenient, that they should be known (as such) and not molested. And God is Oft-Forgiving, Most Merciful" (Qur'ān 33:59). God Almighty also said: "Say to the believing men that they should lower their gaze and guard their modesty: that will make for greater purity for them: and Allah is well acquainted with all that they do. And say to the believing women that they should lower their gaze and guard their modesty; that they should not display their beauty and ornaments except what (must ordinarily) appear thereof; that they should draw their veils over their bosoms and not display their beauty except to their husbands, their fathers, their husbands' fathers" (Qur'ān 24:30–31). The great Companion, 'Abd Allāh b. Mas'ūd (R) rightly explained that the verse: "except what [must ordinarily] appear thereof," refers to a woman's external garb because it is impossible to conceal it without considerable embarrassment. Ibn 'Abbās (R) explained that the intended meaning is her face and both palms, but the stronger position is that of Ibn Mas'ūd (R) because the aforementioned verse about *ḥijāb* points to the obligation of concealing their faces and hands because these are among the most alluring feminine features. Concealing them, therefore, is very important. The *Shaykh* of Islam, Ibn Taymiyyah, may God have mercy on him said:[27] Exposing the face and hands was permitted in the formative period of Islam, then the verse of *ḥijāb* was revealed, mandating their concealment because exposing them to non-*maḥram* men is among the leading causes for temptation and, ultimately, leads to the exposure of other parts of the body. Further, if a woman's face or hands are decorated with dyes, eyeliner, or other types of cosmetics, it is the consensus that exposing [the hands and face] is prohibited. The dominant trend among women today, is toward adornment and beautification, and therefore, the prohibition of exposing the face and hands is based on these two proofs. As to what women do in our day and age of exposing their heads, necks, chests, arms, calves, and thighs, that is prohibited by the consensus of all Muslims, and no one with the least bit of insight would doubt this position. The temptation that results from these corrupt practices is overwhelming and the ensuing sexual promiscuity is even greater. We ask God to grant the Muslim leaders success in effectively bringing an end to these practices, and in returning women to the laws that God ordained for them of wearing the *ḥijāb* and avoiding all avenues that lead to *fitnah*. In this light, God Almighty revealed: "And stay quietly in your houses and make not a dazzling display like that of the former Times of Ignorance." (Qur'ān 33:33). Also: "Such elderly women as are past the prospect of marriage – there is no blame on them if they lay aside their (outer) garments, provided they make not a wanton display of their beauty: but it is best for them to be modest: and God is One Who sees and knows all things" (Qur'ān 24:60). God Almighty, in the previous verse, commanded women to remain in their homes. Their presence in public is a main contributing factor to the spread of *fitnah*. Yes, the *Sharī'ah* permits women to leave their homes only when necessary, provided that they wear the *ḥijāb* and avoid all suspicious situations. However, the general rule is that they should remain at home. This is better for them, more appropriate, and further removed from *fitnah*. God, accordingly, forbade them from exposing themselves as was done in the days of ignorance (pre-Islamic times). At that time, women used to display their adornments and enticements. In the latter verse, God permitted elderly women past the age of menopause to set aside their outer garments, namely, the veil, as long as they do not adorn themselves. Since elderly women must veil themselves when they are adorned, even though they neither tempt nor entice, what about young women who do tempt and entice? Then, God Almighty said that it is better for these elderly women to show modesty by covering with the veil even if they are not beautified. All of this leads to the clear conclusion that women must veil themselves, refrain from exposing themselves, and to avoid all the causes of *fitnah*. We beseech God's assistance.

There is no objection for a woman to work alongside her husband in the fields, factories, and at home, as long as she is working with *maḥram* men and as long as there are no non-*maḥram* men around. She is also permitted to work with women. She is prohibited, however, from working with non-*maḥram* men because this would cause enormous corruptions and a great *fitnah*. [Working with foreign men] allows these male colleagues to be secluded with her and to see some of her charms. The perfect Islamic *Sharīʿah* came to preserve the people's welfare and to maximize it, to ward off corruption and to minimize it, and to cut off all avenues that lead to what God has categorically forbidden. There is no way to happiness, dignity, honor, and success in this life and the next except by adhering to the *Sharīʿah*, binding oneself to its judgments, calling others to abide by it with patience, and being cautious about whatever conflicts with this commitment. May God grant us, you, and the rest of our brethren success in that which pleases God and protect us all from the deviations of *fitnah*. God is Magnanimous and Generous.[28]

## ON THE DANGERS OF WOMEN IN THE WORKPLACES OF MEN

All praise belongs to God and may peace and blessings shower his truthful Messenger, his followers, and Companions. To the point at hand: the call, whether directly or indirectly, for women to join men in their workplaces under the guise of modern necessities and the needs of society, which leads to commingling [of the sexes], is a grave matter, indeed, that leads to a dangerous state of affairs, bitter consequences, and disastrous repercussions. Not to mention the fact that this call contradicts the texts of the *Sharīʿah* that command women to abide in their homes and focus on the work that concerns them at home.

Furthermore, whoever wishes to consider the countless pitfalls of intermingling, then let him reflect upon those societies that have plunged into this heavy calamity, willingly or unwillingly. If such a person maintains objectivity and justly devotes himself to a truthful and honest inquiry, he would discover that people are distressed and dismayed, at the individual and social levels, that women have abandoned their homes and would discover the complete dissolution of the family unit. Moreover, we find clearly on the tongues of many writers, and in all modes of communication, that there is great dismay at the decadence of society and the collapse of its moral fabric.

There are manifold authentic and explicit proofs that forbid one from being secluded with woman, and [forbid] gazing upon a non-*maḥram* woman, and that prohibit the means leading to those actions that God has forbidden. They decisively prohibit intermingling since it leads to disgraceful consequences.

When a woman leaves her home, which is her dominion and place of vivacious liberty in this temporal life, she opposes that which her inherent disposition inclines toward as well as the natural proclivity that God created within her.

In an Islamic society, the call for women to join men in their workplaces is a grave matter, and intermingling with men is among its greatest pitfalls. Loose interaction across gender lines is one of the major causes of fornication, which disintegrates society and destroys its moral values and all sense of propriety.

It is a fact that God Almighty created women with an entirely different physique than that of men. It is well suited for housework and for those vocations particular to women, in general.

In other words, women's intrusion into men's workplaces contradicts their own dispositions and natures. This is a grave offense upon women. It destroys the spirit and sense of worth that is inherited by the next generation of boys and girls who are in want of proper rearing, kindness, and affection. The mother is the one to assume this role, but she has departed from it and completely abandoned the dominion without which she will never attain comfort, tranquility, and contentment. The state of affairs in these societies that have entangled themselves in this disorder is the best testimony in support of our position.

Islam charged each spouse with certain obligations and called upon men and women to assume their respective roles. This assures that society will be strengthened, both inside and outside the home.

The man is responsible for spending and making a living. The woman is responsible for rearing the children with kindness and compassion, breastfeeding, and other endeavors that are appropriate for women and particularly related to women such as teaching children, administering the education of girls, doctoring and nursing women, and so forth. When a woman neglects her household duties, the home and its members fall apart and the family unit actually and symbolically disintegrates. Consequently, we are left with what appears to be a society, but lacks essence and meaning.

God Almighty said: "Men are the protectors and maintainers of women, because Allah has given the one more (strength) than the other, and because they support them from their means" (Qur'ān 4:34). Thus, the *Sunnah* of God in His creation is that the *qiwāmah* (guardianship) belongs to men because of the preference of them over women as supported by this verse. God Almighty commanded women to abide in their homes. The prohibition against women exposing themselves to men, in essence, relates to that of intermingling, which entails the free interaction of foreign men and women in the same place, be it the workplace, marketplace, recreational park, or even while traveling and so forth. The intrusion of women in these places leads to what is forbidden; it contravenes God's command and repudiates His rights, which the *Sharī'ah* expects Muslim women to uphold.

The Qur'ān and the *Sunnah* provide the basis for the prohibition of the mixing of the sexes and all that spawns it. God Almighty said: "And stay quietly in your houses and make not a dazzling display, like that of the former Times of Ignorance; and establish Regular Prayer, and give Regular Charity; and obey Allah and His Messenger. And Allah only wishes to remove all abomination from you, ye Members of the Family, and to make you pure and spotless. And recite what is rehearsed to you in your homes, of the Signs of Allah and His Wisdom: for Allah understands the finest mysteries and is well-acquainted (with them)" (Qur'ān 33:33–34). Thus, God commanded the Mothers of the Faithful, i.e. all women who submit and believe, to abide in their homes for their own protection and in order to distance them from the venues of corruption, since leaving their homes unnecessarily leads to their exposure and other harms. Then God bade them to perform those good deeds that would shield them from promiscuity and evil, such as establishing prayer, giving charity, and obeying God and His Messenger (S). Then God directed them toward what would benefit them in this temporal world and the afterlife: that they be in unison with the noble Qur'ān and the pristine *Sunnah* of the Prophet (S), both of which polish the rusted hearts and purify them from filth and pollution and guide to truth and certainty. God Almighty said: "O Prophet! Tell thy wives and your daughters and the believing women that they should cast their outer garments over their persons (when abroad): That is most convenient, that they should be known (as such) and not molested. And Allah is Oft-Forgiving, Most Merciful" (Qur'ān 33:59). So God ordered His Prophet (S) who speaks on behalf of his Lord, to tell his wives, daughters, and all faithful women to draw their outer garments over their persons. This incorporates covering their full bodies with their outer garments. They are to cover themselves in this manner when leaving their homes. However, they may only leave their homes under circumstances of necessity. This prevents men of diseased hearts from molesting them. Since this is the case, how do you explain their presence in areas that men occupy? They mix with them, express their needs to them in the workplace, relinquish many of their feminine qualities trying to equate themselves with men, and forsake their sense of modesty. All of this results in a lapsing between the genders, which are altogether distinct, inwardly and outwardly?

God Almighty said: "Say to the believing men that they should lower their gaze and guard their modesty: that will make for greater purity for them: and Allah is well acquainted with all that they do. And say to the believing women that they should lower their gaze and guard their modesty; that they should not display their beauty and ornaments except what (must ordinarily) appear thereof; that they should draw their veils over their bosoms" (Qur'ān 24:30–31).

Consider that God commands His Prophet (S) to declare unto believing men and women that they should control their desire to gaze upon one another and should protect their privates from committing fornication. Then God Almighty proclaimed that doing this is more virtuous for them. It is known that preserving the privates from promiscuity can only be achieved by averting the means leading to it. Without doubt, the foremost causes of promiscuity include the staring at the opposite gender and the commingling of women and men in the workplaces and elsewhere. It is impossible to discharge these two commands addressed to men of faith while working and mixing with women, whether as associates or co-workers. When women and men invade each other's workplaces, it is impossible that they would lower their gazes, protect their privates, and increase in spiritual purity and lucidity.

Likewise, God commanded faithful women to lower their gaze, protect their privates, and avoid displaying their ornaments except those ornaments that ordinarily appear. He also commanded them to draw their veils over their *jayb*, which can only be a reference to covering her head and face because the *jayb* is the place of the head and face. So how can a woman withhold her gaze, protect her privates, and conceal her adornments when she is intermingling with men in their workplaces? Mixing of the sexes assures falling into these traps.

How is it possible that a Muslim woman would lower her gaze from her non-*maḥram* male colleague while claiming that she is his co-partner, co-equal in work, and walks side-by-side with him?

Islam has forbidden all ways and means that lead to forbidden matters. Likewise, Islam has forbidden women from speaking softly to men because they might arouse the men. God Almighty said: "O Consorts of the Prophet! Ye are not like any of the (other) women; if ye do fear (Allah), be not too complaisant of speech lest one in whose heart is a disease should be moved with desire." (Qur'ān 33:32). "Disease," here, refers to the disease of longing. So how can there be protection from this where there is loose interaction?

It is self-evident that when a woman is present in the workplaces of men, instances occur in which they exchange dialogue and in which they would speak to each other tenderly. Meanwhile, Satan is behind the scenes, embellishing, titillating, and inviting to lasciviousness until they fall prey to him. God, the Wise and Omniscient, commands women to veil themselves because people could be both righteous and iniquitous, chaste and wanton. By the Will of God, the veil prevents enticements and precludes their causes. It produces pure hearts for both men and women and precludes the misgivings of suspicion. God Almighty said: "and when ye ask (his [the Prophet's] ladies) for anything ye want, ask them from before a screen: that makes for greater purity for your hearts and for theirs" (Qur'ān 33:53). In addition to covering her face, a woman's home is the best way for her to conceal herself. Islam has also forbidden her from interacting with non-*maḥram* men so that she does not expose herself to harm, either directly or indirectly. She was commanded to remain in her home and not to leave it except for a permissible need, and as long as she observes proper prescribed etiquette. In verse 33:33, God described her action of remaining at home as "steady." This connotes various ornately sublime meanings, including spiritual repose, the serenity of her soul, and the contentment of her heart. Thus, were she to desert this "steadiness", her soul would fluctuate, her spirit would be unsettled, her heart would be constricted, and she would be vulnerable to disgraceful consequences. Islam categorically prohibits a man from being in seclusion with a non-*maḥram* woman. There must be present her legal guardian, who must also be present when the woman travels, all in order to inhibit the causes of corruption and to shut the doors of enticement, to hinder the inducements of evil, to protect both parties from the machinations of Satan. To this effect, it has been authentically related that God's Messenger said, "I have not bequeathed a greater *fitnah* for men than women," and the Prophet (S) said, "Be wary of this temporal world and be wary of women, for the first tribulation endured by the Children of Israel was in relation to their women."

Some proponents of intermingling cling to the surface meaning of some legal source texts but whose subtle meanings are accessible only to those whose hearts God has alighted, who acutely understand the religion, and juxtapose all the various proofs until they point to one coherent conclusion. In one report, a group of women fought in battle with God's Messenger (S).

The response to this is:

1) These women at the time of the Prophet (S) must have left their homes with their legal guardians and for noble purposes.
2) It was never feared that these women would commit vile deeds by virtue of their faith and piety.
3) These women were protected by their male guardians.
4) They had been meticulous in veiling themselves after the verse related to veiling was revealed (Qur'ān 24:31). This is in contrast to the practice of most women in our day and age.

Also, it is clear that the case of a woman leaving her home to work is markedly distinct from the circumstances under which the aforementioned women joined God's Messenger (S) in battle. There is an inherent disparity in trying to draw an analogy between these two cases. Furthermore, one should probe the statements of our predecessors regarding this issue – they were certainly the most knowledgeable about the meanings of the source texts and closer to the actual implementation of God's Book and the *Sunnah* of His Messenger (S). So what has been narrated from them with the passing of time? Did they enlarge the circle as called for by the proponents of free interaction and so narrate that women could work in all spheres of life with men, invade one another's space and interact freely? Or did they understand that these circumstances were specific and have no bearing on other cases?

If we examine the Islamic conquests and battles throughout history, we will not find this to be the case. What is claimed nowadays about allowing women to carry weapons and fight like men is nothing more than a source of corruption and the dissolution of proper manners under the guise of boosting the morale of the male soldiers.

Men and women, when they meet in seclusion, tend to be drawn to one another. Proximity and soothing dialogue are exchanged between them, and that attracts them to one another. However, one thing leads to another and suppressing enticement is wiser, more judicious, and prevents future remorse.

Hence, Islam is especially keen about effectuating the welfare of the people, suppressing evils, and shutting those doors that lead to them. Therefore, the intermingling between women and men in the workplace is a major cause of societal decadence and the downfall of people, in general, as we have discussed. Historically, it is well known that the decline and collapse of bygone civilizations, such as the Roman and Greek Empires and so on, was caused by women who forsook their private dwellings and entered the domain of men. This intrusion corrupted men's integrity and prompted them to abandon the defense of their societies and the pursuit of material and moral advancement. A woman's preoccupation outside her home leads to male vagrancy, the regression of society, disintegration of the family unit and destruction of its cornerstone, and the corruption of the character of the children. This is not in line with what God revealed in His Book about men being the guardians of women. Islam was particular about distancing women from all elements that contravene their inherent nature, for example, assuming positions of leadership, such as presiding over a country or being a judge, or other positions of general responsibility. God's Messenger (S) said, "A country led by a woman shall never succeed" (al-Bukhārī in his *Ṣaḥīḥ*). Thus, granting her the option to enter the spheres of men counters the intent of the *Sharī'ah*, which aims to preserve her happiness and stability. Islam prohibits drafting women from their indigenous dwellings to serve in the military. It has been established time and again, especially in mixed societies, that men and women are not equal in essence or nature as clearly and evidently articulated in the Book and the *Sunnah*. Yet, those who call for the equality between men and the weaker sex, who are like those raised among trinkets and are unable to give a clear account in a dispute (Qur'ān 43:18), are either ignorant or feigning ignorance about the fundamental differences between the two sexes. In light of these proofs from the *Sharī'ah*, the material reality of the matter is that mixing is forbidden, as is the presence of women in the workplaces of men. These proofs should be sufficient and convincing for those who seek the truth. However, considering that some people benefit more from the discourses of Eastern and Western scholars than from the words of God, the words of His Messenger (S), and the words of Muslim scholars, it is vital that we cite for them what Eastern and Western scholars admit about the harms and costs of loose interaction. Perhaps, thereby, they might be convinced. They [should] already know that by prohibiting intermingling, their honored religion secured a sense of honor, chastity, and protection for women from all avenues of harm and from the desecration of their dignity.

The English writer, Alidade Cook, [?] said, "Because men are quite fond of mixing with women, women have coveted that which contravenes their own nature. With the proliferation of uninhibited interaction, there is a proportionate increase in the rate of illegitimate childbirth, and this has a devastating effect upon women." She concluded by advising, "Teach the women to distance themselves from men and inform them about the consequences of the hidden dangers that await them."

The German scholar Shopenhauer said, "The call for women to join men in men's high aspirations and lofty eminence is a grievous defect in our present condition. This facilitated for women to raise their voices with lowly demands until they destroyed modern civilization with the strength of their influence and their vile opinions."

Lord Byron said: "O reader! If you reflect upon the actions of women at the time of the Greeks, you would find them in an artificial state that defies nature, itself. If you so reflect, you will find yourself in agreement with me that women should be preoccupied with housework. They should dress appropriately and come and go with modesty, while avoiding mixing with the opposite sex."

Samuel Smiles, the Englishman, said: "The type of thinking that calls for employing women in factories, whatever the economic advancement on a national level, will result in a deterioration of family life because it attacks the very foundation of the home, destroys the pillars of the family unit, and severs social ties. It isolates the wife from her husband and the children from their relatives."

"Specifically, the only tangible result is the degeneration of women's moral conduct, for her appropriate vocation is assuming the responsibilities of the home, such as organizing, raising her children, living according to her means, and replenishing whatever household supplies. But the factories have stripped her from the said responsibilities to the extent that homes have become bereft, children grow up ill-mannered and are cast into the corners of negligence, and the passion between spouses has dwindled away. Women are no longer the charming spouses and beloved supporters of their husbands; rather, they are men's co-workers and colleagues. They come under certain influences that, on the whole, eradicate the restraint of their opinions and the humility of their conduct, both of which compose the foundation of all good virtues."

Dr. Adeline said, "The reason for America's family crisis and the mystery behind the increase in crimes in society is that women have abandoned their homes to boost family income. So while income increased, the standards of morality plummeted." She then remarked, "Experience has proven that the only way to rescue future generations from their current miseries is to return women to their homes."

One of the members of the United States Congress said, "Women can truly serve the country if they stay at home, which is the quintessence of the family, itself."

Another member said, "When God conferred the distinction of childbirth upon women, He did not ask them to abandon their children and work outdoors. Rather, He established that their main concern would be staying at home to raise their children."

Shopenhauer, the German, also said, "Grant women their complete, uninhibited freedom without supervision, then meet me a year from now to see the results. However, bear in mind that you and I will eulogize the loss of moral integrity, piety, and propriety. If it is that I die before that time, then you can say, 'He was mistaken' or 'He was correct with the certainty of truth.'" All the aforesaid was related by Dr. Muṣṭafā al-Sibāʿī, may God have mercy upon him, in his book *Women Between Islamic and Secular Law*.

If we wanted to investigate what the impartial scholars of the West have said regarding the harms of unrestricted mixing that actually resulted from the presence of women in men's workplaces, the discourse would be extensive. Highlighting these harms should suffice in lieu of a lengthy discussion.

In a word, a woman's abiding in her own home and assuming household responsibilities therein, after fulfillment of her religious obligations, is the endeavor that corresponds with her nature, disposition, and essence, for in these matters lay her welfare, the welfare of society, and that of future generations.

If she was given talent [by God], then it is possible that she work in women's fields. Women's education and doctoring or nursing women patients are examples of acceptable vocations for women in their own workplaces as we have pointed out before. This type of work would keep them occupied and cooperating with men in building and developing society. Each gender should specialize in their respective fields. Also, we should not forget the role of the Mothers of the Faithful (R) who contributed to the education, direction, and guidance of the community, conveying to them the laws of God and His Messenger (S). May God reward them with goodness for all they did and multiply amongst Muslims today those, who like them, would veil themselves, preserve their chastity, and avoid mixing with men in their workplaces.

We beseech God to grant us understanding in all obligations, to help us in fulfilling them in a manner pleasing to Him, and to protect us from all forms of enticement, causes of corruption, and machinations of Satan. God is Magnanimous and Generous. May God's peace and blessings be upon His Servant and Messenger, our Prophet, Muhammad, and upon his followers and Companions.[29]

*NOTES*

1 This *fatwā* was issued by Ibn Jibrīn in *Fatāwā al-Lajnah*, p. 205.

2 *Maḥram* relatives are blood relatives such as brothers or sons whom a woman cannot marry. Al-Marghīnānī, *al-Hidāyah*, 1:191; Ibn Rushd, *al-Muqaddimāt al-Mumahhidāt*, 1:455–458.

3 Issued by Ṣāliḥ b. Fawzān in *al-Muntaqā*, 5:383–384.

4 Issued by ʿAbd al-Razzāq ʿAfīfī. ʿAbbāsī, *Fatāwā wa Rasāʾil*, 1/2:478. Presumably, the *responsum* is referring to the Islamic ruling that if two suckle from the same woman in the first two years of their lives they become as if sister and brother. See, al-Marghīnānī, *al-Hidāyah*, 1:223; Ibn Qudāmah, *al-Mughnī*, 6:571–572; Ibn Rushd, *al-Muqaddimāt al-Mumahhidāt*, 1:489–496.

5 *Ẓihār* refers to the pre-Islamic Arabian custom, whereby a husband could divorce his wife by simply declaring, "Thou art [henceforth as unlawful] to me as my mother's back." In pagan Arab society, this mode of divorce was considered final and irrevocable; but a woman thus divorced was not allowed to remarry, and had to remain forever in her husband's custody. Under Islamic law, the husband must perform an act of expatiation before resuming the marital relationship. Al-Marghīnānī, *al-Hidāyah*, 2:17–19; Ibn Rushd, *al-Muqaddimāt al-Mumahhidāt*, 1:599–613; Spectorsky, *Chapters on Marriage and Divorce*, pp. 39–42.

6 Issued by al-ʿUthaymīn. Ibn ʿAbd al-Raḥīm, *Fatāwā al-ʿUthaymīn*, 2:757.

7 In these *fatāwā*, the jurists regularly invoke God's peace and blessings upon the Prophet in the supplication "*ṣallā Allāhu ʿalaihi wa sallam.*" Because of limited space, this supplication shall be denoted hereinafter by '(S)'.

8 The *sutrah* is an object placed in front of a person doing the ritual prayer in order to demarcate the area that the individual is praying in. Al-Kāndahlawī, *Awjaz al-Masālik*, 3:152–159; al-Suyūṭī, *Sunan al-Nasāʾī*, 2:62–66; al-Mubārakfūrī, *Tuḥfat al-Aḥwadhī*, pp. 252–254; Ibn Ḥajar al-ʿAsqalānī, *Fatḥ al-Bārī*, 1:693–696; al-Nawawī, *Sharḥ Ṣaḥīḥ Muslim*, 3/4:439–446.

9 Issued by al-ʿUthaymīn. Ibn ʿAbd al-Raḥīm, *Fatāwā al-ʿUthaymīn*, 1:362–363.

10 Issued by al-ʿUthaymīn. Ibn ʿAbd al-Raḥīm, *Fatāwā al-ʿUthaymīn*, 2:753–754.

11 Issued by Ibn Bāz. Ibn Bāz, *Majmūʿ Fatāwā wa Maqālāt Mutanawwiʿah* (1990), 4:29–30.

12 Issued by al-ʿUthaymīn. Ibn ʿAbd al-Raḥīm, *Fatāwā al-ʿUthaymīn*, 2:854–855.

13 *Maḥram* relatives are blood relatives such as brothers or sons whom a woman cannot marry. A woman does not have to wear a veil in the presence of such relatives anyway. Al-Marghīnānī, *al-Hidāyah*, 1:191; Ibn Rushd, *al-Muqaddimāt al-Mumahhidāt*, 1:455–458;

14 Issued by al-ʿUthaymīn. Ibn ʿAbd al-Raḥīm, *Fatāwā al-ʿUthaymīn*, 2:871–872.

15 Issued by a C.R.L.O committee in, *Fatāwā al-Lajnah*, 4:319–320.

16 Issued by Ibn Bāz. Ibn Bāz, *Majmūʿ Fatāwā*, 1:282.

17 Translations of Qurʾānic verses in the appendix are taken verbatim from Yusuf Ali's translation of the Qurʾān. Additionally, in the original Arabic *fatāwā*, Qurʾānic verses are printed in bold type.

18 Issued by Ibn Bāz. Ibn Bāz, *Majmūʿ Fatāwā wa Maqālāt Mutanawwiʿah* (1990), 4:292–294.

19 Issued by C.R.L.O committee in *Fatāwā al-Lajnah*, 1:457–458.

20 In these *fatāwā*, the jurists regularly invoke God's contentment upon the Prophet's Companions in the supplication "*raḍiya Allāhu ʿanhum*." Because of limited space, this supplication shall be denoted hereinafter by '(R)'.

21 Issued by Ibn Bāz. Ibn Bāz, *Majmūʿ Fatāwā wa Maqālāt Mutanawwiʿah* (1990), 3:351–353.

22 Issued by Ibn Bāz. Ibn Bāz, *Fatāwā*, pp. 193–195.

23 Issued by Ṣāliḥ b. Fawzān, in *al-Muntaqā*, 3:242–243.

24 Issued by Ṣāliḥ b. Fawzān. in *al-Muntaqā*, 5:263.

25 Issued by al-ʿUthaymīn. Ibn ʿAbd al-Raḥīm, *Fatāwā al-ʿUthaymīn*, 1:170.

26 Issued by Ibn Bāz. Ibn Bāz, *Majmūʿ Fatāwā wa Maqālāt Mutanawwiʿah* (1990), 4:254–258.

27 The original does not indicate a beginning and end of quote.

28 Issued by Ibn Bāz. Ibn Bāz, *Majmūʿ Fatāwā wa Maqālāt Mutanawwiʿah* (1990), 4:308–310.

29 Issued by Ibn Bāz. Ibn Bāz, *Majmūʿ Fatāwā wa Maqālāt Mutanawwiʿah* (1987), 1:422–431.

# Glossary of terms

*ʿAbbāsid* The second ruling dynasty of the Muslim empire after the Umayyads. Flourished in Baghdad from 132/750 to 656/1258. Thereafter, it survived as a shadow caliphate until 923/1517. See *Umayyad.*

*ʿabd* A slave; *ʿabd Allāh* means the slave of God.

*adillah* (sing. *dalīl*) See *dalīl.*

*adab* Good manners, humaneness, propriety, good character, decency, social etiquette, proper human conduct.

*adab al-munāẓarah* Appropriate conduct among jurists in the course of argument or dispute over issues of legal import.

*ʿādah* Regular or customary practice. See *ʿurf* and *sunnah.*

*ʿadālah* Trustworthiness of a transmitter of *ḥadīth* reports.

*ʿādat al-nās* Customs of people. See *ʿādah.*

*ʿadl* Justice, impartiality, fairness, uprightness; synonym of *qisṭ*. See *qisṭ.*

*al-ʿadl wa al-tarjīḥ* Complex science documenting and evaluating the authenticity of traditions. See *isnād.*

*āḥād* *Ḥadīth* reported by a singular transmissions whose legal effect is debated by the various schools of Islamic jurisprudence. See *mutawātir.*

*aḥādīth* (sing. *ḥadīth*) Sometimes referred to as *ḥadīths*; the body of reports attributed to the Prophet. See *ḥadīth.*

*aḥkām* (sing. *ḥukm*) Rules of law, positive commandments. See *ḥukm.*

*ahl al-ahwāʾ* Syn. of *ahl al-bidaʿ*; people of whim and caprice. See *ahl al-bidaʿ* and *hawā.*

*ahl al-bidaʿ* Innovators, heretics, people of heterodoxy. See *bidʿah.*

*ahl al-dhikr* People of knowledge who remember God much.

*ahl al-ḥadīth* As distinguished from *ahl al-raʾy*, scholars who favor a literalist approach and de-emphasize the role of reason in the analysis of source texts or *nuṣūṣ*. See *ahl al-raʾy* and *naṣṣ.*

*ahl al-raʾy* As distinguished from *ahl al-ḥadīth*, rationalist scholars who employed reason in legal analysis in contradistinction to literalists. The use of reason was often limited to the use of analogy. However, the parameters and methodology of analogy was ill-defined in early Islam. Also used to refer to Kufan or Ḥanafī jurists. See *ahl al-ḥadīth.*

*ahl al-sunnah wa al-jamāʿah* Adherents to the *Sunnah* of Prophet Muḥammad and the greater community of Muslims.

Synonymous with Sunnīs as opposed to Shīʿīs.

*ajnabī* As distinguished from *maḥram*, a man who cannot serve as the legal guardian of a woman; a marriageable person, according to Islamic law; any man to which the woman could potentially marry.

*āmīn* Expression uttered after a supplication meaning: "Please answer my prayer."

*amīr* (pl. *umarāʾ*) Ruler or prince.

*ʿāmm* Interpretive category used in legal analysis connoting that which is general, as distinguished from *khāṣṣ* or specific. See *khāṣṣ*.

*ʿaqāʾid* (sing. *aqīdah*) See *ʿaqīdah*.

*ʿaqīdah* (pl. *aqāʾid*) Literally, derives from the triliteral *ʿ-qa-da*, "to tie a knot" or "to enter into a contract." Islamic theology: belief system or articles of faith to which one is tied, as in a contract.

*ʿaql* Mind, intellect, reason, rationality. The Qurʾān consistently calls upon men and women to apply their intellects in reflection and analysis.

*asbāb al-nuzūl* Occasions for which Qurʾānic verses were revealed to the Prophet. See *ʿilm asbāb al-nuzūl*.

*Ashʿarī* (*Ashʿariyyah*) Adherent of the theological school named after its eponym Abū Ḥasan al-Ashʿarī (d. 324/936). One of two main Sunnī theological schools, it spread widely during the ʿAbbāsid caliphate. The school argued that the anthropomorphic expressions about God in the Qurʾān are to be interpreted to disallow for any likeness between the Creator and His creatures. The school was attacked by the Ḥanbalīs for using rational arguments and by the Māturīdiyyah for being too conservative. See *Māturīdī*.

*aṣl* (pl. *uṣūl*) Source, origin, root or basis. Islamic law: a theological basic principle upon which disagreement is purportedly not permitted. See *uṣūl*.

*āthār* Inherited wise traditions from the Companions, successors, or scholarly or righteous people; usually distinguished from the Prophetic *ḥadīth*. See *ḥadīth*.

*awqāf* (sing. *waqf*) See *waqf*.

*ʿawrah* Private areas of the human body to be covered in the presence of others with loose and opaque clothing in order to preserve modesty. Whether cultural norms may be considered in defining modesty is subject to debate. The areas that should be covered are different for men and women.

*badhl al-juhd* Expending every possible effort in conscientiously and diligently searching and evaluating the evidence of God's law.

*badhl al-naẓar* See *badhl al-juhd*.

*badhl al-wusʿ* See *badhl al-juhd*.

*bidaʿ* (sing. *bidʿah*) See *bidʿah*.

*bidʿah* (pl. *bidaʿ*) Lit., innovation, often refers to a heretical or illegal innovation in religion. *Bidʿah ḥasanah* is a good or desirable innovation while *bidʿah sayyiʾah* is a bad or undesirable innovation.

*dalīl* (pl. *adillah*) Legal proof, evidence or indicators. Islamic law: the indicators pointing to the law of God.

*dalīl ʿaqlī* Rational proof, an element in the legal analysis dictated by rational proof or evidence.

*dalīl naṣṣī* Textual evidence or proof, evidence from a textual source; also known as *dalīl samʿī*.

*ḍarūrah* (pl. *ḍarūriyyāt*) See *ḍarūriyyāt*.

*ḍarūriyyāt* (sing. *ḍarūrah*) Basic necessities of human beings that the law must fulfill. Necessities are considered more compelling than needs (*ḥājiyyāt*). See *ḥājiyyāt*.

*ḍarūriyyāt ʿaqliyyah* Rational necessities.

*al-ḍarūriyyāt al-khamsah* Five fundamental values that *Sharīʿah* seeks to guard: religion, life, intellect, lineage, property.

*dhū ʿaql* Rationally thoughtful person.

*faḥṣ* Examination, investigation, scrutiny, search, inquiry.

*faqīh* (pl. *fuqahāʾ*) A jurist, one learned in the science of *fiqh*. See *fiqh*.

*farʿ* (pl. *furūʿ*) Branch, sub-division, as distinguished from *aṣl*. Islamic law: a branch or sub-division in which disagreement is permitted; a new and original problem or case. See *aṣl*.

*farḍ* Syn. of *wājib*. Islamic law: one of the five categories or values of *Sharīʿah*, connoting that which is obligatory or mandatory. Some schools of thought distinguish *farḍ* from *wājib*. See *wājib* and *Sharīʿah*.

*farḍ ʿayn* As distinguished from *farḍ kifāyah*, an obligation that is incumbent upon every Muslim in society. See *farḍ kifāyah*.

*farḍ kifāyah* As distinguished from *farḍ ʿayn*, an obligation that must be performed by a sufficient number of people in society. See *farḍ ʿayn*.

*farīḍah* Mandated religious obligation.

*fāsiq* (pl. *fāsiqūn* or *fussāq*) Iniquitous, sinner, corrupt. An impious person.

*fatāwā* (sing. *fatwā*) See *fatwā*.

*fatwā* (pl. *fatāwā*) Non-binding legal opinion issued in response to a legal problem.

*fiqh* Lit., the understanding. Islamic law: the process of jurisprudence by which the rules of Islamic law are derived. The word is also used to refer generally to law.

*fitan* (sing. *fitnah*) See *fitnah*.

*fitnah* (pl. *fitan*) Calamity, corruption, civil discord. Enticement or seduction.

*fiṭrah* Inner essence of an individual or intuitive sense by which one distinguishes right from wrong and moral from immoral.

*fuqahāʾ* (sing. *faqīh*) See *faqīh*.

*furūʿ* (sing. *farʿ*) See *farʿ*.

*fussāq* (sing. *fāsiq*) See *fāsiq*.

*ghalabat al-ẓann* Preponderence of belief or evidence.

*ḥadīth* (pl. *aḥādīth*) Lit., report, account or statement. Islamic law: a Prophetic tradition transmitted through a chain of narrators by which the Prophet or his *Sunnah* is known. The term may also be used to refer to a statement by one of the Companions. See *Sunnah* and *ahl al-ḥadīth*.

*ḥājiyyāt* Basic needs that are less expedient than *ḍarūriyyāt*. See *ḍarūriyyāt*.

*ḥākimiyyah* Sovereignty of God.

*ḥalāl* Syn. of *mubāḥ*. Islamic law: one of the five categories or values of *Sharīʿah*, connoting that which is permitted or allowed. Most schools hold that everything is permitted unless there is evidence declaring it to be prohibited. Most schools adhere to a presumption of permissibility, and so the burden of proof is against the person who is arguing for a prohibition. See *Sharīʿah*.

*Ḥanafī* (*Ḥanafiyyah*) Adherent of the Sunnī juristic school of thought named after its eponym Abū Ḥanīfah al-Nuʿmān (d. 150/767). One of the four main Sunnī jurisprudential schools, it originated in Kūfa and Baṣra, but spread in the Middle East and Indian subcontinent.

*Ḥanbalī* (*Ḥanābilah*) Adherent of the Sunnī juristic school of thought named after its eponym Aḥmad b. Ḥanbal (d. 241/855). One of the four main Sunnī jurisprudential schools, its adherents are found primarily in Saudi Arabia.

*ḥaqīqī* Literal; the apparent meaning of a text, as distinguished from *majāzī*. See *majāzī*.

*ḥarām* Syn. of *maḥẓūr*. Islamic law: one of the five categories or values of *Sharīʿah*, connoting that which is forbidden or sinful. See *Sharīʿah*.

*ḥasanah bi dhātihā* That which has an inherent moral quality, as distinguished from *qabīḥah bi dhātihā*. See *qabīḥah bi dhātihā*.

*hawā* Whim, caprice, or fancy.

*ḥijāb* Lit., obstruction, shield, shelter, protection, cover, screen, seclusion, obscure and hide. The veil with which a Muslim woman covers her head, except her face.

*Hijrah* Lit., migrate, desert, or abandon. Refers to the historical migration of Prophet Muhammad and his Companions from Mecca to Medina in the year 622 C.E.

*ḥukm* (pl. *aḥkām*) Decree of God. Islamic law: a legally binding judgment, ruling, rules of law.

*ḥukm Allāh* The ruling or judgment of God.

*ḥukm muʿayyan* Particular ruling. See *ḥukm*.

*ḥuqūq al-ādamiyyīn* Human rights; lit., the rights of the progeny of Adam.

*ḥuqūq Allāh* As distinguished from *ḥuqūq al-ʿibād*, rights of God upon humanity, the infraction of which may or may not be forgiven. See *ḥuqūq al-ʿibād*.

*ḥuqūq al-ʿibād* As distinguished from *ḥuqūq Allāh*, rights of individuals upon one another, the infraction of which God will not forgive unless the wronged party forgives.

*ḥurriyyah* Freedom, liberty, discretion.

*ḥusn* Lit. the beautiful or good. Islamic law: that which is moral and good.

*iḥsān* Beneficence, moral excellence, the epitome of goodness; described by the Prophet as fulfilling the Divine will as if one actually beholds God.

*ijmāʿ* Lit., consensus, agreement. Islamic law: consensus of legal opinion. Jurists differed, however, about the binding nature of *ijmāʿ*, requirements of eligibility, conditions for its nullification, whether or not it is limited by time and place, etc.

*ijtihād* Lit., exertion. The process of exerting one's utmost in an effort to deduce laws from sources in unprecedented cases. Novel or original legal solutions, the effort of a jurist in searching for and deducing the correct law. See *taqlīd*.

*ikrāh* Compulsion; Islam forbids compulsion in matters pertinent to religion.

*ikhtilāf* Juristic disagreement and diversity of opinion.

*ikhtilāṭ* Mixing, intermingling; often refers to commingling between men and women

*ʿilal* (sing. *ʿillah*) See *ʿillah*.

*ʿillah* (pl. *ʿilal*) Lit., the cause. Islamic law: the operative or effective cause of a ruling, the *ratio legis*. In the language of jurists, "*al-ʿillah tadūr maʿa al-maʿlūl wujūdan wa ʿadaman*" (The rule exists if the operative cause exists and the rule does not exist if the operative cause does not exist).

*ʿilm* Knowledge, learning, science, or religious learning. *ʿIlm* yields *qaṭʿ* (certainty), *ẓann* (probability, likelihood), or *shakk* (doubt). Opposite of *ʿilm* is *jahl* (ignorance).

*ʿilm al-dīn* Religious learning, usually a reference to knowledge of Islam as a science, encompassing its branches.

*ʿilm al-dirāyah* Branch of *ʿilm al-ḥadīth*, also known as *ʿilm al-ḥadīth al-khāṣṣ bi-al-dirāyah*, which evaluates the historical plausibility, social implications, and categories of *ḥadīth* as factors to be considered in a legal decision or in formulating the law. See *ʿilm al-riwāyah*.

*ʿilm al-ḥadīth* Science of *ḥadīth* methodology, comprising the authentication of *ḥadīth* based on chains of transmission and contextual analysis.

*ʿilm al-kalām* Science of theology and dogmatics, scholastic theology. Considered reprehensible in contemporary Wahhābī thought.

*ʿilm al-riwāyah* Science of transmission that includes a keen familiarity of the transmitters of *ḥadīth*, their trustworthiness, and the soundness of reports. A branch of *ʿilm al-ḥadīth*. See *ʿilm al-ḥadīth* and *ʿilm al-dirāyah*.

*ʿilm al-taʿādul wa al-tarjīḥ* See *tarjīḥ*.

*ʿilm al-taʿāruḍ wa al-tarjīḥ* See *tarjīḥ*.

*ʿilm al-tafsīr* Science of Qurʾānic exegesis. See *tafsīr*.

*ʿilm asbāb al-nuzūl* Science of the occasions and situations for which Qurʾānic verses were revealed and concerned with ascertaining God's original Intent, given human limitations, in order to apply the verse in the formulation of law.

*imām* Lit., one who stands out in front. Islamic law: leader of prayer or of a congregation. Commonly used to refer to a religious leader.

*īmān* Lit., belief, faith, conviction. Islamic law: belief in God, His angels, His revealed books including the Qurʾān, the Messengers including Muhammad, and His foreknowledge.

*irjāʾ* Suspension of judgment. See *Murjiʾah*.

*isnād* Chain of transmission for a report or tradition traced back to Prophet Muhammad. One of two prongs tested to establish the authenticity of a *ḥadīth*, the other being contextual analysis of meaning, i.e. *matn* analysis. See *matn*.

*al-istibdād bi al-raʾy* Authoritarianism, intellectual despotism.

*istifrāgh al-wusʿ* See *badhl al-juhd*.

*istiḥsān* Juristic preference, equity, something that is good. Islamic law: a juristic method that considers equity in applying the law. Application of discretion in a legal decision.

*istikhrāj ʿillat al-ḥukm* Islamic law: the derivation of the operative cause of a ruling or judgment.

*istimtāʿ* Enjoyment or pleasure. See *mutʿah*.

*istiṣlāḥ* Islamic law: juristic consideration of equity or public interest in the formulation of a legal decision.

*al-jadal wa al-munāẓarah* See *adab al-munāẓarah*.

*Jaʿfarī (Jaʿfariyyah)* Adherent of the Shīʿī juristic school of thought named after its eponym Jaʿfar al-Ṣādiq (d. 148/765), the sixth Imām in Shīʿī theology. One of the main jurisprudential schools founded in Madīnah.

*jamāʿah* Critical mass or majority of God-fearing Muslims or orthodoxy.

*jayb* Lit., any two objects that conjoin or meet. Bosom of a human being, top of a woman's cleavage, shirt, garment, pocket, all of which comprise the conjunction of two individual parts. Also, meeting of the chest and neck, areas of the human body subject to concealment.

*jihād* Lit., exertion, striving. Struggle for the sake of God, whether for self-discipline and self-purification or against oppression and injustice.

*jizyah* Tax imposed upon non-Muslims citizens of an Islamic State in exchange for protection from internal and external enemies.

*jahd al-qarīḥah* See *badhl al-juhd*.

*kāfir* (pl. *kuffār*) Non-believer, someone who denies God or prophethood of Muḥammad. Someone who is ungrateful towards God. See *kufr*.

*kalām* See *ʿilm al-kalām*.

*kamāliyyāt* See *taḥsīniyyāt*.

*khabar* Narration or report; an assertion.

*al-khabar al-mutawātir* See *mutawātir*.

*al-khabar al-wāḥid* See *āḥād*.

*khafiyy* Inward, concealed, hidden, allegorical, metaphorical. Refers to the allegorical meaning of a source text (*naṣṣ*), as distinguished from the literal (*ẓāhir*). See *ẓāhir* and *naṣṣ*.

*khalīfah* (pl. *khulafāʾ*) Lit., caliph, successive authority, deputy; inheritor, viceroy, agent, successive authority. The Qurʾān charges human beings with being the *khalīfah* on earth (2:30). Refers to the head of the Islamic state after the death of the Prophet.

*khalwah* Seclusion, isolation; often refers to the seclusion of a man and woman who could potentially marry according to Islamic law. See *ajnabī*.

*khānqāh* Convent inhabited by righteous Ṣūfīs and men of learning. Instituted in the 5th/11th century for Ṣūfī recluses to employ themselves therein in the service of God. See *Ṣūfī*.

*khāṣṣ* That which is specific and particular, as distinguished from *ʿāmm* or general. See *ʿāmm*.

*Khawārij* Seditionists who dissented from the supporters of ʿAlī when he agreed to arbitrate with Muʿāwiyah.

*khimār* Lit., scarf, partition, turban, piece of cloth, flowing garb, garb without stitches. Figuratively, spiritual and mental states. See *ḥijāb*.

*khulafāʾ* (sing. *khalīfah*) See *khalīfah*.

*kuffār* (sing. *kāfir*) See *kāfir* and *kufr*.

*kufr* Lit., to cover or bury underground. To this effect, the term is found in the Qurʾān in its plual form (*kuffār*) as a reference to farmers, who bury seeds underground and cover them with earth (57:20). Islamic theology: covering over the truth once one has recognized it as true, i.e. rejecting the message of Islam. Ingratitude or infidelity, not believing in God or ingratitude towards God, an act of disbelief.

*madhāhib* (sing. *madhhab*) See *madhhab*.

*madhhab* (pl. *madhāhib*) School of thought, juristic school, legal guild, orientation, opinion or view. A juristic school of thought is distinguished by its jurisprudential methodology for deducing laws. Disagreements over methodology often distinguish one school from another.

*maḥram* A male relationship to a woman; a husband or a certain blood relative such as a father, brother, son, or uncle.

*maḥẓūr* See *ḥarām* and *Sharīʿah*.

*majāzī* Metaphorical; the figurative meaning of a text, as distinguished from *ḥaqīqī*. See *ḥaqīqī*.

*makrūh* Islamic law: one of the five categories or values of *Sharīʿah*, connoting that which is reprehensible, discouraged, not preferred. See *Sharīʿah*.

*Mālikī* (*Mālikiyyah*) Adherent of the Sunnī juristic school of thought named after its eponym Mālik b. Anas (d. 179/795) and distinguished for its emphasis on the practice of the inhabitants of Madīnah. One of the four main Sunnī jurisprudential schools that later predominated in Muslim Spain. Today, it is widespread in North and sub-Saharan Africa.

*mandūb* See *mustaḥabb* and *Sharīʿah*.

*mansūkh* Qurʾānic verse or *ḥadīth* whose legal effect is abrogated by a Qurʾānic verse or *ḥadīth*. An abrogated law or text. See *naskh*.

*maqāṣid al-Sharīʿah* Lit., purposes or goals. Islamic law: the ideal purposes of Islamic law. See *Sharīʿah*.

*maʿrūf* That which is commonly known to be right; kindness and generosity. Muslims have the dual obligation of practicing it and enjoining others to do the same.

*masānīd* (sing. *musnad*) See *musnad*.

*mashhūr* Syn. of *mushtahirah*. Well-known, generally accepted, vastly circulated.

*mashrūṭ* That which is contingent or dependent upon another.

*maṣlaḥah* Public interest; a juristic assumption that considers public interest, and general welfare in applying the law.

*mathal* Symbol, parable, metaphor, simile.

*matn* Substance. Islamic law: Analysis of the substantive content of a *ḥadīth*; one of two prongs tested to establish the authenticity of a *ḥadīth*, the other being chain of transmission. Accordingly, a *ḥadīth* may be rejected if it contains grammatical or historical errors, contradicts the Qurʾān, conflicts with the laws of nature, common experience, or the dictates of reason, regardless of its chain of transmission.

*Māturīdī (Māturīdiyyah)* Adherent of the theological school named after its eponym Abū Manṣūr al-Māturīdī (c. 333/944). One of two main Sunnī theological schools, it spread widely during the Mamlūk age. The school affirmed the rational basis of good and evil, the freedom of choice in decisions, and faith as assent and confession excluding works. See *Ashʿarī.*

*mawḍūʿ* Fabricated *ḥadīth* that cannot be used as evidence in law.

*miḥnah* Inquisition, trial or tribulation. Historically, theological inquisition imposed by the ʿAbbāsid caliph al-Maʾmūn (r. 197/813–217/833) and lasted until the reign of al-Mutawakkil (r. 232/847–247/861). Under Muʿtazilī influence, the Inquisition punished anyone who declared the Qurʾān to be the uncreated speech of God and not a created revelation, e.g. Aḥmad b. Ḥanbal (d. 241/855).

*misyār* Marriage conceived in which one spouse conceals his or her intent to divorce after a specific period of time. Although forbidden in the major Sunnī schools of jurisprudence, jurists of Saudia Arabia permit this practice. See mutʿah.

*muʾakkid* Report that lends emphasis and support.

*mubāḥ* See *ḥalāl* and *Sharīʿah.*

*mubham* That which is unclear, obscure, vague, such that there is no way of knowing it.

*mubīḥ* Grant of freedom of action.

*mubtadiʿ* One who introduces a *bidʿah*; an innovator. See *bidʿah.*

*mufassar* Unequivocal, specific, clearly explained, as distinguished from *mujmal.* See *mujmal.*

*muftī* Scholar who is qualified to issue legal *responsa.* See *fatwā.*

*muḥaddith* Scholar who memorizes *ḥadīth* with their chains of transmission and transmits them. See *ḥadīth.*

*muḥkam* Inherently clear, beyond doubt, and not susceptible to abrogation or interpretation. Qurʾānic verses whose meanings are clearly intelligible and allow for only one clearly definitive interpretation, as distinguished from the *mutashābih*, which allows for a range of interpretation and a diversity of opinion. See *mutashābih* and *mushkil.*

*muḥtamal* Bearable, probable, tolerable, likely. Refers to the ability to know the meanings of a Qurʾānic verse or passage.

*mujmal* Ambivalent, that which requires explanation, non-specific, summation, general, as distinguished from *mufassar.* See *mufassar.*

*mujtahid* As distinguished from *muqallid*, a jurist who performs *ijtihād* or is qualified to perform *ijtihād.* See *ijtihād* and *muqallid.*

*mujtahid mubtadiʿ* A term used in some sources to describe mujtahid who creates unprecedented doctrines. Arguably, however, every *mujtahid*, by definition, is a *mubtadiʿ*.

*mukhtaṣar* Abridged version of a larger text or a legal hornbook.

*mulk* Dominion, kingdom, royalty, monarchy, dynastic rule, with which the term *mālik* (king) is associated.

*mumāṭalah* Syn. of *tanaṭṭuʿ*. Procrastination, deferment, postponement, delay, pedantic obstructionism.

*munāfiqūn* (sing. *munāfiq*) Hypocrites who profess Islam but behave contrarily, work to undermine it, do not uphold its tenets, and so forth.

*munāẓarah* Legal debates and discussions.

*muqallid* As distinguished from *mujtahid*, one who is bound by precedent by imitating more knowledgeable scholars, usually within a particular school. See *taqlīd* and *mujtahid.*

*muqayyad* Limited, confined, qualified, as distinguished from *muṭlaq*. See *muṭlaq*.

*murīd* Lit., one who yearns or desires. In Ṣūfī tradition, novice or disciple of a Ṣūfī order who yearns or aspires for higher spiritual stations.

*Murji'ah* Branch in early Islam that played a significant political role. Their ideas were often described as politically quietist or passive. The basic tenet of their belief was that those who committed grave sins do not cease to be Muslims. They also believed in the suspension of judgment (*irjā'*) on political conflicts until God resolves all matters in the Hereafter.

*Murji'ī* Adherent of the Murji'ah theological school. See *Murji'ah*.

*mushkil* Source text that is inherently ambiguous or rendered ambiguous by its context, as distinguished from *muḥkam*.

*mushtahirah* See *mashhūr*.

*mushtarak* Homonym; a word or phrase that has more than one meaning.

*musnad* (pl. *masānīd*) Islamic law: a *ḥadīth* with a continuous chain of transmitters; a compilation of reports and traditions from and about the Prophet and the Companions organized by the name of the transmitter. Often distinguished from *sunan*, which is arranged topically.

*mustaḥabb* Islamic law: one of the five categories or values of *Sharī'ah*, connoting that which is recommended, commendable, preferred. See *Sharī'ah*.

*mut'ah* Lit., pleasure, delight, gratification. In *ḥadīth* literature, may refer to a marriage consummated with the mutual intent of both parties to nullify after the agreed time elapses, sexual pleasure, alimony, ritual acts performed during pilgrimage. See *misyār*.

*mutashābih* Equivocal, ambiguous, susceptible to different interpretations because of the lack of precedent in usage. Qur'ānic verses whose meanings are not clearly intelligible and allow for a range of interpretation and a diversity of opinion, as distinguished from the *muḥkam*, which allows for only one clearly definitive interpretation. See *muḥkam*.

*muta'awwilah* Female rebel with a principled cause.

*mutawātir* *Ḥadīth* reported by a large number of people, a report having cumulative authenticity because of the presumption that it could not have possibly been fabricated by such a large number of transmitters. Reports that have been transmitted in this fashion are considered of certain attribution. In the classical tradition, a rejection of such reports (e.g. the Qur'ān) excludes one from Islam.

*Mu'tazilah* Rationalist school of Islamic theology that emphasized the role of reason and the belief in the absolute necessity of God's justice and human free will. The term came to connote a variety of theological and juristic orientations. The basic tenets of the school were the belief that the Qur'ān was created and that the physical attributes of God mentioned in the Qur'ān are allegorical.

*Mu'tazilī* Adherent of the Mu'tazilah theological school. See *Mu'tazilah*.

*muṭlaq* Absolute, unrestricted, without exception, unqualified, as distinguished from *muqayyad*. See *muqayyad*.

*nāsikh* Abrogator; usually, the Qur'ānic verse that abrogated the legal effect or the text of an earlier verse or *ḥadīth*. See *naskh*.

*naskh* Doctrine that God abrogated or repealed the text or legal effect of Qur'ānic verses. It is debated whether a *ḥadīth* can abrogate the legal effect of a Qur'ānic verse. The majority position is that a Qur'ānic verse can abrogate the legal effect of another verse or *ḥadīth*, but that a *ḥadīth* can only abrogate the legal effect of another *ḥadīth*.

*naṣṣ* (pl. *nuṣūṣ*) Text from which the law is derived; an injunction or textual ruling.

*naẓar* Inspection, study, investigation, contemplation, perception, insight, discernment.

*nuṣūṣ* (sing. *naṣṣ*) See *naṣṣ*.

*qabīḥah bi dhātihā* That which has an inherent immoral quality, as distinguished from *ḥasanah bi dhātihā*. See *ḥasanah bi dhātihā*.

*qaḍā'* Judgment of God; the judiciary.

*qāḍī* (pl. *quḍāh)* Judge.

*qānūn* Secular positive law, as distinguished from Islamic law.

*qāri'* (pl. *qurrā'*) Lit., reciters; refers to religious puritans who recited the Qur'ān and lived at the outskirts of Madīnah at the time of the Prophet. They were the progenitors of the Khawārij. See *Khawārij*.

*qaṭ'* Definitive, certain, not speculative.

*qaṭ'ī* See *qaṭ'*.

*qawwāmūna* Those who provide support, protection maintenance, guardianship, sustenance. Refers to the duties of men towards women.

*qillat adab* Lack of good manners, inappropriate behavior, lack of taste or decency.

*qisṭ* Equity, justice, even-handedness, fairness; syn. of *'adl*. See *'adl*.

*qiwāmah* (or *qawāmah*) Support, protection maintenance, guardianship, sustenance.

*qiyās* Deduction by analogy. Islamic law: juristic methodology that relies on the use of analogy for unprecedented cases in which the source texts do not provide a conclusive legal decision. A methodology by which the ruling of a precedent is extended to a new case.

*qubḥ* Ugliness. Islamic law: Immorality.

*quḍāh* (sing. *qāḍī*) See *qāḍī*.

*qudrah* Capacity, capability, ability; strength, aptitude, power.

*Qurayshī* Descendent of the tribe of *Quraysh*, the leading tribe of Mecca from which Prophet Muhammad was born around 570 C.E. *Quraysh* spearheaded the early battles against the Prophet before accepting his message upon his return to Makkah.

*qurrā'* See *qāri'*.

*quṭb* Lit., pole, axis, or pivot. In Ṣūfī tradition, the highest representative of the mystical hierarchy.

*Ramaḍān* Ninth month of the Islamic calendar year. Marks the fourth of five pillars of Islam during which Muslims abstain from food, drink, conjugal relations and all sins and indecencies from dawn to sunset each day.

*ra'y* Opinion, judgment.

*sadd al-dharī'ah* Lit., blocking the means or prevention of harm. Islamic law: juristic assumption used in the formulation of law that prevents the commission of forbidden acts by forbidding the means to those acts. This concept is derived from some doctrinal sources that suggest that it is appropriate to prevent harm before it actually materializes

*ṣaḥābah* Companions of the Prophet.

*ṣaḥīḥ* Lit., authentic, valid, true, correct. Islamic law: report or tradition considered validly traced to the Prophet after rigorous analysis based on chain of transmission and contextual meaning. The six canonical collections (*ṣiḥāḥ*) of *ḥadī*th considered to be authoritative by Sunnī Muslims were compiled by: al-Bukhārī, Muslim, al-Nasā'ī, Ibn Mājah, Abū Dāwūd and al-Tirmidhī.

*Shāfi'ī* (*Shāfi'iyyah*) Adherent of the Sunnī juristic school of thought named after its eponym Muḥammad b. Idrīs al-Shāfi'ī (d. 204/820). One of the four main Sunnī jurisprudential schools, it is widespread in the Muslim world today.

*shar' man qablanā* Precedent legislation of bygone generations; past course of conduct of people, which is considered in investigating the Divine Will.

*Sharīʿah* Lit., water source, the way, the path; Islamic theology and law: the path or way given by God to human beings, the path by which human beings search God's Will. Commonly misinterpreted as "Islamic law," *Sharīʿah* carries a much broader meaning as the sum total of categorizations of all human actions, namely: mandatory (*farḍ* or *wājib*), encouraged (*mustaḥabb* or *mandūb*), permissible (*ḥalāl* or *mubāḥ*), discouraged (*makrūh*), and forbidden (*ḥarām* or *maḥẓūr*). *Sharīʿah* is not restricted to positive law *per se* but includes moral and ethical values, and the jurisprudential process, itself.

*shaykh* Lit., old man, master, leader. Often used to describe a learned man or religious scholar and teacher.

*Shīʿah* Lit., party or faction; historically, a group among the Muslims that called for the caliphate of ʿAlī, the Prophet's cousin, after the Prophet's death. Today, the Shīʿah are the largest group of Muslims after the Sunnīs. See *Sunnī.*

*Shīʿī* As distinguished from *Sunnī*, an adherent of the *Shīʿah*. See *Shīʿah.*

*shirk* Polytheism or the association of partners with God. Believing in gods other than the One God.

*shūrā* Consultative body, council, consultation and advice. The Qur'ān commands that the affairs of the community be run by *shūrā*. In very early Muslim discourses, accusing a leader of abandoning the *shūrā* was the equivalent of claiming that the leader lacked legitimacy.

*sīrah* Lit., derives from *sāra*, he walked. Refers to the biography of the Prophet, i.e. how he walked and the path he tread throughout his life.

*al-ṣirāṭ al-mustaqīm* Straight path which is tread by prophets, the truthful, martyrs, and the righteous (4:68–69).

*subḥān Allāh* See *tasbīḥ*.

*Ṣūfī* Lit., one who wears a coat of wool. This term has been applied to Muslims who seek to achieve higher degrees of spiritual excellence or those who pursue Islamic mysticism or those who belong to a mystical order.

*sunan* (sing. *sunnah*) Islamic law: a compilation of reports and traditions from and about the Prophet and Companions organized by topic, as distinguished from *masānīd*, which are organized by the name of the transmitter. Also, supererogatory acts of worship. The non-binding precedents and acts of the Prophet that are followed in order to gain favor with God. See *sunnah.*

*sunnah* Lit., the way or course or conduct of life. Islamic law: the example of the Prophet embodied in his statements, actions, and those matters that he silently approved or disapproved as reported in *ḥadīth* literature. Also refers to Sunnī Muslims as distinguished from the Shīʿah branch of Islam.

*sunnat al-kawn* Laws through which God sustains the universe, which are considered in investigating the Divine Will.

*sunnat al-khalq* Laws of nature, patterns of creation.

*Sunnī* As distinguished from Shīʿī, the main branch of Islam. Sunnis accept the legitimacy of the caliphate of Abū Bakr, ʿUmar, ʿUthmān, and ʿAlī.

*tābiʿīn* Successors; the immediate Successors to the Companions of Prophet Muḥammad who embraced Islam or were raised as Muslims after the death of the Prophet. See *ṣaḥābah.*

*ṭabīʿat al-khalq* Human nature or the habits and intuitions of human beings which are considered in investigating the Divine Will.

*tafsīr* Exegesis or commentary, particularly as it relates to the Qur'ān. Similar to *ta'wīl*, except that some scholars hold *tafsīr* to refer to the explanation of the literal words of the Qur'ān, as opposed to its underlying interpretations. Other scholars make no such distinction. See *ta'wīl.*

*taghannī* Singing, as in a hymn or a song.

*taḥqīq maṣāliḥ al-ʿibād* To achieve the welfare or good of the people; purpose or object of Islamic law.

*taḥsīniyyāt* Syn. of *kamāliyyāt*; luxuries or embellishments.

*takfīr* Declaring someone to be a disbeliever.

*takhrīj* Extraction and derivation of the law according to systematic principles.

*taklīf* Islamic law: legal charge or obligation set by God upon a discerning person who has reached puberty.

*ṭalab* Request, seeking, asking, searching; usually used for seeking knowledge. See *ṭalab al-ʿilm.*

*ṭalab al-dalīl* Seeking evidence or proof; synonymous with seeking knowledge. See *talab al-ʿilm.*

*ṭalab al-ʿilm* Seeking knowledge, which is a religious obligation upon every Muslim man and woman. See *ʿilm.*

*talfīq* Choosing and mixing between various schools of jurisprudence in order to reach the most prudent and useful results.

*ta'līf* Process of reconciling conflicting evidence.

*tamattuʿ* One of four choices in the performance of pilgrimage in which the major and minor pilgrimages are performed separately with an interruption between them. See *mutʿah.*

*tanaṭṭuʿ* See *mumāṭalah.*

*tanqīḥ* Checking, re-examination, editing, revision. In technical usage, it means to investigate and extract the relevant elements through a process of authentication.

*taqiyyah* Shīʿī doctrine of dissimulation.

*taqlīd* Lit., imitation; Islamic law: the term signifies the imitation of more knowledgeable scholars, usually within a particular school of thought. *Taqlīd* is often considered the opposite of *ijtihād.* See *ijtihād.*

*tarjīḥ* (pl. *tarjīḥāt*) To incline, to prefer more, to give more weight to, to preponderate. Islamic law: to prefer or give more weight to particular evidence or to an opinion according to systematic principles often when the evidence or opinions are conflicting.

*tarjīḥāt* (sing. *tarjīḥ*) See *tarjīḥ.*

*tasbīḥ* Supplication in which a Muslim utters "subḥān Allāh," meaning: God is free and far-removed from all imperfections.

*taṣḥīḥ* Verification, authentication; the process of verifying the authenticity of a report.

*tawātur* See *mutawātir.*

*tawfīq bayn al-mukhtalif* See *ta'līf.*

*ta'wīl* Allegorical interpretation, particularly as it relates to the Qurʿān. Similar to *tafsīr*, except that some scholars hold *ta'wīl* to refer to the interpretation of the concealed, inward meanings of the Qur'ān, as opposed to its outward meanings. Other scholars make no such distinction. *Ta'wīl* also refers to an interpretation or ideology adopted by rebels. See *tafsīr.*

*ta'wīl al-ḥadīth* Interpretation of the meanings of *ḥadīth.* Commonly referred to as *sharḥ al-ḥadīth.*

*al-ta'wīlāt al-muzalzalah* Unsettling or troublesome interpretations of the Qur'ān.

*ʿulamā'* The jurists. Scholars of eminence in one or more of the Islamic sciences.

*ʿulūm al-Qur'ān* Sciences of the Qur'ān, encompassing the fields and subcategories of revelation, oral transmission, recording, textual preservation, memorization, exegesis (*tafsīr*), occasions for revelation (*asbāb al-nuzūl*), abrogation (*naskh*), rules of recitation, dialects of recitation, miracles. See *tafsīr*, *ʿilm asbāb al-nuzūl*, and *naskh*.

*umarāʾ* (sing. *amīr*) Rulers of a country or empire, political leaders. See *amīr*.

*Umayyad* First Muslim dynasty initiated after the death of the rightly guided caliphs. Established by Muʿāwiyah b. Abī Sufyān (d. 60/680) upon the death of ʿAlī b. Abī Ṭālib (d. 40/661), it lasted from 41/661 to 132/750.

*ummah* Community of Muslims; the Muslim nation.

*ʿumūm al-balwā* Of widespread affect, impact, or connotation.

*ʿurf* Local custom. In the absence of anything to the contrary, derivation of the law from the common and approved mores of a people. See *ʿādah*.

*uṣūl* (sing. *aṣl*) Lit., origins or foundations. Islamic law: the principles upon which Islamic jurisprudence is based or the jurisprudential methods of Islamic law. See *aṣl*.

*uṣūl al-fiqh* Islamic jurisprudence. See *uṣūl*.

*uṣūlī* As distinguished from *furūʿī*, a jurist qualified in the science of jurisprudential theory and trained to formulate law from the hermeneutic principles of jurisprudence.

*wāḍiḥ* Clear, lucid, definitive, as distinguished from *mubham*. See *mubham*.

*Wahhābī* (*Wahhābiyyah*) Follower of the strict puritanical teachings of Muḥammad b. ʿAbd al-Wahhāb (d. 1207/1792). Wahhābīs are hostile to the intercession of saints, visiting the tombs of saints, Ṣūfism, Shīʿism, and rational methods of deducing laws. The Wahhābī creed is markedly restrictive of women and dominates in Saudi Arabia and many other parts of the Muslim world.

*wājib* Syn. of *farḍ*. Islamic law: one of the five categories or values of *Sharīʿah*, connoting that which is obligatory, mandatory. In the Ḥanafī school, an obligation drawn from a definitive source text is termed *farḍ* whereas an obligation drawn from a source text of a lesser degree of authenticity is termed *wājib*. See *farḍ* and *Sharīʿah*.

*wakīl* Agent, trustee, authorized representative.

*waqf* (pl. *awqāf*) Religious endowments or charitable trusts; a private endowment to finance the scholarly endeavors of individual jurists or institutional schools of thought. Today, *awqāf* have been largely replaced by state-funded scholars and schools.

*yaqīn* Certainty, certitude, or solid conviction; definitive, certain, and non-speculative legal proof.

*ẓahr* The back end of something, a mount.

*ẓāhir* Lit., apparent, surface. Refers to the literal meaning of a source text (*naṣṣ*), as distinguished from the allegorical (*bāṭin* or *khafiyy*) meaning. See *khafiyy*.

*Ẓāhirī* (*Ẓāhiriyyah*) Adherent of the Sunnī juristic school of thought named after its dominant heuristic method of relying on the literal meaning (*ẓāhir*) of texts. The founder of the school was Dāwūd b. Khalaf (d. 270/884). Its most famous proponent was the jurist Ibn Ḥazm (d. 456/1064)of Muslim Spain. The school is now largely defunct, although the works of Ibn Ḥazm are still in circulation.

*ẓann* Speculative, uncertain, speculation, supposition, likely, probable. The opposite of *yaqīn* (certainty). See *qaṭʿ*.

*ẓannī* See *ẓann*.

*Zaydī* Known as the Shīʿī Seveners; a Shīʿī branch that today predominates in Yemen.

*zaygh* Deviation, departure, error, swerving, wandering.

*ẓālim* Unjust or oppressive person

*ẓulm* Injustice or oppression

*ẓulmat al-taqlīd* Refers to the mental oppression that results from blind obedience and the absence of intellectual exertion.

# Bibliography

## *English and French Sources*


Abdur Rahim, M.A. *The Principles of Muhammadan Jurisprudence According to the Hanafi, Maliki, Shafiʿi and Hanbali Schools.* Lahore: All-Pakistan Legal Decisions, 1958.

Abel, Richard L. *Politics by other Means: Law in the Struggle against Apartheid, 1980–1984.* New York: Routledge, 1995.

Abou El Fadl, Khaled. "Ahkam al-Bughat: A Study of Irregular Warfare and the Law of Rebellion in Islam." In *Cross, Crescent and Sword: The Justification and Limitation of War in Western and Islamic Traditions.* Eds. James Turner Johnson and John Kelsay. Westport, Connecticut: Greenwood Press, 1990.

___. "The Common and Islamic Law of Duress." *Arab Law Quarterly* 2 (1991): 6.

___. *The Conference of the Books.* Lanham, Maryland: University Press of America, 2001.

___. "Islamic Law and Muslim Minorities: The Juristic Discourses on Muslim Minorities from the 2nd/8th to the 11th/17th Centuries." *Journal of Islamic Law and Society* 2 (1994): 1.

___. "The Islamic Law of Rebellion." Ph.D. diss., Princeton University, 1999.

___. "Legal Debates on Muslim Minorities: Between Rejection and Accommodation." *Journal of Religious Ethics* 1 (1994): 22.

___. "Muslim Minorities and Self-Restraint in Liberal Democracies." *Loyola of Los Angeles Law Review* 4 (1996): 29.

___. "Political Crime in Islamic Jurisprudence and Western Legal History." *U.C. Davis Journal of International Law and Policy* 4 (1998):1.

___. *Rebellion and Violence in Islamic Law.* Cambridge: Cambridge University Press, 2001.

Abou El Fadl, Khaled, and Alan Watson. "Fox Hunting, Pheasant Shooting, and Comparative Law." *American Journal of Comparative Law* 1 (2000): 48.

Abrahamov, Binyamin. *Islamic Theology: Traditionalism and Rationalism.* Edinburgh: Edinburgh University Press, 1998.

Abrams, M. H. *Doing Things with Texts: Essays in Criticism and Critical Theory.* New York: W.W. Norton, 1991.

Ahmad, Qeyamuddin. *The Wahabi Movement in India.* Calcutta: Firma K.L. Mukhopadhyay, 1966.

Ahmed, Leila. *A Border Passage: From Cairo to America – A Woman's Journey.* New York: Farrar, Straus and Giroux, 1999.

___. *Women and Gender in Islam.* New Haven: Yale University Press, 1992.

Ajami, Fouad. *The Arab Predicament: Arab Political Thought and Practice Since 1967.* Cambridge: University of Cambridge Press, 1981.

Akhtar, Shabbir. *A Faith for All Seasons: Islam and Western Modernity.* London: Bellew Publishing, 1990.

Algar, Hamid. "The Oppositional Role of the Ulama in Twentieth-Century Iran." In *Scholars, Saints and Sufis: Muslim Religious Institutions in the Middle East Since 1500.* Ed. Nikki R. Keddie. Berkeley and Los Angeles: University of California Press, 1972.

Al-Andalusī, Ṣaʿīd. *Science in the Medieval World: "The Book of the Categories of Nations."* Trans. Semaʿan I. Salem and Alok Kumar. Austin, Texas: University of Texas Press, 1991.

An-Na'im, Abdullahi Ahmad. *Toward an Islamic Reformation: Civil Liberties, Human Rights, and International Law.* Syracuse: Syracuse University Press, 1990.

Al-Azmeh, Aziz. *Muslim Kingship: Power and the Sacred in Muslim, Christian and Pagan Polities.* London: I.B. Tauris, 1997.

ʿAlī, ʿAbdullah Yūsuf., trans. *The Meaning of the Holy Qurʾān.* Brentwood, Maryland: Amana Corporation, 1991.

Ali, Syed Ameer. *Muhammadan Law.* New Delhi: Kitab Bhavan, 1986.

Ali-Karamali, Shaista P., and Fiona Dunne. "The Ijtihad Controversy." *Arab Law Quarterly* 9, no. 3 (1994): 238–257.

Anderson, J.N.D. *Islamic Law in the Modern World.* New York: New York University Press, 1959.

___. *Law Reform in the Muslim World.* London: Athlone Press, 1976.

___. "Modern Trends in Islam: Legal Reform and Modernisation in the Middle East." In *Islamic Law and Legal Theory.* Ed. Ian Edge. New York: New York University Press, 1996. Originally published in *International and Comparative Law Quarterly* 20 (1971): 1–21.

Arendt, Hannah. "What is Authority?" *Between Past and Future.* New York: Viking Press, 1968. Reprint. New York: Penguin Books, 1993.

Arkoun, Mohammed. *Rethinking Islam: Common Questions, Uncommon Answers.* Trans. Robert D. Lee. Boulder: Westview Press, 1994.

Asad, Muhammad. *Islam at the Crossroads.* 7th edn. Lahore: Arafat Publications, 1955.

Avini, Avisheh. "The Origins of the Modern English Trust Revisited." *Tulane Law Review* 70 (1996): 1139–1163.

Azmi, Mohammad Mustafa. *Studies in Early Ḥadīth Literature.* Beirut: al-Maktab al-Islāmī, 1968.

Babuts, Nicolae. "Text: Origins and Reference." *PMLA* 107 (1992): 65–77.

Baghby, Ihsan Abdul. "Utility in Classical Islamic Law: The Concept of 'Maslahah.' 'Usul al-Fiqh'" Ph.D. diss., University of Michigan, 1986.

Bakhash, Shaul. *The Reign of the Ayatollahs: Iran and the Islamic Revolution.* New York: Basic Books, 1984.

Baljon, J.M.S. *Religion and Thought of Shah Wali Allah Dihlawi, 1703–1762.* Leiden: Brill, 1986.

Balkhi, Fasihuddin. *Wahabi Movement.* New Delhi: Classical Publishing Company, 1983.

Barboza, Steven, ed. *American Jihad: Islam after Malcolm X.* New York: Doubleday, 1994.

Barthes, Roland. "Theorie du texte." In *Encyclopaedia Universalis.* Vol. 15. Paris: Encyclopaedia Universalis, 1973.

Barwise, Jon. "On the Circumstantial Relation Between Meaning and Content." In *Meaning and Mental Representations.* Eds. Umberto Eco, Marco Santambrogio, and Patrizia Violi. Bloomington: Indiana University Press, 1988.

Binder, Guyora, and Robert Weisberg. *Literary Criticisms of Law.* Princeton: Princeton University Press, 2000.

Bleich, David. "Epistemological Assumptions in the Study of Response." In *Reader-Response Criticism: From Formalism to Post-Structuralism.* Ed. Jane P. Tompkins. Baltimore: The Johns Hopkins University Press, 1980.

Boisard, Marcel A. "On the Probable Influence of Islam on Western Public and International Law." *International Journal of Middle East Studies* 11 (1980): 429–450.

Bosworth, C.E., trans. *The Sāsānids, the Byzantines, the Lakmids, and Yemen.* Vol. 5 of *The History of al-Ṭabarī.* Albany: State University of New York Press, 1999.

Bowen, H. and C.E. Bosworth. "Niẓām al-Mulk." *Encyclopaedia of Islam.* Eds. C.E. Bosworth, E. van Donzel, W.P. Heinrichs, and Ch. Pellat. 2nd edn. Leiden: E.J. Brill, 1990: 8:69–73.

Brinton, Jasper Yeates. *The Mixed Courts of Egypt.* Rev. ed. New Haven: Yale University Press, 1968.

Brown, Daniel W. *Rethinking Tradition in Modern Islamic Thought.* Cambridge: Cambridge University Press, 1996.

Bulliet, Richard. *The Patricians of Nishapur: A Study in Medieval Islamic Social History.* Cambridge: Harvard University Press, 1972.

Bultmann, Rudolph. "The Problem of Hermeneutics." In *New Testament and Mythology.* Ed. Schubert M. Ogden. Philadelphia: Fortress Press, 1984.

Burnett, Charles. *The Introduction of Arabic Learning into England.* London: The British Library, 1997.

Burns, Gerald L. *Hermeneutics, Ancient & Modern.* New Haven: Yale University Press, 1992.

___. "Law and Language: A Hermeneutics of the Legal Text." In *Legal Hermeneutics: History, Theory and Practice.* Ed. Gregory Leyh. Berkeley: University of California Press, 1992.

Butterworth, Charles E. and Kessel, Blake Andree, eds. *The Introduction of Arabic Philosophy into Europe.* Leiden: E.J. Brill, 1994.

Calder, Norman. *Studies in Early Muslim Jurisprudence.* Oxford: Clarendon Press, 1993.

Chehata, Chafik. *Études de Droit Musulman: La Notion De Responsabilité Contractuelle: Le Concept de Propriété.* Paris: Presses Universitaires de France, 1973.

___. *Théorie Générale de L'Obligation en Droit Musulman Hanéfite: Les Sujets de L'Obligation.* Paris: Éditions Sirey, 1969.

Christelow, Allan. *Muslim Law Courts and the French Colonial State in Algeria.* Princeton: Princeton University Press, 1985.

Cleveland, William L. *A History of the Modern Middle East.* Boulder: Westview Press, 1994.

Cohen, Philip, ed. *Text and Textualities: Textual Instability, Theory, and Interpretation.* New York: Garland, 1997.

Comair-Obeid, Nayla. "Particularity of the Contract's Subject-Matter in the Laws of the Arab Middle East." *Arab Law Quarterly* 11, no. 4 (1996): 331–349.

Conley, John M., and William M. O'Barr. *Just Words: Law, Language, and Power.* Chicago: University of Chicago Press, 1998.

Conrad, Lawrence I. "The Social Structure of Medicine in Medieval Islam." *Society for the Social History of Medicine Bulletin* 37 (December 1985): 11–15.

Corbin, Henry. *History of Islamic Philosophy.* Trans. Liadain Sherrard. London: Kegan Paul International, 1993.

Coulson, N.J. *Conflicts and Tensions in Islamic Jurisprudence.* Chicago: University of Chicago Press, 1969.

___. *A History of Islamic Law.* Edinburgh: Edinburgh University Press, 1964. Reprint, Edinburgh: Edinburgh University Press, 1997.

Crone, Patricia, and Martin Hinds. *God's Caliph: Religious Authority in the First Centuries of Islam.* Cambridge: Cambridge University Press, 1986.

___. *Roman, Provincial and Islamic Law: The Origins of the Islamic Patronate.* Cambridge: Cambridge University Press, 1987.

Crone, Patricia, and Michael Cook. *Hagarism: The Making of the Islamic World.* Cambridge: Cambridge University Press, 1977.

Culler, Jonathan. "In Defence of Overinterpretation." In *Interpretation and Overinterpretation.* Umberto Eco et al. Ed. Stefan Collini. Cambridge: Cambridge University Press, 1992.

___. "Literary Competence." In *Reader-Response Criticism: From Formalism to Post-Structuralism.* Ed. Jane P. Tompkins. Baltimore: The Johns Hopkins University Press, 1980.

Dabashi, Hamid. *Authority in Islam: From the Rise of Muhammad to the Establishment of the Umayyads.* New Brunswick: Transaction Publishers, 1989.

Dallmayr, Fred. "Hermeneutics and the Rule of Law." In *Legal Hermeneutics: History, Theory and Practice.* Ed. Gregory Leyh. Berkeley: University of California Press, 1992.

De Boer, T. J. *The History of Philosophy in Islam.* Trans. Edward R. Jones. Surrey, England: Curzon Press, 1994.

De Jong, F. "Al-Ḳuṭb." *Encyclopaedia of Islam.* Eds. C.E. Bosworth, E. van Donzel, W.P. Heinrichs, and Ch. Pellat. 2nd edn. Leiden: E.J. Brill, 1990: 5:542–543.

Dews, Peter, ed. *Habermas: A Critical Reader.* Oxford: Blackwell Publishers, 1999.

Doi, Abdur Rahman I. *Sharīʿah: The Islamic Law.* London: Ta Ha Publishers, 1984.

___. *Women in Shariʿah (Islamic Law).* London: Ta-Ha Publishers, 1989.

Donoghue, Dennis. *The Practice of Reading.* New Haven: Yale University Press, 1998.

Dorff, Elliot N., and Arthur Rosett. *A Living Tree: The Roots and Growth of Jewish Law.* Albany: State University of New York Press, 1988.

Dowling, William C. *The Senses of the Text: Intentional Semantics and Literary Theory.* Lincoln, Nebraska: University of Nebraska Press, 1999.

Dutton, Yasin. *The Origins of Islamic Law: The Qur'an, the Muwaṭṭaʾ, and Madinan ʿAmal.* Surrey: Curzon Press, 1999.

Duxbury, Neil. "Faith in Reason: The Process Tradition in American Jurisprudence." *Cardozo Law Review* 15 (1993): 601–705.

___. *Patterns of American Jurisprudence.* Oxford: Clarendon Press, 1995.

Eco, Umberto. *The Limits of Interpretation.* Bloomington: University of Indiana Press, 1990.

___. *The Open Work.* Trans. Anna Cancogni. Cambridge: Harvard University Press, 1989.

___. "Overinterpreting Texts." In *Interpretation and Overinterpretation.* Umberto Eco et al. Ed. Stefan Collini. Cambridge: Cambridge University Press, 1992.

___. *The Role of the Reader: Explorations in the Semiotics of Texts.* Bloomington: University of Indiana Press, 1979.

___. "On Truth. A Fiction." In *Meaning and Mental Representations.* Eds. Umberto Eco, Marco Santambrogio, and Patrizia Violi. Bloomington: Indiana University Press, 1988.

Eco, Umberto, Marco Santambrogio, and Patrizia Violi, eds. *Meaning and Mental Representations.* Bloomington: Indiana University Press, 1988.

Eco, Umberto, Richard Rorty, Jonathan Culler, and Christine Brooke-Rose. *Interpretation and Overinterpretation.* Ed. Stefan Collini. Cambridge: Cambridge University Press, 1992.

El-Awa, Mohamed S. *Punishment in Islamic Law.* Indianapolis: American Trust Publications, 1993.

El Guindi, Fadwa. *Veil: Modesty, Privacy and Resistance.* Oxford: Berg, 1999.

Enayat, Hamid. *Modern Islamic Political Thought.* Austin: University of Texas Press, 1982.

Ernst, Carl W. *Sufism: An Essential Introduction to the Philosophy and Practice of the Mystical Tradition of Islam.* Boston: Shambala, 1997.

Esack, Farid. *Qur'an Liberation and Pluralism: An Islamic Perspective of Interreligious Solidarity Against Oppression.* Oxford: Oneworld Press, 1997.

Fadel, Mohammad. "Rules, Judicial Discretion, and the Rule of Law in Naṣrid Granada: An Analysis of *al-Ḥadīqa al-mustaqilla al-naḍra fī al-fatāwā al-ṣadira ʿan ʿulamāʾ al-ḥaḍra.*" In *Islamic Law: Theory and Practice.* Eds. R. Gleave and E. Kermeli. New York: I.B. Tauris, 1997.

___. "The Social Logic of *Taqlīd* and the Rise of the *Mukhataṣar* [sic]." *Islamic Law and Society* 3, no. 2 (1996): 193–233.

___. "Two Women, One Man: Knowledge, Power, and Gender in Medieval Sunni Legal Thought." *International Journal of Middle East Studies* 29 (1997): 185–204.

Fakhry, Majid. *A History of Islamic Philosophy.* 2nd edn. New York: Columbia University Press, 1983.

Al-Farüqi, Lamyaʾ. *Women, Muslim Society, and Islam.* 1988. Reprint, Plainfield, Indiana: American Trust Publications, 1994.

Ferguson, Duncan S. *Biblical Hermeneutics: An Introduction.* London: SCM Press, 1986.

Finnis, John. *Natural Law and Natural Rights.* Oxford: Oxford University Press, 1980.

Fish, Stanley. *Doing What Comes Naturally: Change, Rhetoric, and the Practice of Theory in Literary Legal Studies.* Durham: Duke University Press, 1999.

___. *Is There a Text in This Class? The Authority of Interpretive Communities.* Cambridge: Harvard University Press, 1998.

___. "Literature in the Reader: Affective Sylistics." *Reader-Response Criticism: From Formalism to Post-Structuralism.* Ed. Jane P. Tompkins. Baltimore: The Johns Hopkins University Press, 1980.

___. *The Trouble With Principle.* Cambridge: Harvard University Press, 1999.

Fiss, Owen M. "Objectivity and Interpretation." In *Interpreting Law and Literature: A Hermeneutic Reader.* Eds. Sanford Levinson and Steven Mailloux. Evanston, IL: Northwestern University Press, 1988.

Frei, Hans W. "Conflicts in Interpretation." *Theology Today* 49 (1992): 344–356.

Fried, Charles. "Sonnet LXV and the Black Ink of the Framers' Intention." In *Interpreting Law and Literature: A Hermeneutic Reader.* Eds. Sanford Levinson and Steven Mailloux. Evanston, IL: Northwestern University Press, 1988.

Friedman, R.B. "On the Concept of Authority in Political Philosophy." *Authority.* Ed. Joseph Raz. Oxford: Basil Blackwell, 1990.

Gadamer, Hans-Georg. "Hermeneutics as a Theoretical and Practical Task." *Reason in the Age of Science.* Cambridge: Massachusetts Institute of Technology Press, 1998.

___. *Philosophical Hermeneutics.* Trans. David E. Linge. Berkeley: University of California Press, 1977.

___. *Truth and Method.* 2nd edn., revised. New York: The Continuum Publishing Company, 1998.

Gatje, Helmut. *The Qur'an and its Exegesis.* Trans. Alford T. Welch. Oxford: Oneworld Publicaitons, 1996.

Gaudefroy-Demombynes, Maurice. *Muslim Institutions.* Trans. John P. MacGregor. London: Allen & Unwin 1950. Reprint, London: Allen & Unwin, 1968.

Gaudiosi, Monica M. "The Influence of the Islamic Law of Waqf on the Development of the Trust in England: The Case of Merton College." *University of Pennsylvania Law Review* 136 (1988): 1231–1261.

Gellner, Ernest. *Muslim Society.* Cambridge: Cambridge University Press, 1981.

Ghadbian, Najib. *Democratization and the Islamic Challenge in the Arab World.* Boulder: Westview Press, 1997.

Gibb, H.A.R. "Constitutional Organization." In *Origin and Development of Islamic Law.* Vol. 1 of *Law in the Middle East.* Eds. Majid Khadduri and Herbert J. Liebesny. Washington D.C.: Middle East Institute, 1955.

Gibbs, Raymond W. *Intentions in the Experience of Meaning.* Cambridge: Cambridge University Press, 1999.

Gibson, Walker. "Authors, Speakers, Readers and Mock Readers." In *Reader-Response Criticism: From Formalism to Post-Structuralism.* Ed. Jane P. Tompkins. Baltimore: The Johns Hopkins University Press, 1980.

Gimaret, D. "Muʿtazila." *Encyclopaedia of Islam.* Eds. C.E. Bosworth, E. van Donzel, W.P. Heinrichs, and Ch. Pellat. 2nd edn. Leiden: E.J. Brill, 1990: 7:783–793.

Goldrup, Lawrence Paul. "Saudi Arabia: 1902–1932: The Development of a Wahhabi Society." Ph.D. diss., University of California Los Angeles, 1971.

Goldziher, Ignas. *The Ẓāhirīs: Their Doctrine and Their History.* Leiden: E.J. Brill, 1971.

Gracia, Jorge J. E. *Texts: Ontological Status, Identity, Author, Audience.* Albany: State University of New York Press, 1996.

___. *A Theory of Textuality: The Logic and Epistemology.* Albany: State University of New York Press, 1995.

Graff, Gerald. "*Keep Off the Grass, Drop Dead,* and Other Indeterminacies: A Response to Sanford Levinson." In *Interpreting Law and Literature: A Hermeneutic Reader.* Eds. Sanford Levinson and Steven Mailloux. Evanston: Northwestern University Press, 1988.

Greetham, D.C. *Theories of the Text.* Oxford: Oxford University Press, 1995.

Grigely, Joseph. *Textualterity: Art, Theory, and Textual Criticism.* Ann Arbor: University of Michigan Press, 1995.

Grondin, Jean. *Introduction to Philosophical Hermeneutics.* New Haven: Yale University Press, 1994.

___. *Sources of Hermeneutics.* Albany: State University of New York Press, 1995.

Haddad, Mahmud Osman. "Rashid Rida and the Theory of the Caliphate." Ph.D. diss., Columbia University, 1989.

Haddad, Yvonne Yazbeck. *Contemporary Islam and the Challenge of History.* Albany: State University of New York Press, 1982.

Hallaq, Wael. *A History of Islamic Legal Theories: An Introduction to Sunnī* Uṣūl al-Fiqh. Cambridge: Cambridge University Press, 1997.

___. *Authority, Continuity and Change in Islamic Law.* Cambridge: Cambridge University Press, 2001.

___. "Was the Gate of Ijtihād Closed?" *International Journal of Middle East Studies* 16, no. 1 (1984): 3–41.

___. "Was al-Shāfiʿī the Master Architect of Islamic Jurisprudence?" *International Journal of Middle East Studies* 25 (1993): 587–605.

Hamdi, Mohammed E. *The Making of an Islamic Leader: Conversations with Hasan al-Turabi.* Boulder: Westview Press, 1998.

Hammad, Ahmad Zaki. *Islamic Law: Understanding Juristic Differences.* Indianapolis: American Trust Publications, 1992.

Hasan, Ahmad. *The Doctrine of Ijmāʿ in Islam.* Islamabad: Islamic Research Institute, 1978.

___. *The Early Development of Islamic Jurisprudence.* Delhi, India: Adam Publishers and Distributors, 1994.

Al-Hibri, Azizah Y. "Family Planning and Islamic Jurisprudence." In *Religious and Ethical Perspectives on Population Issues.* Eds. Azizah al-Hibri, Daniel Maguire, and James B. Martin-Schramm. Washington, D.C.: Religious Consultation on Population, Reproductive Health and Ethics, 1993.

___. "Islamic Constitutionalism and the Concept of Democracy." *Case Western Reserve Journal of International Law* 24, no. 1 (Winter 1992): 1–27.

___. "Marriage Laws in Muslim Countries: A Comparative Study of Certain Egyptian, Syrian, Moroccan, and Tunisian Marriage Laws." *International Review of Comparative Public Policy* 4 (1992): 227–244.

___. "A study of Islamic herstory: or how did we ever get into this mess?" In *Women and Islam.* Ed. Azizah al-Hibri. Oxford, New York: Pergamon Press, 1982.

Al-Hibri, Azizah Y. et al. "Symposium on Religious Law: Roman Catholic, Islamic, and Jewish Treatment of Familial Issues, Including Education, Abortion, *In Vitro* Fertilization, Prenuptial Agreements, Contraception and Marital Fraud." *Loyola of Los Angeles International and Comparative Law Journal* 16 (November 1993): 9–95.

Hirsch, E.D. *Validity in Interpretation.* New Haven: Yale University Press, 1967.

___. "Counterfactuals in Interpretation." In *Interpreting Law and Literature: A Hermeneutic Reader.* Eds. Sanford Levinson and Steven Mailloux. Evanston, IL: Northwestern University Press, 1988.

Hodgson, Marshall G.S. *The Classical Age of Islam.* Vol. 1 of *The Venture of Islam: Conscience and History in a World Civilization.* Chicago: University of Chicago Press, 1974.

Hofmann, Murad. *Islam: the Alternative.* Beltsville, MD: Amana, 1997.

Holland, Norman N. "Unity, Identity, Text, Self." In *Reader-Response Criticism: From Formalism to Post-Structuralism.* Ed. Jane P. Tompkins. Baltimore: The Johns Hopkins University Press, 1980.

Horowitz, George. *The Spirit of Jewish Law: A Brief Account of Biblical and Rabbinical Jurisprudence with a Special Note on Jewish Law and the State of Israel.* New York: Central Book Company, 1953.

Hourani, Albert. *Arabic Thought in the Liberal Age, 1798–1939.* London: Oxford University Press, 1962.

___. *A History of the Arab Peoples.* Cambridge: Harvard University Press, 1991.

Hourani, George F. "Divine Justice and Human Reason in Muʿtazilite Ethical Theology." In *Ethics in Islam.* Ed. Richard G. Hovannisian. Malibu: Undena Publications, 1985.

Hoy, David Couzens. "Interpreting the Law: Hermeneutical and Poststructuralist Perspectives." In *Interpreting Law and Literature: A Hermeneutic Reader.* Eds. Sanford Levinson and Steven Mailloux. Evanston, IL: Northwestern University Press, 1988.

Hoyle, Mark S.W. *Mixed Courts of Egypt.* London: Graham & Trotman, 1991.

Hussain, Shaikh Shaukat. *Human Rights in Islam.* New Delhi: Kitab Bhavan, 1990.

Ibn Bāz, ʿAbd al-ʿAzīz b. ʿAbd Allāh b. ʿAbd a-Raḥmān et al. *Islamic Fatawa Regarding Women (Shariʿah Rulings Given by the Grand Mufti of Saudi Arabia Sheikh Ibn Baz, Sheikh Ibn Uthaimin, Sheikh Ibn Jibreen and Others on Matters Pertaining to Women).* Ed. Muḥammad b. ʿAbd al-ʿAzīz al-Musnad. Trans. Jamaal al-Din M. Zarabozo. Riyāḍ: Dār al-Salam, 1996.

Iser, Wolfgang. "The Reading Process: A Phenomenological Approach." In *Reader-Response Criticism: From Formalism to Post-Structuralism.* Ed. Jane P. Tompkins. Baltimore: The Johns Hopkins University Press, 1980. Originally published in Wolfgang Iser. *The Implied Reader: Patterns of Communication in Prose Fiction from Bunyan to Beckett.* Baltimore: Johns Hopkins University Press, 1974.

Işik, Hüseyin Hilmi. *Advice for the Wahhabi.* 2nd edn. Istanbul: Özal Matbaasi, 1978.

___. *The Religion Reformers in Islam.* 3rd edn. Istanbul: Waqf Ikhlas Publications, 1978.

Izutsu, Toshihiko. *Ethico-Religious Concepts in the Qurʾān.* Montreal: McGill University Press, 1966.

___. *God and Man in the Koran.* 1964. Reprint, North Stratford: Ayer Company Publishers, 1995.

Jackson, Sherman. "From Prophetic Actions to Constitutional Theory: A Novel Chapter in Medieval Muslim Jurisprudence." *International Journal of Middle East Studies* 25 (1993): 71–90.

___. *Islamic Law and the State: The Constitutional Jurisprudence of Shihāb al-Dīn al-Qarāfī.* Leiden: E.J. Brill, 1996.

___. "*Taqlīd*, Legal Scaffolding and the Scope of Legal Injunctions in Post-Formative Theory: *Muṭlaq and ʿĀmm* in the Jurisprudence of Shihāb al-Dīn al-Qarāfī." *Islamic Law and Society* 3, no 2 (1996): 165–192.

Jayusi, Salma Khadrar, ed. *The Legacy of Muslim Spain.* Leiden: E.J. Brill, 1992.

Johnson-Laird, Philip N. "How is Meaning Mentally Represented." In *Meaning and Mental Representations.* Eds. Umberto Eco, Marco Santambrogio, and Patrizia Violi. Bloomington: Indiana University Press, 1988.

Juhl, P. D. *Interpretation: An Essay in the Philosophy of Literary Criticism.* Princeton: Princeton University Press, 1986.

Kaba, Lansiné. *The Wahhabiyya: Islamic Reform and Politics in French West Africa.* Evanston: Northwestern University Press, 1974.

Kabbani, Muhammad Hisham. *Forgotten Aspects of Islamic Worship*. Vol. 7 of *Encyclopedia of Islamic Doctrine*. 2nd edn. Mountain View, California: As-Sunna Foundation of America, 1998.

Kamali, Mohammad Hashim. *Freedom of Expression in Islam*. Cambridge: Islamic Texts Society, 1997.

___. *Principles of Islamic Jurisprudence*. Rev. ed. Cambridge: Islamic Texts Society, 1991.

Keller, Nuh Ha Mim. *Reliance of the Traveller: A Classical Manual of Islamic Sacred Law*. Rev. ed. Evanston, IL: Sunna Books, 1994.

Kennedy, Hugh. *The Prophet and the Age of the Caliphates: The Islamic Near East from the Sixth to the Eleventh Century*. London: Longman Group, 1986.

Khadduri, Majid. *The Islamic Conception of Justice*. Baltimore: Johns Hopkins University Press, 1984.

___. *Political Trends in the Arab World: The Role of Ideas and Ideals in Politics*. Baltimore: Johns Hopkins University Press, 1970.

Kristeva, Julia. "Theory of the Text." Trans. Ian McLeod. In *Untying the Text*. Ed. Robert Young. London: Routledge, Kegan Paul, 1981.

Lambton, Ann K.S. *State and Government in Medieval Islam: An Introduction to the Study of Islamic Political Theory: The Jurists*. Oxford: Oxford University Press, 1981.

Lane, E.W. *Arabic-English Lexicon*. Cambridge, England: Islamic Texts Society, 1984.

Lang, Jeffrey. *Even Angels Ask: A Journey to Islam in America*. Beltsville, MD: Amana Publications, 1997.

___. *Struggling to Surrender: Some Impressions of an American Convert to Islam*. Beltsville, MD: Amana Publications, 1994.

Lapidus, Ira M. *A History of Islamic Societies*. Cambridge: Cambridge University Press, 1988.

Laslett, P., W. Runciman, and Q. Skinner, eds. *Philosophy, Politics and Society*. Oxford: Oxford University Press, 1972.

Leaman, Oliver. *An Introduction to Medieval Islamic Philosophy*. London: Cambridge University Press, 1985.

Levinson, Sanford and Steven Mailloux, eds. *Interpreting Law and Literature: A Hermeneutic Reader*. Evanston, IL: Northwestern University Press, 1988.

Leyh, Gregory, ed. *Legal Hermeneutics: History, Theory and Practice*. Berkeley and Los Angeles: University of California Press, 1992.

Liebesny, Herbert J. "Impact of Western Law in the Countries of the Near East." *George Washington Law Review* 22 (1953): 127–141.

Lings, Martin. *Muḥammad: His Life Based on the Earliest Sources*. London: George Allen & Unwin, 1983.

Lukes, Steven. *Power: A Radical View*. London: Macmillan, 1974.

Lyon, Arabella. *Intentions: Negotiated, Contested and Ignored*. University Park, Pennsylvania: The Pennsylvania State University Press, 1998.

Lyotard, Jean François. *The Postmodern Condition: A Report on Knowledge*. Trans. Geoff Bennington and Brian Massumi. Minneapolis: University of Minnesota Press, 1984.

MacIntyre, Alasdair. *After Virtue: A Study in Moral Theory*. 2nd edn. Notre Dame, Indiana: University of Notre Dame Press, 1984.

___. *Whose Justice? Which Rationality?*. Notre Dame: University of Notre Dame Press, 1988.

Macleod, Arlene Elowe. *Accommodating Protest: Working Women, The New Veiling, and Change in Cairo.* New York: Columbia University Press, 1991.

Madelung, Wilfred. "Māturīdiyya." *Encyclopaedia of Islam.* eds. C.E. Bosworth, E. van Donzel, W.P. Heinrichs, and Ch. Pellat. 2nd edn. Leiden: E.J. Brill, 1990: 6:847–848.

___. "Murdji'a." *Encyclopaedia of Islam.* Eds. C.E. Bosworth, E. van Donzel, W.P. Heinrichs, and Ch. Pellat. 2nd edn. Leiden: E.J. Brill, 1990: 7:605–607.

___. *The Succession to Muhammad: A Study of the Early Caliphate.* Cambridge: Cambridge University Press, 1997.

Makdisi, George. "Ashʿarī and the Ash'arites in Islamic Religious History." Parts 1 and 2. *Studia Islamica* 17 (1962): 37–80; 18 (1963): 19–39

___. "The Guilds of Law in Medieval Legal History: An Inquiry into the Origins of the Inns of Court." *Zeitschrift für Geschichte der arabisch-islamischen Wissenschaften.* Ed. Fuat Sezgin. Frankfurt: Institut für Geschichte der arabisch-islamischen Wissenschaften, 1984.

___. *Ibn 'Aqil: Religion and Culture in Classical Islam.* Edinburgh: Edinburgh University Press, 1997.

___. "Al-Kundūrī." *Encyclopaedia of Islam.* Eds. C.E. Bosworth, E. van Donzel, W.P. Heinrichs, and Ch. Pellat. 2nd edn. Leiden: E.J. Brill, 1990: 5:387–388.

___. "La Corporation à l'époque classique de l'Islam." *Présence de Louis Massignon: Hommages et témoignages.* Paris: Maisonneuve & Larose, 1987.

___. *The Rise of Colleges: Institutions of Learning in Islam and the West.* Edinburgh: Edinburgh University Press, 1981.

Makdisi, John. "An Inquiry into Islamic Influences during the Formative Period of the Common Law." In *Islamic Law and Jurisprudence: Studies in Honor of Farhat J. Ziadeh.* Ed. Nicholas Heer. Seattle: University of Washington Press, 1990.

___. "The Islamic Origins of the Common Law." *North Carolina Law Review* 77 (1999): 1635–1739.

___. "Legal Logic and Equity in Islamic Law." *American Journal of Comparative Law* 33 (1985): 63–92.

Marsot, Afaf Lutfi al-Sayyid. *Women and Men in Late Eighteenth-Century Egypt.* Austin: University of Texas Press, 1995.

Martin, Richard C., Mark R. Woodward, and Dwi S. Atmaja. *Defenders of Reason in Islam: Mu'tazilism from Medieval School to Modern Symbol.* Oxford: Oneworld Publications, 1997.

Masud, Muhammad Khalid. *Islamic Legal Philosophy: A Study of Abū Isḥāq al-Shāṭibī's Life and Thought.* New Delhi: International Islamic Publishers, 1989.

Masud, Muhammad Khalid, Brinkley Messick, and David S. Powers, eds. *Islamic Legal Interpretation: Muftis and Their Fatwas.* Cambridge, MA: Harvard University Press, 1996.

Al-Mawdūdī, Sayyid Abū al-Aʿlā. *Towards Understanding the Qur'ān.* Trans. Zafar Ishaq Ansari. Delhi, India: Markazi Maktaba Islami, 1988.

McGann, Jerome. *The Textual Condition.* Princeton: Princeton University Press, 1991.

Melchert, Christopher. *The Formation of the Sunni Schools of Law, 9th–10th Centuries, C.E.* Leiden: Brill, 1997.

Mernissi, Fatima. *The Veil and the Male Elite: A Feminist Interpretation of Women's Rights in Islam.* New York: Addison-Wesley Publishing Company, 1991.

Merryman, John Henry. *The Civil Law Tradition: An Introduction to the Legal System of Western Europe and Latin America.* 2nd edn. Stanford: Stanford University Press, 1985.

Merryman, John Henry et al. *The Civil Law Tradition: Europe, Latin America, and East Asia.* Charlottesville: The Michie Company, 1994.

Messick, Brinkley. *The Calligraphic State: Textual Domination and History in a Muslim Society.* Berkeley and Los Angeles: University of California Press, 1993.

Metlitzki, Dorothee. *The Matter of Araby in Medieval England.* New Haven: Yale University Press, 1977.

Michels, Robert. *Political Parties: A Sociological Study of the Oligarchical Tendencies of Modern Democracy.* New York: The Free Press, 1962.

Mikhail, Hanna. *Politics and Revelation: Māwardī and After.* Edinburgh: Edinburgh University Press, 1995.

Milgrom, Jacob, ed. *The JPS Torah Commentary: Numbers.* Philadelphia: Jewish Publication Society, 1990.

Minces, Juliette. *Veiled Women in Islam.* Trans. S.M. Berrett. Watertown, MA: Blue Crane Books, 1994.

Mir-Hosseini, Ziba. *Islam and Gender: The Religious Debate in Contemporary Iran.* Princeton: Princeton University Press, 1999.

Mitchell, Ruth. "Family Law in Algeria before and after the 1404/1984 Family Code." In *Islamic Law: Theory and Practice.* Eds. R. Gleave and E. Kermeli. London: I.B. Tauris, 1997.

Modarressi, Hossein. *Crisis and Consolidation in the Formative Period of Shi'ite Islam.* Princeton: Darwin Press, 1993.

___. "Early Debates on the Integrity of the Qur'ān." *Studia Islamica* 77 (1993): 5–39.

Moore-Gilbert, Bart. *Postcolonial Theory: Contexts, Practices, Politics.* London: Verso Press, 1997.

Mottahedeh, Roy. *Loyalty and Leadership in an Early Islamic Society.* Princeton: Princeton University Press, 1980.

Müller, Christian. "Judging with God's Law on Earth: Judicial Powers of the Qāḍī al-Jamāʿa of Cordoba in the Fifth/Eleventh Century." *Islamic Law and Society* 7, no. 2 (2000): 159–186.

Musallam, B.F. *Sex and Society in Islam.* Cambridge: Cambridge University Press, 1983.

Nagel, Tilman. *History of Islamic Theology: From Muhammad to the Present.* Trans. Thomas Thornton. Princeton: Markus Wiener Publishers, 2000.

Nakosteen, Mehdi Khan. *History of Islamic Origins of Western Education, A.D. 800–1350.* Boulder: University of Colorado Press, 1964.

Nasr, Seyyed Hossein. *Science and Civilization in Islam.* Cambridge, MA: Harvard University Press, 1968. Reprint. New York: Barnes and Noble, 1992.

Neusner, Jacob. *The Talmud: A Close Encounter.* Minneapolis: Fortress Press, 1991.

Noll, Mark A. *The Scandal of the Evangelical Mind.* Leicester, England: Inter-Varsity Press, 1994.

Onar, S.S. "The Majalla." In *Origin and Development of Islamic Law.* Vol. 1 of *Law in the Middle East.* Eds. Majid Khadduri and Herbert J. Liebesny. Washington, D.C.: Middle East Institute, 1955.

Osman, Fathi. *Sharia in Contemporary Society: The Dynamics of Change in the Islamic Law.* Los Angeles: Multimedia Vera International, 1994.

Page, Carl. "Historicistic Finitude and Philosophical Hermeneutics." In *The Philosophy of Hans-Georg Gadamer*. Ed. Lewis Edwin Hahn. Chicago: Open Court Publishers, 1997.

Palmer, Richard. "Habermas versus Gadamer?" In *Perspectives on Habermas*. Ed. Lewis Edwin Hahn. Chicago: Open Court Press, 2000.

Perlmutter, Amos. *Egypt: The Praetorian State*. New Brunswick: Transaction Books, 1974.

Poulet, Georges. "Criticism and the Experience of Interiority." In *Reader-Response Criticism: From Formalism to Post-Structuralism*. Ed. Jane P. Tompkins. Baltimore: The Johns Hopkins University Press, 1980.

Prince, Gerald. "Introduction to the Study of the Narratee." In *Reader-Response Criticism: From Formalism to Post-Structuralism*. Ed. Jane P. Tompkins. Baltimore: The Johns Hopkins University Press, 1980.

Rahman, Afzalur. *Role of Women in Society*. London: Seerah Foundation, 1986.

Rahman, Fazlur. *Revival and Reform in Islam: A Study of Islamic Fundamentalism*. Ed. Ebrahim Moosa. Oxford: Oneworld Publications, 2000.

___. *Islam*. New York: Holt, Reinhart, and Winston, 1966

___. *Islam*. Garden City, New York: Anchor Books, 1968.

___. *Islamic Methodology in History*. Islamabad: Islamic Research Institute, 1965.

___. *Major Themes of the Qurʾān*. 2nd edn. Minneapolis: Bibliotheca Islamica, 1994.

Rakover, Nahum. *A Guide to the Sources of Jewish Law*. Jerusalem: Library of Jewish Law, 1994.

Rawls, John. *Political Liberalism*. New York: Columbia University Press, 1993.

___. *A Theory of Justice*. Rev. ed. Cambridge: Harvard University Press, 1999.

Raz, Joseph, ed. *Authority*. Oxford: B. Blackwell, 1990.

Raz, Joseph. "Authority and Justification." In *Authority*. Ed. Joseph Raz. Oxford: B. Blackwell, 1990.

___. *The Authority of Law: Essays on Law and Morality*. Oxford: Oxford University Press, 1986.

___. *Practical Reason and Norms*. London: Hutchinson, 1975. Reprint. Princeton: Princeton University Press, 1990.

Reinhart, A. Kevin. *Before Revelation: The Boundaries of Muslim Moral Thought*. Albany: State University of New York Press, 1995.

Robson, J. "Abū Dāʿūd al-Sidjistānī." *Encyclopaedia of Islam*. Eds. C.E. Bosworth, E. van Donzel, W.P. Heinrichs, and Ch. Pellat. 2nd edn. Leiden: E.J. Brill, 1990: 1:114.

___. "Al-Bukhārī, Muḥammad b. Ismāʿīl." *Encyclopaedia of Islam*. Eds. C.E. Bosworth, E. van Donzel, W.P. Heinrichs, and Ch. Pellat. 2nd edn. Leiden: E.J. Brill, 1990: 1:296–297.

Rorty, Richard. *Contingency, Irony and Solidarity*. Cambridge: Cambridge University Press, 1989.

___. "The Pragmatist's Progress." In *Interpretation and Overinterpretation*. Umberto Eco et al. Ed. Stefan Collini. Cambridge: Cambridge University Press, 1992.

Rosenthal, Franz. *Science and Medicine in Islam: A Collection of Essays*. Hampshire, Great Britain: Variorum, 1990.

Roy, Olivier. *The Failure of Political Islam*. Trans. Carol Volk. Cambridge: Harvard University Press, 1994.

Said, Edward. *Orientalism*. New York: Pantheon Books, 1978.

___. *Out of Place: A Memoir*. New York: Knopf, 1999.

Salahi, M.A. *Muḥammad: Man and Prophet.* Rockport, MA: Element, 1995.
Saleh, Nabil. *The Qadi and the Fortune Teller.* London: Quartet Books, 1996.
Sanad, Nagaty. *The Theory of Crime and Criminal Responsibility in Islamic Law: Shari'a.* Chicago: Office of International Criminal Justice, 1991.
Sartain, E.M. *Jalāl al-Dīn al-Suyūṭī: Biography and Background.* Cambridge: Cambridge University Press, 1975.
Schacht, Joseph. *An Introduction to Islamic Law.* London: Oxford University Press, 1964. Reprint, Oxford: Clarendon Press, 1993.
Schacht, Joseph, and C.E. Bosworth. "Al-Subkī." *Encyclopaedia of Islam.* Eds. E. Van Donzel, B. Lewis, Ch Pellat and C.E. Bosworth. 2nd edn. Leiden: E.J. Brill, 1978: 9:743–745.
Schimmel, Annemarie. *Mystical Dimensions of Islam.* Chapel Hill: University of North Carolina Press, 1975.
Schleiermacher, Friedrich. *Hermeneutics and Criticism and Other Writings.* Ed. Andrew Bowie. Cambridge: Cambridge University Press, 1998.
Secall, M. Isabel Calero. "Rulers and Qāḍīs: Their Relationship During the Naṣrid Kingdom." *Islamic Law and Society* 7, no. 2 (2000): 235–255.
Shahin, Emad Eldin. *Political Ascent: Contemporary Islamic Movements in North Africa.* Boulder: Westview Press, 1997.
Shayegan, Daryush. *Cultural Schizophrenia: Islamic Societies Confronting the West.* London: Saqi Books, 1992.
Siddīqī, Muhammad Zubayr. *Hadīth Literature: Its Origin, Development, Special Features and Criticism.* Calcutta, India: Calcutta University Press, 1961.
Singha, Radhika. *A Despotism of Law: Crime & Justice in Early Colonial India.* Delhi, India: Oxford University Press, 1998.
Siraisi, Nancy G. *Avicenna in Renaissance Italy: The Canon and Medical Teaching in Italian Universities After 1500.* Princeton: Princeton University Press, 1987.
Smith, Wilfred Cantwell. *Islam in Modern History.* Princeton: Princeton University Press, 1957.
Soroush, ʿAbd al-Karīm. *Reason, Freedom, & Democracy in Islam: Essential Writings of ʿAbdolkarim Soroush.* Trans. Mahmoud Sadri and Ahmad Sadri. New York: Oxford University Press, 2000.
Spectorsky, Susan. *Chapters on Marriage and Divorce: Responses of Ibn Ḥanbal and Ibn Rāhwayh.* Austin: University of Texas Press, 1993.
Spellberg, D.A. *Politics, Gender, and the Islamic Past: The Legacy of ʿAʾisha Bint Abī Bakr.* New York: Columbia University Press, 1994.
Spiegel, Gabrielle M. *The Past as Text: The Theory and Practice of Medieval Historiography.* Baltimore: The John Hopkins University Press, 1997.
Spivak, Gayatri Chakravorty. *A Critique of Postcolonial Reason: Toward a History of the Vanishing Past.* Cambridge, MA: Harvard University Press, 1999.
Stewart, Devin J. *Islamic Legal Orthodoxy: Twelver Shi'ite Responses to the Sunni Legal System.* Salt Lake City: University of Utah Press, 1998.
Stock, Brian. *Listening for the Text: On the Uses of the Past.* Philadelphia: University of Pennsylvania Press, 1990.
Stone, Jerry H. "Christian Praxis as Reflective Action." In *Legal Hermeneutics: History, Theory and Practice.* Ed. Gregory Leyh. Berkeley and Los Angeles: University of California Press, 1992.

Theunissen, Michael. "Society and History: A Critique of Critical Theory." In *Habermas: A Critical Reader.* Ed. Peter Dews. Oxford: Blackwell Publishers, 1999.

Tibi, Bassam. *The Crisis of Modern Islam: A Preindustrial Culture in the Scientific-Technological Age.* Trans. Judith von Sivers. Salt Lake City: University of Utah Press, 1988.

___. *Islam and the Cultural Accommodation of Social Change.* Trans. Clare Krojzl. Boulder: Westview Press, 1991.

Tolhurst, W.E. "On What a Text Is and How it Means." *British Journal of Aesthetics* 19 (1979): 3–14.

Tompkins, Jane P. "The Reader in History: The Changing Shape of Literary Response." In *Reader-Response Criticism: From Formalism to Post-Structuralism.* Ed. Jane P. Tompkins. Baltimore: The Johns Hopkins University Press, 1980.

Tompkins, Jane P., ed. *Reader-Response Criticism: From Formalism to Post-Structuralism.* Baltimore: The Johns Hopkins University Press, 1980.

Tuck, Richard."Why is Authority Such a Problem?" In *Philosophy, Politics and Society.* Eds. P. Laslett, W. Runciman and Q. Skinner. Oxford: Oxford University Press, 1972.

Tyser, C. R., trans. *The Mejelle: Being an English Translation of Majallahel-Ahkam-Adliya and a Complete Code on Islamic Civil Law.* Lahore, Pakistan: Punjab Educational Press, 1967.

Ulrich Rebstock. "A Qāḍī's Errors." *Islamic Law and Society* 6, no. 1 (1999): 1–37.

Urvoy, Dominique. "The ʿUlamāʾ of al-Andalus." In *The Legacy of Muslim Spain.* Ed. Salma Khadrar Jayusi. Leiden: E.J. Brill, 1992.

Vida, Levi Della. "Khāridjites." *Encyclopaedia of Islam.* eds. E. Van Donzel, B. Lewis, Ch Pellat, and C.E. Bosworth. 2nd edn. Leiden: E.J. Brill, 1978: 4:1074–1077.

Vining, Joseph. *The Authoritative and the Authoritarian.* Chicago: University of Chicago Press, 1986.

Voll, John Robert. *Islam: Continuity and Change in the Modern World.* 2nd edn. Syracuse: Syracuse University Press, 1992.

Von Denffer, Ahmad. *ʿUlūm al-Qurʾān: An Introduction to the Sciences of the Qurʾān.* Rev. ed. Leicester, England: The Islamic Foundation, 1994.

Wadud, Amina. *Qurʾan and Woman.* New York: Oxford University Press, 1999.

Wahba, Mourad, and Mona Abousenna. *Averroes and the Enlightenment.* Amherst: Prometheus Books, 1996.

Wansbrough, John. *Qurʾānic Studies: Sources and Methods of Scriptural Interpretation.* Oxford: Oxford University Press, 1977.

Watson, Alan. *Failures of the Legal Imagination.* Philadelphia: University of Pennsylvania Press, 1988.

___. *Legal Transplants: An Approach to Comparative Law.* 2nd edn. Athens: University of Georgia Press, 1993.

___. *The Making of the Civil Law.* Cambridge: Harvard University Press, 1981.

___. *The Nature of Law.* Edinburgh: Edinburgh University Press, 1977.

Watt, W. Montgomery. "Ashʿariyya." *Encyclopaedia of Islam.* Eds. H.A.R. Gibb, J.H. Kramers, E. Lévi-Provençal, J. Schacht, B. Lewis, and Ch. Pellat. 2nd edn. Leiden: E.J. Brill, 1960: 1:696.

___. *The Formative Period.* Edinburgh: Edinburgh University Press, 1973. Reprint. Oxford: Oneworld Publications, 1998.

___. *Islamic Philosophy and Theology: An Extended Survey.* 2nd edn. Edinburgh: Edinburgh University Press, 1985. Reprint, Edinburgh: Edinburgh University Press, 1992.

___. *Islamic Political Thought: The Basic Concepts.* Edinburgh: Edinburgh University Press, 1968.

___. *Muhammad: Prophet and Statesman.* 1961. Reprint, Oxford: Oxford University Press, 1964.

Watt, W. Montgomery, and Richard Bell. *Introduction to the Qur'an.* Edinburgh: Edinburgh University Press, 1970. Reprint. Edinburgh: Edinburgh University Press, 1994.

Weiss, Bernard G. *The Search for God's Law: Islamic Jurisprudence in the Writings of Sayf al-Dīn al-Āmidī.* Salt Lake City: University of Utah Press, 1992.

___. *The Spirit of Islamic Law.* Athens: University of Georgia Press, 1998.

White, G. Edward. "The Evolution of Reasoned Elaboration: Jurisprudential Criticism and Social Change." *Virginia Law Review* 51 (1973): 279–302.

White, James Boyd. *Heracles' Bow: Essays on the Rhetoric and Poetics of the Law.* Madison: University of Wisconsin, 1985.

Wolfe, Alan. "The Opening of the Evangelical Mind." *The Atlantic Monthly* 286, no. 4 (October 2000): 55–76.

Wolfson, Harry Austryn. *The Philosophy of the Kalam.* Cambridge, MA: Harvard University Press, 1976.

Yanagihashi, Hiroyuki. "The Judicial Functions of the Sulṭān in Civil Cases According to the Mālikīs up to the Sixth/Twelfth Century." *Islamic Law and Society* 3, no. 1 (1996): 41–74.

Yeğenoğlu, Meyda. *Colonial Fantasies: Towards a Feminist Reading of Orientalism.* Cambridge: Cambridge University Press, 1998.

Zaman, Iftikhar. "The Evolution of a Hadith: The Transmission, Growth and the Science of Rijāl in Ḥadīth of Saʿd b. Abī Waqqās." Ph.D. diss., University of Chicago, 1991.

Zaman, Muhammad Qasim. "The Caliphs, the ʿUlamāʾ, and the Law: Defining the Role and Function of the Caliph in the Early ʿAbbāsid Period." *Islamic Law and Society* 4, no. 1 (1997): 1–36.

___. *Religion and Politics Under the Early ʿAbbasids: The Emergence of the Proto-Sunni Elite.* Leiden: E.H. Brill, 1997.

Zebiri, Kate. *Mahmud Shaltut and Islamic Modernism.* Oxford: Clarendon Press, 1993.

## *Arabic and Persian Sources*

ʿAbbāsī, Muḥammad ʿĪd., ed. *Fatāwā wa Rasāʾil Samāḥat al-Shaykh ʿAbd al-Razzāq ʿAfīfī.* 2nd edn. Beirut: Dār Ibn Ḥazm, 1999.

ʿAbd al-ʿAzīz, Amīr. *Dirāsāt fī ʿUlūm al-Qurʾān.* Beirut: Muʾassasat al-Risālah, 1983.

ʿAbd al-Razzāq, Abū Bakr al-Ṣanʿānī. *al-Muṣannaf.* Ed. Ḥabīb al-Raḥmān al-Aʿẓamī. Beirut: al-Maktab al-Islāmī, 1983.

ʿAbduh, Muḥammad. *al-Aʿmāl al-Kāmilah li al-Imām Muḥammad ʿAbduh: al-Kitābāt al-Siyāsiyyah.* Ed. Muḥammad ʿImārah. Beirut: Muʾassasat al-ʿArabiyyah li al-Dirāsāt wa al-Nashr, 1972.

Abū Ḥayyān al-Andalusī, Muḥammad b. Yūsuf. *Tafsīr al-Baḥr al-Muḥīṭ.* Eds. ʿĀdil ʿAbd al-Mawjūd and ʿAlī Muḥammad Muʿawwaḍ. Beirut: Dār al-Kutub al-ʿIlmiyyah, 1993.

Abū al-Nūr, Muḥammad al-Aḥmadī. *al-Muntakhab fī Tafsīr al-Qurʾān al-Karīm.* Cairo: Lajnat al-Qurʾān wa al-Sunnah, 1985.

Abū Shuqqah, ʿAbd al-Ḥalīm. *Taḥrīr al-Marʾah fī ʿAṣr al-Risālah*. Kuwait: Dār al-Qalam, 1990.

Abū Zahrah, Muḥammad. *Uṣūl al-Fiqh*. Cairo: Dār al-Fikr al-ʿArabī, n.d.

Abyaḍ, Anīs. *Rashīd Riḍā: Taʾrīkh wa Sīrah*. Tarabulus: Jarrus Bris, 1993.

al-ʿAjilānī, Munīr. *ʿAbqariyyat al-Islām fī Uṣūl al-Ḥukm: Baḥth fī Taʾrīkh al-Ḥukm al-Islāmī min ʿAhd al-Nubuwwah ilā Ākhir al-ʿAhd al-Islāmī*. Beirut: Dār al-Kitāb al-Jadīd, 1965.

al-Albānī, Muḥammad Nāṣir al-Dīn. *Ḥijāb al-Marʾah al-Muslimah*. Cairo: al-Maktabah al-Salafiyyah, 1374 A.H.

___. *Silsilat al-Aḥādīth al-Ḍaʿīfa wa al-Mawḍūʿa wa Atharahā al-Sayyiʾ fī al-Umma*. Riyad: Maktabat al-Maʿārif, 1408 A.H.

al-ʿĀlim, Yūsuf Ḥāmid. *al-Maqāṣid al-ʿĀmmah li al-Sharīʿah al-Islāmiyyah*. Herndon, Virginia: International Institute of Islamic Thought, 1991.

al-Alūsī, Abū al-Faḍl Shihāb al-Dīn al-Sayyid Maḥmūd. *Rūḥ al-Maʿānī fī Tafsīr al-Qurʾān al-ʿAẓīm wa al-Sabʿ al-Mathānī*. Beirut: Dār Iḥyāʾ al-Turāth al-ʿArabī, 1985.

___. *Rūḥ al-Maʿānī fī Tafsīr al-Qurʾān al-ʿAẓīm wa al-Sabʿ al-Mathānī*. Damascus: Idārat al-Ṭibāʿah al-Munīriyyah, n.d.

al-ʿAlwānī, Ṭāhā Jābir. *Adab al-Ikhtilāf fī al-Islām*. Herndon, Virginia: The International Institute for Islamic Thought, 1992.

al-Āmidī, Sayf al-Dīn Abū al-Ḥasan ʿAlī b. Abī ʿAlī b. Muḥammad. *al-Iḥkām fī Uṣūl al-Aḥkām*. Ed. ʿAbd al-Razzāq ʿAfīfī. 2nd edn. Beirut: al-Maktab al-Islāmī, 1402 A.H.

___. *al-Iḥkām fī Uṣūl al-Aḥkām*. Ed. Sayyid al-Jamīlī. Beirut: Dār al-Kitāb al-ʿArabī, 1984.

___. *al-Iḥkām fī Uṣūl al-Aḥkām*. Cairo: Muḥammad ʿAlī Ṣabī, 1968.

ʿĀmilī, Muṣṭafā Qaṣr. *al-Wajīz fī ʿUlūm al-Qurʾān wa Taʾrīkhihi*. Beirut: Dār al-Islāmiyyah, 1998.

al-Andalūsī, Athīr al-Dīn Muḥammad b. Yūsuf Abī Ḥayyān. *Tafsīr al-Nahr al-Mādd min al-Baḥr al-Muḥīṭ*. Beirut: Dār al-Jinān, n.d.

al-Anṣārī, ʿAbd Allāh b. Ibrāhīm. *Tajrīd al-Bayān li Tafsīr al-Qurʾān min Ṣafwat al-Tafāsīr*. n.p.: al-Dawḥah al-Ḥadīthah, 1984.

al-Asʿadī, Muḥammad ʿUbayd Allāh. *al-Mūjaz fī Uṣūl al-Fiqh*. n.p.: Dār al-Salām, 1990.

al-ʿAṣfarī, Abū ʿUmar Khalīfah b. Khayyāṭ. *Taʾrīkh Ibn Khayyāṭ*. al-Najaf: Maṭbaʿat al-Ādāb, 1967.

al-Ashʿarī, Abū al-Ḥasan ʿAlī b. Ismāʿīl. *Maqālāt al-Islāmiyyīn wa Ikhtilāf al-Muṣallīn*. Ed. Muḥammad Muḥyī al-Dīn ʿAbd al-Ḥamīd. Beirut: al-Maktabah al-ʿAṣriyyah, 1990.

al-Asmandī, Muḥammad b. ʿAbd al-Ḥamīd. *Badhl al-Naẓar fī al-Uṣūl*. Ed. Muḥammad Zakī ʿAbd al-Barr. Cairo: Maktabat Dār al-Turāth, 1992.

al-Asnawī, Jamāl al-Dīn Abī Muḥammad ʿAbd al-Raḥīm b. al-Ḥasan. *Nihāyat al-Sūl fī Sharḥ Minhāj al-Wuṣūl ilā ʿIlm al-Uṣūl*. Ed. Shaʿbān Ismāʿīl. Beirut: Dār Ibn Ḥazm, 1999.

___. *al-Tamhīd fī Takhrīj al-Furūʿ ʿalā al-Uṣūl*. 3rd edn. Beirut: Muʾassasat al-Risālah, 1984.

al-ʿAṭṭār, Ḥasan. *Ḥāshiyat al-ʿAṭṭār ʿalā Jamʿ al-Jawāmiʿ*. Beirut: Dār al-Kutub al-ʿIlmiyyah, n.d.

ʿAwdah, ʿAbd al-Qādir. *al-Tashrīʿ al-Jināʾī al-Islāmī Muqāranan bi al-Qānūn al-Waḍʿī*. 5th ed. Beirut: Dār al-Kitāb al-ʿArabī, 1968.

ʿAwdah, Salmān b. Fahd. *Fī Ḥiwār Hādī maʿa Muḥammad al-Ghazālī*. Saudi Arabia: n.p., 1989.

Aybash, Yūsuf. *Nuṣūṣ al-Fikr al-Siyāsī al-Islāmī: al-Imāmah ʿind al-Sunnah.* Beirut: Dār al-Ṭalīʿah, 1966.

al-ʿAyīnī, Abū Muḥammad Maḥmūd b. Aḥmad. *al-Bināyah fī Sharḥ al-Hidāyah.* Beirut: Dār al-Fikr, 1990.

al-ʿAzzī, ʿAbd al-Munʿim Ṣāliḥ. *Difāʿ ʿan Abī Hurayrah.* Beirut: Dār al-Qalam, n.d.

al-Badakhshī, Muḥammad b. al-Ḥasan. *Sharḥ al-Badakhshī Manāhij al-ʿUqūl maʿa Sharḥ al-Asnawī Nihāyat al-Sūl.* Beirut: Dār al-Kutub al-ʿIlmiyyah, 1984.

Badrān, Badrān Abū al-ʿAynayn. *Uṣūl al-Fiqh.* Cairo: Dār al-Maʿārif, 1965.

al-Baghawī, Abū Muḥammad al-Ḥusayn b. Masʿūd b. Muḥammad al-Farrāʾ. *Maṣābiḥ al-Sunnah.* Eds. Yūsuf ʿAbd al-Raḥmān al-Marʿashlī, Salīm Ibrāhīm Samārah, and Jamāl Ḥamdī al-Dhahabī. Beirut: Dār al-Maʿrifah, 1987.

___. *Sharḥ al-Sunnah.* Ed. Muʿawwaḍ al-Laḥḥām. Beirut: Dār al-Fikr, 1994.

al-Baghdādī, ʿAbd al-Qāhir b. Ṭāhir b. Muḥammad. *al-Farq bayn al-Firaq.* Ed. Muḥammad Muḥyī al-Dīn ʿAbd al-Ḥāmid. Egypt: Muḥammad ʿAlī Subayḥ, 1964.

al-Baghdādī, Abū al-Fatḥ Aḥmad b. ʿAlī b. Burhān. *al-Wuṣūl ilā al-Uṣūl.* Ed. ʿAbd al-Ḥamīd ʿAlī Abū Zanid. Riyāḍ: Maktabat al-Maʿārif, 1984.

al-Bahūtī, Manṣūr b. Yūnus. *Kashshāf al-Qināʾ ʿan Matn al-Iqnāʾ.* Ed. Abū ʿAbd Allāh Muḥammad Ḥasan Muḥammad Ḥasan Ismāʿīl. Beirut: Dār al-Kutub al-ʿIlmiyyah, 1997.

___. *al-Rawḍ al-Murbiʿ Sharḥ Zād al-Mustaqniʿ.* Beirut: Muʾassasat al-Risālah, 1996.

al-Bājī, Abū al-Walīd Sulaymān b. Khalaf. *Iḥkām al-Fuṣūl fī Aḥkām al-Uṣūl.* Ed. ʿAbd Allāh Muḥammad al-Jabūrī. Beirut: Muʾassasat al-Risālah, 1989.

___. *Iḥkām al-Fuṣūl fī Aḥkām al-Uṣūl.* Ed. ʿAbd al-Majīd al-Turkī. 2nd edn. Beirut: Dār al-Gharb al-Islāmī, 1995.

Bāliq, ʿIzz al-Dīn. *Minhāj al-Ṣāliḥīn.* Beirut: Dār al-Fatḥ, 1978.

al-Barazī, Muḥammad Fuʾād. *Ḥijāb al-Muslimah bayn Intiḥal al-Mubṭilīn wa Taʾwīl al-Jāhilīn.* Riyadh: Aḍwāʾ al-Salaf, 2000.

al-Baṣrī, Abū al-Ḥusayn Muḥammad b. ʿAlī b. al-Ṭayyib. *Al-Muʿtamad fī Uṣūl al-Fiqh,* Ed. Khalīl al-Mays. Beirut: Dār al-Kutub al-ʿIlmiyyah, 1983.

___. *Kitāb al-Muʿtamad fī Uṣūl al-Fiqh.* Eds. Muḥammad Ḥamīd Allāh, Muḥammad Bakr, and Ḥasan Ḥanafī. Damascus: Institut Français, 1964.

al-Bayḍāwī, Nāṣir al-Dīn Abī Saʿīd ʿAbd Allāh b. ʿUmar b. Muḥammad. *Anwār al-Tanzīl wa Asrār al-Taʾwīl: Tafsīr al-Bayḍāwī.* Beirut: Muʾassasat al-Shaʿbān, n.d.

al-Bayhaqī, Abū Bakr Aḥmad b. al-Ḥusayn b. ʿAlī. *Kitāb al-Sunan al-Kubrā.* Beirut: Dār al-Maʿrifah, n.d.

al-Birrī, Zakariyyā. *Uṣūl al-Fiqh al-Islāmī.* 3rd edn. Cairo: Dār al-Nahḍah al-ʿArabiyyah, 1974.

al-Bukhārī, Abū ʿAbd Allāh Ismāʿīl b. Ibrāhīm al-Jaʿafī. *Kitāb al-Taʾrīkh al-Kabīr.* n.p.: Muʾassasat al-Kutub al-Thaqāfiyyah, n.d.

al-Bukhārī, ʿAlāʾ al-Dīn ʿAbd al-ʿAzīz b. Aḥmadī. *Kashf al-Asrār ʿan Uṣūl Fakhr al-Islām al-Bazdāwī.* Ed. Muḥammad al-Muʿtaṣim bi Allāh al-Baghdādī. 3rd ed. Beirut: Dār al-Kitāb al-ʿArabī, 1997.

al-Burūsī, Ismāʿīl Ḥaqqī. *Tanwīr al-Adhhān min Tafsīr Rūḥ al-Bayān.* Ed. Muḥammad ʿAlī al-Ṣābūnī. Damascus: Dār al-Qalam, 1989.

al-Būṣayrī, Abū al-ʿAbbās Shihāb al-Dīn Aḥmad b. Abī Bakr b. ʿAbd al-Raḥmān b. Ismāʿīl. *Zawāʾid Ibn Mājah ʿalā al-Kutub al-Khamsah.* Beirut: Dār al-Kutub al-ʿIlmiyyah, 1993.

al-Būṭī, Muḥammad Saʿīd Ramaḍān. *Ḍawābiṭ al-Maṣlaḥah fī al-Sharīʿah al-Islāmiyyah.* 6th edn. Beirut: Mu'assasat al-Risālah, 1992.

al-Dabbāb, ʿAlī b. Hilāl. *al-Shuʿāb al-Fā'iḍ Sharḥ Mukhtaṣar ʿIlm al-Farā'iḍ.* 2nd edn. Cairo: al-Maṭbaʿah al-Salafiyyah, 1397 A.H.

Al-Dārquṭnī,ʿAlī b. ʿUmar. *Sunan al-Dārquṭnī.* Ed. Majdī b. Sayyid al-Shūrī. Beirut: Dār al-Kutub al-ʿIlmiyyah, 1996.

al-Dawālībī, Muḥammad Maʿrūf. *Madkhal ilā ʿIlm Uṣūl al-Fiqh.* 5th edn. n.p.: Dār al-ʿIlm li al-Malāyīn, 1965.

___. al-Dawīsh, Aḥmad b. ʿAbd al-Razzāq. Ed. *Fatāwā al-Lajnah al-Dā'imah li al-Buḥūth al-ʿIlmiyyah wa al-Iftā'.* Riyāḍ: Ri'āsat Idārat al-Buḥūth al-ʿIlmiyyah wa al-Iftā', 1996.

al-Dhahabī, Shams al-Dīn Muḥammad b. Aḥmad b. ʿUthmān. *Kitāb al-Kabā'ir.* Beirut: Dār al-Kutub al-Shaʿbiyyah, n.d.

___. *Siyar Aʿlām al-Nubalā'.* 4th edn. Beirut: Mu'assasat al-Risālah, 1986.

al-Dībānī, ʿAbd al-Majīd ʿAbd al-Ḥamīd. *al-Minhāj al-Wāḍiḥ fī ʿIlm Uṣūl al-Fiqh wa Ṭuruq Istinbāṭ al-Aḥkām.* Binghāzī: Dār al-Kutub al-Waṭaniyyah, 1995.

al-Dimashqī, ʿAbd al-Qādir b. Aḥmad b. Muṣṭafā Badran al-Dawmī. *Nuzhat al-Khāṭir al-ʿĀṭir.* 2nd edn. Beirut: Dār Ibn Ḥazm, 1995.

al-Dimashqī, Abū ʿAbd Allāh ʿAbd al-Raḥmān. *Raḥmat al-Ummah fī Ikhtilāf al-A'immah.* Kuwait: Maktabat al-Bukhārī, n.d.

al-Dimashqī, Abū Ḥafṣ ʿUmar b. ʿAlī Ibn ʿĀdil. *al-Lubāb fī ʿUlūm al-Kitāb.* Eds. ʿĀdil Aḥmad ʿAbd al-Mawjūd and ʿAlī Muḥammad Muʿawwaḍ. Beirut: Dār al-Kutub al-ʿIlmiyyah, 1998.

al-Farrā', al-Qāḍī Abū Yaʿlā Muḥammad b. al-Ḥusayn. *al-Aḥkām al-Sulṭāniyyah.* Beirut: Dār al-Kutub al-ʿIlmiyyah, 1983.

___. *al-ʿUddah fī Uṣūl al-Fiqh.* Ed. Aḥmad b. ʿAlī Sayyid al-Mubārakī. Riyāḍ: n.p., 1990.

al-Fāsī, ʿAllāl. *Maqāṣid al-Sharīʿah al-Islāmiyyah wa Makārimuhā.* 5th edn. Beirut: Dār al-Gharb al-Islāmī, 1993.

*al-Fatāwā al-Hindiyyah* [a.k.a. *al-Fatāwā al-ʿĀlamjīriyyah*]. Beirut: Dār Iḥyā' al-Turāth al-ʿArabī, 1986.

*Fatāwā al-Lajnah al-Dā'imah li al-Buḥūth al-ʿIlmiyyah wa al-Iftā'.* Ed. Aḥmad b. ʿAbd al-Razzāq al-Dawīsh. Riyāḍ: Dār ʿĀlam al-Kutub, 1991.

*Fatāwā al-Mar'ah al-Muslimah.* Ed. Abū Muḥammad Ashraf b. ʿAbd al-Maqṣūd. Riyāḍ: Adwā' al-Salaf, 1996.

*Fatāwā al-Mar'ah al-Muslimah.* Ed. Abū Muḥammad Ashraf b. ʿAbd al-Maqṣūd. Riyāḍ: Maktabah Ṭabariyyah, 1995.

al-Ghazālī, Abū Ḥāmid Muḥammad b. Muḥammad. *Iḥyā' ʿUlūm al-Dīn.* Beirut: Dār al-Maʿrifah, n.d.

___. *al-Mankhūl min Taʿlīqāt al-Uṣūl.* Damascus: Dār al-Fikr, 1980.

___. *al-Mustaṣfā min ʿIlm al-Uṣūl.* Ed. Ibrāhīm Muḥammad Ramaḍān. Beirut: Dār al-Arqam, n.d.

___. *al-Mustaṣfā min ʿIlm al-Uṣūl.* Baghdad: Maktabat al-Muthannā, n.d.

___. *al-Wajīz fī Fiqh al-Imām al-Shāfiʿī.* Eds. ʿAlī Muʿawwaḍ and ʿĀdil ʿAbd al-Mawjūd. Beirut: Dār al-Arqām, 1997.

al-Ghazālī, Muḥammad. *Dustūr al-Wiḥdah al-Thaqāfiyyah bayn al-Muslimīn.* 2nd edn. Damascus: Dār al-Qalam, 1996.

___. *al-Sunnah al-Nabawiyyah bayn Ahl al-Fiqh wa Ahl al-Ḥadīth*. Cairo: Dār al-Shurūq, 1989.

al-Ghazzī, Muḥammad Ṣidqī b. Aḥmad al-Būrnū Abū al-Ḥārith. *Mawsū'at al-Qawā'id al-Fiqhiyyah*. Beirut: n.p., 1995.

al-Ghiṭā', Muḥammad al-Ḥusayn Āl Kāshif. *Naqḍ Fatāwā al-Wahhābiyyah*. Beirut: Markaz al-Ghadīr, 1999.

Ḥammād, Nafīdh Ḥusayn. *Mukhtalaf al-Ḥadīth bayn al-Fuqahā' wa al-Muḥaddithīn*. al-Manṣūrah: Dār al-Wafā', 1993.

al-Ḥarīrī, Abū Mūsā. *'Ālam al-Mu'jizāt: Baḥth fī Ta'rīkh al-Qur'ān*. Beirut: n.p., 1982.

Harrās, Muḥammad Khalīl. *al-Ḥarakah al-Wahhābiyyah: Radd 'alā Maqāl li al-Duktūr Muḥammad al-Bahā fī Naqd al-Wahhābiyyah*. Beirut: Dār al-Kātib al-'Arabī, n.d.

al-Harawī, Abū 'Ubayd al-Qāsim b. Salām. *Gharīb al-Ḥadīth*. Beirut: Dār al-Kutub al-'Ilmiyyah, 1986.

Ḥasab Allāh, 'Alī. *Uṣūl al-Tashrī' al-Islāmī*. 3rd edn. Cairo: Dār al-Ma'ārif, 1964.

al-Ḥasan, Muḥammad b. 'Alī and Sulaymān b. Ṣāliḥ al-Qar'āwī. *al-Bayān fī 'Ulūm al-Qur'ān ma'a Madkhal fī Uṣūl al-Tafsīr wa Maṣādirihi*. Saudi Arabia: Maktabat al-Ẓilāl, 1994.

Ḥassān, Ḥusayn Ḥāmid. *Naẓariyyat al-Maṣlaḥah fī al-Fiqh al-Islāmī*. Cairo: Dār al-Nahḍāh al-'Arabiyyah, 1971.

al-Ḥaṭṭāb, Abū 'Abd Allāh Muḥammad b. Muḥammad b. 'Abd al-Raḥmān al-Maghribī al-Ra'īnī. *Mawāhib al-Jalīl li Sharḥ Mukhtaṣar Khalīl*. Beirut: Dār al-Kutub al-'Ilmiyyah, 1995.

al-Ḥawālī, Ṣafar b. 'Abd al-Raḥmān. *Ẓāhirat al-Irjā' fī al-Fikr al-Islāmī*. Cairo: Maktab al-Ṭayyib, 1417 A.H.

Ḥawwā, Sa'īd. *al-Asās fī al-Tafsīr*. Cairo: Dār al-Salām, 1985.

al-Ḥijāzī, Muḥammad Maḥmūd. *al-Tafsīr al-Wāḍiḥ*. Beirut: Dār al-Kitāb al-'Arabī, 1982.

al-Ḥillī, Abū al-Qāsim Najm al-Dīn Ja'far b. al-Ḥasan. *al-Mukhtaṣar al-Nāfi' fī Fiqh al-Imāmiyyah*. Najaf: Maṭba'at al-Nu'mān, 1964.

al-Hindī, 'Alā' al-Dīn 'Alī al-Muttaqī b. Ḥusām al-Dīn al-Burhān Fawzi. *Kanz al-'Ummāl fī Sunan al-Aqwāl wa al-Af'āl* Beirut: Mu'assasat al-Risāla, 1985.

Ḥusayn, Aḥmad Farrāj. *Uṣūl al-Fiqh al-Islāmī*. Lebanon: al-Dār al-Jāmi'iyyah, 1986.

al-Huwwāriyy, Hūd b. Muḥkam. *Tafsīr Kitāb Allāh al-'Azīz*. Beirut: Dār al-Gharb al-Islāmī, 1990.

Ibn 'Abd al-Barr, Abū 'Umar Yūsuf b. 'Abd Allāh b. Muḥammad al-Namri. *al-Tamhīd li-mā fī al-Muwaṭṭa' min al-Ma'ānī wa al-Asānīd*. Eds. Muṣtafā al-'Alawī and Muḥammad al-Bakrī. Morroco: Maktabat Faḍālah, 1982.

Ibn 'Abd al-Raḥīm, Ashraf b. 'Abd al-Maqṣūd. *Jināyat al-Shaykh Muḥammad al-Ghazālī 'alā al-Ḥadīth wa Ahlihi*. al-Ismā'īliyyah, Egypt: Maktabat al-Imām al-Bukhārī, 1989.

Ibn 'Abd al-Salām, Abū Muḥammad 'Izz al-Dīn b. 'Abd al-'Azīz. *Qawā'id al-Aḥkām fī Maṣāliḥ al-Anām*. Beirut: al-Mu'assasat al-Rayyān, 1990.

Ibn 'Abd al-Wahhāb, Muḥammad. *Kitāb al-Tawḥīd alladhī huwa Ḥaqq Allāh 'alā al-'Abīd*. Cairo: Dār al-Ma'ārif, 1974.

Ibn 'Abd al-Wahhāb, Sulaymān. *al-Ṣawā'iq al-Ilāhiyyah fī al-Radd 'alā al-Wahhābiyyah*. Ed. Bassām 'Amqiyah. Damascus: Maktabat Ḥarrā', 1997.

Ibn Abī al-Damm, Shihāb al-Dīn Ibrāhīm b. 'Abd Allāh. *Kitāb Adab al-Quḍā' aw al-Durar al-Manẓūmāt fī al-Aqḍiyyah wa al-Ḥukūmāt*. Ed. Muḥammad 'Abd al-Qādir 'Aṭā. Beirut: Dār al-Kutub al-'Ilmiyyah, 1987.

Ibn Abī al-Ḥadīd al-Madā'inī, ʿIzz al-Dīn Abū Ḥāmid ʿAbd al-Ḥamīd b. Hibat Allāh. *Sharḥ Nahj al-Balāghah.* Ed. Ḥasan Tamīm. Beirut: Dār Maktabat al-Ḥayāh, 1963.

Ibn Abī Shaybah, Abū Bakr ʿAbd Allāh b. Muḥammad. *al-Kitāb al-Muṣannaf fī al-Aḥādīth wa al-Āthār.* Ed. Muḥammad ʿAbd al-Salām Shāhīn. Beirut: Dār al-Kutub al-ʿIlmiyyah, 1995.

Ibn ʿĀbidīn, Muḥammad Amīn b. ʿUmar. *Ḥāshiyat Radd al-Muḥtār.* Beirut: Dār al-Kutub al-ʿIlmiyyah, 1994.

___. *Ḥāshiyat Radd al-Muḥtār.* 2nd edn. Cairo: Muṣṭafā al-Bābī al-Ḥalabī, 1966.

___. "Nashr al-ʿArf fī Binā' Baʿḍ al-Aḥkām ʿalā al-ʿUrf." *Majmūʿat Rasā'il Ibn ʿĀbidīn.* Beirut: Dār Iḥyā' al-Turāth al-ʿArabī, 1970.

Ibn al-ʿArabī, Abū Bakr Muḥammad b. ʿAbd Allāh. *Aḥkām al-Qur'ān.* Ed. ʿAlī Muḥammad al-Bajāwī. Beirut: Dār al-Jīl, 1987.

___. *Aḥkām al-Qur'ān.* Ed. ʿAlī Muḥammad al-Bajāwī. Beirut: Dār al-Maʿrifah, n.d.

Ibn Aʿtham, Abū Muḥammad Aḥmad. *al-Futūḥ.* Beirut: Dār al-Kutub al-ʿIlmiyyah, 1986.

Ibn al-Athīr, Abū al-Ḥasan ʿAlī b. Abī al-Karam b. ʿAbd al-Waḥīd. *al-Kāmil fī al-Ta'rīkh.* Ed. Abū al-Fidā' ʿAbd Allāh al-Qāḍī. Beirut: Dār al-Kutub al-ʿIlmiyyah, 1987.

___. *Usud al-Ghābah fī Maʿrifat al-Ṣaḥābah.* Beirut: Dār Iḥyā' al-Turāth al-ʿArabī, n.d.

Ibn al-Athīr, Abū al-Saʿādāt al-Mubārak b. Muḥammad al-Jazrī. *al-Nihayah fī Gharīb al-Ḥadīth wa al-Athar.* Ed. Abū ʿAbd al-Raḥmān b. ʿUwīḍah. Beirut: Dār al-Kutub al-ʿIlmiyyah, 1997.

Ibn ʿAṭiyyah, Abū Muḥammad ʿAbd al-Ḥaqq b. Ghālib al-Andalusī. *al-Muḥarrar al-Wajīz fī Tafsīr al-Kitāb al-ʿAzīz.* Ed. ʿAbd al-Salām ʿAbd al-Shāfī. Beirut: Dār al-Kutub al-ʿIlmiyya, 1993.

Ibn al-Bannā, Abū ʿAlī al-Ḥasan b. Aḥmad b. ʿAbd Allāh. *Kitāb al-Muqniʿ fī Sharḥ Mukhtaṣar al-Khiraqī.* Ed. ʿAbd al-ʿAzīz b. Sulaymān b. Ibrāhīm al-Buʿaymī. Riyāḍ: Maktabat al-Rushd, 1993.

Ibn Bāz, ʿAbd al-ʿAzīz b. ʿAbd Allāh b. ʿAbd al-Raḥmān. *Majmūʿ Fatāwā wa Maqālāt Mutanawwiʿah.* Ed. Muḥammad b. Saʿd al-Shawīʿ. 2nd edn. n.p.: Muḥammad b. Saʿd al-Shawīʿ, 1990.

___. *Majmūʿ Fatāwā wa Maqālāt Mutanawwiʿah.* Ed. Muḥammad b. Saʿd al-Shawīʿ. Riyāḍ: Maktabat al-Maʿārif li al-Nashr wa al-Tawzīʿ, 1992.

___. *Majmūʿ Fatāwā wa Maqālāt Mutanawwiʿah.* Ed. Muḥammad b. Saʿd al-Shawīʿ. Cairo: Maktabat Ibn Taymiyyah, 1990.

___. *Majmūʿ Fatāwā wa Maqālāt Mutanawwiʿah.* Saudi Arabia: Idārat al Buḥūth al ʿIlmiyyah wa al-Iftā' wa al-Daʿwah wa al-Irshad, 1987.

___. *Majmūʿ Fatāwā.* Ed. ʿAbd Allāh b. Muḥammad b. Aḥmad al-Ṭayyār. Riyāḍ: Dār al-Waṭan, 1416 A.H.

___. *al-Fatāwā.* 3rd edn. Saudi Arabia: Kitāb al-Daʿwah, 1409 A.H.

Ibn Bāz, ʿAbd al-ʿAzīz b. ʿAbd Allāh b. ʿAbd al-Raḥmān, ʿAbd al-ʿAzīz, Muḥammad b. Ṣāliḥ al-ʿUthaymīn, and ʿAbd Allāh b. Jibrīn. *Fatāwā Islāmiyyah.* Ed. Qāsim al-Shamāʿī al-Rifāʿī. Beirut: Dār al-Qalam, 1988.

Ibn al-Bazzāz, Muḥammad b. Muḥammad b. Shihāb al-Kurdarī. *al-Fatāwā al-Bazzāziyyah.* Printed in the margins of *al-Fatāwā al-Hindiyyah.* 3rd edn. Beirut: Dār al-Maʿrifah, 1973.

Ibn Ḍawayyān, Ibrāhīm b. Muḥammad b. Sālim. *Manār al-Sabīl fī Sharḥ al-Dalīl.* Ed. Muḥammad ʿĪd al-ʿAbbāsī. Riyāḍ: Maktabat al-Maʿārif, 1996.

Ibn Fawzān, Ṣāliḥ b. Fawzān b. ʿAbd Allāh. *al-Muntaqā min Fatāwā Faḍīlat al-Shaykh Ṣāliḥ b. Fawzān b. ʿAbd Allāh al-Fawzān.* Ed. ʿĀdil b. ʿAlī b. Aḥmad al-Farīdān. 2nd edn. Medina: Maktabat al-Ghurbān al-Athariyyah, 1997.

Ibn Hādī Madkhalī, Rabīʿ. *Kashf Mawqif al-Ghazālī min al-Sunnah wa Ahlihā wa Naqd Baʿḍ Ārāʾihi.* 2nd edn. Cairo: Maktabat al-Sunnah, 1410 A.H.

Ibn Ḥajar al-ʿAsqalānī, Shihāb al-Dīn Aḥmad b. ʿAlī. *Fatḥ al-Bārī bi Sharḥ Ṣaḥīḥ al-Bukhārī.* Beirut: Dār al-Fikr, 1993.

___. *Fatḥ al-Bārī: Sharḥ Ṣaḥīḥ al-Bukhārī.* Beirut: Dār al-Maʿrifah, n.d.

___. *Taqrīb al-Tahdhīb.* Ed. ʿAbd al-Wahhāb ʿAbd al-Laṭīf. Cairo: n.p., 1975.

Ibn Ḥajjāj, Muslim. *Ṣaḥīḥ Muslim.* Beirut: Dār al-Maʿrifah, n.d.

Ibn Ḥanbal, Aḥmad. *Musnad al-Imām Aḥmad b. Ḥanbal.* Eds. ʿAlī Ḥasan al-Ṭawīl, Samīr Ṭāhā al-Majdhūb, and Samīr Ḥusayn Ghāwī. Beirut: al-Maktab al-Islāmī, 1993.

Ibn Ḥazm al-Ẓāhirī, Abū Muḥammad ʿAlī b. Aḥmad b. Saʿīd. *Asmāʾ al-Ṣaḥābah al-Ruwāḥ.* Ed. Sayyid Kisrawī Ḥasan. Beirut: Dār al-Kutub al-ʿIlmiyyah, n.d.

___. *al-Faṣl fī al-Milal wa al-Ahwāʾ wa al-Niḥal.* 5 vols. Cairo: Muḥammad ʿAlī Subayḥ, 1964.

___. *al-Iḥkām fī Uṣūl al-Aḥkām.* Cairo: Dār al-Ḥadīth, 1984.

___. *Kitāb al-Faṣl fī al-Milal wa al-Ahwāʾ wa al-Niḥal.* Egypt: al-Maṭbaʿah al-Adabiyyah, 1317 A.H.

___. *Marātib al-Ijmāʿ fī al-ʿIbādāt wa al-Muʿāmalāt wa al-Iʿtiqādāt.* Beirut: Dār al-Kutub al-ʿIlmiyyah, 1970.

___. *al-Muḥallā bi al-Āthār.* Ed. ʿAbd al-Ghaffār Sulaymān al-Bandārī. Beirut: Dār al-Kutub al-ʿIlmiyyah, n.d.

___. *al-Nubadh fī Uṣūl al-Fiqh al-Ẓāhirī.* Ed. Muḥammad Ṣubḥī Ḥasan Ḥallāq. Beirut: Dār Ibn Ḥazm, 1993.

Ibn Ḥibbān, Muḥammad. *al-Majrūḥīn min al-Muḥaddithīn wa al-Ḍuʿafāʾ wa al-Matrūkīn.* Aleppo: Dār Waʿy, 1397 A.H.

Ibn Hishām. *al-Sīrah al-Nabawiyyah.* Beirut: Dār al-Maʿrifah, n.d.

Ibn Hubayrah, Yaḥyā b. Muḥammad. *al-Ijmāʿ ʿind Aʾimmat Ahl al-Sunnah al-Arbaʿah.* Cairo: Dār al-Nahḍah al-ʿArabiyyah, 1993.

Ibn al-ʿImād, Abū al-Falāḥ ʿAbd al-Ḥayy. *Shadharāt al-Dhahab fī Akhbār man Dhahab.* Beirut: Dār al-Kutub al-ʿIlmiyyah, n.d.

Ibn Jār Allāh, Muḥammad b. Aḥmad al-Ṣaʿadī al-Yamānī. *al-Nawāfiḥ al-ʿAṭirah fī al-Aḥādīth al-Mushtahirah.* Ed. Muḥammad ʿAbd al-Qādir Aḥmad ʿAṭā. Beirut: Muʾassasat al-Kutub al-Thaqāfiyyah, 1992.

Ibn al-Jawzī Jamāl al-Dīn, Abū al-Faraj ʿAbd al-Raḥmān b. ʿAlī b. Muḥammad. *Kitāb Aḥkām al-Nisāʾ.* Beirut: Muʾassasat al-Kutub al-Thaqāfiyyah, 1992.

___. *Kitāb al-Mawḍūʿāt.* Beirut: Dār al-Kutub al-ʿIlmiyyah, 1995.

___. *al-Muntaẓam fī Taʾrīkh al-Umam wa al-Mulūk.* Ed. Muḥammad ʿAbd al-Qādir ʿAṭā and Muṣṭafā ʿAbd al-Qādir ʿAṭā. Beirut: Dār al-Kutub al-ʿIlmiyyah, 1992.

___. *al-Shifāʾ fī Mawāʿiẓ al-Mulūk wa al-Khulafāʾ.* Ed. Fuʾād ʿAbd al-Munʿim Aḥmad. Alexandria: Dār al-Daʿwah, n.d.

___. *Tablīs Iblīs.* Jeddah: Dār al-Madanī, 1983.

___. *Zād al-Masīr fī ʿIlm al-Tafsīr.* Ed. Aḥmad Shams al-Dīn. Beirut: Dār al-Kutub al-ʿIlmiyyah, 1994.

Ibn Kathīr, ʿImād al-Dīn Abū al-Fidāʾ b. ʿUmar. *al-Bidāyah wa al-Nihāyah.* Ed. Aḥmad Abū Mulḥim. et al. Beirut: Dār al-Kitāb, 1985.

___. *Mukhtaṣar Tafsīr Ibn Kathīr*. Ed. Muḥammad ʿAlī al-Ṣābūnī. 7th edn. Beirut: Dār al-Qurʾān al-Karīm, 1981.

___. *Tafsīr al-Qurʾān al-ʿAẓīm*. Beirut: Dār al-Khayr, 1990.

Ibn Khaldūn, Abū Zayd ʿAbd al-Raḥmān b. Muḥammad. *al-Muqaddimah*. Beirut: Dār Iḥyāʾ al-Turāth, n.d.

Ibn Khallikān, Abū al-ʿAbbās Shams al-Dīn Aḥmad b. Muḥammad b. Abī Bakr. *Wafayāt al-Aʿyān wa Anbāʾ Abnāʾ al-Zamān*. Eds. Yūsuf ʿAlī Ṭawīl and Maryam Qāsim Ṭawīl. Beirut: Dār al-Kutub al-ʿIlmiyyah, 1998.

___. *Wafayāt al-Aʿyān wa Anbāʾ al-Zamān*. Ed. Iḥsān ʿAbbās. Beirut: Dār Ṣādir, n.d.

Ibn al-Laḥḥām, Abū al-Ḥasan ʿAlāʾ al-Dīn b. Muḥammad b. ʿAbbās. *al-Qawāʿid wa al-Fawāʾid al-Uṣūliyyah wa mā Yataʿallaq bihā min al-Aḥkām al-Farʿiyyah*. Ed. ʿAbd al-Karīm al-Faḍīlī. Beirut: al-Maktabah al-ʿAṣriyyah, 1998.

Ibn Mājah, Abū ʿAbd Allāh Muḥammad b. Yazīd al-Qazwīnī. *Sunan al-Ḥāfiẓ Ibn Mājah*. Ed. Muḥammad Fuʾād ʿAbd al-Bāqī. Cairo: ʿĪsā al-Bābī al-Ḥalabī, 1972.

___. *Sunan Ibn Mājah*. Ed. Muḥammad Fuʾād ʿAbd al-Bāqī. Cairo: Dār al-Ḥadīth, n.d.

Ibn Manẓūr, Abū al-Faḍl Jamāl al-Dīn Muḥammad b. Makram. *Lisān al-ʿArab*. Beirut: Dār Ṣādir, n.d.

Ibn Mufliḥ, Abū Isḥāq Burhān al-Dīn Ibrāhīm b. Muḥammad b. ʿAbd Allāh b. Muḥammad. *al-Mubdiʿ fī Sharḥ al-Muqniʿ*. Ed. ʿAlī b. ʿAbd Allāh Āl Thānī. Beirut: al-Maktab al-Islāmī, 1977.

Ibn al-Mundhir, Muḥammad b. Ibrāhīm. *al-Ijmāʿ: yataḍamman al-Masāʾil al-Fiqhiyyah al-Muttafaq ʿalayhā ʿind Akthar ʿUlamāʾ al-Muslimīn*. Ed. Fuʾād ʿAbd al-Munʿim Aḥmad. 3rd edn. n.p.: Dār al-Daʿwah, 1402 A.H.

Ibn Muslim, Abū al-Ḥusayn Muslim b. al-Ḥajjāj. *al-Jāmiʿ al-Ṣaḥīḥ*. Beirut: Dār al-Maʿrifah, n.d.

Ibn al-Najjār, Muḥammad b. Aḥmad b. ʿAbd al-ʿAzīz b. ʿAlī al-Fatūḥī. *Sharḥ al-Kawkab al-Munīr al-Musammā Mukhtaṣar al-Taḥrīr aw al-Mukhtabar al-Mubtakar Sharḥ al-Mukhtaṣar fī Uṣūl al-Fiqh*. Eds. Muḥammad al-Zuḥaylī and Nazīr Ḥammād. Riyāḍ: Maktabat al-ʿUbaykān, 1993.

Ibn Nujaym, Zayn al-ʿĀbidīn b. Ibrāhīm. *al-Ashbāh wa al-Naẓāʾir*. Beirut: Dār al-Kitāb al-ʿIlmiyyah, 1980.

____. *al-Baḥr al-Rāʾiq Sharḥ Kanz al-Daqāʾiq*. Beirut: Dār al-Kutub al-ʿIlmiyyah, 1997.

Ibn al-Qaṣṣār, Abū al-Ḥasan ʿAlī b. ʿUmar. *al-Muqaddimah fī al-Uṣūl*. Ed. Muḥammad b. al-Ḥusayn al-Sulaymānī. Beirut: Dār al-Gharb al-Islāmī, 1996.

Ibn Qayyim al-Jawziyyah, Shams al-Dīn Abī ʿAbd Allāh Muḥammad b. Abī Bakr. *ʿAwn al-Maʿbūd Sharḥ Sunan Abī Dāwūd*. Ed. ʿAbd al-Raḥmān Muḥammad ʿUthmān. 2nd edn. Medina: al-Maktabah al-Salafiyyah, 1968/1969.

___. *Iʿlām al-Muwaqqiʿīn ʿan Rabb al-ʿĀlamīn*. Ed. Ṭāhā ʿAbd al-Raʾūf Saʿd. Beirut: Dār al-Jīl, n.d.

___. *Iʿlām al-Muwaqqiʿīn ʿan Rabb al-ʿĀlamīn*. Ed. ʿAbd al-Raḥman al-Wakīl. Cairo: Maktabat Ibn Taymiyyah, n.d.

___. *Rawḍat al-Muḥibbīn wa Nuzhat al-Mushtāqīn*. Ed. al-Sayyid al-Jamīlī. 6th edn. Beirut: Dār al-Kitāb al-ʿArabī, 1999.

Ibn Qudāmah, Abū Muḥammad ʿAbd Allāh b. Aḥmad b. Muḥammad. *al-Mughnī*. Beirut: Dār Iḥyāʾ al-Turāth al-ʿArabī, n.d.

___. *al-Mughnī.* Beirut: Dār al-Kutub al-ʿIlmiyyah, n.d.

Ibn Qudāmah al-Maqdisī, Muwaffaq al-Dīn Abū Muḥammad ʿAbd Allāh b. Aḥmad. *Rawḍat al-Nāẓir wa Jannat al-Munāẓir.* Riyāḍ: Maktabat al-Maʿārif, 1990.

Ibn Qutaybah, Abū Muḥammad ʿAbd Allāh b. Muslim al-Daynūrī. *Kitāb Taʾwīl Mukhtalaf al-Ḥadīth.* Beirut: Dār al-Kitāb al-ʿArabī, n.d.

Ibn Rushd (al-ḥafīd), Abū al-Walīd Muḥammad b. Aḥmad b. Muḥammad b. Aḥmad al-Qurṭubī. *Bidāyat al-Mujtahid wa Nihāyat al-Muqtaṣid.* Beirut: Dār al-Kutub al-ʿIlmiyyah, 1997.

Ibn Rushd (al-jadd), Abū al-Walīd Muḥammad b. Aḥmad al-Qurṭubī. *al-Bayān wa al-Taḥṣīl wa al-Sharḥ wa al-Tawjīh wa al-Taʿlīl fī al-Masāʾil al-Mustakhrajah.* Ed. Muḥammad Ḥajjī. 2nd edn. Beirut: Dār al-Gharb al-Islāmī, 1988.

___. *al-Muqaddimāt al-Mumahhidāt.* Ed. Muḥammad Ḥujjī. Beirut: Dār al-Gharb al-Islāmī, 1988.

Ibn Saʿd, Abū ʿAbd Allāh Muḥammad. *al-Ṭabaqāt al-Kubrā.* Beirut: Dār Ṣādir, 1985.

___. *Al-Ṭabaqāt al-Kubrā.* Beirut: Dār Ṣādir, n.d.

Ibn Saʿīd, Abū Saʿīd ʿUthmān. *Naqd al-Marīsī al-Jahamī al-ʿAnīd.* Riyāḍ: Maktabat al-Rashshād, 1998.

Ibn al-Ṣalāḥ, Abū ʿAmr ʿUthmān b. ʿAbd al-Raḥmān al-Shahrazūrī. *Adab al-Muftī wa al-Mustaftī.* Ed. Muwaffaq b. ʿAbd Allāh b. ʿAbd al-Qādir. n.p.: Maktabat al-ʿUlūm wa al-Hikam, 1986.

___. *ʿUlūm al-Ḥadīth.* Damascus: Dār al-Fikr, 1986.

Ibn Sīnā, Abū ʿAlī al-Ḥusayn b. ʿAbd Allāh. *al-Qānūn fī al-Ṭibb.* Beirut: Dār al-Ṣādir, 1970.

Ibn Taymiyyah, Taqī al-Dīn Aḥmad b. ʿAbd al-Ḥalīm. *al-Ḥisbah fī al-Islām aw Waẓīfat al-Ḥukūmah al-Islāmiyyah.* Beirut: Dār al-Kutub al-ʿIlmiyyah, 1992.

___. *Iqtiḍāʾ al-Ṣirāṭ al-Mustaqīm Mukhālafat Aṣḥāb al-Jaḥīm.* Beirut: Dār al-Kutub al-ʿIlmiyyah, n.d.

___. *Majmūʿ al-Fatāwā.* Ed. ʿAbd al-Raḥmān b. Muḥammad b. Qāsim. Cairo: Maktabat Ibn Taymiyyah, n.d.

___. *al-Siyāsah al-Sharʿiyyah fī Iṣlāḥ al-Rāʿī wa al-Raʿiyyah.* Beirut: Dār al-Kutub al-ʿIlmiyyah, 1988.

___. *al-Tafsīr al-Kabīr.* Ed. ʿAbd al-Raḥmān ʿUmīra. Beirut: Dār al-Kutub al-ʿIlmiyyah, n.d.

Ibn al-Wardī, Zayn al-Dīn ʿUmar b. Muẓaffar. *Taʾrīkh Ibn al-Wardī.* Beirut: Dār al-Kutub al-ʿIlmiyyah, 1996.

al-ʿĪd, Taqī al-Dīn Abū al-Fatḥ b. Daqīq. *Iḥkām al-Aḥkām Sharḥ ʿUmdat al-Aḥkām.* Beirut: Dār al-Kutub al-ʿIlmiyyah, n.d.

ʿImārah, Muḥammad. *al-Shaykh Muḥammad al-Ghazālī: al-Mawqif al-Fikrī wa al-Maʿārik al-Fikriyyah.* Cairo: al-Ḥayāh al-Miṣriyyah al-ʿĀmmah li al-Kitāb, 1992.

ʿĪsā, ʿAbd al-Jalīl. *Mā lā yajūz fihi al-Khilāf bayn al-Muslimīn.* Kuwait: Dār al-Bayān, 1969.

al-Iṣbahānī, Abū al-Faraj. *al-Qiyān.* Ed. Jalīl al-ʿAṭiyyah. London: Riyāḍ al-Raʾīs li al-Kutub wa al-Nashr, 1989.

al-Iṣfahānī, Shams al-Dīn Maḥmūd b. ʿAbd al-Raḥmān. *Sharḥ al-Minhāj li al-Bayḍāwī fī ʿIlm al-Uṣūl.* Ed. ʿAbd al-Karīm b. ʿAlī b. Muḥammad al-Namlah. Riyāḍ: Maktabat al-Rushd, 1410 A.H.

Ismāʿīl, ʿAbd al-Ḥamīd Abū al-Makārim. *al-Adillah al-Mukhtalaf fīhā wa Āthāruhā fī al-Fiqh al-Islāmī.* Cairo: Dār al-Muslim, n.d.

ʿItr, Nūr al-Dīn. *Manhaj al-Naqd fī ʿUlūm al-Ḥadīth*. Damascus: Dār al-Fikr, 1981.

al-Jabrī, ʿAbd al-Mutaʿāl Muḥammad. *al-Mushtahir min al-Ḥadīth: al-Mawḍūʿ wa al-Ḍaʿīf wa al-Badīl al-Ṣaḥīḥ*. n.p.: Maktabah Wahbah, 1987.

Jaʿīṭ, Hishām. *al-Fitnah: Jadaliyyat al-Dīn wa al-Siyāsah fī al-Islām al-Mubakkir*. Beirut: Dār al-Ṭalīʿah, 1989.

Jalālī, Muḥammad Reza. *Taʾrīkh Jamʿ al-Qurʾān al-Karīm*. n.p.: Nokre, 1365 A.H.

al-Jaṣṣāṣ, Abū Bakr Aḥmad b. ʿAlī al-Rāzī. *Aḥkām al-Qurʾān*. Beirut: Dār al-Kitāb al-ʿArabī, 1986.

___. *Aḥkām al-Qurʾān*. Beirut: Dār al-Kutub al-ʿImiyyah, 1994.

___. *al-Ijmāʿ*. Ed. Zuhayr Shafīq Kabbī. Beirut: Dār al-Muntakhab al-ʿArabī, 1993.

al-Jīlānī, ʿAbd al-Qādir b. Abī Ṣāliḥ. *al-Ghunyah li Ṭālibī Ṭarīq al-Ḥaqq ʿAzza wa Jalla fī al-Akhlāq wa al-Taṣawwuf wa al-Ādāb al-Islāmiyyah*. Beirut: Dār al-Kutub al-ʿIlmiyyah, 1997.

al-Jirāḥī, Ismāʿīl b. Muḥammad al-ʿAjlūnī. *Kashf al-Khafāʾ wa Muzīl al-Ilbās ʿan mā ishtahar min al-Aḥādīth ʿalā Alsinat al-Nās*. 2nd edn. Beirut: Dār Iḥyāʾ al-Turāth al-ʿArabī, 1968.

___. *Kashf al-Khafāʾ wa Muzīl al-Ilbās*. Beirut: Muʾassasat al-Risālah, 1983.

al-Jundī, Khalīl b. Isḥāq. *Mukhtaṣar Khalīl*. Cairo: Dār Iḥyāʾ al-Kutub al-ʿArabiyyah, n.d.

al-Jurjānī, Abū Aḥmad ʿAbd Allāh b. ʿUdayy. *al-Kāmil fī Ḍuʿafāʾ al-Rijāl*. Ed. ʿĀdil Aḥmad ʿAbd al-Mawjūd and ʿAlī Muḥammad Muʿawwaḍ. Beirut: Dār al-Kutub al-ʿIlmiyyah, 1997.

al-Juwaynī, Abū al-Maʿālī ʿAbd al-Malik b. ʿAbd Allāh b. Yūsuf. *al-Burhān fī Uṣūl al-Fiqh*. Ed. Sāliḥ b. Muḥammad b. ʿUwaydah. Beirut: Dār al-Kutub al-ʿIlmiyyah, 1997.

___. *Kitāb al-Ijtihād min Kitāb al-Talkhīṣ*. Damascus: Dār al-Qalam, 1987.

al-Kabīr, Abū Ismāʿīl b. ʿAbd al-Raḥmān al-Suddī. *Tafsīr al-Suddī al-Kabīr*. Ed. Muḥammad ʿAṭā Yūsuf. Riyāḍ: Dār al-Wafāʾ, 1993.

al-Kalūzānī, Maḥfūẓ b. Aḥmad b. al-Ḥasan Abū al-Khaṭṭāb. *al-Tamhīd fī Uṣūl al-Fiqh*. Ed. Muḥammad b. ʿAlī b. Ibrāhīm. Mecca: Markaz al-Baḥth al-ʿIlmī wa Iḥyāʾ al-Turāth al-Islāmī, 1985.

Kamāl, ʿAbd Allāh. *al-Dāʾirah al-Ḥalāl: al-Muʾassasah al-Ḥādithah lī al-Zawāj fī Miṣr wa al-Suʿūdiyyah wa Irān*. Beirut: al-Maktabah al-Thaqāfiyyah, 1997.

al-Kāndahlawī, Muḥammad Zakariyyā. *Awjaz al-Masālik ilā Muwaṭṭaʾ Mālik*. 3rd edn. Mecca: al-Maktabah al-Amradiyyah, 1984.

al-Kāsānī, Abū Bakr b. Masʿūd. *Badāʾiʿ al-Ṣanāʾiʿ fī Tartīb al-Sharāʾiʿ*. Eds. ʿAlī Muḥammad Muʿawwaḍ and ʿĀdil Aḥmad ʿAbd al-Mawjūd. Beirut: Dār al-Kutub al-ʿIlmiyyah, 1997.

al-Kāshānī, Muḥsin al-Fayḍ. *Tafsīr al-Ṣāfī*. Beirut: Muʾassasat al-Aʿlāmī, 1982.

Khān, Muṣṭafā, Muṣṭafā Bāghā, et. al. *Nuzhat al-Muttaqīn Sharḥ Riyāḍ al-Ṣāliḥīn*. Beirut: Muʾassasat al-Risālah, 1987.

al-Khaṭīb, Muḥammad ʿAjāj. *al-Mukhtaṣar al-Wajīz fī ʿUlūm al-Ḥadīth*. 5th edn. Beirut: Muʾassasat al-Risālah, 1991.

al-Khaṭīb al-Baghdādī, Abū Bakr Aḥmad b. ʿAlī b. Thābit. *Kitāb al-Faqīh wa al-Mutafaqqih wa Uṣūl al-Fiqh*. Cairo: Zakariyyā ʿAlī Yūsuf, 1977.

___. *Kitāb al-Faqīh wa al-Mutfaqqih*. n.p.: Maṭbaʿat al-Imtiyāz, 1977.

___. *Taʾrīkh Baghdād*. Beirut: Dār al-Kutub al-ʿIlmiyyah, 1997.

al-Khiraqī, ʿUmar b. al-Ḥusayn. *Mukhtaṣar al-Khiraqī*. n.p.: n.p., 1964.

Kishk, Muḥammad Jalāl. *al-Ghazw al-Fikrī*. Cairo: Maktabat Dār al-ʿUrūbah, 1964.

___. *Ḥaqq al-Murr*. Cairo: Dār al-Maʿārif, 1978.

___. *Al-Shaykh Muḥammad al-Ghazālī bayn al-Naqd al-ʿĀtib wa al-Madḥ al-Shāmit*. Cairo: Maktabat al-Turāth al-Islāmī, 1990.

al-Kiyyā al-Harrāsī, ʿImād al-Dīn b. Muḥammad. *Aḥkām al-Qurʾān*. Eds. Mūsā Muḥammad ʿAlī and ʿIzzat ʿAlī ʿĪd ʿAṭiyyah. Cairo: Dār al-Kutub al-Ḥadītha, 1974.

___. *Aḥkām al-Qurʾān*. Beirut: Dār al-Kutub al-ʿIlmiyyah, 1985.

al-Kūrānī, Ṭāhā b. Aḥmad b. Muḥammad b. Qāsim. *Sharḥ Mukhtaṣar al-Manār fī Uṣūl al-Fiqh*. Ed. Shaʿbān Ismāʿīl. Cairo: Dār al-Salām, 1988.

al-Lāmishī, Abū al-Thanāʾ Maḥmūd b. Zayd. *Kitāb fī Uṣūl al-Fiqh*. Ed. ʿAbd al-Majīd Turkī. Beirut: Dār al-Gharb al-Islāmī, 1995.

Madkhalī, Rabīʿ b. Hādī. *Kashf Mawqif al-Ghazālī min al-Sunnah wa Ahlihā wa Naqd Baʿḍ Ārāʾihi*. 2nd edn. Cairo: Maktabat al-Sunnah, 1410 A.H.

Maḥmaṣānī, Ṣubḥī. *Falsafat al-Tashrīʿ fī al-Islām: Muqaddimah fī Dirāsat al-Sharīʿah al-Islāmiyyah ʿalā Ḍawʾ Madhāhibihā al-Mukhtalifah wa Ḍawʾ al-Qawānīn al-Ḥadīthah*. 3rd edn. Beirut: Dār al-ʿIlm li al-Malāyīn, 1961.

Maḥmūd, Ibrāhīm. *Jughrāfiyā al-Maladhdhāt: al-Jins fi al-Jannah*. Beirut: Riyāḍ al-Raʾīs lī al-Kutub wa al-Nashr, 1998.

al-Makkī, Ibn Aḥmad. *Manāqib Abī Ḥanīfah*. Beirut: Dār al-Kitāb al-ʿArabī, 1981.

al-Maqdisī, Shams al-Dīn Muḥammad b. Mufliḥ. *Uṣūl al-Fiqh*. Ed. Fahd b. Muḥammad al-Sadhān. Riyāḍ: Maktabat al-ʿUbaykān, 1999.

al-Marghīnānī, Abū al-Ḥasan ʿAlī b. Abī Bakr b. ʿAbd al-Jalīl. *al-Hidāyah Sharḥ Bidāyat al-Mubtadī*. Egypt: Muṣṭafā al-Bābī al-Ḥalabī, 1975.

al-Masʿūdī, Abū al-Ḥasan ʿAlī b. al-Ḥusayn b. ʿAlī. *Murūj al-Dhahab wa Maʿādin al-Jawhar*. Ed. Shārik Pallā. Beirut: Manshūrāt al-Jāmiʿah al-Lubnāniyyah, 1965.

___. *Murūj al-Dhahab wa Maʿādin al-Jawhar*. Ed. Muḥammad Muḥyī al-Dīn ʿAbd al-Ḥamīd. Cairo: Kitāb al-Taḥrīr, 1966.

al-Māwardī, Abū al-Ḥasan ʿAlī b. Muḥammad b. Ḥabīb. *Adab al-Qāḍī*. Ed. Muḥyī Hilāl al-Sarḥān. Baghdad: Matbaʿat al-Irshād, 1971.

___. *al-Aḥkām al-Sulṭāniyyah wa al-Wilāyah al-Dīniyyah*. Beirut: Dār al-Kutub al-ʿIlmiyyah, 1985.

___. *al-Ḥāwī al-Kabīr fī Fiqh Madhhab al-Imām al-Shāfiʿī*. Eds. ʿAlī Muḥammad Muʿawwaḍ and ʿĀdil Aḥmad ʿAbd al-Mawjūd. Beirut: Dār al-Kutub al-ʿIlmiyyah, 1994.

___. *al-Nukat wa al-ʿUyūn*. Ed. al-Sayyid b. ʿAbd al-Maqṣūd b. ʿAbd al-Raḥīm. Beirut: Dār al-Kutub al-ʿIlmiyyah, 1992.

al-Mawdūdī, Abū al-Aʿlā. *al-Ḥijāb*. Cairo: Dār al-Anṣār, 1977.

al-Mazzī, Jamāl al-Dīn Abī al-Ḥajjāj Yūsuf. *Tahdhīb al-Kamāl fī Asmāʾ al-Rijāl*. Ed. Bashshār Maʿrūf. Beirut: Muʾassasat al-Risālah, n.d.

al-Mināwī, ʿAbd al-Raʾūf. *Fayḍ al-Qadīr Sharḥ al-Jāmiʿ al-Ṣaghīr*. Beirut: Dār al-Maʿrifah, 1972.

al-Mubārakfūrī, Muḥammad ʿAbd al-Raḥmān b. ʿAbd al-Raḥīm. *Tuḥfat al-Aḥwadhī bi Sharḥ Jāmiʿ al-Tirmidhī*. Beirut: Dār al-Kutub al-ʿIlmiyyah, n.d.

Muḥammadī, Abū al-Faḍl Mīr. *Buḥūth fī Taʾrīkh al-Qurʾān wa ʿUlūmihi*. Lebanon: Dār al-Taʿāruf, 1980.

al-Muqaddim, Muḥammad Aḥmad Ismāʿīl. *ʿAwdat al-Ḥijāb*. Riyāḍ: Dār Ṭaybah, 1996.

al-Mūsawī, ʿAbd al-Ḥusayn Sharaf al-Dīn. *Abū Hurayrah*. Beirut: Dār al-Zahrāʾ, 1977.

Mutahhari, Murtaza. *Mas'ala-i Hijāb.* Tehran: Anjuman-i Islām-yi Pizhishkan, 1969.
al-Nadhwī, 'Alī Aḥmad. *al-Qawā'id al-Fiqhiyyah: Mafhūmuhā, Nasha'tuhā, Taṭawwuruhā, Dirāsat Mu'allafātihā, Adillatuhā, Muhimmatuhā, Taṭbīqātuhā.* 3rd edn. Damascus: Dār al-Qalam, 1994.
al-Namarī, Abū 'Umar Yūsuf b. 'Abd al-Barr. *Jāmi' Bayān al-'Ilm wa Faḍlihi wa mā yanbaghī fī Riwāyatihi wa Ḥamlihi.* Beirut: Dār al-Kutub al-'Ilmiyyah, n.d.
al-Nasafī, Abū al-Barakāt 'Abd Allāh b. Aḥmad b. Maḥmūd Ḥāfiẓ al-Dīn. *Tafsīr al-Nasafī: Madārik al-Tanzīl wa Ḥaqā'iq al-Ta'wīl.* Ed. Marwān Muḥammad al-Shi'ār. Beirut: Dār al-Nafā'is, 1996.
___. *Tafsīr al-Nasafī.* Cairo: 'Īsā al-Bābī al-Ḥalabī, n.d.
___. *Tafsīr al-Nasafī.* Cairo: Dār Iḥyā' al-Kutub al-'Arabiyyah, n.d.
al-Nasā'ī, Abū 'Abd Allāh 'Abd al-Raḥmān Aḥmad b. Shu'ayb b. 'Alī. *Sunan.* Beirut: Dār al-Qalam, n.d.
___. *Ishārat al-Nisā'.* Beirut: Mu'assasat al-Kutub al-Thaqāfiyyah, 1989.
al-Nawawī, Abū Zakariyyā Muḥyī al-Dīn b. Sharaf. *Majmū' Sharḥ al-Muhadhdhab.* Beirut: Dār al-Fikr, n.d.
___. *Rawḍat al-Ṭālibīn wa 'Umdat al-Muftīn.* Ed. Zuhayr al-Shāwīsh. 3rd edn. Beirut: al-Maktab al-Islāmī, 1991.
___. *Sharḥ Ṣaḥīḥ Muslim al-Musammā al-Minhāj Sharḥ Ṣaḥīḥ Muslim b. Ḥajjāj.* Beirut: Dār al-Ma'rifah, 1996.
___. *Sharḥ Ṣaḥīḥ Muslim.* Beirut: Dār al-Qalam, n.d.
al-Nīfāsh, Shihāb al-Dīn Aḥmad. *Nuzhat al-Albāb fī mā lā yūjad fī Kitāb.* Ed. Jamāl Jum'ah. London: Riyāḍ al-Ra'īs lī al-Kutub wa al-Nashr, 1992.
al-Nīsābūrī, Abū 'Abd Allāh al-Ḥākim. *al-Mustadrak 'alā al-Ṣaḥīḥayn.* Beirut: Dār al-Ma'rifah, n.d.
al-Qaddūrī, Abū al-Ḥasan Aḥmad b. Muḥammad b. Aḥmad b. Ja'far. *Mukhtaṣar al-Qaddūrī fī al-Fiqh al-Ḥanafī.* Beirut: Dār al-Kutub al-'Ilmiyyah, 1997.
al-Qaffāl, Abū Bakr Muḥammad b. Aḥmad al-Shāshī. *Ḥulyat al-'Ulamā' fī Ma'rifat Madhāhib al-Fuqahā'.* Amman: Maktabat al-Risālah al-Ḥadīthah, 1988.
al-Qaraḍāwī, Yūsuf. *Al-Imām al-Ghazālī bayn Mādiḥīh wa Nāqidīh.* Beirut: Mu'assasat al-Risālah, 1994.
al-Qarāfī, Shihāb al-Dīn Abū al-'Abbās Aḥmad b. Idrīs. *al-Dhakhīrah.* Ed. Sa'īd A'rāb. Beirut: Dār al-Gharb al-Islāmī, 1994.
___. *al-Furūq.* Ed. Muḥammad Rawwās Qal'ah Jī. Beirut: Dār al-Ma'rifah, n.d.
___. *al-Iḥkām fī Tamyīz al-Fatāwā 'an al-Aḥkām wa Taṣarrufāt al-Qāḍī wa al-Imām.* Beirut: Dār al-Bashā'ir al-Islāmiyyah, 1995.
___. *al-Iḥkām fī Tamyīz al-Fatāwā 'an al-Aḥkām wa Taṣarrufāt al-Qāḍī wa al-Imām.* Ed. Abū Bakr 'Abd al-Rāziq. Cairo: al-Maktab al-Thaqāfī lī al-Nashr wa al-Tawzī', 1989.
___. *Sharḥ Tanqīḥ al-Fuṣūl fī Ikhtiṣār al-Maḥṣūl fī al-Uṣūl.* Ed. Ṭāhā 'Abd al-Ra'ūf Sa'd, Beirut: Dār al-Fikr, 1973.
al-Qārī, 'Alī b. Sulṭān Muḥammad. *Marqāt al-Mafātīḥ Sharḥ Mishkāt al-Maṣābīḥ.* Ed. Ṣidqī Muḥammad Jamīl al-'Aṭṭār. Beirut: Dār al-Fikr, n.d.
al-Qaṭṭān, Mannā'. *Mabāhith fī 'Ulūm al-Qur'ān.* Beirut: Mu'assasat al-Risālah, 1986.
___. *Ta'rīkh al-Tashrī' al-Islāmī: al-Tashrī' wa al-Fiqh.* 24th edn. Beirut: Mu'assasat al-Risālah, 1996.

al-Qayrawānī, Abū Muḥammad ʿAbd Allāh b. Abī Zayd. *al-Nawādir wa al-Ziyādāt.* Ed. ʿAbd al-Fattāḥ al-Ḥilw. Beirut: Dār al-Gharb al-Islāmī, 1999.
al-Qurṭubī, Abū ʿAbd Allāh Muḥammad b. Aḥmad al-Anṣārī. *al-Jāmiʿ li Aḥkām al-Qurʾān.* Beirut: Dār al-Fikr, 1987.
___. *al-Jāmiʿ li Aḥkām al-Qurʾān.* Beirut: Dār al-Kutub al-ʿIlmiyyah, 1993.
___. *al-Jāmiʿ li Aḥkām al-Qurʾān.* Cairo: n.p., 1952.
Quṭb, Muḥammad. *Shubuhāt ḥawl al-Islām.* 14th edn. Cairo: Dār al-Shurūq, 1981.
Quṭb, Sayyid. *Fī Ẓilāl al-Qurʾān.* 10th edn. Beirut/Cairo: Dār al-Shurūq, 1981.
al-Raḥbī al-Simnānī, Abū al-Qāsim ʿAlī b. Muḥammad. *Rawḍat al-Quḍāh wa Ṭarīq al-Najāḥ.* Beirut: Muʾassasat al-Risālah, 1984.
al-Ramlī, Shams al-Dīn Muḥammad b. Abī al-ʿAbbās Aḥmad b. Ḥamzah b. Shihāb al-Dīn al-Anṣārī. *Nihāyat al-Muḥtāj ilā Sharḥ al-Minhāj fi al-Fiqh ʿalā Madhhab al-Imām al-Shāfiʿī.* 3rd edn. Beirut: Dār Iḥyāʾ al-Turāth al-ʿArabī, 1992.
___. *Nihāyat al-Muḥtāj ilā Sharḥ al-Minhāj.* Cairo: Maktabat Muṣṭafā al-Ḥalabī, 1967.
al-Rāwandī, Quṭb al-Dīn Saʿīd b. Hibat Allāh. *Fiqh al-Qurʾān.* Ed. al-Sayyid Aḥmad al-Ḥusaynī. Qum: Maṭbaʿat al-Wilāyah, 1405 A.H.
al-Rāzī, Abū Muḥammad ʿAbd al-Raḥmān. *ʿIlal al-Ḥadīth.* Beirut: Dār al-Maʿrifah, 1985.
al-Rāzī, Fakhr al-Dīn Muḥammad b. ʿUmar b. al-Ḥusayn. *al-Maḥṣūl fī ʿIlm Uṣūl al-Fiqh.* Ed. Ṭāhā Jābir Fayyāḍ al-ʿAlwānī. 3rd edn. Beirut: Muʾassasat al-Risālah, 1997.
___. *al-Maḥṣūl fī ʿIlm Uṣūl al-Fiqh.* Beirut: Dār al-Kutub al-ʿIlmiyyah, 1988.
___. *al-Maḥṣūl fī ʿIlm Uṣūl al-Fiqh.* Beirut: Dār al-Kutub al-ʿIlmiyyah, n.d.
___. *al-Tafsīr al-Kabīr li al-Imām Fakhr al-Dīn al-Rāzī.* 3rd ed. Beirut: Dār Iḥyāʾ al-Turāth al-ʿArabī, 1999.
___. *al-Tafsīr al-Kabīr (a.k.a Mafātīḥ al-Ghayb).* Beirut: Dār al-Kutub al-ʿIlmiyyah, 1990.
Riḍā, Muḥammad Rashīd. *Fatāwā al-Imām Muḥammad Rashīd Riḍā.* Beirut: Dār al-Kitāb al-Jadīd, 1971.
___. *Tafsīr al-Qurʾān al-Ḥakīm al-Shahīr bi Tafsīr al-Manār.* 2nd edn. Beirūt: Dār al-Maʿrifah, n.d.
al-Rustāqī, Khamīs b. Saʿīd al-Shaqaṣī. *Manhaj al-Ṭālibīn wa Balāgh al-Rāghibīn.* Oman: Wizārat al-Turāth al-Qawmī wa al-Thaqāfī, n.d.
Sābiq, al-Sayyid. *Fiqh al-Sunnah.* 13th edn. Cairo: al-Fatḥ li al-Aʿlām al-ʿArabī, 1996.
al-Ṣaghīr, Muḥammad Ḥusayn ʿAlī. *Taʾrīkh al-Qurʾān.* Lebanon: al-Dār al-ʿĀlamiyyah, 1983.
Saḥnūn b. Saʿīd al-Tanūkhī. *Al-Mudawwanah al-Kubrā.* Egypt: Maṭbaʿat al-Saʿāda, n.d.
___. *al-Mudawwanah al-Kubrā.* Beirut: Dār al-Kutub al-ʿIlmiyyah, 1994.
___. *al-Mudawwanah al-Kubrā.* Beirut: Dār Ṣādir, n.d.
al-Sakhāwī, Muḥammad ʿAbd al-Raḥmān. *al-Maqāṣid al-Ḥasanah fī Bayān Kathīr min al-Aḥādīth al-Mushtahirah ʿalā al-Alsinah.* Ed. Muḥammad ʿUthmān al-Khasht. 2nd edn. Beirut: Dār al-Kitāb al-ʿArabī, 1994.
al-Ṣāliḥ, Ṣubḥī. *Maʿālim al-Sharīʿah al-Islāmiyyah.* Beirut: Dār al-ʿIlm li al-Malāyīn, 1975.
___. *Mabāḥith fī ʿUlūm al-Qurʾān.* 19th edn. Beirut: Dār al-ʿIlm li al-Malāyīn, 1996.
___. *ʿUlūm al-Ḥadīth.* Beirut: Dār al-ʿIlm, 1991.
Āl Salmān, Abū ʿUbaydah b. Ḥasan. *Kutub ḥadhdhara minhā al-ʿUlamāʾ.* Riyāḍ: Dār al-Ṣamīʿī, 1995.
Salqīnī, Ibrāhīm Muḥammad. *al-Muyassar fī Uṣūl al-Fiqh al-Islāmī.* Beirut: Dār al-Fikr al-Muʿāṣir, 1991.

Al-Ṣanʿānī, Abū Bakr ʿAbd al-Razzāq. *Tafsīr al-Qurʾān al-ʿAzīz*. Beirut: Dār al-Maʿrifah, 1991.

al-Sanhūrī, ʿAbd al-Razzāq. *Maṣādir al-Ḥaqq fī al-Fiqh al-Islāmī: Dirāsah Muqārinah bi al-Fiqh al-Gharbī*. Beirut: Dār Iḥyāʾ al-Turāth al-ʿArabī, n.d.

al-Sarakhsī, Abū Bakr Muḥammad b. Aḥmad b. Abī Sahl. *al-Muḥarrar fī Uṣūl al-Fiqh*. Beirut: Dār al-Kutub al-ʿArabiyyah, 1996.

___. *Uṣūl al-Sarakhsī*. Ed. Abū Wafāʾ al-Afghānī. Beirut: Dār al-Kutub al-ʿIlmiyyah, 1993.

al-Ṣāwī, Aḥmad b. Muḥammad. *Ḥāshiyat al-ʿAllāmah al-Ṣāwī ʿalā Tafsīr al-Jalālayn*. Beirut: Dār Iḥyāʾ al-Turāth al-ʿArabī, n.d.

Shaʿbān, Zakī al-Dīn. *Uṣūl al-Fiqh al-Islāmī*. Egypt: Maṭbaʿat Dār al-Taʾlīf, 1965.

al-Shāfiʿī, Abū ʿAbd Allāh Muḥammad b. Idrīs. *Ikhtilāf al-Ḥadīth*. Printed in the margins of *al-Umm*, by al-Shāfiʿī, Muḥammad b. Idrīs. Vol. 7. Cairo: Maṭbaʿat Būlāq, 1325 A.H.

___. *Kitāb al-Umm*. Beirut: Dār al-Fikr, 1990.

___. *al-Umm*. Beirut: Dār al-Fikr, n.d.

___. *al-Risālah*. Ed. Aḥmad Muḥammad Shākir. n.p.: Dār al-Fikr, n.d.

Shāh Walī Allāh, Aḥmad b. ʿAbd al-Raḥīm al-Fārūqī al-Dahlawī. *al-Inṣāf fī Bayān Sabab al-Ikhtilāf fī al-Aḥkām al-Fiqhiyyah*. Cairo: al-Maṭbaʿah al-Salafiyyah, 1385 A.H.

al-Shahrastānī, Muḥammad b. ʿAbd al-Karīm Abī Bakr Aḥmad. *al-Milal wa al-Niḥal*. Eds. Amīr ʿAlī Mihannā and ʿAlī Ḥasan Fāʿūr. 5th edn. Beirut: Dār al-Maʿrifah, 1996.

Shaʿlabī, Raʾūf. *Shaykh al-Islām ʿAbd al-Ḥalīm Maḥmūd: Sīratuhu wa Aʿmāluhu*. Kuwait: Dār al-Qalam, 1982.

Shaltūt, Maḥmūd. *al-Islām: ʿAqīdah wa Sharīʿah*. 17th edn. Cairo: Dār al-Shurūq, 1991.

Sharaf, Muḥammad Jalāl and ʿAlī ʿAbd al-Muʿṭī Muḥammad. *al-Fikr al-Siyāsī fī al-Islām: Shakhṣiyāt wa Madhāhib*. Alexandria: Dār al-Jāmiʿāt al-Miṣriyyah, 1978.

Sharīf, Hāshim. *al-Marʾah al-Muslimah bayn Ḥaqīqat al-Sharīʿah wa Zayf al-Abāṭil*. Alexandria: Dār al-Maʿrifah al-Jamiʿiyyah, 1987.

al-Shāṭibī, Abū Isḥāq Ibrāhīm b. Mūsā. *al-Muwāfaqāt fī Uṣūl al-Fiqh*. Eds. ʿAbd Allāh Darāz and Muḥammad ʿAbd Allāh Darāz. Beirut: Dār al-Kutub al-ʿIlmiyyah, n.d.

al-Shawkānī, Muḥammad b. ʿAlī b. Muḥammad. *Fatḥ al-Qadīr: al-Jāmiʿ bayn Fannay al-Riwāyah wa al-Dirāyah min ʿIlm al-Tafsīr*. Beirut: Dār al-Maʿrifah, 1996.

___. *Irshād al-Fuḥūl ilā Taḥqīq al-Ḥaqq min ʿIlm al-Uṣūl*. Beirut: Dār al-Kutub al-ʿIlmiyyah, n.d.

___. *Nayl al-Awṭār*. Cairo: Dār al-Ḥadīth, n.d.

___. *al-Qawl al-Mufīd fī Adillat al-Ijtihād wa al-Taqlīd*. Cairo: Maktabat al-Qurʾān, 1988.

___. *Ṭalab al-ʿIlm wa Ṭabaqāt al-Mutaʿallimīn: Adab al-Ṭalab wa Muntahā al-Arab*. n.p.: Dār al-Arqām, 1981.

al-Shaybānī, ʿAbd al-Raḥmān b. ʿAlī b. Muḥammad b. ʿUmar. *Kitāb Tamyīz al-Ṭayyib min al-Khabīth fī mā yadūr ʿalā Alsinat al-Nās min al-Ḥadīth*. Beirut: Dār al-Kitāb al-ʿArabī, n.d.

al-Shaybānī al-Khaṣṣāṣ, Abū Bakr Aḥmad b. ʿAmr b. Muhīr. *Kitāb Adab al-Qāḍī*. Ed. Farḥāt Ziyādah. Cairo: American University of Cairo Press, 1978.

al-Shinqīṭī, Muḥammad al-Amīn b. Muḥammad al-Mukhtār. *Mudhakkirah fī Uṣūl al-Fiqh*. Cairo: Maktabat Ibn Taymiyyah, 1989.

___. *Aḍwāʾ al-Bayān fī Īḍāḥ al-Qurʾān bi al-al-Qurʾān*. Beirut: ʿĀlam al-Kutub, n.d.

al-Shīrāzī, Abū Isḥāq Ibrāhīm b. ʿAlī b. Yūsuf al-Fayrūzābādī. *al-Muhadhdhab fī Fiqh al-Imām al-Shāfiʿī*. Beirut: Dār al-Kutub al-ʿIlmiyyah, 1995.

___. *Sharḥ al-Lumʿah*. Ed. ʿAbd al-Majīd Turkī. Beirut: Dār al-Gharb al-Islāmī, 1988.

___. *al-Tabṣirah fī Uṣūl al-Fiqh*. Ed. Muḥammad Ḥasan Haytū. Damascus: Dār al-Fikr, 1980.

Shukrī, Murād. *Taḥqīq al-Wuṣūl ilā ʿIlm al-Uṣūl: Sharḥ al-Muḥaqqiqah al-Nūniyyah*. ʿAmmān: Dār al-Ḥasan, 1991.

al-Sijistānī, Abū Bakr ʿAbd Allāh b. Abī Dāwūd Sulaymān b. al-Ashʿath. *Kitāb al-Maṣāḥif*. Beirut: Dār al-Kutub al-ʿIlmiyyah, 1985.

al-Simʿānī, Abū al-Muẓaffar Manṣūr b. Muḥammad b. ʿAbd al-Jabbār. *Qawāṭiʿ al-Adillah fī al-Uṣūl*. Ed. Muḥammad Ḥasan Ismāʿīl. Beirut: Dār al-Kutub al-ʿIlmiyyah, 1997.

al-Subkī, Tāj al-Dīn Abī Naṣr ʿAbd al-Wahhāb b. ʿAlī b. ʿAbd al-Kāfī and ʿAlī b. ʿAbd al-Kāfī al-Subkī. *al-Ibhāj fī Sharḥ al-Minhāj ʿalā Minhāj al-Wuṣūl ilā ʿIlm al-Uṣūl*. Ed. Shaʿbān Muḥammad Ismāʿīl. Cairo: al-Kulliyyah al-Azhariyyah, 1981.

al-Subkī, Tāj al-Dīn Abī Naṣr ʿAbd al-Wahhāb b. ʿAlī b. ʿAbd al-Kāfī. *Rafʿ al-Ḥājib ʿan Mukhtaṣar Ibn al-Ḥājib*. Eds. ʿAlī Muḥammad Muʿawwaḍ and ʿĀdil Aḥmad ʿAbd al-Mawjūd. Beirut: ʿĀlam al-Kutub, 1999.

___. *Ṭabaqāt al-Shāfiʿiyyah al-Kubrā*. Egypt: al-Maṭbaʿah al-Ḥusayniyyah, 1906.

Sulṭān, Jamāl. *Azmat al-Ḥiwār al-Dīnī: Naqd Kitāb al-Sunnah al-Nabawiyyah bayn Ahl al-Fiqh wa Ahl al-Ḥadīth li Muʾallifihi Muḥammad al-Ghazālī*. Cairo: Dār al-Ṣafāʾ, 1990.

Susāwah, ʿAbd al-Majīd Muḥammad Ismāʿīl. *Manhaj al-Tawfīq wa al-Tarjīḥ bayn Mukhtalaf al-Ḥadīth wa Āthārihi fī al-Fiqh al-Islāmī*. Amman, Jordan: Dār al-Nafāʾis, 1997.

al-Suyūṭī, Jalāl al-Dīn ʿAbd al-Raḥmān b. Abī Bakr and al-Maḥallī, Jalāl al-Dīn Muḥammad b. Aḥmad. *Tafsīr al-Jalālayn*. Istanbul: Maktabat Arsilān, n.d.

al-Suyūṭī, Jalāl al-Dīn ʿAbd al-Raḥmān b. Abī Bakr. *al-Durar al-Muntathirah fī al-Aḥādīth al-Mushtahirah*. Ed. Muḥammad ʿAbd al-Qādir al-ʿAṭā. Cairo: Dār al-Iʿtiṣām, 1987.

___. *al-Durr al-Manthūr fī al-Tafsīr bi al-Maʾthūr*. Cairo: Maṭbaʿat al-Anwār al-Muḥammadiyyah, n.d.

___. *Ikhtilāf al-Madhāhib*. Ed. ʿAbd al-Qayyūm Muḥammad Shafīʿ al-Basṭawī. Cairo: Dār al-Iʿtiṣām, 1404 A.H

___. *al-Itqān fī ʿUlūm al-Qurʾān*. Ed. Muḥammad Abū al-Faḍl Ibrāhīm. Cairo: al-Mashhad al-Ḥusaynī, 1967.

___. *al-Jāmiʿ al-Ṣaghīr min Ḥadīth al-Bashīr al-Nadhīr*. Ed. Muḥammad Muḥyī al-Dīn ʿAbd al-Ḥamīd. Cairo: Dār Khadamāt al-Qurʾān, n.d.

___. *al-Laʾālī al-Maṣnūʿa fī al-Aḥādīth al-Mawḍūʿa*. Egypt: al-Maktaba al-Tijāriyya al-Kubrā, 1960.

___. *Rashf al-Zulāl min al-Siḥr al-Ḥalāl*. Beirut: al-Intishār al-ʿArabī, n.d.

___. *Sharḥ Sunan al-Nasāʾī*. n.p.: Dār al-Kitāb al-ʿArabī, n.d.

___. *Tanwīr al-Ḥawālik Sharḥ Muwaṭṭaʾ Mālik*. Beirut: Dār al-Kutub al-ʿIlmiyyah, n.d.

al-Ṭabarī, Abū Jaʿfar Muḥammad b. Jarīr. *Jāmiʿ al-Bayān fī Tafsīr al-Qurʾān*. Beirut: Dār al-Maʿrifah, 1989.

___. *Tafsīr al-Ṭabarī min Kitābihi Jāmiʿ al-Bayān ʿan Taʾwīl Āyāt al-Qurʾān*. Eds. Bashshār ʿAwwād Maʿrūf and ʿIṣām Fāris al-Ḥarastānī. Beirut: Muʾassasat al-Risālah, 1994.

___. *Taʾrīkh al-Ṭabarī: Taʾrīkh al-Umam wa al-Mulūk*. Beirut: Dār al-Kutub al-ʿIlmiyyah, n.d.

al-Ṭabarānī, Abū al-Qāsim Sulaymān b. Aḥmad. *al-Muʿjam al-Kabīr*. Ed. Ḥamdī ʿAbd al-Majīd al-Salafī. Beirut: Dār Iḥyāʾ al-Turāth al-ʿArabī, 1985.

al-Ṭabaʾtabāʾī, al-Sayyid Muḥammad Ḥusayn. *al-Mīzān fī Tafsīr al-Qurʾān*. Qum: Maṭbaʿat al-Ismāʿīliyān, 1412 A.H.

al-Ṭabrīsī, Abū ʿAlī al-Faḍl b. al-Ḥasan. *Majmaʿ al-Bayān fī Tafsīr al-Qurʾān*. Beirut: Dār Maktabat al-Ḥayāh, n.d.

al-Taftazānī, Saʿd al-Dīn Masʿūd b. ʿUmar. *Ḥāshiyah ʿalā Mukhtaṣar al-Muntahā al-Uṣūlī li al-Imām Ibn Ḥājib*. Ed. Shaʿbān Muḥammad Ismāʿīl. Cairo: Maktabat al-Kulliyyah al-Azhariyyah, 1983.

____. *Sharḥ al-Talwīḥ ʿalā al-Tawḍīḥ li Matn al-Tanqīḥ fī Uṣūl al-Fiqh*. Beirut: Dār al-Kutub al-ʿIlmiyyah, n.d.

al-Ṭaḥāwī, Abū Jaʿfar Aḥmad b. Muḥammad b. Salāmah. *Sharḥ Mushkil al-Ḥadīth*. Ed. Shuʿayb al-Arnaʾūṭ. Beirut: Muʾassasat al-Risālah, 1994.

Ṭanṭāwī, Muḥammad Sayyid. *Mabāḥith fī ʿUlūm al-Qurʾān*. Cairo: Dār al-Shurūq, 1998.

al-Thaʿālibī, ʿAbd al-Raḥmān b. Muḥammad b. Makhlūf. *al-Jawāhir al-Ḥisān fī Tafsīr al-Qurʾān*. Beirut: Muʾassasat al-Aʿlamī li al-Maṭbūʿāt, n.d.

al-Tijānī, Ibn Abī al-Qāsim. *Tuḥfat al-ʿArūs wa Nuzhat al-Nufūs*. Eds. Fuʾād Shākir and Abū Hājir Muḥammad al-ʿĪd Zaghlūl. Cairo: Maktabat al-Turāth al-Islāmī, n.d.

al-Tirmidhī, Abū ʿAbd Allāh Muḥammad al-Ḥakīm. *Nawādir al-Uṣūl fī Maʿrifat Aḥādīth al-Rasūl*. Beirut: Dār Ṣādir, n.d.

al-Ṭūfī, Najm al-Dīn. "Al-Ḥadīth al-Thānī wa al-Thalāthūn." In *al-Maṣlaḥah fī al-Tashrīʿ al-Islāmī wa Najm al-Dīn al-Ṭūfī*. Muṣṭafā Zayd. 2nd edn. Cairo: Dār al-Fikr al-ʿArabī, 1964.

al-Turābī, Ḥasan. *Tajdīd al-Fikr al-Islāmī*. Morocco: Dār al-Qarāfī li al-Nashr wa al-Tawzīʿ, 1993.

al-Ṭūṣī, Abū Jaʿfar Muḥammad b. al-Ḥasan b. ʿAlī. *al-Mabsūṭ fī Fiqh al-Imāmiyyah*. Tehran: al-Maṭbaʿah al-Ḥaydariyyah, 1387 A.H.

al-ʿUkbarī, Abū ʿAlī al-Ḥasan b. Shihāb al-Ḥasan. *Risālah fī Uṣūl al-Fiqh*. Ed. Muwaffaq b. ʿAbd Allāh b. ʿAbd al-Qādir. Mecca: al-Maktabah al-Makkiyyah, 1992.

al-Urmawī, Sirāj al-Dīn Maḥmūd b. Abī Bakr. *al-Taḥṣīl min al-Maḥṣūl*. Ed. ʿAbd al-Ḥamīd ʿAlī Abū Zaynad. Beirut: Muʾassasat al-Risālah, 1988.

al-Ushayqir, Muḥammad ʿAlī. *Lamaḥāt min Taʾrīkh al-Qurʾān*. Karbala: Dār al-Muḥīṭ, n.d.

al-ʿUthaymīn, Muḥammad al-Ṣāliḥ. *Fatāwā al-Shaykh Muḥammad al-Ṣāliḥ al-ʿUthaymīn*. Ed. Ashraf b. ʿAbd al-Maqṣūd ʿAbd al-Raḥīm. Riyāḍ: Dār ʿĀlam al-Kutub, 1991.

Wakīʿ Ibn Ḥayyān, Muḥammad b. Khalaf. *Akhbār al-Quḍāh*. Egypt: Maṭbaʿat al-Saʿādah, 1947.

al-Wansharīsī, Aḥmad b. Yaḥyā. *al-Miʿyār al-Muʿrib wa al-Jāmiʿ al-Maghrib ʿan Fatāwā ʿUlamāʾ Ifrīqiyah wa al-Andalus wa al-Maghrib*. Ed. Muḥammad Ḥajjī. Beirut: Dār al-Gharb al-Islāmī, 1981.

al-Warjalānī, Abū Yaʿqūb Yūsuf b. Ibrāhīm. *al-ʿAdl wa al-Inṣāf fī Maʿrifat Uṣūl al-Fiqh wa al-Ikhtilāf*. Oman: Wizārat al-Turāth, 1983.

al-Wazīr, Muḥammad b. Ibrāhīm al-Yamānī. *al-ʿAwāṣim wa al-Qawāṣim fī al-Dhabb ʿan Sunnat Abī al-Qāsim*. Beirut: Muʾassasat al-Risālah, 1992.

al-Yamanī, Abū Muḥammad. *ʿAqāʾid al-Thalāth wa al-Sabʿīn Firqah*. Medina: Maktabat al-ʿUlūm wa al-Ḥikam, 1414 A.H.

al-Yamānī, Muḥammad b. Aḥmad b. Jār Allāh al-Ṣaghrī. *al-Nawāfiḥ al-ʿAṭirah fī al-Aḥādīth al-Mushtahirah*. Ed. Muḥammad ʿAbd al-Qādir Aḥmad ʿAṭā. Beirut: Muʾassasat al-Kutub al-Thaqāfiyyah, 1992.

al-Zāhidī, Ḥāfiẓ Thanā' Allāh. *Taysīr al-Uṣūl.* 2nd edn. Beirut: Dār Ibn Ḥazm, 1997.

al-Zamakhsharī, Abū al-Qāsim Jār Allāh Maḥmūd b. ʿUmar. *al-Kashshāf ʿan Ḥaqā'iq al-Tanzīl wa ʿUyūn al-Aqāwīl fī Wujūh al-Ta'wīl. n.p.*: Dār al-Fikr, n.d.

___. *al-Kashshāf ʿan Ḥaqā'iq al-Tanzīl wa ʿUyūn al-Aqāwīl fī Wujūh al-Ta'wīl.* Beirut: Dār al-Fikr, n.d.

al-Zanjānī, Abū ʿAbd Allāh. *Ta'rīkh al-Qur'ān.* Lebanon: Mu'assasat al-ʿĀlam li al-Maṭbūʿat, 1969.

al-Zarʿī, ʿAbd al-Raḥmān ʿAbd Allāh. *Abū Hurayrah wa Aqlām al-Ḥāqidīn.* Kuwait: Dār al-Qalam, 1984.

al-Zarkashī, Shams al-Dīn Muḥammad b. ʿAbd Allāh. *al-Baḥr al-Muḥīṭ fī Uṣūl al-Fiqh.* Cairo: Dār al-Ṣafwā, 1988.

___. *Sharḥ al-Zarkashī ʿalā Mukhtaṣar al-Khiraqī fī al-Fiqh ʿalā Madhhab al-Imām Aḥmad b. Ḥanbal.* Ed. ʿAbd Allāh b. ʿAbd al-Raḥmān b. ʿAbd Allāh al-Jibrīn. Riyāḍ: Sharikat al-ʿUbaykān, 1983.

al-Zarqā, Aḥmad b. Muḥammad. *Sharḥ al-Qawāʿid al-Fiqhiyyah.* Ed. Muṣṭafā Aḥmad al-Zarqā. 4th edn. Damascus: Dār al-Qalam, 1996.

Zayd, Muṣṭafā. *al-Maṣlaḥah fī al-Tashrīʿ al-Islāmī wa Najm al-Dīn al-Ṭūfī.* 2nd edn. Cairo: Dār al-Fikr al-ʿArabī, 1964.

Zaydān, ʿAbd al-Karīm. *Aḥkām al-Dhimmiyīn wa al-Musta'minīn fī Dār al-Islām.* Baghdad: n.p., 1963.

___. *al-Madkhal li Dirāsat al-Sharīʿah al-Islāmiyyah.* 14th edn. Beirut: Mu'assasat al-Risālah, 1996.

___. *al-Mufaṣṣal fī Aḥkām al-Mar'ah wa al-Bayt al-Muslim fī al-Sharīʿah al-Islāmiyyah.* Beirut: Mu'assasat al-Risālah, 1994.

___. *al-Mufaṣṣal fī Aḥkām al-Mar'ah.* Beirut: Mu'assasat al-Risālah, 1993.

al-Zaylaʿī, Fakhr al-Dīn ʿUthmān b. ʿAlī. *Tabyīn al-Ḥaqā'iq: Sharḥ Kanz al-Daqā'iq.* Medina: Dār al-Kitāb al-Islāmiyyah, n.d.

al-Ziriklī, Khayr al-Dīn. *al-Aʿlām: Qāmūs Tarājim li Ashhar al-Rijāl wa al-Nisā' min al-ʿArab wa al-Mustaʿribīn wa al-Mustashriqīn.* 12th edn. Beirut: Dār al-ʿIlm li al-Malāyīn, 1997.

Ziyādah, Aḥmad. *al-Imām ʿAbd al-Ḥalīm Maḥmūd: Ākhir al-ʿUlamā' al-Awliyā'.* Mecca: Dār al-Amīn, 1998.

al-Zuḥaylī, Wahbah. *Naẓariyyat al-Ḍarūrah al-Sharʿiyyah.* 5th edn. Beirut: Mu'assasat al-Risālah, 1997.

___. *al-Wasīṭ fī Uṣūl al-Fiqh al-Islāmī.* 2nd edn. Beirut: Dār al-Fikr, 1969.

# Index

G



H

XYZ